Contents

Foreword

The pace of change in further and higher education has been nothing short of dizzying in the last decade, and it shows little sign of abating as the present Westminster government's reforms are enacted. Since the last general election we've seen fees for undergraduates nearly treble, the abolition of the Education Maintenance Allowance and the introduction of a discretionary bursary system as its replacement, and difficult reforms to NHS and social work bursaries. And this is just in England: the three devolved administrations continue to determine their own policies and become ever more distinct.

It should be no surprise that at a time of public austerity students are feeling the impact as grant and loan rates are frozen and cuts to hardship funds bite. The National Union of Students (NUS) commissioned a major piece of research last year, *The Pound in Your Pocket*, and this found that many were being pushed to the brink of dropping out due to inadequate student support, and that disabled students, student parents and adults in further education are most vulnerable in the current system.

Access to student support is becoming more fragmented, more reliant on institutional discretion and in many cases less generous, yet it's clear that adequate support is critical for the retention and attainment of students.

All this makes *The Guide to Educational Grants* as important a resource as ever. The NUS has happily recommended the directory to students, their families and advisers for many years and this twelfth edition is no exception. It's an incredibly accessible way to identify potential funds from a huge range of trusts and charities that might otherwise remain obscure – and that may make all the difference to a struggling student.

I've made student support a key priority of my time as President of the NUS, and I know we will continue to campaign for a fair and comprehensive system of student support in the years ahead. We'd urge all students to both make best use of this directory and join us in that fight.

Liam Burns
NUS National President 2011–2013

Introduction

Welcome to *The Guide to Educational Grants 2013/14*. The core purpose of this guide is to provide up-to-date information on charitable trusts and foundations which offer financial support for people who are in education or training. This is the twelfth edition of the guide, which is designed to be a practical and valuable tool with which to find funding for educational needs.

This guide contains 1,447 grantmaking trusts and foundations, which gave around £54 million in grants to individuals for educational purposes in the last financial year. Many of the organisations included in this guide also give grants to individuals in need for welfare purposes. These are detailed in the guide's sister publication *The Guide to Grants for Individuals in Need 2013/14*, also published by the Directory of Social Change.

Throughout the research for this edition, we have been collecting detailed financial figures from annual reports and accounts, and gathering comments and feedback about grantmaking from trusts. We also carried out the Grants for Individuals in Need and Education survey, examining a sample of the grantmaking trusts and foundations contained in the guide. This bore additional statistics, along with many interesting comments on the current climate for grantmaking and the recent experiences of the trusts themselves.

Current climate

The biggest influence on the grantmaking climate since the last edition of the guide has undoubtedly been the ongoing effects of the recession and the implementation of severe public sector cuts, the consequences of which had not been fully realised during the research for the last edition, but are now having an acute impact on the lives of people across the UK.

When the coalition government came into power it implemented a series of measures to reduce public spending. There were reductions in central government spending of £6 billion in 2010/11 and a further 19% reduction planned for the following four years (Committee of Public Accounts 2012). Local authorities began their programmes of cuts in 2011/12, reducing expenditure on average by 9.4% (excluding education) since 2009/10. In the 2010 Spending Review, funding from the Department for Communities and Local Government was planned to be cut by 27.4% between 2011 and 2015. These reductions in local government funding have disproportionally hit poorer, more urban areas which are more reliant on grants from central government (Crawford and Phillips 2012).

Clearly these changes have had an impact on the voluntary sector as well. According to NCVO, employment and training charities are the most vulnerable to cuts in public spending because they derive 70% of their income from this source (Funding Commission 2010). Charities' income in the education sector is around £940 million, equivalent to around 2% of the total spend on schools and colleges (Horgan 2007). Along with the tuition fee rises and the rapid expansion of the academy programme this has shaped the changes in the way education in the UK functions and is funded.

Trusts and foundations

These issues have been discussed by many grantmaking trusts and foundations in their annual reports and accounts, and directly to us via our survey. By far the main issue was the grim economic climate and its knock-on effects. Many trusts were experiencing an increase in applications: '[We] witnessed a very large increase in applications from needy people as a result of the continuing economic recession in the UK' (Hereford Municipal Charities 2011) and '252 people applied, a 28% increase on the previous year' (Lawrence Atwell's Charity 2011). Conversely, some trusts experienced a drop in applications. A possible cause for this was put forward by a representative of The Jonathon Young Memorial Trust: 'I think it possible that the number of referrals from state-funded professionals … is falling, and wonder if this is because jobs in support services are being cut.'

However, most trusts reported an increase in applications and were reacting to this in a variety of ways. Some trusts had increased the amount of funding available: 'The trustees, having noted the difficult economic climate for the annual awardees, were able to increase the annual award payments' (St Andrew Holborn Charity 2011). Charities have also been reaching out to beneficiaries in order to increase the amount of support they provide: 'As students have found it harder to obtain grants for further education the trustees have endeavoured to publicise the availability of the Charity in the principal areas where help can be given' (Bishop Laney's Charity 2010/11). Others have chosen to focus their giving on existing beneficiaries: 'Trustees were unable to expand their charitable giving and, instead, concentrated on the areas which they have committed to in the past' (Miss E.B. Wrightson's Trust 2011). This information is supported by evidence we gathered in our survey, see page vi for more details.

We collected extensive financial information throughout the research for this book, recording asset, income, total charitable expenditure, grant and governance figures wherever possible. It has been feasible to compare some of this data with the data collected during the research for the last edition of this guide. However, as some of the methodology was different for this edition, we cannot compare all of the data.

The median financial year was 2011 (2009 in the last edition). The median grant total of the organisations stayed the same at £10,000 per annum. The modal grant total also remained the same at £1,000; this indicates the large number of smaller trusts in the guide. Overall, grant totals had increased by 4% from the last edition. Some figures relate only to those trusts for which we were able to obtain more detailed financial information (these tend to be the larger trusts). For example, grants to individuals for education account for just 11.7% of the total charitable expenditure of the trusts for which we have full financial information. However, it is likely that the smaller trusts have fewer grantmaking priorities and so more, if not all, of their charitable expenditure is for educational grants. The mean assets increased from £6.5 million (adjusted for inflation) to £7.1 million, an increase of £0.6 million. Governance costs decreased on average by 0.8%, perhaps showing evidence that charities are tightening their belts and finding ways to make savings.

Higher education

University tuition fee rises to an upper limit of £9,000 had just been confirmed when the last edition of this guide was published. The government expected that the average fees would be £7,500 but most universities chose to charge the highest fee level, making the average fees paid by a student starting in 2012 nearly £8,400. This is set to rise again in 2013. In 2012 there was an 11% fall in students accepted onto courses, which is widely attributed to the tuition fee rise. Yet this is measured against 2011 levels of acceptances which were substantially above trend in the rush for students to start their degree courses before the fee rise (UCAS 2012). Along with this, universities had to make agreements with the Office for Fair Access as to how they would take measures to improve participation from disadvantaged students if they charge over £6,000. This led to the National Scholarship Programme which both central government and universities put resources into. Since universities can determine their own systems for using this, it has led to a considerable range in generosity to students from the lowest income backgrounds (Hills and Richards 2012).

Many of the trusts in this guide have recognised the escalating costs of attending university and will give to students who are studying in higher education: 'Students have become much more reliant on charitable support with the decline in support available from the government and through local authorities, and the move into students loans. With further cuts in funding to be made available to universities, and the likelihood therefore of increases in tuition fees to be paid by students, the situation will be exacerbated' (The Miners' Welfare National Educational Fund 2011).

Although it is unlikely that a trust would fund a significant portion of tuition fees or living expenses, they may make a contribution, and grants are also available for travel, books, equipment, instruments, materials and trips. See the 'How to make an application' section on page xii for more details on obtaining support.

Schools

By far the biggest change for schools in the last two years has been the academies programme, instigated by Labour but rapidly expanded by the coalition government under education secretary, Michael Gove. As of January 2013, over half of all secondary schools had become or were becoming academies, which are independent of local authority control, funded directly by central government and can choose how to spend their own budgets (Department for Education 2013). Charities can sponsor and make financial contributions to academies.

It is yet to be seen what the long-term effects of the academies programme on education and schools will be. One trust mentioned in its annual report that school clothing grants fell in part because of 'newly established academies which provided uniforms to their own new students'. This is one area which has fallen victim to public sector cuts. As the provision of uniforms is not a statutory duty, many local authorities have scrapped the grants that have previously helped parents to buy them (Citizens Advice 2012). Fortunately, this is an area in which trusts are glad to fund, along with the costs of school trips and those relating to special educational needs, amongst many other expenses. See the advice in the 'How to make an application' section on page xii for more information on how to get support.

Further and vocational education

Scrapping the Education Maintenance Allowance (EMA) was another coalition decision implemented at the same time as the tuition fee rises, despite extensive and vociferous opposition from students. This meant that further education students from low-income backgrounds would no longer receive grants of up to £30 a week from the government to help with the costs of education such as books, travel and trips. The decision has incurred considerable criticism for impeding social mobility (Milburn 2012). Nevertheless, grants are available from the trusts in this guide for further education students for items that the EMA might have previously paid for, such as books, equipment, travel, sustenance and uniforms. See the 'How to make an application' section on page xii for more advice on applying for funding.

The majority of trusts in this guide are also pleased to fund vocational education, including apprenticeships and courses that are likely to lead to employment. This is particularly relevant given the rise in demand for apprenticeships; in 2012, there were over one million applications for apprenticeships (National Apprenticeship Service 2013). In addition, trusts will often fund equipment, travel and uniforms for people starting work.

Grants for Individuals in Need and Education survey

In 2012 the Directory of Social Change carried out the first ever Grants for Individuals in Need and Education survey. We invited a sample of the trusts and foundations in *The Guide to Educational Grants* and *The Guide to Grants for Individuals in Need* to participate in order to gather more detailed information than is contained in annual reports and accounts. This was with the aim of further illuminating the essential information we provide to our readers, and to obtain the most accurate and up-to-date picture of the funding environment.

What we found supported the anecdotal information that we had been hearing from trusts throughout the research for the guide, and the information garnered from their annual reports and accounts. Concerns about the recession and the economic climate dominated the responses. Most trusts had experienced a drop in income (although investments were recovering), coupled with an increase in demand as beneficiaries' needs grew. They have reacted to this in a variety of ways: some trusts reduced the amount of funding given out, in line with reductions in income, whereas others focused on trying to meet the rising demand. A few said that they were unaffected by the recession. We asked the trusts:

What impact, if any, do you feel the recession has had on your charity?

'Far less investment income and hence restricted ability to give grants.'

'More demand for our support services as support is no longer available from some other sources.'

'Income is down slightly but not substantially; applications were up in the last year.'

'Negligible.'

We also asked trusts about the number of applications they received. 84% said that they had received the same or more applications than the previous financial year.

Of the applications received in the last financial year did you receive fewer, about the same, or more applications than the previous year?

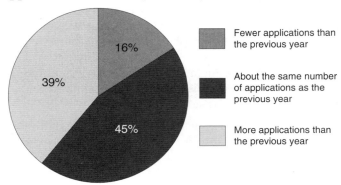

- Fewer applications than the previous year
- About the same number of applications as the previous year
- More applications than the previous year

Although some said that they had had fewer applications, they gave possible explanations for this:

'A lower number of applications [may be a result of there being] fewer front-line workers?'

'Our charity has difficulty reaching the people in need we aim to help.'

Of those that had experienced a rise in applications, we asked them what their reaction was.

How are you reacting to this increased demand from applicants?

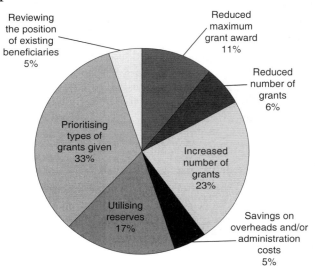

Norwich and Norfolk Grant-Makers' Forum

A group of grantmaking forums in the greater-Norwich area meet three times a year to 'exchange intelligence with a view to promoting more co-ordinated action where the individual Trustee bodies concur'.

David Walker, chair of Anguish's Educational Foundation, takes part in the forum and said they were:

'Directly involved with senior representatives of Norfolk County Council and the City Council in discussing priority needs in the local community and exploring how the Charities might respond collaboratively.'

DSC believes that grantmakers should engage with other organisations and learn from each other in order to do the best for their beneficiaries; therefore we were also interested in levels of collaboration between funders. Of the survey respondents, 55% said that they collaborated with other organisations. This figure may be skewed by the fact that trusts which chose to complete the survey are probably more inclined to engage with other organisations. Descriptions of the collaborations mainly referred to organising the best way of funding shared beneficiaries:

> *'Co-operative liaison with trusts whose criteria are similar to ours re putting together 'packages' of funding for individual pupils.'*

> *'Share funding for dually eligible beneficiaries.'*

If you are interested in the full results and a discussion of this survey, please contact us or visit www.grantsforindividuals.org.uk.

Finally . . .

This discussion may paint a fairly pessimistic picture of the current grantmaking environment, but it is not all doom and gloom. Trusts and foundations are still active and still making grants and they are doing their best in various ways to support their beneficiaries. The following sections include:

- ▶ 'Grantmaking trusts – their processes and effectiveness': our recommendations for grantmaking trusts
- ▶ 'About this guide': a description of the types of trusts that are included, how they are ordered in the guide and the type of help that they give
- ▶ 'How to use this guide': an explanation of a typical trust entry and a flowchart to show you how to identify sources of help
- ▶ 'How to make an application': some advice on making applications, including an application form template

Most importantly, ensure that you read eligibility criteria accurately. Do not apply if you are not eligible because the charities will not be able to fund you and it merely wastes everyone's time. Follow application procedures precisely and make sure that you meet any deadlines. More and more, we are seeing organisations expanding their support beyond just financial grants, and many are offering advice services as well, so take full advantage of these.

We wish you the best of luck in your search for funding.

Acknowledgements

We are extremely grateful to the many trust officers and others who have helped to compile this guide. To name them all individually would be impossible. Where possible, drafts were sent to individual trusts and any corrections were noted and incorporated. Special thanks specifically go to the trusts that responded to our Grants for Individuals in Need and Education survey.

Requests for further information

The research for this guide was done as carefully and thoroughly as we were able, but there will still be relevant charities that we have missed and some of the information may be incomplete or will become out of date. If you come across omissions or mistakes in this guide please let us know by calling or emailing the Directory of Social Change's research team (0151 708 0136; email: research@dsc.org.uk) so that we can rectify them for the future.

We are always looking to improve our guides and would appreciate any comments, positive or negative, about this guide, or suggestions on what other information would be useful for inclusion when we research the next edition.

References

Bishop Laney's Charity (2011), annual report and accounts 2010/11, www.charity-commission.gov.uk, accessed 31 January 2013

Citizens Advice (2012), 'Adding up campaign', www.citizensadvice.org.uk/addingupcampaign, accessed 10 December 2012

Committee of Public Accounts (2012), *Cost reduction in central government: summary of progress: Eightieth Report of Session 2010–12*, London, The Stationery Office

Crawford, Rowena and David Phillips (2012), *Local government spending: where is the axe falling?*, London, Institute for Fiscal Studies

Department for Education (2013), 'Publication list for converter academies' [downloadable Excel sheet], www.education.gov.uk, accessed 30 January 2013

Funding Commission (2010), *Funding the Future: A 10-year framework for civil society*, London, National Council for Voluntary Organisations

Hereford Municipal Charities (2011), annual report and accounts 2011, www.charity-commission.gov.uk, accessed 31 January 2013

Hills, J., and B. Richards (2012), 'Localism and the Means Test: A Case Study of Support for English Students from Autumn 2012', Welfare Policy and Analysis Seminar

Horgan, Goretti (2007), *The impact of poverty on young children's experience of school*, York, Joseph Rowntree Foundation

Lawrence Atwell's Charity (2011), annual report and accounts 2010/11, www.charity-commission.gov.uk, accessed 31 January 2013

Milburn, Alan (2012), *University Challenge: How Higher Education Can Advance Social Mobility*, London, Cabinet Office

Miners' Welfare National Educational Fund (2011), annual report and accounts 2010/11, www.charity-commission.gov.uk, accessed 4 February 2013

Miss E.B. Wrightson's Trust (2011), annual reports and accounts 2010/11, www.charity-commission.gov.uk, accessed 4 February 2013

National Apprenticeship Service (2013), 'Over One Million Apprenticeship Applications Generated online in 2012' [online press release], www.apprenticeships.org.uk, dated 2 January 2013, accessed 31 January 2013

St Andrew Holborn Charity (2011), annual report and accounts 2011, www.charity-commission.gov.uk, accessed 31 January 2013

UCAS (2012), *End of Cycle Report*, Cheltenham, UCAS

Grantmaking trusts – their processes and effectiveness

The Directory of Social change has a vision of an independent voluntary sector at the heart of social change. Based upon this vision and our experience of researching this publication for the past 25 years, we would like to suggest some ways in which trusts which give grants to individuals could seek to encourage greater fairness and more effective practices in grantmaking:

- Trusts and foundations should seek to collaborate with others that have similar objectives. By sharing knowledge and best practice, organisations can contribute towards improving the wider grantmaking landscape. Of the respondents to our survey, 55% collaborated with organisations, mostly by jointly funding individuals and sharing information.
- Trusts should do as much as possible to decrease the amount of ineligible applications they receive. This is a joint responsibility with applicants, who should make sure that they read criteria carefully and not apply to trusts for which they are not eligible. However, trusts should facilitate this by ensuring that eligibility criteria and applications guidelines are transparent and easily available.
- Local trusts should ensure they are very well known within their area of benefit by writing to local Citizens Advice branches, local authorities, schools and other educational establishments and community centres.
- Ideally, trusts should aim to ensure that needs can be met as rapidly as possible; for example, by empowering the clerk or a small number of trustees to make small emergency grants. If trustees can only meet twice a year to consider applications these should cover the peak times, namely May to June when people are running out of money at the end of the academic year or looking forward to funding courses beginning in September, and November to December when people who have started their courses have a much clearer picture of how much money they need.
- One or two trusts in this guide are restricted to making grants to inhabitants of relatively wealthy parishes and appear to have great difficulty finding individuals in need of financial support. The majority, however, receive constant applications for worthy causes. Where the objects of the trusts permit it, we would like to see trusts forming clear policies on who they can support and what they can fund, targeting those most in need.

About this guide

What trusts are included?

We have included in this guide trusts and foundations that give:

- At least £500 a year in educational grants (most give considerably more)
- Grants based upon need rather than academic performance
- Funding for levels of education from primary school to first degree level. 'Education' is defined in its loosest sense, and therefore includes all types of vocational education and training, extracurricular activities and personal development
- Grants to students of more than one educational establishment

We have not included those that give:

- Grants that are solely for postgraduate study
- Awards or scholarships for academic excellence, except where these appear to be particularly relevant to people in need

About 30% of the trusts in this guide also give grants to individuals in need for the relief of poverty and hardship. These, along with many other trusts, are included in the guide's sister publication *The Guide to Grants for Individuals in Need 2013/14*. The trusts in this guide often support educational charities, youth organisations and schools as well; however, the information given relates only to that which is relevant for individuals. *The Directory of Grantmaking Trusts*, also published by the Directory of Social Change, contains funding for organisations.

How trusts are ordered

The trusts are listed in two sections:

1) National trusts classified according to:

- **Need:** for example, disability, independent schools, overseas students (see page 3)
- **Occupation** of parent or applicant (see page 49)
- **Subject** being studied (see page 71)

Within each of these sections there is a General section which lists trusts that do not fall into a specific category.

2) Local trusts classified by region, county, borough or parish; see page 111 for details about how to use this section.

What are grants given for?

Most of the trusts in this guide can give supplementary help with small grants for:

- Uniforms, books, equipment and materials relating to a course
- Small-scale fees such as exam fees and supplementary awards
- Travel, including for field studies or educational trips, both in and outside the UK
- Course fees, particularly those for professional, technical or vocational courses and qualifications

- Extra-curricular activities aimed at the physical and social development of the individual, such as outdoor education or voluntary work overseas
- Musical instruments; this can take the form of loans
- Extra equipment related to disability that cannot be funded from statutory sources
- Childcare costs for students with children
- Costs relating to apprenticeships or people entering a trade or profession

Grants can be one-off – just to fund a particular item – or recurring, to support an individual throughout their course. Grants may also be given in the form of vouchers; for the local school uniform shop, for example.

Supporting information and advice

This guide also contains supporting information and advice on:

- Statutory grants and student support (see page 359)
- Types of schools in the UK and their funding (see page 363)
- Company sponsorship and career development loans (see page 367)
- Funding for gap years and overseas voluntary work (see page 371)
- Contacts and sources of further information (see page 375)
- Education authority contacts (see page 379)

How to use this guide

Below is a typical trust entry, showing the format we have used to present the information obtained from each of the trusts.

On the following page is a flowchart. We recommend that you follow the order indicated in the flowchart to look at each section of the guide and find trusts that are relevant to you. You can also use the information in the sections 'About this guide' and 'How to make an application' to help inform your applications.

The Fictitious Trust

£24,000 (120 grants)

Correspondent: Ms I M Helpful, Charities Administrator, 7 Pleasant Road, London SN0 0ZZ (020 7123 4567; email: admin@fictitious.org.uk; website: www.fictitious.org.uk).

Trustees: Annette Curtain; Felix Cited; Paige Turner; Russell Ingleaves.

CC Number: 112234

Eligibility
Children or young people up to 25 years of age who are in need. Preference is given to children of single parent families and/or those who come from a disadvantaged family background.

Types of grants
Small one-off grants of up to £250 for a wide range of needs, including school uniforms, books, equipment and educational trips in the UK and abroad. Grants are also available for childcare costs.

Annual grant total
In 2011 the trust had an income of £25,000 and an expenditure of £27,000. Grants to 120 individuals totaled £24,000.

Other information
The trust also gives relief-in-need grants to individuals.

Exclusions
No grants for private school or university fees.

Applications
On a form available from the correspondent, submitted either directly by the individual or by the parent or guardian for those under 18. Applications are considered in January, April, July and October.

Award and no. of grants
Total amount given in grants to individuals for education and how many individual grants were made, if this information was available.

Correspondent
The main person to contact, nominated by the trustees.

Trustees
Note: information on the trustees of Scottish trusts is often unavailable.

Charity Commission number
Note: occasionally some of the smallest Scottish organisations are not registered charities.

Eligibility
This states who is eligible to apply for a grant. This can include restrictions on age, family circumstances, occupation of parent, subject to be studied, stage of education, ethnic origin, or place of residence.

Types of grants
Specifies whether the trust gives one-off or recurrent grants, the size of grants given and for which items or costs grants are actually given. This section will also indicate if the trust runs various schemes.

Annual grant total
This shows the total amount of money given in grants to individuals in the last financial year for which there were figures available. Other financial information may be given where relevant.

Other information
This contains miscellaneous further information about the trust, including if they give grants to individuals for relief-in-need, or to organisations.

Exclusions
This field gives information, where available, on what the trust will not fund.

Applications
Including how to apply, who should make the application (i.e. the individual or a third party) and when to submit an application.

How to identify sources of help - a quick reference flowchart

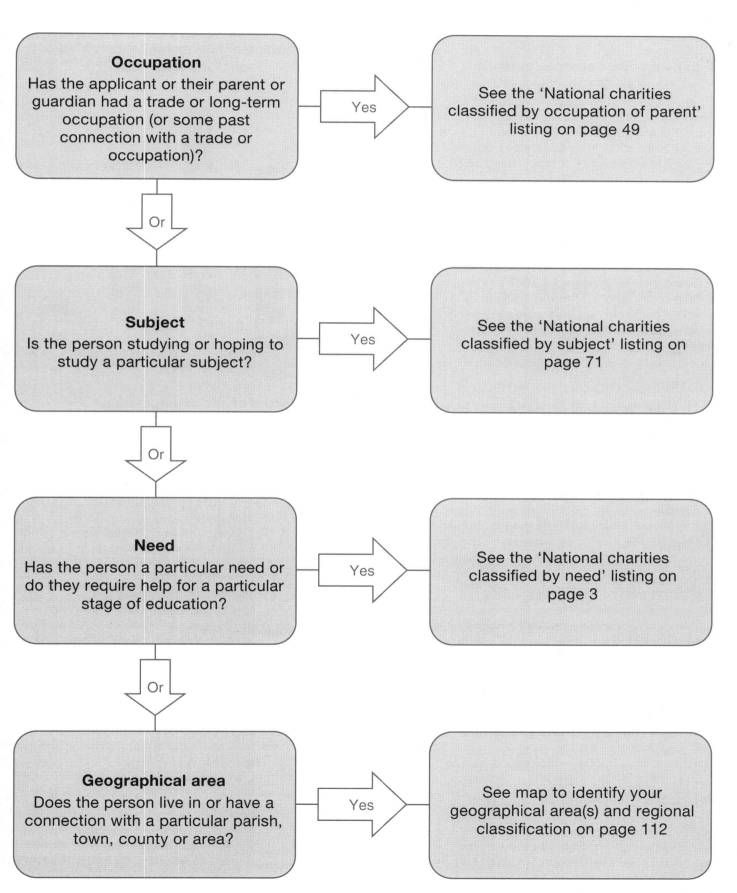

Occupation
Has the applicant or their parent or guardian had a trade or long-term occupation (or some past connection with a trade or occupation)?

Yes → See the 'National charities classified by occupation of parent' listing on page 49

Or

Subject
Is the person studying or hoping to study a particular subject?

Yes → See the 'National charities classified by subject' listing on page 71

Or

Need
Has the person a particular need or do they require help for a particular stage of education?

Yes → See the 'National charities classified by need' listing on page 3

Or

Geographical area
Does the person live in or have a connection with a particular parish, town, county or area?

Yes → See map to identify your geographical area(s) and regional classification on page 112

How to make an application

This section gives you some information on how to make an application, with additional tips from funders' perspectives.

1. Exhaust other sources of funds

All sources of statutory funding should have been applied for and/or received before applying to a charity. Applications, therefore, should include details of these sources and any refusals. Where statutory funding has been received but is inadequate, an explanation that this is the case should be made. A supporting reference from a relevant agency may also be helpful.

If the applicant attends an educational establishment this should also have been approached to see if it has any funds or can give a reduction in fees.

> '*The best way to get help for individual funding is to start by helping yourself – try every avenue to raise as much of the money yourself before and while you approach others for a contribution to your cause. If they can see how determined you are and how hard you've worked already, they'll naturally feel motivated to help you find the remainder.*'
> *BBC Performing Arts Fund*

Other possible sources of funding and advice are included at the back of this guide.

2. Use the flowchart on page xi to identify potential sources of funding

Once you have found a trust that may be relevant to you...

3. Check eligibility criteria

Submitting ineligible applications is the biggest mistake that applicants make. A charity cannot fund you if you are not eligible and you merely waste both your time and theirs by applying. If you are in any doubt, contact the trust for clarification. Of the applications received by respondents to our grantmakers survey, 25% of all applications were ineligible.

> '*Always read carefully a charity's criteria for eligibility. We, for example, are only allowed to help the children of actors, but three quarters of the applications I receive do not match this basic requirement. You are wasting your time and hopes by applying to a trust which clearly is not allowed to help you.*'
> *TACT*

4. Follow the application procedures precisely

Wherever they are available, we have included application procedures in the entries; applicants should take great care to follow these. If there is an application form, use it! Read any guidelines thoroughly and take note of deadlines. Some charities can consider applications throughout the year; others may meet monthly, quarterly or just once a year. Very urgent applications can sometimes be considered between the main meetings. Make sure that the appropriate person submits the application; this could be

the individual, their parent or guardian or some professional such as a social worker.

Evidence from our survey of grantmakers shows that a large majority of trusts welcome initial contact before a full application is made, so if you are unsure about anything, get in touch with them.

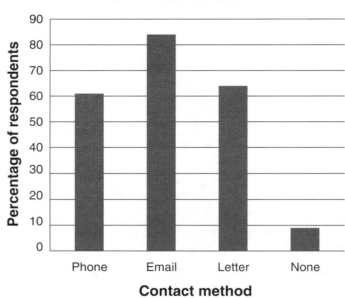

Percentage of survey respondents open to informal contact

5. Give details of any extenuating or unforeseen circumstances

Potential applicants should think carefully about any circumstances which put them at a disadvantage from other families or students, such as coming from a low-income background, being in receipt of state benefits, being a single parent, having a health problem or disability and so on. Where relevant, try and show how the circumstances you are now in could not have been foreseen (for example, illness, family difficulties, loss of job and so on). Charities are often more willing to help if financial difficulties are a result of unforeseen circumstances rather than a lack of forward planning. The funding in this guide is aimed at those facing the most barriers to education or training.

6. Give clear, honest details about your circumstances, including any savings, capital or compensation

Most trustees will consider the applicant's savings when they are awarding a grant, although sometimes this does not need to affect trustees' calculations. In circumstances where you are certain that your savings are not relevant to grant calculations, you should explain this in the application.

> '*Be open and honest about your circumstances. We have to ensure that we have all the information we need to put your case forwards. If essential details emerge at a later date, this can affect your application. Be honest about how much you want to apply for and don't ask for the most*

expensive item. If you show that you've done your research, then that helps us too.'

Fashion and Textile Children's Trust

7. Tailor the application to suit the particular charity

For example, if someone is applying to a trade charity on behalf of a child whose father had lengthy service in that particular trade, then a detailed description (and, where possible, supporting documentation) of the father's service would be highly relevant. If an application for the same child was being made to a local charity on another occasion, it would not be relevant.

8. Ask for a suitable amount

Ask for an amount that the trust is able to give. Most grants are for under £300, and local charities often give much less. If a trust only makes small grants, try asking for help with books, travel, childcare expenses and such like, and apply for fees elsewhere.

9. Mention applications to other charities

Explain that other charities are being approached, when this is the case, and state that any surplus money raised will be returned.

10. Offer to supply references

For example, from a teacher, college tutor, support worker and/or another independent person. If the individual has disabilities or medical needs then a report from a doctor would be necessary.

11. Be honest and realistic, not moralising and emotional

Some applications try to morally bribe trustees into supporting the application, or launch into tirades against the current political regime. It is best to confine your application to clear and simple statements of fact.

12. Be clear, concise and provide sufficient detail

Give as much relevant information as possible, in the most precise way. For example, 'place of birth' is sometimes answered with 'Great Britain', but if the trust only gives grants in Liverpool, to answer 'Great Britain' is not detailed enough and the application will be delayed pending further information. Make sure that you write clearly and do not use jargon so your application is easily understood.

13. Say thank you!

Charitable trusts generally like to be kept informed of how their grants have made a difference. It is also important to keep in touch if you are in need of recurrent funding. Feedback also helps trusts for future grant giving.

'Don't consider the moment the grant appears in your bank account as the end of your relationship with the grantmaker – try to provide updates on the work the grant has helped you to undertake, including photos, videos and other resources.' *Royal Geographical Society*

So remember to thank trusts for their support and let them know how their funding has helped you.

See page xvi for notes on the application form template.

Application form template

Purpose for which grant is sought	Amount sought from this application £
Applicant (name)	Occupation/School
Address Telephone no.	
Date of birth	Age	Place of birth
Nationality	Religion (if any)

☐ Single   ☐ Married   ☐ Divorced   ☐ Partnered   ☐ Separated   ☐ Widow/er

Family details: Name	Age	Occupation/School
Parents/ Partner	. . . . . .	. . . .
Brothers/Sisters/ Children	. . . . . .	. . . .
. . . .	. . . . . .	. . . .
. . . .	. . . . . .	. . . .
Others (specify)		. . . .

Income (weekly)	£	p	Expenditure (weekly – *excluding course fees*)	£	p
Father's/husband's wage	. . . . . .		Rent/mortgage	. . . . . .	
Mother's/wife's wage	. . . . . .		Council tax	. . . . . .	
Partner's wage	. . . . . .		Water rate	. . . . . .	
Income Support	. . . . . .		Electricity	. . . . . .	
Jobseeker's Allowance	. . . . . .		Gas	. . . . . .	
Employment and Support Allowance	. . . . . .		Other fuel	. . . . . .	
Pension Credit	. . . . . .		Insurance	. . . . . .	
Working Tax Credit	. . . . . .		Fares/travel	. . . . . .	
Child Tax Credit	. . . . . .		Household expenses (food, laundry etc.).	. . . . . .	
Child Benefit	. . . . . .		Clothing	. . . . . .	
Housing Benefit	. . . . . .		School dinners	. . . . . .	
Attendance Allowance	. . . . . .		Childcare fees	. . . . . .	
Disability Living Allowance	. . . . . .		HP commitments	. . . . . .	
Universal Credit	. . . . . .		Telephone	. . . . . .	
Personal Independence Payments	. . . . . .		TV rental	. . . . . .	
Maintenance payments	. . . . . .		TV licence	. . . . . .	
Pensions	. . . . . .		Other expenditure (specify)	. . . . . .	
Other income (specify)	. . . . . .		. . . .	. . . . . .	
. . . .	. . . . . .		. . . .	. . . . . .	
. . . .	. . . . . .		. . . .	. . . . . .	
. . . .			. . . .		

Total weekly income £ _____   **Total weekly expenditure** £ _____

Name of school/college/university:

Address

Date of starting course:

Course:

Is the course ☐ full-time? ☐ part-time?

Date of finishing course:

Name of local education authority:

Have you applied for a grant? ☐ YES ☐ NO

What was the outcome of the application?

Give details of any other grants or scholarships awarded:

Have you applied to your school/college/university for help? ☐ YES ☐ NO

What was the outcome of the application?

Have you applied to any other trusts? ☐ YES ☐ NO

What was the outcome of the application?

Have you applied for any loans? ☐ YES ☐ NO

What was the outcome of the application?

How much are your school/college fees?
£

Have they been paid in full? ☐ YES ☐ NO

If NO, please give details:

Other costs (e.g. books, clothing, equipment, travel etc.):

How much money do you need to complete the course? £

Examinations passed and other qualifications

Previous employment (with dates)

Any other relevant information (please continue on separate sheet if necessary)

Signature:

Date:

Notes: application form template

1. Because this form is designed to be useful to the wide range of people who apply for education grants, not all the information asked for will be relevant to every application. If, for example, you are not in receipt of state benefits, or do not have credit debts, you should write 'N/A' (not applicable) in the box or line in question.

2. If, similarly, you do not have answers for all the questions at the time of applying – for example, if you have applied to other trusts and are still waiting for a reply – you should write 'Pending' under the question: 'Have you written to any other trusts? What was the outcome of the application?'

3. The first page is relevant to all applications; the second page is only relevant to people applying for school or college fees. If you are applying for clothing or books for a schoolchild then it may be worth filling out only the first page of the form and submitting a covering letter outlining the reasons for the application.

4. Filling out the weekly income and expenditure parts of the form can be worrying or even distressing. Expenditure when itemised in this way is usually far higher than people expect. It is probably worth filling out this form with the help of a trained welfare rights worker.

5. You should always keep a copy of the completed form in case the trust has a specific query.

6. This form should not be used when the trust has its own form that must be completed.

About the Directory of Social Change

DSC has a vision of an independent voluntary sector at the heart of social change. The activities of independent charities, voluntary organisations and community groups are fundamental to achieve social change. We exist to help these organisations and the people who support them to achieve their goals.

We do this by:

- providing practical tools that organisations and activists need, including online and printed publications, training courses, and conferences on a huge range of topics
- acting as a 'concerned citizen' in public policy debates, often on behalf of smaller charities, voluntary organisations and community groups
- leading campaigns and stimulating debate on key policy issues that affect those groups
- carrying out research and providing information to influence policymakers.

DSC is the leading provider of information and training for the voluntary sector and publishes an extensive range of guides and handbooks covering subjects such as fundraising, management, communication, finance and law. We have a range of subscription-based websites containing a wealth of information on funding from trusts, companies and government sources. We run more than 300 training courses each year, including bespoke in-house training provided at the client's location. DSC conferences, many of which run on an annual basis, include the Charity Management Conference, the Charity Accountants' Conference and the Charity Law Conference. DSC's major annual event is Charityfair, which provides low-cost training on a wide variety of subjects.

For details of all our activities, and to order publications and book courses, go to www.dsc.org.uk, call 08450 777707 or email publications@dsc.org.uk

National and general sources of help

The entries in this first section are arranged in three groups: 1) classified by need, 2) classified by occupation of parent or applicant, and 3) classified by subject. Trusts appear in full in the section that is most relevant (usually the section which occurs first) and are then cross referenced should they also apply in another section.

This breakdown is designed to be the easiest way to identify trusts which might be of relevance and as such we have attempted to make the terms as specific as possible. In doing so, this means that there is some crossover between sections. For instance, mature university students could identify trusts in the 'Adult and continuing education' and 'Further and higher education' sections, with various other categories possibly being relevant dependent on personal circumstances.

There are a number of trusts which do not fall into any specific category; these appear first in the 'General' section.

Trusts are arranged alphabetically within each category. We always caution against using these lists alone as a guide to sources of money. Read each main entry carefully as there will usually be other criteria that must be met; for example, someone who is blind should not simply apply to all the trusts in the 'blindness' section. See the advice in the 'How to make an application' section on page xii for more information on how to apply.

Classification by subject

National charities classified by need

General

The British and Foreign School Society – Alfred Bourne Trust

£1,000

Correspondent: Imogen Wilde, Director, Maybrook House, Godstone Road, Caterham, Surrey CR3 6RE (01883 331177; email: director@bfss.org.uk; website: www.bfss.org.uk)

Trustees: Graham Kingsley; Stephen Orchard; David Swain; Steve Hodkinson; Roger Howarth; David Tennant; Brian York; Stephen Ross; Emily Tomlinson; David Zahn; David Stephens; Shubhi Rao; Jaz Saggu; Ben Ramm; E. J. Weale.

CC Number: 314286

Eligibility
Students aged under 30, who are in the final stage of an initial teacher training course leading to qualified teacher status, and have run into unexpected financial difficulties for reasons outside their control.

Types of grants
Grants are one-off and there is no maximum amount.

Annual grant total
About £1,000 is available each year for individuals.

Applications
At the time of publication (March 2013) the British and Foreign School society who administer this fund, was undertaking a review of the requirements for the fund, and not currently accepting applications. Contact the trust or check the website for the latest information.

Al-Mizan Charitable Trust

£4,500

Correspondent: Mohammed Sadiq Mamdani, 2 Burlington Gardens, London W3 6BA (email: admin@almizantrust.org.uk; website: www.almizantrust.org.uk)

Trustees: Rukaiya Jeraj; Mohammad Musa; Ali Orr; Sanjana Deen; Sonia Malik; Karim Farrag; Fatema Bendali; Amir Rizwan; Afshaan Hena; Sarfaraz Hussein.

CC Number: 1135752

Eligibility
British citizens, those granted indefinite leave to remain in the UK and asylum seekers who are living in a condition of social or economic deprivation. Preference is given to the following groups:
- Orphans (a child who has lost either both parents or one parent who was the main bread-winner in the family)
- Children and young people under the age of 19 years (particularly those in care or who are carers)
- Individuals who are disabled, incapacitated or terminally ill (particularly those who are severely mentally disabled)
- Single parents (particularly divorcees and widows/widowers with children)
- Estranged or isolated senior citizens
- Individuals with severe medical conditions or their families
- Ex-offenders or reformed drug addicts or alcoholics
- Victims of domestic violence and/or physical or sexual abuse
- Victims of crime, anti-social behaviour and/or terrorism

Types of grants
Mainly one-off grants ranging from £200–£250, though in some cases up to £500 may be awarded. Grants are available both for subsistence costs and those which help break the cycle of poverty by encouraging educational attainment and employability.

Annual grant total
In 2010/11 the trust had both an income and total charitable expenditure of £10,500.

Exclusions
No grants for: general appeals; applicants who are not claiming all available benefits; retrospective funding; expenses relating to the practice or promotion of religion; debt, including council tax arrears; fines or criminal penalties; university tuition fees; gap year trips; building work or construction projects; funeral expenses; gifts (including birthdays and festivals); vehicles; and, holidays or recreational outings, unless they serve a medical, social or educational need. No support is given to those who have received a grant in the last twelve months.

Applications
All applications for grant funding must be submitted using the trust's online application system.

Other information
The trust has an informative website.

Lawrence Atwell's Charity

£171,000 (133 grants)

Correspondent: Louise Pooley, Atwell Administrator, The Skinners' Company, Skinners' Hall, 8 Dowgate Hill, London EC4R 2SP (020 7236 5629; fax: 020 7236 5629; email: atwell@skinners.org.uk; website: www.skinnershall.co.uk/charities/lawrence-atwell-charity.htm)

Trustee: The Worshipful Company of Skinners.

CC Number: 210773

Eligibility

Young people aged between 16 and 26 (inclusive) who come from low-waged families, i.e. applicants whose parent/s' total gross income is less than £26,000 a year and has been for some time. Applicants must be British citizens, refugees with leave to remain in the UK or asylum seekers in the process of obtaining leave to remain.

Preference is given to applicants who face additional barriers in life, work and training. For example those who: have no or few qualifications after leaving secondary education; have very limited or no support from their families; have a physical or mental disability; are lone parents; have fled persecution in their home countries; or, are ex-offenders or at risk of offending.

Types of grants

One-off and recurrent grants in the range of £100 to £1,000. Support is offered towards:

- Vocational training below the level of a first undergraduate degree – for example, NVQ Level 3, BTEC National Diplomas and City and Guilds courses
- 'first step' qualifications that help people to become qualified for work – e.g. NVQ Level 1/2, BTEC First Diplomas/Certificates and access and foundation courses
- The costs of finding a job – e.g. the costs of attending an interview or buying tools to get someone started

Support may be given towards tuition, enrolment, registration and examination fees; general living expenses; and specific items and one-off costs, e.g. essential tools and childcare costs.

Grants can be made for courses lasting more than one year. If the applicant is on a two or three year course, he/she may be asked to re-apply before the start of each year. If the applicant's costs are very high, they will be expected to show how they intend to raise the funds needed. The trustees will not make an award if they feel that finances are not feasible. Loans are rarely made.

The majority of recipients receive grants towards their tuition fees and maintenance costs whilst undertaking study. Support is also given towards the purchase of equipment, tools and occasionally clothes for attending interviews or college.

Annual grant total

In 2010/11 the charity had assets of £13.7 million and an income of £377,000. Grants were made to 133 individuals totalling £171,000.

Exclusions

No grants for: international or foreign students (this includes people from EU countries); non-vocational courses such as GCSEs, A-levels, or GNVQs; higher education courses or courses for which government funding, such as a student loan, is available; dance and drama courses which take place at private schools and colleges; individuals who are already qualified to work or who have had significant work experience; payment of any already existing fees or debts (including loans); cases where it is unclear that the applicant will realistically be able to raise the balance of funds to complete the entire course; expeditions, travel or study abroad; business enterprises or startup costs.

Applications

Applicants should first complete a short pre-application questionnaire, available on request from the correspondent or to download from the charity's website. Eligible applicants will then be provided with a full application pack. Guidelines for applicants and a useful FAQ section are also available to view on the website.

Applications are from February each year and the deadline is mid-September.

The charity welcomes informal contact via phone or email to discuss applications.

Other information

The charity also provides financial support to the Skinner's Company's voluntary-aided schools.

Black Family Charitable Trust

£31,000

Correspondent: The Trustees, PO Box 232, Petersfield, Hampshire GU32 9DQ (email: enquires@bfct.org.uk)

Trustees: Ann Black; Thomas Black; Alexandra Black; Emily Black.

CC Number: 1134661

Eligibility

Schoolchildren, further and higher education students in financial need in England and Wales.

Types of grants

Bursaries, scholarships, prizes and awards to support education.

Annual grant total

In 2010/11 the trust had assets of £455,000. £55,000 was given in grants to organisations, no grants were made directly to individuals but a grant of £31,000 was made to the University of Strathclyde to provide bursaries.

Applications

In writing to the correspondent either by post-or email.

Other information

Grants are also given to schools.

The Chizel Educational Trust

£2,000

Correspondent: Geoffrey Bond, Burgage Manor, Southwell, Nottingham NG25 0EP

Trustees: Alistair MacDiarmid; David Stephens; Geoffrey Bond; Bill Russell.

CC Number: 1091574

Eligibility

People under 25 in the UK.

Types of grants

Grants towards equipment, instruments, books, travel, bursaries and maintenance allowances.

Annual grant total

In 2010/11 the trust had an income of £4,500 and an expenditure of £4,700.

Applications

In writing to the correspondent. Applications are considered twice a year.

Other information

Donations are also made towards the maintenance of Ackworth School, Yorkshire and the Inverness Royal Academy Mollie Stephens Trust.

The Coffey Charitable Trust

£1,000

Correspondent: Christopher Coffey, Oaktree House, Over the Melbourne Road, Denham, Uxbridge, Middlesex UB9 5DR (01895 831381)

Trustees: Christopher Coffey; Wendy Coffey; Christopher Green.

CC Number: 1043549

Eligibility

People in need in the UK.

Types of grants

Occasional one-off and recurrent grants according to need.

Annual grant total

In 2010/11 the trust had an income of £15,000 and a total expenditure of £21,000.

Applications

In writing to the correspondent.

Other information

This trust mainly provides grants to Christian organisations and events.

Conservative and Unionist Agents' Benevolent Association

£10,000

Correspondent: Sally Smith, Conservative Campaign Headquarters, Millbank Tower, 30 Millbank, London SW1P 4DP (020 7984 8172; email: sally. smith@conservatives.com)

Trustees: Sir David Kelly; Sir Anthony Garrett; Donald Porter.

CC Number: 216438

Eligibility

Children of deceased Conservative or Unionist Agents or Women Organisers.

Types of grants

One-off and recurrent grants towards books, equipment, instruments and fees for schoolchildren.

Annual grant total

In 2010/11 the association had assets of £2.5 million and an income of £101,000. Grants were made totalling £56,000.

Applications

Initial telephone calls are welcomed and application forms are available on request. Applications can be made either directly by the individual or their parent/guardian, or through a member of the management committee or local serving agent. All beneficiaries are allocated a 'visiting agent'.

Other information

The majority of the association's grants are made for relief-in-need purposes.

Peter Alan Dickson Foundation

See entry on page 29

The Fenton Trust

£4,000

Correspondent: Fiona Macgillivray, Family Action, 501–505 Kingsland Road, Dalston, London E8 4AU (020 7241 7609; fax: 020 7249 5443; email: grants. enquiry@family-action.org.uk; website: www.family-action.org.uk)

Trustee: Family Action.

CC Number: 247552

Eligibility

British-born subjects who are dependents of a member of the professional classes and are undergoing a course of education or training approved by the trustees; or poor members of the professional or middle classes.

Types of grants

Grants are one-off and range between £100 and £500. They are only intended to be supplementary, therefore applicants are only considered if they are in the final year of a course and if they have managed to raise almost the whole amount needed, or if they encounter unexpected difficulty. Grants can go to students and mature students for help with costs of books, fees, living expenses, travel and childcare.

Annual grant total

In 2010/11 the trust had an income of £17,000 and an expenditure of £4,500 which is much lower than previous years.

Exclusions

Grants are not given towards postgraduate study.

Applications

On a form available from the correspondent or the website, to be submitted directly by the individual and supported by an academic reference. Trustees meet monthly.

The General Federation of Trade Unions Educational Trust

£1,500

Correspondent: Judith Jackson, Head of Educational Services, Headland House, 308–312 Gray's Inn Road, London WC1X 8DP (020 7520 8340; fax: 020 7520 8350; email: judith@gftu.org.uk; website: www.gftu.org.uk)

Trustees: Chris Wilkes; David Spooner; Marion Colverd; John Fray; Joseph Marino; Anthony Jowitt; Joseph Mann.

CC Number: 313439

Eligibility

Members of a trade union. Grants will only be considered for the subjects of economic history and theory; industrial law; and the history and principles of industrial relations.

Types of grants

Full-time and part-time students undertaking a course nominated by the recipient's trade union receive a grant of up to £150 (full-time), £50 (part-time) or £100 (Open University). Open University students will be supported after completing the first year. Grants may be paid annually.

Annual grant total

In 2011 the trust had assets of £2.3 million and an income of £1.1 million. Grants are given to around 15 individuals totalling about £1,500 annually.

Applications

A nomination form is available from the correspondent and must be signed by the general secretary from the applicant's trade union. Applications are considered quarterly. Proof of trade union membership may be required. Forms signed by lay representatives and local officials are not valid.

Global Educational Trust

£0

Correspondent: Mohammad Yusuf Adrian Bashforth, 78 York Street, London W1H 1DP (020 7692 4076; fax: 02076924077; email: info@ globaleducationaltrust.org; website: www.globaleducationaltrust.org)

Trustees: Morad Khan; Junaid Rahim; Simon Jennings.

CC Number: 1144969

Eligibility

People in the UK and overseas.

Types of grants

Scholarships and bursaries to allow people to attend school, college or university.

Annual grant total

This trust is newly registered so no financial information is available.

Applications

In writing to the correspondent.

Other information

The trust also gives grants to organisations in the UK and overseas. It aims to increases literacy rates.

The Eleanor Hamilton Educational Trust

£161,000 (194 grants)

Correspondent: The Secretary, 65 Bolsover Road, Hove BN3 5HQ (01273 279352; email: ehamiltonet@ virginmedia.com)

Trustees: John Miles; Jennifer Nyiri; Polly Brandon; Ronald Orr; William Brandon; Ingo Hippisley.

CC Number: 309997

Eligibility

Priority is given to children who are either in their second year of GCSEs or their second year at A-level depending on social, health and financial need. Consideration is also given to students (under 30) who are dyslexic, have other special needs or are estranged from their parents.

Types of grants

One-off grants in the range of £100 and £500 towards fees for schoolchildren and people with special educational needs and towards living expenses for college students, undergraduates, vocational students and people with special educational needs.

Annual grant total

In 2010 grants to individuals totalled £161,000.

Applications

On a form available from the correspondent at any time.

Other information

The trust also gives to organisations.

Horizons Your Education

£200,000

Correspondent: EGAS, Family Action, 501–505 Kingsland Road, London E8 4AU (020 7254 6251; email: horizons@family-action.org.uk; website: www.yourhorizons.com/education-advice-for-lone-parents)

Trustees: Iain Harris; Peter Stoakley; Brent Thomas; Hilary Seal; Gillian Keene; Martin Barnes; Sean O'Callaghan; Bryan Portman; John Rowlands; Sally Shire.

CC Number: 264713

Eligibility

Lone parents living in the UK, on a low income with sole responsibility for dependent children. Applicants must be British citizens or have refugee status, indefinite leave to remain, discretionary leave to remain or have been granted humanitarian protection.

Types of grants

£500 to £1,000 for expenses associated with a course of education or training, such as fees, books, equipment, travel and childcare.

Annual grant total

The fund gives about 350 grants a year totalling around £200,000.

Applications

On a form available to download by completing the grants search (to check eligibility) on the family action website. The fund is open to applications for approximately six weeks in October/November.

The Leverhulme Trade Charities Trust

£724,000

Correspondent: Reena Mistry, 1 Pemberton Row, London EC4A 3BG (020 7042 9883; fax: 020 7042 9889; email: rmistry@leverhulme.ac.uk; website: www.leverhulme-trade.org.uk)

Trustees: Michael Perry; Ashok Ganguly; Niall Fitzgerald; Patrick Cescau; Paul Polman.

CC Number: 288404

Eligibility

Undergraduates who are in need and are the dependents of people who have been employed for at least five years as commercial travellers, chemists (members of the Royal Pharmaceutical Society) or grocers. This includes the offspring, spouses, widows and widowers of such people.

Types of grants

Grants of up to £3,000 a year to full-time first degree students for needs such as tuition fees, books, travel costs and accommodation. Grants can be one-off or last for the duration of the course.

Annual grant total

In 2011 the trust had assets of £52 million and an income of £2 million. Undergraduate bursaries totalled £563,000 and postgraduate bursaries amounted to £161,000.

Applications

Undergraduate applications must be made through their university rather than directly by the individual, with the grants paid to the institutions to pass through to the successful applicants. The deadlines for the trust receiving the completed applications are 1 March and 1 November, with decisions made and funds available by the end of the month. Forms, terms and conditions are available on the website.

P. and M. Lovell Charitable Settlement

£1,300 (5 grants)

Correspondent: The Trustees, KPMG, 100 Temple Street, Bristol BS1 6AG (01179 054000)

Trustees: Benjamin Lovell; Martin Lovell; William Lovell.

CC Number: 274846

Eligibility

People in education who are in need.

Types of grants

One-off grants of £50 to £500.

Annual grant total

In 2010/11 the trust had assets of £1.8 million, an income of £54,000 and made five grants to individuals totalling £1,300.

Applications

In writing to the correspondent.

Other information

Grants are mostly made to organisations.

Open Wing Trust

£10,000

Correspondent: Jennifer Kavanagh, Clerk, 44 Langham Street, London W1W 7AU (email: Online contact form; website: www.openwing.org.uk)

Trustees: Jennifer Kavanagh; Penny Markell; Mirabai Swingler; Stephen Petter; Alexandra Porter; Maggie Waterworth.

CC Number: 1149773

Eligibility

Individuals at the beginning of their career and those contemplating a radical re-orientation of their life's work or the deepening of an existing vision. The trustees advise: 'we expect applicants to be in a process of inner change leading to a socially engaged commitment to working with those in need.'

Types of grants

One-off grants according to need. 'Trustees will consider funding specific living costs such as food and rent, training programmes, or offering support during voluntary work or an internship. We will not fund holidays or unspecified thinking time.'

Annual grant total

This newly established trust expects to fund up to three small grants each year, up to a maximum of £4,000.

Exclusions

No re-applications for further funding will be considered within five years of an initial grant.

Applications

On an application form available to download from the website. Applications should be accompanied by two supporting letters from referees who have known the applicant for at least five years. Applicants will need to demonstrate commitment to their purpose, and that they are in need of financial support to make it feasible. Consult the guidance notes on the trust website before applying to ensure that your application is in line with the aims and values of the trust.

Trustees meet twice a year to consider applications, but can make decisions between meetings. Suitable applicants will be invited to meet the trustees.

The Osborne Charitable Trust

£1,000

Correspondent: John Eaton, 57 Osborne Villas, Hove, East Sussex BN3 2RA (01273 732500; email: john@eaton207. fsnet.co.uk)

Trustees: John Head; David Goldin; John Eaton.

CC Number: 326363

Eligibility

People in education in the UK and overseas.

Types of grants

One-off and recurrent grants according to need and one-off grants in kind. Grants are given to schoolchildren for equipment/instruments and special needs education for fees and equipment/ instruments.

Annual grant total

In 2010/11 the trust had an income of £6,200 and a total expenditure of £13,000. Grants are made to organisations and individuals.

Exclusions

No grants for religious or political purposes.

Applications

This trust does not respond to unsolicited applications.

The Tim Rice Charitable Trust

£750 (2 grants)

Correspondent: Eileen Heinink, Trustee, Ivy House, 31 The Terrace, Barnes, London SW13 0NR (020 7580 7313)

Trustees: Eileen Heininck; Neil Benson; Tim Rice.

CC Number: 1049578

Eligibility

People in need in the UK on academic or cultural courses.

Types of grants

One-off and recurrent grants of up to £1,000, but typically £250 to £500 each. Grants can be for the costs of music and sport, school fees and for other educational purposes.

Annual grant total

In 2010/11 the trust had an income of £257,000 and made grants totalling £243,000, mostly to organisations but including £750 in two grants to individuals.

Applications

In writing to the correspondent.

Scarr-Hall Memorial Trust

£10,000

Correspondent: Donna Thorley, Baker Tilley, Festival Way, Stoke-on-Trent, Staffordshire ST1 5BB

Trustees: Margaret Hall; Ruth Scarr-Hall; Ian Scarr-Hall; Kirsteen Scar-Hall; Rachel Scarr-Hall.

CC Number: 328105

Eligibility

People in education in the UK.

Types of grants

One-off grants according to need, usually in the range of £100 and £500.

Annual grant total

About £10,000.

Applications

In writing to the correspondent, including details on the individual circumstances, why the grant is required and how much is needed.

Victoria Shardlow's Children's Trust

£10,000

Correspondent: Mrs Liz Clifford, Charities Administrator, 9 Menin Way, Farnham GU9 8DY (email: Victoriashardlowtrust@googlemail.com)

Eligibility

Children or young people up to 18 years of age who are 'living in difficult circumstances and under general disadvantage to participate in and benefit from formal or non-formal education'.

Types of grants

Small one-off grants to assist with the provision of equipment, fees, transportation costs and educational trips in the UK and abroad. The maximum grant is £3,000.

Annual grant total

In 2010/11 the trust gave £10,000 in grants.

Exclusions

No grants for university fees.

Applications

On a form available from the correspondent, submitted either directly by the individual or by the parent or guardian. Applications are considered in January, April, July and October.

Other information

This trust is very small and therefore is not registered with the Charity Commission.

Southdown Trust

£25,000 (96 grants)

Correspondent: John Wyatt, Holmbush, 64 High Street, Findon, West Sussex BN14 0SY

Trustees: Hugh Wyatt; John Wyatt; Meriel Buxton, John McBeath.

CC Number: 235583

Eligibility

People aged between 17 and 26 for individual ventures of general educational benefit.

Types of grants

One-off and recurrent grants and loans ranging from £20 to £1,000. Grants are to 'support individual ventures of general educational benefit'. Previously grants have been made, for example, to fund a teaching assistant at a primary school, and to provide a scholarship for a university student.

Annual grant total

In 2010/11 the trust had assets of £929,000 and an income of £71,000. Grants to individuals totalled £25,000.

Exclusions

No grants are made for art, dance, sociology, theatre, law, journalism, counselling, media studies, PhDs or materials.

Applications

In writing to the correspondent enclosing full information and an sae. Applications should be made directly by the individual.

The Stanley Stein Charitable Trust

£20,000

Correspondent: Michael Lawson, Trustee, Burwood House, 14–16 Caxton Street, London SW1H 0GY (020 7873 1000)

Trustees: Michael Lawson; Walter Felman; Brian Berg.

CC Number: 1048873

Eligibility

People under the age of 21 who are sick and in need.

Types of grants

One-off and recurrent grants according to need.

Annual grant total

The latest figures were for 2009/10 when the trust had an income of £20,000 and an expenditure of £44,000.

Applications

On a form available from the correspondent.

Other information

Grants are given for welfare and education.

The Talisman Charitable Trust

£22,000 (10 grants)

Correspondent: Philip Denman, Lower Ground Floor Office, 354 Kennington Road, London SE11 4LD (020 7820 0254; website: www.talismancharity.org)

Trustees: Philip Denman; Dr Francesca Marie-Carola Denman; Nicholas Caine.

CC Number: 207173

Eligibility

People in the UK who are living on a very low income.

Types of grants

One-off and recurrent grants according to need.

Annual grant total

In 2010/11 the trust had assets of £8.6 million and an income of £155,000. Ten grants for education were made totalling £22,000.

Grants were also made to organisations totalling £50,000 and to individuals for welfare purposes totalling £95,000.

Applications

In writing to the correspondent through a social worker, Citizens Advice or similar third party.

Applications should be on headed paper and include the individual's full name and address, a summary of their financial circumstances, what is needed and how much it will cost. A brief history of the case and a list of any other charities approached should be included as well. Supporting evidence such as medical documentation, a letter from the applicant's school and written quotations would also be helpful. Applications are considered throughout the year. Only successful applications will receive a reply.

Note: applications should not be sent by recorded delivery or any 'signed for' services.

Other information

This trust was previously called The Late Baron F A D'Erlanger's Charitable Trust.

Madeleine Mary Walker Foundation

£29,000

Correspondent: Paul Benfield, Trustee, 1 Levington Wynd, Nunthorpe, Middlesbrough TS7 0QD (email: m100pfb@yahoo.co.uk)

Trustees: Paul Benfield; Mary Frankland; Thomas Power; Paul Hutchinson; Lynn Smith; Michael Westgarth-Taylor.

CC Number: 1062657

Eligibility

People in need in the UK who are in education up to first degree level. Priority is given to those living within a 30 mile radius of Stokesley, North Yorkshire.

Types of grants

Grants usually range from £250 to £750 and are given for a variety of educational needs including books, equipment, tools, fees, instruments and travel abroad.

Annual grant total

In 2010/11 the foundation gave grants totalling £29,000.

Applications

In writing to the correspondent including an sae and contact telephone number. Trustees meet three/four times per year. Applicants may be interviewed.

S. C. Witting Trust

£1,000

Correspondent: Christopher Gregory, Secretary, Friends House, 173 Euston Road, London NW1 2BJ

Trustees: Ronald Barden; Richard Bloomfield; Mark Tod; David Stanton; Rod Usher; Philip Hills; Delia Suffling; Steven Pullan; Ian Watson; Colin Hulse.

CC Number: 237698

Eligibility

Students following or intending and preparing to follow a course of study at university, ordinarily resident in England.

Types of grants

One-off grants are made for uniforms/clothing, books and equipment/instruments.

Annual grant total

In 2011 the trust gave £15,000 to individuals in England, Germany and Poland for educational and welfare purposes. About £6,000 is available each year for distribution to individuals in England and grants are mostly made for welfare.

Exclusions

No grants towards debts or loans.

Applications

In writing to the correspondent, through a third party such as a social worker or teacher including a short case history, reason for need and the amount required. University students must have a letter of support indicating financial need. Unsuccessful applications are not acknowledged unless an sae is included.

Other information

Grants are also made to individuals for welfare purposes.

Toby and Regina Wyles Charitable Trust

£7,000

Correspondent: Ross Badger, Trustee, 3rd Floor, North Dukes Court, 32 Duke Street, St James' London, London SW1Y 6DF (020 7930 7797; email: ross.badger@hhllp.co.uk)

Trustees: Ross Badger; Andrew Wyles; Regina Wyles.

CC Number: 1118376

Eligibility

People in need of assistance to continue their education in the UK.

Types of grants

Grants towards educational costs.

Annual grant total

In 2010/11 the trust had an income of £12,000 and an expenditure of £50,000. Previously, grants to individuals have totalled £7,000.

Applications

In writing to the correspondent.

The Zobel Charitable Trust

£1,500

Correspondent: S D Scott, Tenison House, Tweedy Road, Bromley, Kent BR1 3NF (020 8464 4242)

Trustees: Stephen Scott; Joy Pennells; Marie Zobel; Reginald Botley.

CC Number: 1094186

Eligibility

People in education in the UK, particularly in the Christian field.

Types of grants

One-off and recurrent grants according to need.

Annual grant total

About £1,500 a year.

Exclusions

No grants for fees.

Applications

This trust does its own research and does not always respond to unsolicited applications.

Other information

Grants are also made to organisations.

Adult and continuing education

The Adult Education Bursary Scheme

£250,000

Correspondent: Christine Francis, Awards Officer, Adult Education Bursaries, c/o Ruskin College, Walton Street, Oxford OX1 2HE (01865 554331; fax: 01865 556362; email: awards@ruskin.ac.uk)

Eligibility

People over 19, attending full-time certificate or diploma courses of at least one year at one of the following residential colleges: Fircroft College, Birmingham; Hillcroft College, Surbiton, London; Northern College, Barnsley; and Ruskin College, Oxford. Applicants must have been offered a place on the course, and have been recommended for a bursary by the college.

Types of grants

These colleges offer to relatively small numbers each year the opportunity of full-time university-type education in the broad field of social sciences and liberal studies. Students accepted by the colleges for one year courses are normally eligible for the bursaries covered by this scheme. These cover tuition fees and a maintenance grant. Grants for travel of over £80 a year are considered for the journey between the home and the residential college, or daily travel fees for students living at home during term-time. Grants are also available to students who have a disability or a specific learning difficulty. Students with dependent children can apply for a parents learning allowance and childcare grant.

Annual grant total

Grants total about £250,000 each year.

Note: The scheme correspondent has informed us that the scheme is currently undergoing a governmental review therefore there are likely to be significant changes from 2013/14.

Applications

Most of the colleges have an annual intake of students each September or October, with some offering intakes in January or April. Intending applicants should write initially to the college of their choice for a guideline to applying. Students' application forms will be allocated by the college once they have been accepted on the course.

Other information

The addresses of the colleges are as follows:

Fircroft College, 1018 Bristol Road, Selly Oak, Birmingham B29 6LH (01214 720116).

Hillcroft College, South Bank, Surbiton, Surrey KT6 6DF (020 8399 2688).

Northern College, Wentworth Castle, Stainborough, Barnsley, South Yorkshire S75 3ET (01226 776000).

Ruskin College, Walton Street, Oxford OX1 2HE (01865 554331).

Diamond Education Grant

See entry on page 43

Monica Eyre Memorial Foundation

£2,000

Correspondent: Michael Bidwell, 5 Clifton Road, Winchester, Hampshire SO22 5BN

Trustees: Barbara Miller; Michael Bidwell; Sheila Laxman.

CC Number: 1046645

Eligibility

Mature students in need, particularly those with disabilities/special needs in the UK.

Types of grants

Grants towards fees to enable mature students to start or continue courses.

Annual grant total

In 2010/11 the trust had an income of £4,500 and a total expenditure of £6,000.

Applications

In writing to the correspondent. The trust vets course content and validates enrolment before awarding any funding.

Other information

The trust also makes grants to organisations and to individuals for welfare purposes.

The Gilchrist Educational Trust

£32,000

Correspondent: Val Considine Acis, 20 Fern Road, Storrington, Pulborough, West Sussex RH20 4LW (01903 746723; email: gilchrist.et@blueyonder.co.uk; website: www.gilchristgrants.org.uk)

Trustees: John Hemming; F. L. Pearce; Lord Shuttleworth; Charles Whitebread; Stuart Harrop.

CC Number: 313877

Eligibility

Full-time students at a UK university who:

(i) have made proper provision to fund a degree or higher education course but find themselves facing unexpected financial difficulties which may prevent the completion of it. Applicants will normally be in the last year of the course, or
(ii) as part of their degree course, are required to spend a short period studying in another country. Examples are the fieldwork necessary for a thesis or dissertation, or medical students' elective periods study.

Types of grants

Adult Study Grants are up to £1,000. Travel Study Grants are up to £500.

Annual grant total

Grants to individuals totalled £32,000 comprising of £12,000 in adult study grants and £20,000 in travel study grants.

Exclusions

Assistance cannot be offered to the following: part-time students; those seeking funds to enable them to take up a place on a course; students seeking help in meeting the cost of maintaining dependents; students who have, as part of a course, to spend all or most of an academic year studying in another country; those wishing to go abroad under the auspices of independent travel, exploratory or educational projects.

Applications

There is no application form. In response to an initial enquiry, the trust sends a sheet listing the information required to enable an application to be considered. They can be submitted at any time of the year.

Other information

The trust also gives grants to organisations and expeditions.

Business start-up and apprentices/ vocational training

The Oli Bennett Charitable Trust

£10,000

Correspondent: Joy Bennett, Camelot, Penn Street, Amersham, Buckinghamshire HP7 0PY (01494 717702; email: info@olibennett.org.uk; website: www.olibennett.org.uk)

Trustees: Edward Weiss; Joy Bennett; Luke Mugliston; Sally Taber; Thomas Patrick; Kieron Connolly; Peregrine Hill; R. Gwinner; Edward Stern; Adrian Bennett; Debs Gwinner.

CC Number: 1090861

Eligibility
Young people between 18 and 30, who are self-employed and are UK residents.

Types of grants
Grants in the range of £1,000 and £1,500 for people starting up their own businesses.

Annual grant total
In 2011 the trust had an income of £15,000 and an expenditure of £13,000.

Applications
Application forms are available on the trust's website. Applications are considered every three months. A business plan is required to assess the viability of the idea.

Other information
The trust was set up in memory of Oli Bennett, who died in the September 11 2001 attacks in New York.

City and Guilds Bursaries

£24,000

Correspondent: Bursaries, Policy and Corporate Affairs, 1 Giltspur Street, London EC1A 9DD (0844 543 0033; email: bursaries@cityandguilds.com)

Trustees: David Illingworth; Richard Sermon; David Wilbraham; John Randall; Pat Stringfellow; Michael Howell; Valerie Bayliss; Allan Johnston; Tim Strickland; John Armitt.

CC Number: 312832

Eligibility
UK residents who wish to study or are studying a City and Guilds qualification to improve their financial security.

Types of grants
Grants for course fees and course related expenses such as living costs, books/ equipment, travel costs and childcare. Between 40 and 60 awards are made each year, amounts are agreed on a case by case basis and determined by the individual course costs.

Annual grant total
In 2010/11 the charity had assets of £430 million and an income of £118 million. 48 bursaries were awarded during the year.

Applications
On an online form on the website. Applications are considered twice a year, in May and October, and can be submitted up to three months before the closing date. For deadlines see the website.

Other information
City and Guilds primarily exists to provide qualifications, awards, assessments and support across a range of occupations in industry, commerce and the public services.

Go Make it Happen

Correspondent: Keith Harding, 28 Lightfoot Road, London N8 7JN (020 8348 3197; email: info@gomakeithappen. co.uk; website: www.gomakeithappen.co. uk)

Trustees: Julie Cometa; Robert Harding; Stewart MacDonald; Rachael Bonfiglioli; Mary Harding; Sam Jackson.

CC Number: 1145369

Eligibility
People aged 18 to 30 to who want to 'achieve things in their lives that they would not otherwise be able to achieve, in particular in the area of travel and tourism'.

The trust has a particular focus on young people who have not necessarily followed a 'conventional' academic route.

Types of grants
Funding is available for training courses and travel and education in the UK and overseas, plus related expenses.

Annual grant total
As the trust is newly registered, no financial information is available.

Applications
On a form available to download from the website. The trust will make contact within two weeks and may arrange for an interview.

Other information
The trust also provides information on opportunities for working overseas, and for working in travel and tourism generally, both in the UK and overseas by supplying advice and guidance on how people can realise these opportunities.

They also campaign for cycling safety and driver awareness.

The N. and P. Hartley Memorial Trust

£2,000

Correspondent: Virginia Watson, Trustee, 24 Holywell Lane, Leeds LS17 8HA

Trustees: Gwendolyn Proctor; James Proctor; John Kirman; Virginia Watson.

CC Number: 327570

Eligibility
Priority is firstly given to those living in West Yorkshire, secondly to individuals living in the north of England and thirdly to those elsewhere in the UK and overseas.

Types of grants
One-off grants for vocational training for vocational employment.

Annual grant total
Grants to individuals total between £3,000 and £4,000 each year.

Applications
In writing to the correspondent, preferably through a social worker, Citizens Advice or other welfare agency, for consideration twice yearly. Re-applications from previous beneficiaries are welcomed.

Other information
The trust also makes a number of grants to organisations and to individuals for welfare purposes.

The Prince's Trust

£1.8 million (6,255 grants)

Correspondent: Sarah Haidry, 18 Park Square East, London NW1 4LH (0800 842 842; fax: 020 7543 1300; email: sarah.haidry@princes-trust.org.uk; website: www.princes-trust.org.uk)

Trustees: Patrick Passley; Charles Dunstone; H. J. Hancock; John Marks; Lloyd Dorfman; William Eccles.

CC Number: 1079675

Eligibility
Young people between the ages of 14 and 25 who are not expecting to achieve

five GCSEs grades A–C or who are not in education, training or not working more than 16 hours a week. The Prince's Trust works with individuals who have experienced difficulties at school, have been in trouble with the law, are long-term unemployed or have been in care.

Types of grants

The Prince's Trust aims to change the lives of young people, helping them to develop confidence in themselves, learn new skills and get practical and financial support.

- Development awards: grants of up to £500 to assist young people with getting into education, training or employment. Examples of support include grants for equipment, clothing, travel costs, fees (including licence fees) or childcare costs
- Community cash awards: grants of up to £3,000 to design and set up a youth led community project
- Enterprise programme: Start-up loan funding for unemployed young people to start a business. This fund is available for those aged 18 to 30

Annual grant total

In 2010/11 the trust had assets of £34 million and an income of £40 million. £1.8 million was distributed in 6,255 grants to individuals, broken down as follows:

Enterprise Programme Grants	448	502,000
Development awards	4,428	788,000
Community Cash Awards	1,379	552,000

Exclusions

No grants for university course fees, trips, gap year funding or welfare.

Applications

On forms available on the trust's website, which should be returned to the local regional office, details of which are also available on the website. Potential applicants are also welcome to phone, or text 'Call Me' to 07983 385418 to discuss an application.

Other information

The Prince's Trust also runs many programmes which provide young people with personal development, training and opportunities to help them move into work. Details of these can be found on the website.

The Thomas Wall Trust

£44,000 (44 grants)

Correspondent: Sue Ellis, Charities Officer, Thomas Wall Trust, Skinners' Hall, 8 Dowgate Hill, London EC4R 2SP (020 7213 0564; email: information@ thomaswalltrust.org.uk; website: www. thomaswalltrust.org.uk)

Trustees: Ralph Waller; Geoffrey Copland; Ann Kennedy; Colin Broomfield; Ann Mullins; Anne-Marie Martin; Paul Bellamy; Mary Barrie.

CC Number: 206121

Eligibility

UK nationals in financial need, who wish to undertake educational studies which are vocational, short courses of professional training, or in a broad sense are concerned with social service and which will lead to paid employment.

Types of grants

One-off grants, up to £1,000, to supplement assistance from other sources. Interest free loans can also be made. Both full-time and vocational part-time courses are considered for support.

Annual grant total

In 2010/11 the trust had assets of £2.8 million and an income of £116,000. Grants were made to 44 individuals totalling £44,000.

Exclusions

Grants are not given: to those who qualify for support from the Student Loan Company for undergraduate study; for travel, study or work experience abroad; for elective periods or intercalated courses; for attendance at conferences; for research or study for higher degrees by research; or to schoolchildren.

Applications

Applications can be made online at the trust's website. Applications are considered from January until September, or until funds run out. Only successful applicants will be notified by the trust. All information on the trust is available on its website.

Other information

Grants are also given to charitable organisations in the fields of education and social welfare, especially those that are small or of a pioneering nature.

Carers

The Princess Royal Trust for Carers

£46,000

Correspondent: The Clerk, Unit 14, Bourne Court, Southend Road, Woodford Green, Essex IG8 8HD (0844 800 4361; email: info@carers.org; website: www.carers.org)

Trustees: Ray Robertson; Andrew Cozens; Tim Poole; Andrew Robertson; Edward Wojakovski; Josephine Barrett;

Dr David Gabbay; Tanya Fitzgerald; Stuart Taylor; Lynne Powrie.

SC Number: SC015975

Eligibility

Unpaid carers in the UK, especially those who live near a Princess Royal Trust for Carers Centre.

Types of grants

One-off grants. The Explore More Fund enables young carers to apply for up to £300 for activities that will have an impact on their lives.

Annual grant total

In 2010/11 the trust gave 399 grants to individuals totalling £92,000 for both education and welfare.

Applications

Applications are made via your local Princess Royal Trust for Carers Centre. Direct applications will not be considered.

Children and young people

The French Huguenot Church of London Charitable Trust

£103,000

Correspondent: Duncan McGowan, c/o Haysmacintyre, Fairfax House, 15 Fulwood Place, London WC1V 6AY (email: dmcgowan@haysmacintyre.com)

Trustees: Charles Martineau; Alethea Phelips; Henry Martineau; Peter Duval; Alexander Duval; Marin Williams; Natasha Martineau; Herve Gilg; Stephen Champion de Crespigny; Anthony Wilson; Laurence Colchester; Denis Faure; Thibault Lavergne.

CC Number: 249017

Eligibility

People under 25. For all categories, where there are two or more claimants of equal merit, the trustees have the following order of priority:

(a) people who, or whose parents are, members of the Church
(b) people of French Protestant descent
(c) other people as trustees think fit.

Grants can be given for the education of:
(i) children of members of the church
(ii) French Protestant children attending French schools in London
(iii) those under 25 of proven French Protestant descent
(iv) girls at schools of the Girls' Public

Day School Trust and the Church Schools Company Ltd
(v) boys at selected independent day schools
(vi) choristers at schools of the Choir Schools Association
(vii) people under 25 for individual projects, at home or abroad.

Types of grants

Allowances, bursaries and emergency grants for students at boys and girls day schools, choir schools and various colleges. Grants are also made for overseas projects.

Annual grant total

In 2011 the trust had assets of £10.4 million and an income of £352,000. Educational grants and bursaries to 50 individuals totalled £103,000, including grants to eight young people totalling £1,500 for overseas projects.

Applications

Applications for categories (i) and (ii) above should be made to the Secretary of the Consistory, 8–9 Soho Square, London W1V 5DD. Correspondence regarding categories (iii) and (vii) should be sent to the correspondent. Applications for categories (iv), (v) and (vi) should be sent to the head of the school concerned, mentioning the applicant's connection (if any) with the French Protestant Church.

Other information

The trust also awards an annual scholarship for Huguenot Research at the Institution of Historical Research at the University of London, and has endowed an annual scholarship to support students under 25 wishing to undertake projects relevant to modern Europe (Peter Kirk Memorial Fund).

Grants are also given in support of the church and to organisations for the relief of hardship.

The William Gibbs Trust

£11,000

Correspondent: A Johnson, 40 Bathwick Hill, Bath BA2 6LD

Trustees: Mary Aldenham; Antonia Johnson.

CC Number: 282957

Eligibility

Young people in education who are of British nationality.

Types of grants

One-off and recurrent grants according to need.

Annual grant total

In 2011 the trust had an income of £8,700 and an expenditure of £11,000.

Applications

This trust states that it does not respond to unsolicited applications as the funds are already allocated. Any enquiries should be made in writing.

The Marillier Trust

£17,000

Correspondent: William Stisted, Trustee, 38 Southgate, Chichester, West Sussex PO19 1DP (01243 787899; email: ws@alhlaw.co.uk)

Trustees: William Stisted; Dave Miller; Chris Fitton; Jo Lambert.

CC Number: 1100693

Eligibility

Educational grants for boys between the ages of 5 and 13 years in the UK.

Types of grants

Equipment, residential trips and after school activities. Loans are also made to individuals.

Annual grant total

In 2010/11 the trust had assets of £1.6 million and an income of £49,000. Grants to individuals were made totalling £17,000, broken down as follows:
- Residential trips £2,300
- After school activities £12,000
- Provision of equipment £2,000

Applications

In writing to the correspondent.

Other information

Grants to institutions were made totalling £62,000 in 2010/11.

Professionals Aid Council

£19,000 (75 grants)

Correspondent: Fiona McNicholl, 10 St Christopher's Place, London W1U 1HZ (020 7935 0641; email: admin@professionalsaid.org.uk)

Trustees: Christopher Everett; Jennifer Anderson; Peter Dixon; Beryl Greenslade; Robert Caton; Mary Springham; Lucy Carmichael; Astrid Lewis.

CC Number: 207292

Eligibility

The dependents of people who are graduates or have worked in a professional occupation requiring that level of education, or those who have a first degree themselves, studying in the UK.

Types of grants

One-off and recurring. Children's education grants for uniforms, travel, equipment/books and educational outings. College or university student grants of £300 to £500 for tuition fees in the final months of a course, medical, dental and veterinary courses in the final two years, degree shows, travel expenses and equipment/books.

Annual grant total

In 2011 the charity had assets of £2.1 million and an income of £108,000. During the year there were 20 grants for children's education and 55 grants for further/higher education students, totalling £19,000.

Exclusions

No grants for private tutors, study abroad, ordination or conversion courses, medical electives, IELTS or PLAB tests.

Applications

Initially by filling in the enquiry form on the website or writing to the correspondent.

Other information

The organisation also offers advice and assistance. Grants are also made for welfare purposes.

Red House Youth Projects Trust

£0

Correspondent: Marguerite Smith, The Grants Administrator, 12 Spruce Avenue, Ormesby, Great Yarmouth, Norfolk NR29 3RY (01493 731976; email: grants@redhouseyouthprojects.co.uk; website: www.redhouseyouthprojects.co.uk)

Trustees: Richard Gurney; N. G. Sparrow; Ray Hollands; James Kearns; Richard Butler; Rodney Matless; Michael Falcon; Sara Cator; Lorraine Bliss; Louise Barber.

CC Number: 1092828

Eligibility

People under 21 who are resident in Norfolk.

Types of grants

Grants of up to £750 for young people to follow personal ambitions, undertake arts/citizenship projects.

Grants are also available to support the training of adults in charity and voluntary organisations. These would be for up to 50% of costs to a maximum of £2,500.

Annual grant total

In 2010/11 the trust had assets of £799,000 and an income of £30,000. Grants to organisations totalled £10,000. No grants to individuals were made during the year but previously around £4,500 has been given.

Exclusions

No grants for trips abroad or core costs.

Applications

On forms available from the website. Trustees or staff are willing to help individuals complete forms. Grants are considered four times a year in March, June, September and December.

Other information

Grants are also made to organisations.

Dr M. Clare Roberts Memorial Fund

£1,000

Correspondent: Sarah Roberts-Penn, 52 Stubbington Way, Fair Oak, Eastleigh, Hampshire SO50 7LR

Trustees: Sarah Roberts-Penn; Derrick Roberts; Kathleen Roberts; Amanda Roberts; Andrew Mills; Colin McGuiness; Annette Lake; Claire; Burnill; Jean Fitch; Joyce Thornhill; Sarah Irwin.

CC Number: 1101006

Eligibility

Children and young people in the UK looking to expand their 'educational horizons'.

Types of grants

Provision of facilities, equipment or financial assistance.

Annual grant total

Grants average around £1,000 per year.

Applications

In writing to the correspondent.

The T. A K. Turton Charitable Trust

£14,000

Correspondent: R M Fullerton, 47 Lynwood Road, London W5 1JQ (020 8998 1006)

Trustees: I. Ewing; R. Fullerton; R. M. Fullerton.

CC Number: 268000

Eligibility

The trust usually supports three pupils in the UK and three in South Africa where TAK Turton, the founder of the trust, spent the final years of his life. Candidates should have a good academic record, e.g. good GCSE results or equivalent.

Applications are only accepted from schools which have awarded the candidate a bursary of at least 25% of the fees.

Types of grants

Grants are given for a two year period to cover up to 25% of school fees, usually to enable applicants to study for A-levels or equivalent university entrance qualifications.

Annual grant total

In 2010/11 the trust had an income of £14,000 and an expenditure of £16,000. Grants are usually distributed evenly between students in South Africa and students in the UK.

Applications

Applications should be submitted through the school where the candidate proposes to study, to the above address.

Other information

Grants are normally given for a two year period, so new applications from UK students can now only be considered every two years.

Further and higher education

2 Study Foundation

Correspondent: Office Administrator, 152 City Road, London EC1V 2NX (0844 318 7883; fax: 0844 318 7884; email: info@2studyfoundation.org; website: www.2studyfoundation.org.uk)

Trustees: Atul Kochhar; Michael Blasebalk; Mitesh Soma; Tracy Ferrier; Natasha Makhijani.

CC Number: 1144500

Eligibility

Higher education students in England and Wales.

Types of grants

One-off grants of £500 to £3,000 to alleviate students in financial hardship. Grants are means tested.

Annual grant total

No financial information is available yet as this is a new charity. They stated that they have been inundated with 1251 applications in 12 days.

Applications

Request an application form on the website, using a valid UK university email ID (.ac.uk). Applications can be submitted at any time and will be checked with the university for verification. Grants are awarded at the beginning of every term.

Buttle UK – Student and Trainee Grant Scheme

£312,000 (208 grants)

Correspondent: Alan Cox, Audley House, 13 Palace Street, London SW1E 5HX (020 7798 6227; email: info@ buttleuk.org; website: www.buttleuk.org)

Trustees: David Anderson; Elizabeth Stearns; Keith Mullins; Richard Buttle; Stephen Fielding; Gordon Anderson; Clare Montagu; Trevor Reaney; Dominic Vallely; Julia Ogilvy.

CC Number: 313007

Eligibility

Young people estranged from their family; orphans; those who have been adopted or cared for by relatives or friends; young people caring for a severely sick or disabled single parent; and, refugees with full refugee status or Indefinite Leave to Remain in the UK. Support is usually limited to those who are over 16 and under 21. However, assistance will be given to those over the age of 21 when both the course being followed and the financial support from the trust began before the applicant was 21.

Note: The trust expects applicants in higher education to apply for the maximum student loan and students in further or higher education are also expected to apply for any additional help that may be available from the institution, e.g. bursaries and hardship funds.

Types of grants

Support is given to young people aged 16–20 facing severe social, emotional or health problems to gain academic, trade, professional or vocational qualifications. Grants are mainly given towards living costs such as rent, food, clothing, transport, books and other materials needed for the course.

Annual grant total

In 2010/11 208 grants totalling £312,000 were made for support for students and trainees

Exclusions

Grants are not usually made for: second degrees, postgraduate courses or studying overseas; students being looked after by a local authority or Health Board in Northern Ireland; and, students living outside the UK. No assistance is available under any circumstances to students who have reached the age of 25.

Applications

Initial enquiries should be made by telephone or email to the trust with the following information: Name, date of birth, contact address, course and place of study or training including start and end date, grounds of eligibility with reference to our criteria, a full account of the problems and family circumstances that might make it possible for the trust to offer assistance.

The applicant will then be provided with an application form if the trust believes they can help.

Contact details for applicants resident in:

England: Audley House, 13 Palace Street, London SW1E 5HX, infor@buttleuk.org, 020 7828 7311

Scotland: PO Box 5075, Glasgow G78 4WA, annmariep@buttleuk.org, 01505 850437

Wales: PO Box 224, Caerphilly CF83 9EE, wales@buttleuk.org, 01633 440052

Northern Ireland: PO Box 484, Belfast BT6 0YA, nireland@buttleuk.org, 02890 641164

Further information is available on the website.

Other information

The trust was founded by the Revd W F Buttle in 1953.

Grants are also given to children and young people for school fees (see *The Frank Buttle Trust – School Fees Grants Scheme*) and for welfare purposes.

The Follett Trust

£5,200

Correspondent: Brian Mitchell, Trustee, PO Box 4, Knebworth, Hertfordshire SG3 6UT (01438 222908)

Trustees: Barbara Follett; Ken Follett; Brian Mitchell.

CC Number: 328638

Eligibility

Students in higher education.

Types of grants

One-off and recurrent grants according to need.

Annual grant total

In 2010/11 the trust made grants to individuals totalling £5,200.

Applications

The trust states: 'The Trust is unable to accept unsolicited applications.'

The majority of successful applications come from persons known to the trustees or in which the trustees have a particular interest.

George Heim Memorial Trust

£2,000

Correspondent: Paul Heim, Wearne Wyche, Picts Hill, Langport, Somerset TA10 9AA (01458 252097)

Trustees: Paul Heim; Andrea Pyle; John Board; Susan Board.

CC Number: 1069659

Eligibility

People aged under 30 who are in further education.

Types of grants

Grants range from £100 to £1,000.

Annual grant total

In 2010/11 the trust had an income of £3,000 and an expenditure of £2,000.

Applications

In writing to the correspondent.

The Hockerill Educational Foundation

£49,000

Correspondent: Derek Humphrey, 3 The Swallows, Harlow, Essex CM17 0AR (01279 420855; fax: 05603 140931; email: info@hockerillfoundation.org.uk; website: www.hockerillfoundation.org.uk)

Trustees: H. Potter; Jonathan Reynolds; Elwin Cockett; Lesley Barlow; Colin Bord; T. P. Jones; Harry Marsh; Paul Bayes; The Bishop of Colchester; Coralie McCluskey; Janet Scott; Jonathan Longstaff; Alan Smith; Rob Fox; Stephen Cottrell.

CC Number: 311018

Eligibility

The trust awards grants widely for causes related to religious education, which are usually given under the following categories:

- Students and teaching assistants taking teaching qualifications, or first degrees leading to teaching
- Teachers, teaching assistants and others in an educational capacity seeking professional development through full-time or part-time courses
- Those undertaking research related to the practice of Religious Education in schools or further education
- Students taking other first degree courses, or courses in further education
- Others involved in teaching and leading in voluntary, non-statutory education, including those concerned with adult and Christian education

Grants are also made for gap year projects with an educational focus to those whose home or place of study is in the Dioceses of Chelmsford and St Albans.

Types of grants

Grants of £500 to £1,000 are available for students for help with fees, books, living expenses and travel. Priority is given to those training to be teachers, with a priority to teaching religious education but if funds are available other students with financial difficulties will be funded.

Annual grant total

In 2010/11 grants totalling £49,000 were made to 89 individuals consisting of:

- 52 training for primary education
- 26 for secondary education
- 4 for higher or degrees or diplomas in education
- 1 for a gap year student

Of the 88 education students, 20 were following courses either partly or directly relating to the teaching of religious education and 68 were taking other education courses or professional development in education.

Exclusions

No grants to schoolchildren, those studying for Christian ministry or mission unless continuing in teaching, and for visits, study or conferences abroad, gap year activities, courses in counselling, therapy or social work, or for courses leading specifically to non-teaching careers such as medicine, law or accountancy. Grants are no longer made to overseas students.

Applications

On a form available from the website, to be returned by 1 March.

Other information

The charity states that the majority of annual funding is committed to long-term projects or activities in education, but funding is also given to other projects, namely:

- Training and support for the church's educational work in the dioceses of Chelmsford and St Albans
- Research, development and support grants to organisations in the field of Religious Education

The charity also supports conferences for new RE teachers and a 'Prize for Innovation in the Teaching of RE'.

The Humanitarian Trust

£0

Correspondent: The Trustees, 2 Grosvenor Gardens, London SW1W 0DH (020 3262 1056)

CC Number: 208575

Eligibility

British citizens and overseas students under 30 years old on a recognised course of study in the UK and who hold a basic grant for the course.

Types of grants

Grants of £200 are available to graduates and postgraduates and are awarded for 'academic subjects only', and top up fees.

Annual grant total

In 2010/11 grants to organisations totalled £87,000, although no grants were made to individuals this year.

Exclusions

No grants for domestic expenses such as childcare, overseas courses, fieldwork or travel, theatre, music, journalism or art, drama, sociology, youth work or sports.

Applications

In writing to the correspondent including a CV, income and expenses and total shortfall and two references (from course tutor and head of department). Applications are considered twice a year in March and October.

Helena Kennedy Foundation

£131,000 (125 grants)

Correspondent: Rachel Watters, Development and Fundraising Officer, Zenith House, 155 Curtain Road, London EC2A 3QE (020 7729 4584; email: enquires@hkf.org.uk; website: www.hkf.org.uk)

CC Number: 1074025

Eligibility

Students attending a further education college or sixth form in the UK who are progressing to university education and who may be disadvantaged in some way. Applicants must be intending to undertake a higher diploma or undergraduate degree for the first time.

Types of grants

One-off bursaries of up to £1,500. There are a large number of specific awards, see the website for details.

Annual grant total

In 2010/11 the foundation had assets of £353,000 an income of £237,000 and awarded bursaries totalling £131,000.

Exclusions

Anyone who has already undertaken a higher education course.

Applications

Applicants are encouraged to visit the website, or send a short email to enquire about eligibility criteria. The trust is usually only open to applications January to March.

Other information

The charity also provides mentoring, information and advice, specialist and practical support and work experience opportunities.

The Leathersellers' Company
See entry on page 96

The Sidney Perry Foundation

£129,000 (156 grants)

Correspondent: L A Owens, PO Box 2924, Faringdon SN7 7YJ

CC Number: 313758

Eligibility

The trust aims primarily to help first degree students. Students must be younger than 35 when the course starts. Eligible foreign students studying in Britain can also apply. Postgraduates may also receive support (see under Types of grants).

Types of grants

One-off and recurrent grants for around £800 with the maximum award of £1,200 reserved for exceptional cases. Grants are usually towards books and equipment/instruments. Applicants can reapply in further years.

Distance learning, correspondence, part-time and short-term courses may be considered according to circumstances, in particular Open University engineering courses.

Annual grant total

In 2010/11 the foundation made grants to individuals totalling £129,000. This consisted of 134 basic grants including thirty 'super grants' for £1,000 to £1,2000, fifteen awards of £1,000 to young musicians, three awards of £3,000 to vocal students of the Guildhall School of Music and four awards totalling £3,000 to Open University Students studying engineering

Exclusions

The foundation is unable to assist:

- The first year of a (three or four year) first degree save in exceptional circumstances
- Medical students during their first year if Medicine is their second degree. Medical students during elective periods and intercalated courses
- Second degree courses where the grade in the first is lower than a 2:1 save in exceptional circumstances
- Second degree courses or other postgraduate study unrelated to the first unless they are a necessary part of professional training (e.g. medicine, dentistry)
- Expeditions overseas, emergency funding or clearance of existing debts
- Students over the age of 35 years when their course of study commences save in the most exceptional circumstances
- A-level and GCSE examinations. Students on Access, ESOL, HNC, HND, BTEC, GNVQ and NVQ
- Levels 1–4 and Foundation courses nor, except in exceptional circumstances, those with LEA/SAAS funding
- Distance learning, correspondence, part-time and short-term courses may be considered according to circumstances and in particular Open University engineering courses

Applications

Applications can be made at any time on official forms available from the correspondent and directly by the individual. Incomplete forms will be disregarded. Enclosure of an sae would be appreciated. 'Students are expected to have a confirmed placement at college and have the bulk of their funding before approaching the foundation. We will not contact referees on an applicant's behalf: candidates should ensure an academic reference (not a photocopy) is included'. Previous beneficiaries of grants should include details of the previous grant i.e. amount of grant, year received and grant number.

Other information

The foundation is unable to deal with student debt or financial problems needing a speedy resolution.

Thornton-Smith and Plevins Trust
See entry on page 27

Williamson Memorial Trust

£4,000

Correspondent: Colin Williamson, 6 Windmill Close, Ashington, Pulborough, West Sussex RH20 3LG (01903 893649)

Trustees: Colin Williamson; Dr Roger Williamson; John Clark; Philip Cutts.

CC Number: 268782

Eligibility

Students on first degree courses.

Types of grants

Grants of not more than £200 a year are made for help with books, fees, living expenses and study or travel abroad. Grants limited to £200 a year to overseas students; the trust is not able to make a more significant contribution towards the higher fees and living expenses that overseas student incur.

Annual grant total

In 2010/11 the trust had both an income and total expenditure of £9,000. Grants are made for education and welfare purposes.

Exclusions

Grants are not made for postgraduate study.

Applications

Due to a reduction of its funds and the instability of its income, the trust regrets that very few new applications will be considered to ensure it can meet its existing commitments. Support will generally only be given to cases known personally to the trustees and to those individuals the trust has existing commitments with.

Gap year/ voluntary work overseas

The Melanie Akroyd Trust

£5,000

Correspondent: Jonny Bealby, 3A Thorpebank Road, London W12 0PG (07787 521277; email: jonnybealby@ hotmail.com)

Trustees: Ann Llewellyn; Nicola Joseph; Robert Tasher; Jonny Bealby.

CC Number: 1001499

Eligibility

Young people aged 22 to 27 living in the UK.

Types of grants

Travel scholarships for educational or personal development purposes, up to a maximum of £1,500. The applicant must begin their journey alone and will have to demonstrate that (i) they have been earning their own living for some years, (ii) that there are no financial resources available to them from their family which could go towards the trip, and (iii) that they have earned and saved funds for the trip which are equal to the funds which the trust will provide. Candidates' trips must cover a period of at least six months and must be in developing countries.

Annual grant total

In 2010/11 the trust had an income of £14,000 and an expenditure of £5,800.

Applications

This trust does not accept unsolicited applications.

The Alchemy Foundation

£3,200

Correspondent: R Stilgoe, Trevereux Manor, Limpsfield Chart, Oxted, Surrey RH8 0TL (01883 730600; fax: 01883 730800)

Trustees: Dr Jemima Stilgoe; Holly Stilgoe; Jack Stilgoe; Rufus Stilgoe; Richard Stilgoe; Alexander Armitage; Andrew Murison; Annabel Stilgoe; Esther Rantzen; Joseph Stilgoe; Antoun Elias.

CC Number: 292500

Eligibility

Enterprising individuals in need in the UK.

Types of grants

Grants are made to support voluntary work overseas.

Annual grant total

In 2010/11 the trust had assets of £2.4 million and an income of £335,000. Approximately £6,500 was given in grants to individuals for relief-in-need and educational purposes, distributed through other charities.

Applications

In writing to the correspondent. Applications from individuals will only be considered if they are for worthwhile and enterprising voluntary work by young people in the developing world under the auspices of Raleigh International or The Project Trust.

Other information

The trust gives grants mostly to organisations, namely overseas development, social welfare and disability projects.

John Allatt's Educational Foundation
See entry on page 234

Lady Allen of Hurtwood Memorial Trust
See entry on page 45

The Alvechurch Grammar School Endowment
See entry on page 251

Angus Educational Trust
See entry on page 128

The Arrol Trust

£25,000

Correspondent: C S Kennedy, Lindsays, Caledonian Exchange, 19a Canning Street, Edinburgh EH3 8HE (01312 291212)

SC Number: SC020983

Eligibility

Young people aged 16 to 25. Priority is given to those who have physical or mental disabilities and those in need.

Types of grants

Grants are given to people wishing to broaden their horizons through travel in the UK or overseas for gap years and educational trips.

Annual grant total

In 2010/11 the trust had an income of £29,000.

Exclusions

No grants are made for course fees or other educational expenses.

Applications

Application forms may be obtained from the correspondent and must be supported by a reference from the applicant's teacher or employer. Applicants must be willing to attend an interview with the trustees and be willing to report back on the completion of their trip.

The Barnabas Trust
See entry on page 103

Jim Bishop Memorial Fund

£2,000

Correspondent: Miss M A Brown, Fund Secretary, c/o Young Explorers Trust, 10 Larch Close, Bingham, Nottinghamshire NG13 8GW (email: m.brown@dayncourt.notts.sch.uk; website: www.theyet.org)

Trustees: Christopher Blessington; Robert Schroter; Graham Derrick; Edward Grey.

CC Number: 1006211

Eligibility

People under 19 who wish to participate in any adventure activity.

Types of grants

Grants of between £50 and £150. Recent grants have been given to enable participation in expeditions abroad, at sea and in the UK.

Annual grant total

Around £2,000.

Exclusions

University expeditions will not be supported.

Applications

On a form available from the correspondent or to download from the Young Explorers' Trust website. Applications should include an sae and be submitted by the end of March.

The Challenger Trust Bursary Scheme

£5,700 (13 grants)

Correspondent: Sebastian Hare, Challenger Trust, The Lido Centre, 63 Mattock Lane, London W13 9LA (020 8133 6457; email: info@challengertrust.org; website: www.challengertrust.org)

Trustees: Max Bilsborough; Charles Rigby; Jeremy Witcher; Graeme Guthrie.

CC Number: 1068226

Eligibility

Young people taking part in overseas expeditions whose family or financial circumstances have changed dramatically, preventing them from continuing with their project.

Types of grants

'The Trust offers bursaries to young people who have signed up for an overseas expedition experience and subsequently suffer a significant change in family circumstances and finances which will prevent them from continuing with this opportunity. These may arise from parental separation, job loss, illness or bereavement. Preference is given to those who demonstrate their determination to succeed despite such adversity'

Previously the trust has supported young people taking in part in expeditions with the British Schools Exploring Society, World Challenge and Yorkshire Schools Exploring Society. Applications will be considered on behalf of any approved organisation that promotes personal development through outdoor education.

Annual grant total

In 2010/11 the trust had assets of £101,000, an income of £148,000 and gave 13 grants to young people totalling £5,700.

Applications

Applications are considered once a year at the end of May and successful applicants will be notified by mid-June. Application forms and guidelines can be downloaded from the trust's website.

The Church Burgesses Educational Foundation
See entry on page 169

Churchill University Scholarships Trust for Scotland

£20,000

Correspondent: Kenneth MacRae, McLeish Carswell, 6th floor, 45 Hope Street, Glasgow G2 6AE (01412 484134)

SC Number: SC013492

Eligibility

Students in Scotland.

Types of grants

Grants are given for one-off educational projects of benefit to the community, for example, medical electives or voluntary work overseas in a student's gap year or holiday.

Annual grant total

In 2010/11 the trust had an income of £21,000.

Exclusions

Grants are not made for any other educational needs, such as course fees, books or living expenses.

Applications

In writing to the correspondent.

The Cross Trust
See entry on page 120

Crowthorne Trust

£10,000

Correspondent: John Ferns, 55 Manor Road, Tongham, Farnham GU10 1BA (01252 319788; email: CMSTGP@wellingtoncollege.org.uk)

Trustees: James Finnie; Justin Yeldham; Robin Dyer; Anthony Seldon; Lisa Cornwell; Chris Potter; Ian Frayne; Tim Novis.

CC Number: 277491

Eligibility

People in need who live in the parishes of Crowthorne, Finchampstead, Sandhurst and Wokingham Without, all in Berkshire. Preference is given to applicants under 25.

Types of grants

Grants are towards the spiritual, moral, mental and physical well-being of recipients. Previously grants have been awarded for a wide range of overseas gap year projects, outward bound expeditions and school trips.

Annual grant total

The trust awards grants usually totalling around £10,000 a year to individuals.

Applications

In writing to the correspondent by downloading the form on the website or submitting it online. Meetings are held three times a year, although in urgent cases applications can be considered between meetings.

Other information

The trust also gives £5,000 a year to local youth organisations.

Frank Denning Memorial Charity
See entry on page 347

Reg Gilbert International Youth Friendship Trust (GIFT)

£6,000 (18 grants)

Correspondent: The Secretary, 19 Church Street, Beckington, Frome, Somerset BA11 6TG (01373 830232; website: giftfriendshiptrust.org.uk)

Trustees: Peter Starkie; Hilary Daniel; Derek Trick; Peter Smith; Kenneth Bateson; David Gerhardt.

CC Number: 327307

Eligibility

UK residents who are aged 16 to 25 and are visiting a developing country on a trip lasting at least six weeks. Applicants must be unable to afford the cost, be planning to live with an indigenous family in the host country as an ordinary member of the family, and be aiming to develop friendship. The trust stresses that there must be an indigenous homestay element within the programme to be eligible for any funding.

Types of grants

The aim of the trust is to help with the personal development of young people by assisting them in gaining first-hand experience of a different culture, thereby developing friendships with, and an understanding of, people of that culture. The more applicants can show they will have a clear association with indigenous people, the more likely they are to get a bursary. Grants are for up to £500.

Annual grant total

In 2010/11 the trust had an income of £5,600 and an expenditure of £6,400.

Exclusions

No grants for proposals leading to academic or vocational qualifications.

Applications

Potential applicants should complete the eligibility questionnaire on the website in order to access the downloadable application form.

Applications are considered in November and June.

The Mary Grave Trust
See entry on page 184

Hazel's Footprints

£40,000

Correspondent: The Clerk, Legerwood, Earlston, Berwickshire TD4 6AS (01896 849677; fax: 01896 849677; email: info@hazelsfootprints.org; website: www.hazelsfootprints.org)

SC Number: SC036069

Eligibility

People from the UK and Europe who want to take part in voluntary projects abroad. Proposed projects must be of an educational nature, i.e. teaching, community development work, and should last no less than six months.

Types of grants

The trust gives funding to people of any age who want to take part in voluntary work abroad but are struggling to cover the whole costs themselves.

Annual grant total

In 2010/11 the trust had an income of £109,000. Expenditure in grants can vary from year to year, and the trust aims to help on average 15 to 20 individuals per year.

Applications

On a form available to download from the website. Grants are awarded three times a year in November, early May and June. Applications can be considered throughout the year; however grants are usually awarded on a mostly first-come-first-served basis.

Other information

The trust also makes annual donations to the Otjikondo village school in Namibia and other educational establishments in need in developing countries.

The Hertfordshire Educational Foundation
See entry on page 304

The Holywood Trust
See entry on page 135

The Leadership Trust Foundation

£0

Correspondent: Robert Noble, The Leadership Trust, Weston Under Penyard, Ross-on-Wye, Herefordshire HR9 7YH (01989 767667; email: enquiries@leadership.org.uk; website: www.leadership.org.uk)

Trustees: Simon Bentley; Michael Aiken; W. Colacicchi; Tim Cross.

CC Number: 1063916

Eligibility

Young people, primarily those aged 16 to 25, living within 25 miles of the trust's office who are undertaking activities designed to enhance their personal development and leadership training with an established and recognised charity.

Types of grants

Bursaries to enable individuals from the charitable sector to undertake training in leadership development. Grants are given to individuals embarking on activities with Raleigh International, Duke of Edinburgh's Award, GAP, British Schools Expedition Society, Jubilee Sailing Trust, Global Young Leaders Conference and so on.

Annual grant total

In 2010 the foundation had assets of £4.4 million and an income of £2.8 million. Bursaries totalled £101,000, directly to the foundation's training company to allow 33 individuals to attend programmes. No small grants were awarded in the year.

Applications

Initially in writing to the correspondent, who will then send an application form to relevant applicants. Completed forms are considered quarterly.

Roger and Miriam Pilkington Charitable Trust

£2,500 (4 grants)

Correspondent: Jane Fagan, c/o Brabners Chaffe Street, Horton House, Exchange Flags, Liverpool L2 2ET (01516 003000)

Trustees: Cynthia Rumboll; Robin Rumboll; Julia Chapman; Jack Worrall; Robin Dupre.

CC Number: 261804

Eligibility

One-off grants are given to 'enterprising' people aged 16 to 25, particularly those who are undertaking imaginative projects abroad which could be said to broaden horizons, giving them experiences which they may not otherwise have; increase awareness of other cultures and ways of living; or help them understand something of social problems outside their immediate environment. Suitable projects include British Schools Exploring Society, Raleigh International, Project T and Trek Aid.

Types of grants

Grants of £500 to £1,000.

Annual grant total

In 2010/11 the trust had an income of £32,000. Four grants to individuals were made totalling £2,500.

Exclusions

The trustees favour making awards for medical electives and VSO projects. The trustees do not take on responsibilities which are properly those of the education authorities. Long-term funding is not given.

Applications

In writing, directly by the individual to the correspondent at any time, for consideration in March and August. All grants are contingent on the applicant raising a significant proportion of the funds through their own efforts.

Other information

Grants are also made to schools.

The Prince Philip Trust Fund
See entry on page 285

Provincial/Walsh Trust for Bolton

£10,000

Correspondent: Joan Bohan, 237 Ainsworth Lane, Bolton BL2 2QQ

Trustees: Leslie Grant; Sandra Badland; Irene Simpson; David Porter; Jeremy Glover; Peter Steele.

CC Number: 222819

Eligibility

People who live in Bolton Metropolitan Borough.

Types of grants

Grants are mainly one-off and are for between £100 and £1,000. Grants are not made for relief-in-need, but are given to individuals towards character development and 'helping others', for example, Operation Raleigh, Health Projects Abroad.

Annual grant total

About £25,000 to organisations and individuals.

Exclusions

No grants to students or recent ex-students of Bolton School, building works, commercial ventures or for personal loans.

Applications

On a form available from the correspondent. Applications are usually considered in March/April and September/October and should be submitted at least two to four weeks before those meetings.

Other information

The trust also makes grants to organisations.

The Sir Philip Reckitt Educational Trust Fund

£31,000

Correspondent: The Trustees, Trust's principle address:, Rollits, Wilberforce Court, High Street, Hull HU1 1JY (email: spretrust@googlemail.com; website: www.spret.org)

Trustees: Martin Needler; John Ayre; John Lane; Philip Holt; Philip Strachan; Vincent Lachowycz; Glynis Witham.

CC Number: 529777

Eligibility

People in full-time education who live in Kingston upon Hull, the East Riding of Yorkshire, or the county of Norfolk.

Types of grants

Grants are given towards educational travel such as Raleigh International, working in the developing world, outward bound type courses and so on. Travel must be connected with the extracurricular projects of the course. Grants can also be used to help with residence and attendance at conferences, lectures and short educational courses.

Annual grant total

In 2011 the trust had assets of £871,000 and an income of £34,000. Grants totalled £31,000 with £13,000 given in Hull and East Riding of Yorkshire and £18,000 given in Norfolk.

Exclusions

Awards will not normally be made to persons under the age of 14 on the date of travel.

Applications

On a form available from the correspondent or the website along with a reference from the head of the institution of study or an employer or other suitable referee.

Other information

Contacts: Kingston upon Hull, the East Riding of Yorkshire – Rollits, Wilberforce Court, High Street, Hull HU1 1JY (email: hull@spret.org).

Norfolk – Mrs J. Pickering, 99 Yarmouth Road, Ellingham, Bungay NR35 2PH (email: jpickering@spretrust.freeserve.co.uk).

The Saint George's Trust

See entry on page 39

The Bassil Shippam and Alsford Charitable Trust

£6,800 (17 grants)

Correspondent: Iain MacLeod, Thomas Eggar, The Corn Exchange, Baffins Lane, Chichester, West Sussex PO19 1GE (01243 786111)

Trustees: Christopher Doman; John Shippam; Molly Hanwell; Susan Trayler; Richard Tayler; Stanley Young; Simon MacFarlane; Janet Bailey.

CC Number: 256996

Eligibility

Students in need who live in West Sussex.

Types of grants

One-off grants of £250 to £1,500 for projects undertaken voluntarily, such as gap year activities, for example, Operation Raleigh.

Annual grant total

In 2010/11 the trust had assets of £3.8 million and an income of £141,000. Grants were made to 17 individuals totalling £6,800.

Exclusions

No grants for expenses related to academic courses.

Applications

In writing to the correspondent, for consideration at any time. Applications should indicate the nature and location of the project and should give as much notice as possible.

W. W. Spooner Charitable Trust

£16,000

Correspondent: Michael Broughton, Tree Tops, Main Street, Hawksworth, Leeds LS20 8NX

Trustees: James Hill; John Priestley; Jonathan Wright; Julia McKiddie; Michael Broughton; Thomas Ramsden.

CC Number: 313653

Eligibility

Young people who are taking part in voluntary overseas projects and expeditions, with a preference for those living in Yorkshire – especially West Yorkshire.

Types of grants

One-off and recurrent grants towards voluntary work overseas.

Annual grant total

In 2010/11 the trust had assets of £1.7 million and an income of £67,000. 'charitable donations and grants' totalled £41,000. Previously around £16,000 was given in grants to individuals.

Applications

In writing to the correspondent by the end of March, July or October.

The Erik Sutherland Gap Year Trust

£1,000

Correspondent: Viki Sutherland, Erik's Gap Year Trust, Torren, Glencoe, Argyll, Scotland PH49 4HX (01855 81107; fax: 01855 811338; email: info@eriks-gap-year-trust.com; website: www.eriks-gap-year-trust.com)

Trustees: Norman Drummond; Jane Maclure; Louisa Gardiner; Andrew Sutherland.

SC Number: SC028293

Eligibility

Young people living in the UK

Types of grants

Grants for young people who wish to take a gap year or take part in voluntary work overseas before entering higher education. Loans are also available.

Annual grant total

In 2010/11 the trust had an income of £1,000. Several awards are given each year to individuals.

Applications

On a form available from the correspondent.

The Vandervell Foundation

£4,300 (3 grants)

Correspondent: Valerie Kaye, Administrator, Hampstead Town Hall Centre, 213 Haverstock Hill, London NW3 4QP (020 7435 7546)

Trustee: The Vandervell Foundation Ltd.

CC Number: 255651

Eligibility

Medical students and other gap year students.

Types of grants

One-off grants averaging £300 to £1,000 towards students taking medical electives and gap year projects.

Annual grant total

In 2010 the foundation had assets of £6.7 million and an income of £258,000. Three grants to individuals were made totalling £4,300.

Exclusions

Grants are not made where the foundation already makes a major grant directly to the organisation, such as Raleigh International.

Applications

In writing to the correspondent, enclosing a CV and a budget. Applications are reviewed every two months.

Other information

The foundation primarily makes grants to organisations (92 grants totalling £387,000 in 2010).

Warwick Apprenticing Charities

See entry on page 241

Illness and disability

Crohn's and Colitis UK

£1,400 (5 grants)

Correspondent: Julia Devereux, Personal Grants Fund Secretary, PO Box 334, St Albans, Herts AL1 2WA (01727 759654 or 01727 830038 (main switchboard); fax: 01727 759654; email: julia.devereux@nacc.org.uk; website: www.crohnsandcolitis.org.uk)

Trustees: John Stanley; Denise Cann; John Clarke; Martin Gay; Stuart Berliner; Tim Mutum; Kati Simpson; Michael Hilton; Peter Stewart; Deborah Hodges; Alan Thackrey.

CC Number: 1117148

Eligibility

People in need aged between 15 and 25, who have ulcerative colitis, Crohn's Disease or related inflammatory bowel diseases. Individuals must be in full or part time education and have been resident in the UK for at least six months.

Annual grant total

In 2011 the charity had assets of £2.3 million and an income of £2.8 million. There were five grants for education or training and 237 for welfare, altogether totalling £66,000.

Applications

On a form available from the correspondent or to download from the website. The form has two extra sections, one which should be completed by a doctor to confirm the individual's illness and one to be filled in by a social worker (or health visitor, district nurse or CAB advisor). Applications are considered every six to eight weeks.

Other information

Grants are also made for welfare purposes and to institutions for research. However, the association's main role is providing information and advice to people living with IBD.

The MFPA Trust Fund for the Training Of Handicapped Children in the Arts

£350

Correspondent: Tom Yendell, Trustee, 90 London Road, Holybourne, Alton, Hampshire GU34 4EL (01420 80560)

Trustees: Trevor Wells; Tom Yendell; Keith Jansz.

CC Number: 328151

Eligibility

Children with physical or mental disabilities living in the UK between the ages of 5 and 18.

Types of grants

One-off and recurrent grants towards participation in painting, music, or drama, for example, books, educational outings and school fees. The maximum grant available is £6,000.

Annual grant total

Grants to individuals are erratic, with £10,000 to £30,000 being given previously, but in 2010/11, £350.

Applications

In writing to the correspondent for consideration throughout the year. Applications can be made directly by the individual or through a third party such as their school, college or educational welfare agency. Applications should enclose a letter explaining their needs and a doctor's letter confirming disability.

Other information

The trust also gives grants to charities (£18,000 in 2010/11).

The Adam Millichip Foundation

£20,000

Correspondent: Paul Millichip, Trustee, 17 Boraston Drive, Burford, Tenbury Wells WR15 8AG (07866 424286; email: paul@adammillichipfoundation.org; website: www.adammillichipfoundation.org)

Trustees: Stuart Millichip; Mark Benbow; Mark Fish; Paul Millichip.

CC Number: 1138721

Eligibility

Disabled people in the UK who wish to participate in sports, with the aim of improving the quality of their lives.

Types of grants

Grants have previously been awarded for riding lessons; a specialist bike; ski lessons and a ski slope pass and swimming lessons.

Annual grant total

About £20,000 to individuals in 2011/12.

Exclusions

Grants cannot be awarded for competitive purposes.

Applications

There is a six stage application process which is begun on the website. Applications are processed on a first come first served basis and can take up to two months once all the information has been gathered.

Other information

This foundation was established in memory of Adam Millichip.

Richard Overall Trust

£3,000

Correspondent: Nicholas Overall, New Barn Cottage, Honey Lane, Selbourne, Alton GU34 3BY (01420 511175)

Trustees: Nicholas Overall; Barbara Overall; Michael Lee; Patrick Cuss; Richard Blair; Trevor Faris; William Marshal; Lincoln Small; Jeremy Davies.

CC Number: 1088640

Eligibility

Young people with disabilities participating in physical education.

Types of grants

Grants given according to need.

Annual grant total

About £3,000 per year.

Applications

In writing to the correspondent.

The Silverwood Trust

£10,000

Correspondent: John Shergold, Trustee, 35 Orchard Grove, New Milton, Hampshire BH25 6NZ

Trustees: Jean Shergold; John Shergold; Gary Bowes-Read; Diane Bowes-Read; J. Wentzel; Martyn Travers.

CC Number: 292372

Eligibility

Children and young people of school age with physical or learning disabilities.

Types of grants

One-off or small recurrent grants according to need. (Normally restricted to people known to the trustees.)

Annual grant total

In 2011 the trust had assets of £37,000 and an income of £50,000. Grants to individuals totalled £19,000 for welfare and education.

Exclusions

No grants for computers or school fees.

Applications

In writing to the correspondent.

The Snowdon Award Scheme

£153,000 (91 grants)

Correspondent: Paul Alexander, Unit 18, Oakhurst Business Park, Wilberforce Way, Southwater, West Sussex RH13 9RT (01403 732899; email: info@snowdonawardscheme.org.uk; website: www.snowdonawardscheme.org.uk)

Trustees: Stephen Bradshaw; Lord Snowdon; Viscount Linley; John Hannam; Peter Holland; Renny Leach; Richard Lansdown; Robert Edwards; Jane McLarty; Anji Hunter; Dan Norris; Sidney Hunt; Andrew Farquhar; Tanni Grey-Thompson; Simon Preece; Wendy Piatt; Amber Rudd; Colin Low; Frances von Hofmannsthal.

CC Number: 282754

Eligibility

Students with physical or sensory disabilities who are in or about to enter further or higher education or training in the UK and because of their disability have financial needs which are not met elsewhere.

Types of grants

Grants are given towards costs which cannot be met in full from statutory sources, including: human help such as sign language interpreters or people to take notes; computer equipment; adapted or additional accommodation; travel costs; mobility equipment; and other costs which relate solely to disability. Grants are normally between £250 and £2,000.

Annual grant total

In 2010/11 the scheme had assets of £560,000 and an income of £188,000. Grants were made to 91 students totalling £153,000.

Applications

Application forms are available from the trust's website, along with full guidance notes or by contacting the trust directly. Applications are also available as an MP3 file with a spoken application form. The closing date for completed applications is 31 May for consideration in July; late applications will be accepted until 31 August for consideration in October, funds permitting.

Other information

This scheme also provides mentoring support and advice to beneficiaries.

Student Disability Assistance Fund

£11,000

Correspondent: c/o Sandra Furmston, Administrative Secretary, BAHSHE Office, 35 Hazelwood Road, Bush Hill Park, Enfield EN1 1JG (email: s.furmston@mdx.ac.uk; website: www.bahshe.co.uk)

Trustees: Lisa Green; Daniel Hammersley; Alison James.

CC Number: 253984

Eligibility

Students engaged in a course of study, in any subject, at a higher or postgraduate level, who are affected by illness, disease, injury or physical infirmity. Priority will be given to those who are not eligible for funding from LEAs. Mature students can also be supported. The fund expects students to apply for the Disabled Students' Allowance before applying and preference is given to those who do not qualify for DSA.

Types of grants

One-off grants of up to £500 towards educational aids made necessary by the student's disability, for example special computer equipment, extra travel costs for those with mobility problems, cost of note-takers or signers and other special equipment.

Annual grant total

In 2010/11 the fund had an income of £9,200 and an expenditure of £12,000.

Exclusions

No funding for expenses incurred by all students including fees, living costs or books needed by all. No grants for medical treatment or equipment unless it is specific to study problems.

Applications

Eligible applicants are now asked to apply online. Students are expected to apply for Disabled Students Allowance before applying to the fund, and to note the outcome of this in their application. Deadlines for applications are 1 March, 1 June and 1 November each year.

Blindness

The Amber Trust

£96,000 (124 grants)

Correspondent: Roderic Hill, Chair, 19 Scarsdale Villas, London W8 6PT (020 7937 9567; email: info@ambertrust.org; website: www.ambertrust.org)

Trustees: Roderic Gordon Hill; Gavin Nicholas Tait; Michael David Finniston; Lucy Ann Heber-Percy; Isambard Henry

Sidley Panton Corbett; Elizabeth Rebecca Offord; George Adam Ocelford.

CC Number: 1050503

Eligibility

Children and young people (up to and including the age of 18) who are blind or partially sighted.

Types of grants

One-off and recurrent grants of up to one year to pay for music lessons, music therapy, musical instruments, music software, concert tickets or for travel to musical activities. After one year parents may apply again but using a re-application form which allows the trust to monitor the impact of their funding.

Annual grant total

In 2010/11 the trust held assets of £233,000 and had an income of £160,000 primarily from general donations. Grants to 124 children totalled £96,000.

Exclusions

No retrospective grants.

Applications

On an application form available to download from the trust website. Applications should be completed by the child's parents or carers, but can be prepared by a support worker or teacher. Applications for instruments or software should include prices and supplier details. Applications for lessons or music therapy sessions must include details of the teacher's or therapists qualifications, experience and CRB clearance.

Trustees meet three times a year in March, July and November. Applications should be received by the trust by the month preceding the meeting to be considered. Receipt of applications will be acknowledged in writing.

Parents or carers re-applying must use a different re-application form, also available on the website.

Elizabeth Eagle-Bott Memorial Awards

£28,000

Correspondent: Music Advisory Service, RNIB, 105 Judd Street, London WC1H 9NE (020 7391 8873; email: mas@rnib.org.uk; website: www.rnib.org. uk)

Trustee: RNIB.

Eligibility

Applicants must be:
- Registered as sight impaired or seriously sight impaired, and
- A UK citizen

Preference is given to classical musicians, especially organists.

Types of grants

Grants of up to £10,000 to blind or partially sighted musicians, for musical study, projects and events for the benefit of local, national and international communities; and third parties supporting blind or partially sighted musicians in their music making. Recent grants have been made for instrument and vocal tuition; tuition fees for a music course; transcriber and reader costs; purchasing music technology; costs associated with staging concerts; and developing accessible and assistive music technology.

Annual grant total

In 2010/11 the fund held assets of £92,000 and had an income of £25,000. Expenditure totalled £31,000.

Applications

Application forms are available by contacting RNIB's music advisory service and should be submitted by email by 31 March each year. Applications are assessed in May although the grants panel may meet more than once a year to consider exceptional applications. Interview and audition expenses will be met by the fund. Applicants may receive up to three successful bids (each in a different year). The award may be used within or outside the UK.

Gardner's Trust for the Blind

£14,000

Correspondent: Angela Stewart, 117 Charterhouse Street, London EC1M 6AA (020 7253 3757)

Trustees: Viscount Gough; D. R. Beardsley; R. Forster; J. W. Hawkins; S. C. Jones.

CC Number: 207233

Eligibility

Registered blind or partially-sighted people who live in the UK.

Types of grants

Grants are mainly for computer equipment, music equipment and course fees.

Annual grant total

In 2010/11 the trust had assets of £2.8 million and an income of £87,000. Education and trade grants totalled £14,000 and music grants £50.

Exclusions

No grants for loan repayments.

Applications

In writing to the correspondent. Applications can be submitted either directly by the individual or by a third party, but they must also be supported by a third party who can confirm the disability and that the grant is needed. They are considered in March, June, September and December and should be submitted at least three weeks before the meeting.

Other information

The trust also gives grants for welfare purposes and pensions.

The Webster and Davidson Mortification for the Blind

£8,000

Correspondent: N Barclay, Trust Agent, Thorntons Law LLP, Whitehall House, 33 Yeaman Shore, Dundee DD1 4BJ (email: nbarclay@thorntons-law.co.uk; website: www.thorntons-law.co.uk/ Services/PrivateClient/Trusts/Webster_ and_Davidson_Mortification_for_the_ Blind.asp)

SC Number: SC004920

Eligibility

People who are blind or partially sighted studying music at secondary school, or at further or higher education. Applicants must be resident or normally resident in Britain. Preference will be given to those living in Dundee, Tayside or Scotland.

Types of grants

Grants of around £1,000 to support the learning and appreciation of music and for specific musical purposes. Bursaries are tenable for one year but may be renewable.

Annual grant total

About £6,000 to £7,000 a year.

Exclusions

The bursary is not intended to take the place of or supplement Scottish Students' Allowances or other awards derived from public funds.

Applications

Application and referee forms (also available in Braille) are available from the correspondent or to download from the website, to be submitted by 31 March each year.

Cancer

CLIC Sargent (formerly Sargent Cancer Care for Children)

£6,000

Correspondent: Grants Department, Griffin House, 161 Hammersmith Road,

London W6 8SG (020 8752 2800; website: www.clicsargent.org.uk)

Trustees: Daphne Pullen; Rachel Billsberry-Grass; Tim Holley; Meriel Jenney; Henry Kenyon; Jonathan Plumtree; Chris Wathen; Dr Hamish Wallace; Alison Arnfield; Keith Wexford.

CC Number: 1085616

Eligibility

Children and young people under the age of 24 living in the UK who have cancer or have been under treatment in the past six months.

Types of grants

Grants of up to £170 to alleviate crises or help with the quality of life of the child and/or family during treatment. Exceptional grants of up to £400 may be issued where no other support is available. Community Support Grants and Compassionate Grants are also available to some.

Annual grant total

Previously the charity made 25 educational grants totalling £6,000. Grants are also made for welfare purposes.

Applications

On a form, to be completed by the CLIC Sargent Care Professional working with the family.

Other information

The charity also provides respite holidays. Details of grants holidays and other services are available from the CLIC Sargent Care Professional.

Cystic Fibrosis

The James Levy Memorial Trust

£55,000

Correspondent: Peter Levy, Pegasus House, 37/43 Sackville Street, London W1S 3DL (020 7333 8118; email: elizabeth.neville@shaftesbury.co.uk; website: www.cftrust.org.uk/aboutus/what_we_do/support/welfaregrants)

Trustee: The Cystic Fibrosis Trust.

CC Number: 1079049

Eligibility

18–25 year olds with cystic fibrosis.

Types of grants

Grants for tuition fees, examination fees and living expenses.

Annual grant total

In 2010/11 the trust had assets of £41,000 and an income of £38,000. Expenditure totalled £58,000.

Applications

In writing to the correspondent by post- or email. The deadline for applications is 31 March and awards are decided in mid-June.

Deafness

The Peter Greenwood Memorial Trust for Deaf People

£2,500

Correspondent: Nicola Storey, Bursary Secretary, Westbrook Building, Great Horton Road, Bradford BD7 1AY (01274 436414 (voice) 01274 433223 (text); email: davemarshall@blueyonder.co.uk; website: www.pgmtrust.org.uk)

Trustees: Peter Harrison; Pat Anderson; Louise Hart; David Marshall; Clive Robinson; Nicola Storey.

CC Number: 327262

Eligibility

Post-school (over 16) students living in England and Wales who are deaf or whose hearing is impaired and who live in England and Wales. Grants are tenable for any higher or further education course or training and mature students and postgraduates can also be supported.

Types of grants

Grants of under £200 towards books, videos, software and equipment than cannot be provided from other sources.

Annual grant total

Around £2,000 to £3,000 is distributed in grants annually

Applications

On a form available from the correspondent, to be received before 25 September (check the website for the closing date), together with a letter from a sponsor who can verify the applicant's deafness and need. The sponsor must be someone who knows the applicant well and works with them professionally such as a lecturer, teacher, social worker or doctor. Late applications will not be considered.

Other information

Applicants are requested to ask their LEA for assistance before contacting the trust as they often offer special help to deaf students.

Dyslexia

Dyslexia Action

£200,000 (403 grants)

Correspondent: The Learning Fund Manager, Park House, Wick Road, Egham, Surrey TW20 0HH (01784 222300; fax: 01784 222333; email: info@dyslexiaaction.org.uk; website: www.dyslexiaaction.org.uk)

Trustees: Anna Taylor; Lawrence Bailey; Judith Bloomer; Anneli Collins; Judy Baker; Brian Patman; Stanley Levin; Richard Green.

CC Number: 268502

Eligibility

Children, young people and adults living in England, Wales and Scotland who have dyslexia or literacy difficulties and are from families on a low income.

Types of grants

Grants are made from the learning fund for specific periods of tuition based on educational needs related to dyslexia and literacy difficulties. Grants for one term's tuition are for approximately £400, totalling £2,400 for six term's tuition. A contribution from the individual or their family is required at a minimum of £5 per week.

The majority of bursary-funded pupils attend the nationwide centres of Dyslexia Action for one and a half or two hours multi-sensory tuition each week during the academic year.

Annual grant total

In 2010/11 the trust had assets of £1.7 million and an income of £8.2 million. The fund provided support for 403 children during the year and grants have previously totalled £200,000.

Exclusions

Applicants from families where joint annual income is in excess of £22,000 will not be considered without evidence of exceptional circumstances.

Applications

In writing via the Dyslexia Action Centre at which the applicant wishes to have tuition. Applications are considered by the Learning Fund Allocations Committee three times a year (one meeting each academic term). Grants are awarded on the basis of educational need. Applicants for tuition grants should indicate family income and severity of dyslexia – a full educational psychologist's assessment is required.

Note that whilst a grant is awarded to an individual, the payment of fees for tuition is made directly to the Dyslexia Action centre where the tuition will take place.

Meningitis

Meningitis Trust

£104,000

Correspondent: Financial Grants Officer, Fern House, Bath Road, Stroud GL5 3TJ (01453 769043; fax: 01453 768001; email: info@meningitis-trust. org; website: www.meningitis-trust.org)

Trustees: Mr A. Irvine; Miss G. Noble; Mr M. Wolfe; Ms B. McGhie; Mr R. Johnson; Mr L. Green; Mr E. Wilson; Mr J. Kilmister; Mr R. Greenhalgh; Mr M. Hall; Mr P. Johnson; Prof. K. Cartwright.

CC Number: 803016

Eligibility

People in need who have meningitis or who are disabled as a result of meningitis.

Types of grants

One-off and recurrent grants are given towards equipment, re-education and special training, such as sign language lessons.

Annual grant total

In 2010/11 the trust had assets totalling £1.6 million and an income of £3.2 million. Grants for educational and welfare purposes were made to 151 families totalling £208,000.

Applications

On a form available from the correspondent or downloaded from the website, where criteria is also posted. An initial telephone call to the grants financial officer on 01453 769043 or the 24-hour helpline on 0800 028 1828 to discuss the application process is welcomed. Applications should be submitted through a third party and are reviewed on a monthly basis.

Other information

The trust runs a 'family day' for children who have meningitis and their families. The day includes arts, crafts and music for children and gives parents an opportunity to meet the trust's staff and other families. The trust also supports a range of professional counselling, home visits, therapy and information services. The trust has an informative website.

Renal

The British Kidney Patient Association

£321,000

Correspondent: Susan Lee, 3 The Windmills, St Mary's Close, Turk Street, Alton GU34 1EF (01420 541424; fax: 01420 89438; email: info@britishkidney-pa.co.uk; website: www.britishkidney-pa.co.uk)

Trustees: David Oliveira; Chris Rudge; Sally Taber; Robin Eady; Richard Chapman Jones; Marcelle De Sousa; Margaret Mitchell; Kathleen Shipton; David Sawyer; Lesley Rees; Sandra Verkuyten.

CC Number: 270288

Eligibility

Kidney patients and their families on low incomes, patients about to start dialysis, and those within six months of having had a transplant and other patients whose renal condition is having a serious impact on their health and quality of life.

Types of grants

Grants to help with the cost of books and materials, computers, board and lodgings, university and college fees and other expenses involved with educational and job opportunities.

Annual grant total

In 2011 the trust had an income of £2.6 million and an expenditure of £3.8 million, including £642,000 in patient grants for both educational and welfare purposes.

Exclusions

The association will not pay loans, court fines or bills already paid.

Applications

Via a kidney unit social worker or a member of the kidney care team on a form available from the correspondent, or to download from the BKPA website. Applications are considered on an ongoing basis.

Other information

The trust also makes grants to hospitals and supports the Ronald McDonald Houses at the Alder Hey Children's Hospital, Liverpool, Bristol Royal Hospital for Children, Evelina Children's Hospital, London and the Royal Hospital for Sick Children, Yorkhill which provide support for the families of young renal patients attending the units at these hospitals.

They also fund non-laboratory research and provide support services, information and advice to kidney patients, amongst other projects.

Independent and boarding schools

The Athlone Trust

£10,000

Correspondent: Peter Canney, Stoakes Cottage, Hastingleigh, Ashford, Kent TN25 5HG (01233 750216; email: peter.canney1@btinternet.com)

Trustees: David King-Farlow; Anita Loring; Jacqueline Barrow; Peter Canney; Mohaia Amin; Matthew Smallwood.

CC Number: 277065

Eligibility

Adopted children under the age of 18 who are in need.

Types of grants

The trust gives grants for school fees, but not for people at college or university. Occasionally one-off grants are given to help with the cost of education essentials for schoolchildren.

Annual grant total

In 2011 the trust had an income of £16,000 and an expenditure of £12,000.

Applications

In writing to the correspondent. Applications should be submitted by the applicant's parent/guardian and are usually considered in May and November.

Other information

Occasionally the trust will consider people who are 19 years old providing they are still at school.

The BMTA Trust Ltd

£91,000 (90 grants)

Correspondent: Carol Wildig, 4 Oak Way, Ashtead, Surrey KT21 1LG (01372 210124; email: bmtatrust@yahoo.co.uk)

Trustees: S. G. M. Caffyn; A. Pearson; P. N. Guy; Susanne Croucher; David Evans.

CC Number: 273978

Eligibility

Children aged 13 to 16 who are already attending an independent school with a preference for those whose families are connected with the motor industry. Children in exceptional circumstances of social need are occasionally supported to begin attending an independent or boarding school.

Types of grants

Short-term grants of a maximum of two years at £500 a term to enable children to complete their current stage of schooling when families have suffered unforeseen financial difficulties. Help is given for children attending fee-paying schools.

Annual grant total

In 2010/11 the trust has assets of £4.3 million and an income of £166,000. Educational grants to individuals totalled £91,000.

Applications

By email, letter or phone call to the correspondent.

Other information

£16,000 was also given to individuals for welfare purposes.

Buttle UK – School Fees Grants Scheme

£772,000 (327 grants)

Correspondent: Alan Cox, Audley House, 13 Palace Street, London SW1E 5HX (020 7798 6227; email: info@buttleuk.org; website: www.buttleuk.org)

Trustees: David Anderson; Elizabeth Stearns; Keith Mullins; Richard Buttle; Stephen Fielding; Gordon Anderson; Clare Montagu; Trevor Reaney; Dominic Vallely; Julia Ogilvy.

CC Number: 313007

Eligibility

Children and young people with acute needs that cannot in practice be met within the state education system. The following groups are eligible to apply: adopted children and young people; children and young people cared for by grandparents, other relatives or friends; children and young people from single parent families; children and young people with two carers, where one is severely incapacitated through illness or disability, or is terminally ill. In the majority of cases, help is given during the secondary phase of education.

Types of grants

Funding for places within a UK boarding or independent day school. Support can be given either for boarding fees, or for independent day fees.

Annual grant total

In 2010/11 this scheme gave £772,000 in 327 grants to 295 children. Of these, 94 were for new applicants, eight of whom were adopted children.

Exclusions

The trust does not assist: children or young people who are looked after by a local authority or other statutory body;

where a school has been chosen because of special facilities for a learning or developmental difficulty; where needs could be met within the state day system; children or young people who do not have settled status in the UK or who are normally resident abroad; or children or young people whose parental preference is for a particular type of education.

Applications

In writing, through a statutory agency or voluntary organisation that is capable of assessing the needs of the child and that can also administer a grant on behalf of the trust; where no such organisation exists, the trust will discuss alternative arrangements. Applications should include the facts of the case, outlining how the applicant meets the criteria, and including details of the health, emotional, social or family difficulties that mean the child/young person cannot be educated at a state day school. Eligible applicants will be sent an application form.

Contact details for applicants resident in:

England: Audley House, 13 Palace Street, London SW1E 5HX, info@buttleuk.org, 020 7828 7311

Scotland: PO Box 5075, Glasgow G78 4WA, scotland@buttleuk.org, 01505 850437

Wales: PO Box 224, Caerphilly CF83 9EE, wales@buttleuk.org, 01633 440052

Northern Ireland: PO Box 484, Belfast BT6 0YA, nireland@buttleuk.org, 02890 641164

Further information is available on the website.

Other information

The trust was founded by the Revd W F Buttle in 1953. Grants are also made through other schemes, to students and trainees and for welfare purposes.

The Emmott Foundation Ltd

£392,000 (111 grants)

Correspondent: Mr and Mrs Spillane, Education Officers, 136 Browns Lane, Stanton-on-the-Wolds, Nottinghamshire NG12 5BN (01159 376526; email: emmottfoundation@btinternet.com)

Trustees: Deborah Jane Forbes; Gillian Hylson-Smith; Prof. John Barry Dent; Richard Charles Dick; Timothy Edwin Paul Stevenson; Prof. Roger Ainsworth.

CC Number: 209033

Eligibility

The pupils' parents or guardians will no longer be able to meet their planned financial commitments for education at the school currently attended as a result of a sudden or unexpected family crisis such as death, accident, severe illness, divorce, desertion or loss of employment.

Grants are made only where the school is willing to make a significant contribution to the fees.

The pupils will normally have high academic achievement (a majority of actual or predicted A*s or As at GCSE). In exceptional cases, where need is demonstrably great, the trustees will consider applicants from those with lower grades. Consideration will also be given to cases where there is a major educational, social or pastoral problem.

Types of grants

Grants are for Sixth Form only. Their purpose is to enable pupils to enter or remain in the Sixth Form in their present school. The grants help only with basic fees in fee-paying schools (including state boarding schools), not with incidental expenses, music lessons, travel, books, expeditions etc. Grants are usually of between £500 and £1,500 per term, paid directly to the school at the start of each Sixth Form term.

Annual grant total

In 2010/11 the foundation held assets of £8.3 million and had an income of £541,000. Direct support to 83 individuals for sixth-form fee assistance amounted to £246,000. In 2011/12 111 grants were made totalling £392,000.

Applications

Application forms are sent to parents or guardians if there is the possibility of a grant being made. The trustees meet in March and June to consider applications.

Other information

The trust also gives annual grants to organisations (£9,000 in 2010/11).

The Fishmongers' Company's Charitable Trust

£33,000

Correspondent: The Clerk, Fishmongers' Hall, London Bridge, London EC4R 9EL (020 7626 3531; fax: 020 7929 1389; email: clerk@fishhall.co.uk; website: www.fishhall.co.uk)

Trustee: Worshipful Company of Fishmongers.

CC Number: 263690

Eligibility

Children/young people up to 19 years of age in need of a sum of money to complete schooling. Preference is given to children of single-parent families and/or those with a learning difficulty or disability, or those who come from a disadvantaged or unstable family background. Preference is also given to those studying fishery related education.

Types of grants

Small, one-off grants to assist in cases of short-term need. The company gives assistance with school fees. The maximum grant is £1,800.

Annual grant total

In 2011 the company had assets of £17 million, an income of £933,000 and gave £1,400 for general education grants to individuals and £32,000 in grants to individuals for fishery related education.

Applications

On a form available from the correspondent, to be submitted directly by the individual or by the parent or guardian for those under 18.

Other information

The company also gives to organisations for welfare, environment and heritage causes and administers Gresham's School in Norfolk, a fee-paying public school.

IAPS Charitable Trust

Correspondent: Richard Flower, 11 Waterloo Place, Warwick Street, Leamington Spa CV32 5LA (07818 217327)

Trustees: Richard Tovey; Edward Bradby; Charles Abram; Kevin Douglas; Joanna Pardon; David Hanson; Richard Flower.

CC Number: 1143241

Eligibility

People up to the age of 18 in the UK and teachers. Preference is given to members and former members of the Independent Association of Prep Schools (IAPS) and their dependents.

Types of grants

Grants are available to support children's education and also to teachers for training and research.

Annual grant total

This trust is newly registered so no financial information is available.

Applications

In writing to the correspondent.

Other information

The trust also gives welfare grants to members and former members of the Independent Association of Prep Schools (IAPS) and their dependents.

The Lloyd Foundation

£100,000 (60 grants)

Correspondent: Margaret Fairway, Fairway, Round Oak View, Tillington, Herefordshire HR4 8EQ (01432 760409; email: lloymit@borderoffice.net)

Trustees: Joan Caesar; Margaret Swinley; Arthur Pont; Brian Howes; Hilary Dibble; Soloman Green; David Taylor; Margaret McIntosh; Andrew Mackay; Valerie Pike.

CC Number: 314203

Eligibility

The children (between 5 and 25 years old) of British citizens where the family are necessarily living/working overseas.

Types of grants

Grants ranging between £300 and £3,000 a year to enable such children to attend the nearest English-medium school. Where no such school exists the foundation may give some help with fees for a school in the UK. Grants for schoolchildren, further/higher education and special educational needs are for educational expenses, such as fees, books, equipment and living expenses.

Annual grant total

In 2010/11 the foundation had assets of £2.7 million and an income of £132,000 and gave awards totalling £100,000 to 60 beneficiaries.

Exclusions

No help can be given for children under the age of five or for those taking postgraduate courses.

Applications

On a form available from the correspondent, to be submitted directly by the individual or through a third party. Applications are considered quarterly.

The McAlpine Educational Endowments Ltd

£100,000

Correspondent: Brian Arter, Eaton Court, Maylands Avenue, Hemel Hempstead, Hertfordshire HP2 7TR (01442 233444)

Trustees: Andrew McAlpine; Kenneth McAlpine; Brian Arter.

CC Number: 313156

Eligibility

Schoolchildren aged 13 to 18 who are in need.

Types of grants

Grants of up to £1,800 a year, mainly towards the cost of independent school fees for children of academic ability, sound character and leadership potential who, for reasons of financial hardship, would otherwise have to leave the school. Grants are paid each term while the child is at school (subject to an annual review) and are limited to children attending ten schools selected by the trustees.

Annual grant total

Income has increased steadily in recent years, culminating in an expenditure of £104,000 in 2010/11 despite having an income of £4,000.

Exclusions

There are no grants for students at college or university, nor for people at specialist schools (such as ballet or music schools, or schools for children with learning difficulties).

Applications

In writing to the correspondent. Applications must be submitted through one of the ten schools where applicants are supported by the trust but, because of the long-term nature of the trust's commitments, very few new grants can be considered each year. Applications are considered during the summer before the new academic year. A list of the schools involved is available from the correspondent.

The Ogden Trust

£618,000 (68 grants)

Correspondent: Tim Simmons, Chief Executive, Hughes Hall, Wollaston Road, Cambridge CB1 2EW (01223 518164; email: office@ogdentrust.com; website: www.ogdentrust.com)

Trustees: Peter Ogden; Cameron Ogden; Edward Ogden; Tiffany Ogden; Lady Ogden.

CC Number: 37570

Eligibility

Academically gifted young people in the areas of science and maths who have previously been educated in the state sector and who wish to attend a selection of independent secondary schools at sixth form level to study science subjects at A-level with the intention of studying physics at university. Applicants must be of British nationality and have a combined parental income of less than £50,000.

Grants are also made to undergraduates studying physics who have achieved a minimum of AAB.

Types of grants

(i) Educational scholarships covering at least 50% of school fees, paid half by the trust and matched by the school, which is a condition of their participation. The bursaries fund the pupils through the two years of their A-levels. (ii) Undergraduate scholarships of £1,500 per annum for up to four years of undergraduate study and are payable in two annual instalments (October and February).

Annual grant total

In 2010/11 the trust had assets of £39.6 million and an income of £285,000. Forty five bursaries totalling £449,000 and twenty three undergraduate scholarships totalling £169,000 were made.

Applications

The sixth form scholarships operate through schools associated with the trust, a list of which can be found on its website. The list is not closed and new schools may submit candidates. Applicants should apply to the school directly.

Applications for schools that are not on the current list should be made by approaching the trust directly. Applicants should already have secured a place at the school and a means tested scholarship or bursary worth at least part of the fees.

Undergraduate scholarships are only open to specific categories of candidate. See the trust's website for further details.

Other information

The trust also offers scholarships of £2,500 or £4,000 for PGCE students specialising in physics.

The Reedham Trust

£322,000 (131 grants)

Correspondent: Jean Watkins, Trust Secretary, The Lodge, 23 Old Lodge Lane, Purley, Surrey CR8 4DJ (020 8660 1461; email: info@reedham-trust.org.uk; website: www.reedham-trust.org.uk)

Trustees: William Rymer; Charles Link; Douglas Reed; Gerald Tubb; Michael Paterson; Peter Coleman; Mary Thompson; Paul Julius; Peter Allen; Darien Fyfield; Judith Kidd.

CC Number: 312433

Eligibility

Children aged up to 16 who, due to the death, disability or absence of one or both of their parents (whether natural or through adoption) or of their own disablement or other domestic or personal circumstances, are in need of boarding care. Help will continue after the age of 16 only in exceptional circumstances.

The trust does not support day pupils or children of two-parent families, unless one or both parents are totally incapacitated in some way.

Grants are only given where there is a social need for boarding, not an educational need. Assistance is only available where the Local Educational Authority has no statutory duty to help.

Types of grants

Grants towards boarding fees, of around £2,000 per year.

There is also a small fund for one-off assistance for items such as uniforms, trip and equipment.

Annual grant total

In 2010/11 the trust had assets of £6.5 million and an income of £677,000. Grants were awarded totalling £322,000 in support of 131 children. 27% of grants were awarded for children attending state schools.

Exclusions

Grants are not given for children who have already been placed within a school without any means of meeting the fees.

Applications

On a form available from the trust along with guidelines. Applications may be submitted directly by the individual, a parent/guardian, through the applicant's school or an educational welfare agency. They are considered throughout the year. Applications need confirmation from a professional that boarding school education is in the best interests of the applicant. Applications are considered five times a year.

To apply for a small grant contact the trust with full details of the need.

Royal National Children's Foundation

£774,000 (337 grants)

Correspondent: Mrs Chris Hughes, Director, Sandy Lane, Cobham, Surrey KT11 2ES (01932 868622; fax: 01932 866420; email: admin@rncf.org.uk; website: www.rncf.org.uk)

Trustees: David Oxon; Thomas Shields; June Taylor; Colin Morrison; John Spinks; Kevin Parry; Mary Seller; Douglas Brule; H. C. Cameron; Helen Starkie; Helen Pernelet; Jonathan Exten-Wright; Bob Dwyer; Darrell Farrant; Clive Richardson; Michael Connell; Andrew Corbett.

CC Number: 310916

Eligibility

Children aged between 7 and 18 who have suffered real trauma, tragedy or neglect or are at risk in some way, and are from a family who cannot meet the costs of boarding education unaided.

Types of grants

Grants towards school fees.

Emphasis is on boarding need rather than on educational need. The foundation does not discriminate between state and independent education and where a place is secured at a state boarding school, the foundation is prepared to consider help with the boarding element of the fees if necessary.

Annual grant total

In 2010/11 following a merger, the foundation had assets of £20.5 million and an income of £1.2 million. 337 children were supported with a total of £774,000, the average grant being £3,000. These grants were distributed by age as follows:

- 21 pupils aged under 12
- 155 pupils aged 12 to 14
- 161 pupils aged over 14

Applications

On a form available from the foundation. Initial enquiries can be made to the correspondent.

Other information

The Royal Wanstead Children's Foundation and Joint Educational Trust have recently merged to form Royal National Children's Foundation, retaining the Charity Commission no. of the former.

Thornton-Smith and Plevins Trust

£213,000

Correspondent: Heather Cox, 298 Icknield Way, Luton, Bedfordshire LU3 2JS (email: thornton.smithpt@ ntlworld.com)

Trustees: John Arkell; Fiona Tennick; Hugh Cairns; John Varley; Peter Larkman; Robert Gray; Charles Martyn-Hemphill.

CC Number: 1137196

Eligibility

Children of above average ability already attending fee-paying public schools whose parents have experienced an unexpected change in financial circumstances. Currently the trustees mostly support sixth formers studying A-levels.

Types of grants

Grants follow a means test of the parental resources and are paid per term, subject to reasonable progress. The average award is up to half the total fees. Preference is given to short-term applications primarily in relation to A-levels.

Annual grant total

In 2010/11 the trust had assets of £10.3 million and an income of £320,000. Grants were made totalling £213,000 to 147 beneficiaries, of which £211,000 was given in individual grants and loans to assist with school fees and expenses and £2,000 was given for educational travel abroad.

Exclusions

Grants are not given for first degree courses or in circumstances where parents were not in a position to fund the fees when entering the child for the school.

Applications

In writing to the correspondent, including details of education and parents' financial situation. If an applicant is considered eligible further inquiries are made. Applications are normally considered by 31 March to commence in September.

Other information

This trust was formerly the Thornton-Smith Young People's Trust which has been combined with the Wilfred Maurice Plevin's Trust, Thornton-Smith Plevins Common Investment Fund and The Thornton-Smith Trust for efficiency.

Orders

The Journal Children's Fund (in conjunction with the Royal Antediluvian Order of Buffaloes)

£10,000

Correspondent: C McMahon, Grant Secretary, RAOB GLE Trust Corporation, Grove House, Skipton Road, Harrogate, North Yorkshire HG1 4LA (01423 502438; email: hq@raobgle.org.uk; website: www.raobgle.org.uk)

Trustee: Alan Egan.

CC Number: 529575

Eligibility

'The education and preferment of orphan or necessitous children of deceased members of the Royal Antediluvian Order of Buffaloes Grand Lodge of England.' The fund's activities extend worldwide.

Types of grants

Help with the cost of books, clothing and other essentials for schoolchildren.

Grants may also be available for those at college or university who are eligible.

Annual grant total

In 2010/11 the fund had assets of £331,000 and an income of £47,000. Grants totalled £27,000 which includes grants made for welfare purposes.

Applications

Initial enquiries regarding assistance can only be made through the individual's branch of attendance.

Royal Masonic Trust for Girls and Boys

(1,774 grants)

Correspondent: Kerry Whiteford, Freemasons' Hall, 60 Great Queen Street, London WC2B 5AZ (020 7405 2644; fax: 020 7831 4094; email: info@rmtgb.org; website: www.rmtgb.org)

Trustees: Nicholas Springer; Malcolm Lane; Graham Ives; Keith Emmerson; John Thompson; Joe Roseman; Robert Bethel; Jeremy Aspden; Laurence Bourne; Charles Cadogan; Andrew Ross; Chris White; John Martin; Nicolas Hart; Stephen Shuttleworth; Michael Woodcock; Michael Codd; Jonathan Knopp; Robert Chevin; Colin Harris; James Campbell; Jonathan Winpenny; Andrew Wauchope.

CC Number: 285836

Eligibility

Generally the dependents of Freemasons. The objects of the trust are to relieve poverty and to advance education. The trust also has power, provided sufficient funds are available, to help children who are not the offspring of a Freemason. Such assistance is usually only given by way of grants to other children's charities or via the subsidiary funds.

Types of grants

Any necessary kind of assistance. The children concerned are usually, but not always, in state education. Help with the costs of a boarding education can only be given if there is a specific and demonstrable boarding need. Grants can be one-off or recurring and go towards school uniforms, school clothing, books, educational outings, maintenance costs, living expenses, music and sports tuition, equipment/tools, childcare and study or travel overseas.

Choral bursaries are also available to any child, regardless of Masonic connection. Nominations for these can be submitted by cathedrals.

Annual grant total

In 2011 the trust had assets of £137 million and an income of £5.2 million. There were 1774 beneficiaries during the year (including

246 young people who received support from the subsidiary funds). Grants were broken down as follows:
- Amount awarded for beneficiaries – £5.1 million
- TalentAid – £438,000
- Choral Bursaries – £153,000

Exclusions

No grants are available for student exchanges.

Applications

Applications should be made in the first instance to the nearest Masonic authority or, where that is not known, a preliminary enquiry may be addressed to the correspondent.

Other information

The trust has welfare and case advisers to assist families. Most of the funds are given to individuals with a Masonic connection, hence why a grants total has not been given.

Overseas students (by place of origin)

British Government and British Council Award Schemes – Scholarships for Overseas Students and Trainees

Correspondent: The Association of Commonwealth Universities, Woburn House, 20–24 Tavistock Square, London WC1H 9HF (website: www.acu.ac.uk)

Eligibility

Specified foreign nationals resident outside of the UK.

Types of grants

There are various awards/schemes. The following two scholarships may be awarded to undergraduates:

(i) DFID Shared Scholarship Scheme

Eligibility: Students from developing Commonwealth countries who are of a high academic calibre and intend to study subjects of developmental relevance but who are unable to support their studies in Britain. Normally under 35 years of age; they must be able to speak English fluently.

No grants to people who are employed by their government or by an international organisation.

Types of grants: Awards are for taught courses at postgraduate level. Very exceptionally, awards for undergraduate study may be made available where the course of training satisfies the conditions of the scheme but is not available in the student's own country or at a nearby regional institution.

Applications for awards should be made directly to the participating British institutions. These usually vary from year to year, as can each institution's individual closing date for receipt of applications. A revised list of institutions is normally available from December onwards from the Association of Commonwealth Universities, the Department for International Development, and British High Commissions and British Council representatives in the Commonwealth countries concerned.

Applicants must be resident in a developing Commonwealth country at the time of application and, if successful, are required to return there on completion of their awards.

Further details are available from the correspondent.

(ii) Commonwealth Scholarships and Fellowship Plan (CSFP)

Eligibility: People who live in either a Commonwealth country or a British dependent territory.

Types of Grants: The scholarships are normally for postgraduate study or research, so applicants must have a university degree or equivalent qualification. If there are no undergraduate courses in a particular subject in a country or regional university, it may sometimes be possible to apply to do a first degree course under this scheme.

Grants are for one to three years and usually cover the cost of travel, tuition fees and living expenses. In some cases additional allowances may be available for help with books or clothes. An allowance may be paid to help with the cost of maintaining a spouse.

Applications for awards should be made through the Commonwealth Scholarship Agency in the individual's home country. Agency addresses are listed in the 'Commonwealth Universities Yearbook', available from the address below. If you are already in the UK the ACU can help you with general information concerning the scheme, but it cannot issue application forms to international students.

Further details from the correspondent or the website.

Other postgraduate awards include: British Chevening Scholarships, British Council Fellowship Programmes,

Overseas Research Students Awards Scheme and Royal Society Fellowships.

Other information
This is a government scheme, not a charity.

The British Institute of Archaeology at Ankara
See entry on page 96

Churches' International Student Network: Hardship Fund

£56,000 (87 grants)

Correspondent: David Philpot, Grants Secretary, 2/27 Pentland Drive, Edinburgh EH10 6PX (01312 255722 ext. 300; email: dphilpot@cofscotland.org.uk; website: www.ctbi.org.uk/116)

CC Number: 1113299

Eligibility
Full-time students from developing countries attending British or Irish institutions for first-degree or postgraduate studies lasting a minimum of one academic year, who are within six months of completing their course but face unexpected financial problems. They are required to confirm their intention to return to their home country immediately after their course.

Types of grants
Grants are typically £500 but do not exceed £800; the same person is not funded twice.

Annual grant total
In 2010 97 grants were made to individuals for educational purposes totalling £56,000.

Exclusions
The fund will not consider students from industrialised countries, asylum seekers or refugees, or those whose studies relate to arms manufacture or experimentation on live animals. There will be no funding for students whose fees and living expenses have been covered by major awards.

Applications
Initial enquires should be made to the grants secretary including basic details especially concerning eligibility.

The hardship fund committee decides on grants three times a year, in February (for studies finishing April-July), June (for August-November) and October (for December-March). Requests for forms (including postal address) should be made respectively by mid-December, mid-April and mid-August at the latest.

Peter Alan Dickson Foundation

£5,000

Correspondent: Grant Applications, 91/93 Great Portland Street, London W1W 7NX (email: info@padfoundation. org; website: www.tarncourt.com/index. php?option=com_content&view= article&id=8&Itemid=8#)

Trustees: Pauline Broomhead; Charles Dickson; James Dickson; A. L. Brierley.

CC Number: 1129310

Eligibility
Individuals who face barriers to educational activities through poverty or other circumstance. Preference is given to those in the developing world.

Types of grants
Financial support to enable people to participate in educational activities that provide opportunities to develop skills, capacities and capabilities.

Annual grant total
In 2010/11 the foundation had an income of £24,000 and an expenditure of £37,000, most of which was probably given in grants to organisations.

Applications
On a form available from the website, along with guidelines.

Global Educational Trust
See entry on page 5

Ruth Hayman Trust

£15,000 (201 grants)

Correspondent: The Trustees, PO Box 17685, London N6 6WD (email: trustee@ruthhaymantrust.com; website: www.ruthhaymantrust.com)

Trustees: Frances Weinreich; Margaret Siudek; Gomathi Panchapagesan; Judith Smith; Susan Zagor; Jennifer Wainman; Kathleen Simpson; Lynette Murphy-O'Dwyer; Sheila Rosenberg; Shabibi Shah; Sue Colquhorn; James Lee.

CC Number: 287268

Eligibility
Adults (aged over 16) who live in the UK and who speak a language other than English as their first language. In practice, most beneficiaries are refugees and asylum seekers.

Types of grants
One-off and recurrent grants ranging from £20 to £300. First priority is given to tuition and examination fees, but small grants can also be made towards

books and materials. Grants towards travel costs are also made to people who have disabilities.

Annual grant total

In 2010/11 the trust made £15,000 in grants to 201 individuals.

Exclusions

No grants to overseas students for fees, higher degrees, computers or for childcare or living costs.

Applications

On a form available from the correspondent on request either by letter, email or downloadable from the website. Applications are considered in June, September, December and March. Deadlines for applications are posted on the trust's website. Applicants must provide a reference.

Other information

The trust also gave 63 Oxford English Dictionaries to individuals.

The Nora Henry Trust

£20,000

Correspondent: Fiona Macgillivray, Family Action, 501–505 Kingsland Road, Dalston, London E8 4AU (020 7254 6251; email: grants.enquiry@family-action.org.uk; website: www.family-action.org.uk)

Trustee: Family Action.

CC Number: 313949

Eligibility

Students from any country with a preference for students from developing countries who are studying subjects which will be of use when the student returns to that country.

Types of grants

One-off grants usually ranging from £100 to £200 can be given towards books, fees, living expenses, travel and childcare.

Annual grant total

In 2010/11 the trust had assets of £1.5 million, an income of £48,000 and a total expenditure of £26,000.

Exclusions

No grants for study or travel overseas for British students, or for student exchanges.

Applications

On a form available from the correspondent. Applications should be submitted directly by the individual and supported by an academic referee. They are considered all year round.

The Professor D. G. Montefiore Trust

£2,000

Correspondent: Jean MacDonald Bogaardt, 17 Market Street, Crewkerne, Somerset TA18 7JU (01460 74401)

Trustees: Jean MacDonald Bogaardt; David Goldsmid-Montefiore.

CC Number: 260452

Eligibility

Students from developing countries, principally those undertaking postgraduate medical work in the UK before returning to their own countries. Asylum seekers who need retraining in this country at any level, from language courses to medical exams.

Types of grants

Normally grants are in the form of single payments in time for the start of the academic year and can be for up to £500.

Annual grant total

About £2,000 a year is given in grants to individuals.

Applications

Applications must be made through the university or college and provide details of how all other costs, including living expenses, are going to be met. Applications from individuals will not be considered without confirmation from the university including references and CVs. Applications are considered monthly.

Other information

The trust prefers all correspondence to be received in writing.

The Nurses Association of Jamaica (NAJ) (UK)
See entry on page 99

Prisoners of Conscience Appeal Fund

£27,000

Correspondent: The Grants Officer, PO Box 61044, London SE1 1UP (020 7407 6644; fax: 020 7407 6655; email: info@prisonersofconscience.org; website: www.prisonersofconscience.org)

Trustee: Prisoners of Conscience Appeal Fund (Trustee) Ltd.

CC Number: 213766

Eligibility

Prisoners of conscience and/or their families, who have suffered persecution for their beliefs. The fact that the person is seeking asylum or has been a victim of civil war is not sufficient grounds in itself.

Types of grants

Mainly one-off grants of about £350 each for travel, resources, equipment, vocational conversion courses and re-qualification costs. Bursary grants are also available for tuition fees for postgraduate study and professional conversion courses.

Annual grant total

In 2011 grants made in the UK totalled £52,000, distributed as follows:

- 17 family reunion grants totalling £17,000
- UK relief grants to asylum seekers totalling £7,300
- Refugees Liverpool grants totalling £800
- Bursaries totalling £27,000

Exclusions

No support is given to people who have used or advocated violence or supported a violent organisation.

Applications

Application forms are available from the correspondent and should be submitted by a third party such as human rights organisations, refugee groups, solicitors and organisations in the UK and overseas, from large NGOs to small refugee community organisations. Applicants who do not know of a third party organisation that they can submit an application through should contact the fund for advice. Applications should include evidence of identification of the applicant and of costs.

Other information

The fund was initially established in 1962 as the relief arm of Amnesty International, but is now a charity in its own right.

The Sloane Robinson Foundation

£72,000

Correspondent: Michael Wilcox, c/o WillcoxLewis LLP, The Old Coach House, Bergh Apton, Norwich NR15 1DD (01508 480100; email: info@wilcoxlewis.co.uk)

Trustees: Michael Wilcox; Hugh Sloane; George Robinson.

CC Number: 1068286

Eligibility

Overseas students wishing to study at British universities and British students wishing to study overseas.

Types of grants

Grants are given according to need.

Annual grant total

In 2010/11 the trust had assets of £24 million and an income of £1.8 million, most of which came from donations. Grants made to individuals totalled £72,000.

Applications

In writing to the correspondent. 'Only successful applicants are notified, in order to avoid increased administrative costs for the foundation.'

Other information

The foundation is developing long-term relationships with a number of academic institutions, with the ultimate goal of establishing scholarships and bursary schemes for overseas students to study in the UK.

Grants to organisations in 2010/11 totalled £3.4 million.

The Mary Trevelyan Fund

£8,800

Correspondent: The Welfare Service, International Students House, 229 Great Portland Street, London W1W 5PN (020 7631 8309; email: advice@ish.org.uk; website: www.ish.org.uk)

Trustees: John Ritblat; James Hambro; Baroness Warwick; John Garbutt.

CC Number: 294448

Eligibility

Students from developing countries studying in London who are experiencing unexpected financial difficulties. Students must be in their final year of study and intend to return home on completion of their course. Preference is given where the institution is a member of International Students House. See the website for a list of member institutions and the trusts approved 'developing countries'.

Types of grants

Grants or loans of up to £1,000 are available to those who experience difficulties due to unexpected financial hardship.

Annual grant total

£8,800 in 2010/11.

Exclusions

Students with outstanding tuition fees will not generally be considered and no support for those seeking or granted asylum in the UK.

Applications

On an application form available from the correspondent or the website. Applications can be submitted directly by the individual or through a social worker, Citizens Advice or other welfare

agency at any time. The trust states that an application will have a greater chance of success if it is supported by the student's own college/university advice or welfare service.

Other information

This fund is a subsidiary charity of The International Students Trust.

Africa

Africa Educational Trust

£4,200

Correspondent: Jill Landymore, 18 Hand Court, London WC1V 6JF (020 7831 3283; fax: 020 7242 3265; email: info@africaeducationaltrust.org; website: www.africaeducationaltrust.org)

Trustees: Raschid Desai; Terry Connor; Richard Hodder-Williams; Christopher Beer; Cream Wright; Francis Katamba; Sally Healy; Sally Tomlinson; Richard Dowden; Cisco Magagula.

CC Number: 313139

Eligibility

Students from Africa studying in the UK on a student visa, facing unexpected financial hardship in the last four months of their course.

Types of grants

Emergency small grants are made to enable students who are facing unexpected financial problems in the last few months of a college or university course in the UK to finish their course.

Annual grant total

In 2010/11 the trust has an income of £4.5 million and gave £4,200 from the emergency small grants fund.

Applications

On a form available from the correspondent, at any time. Applications must be supported by a supervisor, tutor or head of course.

Other information

The trust also offers a free educational advice service to migrants and refugees with an African background.

Most of the thrusts work is carried out in Africa. Scholarships and study grants are available for people from Africa who wish to study further and higher education courses in Africa or Europe, with the intention of using their qualifications and skills in Africa.

Armenia

The Armenian General Benevolent Union London Trust

£46,000 (23 grants)

Correspondent: Berge Azadian, c/o Student Loans Committee, 51c Parkside, Wimbledon Common, London SW19 5NE

Trustees: Berge Azadian; Berge Setrakian; Hampar Chakardjian; Aris Atamian; Annie Kouyoumdjian; Noushig Yakoubian Setrakian; Assadour Guzelian; Anahid Manoukian; Arline Medazoumian; Armine Afrikian.

CC Number: 282070

Eligibility

Children of an Armenian parent(s) studying recognised undergraduate or postgraduate courses in British universities or educational institutions, including specific vocational courses. Preference is given to courses in Armenian studies or subjects which may benefit the Armenian community.

Types of grants

Student loans are normally for educational fees; otherwise, a contribution can be made towards the cost of books or some maintenance costs. All loans are interest free and subject to a maximum set by the trustees reflecting the current income available. Student grants are occasionally given to Armenians with significant financial hardship or for refugees in the UK. Grants have also occasionally been given towards teaching, arts and research papers connected with Armenian culture.

Special grants are available for people to attain Armenian university education or to pursue Armenian studies at university.

Annual grant total

In 2010 the charity had assets of £8.8 million and an income of £197,000. Grants were made to individuals totalling £46,000 which included £41,000 in 20 student grants and loans and £5,000 in grants for cultural/academic purposes.

Applications

On a form available from the correspondent, to be submitted by 15 June each year.

Other information

Support is also given to Armenian schools, nurseries and cultural groups in the UK and overseas, usually towards running costs for Armenian language, history and culture classes. Occasionally welfare grants can be given to people in need.

The Armenian Relief Society of Great Britain Trust

£250

Correspondent: The Secretary, 209 Syon Lane, Isleworth TW7 5PU

Trustees: Rubina Boghosian; Silva Beshirian; Mariette Nazloomian; Zovig Haladjian; Sonia Bablanian; Jaqueline Karanfilian; Jabet Kachatourian.

CC Number: 327389

Eligibility

Poor, sick or bereaved Armenians, worldwide.

Types of grants

One-off and recurrent grants of £150 are available to promote the study and research into the history and culture of Armenians or to pay fees or educational costs.

Annual grant total

The majority of grants are usually made to organisations, although the trust does have the capacity to make grants to individuals.

Applications

In writing to the correspondent.

The Benlian Trust

£49,000 (15 grants)

Correspondent: S Ovanessoff, Administrator, 15 Elm Crescent, Ealing, London W5 3JW (020 8567 1210)

Trustees: Paul Gulbenkian; Rita Vartoukian; Sandi Simons; Audrey Selian.

CC Number: 277253

Eligibility

Children of Armenian fathers; applicants must be members of the Armenian Church studying at universities in Great Britain.

Types of grants

Grants for people studying on undergraduate degree courses and apprenticeships. Grants may also be given to help with the cost of articles, but otherwise priority is given to undergraduates.

Annual grant total

In 2010/11 the trust had assets of £2.6 million and an income of £141,000. Grants were made to 15 individuals totalling £49,000.

Applications

On a form available from the correspondent, completed applications must be returned before 30 April.

Other information

This trust also makes grants to Armenian organisations.

The Mihran Essefian Charitable Trust

£33,000 (220 grants)

Correspondent: Stephen Ovanessoff, Administrator, 15 Elm Crescent, Ealing, London W5 3JW (020 8567 1210)

Trustees: Paul Gulbenkian; Rita Vartoukian; Sandi Simons; Audrey Selian.

CC Number: 275074

Eligibility

University students of Armenian origin studying in Armenia. Help can also been given to Armenian university students in the UK.

Types of grants

Scholarship grants are made ranging from £100 to £6,000.

Annual grant total

In 2010/11 the trust had assets of £1.5 million and an income of £48,000. 220 grants were made to individuals totalling £33,000.

Applications

In writing to the correspondent by 30 April each year.

Other information

Grants are also given to organisations (£7,000).

Asia

The Bestway Foundation

£80,000 (97 grants)

Correspondent: M Y Sheikh, Abbey Road, Park Royal, London NW10 7BW (020 8453 1234; email: zulfikaur.wajid-hasan@bestway.co.uk; website: www.bestwaygroup.co.uk/page/Bestway-Foundation.html)

Trustees: M. Y. Sheikh; A. K. Bhatti; A. K. Chaudhary; Anwar Pervez; Zameer Choudrey.

CC Number: 297178

Eligibility

Schoolchildren and students who are of Indian, Pakistani, Bangladeshi or Sri Lankan origin.

Types of grants

One-off and recurrent grants and loans.

Annual grant total

In 2010/11 the foundation had assets of £6.2 million and an income of £991,000. There were 97 grants to individuals which previously have totalled around £80,000.

Applications

In writing to the correspondent enclosing an sae. Applications are considered in March/April. Initial enquiries should be made in writing.

Other information

Grants are also made to organisations in the UK and overseas.

The Hammond Trust

£6,000

Correspondent: Andrew Mackay, Secretary to the British Council, British Council, 10 Spring Gardens, London SW1A 2BN (email: Hammond.Trust@ britishcouncil.org)

Trustee: The British Council.

CC Number: 1001818

Eligibility

Students from Asia between the ages of 18 and 45, who are studying in the UK. Grants are available to students whose studies are at risk of being affected by unexpected financial difficulties, to enable them stay in the UK to finish their course of education. Applicants must be in their final six months of study for a degree, diploma or other professional qualification at a recognised institution. Preference will be given to those following a course of study that will be of benefit to the applicant's own country. Applicants are expected to make every effort to meet their commitments from their own resources

Types of grants

One-off and recurrent grants, generally of £500.

Annual grant total

Grants of £500 are usually given to around 12 individuals.

Exclusions

Grants will not be awarded for help with tuition fees.

Applications

On an application form available from the correspondent. The course tutor or supervisor must give a report on the applicant in part B of the application form which must be sent through the academic institution's authority and be endorsed with the official stamp.

Australia

The Britain-Australia Society Education Trust

£0

Correspondent: Michael Clough, The Britain-Australia Society, Swire House, 59 Buckingham Gate, London SW1E 6AJ (020 7630 1075; fax: 020 7828 2260; email: adm@britain-australia.org.uk; website: www.britain-australia.org.uk)

Trustees: Miles Hobart-Hampden; Dale Eaton; Paula Hardgrave; John Allen.

CC Number: 803505

Eligibility

Individuals 18 or under (usually of secondary school age) living in the UK who have a connection with Australia.

Types of grants

Grants contributing towards the expenses (but not fares) of educational projects leading to better British-Australian understanding. Grants are also given to schoolchildren for uniforms/clothing, fees, study/travel overseas and books. Grants range from between £250 to £500.

Annual grant total

In 2010/11 the trust had an income of £5,300. The expenditure has fluctuated in recent years from £1,000 in 2008/09 to £0 in 2010/11.

Applications

In writing to the correspondent, including details of the funding required. The deadline for applications is 31 March for consideration through May.

Belgium

The Royal Belgian Benevolent Society

£5,000

Correspondent: Patrick Bresnan, 5 Hartley Close, Bromley BR1 2TP (020 8467 8442)

Trustees: Mrs A. Verity; Mrs D. Massaux; Jean Francois-Dor; Mrs S. Ault; Patrick Bresnan; Baronne Van Havre.

CC Number: 233435

Eligibility

Belgian students who are living/studying in Britain and are in need.

Types of grants

One-off grants of £500 to £2,000 towards the costs of further/higher education and postgraduate study.

Annual grant total

In 2010 the society had an income of £620 and a total expenditure of £11,000. The trust has stated that after a period of increased funding commitments in 2010, no scholarships would be awarded in 2011. Applications will continue to be received in 2012.

Applications

On a form available from the correspondent, submitted directly by the individual.

British Commonwealth

The Sir Ernest Cassel Educational Trust: Mountbatten Memorial Grants

£44,000

Correspondent: Kathryn Hodges, Trust Secretary, 121 George Street, Edinburgh EH2 4YN (01312 255722; email: casseltrust@btinternet.com; website: www.casseltrust.co.uk)

Trustees: Amanda Ellingworth; Ann Kennedy; Anne Sofer; Colin Lucas; Francis Robinson; Nicholas Allan; Kit Gordon; Gordon Johnson.

CC Number: 313820

Eligibility

Overseas students from Commonwealth countries studying in the UK who are in the final year of their studies and are experiencing unforeseen financial difficulties. Postdoctoral students who are at university in the UK. Grants are only given to students in higher education (at college or university) in the UK.

Types of grants

The trust has two grants categories for individuals:

- Mountbatten memorial grants for commonwealth students facing financial difficulties in their final year at a UK university
- Postdoctoral travel grants for postdoctoral students who are at a university in the UK undertaking research overseas in the humanities and other fields

Annual grant total

In 2010/11 the trust had assets of £1.3 million and an income of £60,000. Grants made to individuals totalled £44,000

Exclusions

Overseas students who are UK-registered for fees purposes are not eligible; applicants must have paid course fees as an overseas student. Grants are not given for the actual course fees themselves. No retrospective grants are given.

Applications

The Mountbatten memorial grants are administered by the following universities: Birmingham, Cardiff, Glasgow, Leeds, Leicester, Manchester, Nottingham, Reading, Imperial College London and University College London. Potential applicants should consult their student welfare officer for further details. Students at universities and institutions not included in the scheme may also apply through their student welfare officers to the correspondent with the following details:

- Biographical details and a note of the intended career
- Details of the course or research degree and completion date
- The applicants current financial position and the nature of the unforeseen circumstances causing the difficulty
- Any other grants and outstanding applications for financial assistance
- A letter of support/statement of attendance from an academic supervisor

Trustees meet once a year to consider applications.

Applications for the Postdoctoral travel grants should be made directly to the British Academy on the small research grant form and are considered in spring.

Other information

Grants are also made to organisations.

Canada

The Canadian Centennial Scholarship Fund

£37,000 (16 grants)

Correspondent: Mrs Julia Montgomery, Chair, 1 Grosvenor Square, London W1X OAB (075000 008457; email: info@canadianwomenlondon.org; website: www.canadianscholarshipfund.co.uk)

Trustees: Jill Pollock; Julia Montgomery; David Glennie; Michelle Cassidy; Leith McKay.

CC Number: 313966

Eligibility

Canadian post-secondary school students studying in the UK, who are planning to return to Canada after studying and are both in need and of high academic ability. Preference is given to students taking courses which are 'of relevance to Canada'.

Students must already be enrolled in a UK educational institution before applying for a grant.

Types of grants

One-off grants of £500 to £2,500 for fees, study or travel abroad, books, maintenance and living expenses.

Annual grant total

In 2010/11 the fund had assets of £74,000 and an income of £26,000. Grants were made to 16 individuals totalling £37,000.

Applications

Further information and application forms are also available from the fund's website. Applications must be received, with references, by 15 March. Interviews for those shortlisted are the first week of June and scholarships are paid out in late September.

Costa Rica

Ronaldo Falconer Charitable Trust

£2,000

Correspondent: The Manager, Natwest Trust Services, 5th Floor, Trinity Quay 2, Avon Street, Bristol BS2 0PT (01179 403283)

Trustee: Nat West Trust Services.

CC Number: 295853

Eligibility

Further and higher education Costa Rican students, including mature students, who are studying in the UK, with a preference for technical courses. Students of any nationality studying in Costa Rica.

Types of grants

Scholarships and bursaries.

Annual grant total

In 2010/11 the trust had an income of £7,000 and an expenditure of £2,500.

Applications

The Trust does not accept unsolicited applications. Instead, students are recommended to them by a particular university.

Czech Republic

The Anglo-Czech Educational Fund

£48,000

Correspondent: Paul Sheils, Moon Beever Solicitors, 24–25 Bloomsbury Square, London WC1A 2PL (020 7637 0661; email: info@moonbeever.com)

Trustees: Paul Sheils; Veronika Hyks-Dyer; Jan Hasek.

CC Number: 1110348

Eligibility

Students from the Czech Republic who wish to study primarily in the UK, USA and European countries.

Types of grants

Grant and loans.

Annual grant total

In 2010/11 the fund had an income of £20,000 and an expenditure of £71,000. Previously the trust has made one large grant each year to Karlova Univerzita to distribute as grants.

Applications

In writing to the correspondent.

Egypt

Egyptian Community Association in the United Kingdom

£250

Correspondent: Hosni El-Sherif, 100 Redcliffe Gardens, London SW10 9HH (020 7244 8925)

Trustee: Hosni El-Sherif.

CC Number: 289332

Eligibility

People in need who are Egyptian or of Egyptian origin and are living in or visiting the UK.

Types of grants

One-off and recurrent grants towards course fees, clothing, books, and so on.

Annual grant total

Grants usually total around £500 per year.

Applications

In writing to the correspondent.

Other information

The association arranges seminars and national and religious celebrations, as well as offering other services. It also gives grants to individuals for general welfare purposes. Limited information was available due to no accounts being filed at the Charity Commission since 2007.

Greece

The Schilizzi Foundation

£35,000 (16 grants)

Correspondent: The Secretary, Chacombe Priory, Chacombe, Banbury OX17 2AW (01295 710356; email: schilizzifoundation@tiscali.co.uk; website: www.schilizzifoundation.org.uk)

CC Number: 314128

Eligibility

Greek nationals pursuing an undergraduate degree course or vocational training in Great Britain where there is a real need for financial assistance. Priority is given to students in their final year of study, first and second year and postgraduate students will only be considered in exceptional circumstances.

Types of grants

One-off grants ranging from £250 to £2,000, awarded in cases of hardship or special need during the final year of study for books, fees and living expenses. Other cases will be considered only in exceptional circumstances of serious or unforeseen hardship. (Major scholarships for further education in the UK are also awarded to selected students; no direct applications will be considered.)

Annual grant total

In 2010/11 the foundation had assets of £1.9 million and an income of £59,000. Grants and scholarships totalled £35,000.

Exclusions

Postgraduates are not eligible for funding.

Applications

On a form available from the secretary. Applications can be submitted directly by the individual or a parent/guardian, or through an organisation such as a school or an educational welfare agency. They are considered up to 1 April in the final year, although earlier applications are preferred.

India

The Charles Wallace India Trust

£207,000 (51 grants)

Correspondent: Richard Alford, 36 Lancaster Avenue, London SE27 9DZ (020 8670 2825; email: cwit@btinternet.com; website: www.wallace-trusts.org.uk)

Trustees: Colin Perchard; Ingval Maxwell; Yasmin Khan; Caroline Douglas.

CC Number: 283338

Eligibility

People of Indian nationality and citizenship, aged between 25 to 38 and studying in the UK, who are normally resident in India and intending to return to India at the end of their study. Certain short-term awards are available for people aged between 25 to 45.

Types of grants

Only in the arts and humanities, with particular emphasis on fine arts, music, theatre, crafts and design, conservation of historical buildings and materials, anthropology, the preservation of archives, letters, history and the history of ideas.

Most awards are at postgraduate level to supplement other sources of funding or constitute completion of study awards for those whose scholarships have run out. A limited number of postdoctoral or post-professional research grants are awarded.

Annual grant total

In 2010/11 the trust had assets of £5.6 million and an income of £232,000. 51 Scholarships and grants were made totalling £207,000.

Exclusions

Studies relating to economic development or leading to professional legal, business or administrative qualifications are not considered.

Applications

In writing to the correspondent. Detailed information and application forms can be downloaded from the website.

Other information

There are separate, smaller Charles Wallace Trusts for Bangladesh, Burma and Pakistan. All of the trusts are registered charities in the UK with separate and independent boards of trustees.

Iraq

The British Institute for the Study of Iraq

£27,000

Correspondent: Joan MacIver, 10 Carlton House Terrace, London SW1Y 5AH (020 7969 5274; email: bisi@britac.ac.uk; website: www.britac.ac.uk/institutes/iraq)

Trustees: Eleanor Robson; Athem Alsabti; Iain Cheyne; Harriet Martin; Nicholas Postgate; Emile Savage-Smith; Paul Collins; Glen Rangwala; Peter

Davies; Charles Tripp; Teresa Bernheimer; Augusta McMahon; Mark Altaweel; Edward Chaplin.

CC Number: 1135395

Eligibility

UK residents undertaking research, projects, conferences or development events on Iraq. Very occasionally other individuals whose academic research coincides with that of the British Institute for the Study of Iraq. Iraqi scholars visiting the UK for study.

Types of grants

Grants, usually of up to £4,000 but occasionally more, for research and conferences on Iraq and neighbouring countries including anthropology, archaeology, geography, history, language and related disciplines within the arts, humanities and social sciences, concerned with any time period from prehistory to the present day. Up to £8,000 for pilot projects, preliminary to larger research projects, especially on the Theme 'Exile and return'.

Development and outreach grants of up to £500, occasionally more, for development events and projects, such as lectures, study days and popular publications that relate to Iraq and neighbouring countries.

Two or three grants a year are also available for Iraqi scholars visiting the UK and studying archaeology, ancient languages, museum and heritage studies and other disciplines within the humanities and social sciences.

Annual grant total

In 2010/11 the charity had an income of £4 million and made grants to individuals in the UK totalling £27,000, broken down as follows:

- Research, travel and conference grants: £18,000
- Pilot project grants: £4,500
- Development grants: £4,000

The charity also spent £29,000 on its visiting scholars program.

Applications

On a form available from the correspondent. Deadlines are 10 January for research and conference grants, 1 October for development and outreach grants and 1 March for visiting Iraqi scholars grants. Two academic references must also be supplied.

Pakistan

Noon Educational Foundation

£88,000

Correspondent: Paul Flather, Chairman, c/o Mansfield College, University of

Oxford, Mansfield Road, Oxford OX1 3TF (01865 284480; fax: 01865 284481; email: paul.flather@mansfield.ox.ac.uk)

Trustees: Nicholas Barrington; Paul Flather; Lousie Johnson; Haroon Ahmed; Rosemary Raza; Humayun Khan; Ehsan Mani.

CC Number: 1017002

Eligibility

People who are from Pakistan and wish to undertake a higher education course in the natural, applied and social sciences at either Oxford or Cambridge University. Applicants must be able to demonstrate academic merit in that they have been accepted onto a course at one of those Universities and evidence that they have not previously had the opportunity to study abroad at a western university. They must also show that they intend to return to Pakistan on completion of the course.

Types of grants

Full and partial scholarships.

Annual grant total

In 2010/11 the foundation had assets of £600,000 and an income of £32,000. £41,000 was made in grants to Cambridge students and £47,000 to Oxford Students.

Applications

In writing to the correspondent in the first instance. Scholarships are decided upon in June/July of each year, in preparation for the coming academic year.

Poland

The Jeremi Kroliczewski Educational Trust

£14,000

Correspondent: Simeon Emmanuel Arnold, Solicitor, Montage Lambert and Co., 41 Haven Green, Ealing, London W5 2NX (020 8997 2288; email: sarnold@montaguelambert.com)

Trustees: Selwyn Arnold; Simeon Arnold; Krystyna Wilowska; Teresa Robinski.

CC Number: 1051524

Eligibility

Polish students under 25 who are in education and live in England or Wales. The trust has previously stated that all funds are fully committed years in advance.

Types of grants

Grants given according to need.

Annual grant total

In 2010/11 the trust had an income of £14,000 and an expenditure of £15,000.

Applications

The trust states that all funds are fully committed.

Turkey

Hazel Heughan Educational Trust

£400

Correspondent: The Trustees, 14 Camus Avenue, Edinburgh EH10 6QT

SC Number: SC013045

Eligibility

Students and academics in further, higher or postgraduate education who usually live in Turkey and are from poor backgrounds.

Types of grants

One-off and recurrent grants towards education at university, and for trips to the UK (usually Edinburgh) to further studies in the English language and, if possible, gain work experience. This can include grants for travel expenses, books, equipment and instruments, fees and maintenance and living expenses.

Annual grant total

In 2010/11 the trust had an income of £480.

Applications

In writing to the correspondent at any time, for consideration usually in May and November. Applications should be submitted by a third party.

Prisoners/ ex-offenders

The Aldo Trust

£4,750

Correspondent: c/o NACRO, Coast Cottage, 90 Coast Road, West Mersea, Colchester CO5 8LS (01206 383809; fax: 01206 383809; email: owenwheatley@ btinternet.com)

Trustees: Owen Wheatley; Anthony Heaton-Armstrong; Peter Ashman.

CC Number: 327414

Eligibility

People in need who are being held in detention pending their trial or after their conviction. The applicant must still be serving the sentence. Applicants must have less than £25 in private cash.

Types of grants

Education grants of £10 to help with items such as books, course fees, equipment, audio/visual and other training equipment and tools for employment. Those eligible can only receive one grant a year.

Annual grant total

In 2010 the trust had an income of £20,000. Previously 975 grants were made to individuals totalling £9,500.

Applications

On a form available from the correspondent. Applications must be made through prison service personnel (for example, probation, chaplaincy, education), and should include the name and number of the prisoner, age, length of sentence and expected date of release. No applications direct from prisoners will be considered. Applicants may apply once only in each twelve-month period, and applications are considered monthly.

Other information

NACRO also offers a fund for people on probation; see separate entry in this guide.

The Longford Trust

£40,000

Correspondent: Peter Stanford, 42 Callcott Road, London NW6 7EA (020 7625 1097; website: www. longfordtrust.org)

Trustees: Kevin Pakenham; Rachel Billington; Jon Snow; Edward Fitzgerald; Tom Pakenham; John Podmore.

CC Number: 1092825

Eligibility

Ex-offenders or those awaiting release in the near future whose sentence was or is still being served in a UK prison. Applicants must have identified a specific course they want to study at degree level offered by an institute of higher education and have obtained a provisional offer of a place (Eligibility remains open for up to five years after release).

Types of grants

Scholarships are worth a maximum of £5,000 per annum, extendable for up to three years on receipt of suitable reports of academic progress. Grants are intended to cover both the cost of tuition fees on higher education courses and offer a contribution to living expenses for books, course material and basic sustenance.

Annual grant total

In 2010 the trust had an income of £64,000 and gave scholarships totalling £40,000.

Exclusions

No grants for postgraduate study.

Applications

Application forms can be downloaded from the trust's website, or are available by contacting the trust in writing. Applications for courses beginning in the September of any year must be made by 1 June in that year.

Other information

Recipients of scholarships are also assigned a mentor who can offer practical and emotional advice.

The trust also administers the Patrick Pakenham Educational Awards, for ex-prisoners wishing to study law to degree level.

The Prisoners' Education Trust

£561,000 (2,510 grants)

Correspondent: The Director, Wandle House, Riverside Drive, Mitcham, Surrey CR4 4BU (020 8648 7760; email: info@ prisonerseducation.org.uk; website: www.prisonerseducation.org.uk)

Trustees: Norman Franklin; Vanni Teves; Philip Deer; Peter Honey; John Samuels; Charlotte Rendle; Alexandra Ziegler; Geoffrey Wolfson; Lynn Bindman; Hugh Lenon.

CC Number: 1084718

Eligibility

Prisoners aged 18 and above who are in custody in England and Wales and still have at least six months of their sentence to serve.

Types of grants

Grants from the Access to Learning programme to pay fees for distance learning and resettlement courses, including Open University courses (funded by contract from DIUS), A-level, GCSE and vocational qualifications, including both accredited and non-accredited courses. Grants are also available for arts and crafts materials.

Annual grant total

In 2011 the trust awarded 2,490 grants for distance learning courses and creative activities. Additionally, 11 bursaries were awarded and nine resettlement awards. 916 awards were for Open University courses. Grants to individuals altogether totalled £561,000.

Applications

Applications should be submitted on a form available from the trust or through a prison education department, for consideration monthly. Initial telephone enquiries are welcome. Endorsement by a prison education manager is essential.

Other information

The organisation also provides advice about distance learning courses and how they relate to employment paths and possibilities. They support learners in prisons and in some prisons and regions they train people to act as peer learning mentors.

Funding arrangements for prisoner's education changes dramatically in 2012 with funding from the government for distance learning courses being withdrawn, and prisoners also now having to apply for student loans to cover the costs. The impact of this on the trust and on the wider landscape of prisoner learning has yet to be seen.

The Royal London Society

£46,000 (161 grants)

Correspondent: Peter Cox, Grant Administrator, 71a Knightsbridge, London SW1 7RB (01622 230737; fax: 01622 690635; email: office@ royallondonsociety.org.uk; website: www.royallondonsociety.org.uk)

Trustees: Liz Day; Robert Bieber; Peter Timms; John Martin; Robert Kissin; Ian Kirk; Brian Caton; John O'Sullivan; Douglas Connon; Veronica Timm; Margaret Levin; Justin Atkinson; Simone Sandelson.

CC Number: 214695

Eligibility

People in prison and ex-offenders, people under supervision and young people 'at risk' (that is young people under a supervision order or who have come to the attention of the police) who live in or intend to live in Greater London and the South East.

Types of grants

One-off grants, usually of £300, that will help lead to employment in the immediate future or within the next six months. Donations may be made for training, resettlement education, work clothing, tools and equipment and travel expenses.

Annual grant total

In 2011 the society awarded grants to 161 individuals totalling £46,000.

Exclusions

Grants are not given for accommodation/living costs; household items; debts/loans; driving lessons for domestic purposes; distance learning courses not related to employment or clothing not related to employment. The trust does not normally consider grants for hobbies or recreation, unless the applicant still has at least 12 months to serve.

Applications

On a form available from the website. Applications must be supported by a prison officer, probation officer, trade instructor, education department or other agency such as social services or housing trusts. Applications are considered at quarterly meetings however there is a fast track process for urgent applications.

Other information

A small number of grants are also made to organisations, totalling £4,400 in 2011.

SACRO Trust

£6,500

Correspondent: Trust Fund Administrator, 29 Albany Street, Edinburgh EH1 3QN (01316 247270; fax: 01316 247269; email: info@national. sacro.org.uk; website: www.sacro.org.uk)

SC Number: SC023031

Eligibility

People living in Scotland who are subject to a license/court order or who have been released from prison in the last two years.

Types of grants

Grants are usually to a maximum of £300, including those for fees, driving lessons, books and equipment.

Annual grant total

In 2010/11 the trust gave grants to 72 individuals totalling £13,000

Exclusions

No grants are made where financial help from other sources is available.

Applications

On a form available from the correspondent. Applications can only be accepted if they are made through a local authority, voluntary sector worker, health visitor or so on. They are considered every two months. No payment can be made directly to an individual by the trust; payment will be made to the organisation making the application. Other sources of funding should be sought before applying to the trust.

The Paul Stephenson Memorial Trust

£500

Correspondent: Pauline Austin, The New Bridge, 27A Medway Street, London SW1P 2BD

Trustees: Tony Wise; Pauline Austin; Sir Peter Lloyd; Ben Owen; Donna King.

CC Number: 295924

Eligibility

People who have served at least two years of imprisonment and are near the end of their sentence or have been released recently.

Types of grants

One-off grants of up to £100 for tools for work or assistance with college fees.

Annual grant total

Around £1,000.

Exclusions

Grants are not given for recreational activities, setting up small businesses or becoming self-employed, or for existing debts.

Applications

On a form available from the correspondent, which must be submitted via a probation officer, prison education officer or voluntary associate. Applicants should mention other trusts or organisations that have been applied to and other grants promised or received, including any statutory grants. Trustees usually meet twice a year.

Refugees

Aid for Jewish Refugees

£350

Correspondent: Anthony Newton, 22 Fitzjohns Avenue, London NW3 5NB (email: aidforjewishrefugees@gmail.com)

Trustees: Anthony Newton; Irene Newton; Eva Jacobs; David Goldberg; Herman David.

CC Number: 1001059

Eligibility

Refugees and in particular Jewish refugees, who live in the UK and are seeking to re-train in their profession.

Types of grants

Grants may be spent on vocational training courses, fees, books and equipment for any future career.

Annual grant total

In 2010/11 the fund had an income of £70 and an expenditure of £370.

Applications

In writing to the correspondent.

Other information

The trust has informed us that they are fully open and welcoming and encouraging applications from refugees, both Jewish and otherwise.

The Airey Neave Trust

£15,000

Correspondent: Hannah Scott, PO Box 111, Leominster HR6 6BP (email: aireyneavetrust@gmail.com; website: www.aireyneavetrust.org.uk)

Trustees: Hugh Tilney; W. M. McAlpine; Veronica Sutherland; Christopher Andrew; Patrick Sookhdeo; Kevin Tebbit; Brigadier Butler; Marigold Webb; Howard Dawson; Patrick Neave; Miss Robilliard; William Neave; John Giffard; Michael Bottenheim; David Veness.

CC Number: 297269

Eligibility

Research projects that aim to draw attention to terrorist organisations and their motives. Seminars on terrorism.

Types of grants

Grants for research projects or seminars.

Annual grant total

In 2010/11 the trust held assets of £617,000, had an income of £47,000 and made grants totalling £15,000.

Exclusions

The trust has stopped providing financial assistance to refugees.

Applications

In writing to the correspondent using the form available on the trust's website. The trust welcomes informal contact by email prior to application.

Other information

This trust has stopped funding for refugees in order to focus all its funds on research grants.

Ruth Hayman Trust

See entry on page 29

Prisoners of Conscience Appeal Fund

See entry on page 30

Religion

Christian

The Britland Trust

£500

Correspondent: Jeremiah Powlett, 20 Henderson Road, Wandsworth, London SW18 3RR (0870 084 8207; email: jcolman@lineone.net)

Trustees: Jeremiah Colman; Susan Coleman.

CC Number: 1014956

Eligibility

People involved in the advancement of Christianity, mission work and Christian education and training.

Types of grants

One-off and recurrent grants according to need.

Annual grant total

In 2010 the trust had an income of £8,500 and an expenditure of £24,000. Previously, most grants have gone to organisations, with individuals receiving around £500.

Applications

In writing to the correspondent.

The Daily Prayer Union Charitable Trust Ltd

£41,000

Correspondent: C Palmer, 12 Weymouth Street, London W1W 5BY

Trustees: David Jackman; Timothy Sterry; Anne Thompson; Elizabeth Bridger; Fiona Ashton; Joanna Sudell; Giles Rawlinson; Raymond Porter; Carolyn Ash.

CC Number: 284857

Eligibility

Christians undertaking religious training or education.

Types of grants

Grants to support Christian training and education.

Annual grant total

In 2011 the trust had an income of £53,000 and gave £7,300 in education grants and £34,000 in training grants to individuals, totalling £41,000.

Applications

In writing to the correspondent.

Other information

Grants are also given to schools and other organisations.

Medical Service Ministries

£10,000

Correspondent: The Trustees, Box 13, Newton Abbot TQ13 8WZ (01647 440113; email: resources.msm@btopenworld.com; website: www.medicalserviceministries.org.uk)

Trustees: Brian Weller; Keith Cornell; Alan Geddes; Anita Davies; David Ryan; Rosemary Brown; Brian Coupland.

CC Number: 234037

Eligibility

Christians of any nationality who wish to train in healthcare, or gain an additional medical qualification in order to help the group or community they are working with in a developing or marginalised country. Applicants must be sponsored by a recognised Christian society or community. The trust also asks that applicants be in full agreement with its 'Statement of Faith', which is available to view on the website.

Types of grants

Grants towards the costs of training.

Annual grant total

In 2010/11 the trust had an income of £9,600 and an expenditure of £11,000.

Exclusions

No support for basic professional medical training, for example courses leading to qualification as a doctor, nurse, midwife, dentist, and so on, nor training for work which cannot be considered as involving 'hands on' contact with patients for example administrators or pharmacists.

Applications

On a form available from the trust. Applicants should read the guidelines and agree with the statement of faith before requesting an application form. Forms must be returned electronically wherever possible.

Other information

Training courses for groups may also be considered.

The NFL Trust

£44,000 (11 grants)

Correspondent: Margot Chaundler, 9 Muncaster Road, London SW11 6NY (020 7223 7133; email: nfltrust@mail.com; website: www.nfltrust.org.uk)

Trustees: F. J. Pym; Roger Trafford; Christine Caunt; Joanna Peterkin; Ann Sturgis; Iain Cheyne; David Gye.

CC Number: 1112422

Eligibility

Girls aged between 11 to 18 attending schools and colleges which charge fees in the UK. Support is given in line with 'Christian principles'.

Types of grants

'Bursaries awarded by the NFL Trust are subject to means testing and annual financial review, also taking into account the needs of the child and the commitment of her parents.'

Annual grant total

In 2010/11 the trust had assets of £3.4 million and an income of £126,000.

The trust funded five new and six ongoing bursaries totalling £44,000. One application was made and granted from the Diana Matthews Trust Fund totalling £250.

Applications

In writing to the correspondent. Families of applicants should apply in the academic year before the year in which a bursary is sought.

The Podde Trust

£5,000

Correspondent: Peter Godfrey, 68 Green Lane, Hucclecote, Gloucester GL3 3QX (01452 613563; email: podde@supanet. com)

Trustees: Mr P. B. Godfrey; Mrs P. E. Godfrey; Mr A. Gent; Dr D. Maxted.

CC Number: 1016322

Eligibility

Individuals involved in Christian work in the UK and overseas.

Types of grants

One-off and recurrent grants.

Annual grant total

In 2010/11 the trust had assets of £3,800 and an income of £43,000. There were 28 grants to individuals totalling £10,000.

Applications

In writing to the correspondent: note, the trust states that it has very limited resources, and those it does have are mostly already committed. Requests from new applicants therefore have very little chance of success.

Other information

Organisations involved in Christian work are also supported (£33,000 in 2010/11).

The Stewardship Trust Ripon

£8,000

Correspondent: Ann Metcalfe, Trustee, Hutton Hill, Hutton Bank, Ripon, North Yorkshire HG4 5DT (01765 602887)

Trustees: R. Fay; Ann Metcalfe; D. W. Metcalfe; S. P. Metcalfe.

CC Number: 224447

Eligibility

People connected with Christian causes living in the UK, with a preference for Yorkshire.

Types of grants

One-off and recurrent grants, for example, for training in Christian ministry.

Annual grant total

In 2010/11 the trust had an income of £9,000 and a total expenditure of £45,000. Previously grants to individuals have totalled £8,000.

Applications

In writing to the correspondent. The trust's funds are usually fully committed and new applications are only considered if there is 'extreme need'.

Other information

Grants are also made to churches and societies.

Church of England

The Saint George's Trust

£15,000

Correspondent: Geoff Hammond, 83 Victoria Street, Room No. 4.08, London SW1H 0HW (email: geoffhammond@ssje.org.uk)

Trustees: Andrew Malcolm; Charles Card-Reynolds; Ade Ademola; Stephen Anderson.

CC Number: 253524

Eligibility

People involved in work 'for the furtherance of the Church of England and churches in communion with her'.

Types of grants

Grants are small, one-off and made towards a specific project or theological course, e.g. young people undertaking voluntary Christian work abroad and clergymen planning special work during a sabbatical.

Annual grant total

About £15,000 to £18,000 is given in grants each year.

Exclusions

Restoration projects or any long-term financial support.

Applications

In writing to the correspondent, giving details of the project, its likely cost and with a note of any funds available towards it. An sae is required for a reply.

Huguenot

Charities in connection with the Society of St Onge and Angoumois

£1,500

Correspondent: P J Lane-Gilbert, Brook Hill Top, Great Wolford, Shipston-on-Stour, Warwickshire CV36 5NW (01608 674379)

Trustees: Allan Squire; Barbara Lane; Claire Acharya; John Gill; Pauline Lane-Gilbert; Mark Gibbons; Terry Key.

CC Number: 208718

Eligibility

Young people aged 16 to 25 who live in the UK, with preference for those who are descended from French Protestants (Huguenot) and in particular those who have at any time lived in the province of St Onge and Angoumois in France, who are in need, and who are preparing for, entering upon or engaged in any profession, trade or service.

Types of grants

One-off grants to enable beneficiaries to train for a trade or occupation in order to help them to advance in life or earn their living. Grants are only given on proof of purchase, for example, for books, equipment, daily travel and clothing for people on a training course, and for books, equipment and daily travel for students in further or higher education. Grants range from £100 to £400.

Annual grant total

About £1,500.

Exclusions

No grants to foreign students studying in the UK.

Applications

On a form available from Mr A Squire, 26 Blaisdon, Weston-super-Mare, Somerset BS22 8BN. Applications should be submitted directly by the individual or by a parent or guardian. They are considered in April and May.

Jewish

The Anglo Jewish Association

£90,000

Correspondent: Neil Miron, Haskell House, 152 West End Lane, London NW6 1SD (020 7443 5169; email: info@ anglojewish.org.uk; website: www. anglojewish.org.uk)

Trustees: Clemens Nathan; Julia Samuel; Michael Hilsenrath; Alan Philipp; Adam Dawson; David Loewe; Neil Miron; David Jacobs; Jonathan Walker; Michael Newman; Sam Szlezinger.

CC Number: 256946

Eligibility

Jewish students studying a full-time course at a UK university or further education college, regardless of nation of origin, who are in need.

Types of grants

Grants ranging between £500 and £3,000 a year for students at either undergraduate or postgraduate level.

Annual grant total

Educational grants total around £90,000 per year.

Applications

On a form available from the correspondent or from the website, to be submitted by 30 April. Applications must include academic references, a CV and details of the applicant's personal history.

Scholarships are for one academic year and individuals may apply for the part or the whole of an additional academic year by submitting another complete application, prior to the closing date for the relevant year. The award of a second, third or fourth scholarship is not automatic.

Application forms for the Finnart House School Trust and the Stuart Young Foundation are also available from the website.

The trust welcomes applicants to contact them via email to discuss an application.

Other information

The organisation also administers grants from the Finnart House School Trust and the Stuart Young Foundation.

Finnart House School Trust

£124,000 (34 grants)

Correspondent: Peter Shaw, Clerk to the Trustees, PO Box 603, Edgware, Middlesex HA8 4EQ (020 3209 6006; email: info@finnart.org; website: www.finnart.org)

Trustees: Mark Sebba; Robert Cohen; Hilary Blume; Anthony Yadgaroff; Linda Paterson; Sue Leiffer; Gideon Lyons; Gil Cohen.

CC Number: 220917

Eligibility

Jewish children and young people aged between 14 and 21 who are in need. Bursaries and scholarships are for those with ability, who, because of family circumstances, may otherwise be unable to achieve their potential. The course to be studied must be at a UK institution and end in a recognised qualification.

Types of grants

Bursaries are awarded through schools. Awards may be made regularly each term, or may be one-off. Grants range between £100 and £1,500.

Scholarships are awarded for higher education until the completion of the course and range up to £5,000 a year.

Annual grant total

In 2010/11 the trust had assets of £4.5 million and an income of £148,000. 34 scholarships were awarded to individuals totalling £124,000.

Exclusions

Only members of the Jewish faith can be supported.

Applications

Bursaries are awarded via schools. Scholarship applications are made by the individual on an application pack available to download from the website, to be submitted by April.

Other information

This trust also makes grants for relief-in-need purposes and to organisations which work with children and young people of the Jewish faith who are in need, but its main purpose is to award scholarship grants.

Gur Trust

£7,000

Correspondent: The Trustees, 206 High Road, London N15 4NP (020 8801 6038)

Trustees: Sheldon Morgenstern; Mier Mandel; David Cymerman.

CC Number: 283423

Eligibility

People connected to the Jewish faith in the UK.

Types of grants

One-off and recurrent grants according to need.

Annual grant total

In 2010/11 the trust had assets of £1.4 million and an income of £40,000. Charitable expenditure totalled £34,000, to organisations and individuals.

Applications

'Funds are raised by the trustees. All calls for help are carefully considered and help is given according to circumstances and funds then available.'

Other information

The trust also makes grants to organisations and to individuals for relief-in-need.

The Jewish Widows and Students Aid Trust

£51,000 (31 grants)

Correspondent: Alan Philipp, Trustee, 5 Raeburn Close, London NW11 6UG (020 8349 7199)

Trustees: Alan Philipp; Joanna Philipp.

CC Number: 210022

Eligibility

Jewish students from the UK, France, the Commonwealth and Israel who are aged 10 to 30 years old. Grants are also given to widows with young children.

Types of grants

Mainly interest-free loans ranging from £250 to £1,000. Awards are made on the basis of academic excellence and need. Students can be given grants towards fees, living expenses, books or travel. On occasions grants can also be given to schoolchildren.

Annual grant total

In 2010/11 the trust had assets of £659,000 and an income of £92,000. Grants were made to thirty one students totalling £51,000.

Applications

In writing to the correspondent requesting an application form, including a CV and confirmation of acceptance at an educational establishment. Applications should be submitted directly by the individual to be considered at any time.

The Charities of Moses Lara

£20,000

Correspondent: The Secretary, Spanish and Portuguese Synagogue, 2 Ashworth Road, London W9 1JY (0202892573)

Trustees: Susan Kandel; Adam Musikant; Ronald Sassoon; Sabah Zubaida; Barry Musikant; Daniel Ettinghausen; Suzanne Magnus; Alan Mendoza; Howard Martin; Peter Fraiman.

CC Number: 230826

Eligibility

Spanish and Portuguese Jews, born in wedlock and living in the UK. There may be a preference for people whose principal place of worship is a Sephardi Synagogue.

Types of grants

Help with the cost of books, clothing and other essentials for college and university students. Preference may be given to those promoting the study of texts and so on of Judaism involving the

Rabbinic Law. The trust also assists residents in Beth Holim (Wembley).

Annual grant total

In 2010/11 the charity had an income of £18,000 and an expenditure of £22,000.

Applications

In writing to the correspondent.

The Montpellier Trust

£1,000

Correspondent: Michael Allweis, 7 Montpellier Mews, Salford M7 4ZW (01613 083928; email: michaelallweis@ dwyers.net)

Trustees: Michael Allweis; Jonathan Allweis; Shirley Allweis.

CC Number: 1108119

Eligibility

People in education connected to the Orthodox Jewish faith.

Types of grants

Grants given according to need.

Annual grant total

In 2010/11 the trust had an income of £1,500 and an expenditure of £1,300.

Applications

In writing to the correspondent.

The Rank Trust

£1,500

Correspondent: Nikki Spencer, 6 Seatallan Close, 16 Eyres Gardens, Ilkeston DE7 8JE (01158 49216; email: nikki@spenceruk.co.uk)

Trustees: Peter Strauss; Nikki Spencer; Neil Pike.

CC Number: 1091456

Eligibility

Students of the Jewish faith who are either living or studying within a 50-mile radius of Nottingham city centre.

Types of grants

One-off and recurrent grants to students in college or university.

Annual grant total

In 2010/11 the trust had a total expenditure of £1,600.

Applications

In writing to the correspondent.

The Spanish and Portuguese Jews Children's Fund

£24,000 (37,000 grants)

Correspondent: Howard Miller, Secretary, Spanish and Portuguese Jews Congregation, 2 Ashworth Road, London W9 1JY (020 7289 2573)

Trustees: Judith Hassan; Susan Kandel; Julia Samul; Viviane Ettinghausen; Michael Dangoor; Sarah Magnus; Natalie Leon-Gonn; Simon Dangoor; Messody Adler.

CC Number: 313635

Eligibility

People under 26 who are in need and are Sephardi Jews or are accustomed to congregate with them.

Types of grants

One-off and recurrent grants for schoolchildren and people in further and higher education.

Annual grant total

In 2010/11 the fund benefitted from a substantial legacy. Consequently, in 2010/11 the trust has assets of £1.3 million, an income of £703,000 and made educational grants to 37 individuals totalling £24,000.

Applications

In writing to the correspondent. Applications are considered twice a year, and are to be submitted by 31 March or 30 September.

Protestant

William and Mary Hart Foundation

£1,000

Correspondent: David Marshall, 2 Keats Drive, Hucknall, Nottingham NG15 6TE (01159 635428; email: administrator@ embaptists.com)

Trustee: East Midlands Baptists.

CC Number: 510717

Eligibility

Baptist Christians under the age of 25. Preference shall be given to persons who live in the parish of Collingham or who have a parent or parents living there.

Types of grants

One-off and recurrent grants and loans to schoolchildren, undergraduates and vocational students.

Annual grant total

In 2010 the foundation had an income of £1,100 and an expenditure of £1,000.

Applications

In writing to the correspondent.

The Mylne Trust

£35,000

Correspondent: Paul Jenkins, PO Box 530, Farnham GU9 1BP (email: admin@ mylnetrust.org.uk; website: www. mylnetrust.org.uk)

Trustees: Brian Daniels; Elizabeth Barnes; Revd Andrew Tuck; Ian Sargeant; Mrs A. Mansell; Roy Picken.

CC Number: 208074

Eligibility

Members of the Protestant faith who have been engaged in evangelistic work, including missionaries and retired missionaries, and Christian workers whose finances are inadequate. Married ordinands with children are also supported when all other sources of funding have failed to cover their needs.

Types of grants

Grants are given towards educational training at theological colleges, for the cost of books and living expenses to undergraduates and overseas students.

Annual grant total

In 2010/11 grants were made to over 134 people totalling £55,000.

Applications

On a form available from the correspondent. Applications should be returned to: The Mylne Trust, PO Box 530, Farnham GU9 1BP. The trustees meet quarterly to consider applications.

Other information

Grants are also made for welfare purposes.

The Trust's website currently states that applications are suspended until further notice.

Roman Catholic

The Duchess of Leeds Foundation for Boys and Girls

£24,000 (29 grants)

Correspondent: Bernard Cawley, Clerk, 15 High Oaks, Enfield EN2 8JJ (020 8367 1077)

Trustees: Philip Noel; Julian Stourton; Graham Preston; Adrian Randag; Margaret Waddingham.

CC Number: 313103

Eligibility

Orphaned or fatherless Catholic children aged between 11 and 18 who attend fee-paying Catholic schools and are in need. Children must live in England, Wales or the Channel Islands. Help is concentrated on secondary education; children in primary school are helped only in exceptional circumstances.

Types of grants
Recurring grants of between £359 and £416 per term to help with the cost of school fees only, and single payment awards. Grants may continue until the end of an A-level course.

Annual grant total
The latest accounts available were for 2012. During the year the trust had assets of £522,000 and an income of £39,000. There were 29 grants made totalling £24,000.

Applications
On a form available from the correspondent to be submitted directly by the individual or a parent/guardian. The deadline for applications in 31 January.

United Reformed Church

Milton Mount Foundation

£28,000

Correspondent: Erna Stevenson, Secretary, 11 Copse Close, Cippenham, Slough, Berkshire SL1 5DT (01753 748713)

Trustees: June Colley; David Cuckson; Michael Hopkins; Margaret Morris; Kathleen Oliver; Hilary Miles; Raymond Dunnett; Peter Young; Nina Dunne.

CC Number: 306981

Eligibility
The children of ministers of the United Reformed Church, the Congregational Federation, the Evangelical Fellowship of Congregational Churches and the Unaffiliated Congregational Churches; also daughters of members of these churches.

Types of grants
The foundation gives bursaries towards school fees for children aged 11 to 18, both at United Reformed Church and Congregational schools, and at other independent boarding or day schools approved by the trustees. Grants may also be given towards the cost of school uniform for eligible boys or girls on entry to secondary school at both independent and maintained schools. Women taking up further/higher education at a later stage can also receive grants towards books and fees. Up to one third only of the income may be

spent on boys as the funds arise from the sale of a girls' school, thereby limiting the number of bursaries available to the sons of ministers.

Annual grant total
In 2010/11 the trust had assets of £2.8 million and an income of £122,000. Grants to individuals totalled £28,000.

Applications
On a form available from the correspondent, with information about total family income. Applications are considered in May and June.

Sport

The Francis Drake Fellowship

£3,000

Correspondent: Joan Jupp, 24 Haldane Close, London N10 2PB (020 8883 8725)

Trustees: John Fox; Lillian Brett-Golding.

CC Number: 248302

Eligibility
Dependents of deceased flat green bowlers who were members of the fellowship.

Types of grants
Allowances of £52 per month per child is given to children in full-time education, up to the end of their A-levels.

Annual grant total
In 2011 the trust had an income of £2,700 and an expenditure of £6,500.

Applications
In writing to the correspondent, requesting an application form. Applications should be submitted through the bowling club's Francis Drake Fellowship delegate. Applications are accepted two years after the date of the member's death.

Other information
Grants are also given to dependents for welfare.

Vegetarian

The Vegetarian Charity

£10,000

Correspondent: Susan Lenihan, 56 Parliament Street, Chippenham, Wiltshire SN14 0DE (01249 443521; email: grantssecretary@vegetariancharity.org.uk)

Trustees: I. Allen; Ms C. George; J. Hickey; B. Harkison; Mrs S. Lenihan; Miss K. Lee; Mrs B. Holdsworth; Mrs K. Barker; Miss A. Pattenden; Mrs J. Hughes.

CC Number: 294767

Eligibility
People under the age of 26 who are vegetarian or vegan and are sick or in need.

Types of grants
One-off and recurrent grants of £250 to £1,000 for general educational purposes.

Annual grant total
In 2010/11 the charity had assets of £987,000 and an income of £63,000. Grants paid during the year to individuals and organisations totalled £30,000; a further breakdown was not available.

Applications
On a form available from the correspondent, including details of any other grants received, a CV, a letter of recommendation from a tutor, school reports, covering letter and three references. Applications are considered throughout the year.

Other information
Grants are also made to organisations which promote vegetarianism among young people and to vegetarian children's homes.

Volunteers

The Alec Dickson Trust

£3,000

Correspondent: Jessica Garland, 237 Pentonville Road, London N1 9NJ (email: thealecdicksontrust@talk21.com; website: www.alecdicksontrust.org.uk)

Trustees: Louise Pulford; Laura Compton; Natasha Mogashoa.

CC Number: 1076900

Eligibility
Young people under 30 years of age who are involved in volunteering or community service in the UK.

Types of grants
'The trust's mission is to support young people who are able to demonstrate that through volunteering or community service projects they can enhance the lives of others, particularly those most marginalised by society. The trust particularly welcomes applications from innovative projects in the spirit of Alec Dickson [and] projects which young people themselves have devised and which are unlikely to be funded by other

charitable trusts.' Grants of up to £500 are available.

Annual grant total

Grants are mostly given through the charity that administers the fund, Community Service Volunteers which is why the trust has very low income and expenditure figures.

Exclusions

No grants for gap years, projects based outside of the UK or personal development i.e. student course fees.

Applications

On a form available from the correspondent or to download on the website. Applications can be submitted at any time.

Other information

In the spirit of the trust, all the trustees are aged under 30 and have a connection to voluntary or community service.

The Duveen Trust

£6,000

Correspondent: The Trustees, 26 Beechwood Avenue, London N3 3AX (fax: 020 8349 9649; email: administrator@theduveentrust.org.uk; website: www.theduveentrust.org.uk)

Trustees: Peter Shaw; Alan Greenbat; Ian Berkoff; Gillian Murray; Peter Sollosi; Susan Cipin; Alan Kaye; Ben Sollosi.

CC Number: 326823

Eligibility

Individuals aged up to 25 who wish to get involved with projects which require initiative and which give something back to the community, and who are in need of financial support.

Types of grants

One-off grants of £100 to £500.

Annual grant total

In 2010/11 the trust had an income of £14,000 and an expenditure of £6,300.

Exclusions

Grants are unlikely to be made to support formal education, except for courses leading to qualifications in youth and community work.

Applications

Application forms and guidelines are available from the correspondent or on the website and should be accompanied by a report from the organising agency, and a copy of the programme of the scheme that the applicant wishes to participate in. The deadlines for applications are just before the trustees' meetings, three times a year.

The Emmaus Charitable Trust

£6,000

Correspondent: R J Silman, Trustee, 4 Church Avenue, Lancaster LA1 4SP (01524368)

Trustees: Doreen Silman; Richard Silman.

CC Number: 288515

Eligibility

Christians involved in voluntary projects. Grants are given internationally but in practice there is a preference for Greater London.

Types of grants

One-off and recurrent grants according to need.

Annual grant total

In 2010/11 the trust had an income of £5,900 and a total expenditure of £7,100.

Applications

In writing to the correspondent.

Other information

The trust also makes grants to organisations.

The Torch Trophy Trust
See entry on page 108

See entry on page 108

Women

The Altrusa Careers Trust

£24,000

Correspondent: Raye Lennie, 33 Queensferry Street, West End, Edinburgh EH2 4QS

SC Number: SC009390

Eligibility

Women in the UK and Eire who wish to further their career prospects or to retrain after bringing up a family, and who are in extreme need or facing an emergency.

Types of grants

A loan of up to £500 is available. All loans are interest free and should be repaid within two years of completion of course

Annual grant total

In 2010/11 the trust had an income of £26,000. The majority of income is distributed annually in grants to individuals.

Exclusions

Loans are not available to those still at school and there is probably a restriction on those going on to do a second degree.

Applications

On a form available from the correspondent. Applications are reviewed after 31 March each year. A shortlist is drawn up and references taken up. Applicants are requested to keep in touch with the trustees once a year so that their progress can be noted.

Diamond Education Grant

£8,000 (16 grants)

Correspondent: The Trustees, 2nd Floor Beckwith House, 1 Wellington Road North, Stockport, Cheshire SK4 1AF (01614 807686; email: hq@sigbi.org; website: sigbi.org/our-charities/diamond-education-grant/)

Trustees: Margaret Oldroyd; Maureen Maguire; Susan Biggs; Patricia Black; Elizabeth Batten; Jennifer Vince; Jane Slatter; Denise Staplehurst; Ann Hodgson; Jean Campbell; Constance Mutunhu; Angela Giwa-Osagie.

CC Number: 1139668

Eligibility

Women who are permanently resident in a country in the Federation of Soroptimist International Great Britain and Ireland and wish to refurbish their skills after an employment break or acquire new skills to improve their opportunities of employment and promotion. For a full list of countries visit the website.

Types of grants

Grants of around £500 towards the cost of course fees, books or equipment.

Annual grant total

Approximately £8,000 is available for distribution across the world each year. Around 16 grants of £500 are made each year.

Exclusions

No grants for living expenses.

Applications

Apply through the nearest local branch of Soroptimist International by 15 April.

The Hilda Martindale Educational Trust

£23,000

Correspondent: Clare Munton, The Secretary to the Trustees, Royal Holloway, University of London, Egham,

Surrey TW20 0EX (email: hildamartindaletrust@rhul.ac.uk)

Eligibility
British women pursuing a profession or career in which women are underrepresented.

Types of grants
One-off awards of up to £3,000 which are paid in three instalments in October, January and April. Awards can be used for books, equipment, fees, living expenses or childcare.

Annual grant total
The trust generally gives awards to about ten women totalling £20,000 to £25,000 a year.

Exclusions
Assistance is not given for short courses, access courses, elective studies, courses abroad or first year undergraduates. Funding can only be given to women seeking training/qualifications in areas in which women are underrepresented.

Applications
On a form available from the correspondent in October, to be returned by 1 March for the following academic year. Applicants are informed of the result in mid-June. Applications should be submitted by the individual and must include a reference and a personal statement.

Other information
People who do not exactly suit the eligibility criteria are asked not to apply. The trust has recently revised its eligibility criteria to take into consideration changes in equal opportunities legislation.

President's Fund

£10,000

Correspondent: The Secretary, 6/5 Craigleith Avenue South, Edinburgh EH4 3LQ

SC Number: SC004501

Eligibility
Women in their final year of study for a degree (postgraduate or undergraduate) at a British university who face unexpected financial hardship.

Types of grants
One-off grants between £150 and £500. Applicants receive only one award which is for current study. Grants are intended to help with costs of books, equipment and maintenance/living expenses.

Annual grant total
The trust has an annual income of about £15,000.

Exclusions
Grants are not given towards access courses, diplomas, certificates, study or work outside the UK, childcare, any year of study other than final year, one year undergraduate and one year postgraduate degrees.

Applications
On a form only available by writing to the correspondent. Requests for application forms must be submitted directly by the applicant (not third parties). The trustees meet to consider applications in February, April/May, October and November.

Other information
The trust stated that 'applications which disregard the exclusions listed above will not be acknowledged'.

The Women's Careers Foundation (Girls of The Realm Guild)

£10,000

Correspondent: Beth Hayward, Secretary, 2 Watchoak, Blackham, Tunbridge Wells, Kent TN3 9TP (01892 740602)

Trustees: Barbara Reckman; Elspeth Crail; Hilary Pearson; Diana Morgan; Sheila Henwood; Alexandra Eversole; Maurine Lewin; Rowena Meager; Maggie Goodall; Judith Mortimer-Sykes.

CC Number: 313159

Eligibility
Women only, who are UK citizens. Applicants should be seeking assistance to begin or continue studies for a career and should be 21 or over, except for music or dancing when the minimum age is 16.

Types of grants
One-off grants and loans to help with any costs relating to further education relevant to a career. Average grants usually total around £250. The maximum amount for loans is £1,000.

Annual grant total
The foundation has an average income of £11,000. Grants to students usually total around £10,000 per year.

Exclusions
Grants are not given for PhD study or postgraduate studies if the subject indicates a complete change of direction.

Applications
In writing to the correspondent. Applications should be submitted between 1 September and 31 January for the following academic year. An sae is essential. The correspondent has stated that timing is crucial: 'so many people write for immediate help which we cannot give'. Applications must be submitted well in advance.

Yorkshire Ladies' Council of Education (Incorporated)

£11,000

Correspondent: Phillida Richardson, Flat 4 Forest Hill, 11 Park Crescent, Leeds LS8 1DH (01132 691471; email: ylce411@btinternet.com; website: www.ylce.org.uk)

Trustees: Barbara Neale; Gwynneth Owen; Liz Arnold; Margaret Bradbury; Eva Herbert; Francoise Logan; Jillian Rennie; Nancy Donner; Rosemary Stephens; Rosemary Ward; Gill Milner; Kim Knowles; Isobel Jenkins; Elizabeth Thring; Anne Taylor; Peggy Pullan.

CC Number: 529714

Eligibility
British women who are aged 21 or over 'who can present a case of special need in funding their further or higher education at a British institution'. Applicants must not qualify for Local Authority support. A separate fund has been set up in association with the Sir James Knott Trust, to enable grants to be offered exclusively to applicants from the North East of England (defined as Tyne and Wear, Northumberland, County Durham inclusive of Hartlepool but exclusive of Darlington, Stockton-on-Tees, Middlesbrough, Redcar and Cleveland).

Types of grants
About 60 grants of £100 to £500 (generally being £200 to £300) a year for fees.

Annual grant total
In 2010/11 the trust had assets of £446,000 and an income of £30,000. Grants to individuals totalled £11,000.

Exclusions
YLCE members and their dependents are not eligible for support.

Applications
Application forms can be requested from the correspondent, or are available to download from the charity's website along with guidelines. Completed forms should be submitted directly by the individual by the first of January, March, June or September for consideration later in the month. Applicants for grants from the Sir James Knott Trust (who may be asked for proof of residency) should label their form 'SPECIAL FUND'.

Work/study overseas

Lady Allen of Hurtwood Memorial Trust

£2,000

Correspondent: Caroline Richards, Chatsworth Cottage, Collington Lane West, Bexhill-on-Sea TN39 3TA (01424 844017; email: lamt@hotmail.co.uk)

Trustees: Caroline Richards; Dorothy Whitaker; Dorothy Selleck; Heather Ewart; Paul Soames; Peter Allen; Edwina Mitchell.

CC Number: 277942

Eligibility

Individuals wishing to carry out a specific travel project that will help them gain specific additional knowledge and experience which will enhance the quality and the nature of their work with young children (particularly children with disabilities or children from disadvantaged backgrounds) and their families.

Types of grants

In the region of £1,000.

Annual grant total

In 2010/11 the trust had an income of £1,000 and an expenditure of £2,200.

Exclusions

No grants for: academic course fees; attendance at specific conferences; building and equipping centres; gap year, sixth form projects or similar travel proposals; medical electives; supporting individual children.

Applications

On a form available, with guidelines for applicants, from the correspondent or to download from the website. Guidance notes are also available from the website. Applicants must have a specific project in mind and offer positive evidence of how the award will help them, and how the knowledge gained will be shared with others. The closing date for applications is 31 January each year. Shortlisting is in February and awards are distributed in March.

Captain F. G. Boot Scholarships

£5,000 (8 grants)

Correspondent: John Allen, The Worshipful Company of Cutlers, Cutlers' Hall, 4 Warwick Lane, London EC4M 7BR (020 7248 1866; email: clerk@cutlerslondon.co.uk; website: www.cutlerslondon.co.uk)

Trustees: Christopher Robinson; Christopher Fisher; Adam Traill.

CC Number: 283096

Eligibility

Young people aged 17 to 25.

Types of grants

These scholarships enable school leavers to spend at least six months abroad to learn a foreign language or a certain foreign culture prior to further education. Scholarships are generally for between £500 and £1,000. Grants are not given to Project Trust applicants.

Annual grant total

Around £5,000 a year is awarded in grants.

Applications

Application forms can be downloaded from the Worshipful Company of Cutlers website.

The Winston Churchill Memorial Trust

£561,000 (105 grants)

Correspondent: Alexandra Sibun, Trust Secretary, 29 Great Smith Street (South Door), London SW1P 3BL (020 7799 1660; fax: 020 7581 0410; email: office@wcmt.org.uk; website: www.wcmt.org.uk)

Trustees: Brian Clarke; Brian Williamson; Robert Fellowes; Harry Henderson; Jeremy Soames; Merlyn Lowther; Randolph Churchill; Alan Brooke; Anne Boyd; John Baker; Dinesh Dhamija.

CC Number: 313952

Eligibility

British citizens resident in the UK who are over 18.

Types of grants

Categories supported change each year but in general grants are made to people with a specific project which involves them travelling overseas, in order to bring back knowledge and best practice for the benefit of others in their UK professions and communities. Grants cover return airfare, daily living, insurance, travel within the countries being visited and occasionally assistance with home expenses. People are expected to travel for four to eight weeks (however fellowships have been awarded for up to 13 weeks). Amounts range from £2,300 to £11,000 with an average grant of £5,200.

Categories are drawn from the following fields: science, engineering and technology; business, industry and commerce; education and vocational training; environment, food and rural affairs; medical and health; communities that work; discovery and exploration; the arts and older people; professions and the public services; and other.

Annual grant total

In 2010/11 the charity had assets of £29 million and an income of £1 million. 105 scholarships were awarded totalling £561,000.

Exclusions

No awards for attendance of courses, academic studies, student grants or gap year projects.

Applications

On a form available on the website or as a hard copy from the correspondent. Applications are open in May of each year and should be received by the end of October for travel in the following year.

Other information

The charity also awards up to ten bursaries a year of £2,000 to undergraduates at Churchill College, Cambridge. Contact the college for further information.

The Gilchrist Educational Trust
See entry on page 9

Go Make it Happen
See entry on page 10

The Rotary Foundation Scholarships

£1 million

Correspondent: The Secretary, Rotary International in Great Britain and Ireland, Kinwarton Road, Alcester, Warwickshire B49 6PB (01789 765411; fax: 01789 756570; email: info@ribi.org; website: www.ribi.org)

Eligibility

Scholarships overseas to further international understanding, for vocational study, graduates, undergraduates who have completed two years of university study, teachers of people with disabilities or professional journalists.

Types of grants

The purpose of the scholarships is to further international understanding and friendly relations among peoples of different countries, rather than to enable beneficiaries to achieve any particular qualification.

Annual grant total

Previously about £1 million.

Applications

Applications can only be made through a rotary club in the district where the applicant lives, studies or works.

Other information

Not a registered charity.

The Sloane Robinson Foundation

See entry on page 30

The Tropical Agricultural Association Award Fund

£11,000

Correspondent: Elizabeth Warham, General Secretary, 144 Mostyn Road, London SW19 3LR (020 8543 7563; email: general_secretary@taa.org.uk; website: www.taa.org.uk)

Trustees: Elizabeth Warham; John Davies; Jim Ellis-Jones; Christopher Garforth; Paul Harding.

CC Number: 800663

Eligibility

UK graduates, people with a diploma or senior students up to the age of 30 wishing to spend at least six months working on a rural development project in a developing country. Usually grant recipients have had training in agriculture, forestry, agroforestry, environmental science or geography.

Types of grants

Grants of up to a maximum of £2,000 to help with airfares or living costs arising from their proposed projects (paid or unpaid).

Annual grant total

In 2010/11 the fund had an income of £19,000 and made grants totalling £11,000, including expenses.

Exclusions

People with more than two years prior experience working overseas.

Applications

Application forms are available from the association's website. Applications are considered every two months.

Other information

Successful applicants will also gain access to the TAA networks and journal, professional advice from a mentor and two years free membership of the TAA.

The WR Foundation

£2,500

Correspondent: John Malthouse, Trustee, Malthouse and Co., America House, 8B Rumford Place, Liverpool L3 9DD (01512 842000)

Trustees: Anne Russell; John Malthouse; William Russell.

CC Number: 1003546

Eligibility

Undergraduates and people undertaking educational trips overseas.

Types of grants

One-off grants of around £1,000.

Annual grant total

In 2010/11 the foundation had an income of £51,000 and sponsored two students to a total of £2,500.

Applications

In writing to the correspondent.

Other information

The foundation mostly makes grants to organisations.

Antarctic

The Trans-Antarctic Association

£14,000

Correspondent: Peters Elworthy and Moore, Salisbury House, 2–3 Salisbury Villas, Cambridge CB1 2LA (01223 728222; fax: 01223 362616; email: taagrants@bas.ac.uk; website: www.transantarctic.org.uk)

Trustees: Julian Paren; Harry Atkinson; Peter Clarkson; A. Clarke; Colin Harris.

CC Number: 205773

Eligibility

Citizens of the UK, Australia, South Africa and New Zealand seeking to further knowledge or exploration of the Antarctic.

Types of grants

Cash grants of up to £1,500 to support field work or travel to Antarctica, as well as equipment and other research activities. One third of the £10,000–£15,000 available each year is awarded to New Zealand nationals.

Annual grant total

In 2011 the Association had an income of £12,000 and an expenditure of £14,000.

Exclusions

No grants for Arctic work or for people who are not nationals of the countries named above.

Applications

Applications should be made by 31 January each year on a form available from the correspondent.

Europe

Erasmus Mobility Grants

£10,000,000

Correspondent: The Erasmus Team, British Council, Bridgewater House, Manchester M1 6LT (02920 397405; email: erasmus@britishcouncil.org; website: www.britishcouncil.org/erasmus)

CC Number: 209131

Eligibility

Students from the EU who wish to study and work abroad for a period of between three months and one year. (Support is also available to professors and business staff who want to teach abroad and for university staff who want to be trained abroad.)

Types of grants

Grants for students carrying out study or work placements, based on the duration of period abroad, for travel costs, foreign language preparation and living costs abroad. Students can receive one grant for and Erasmus study period, an Erasmus work placement and Erasmus Mundus mobility.

Annual grant total

The annual budget is in excess of €400 million; more than 3,100 higher education institutions in 31 countries participate. (This budget relates to all of the participating countries not just the UK.)

Applications

Students should enquire about the programme at their home university department or International/European office.

The Peter Kirk Memorial Fund

£20,000

Correspondent: Gillian King, 11 Luttrell Avenue, Putney, London SW15 6PA (020 8789 7927; email: mail@kirkfund.org.uk; website: www.kirkfund.org.uk)

Trustees: Terry Marsh; David Peacock; David Kirk; Margaret Whiteside; Simon Cox; William Sampson; Philip Hegarty; Gareth Sibson; Barney Holbeche.

CC Number: 1049139

Eligibility

Citizens of any European country aged between 17 and 29 years. Applicants must have been in full-time education at some time during the 12 months preceding the application.

Annual grant total

In 2011 the trust had an income of £20,000 and an expenditure of £21,000. Previously 10 to 12 scholarships a year have totalled around £20,000.

Applications

On a form available from the correspondent, by email or on receipt of an sae. Application forms can also be downloaded from the website. Projects must be submitted by 5 November, with selection/interviews normally being completed by the end of December (check the website for the most up to date deadlines). Interviews take place in London at the applicant's expense. The fund would prefer applications to be submitted by email if possible.

The Trades Union Congress Educational Trust

£5,500

Correspondent: Jean Scott, Congress House, 23–28 Great Russell Street, London WC1B 3LQ (020 7467 1344; email: jscott@tuc.org.uk)

Trustees: Brendan Barber; Alison Shepherd; Gloria Mills; Dave Prentis; Sheila Bearcroft; Michael Leahy.

CC Number: 313741

Eligibility

Members of TUC affiliated trade unions who are attending a course and are not in receipt of other grants.

Types of grants

Scholarships and bursaries for: Ruskin College, Coleg Harlech and Northern College; trade union and industrial relations students at Keele, Birkbeck and Middlesex universities; European Study Bursaries; trade union learners working online; a Harvard bursary and support for female trade unionists.

Annual grant total

In 2010 scholarships and bursaries totalled £5,500.

Applications

Applications should be made through the participating colleges.

New Zealand
The Link Foundation

£34,000

Correspondent: Stephen Rowland-Jones, 2 Sovereign Close, Quidhampton, Salisbury SP2 9ES (020 7839 3423; email: nz-uk.link@hotmail.co.uk)

Trustees: Graham Lovelock; Richard Fell; Jenny Stevens; Dorothy Garland; Derek Leask; Sjoerd Post; David Thompson.

CC Number: 802457

Eligibility

People wishing to participate in a vocational exchange between the UK and New Zealand, through specific joint schemes such as Equine Fertility, Hospitality Awards and Social Sciences Awards. The schemes are advertised through the governing bodies and specialist press belonging to these areas.

Types of grants

Grants of between £200 and £10,000 towards educational and cultural exchange linked to a vocation, including for research.

Annual grant total

In 2010/11 £34,000 was given in scholarships and fellowships.

Exclusions

Grants are not made to individuals seeking funds for one-off trips such as medical residencies or to applicants wishing to visit countries other than Britain or New Zealand. Grants are not usually made for study.

Applications

In writing to the correspondent using the application forms available on the website, or to the organisation with which the foundation is jointly offering the award. Applications can be submitted directly by the individual or through the school/college or educational welfare agency.

Scandinavia
CoScan Trust Fund

£1,400

Correspondent: Dr Brita Green, 103 Long Ridge Lane, Nether Poppleton, York YO26 6LW (01904 794438; email: PSGBEG@aol.com; website: www.coscan.org.uk/side7.html)

Trustee: Executive Committee, CoScan Officers.

Eligibility

British people aged between 15 and 25 who are undertaking a project of an educational nature involving travel between the UK and Scandinavia and within Scandinavia. Only short visits will be considered.

Types of grants

One-off grants of between £75 and £150.

Annual grant total

In previous years approximately 15 grants have been awarded annually through the travel awards scheme.

Applications

On a form available from the correspondent, accompanied by a personal letter. Applications are considered once a year and should be submitted by March for consideration in April/May.

Sweden
Anglo-Swedish Literary Foundation

£10,000

Correspondent: c/o Swedish Embassy, Swedish Embassy, 11 Montagu Place, London W1H 2AL (020 7917 6400)

Trustees: Carl Werkelid; Nicola Clase; Helena Reitberger.

CC Number: 230622

Eligibility

Individuals wishing to participate in study visits connected to research on Swedish literature. The foundation aims to encourage cultural exchange between Sweden and the British Isles by promoting and diffusing knowledge and the appreciation of Swedish art and literature in the UK.

Types of grants

Grants may be spent on study visits connected with research on Swedish literature. Grants may also be used for translations and publishing subsidies and so on.

Annual grant total

In 2010/11 the foundation had an income of £12,000 and an expenditure of £11,000.

Applications

In writing to the correspondent, outlining your project or activity and stating required funding and any other sources of funding. Applications must be received by 1 May or 1 November.

Other information

The foundation established the Bernard Shaw Translation Prize which awards £2,000 every three years for the best translation into English of a Swedish Work. This prize is administered by the Society of Authors.

National charities classified by occupation of parent

Airline Pilots

The British Airline Pilots' Association Benevolent Fund (BALPA)

£19,000

Correspondent: Carolyn Evans, BALPA House, 5 Heathrow Boulevard, 278 Bath Road, West Drayton UB7 0DQ (020 8476 4000; fax: 020 8476 4077; email: balpa@balpa.org)

Trustees: Andrew Gooch; Capt. Anthony Pell; Capt. David Marshall; Capt. Henry Hopkins; Capt. Dave Smith; David Hogg; Robin Keegan.

CC Number: 229957

Eligibility

Dependents of retired or deceased commercial pilots and flight engineers, who are or have been members of BALPA.

Types of grants

Limited grants are made towards the cost of books, uniforms and associated educational expenses.

Annual grant total

In 2010/11 the trust had an income of £35,000 and a total expenditure of £69,000. The trust made grants of approximately £19,000 and gave about £39,000 in interest-free loans.

Exclusions

Grants are not given for school fees.

Applications

In writing to the correspondent requesting an application form. Applications are considered quarterly.

Artists

The Artists' Orphan Fund

£72,000 (21 grants)

Correspondent: Brad Feltham, Burlington House, Piccadilly, London W1J 0BB (020 7734 1193)

Trustees: Laurie Bray; David Gentleman; Gerald Libby; Jacqueline Rizvi; Martin Bailey; Nicola Hicks; Phillip Hicks; Richard Grasby; Ronald Maddox; Bernard Dunstan; Ken Howard.

CC Number: 219356

Eligibility

Children of a professional artist (for example painter, sculptor, illustrator or designer), where either one or both parents have died. Applicants must be under the age of 25 and/or in full-time education.

Types of grants

Grants for maintenance expenses, educational costs and extra-curricular activities. Individuals can be supported throughout their education but they must reapply each year.

Annual grant total

In 2010/11 the fund had assets of £1.3 million and an income of £80,000. 21 individuals were supported totalling £72,000.

Exclusions

Funding is rarely provided for private or boarding education, but will be considered when a child has a scholarship, considerable bursary or the family circumstances present a genuine need for the child to be living outside of the family unit.

Applications

In writing to the correspondent, including career details of qualifying parent and the present financial position of the family. Appropriate applicants will receive a form which they will need to complete, and are considered upon receipt.

Dancers' Career Development

£387,000 (122 grants)

Correspondent: Linda Yates, Secretary, Plouviez House, 19–20 Hatton Place, London EC1N 8RU (020 7831 1449; fax: 020 7242 1462; email: admin@thedcd.org.uk; website: www.thedcd.org.uk)

Trustees: Russell Brown; Janet Eager; Colin Nears; Gerry Weiss; Gillian Raine; Anthony John Dyson; Hilary Hadley; Felicity Clarke; Panton Corbett; Kenneth James Marchant; Charles Glanville; Marguerite Porter; Robert Robson; Maxine Room; Paul Mitchell; Victoria Mather; Alison Beckett; Fred Emden; Paul Mead.

CC Number: 327747

Eligibility

Professional and independent dancers in the UK, regardless of their artistic background. There are slightly different eligibility criteria for different sorts of dancers.

Independent dancers must have worked:
- As a professional dancer for a minimum of eight years
- A minimum of five years in the UK
- For at least four months during each of the last three years of employment

Company dancers must have been a professional dancer for a minimum of eight years and spent at least five with one or more of the following companies affiliated to the organisation: Adzido Pan African Dance Company, Birmingham Royal Ballet, Northern Ballet, Phoenix Dance Theatre, Rambert Dance Company, Richard Alston Dance Company, Scottish Ballet, Siobhan Davies Dance Company and The Royal Ballet. However, DCD has introduced a second-tier funding system which allows dancers working with one of these companies from one to four years to apply for a lower level of retraining grant.

The trustees may be able to exercise discretion in cases where dancers do not meet any of the above criteria because they have had to retire on medical grounds.

Types of grants

One-off payments and financial support for re-training are given to dancers at the end of their career. Business start-up grants are also available. Support may be used for: course/training fees, equipment, maintenance, travel costs and childcare costs.

Annual grant total

In 2010/11 the trust held assets of £1.2 million and had an income of £747,000 the majority of which was in contributions from member companies. 122 new awards were made totalling £387,000: 63 to company dancers and 59 to independent dancers. Meanwhile DCD continued to support a further 121 dancers during the year.

Applications

Applications may be obtained from the correspondent or downloaded from the DCD website and should be submitted by the individual. Although individuals may access the application forms themselves, they are encouraged to arrange a personal or telephone appointment with DCD prior to applying. DCD can assist with travel costs for any such meeting.

Applications must also include a dance career CV, covering letter addressed to the trustees, information on the course or equipment and a detailed application budget. Applications should be submitted at a minimum of three months prior to the beginning of any training. Trustees meet five times per year to consider applications. Deadline dates are publicised in DCD's monthly e-newsletter.

Other information

DCD also provide careers advice and counselling services regardless of an applicant's funding status.

The DCD website contains a lot of useful information including application guidelines, sample budgets and links to organisations which may be able to help individuals who have not spent enough time dancing in the UK to qualify for help from DCD.

DCD is a founding member of the International Organisation for the Transition of Professional Dancers (IOTPD).

Equity Trust Fund

£117,000 (44 grants)

Correspondent: Keith Carter, Secretary, Plouviez House, 19–20 Hatton Place, London EC1N 8RU (020 7831 1926; email: keith@equitycharitabletrust.org.uk; website: www.equitycharitabletrust.org.uk)

Trustees: James Bolam; Anne Bright; Glen Barnham; Robin Browne; David Cockayne; Oliver Ford Davies; Bryn Evans; Ryan Losco; Graham Hamilton; Frank Hitchman; Barbara Hyslop; Milton Johns; Ian McGarry; Harry Landis; Gillian Rayne; Frederick Pyne; Rosalind Shanks; John Rubinstein; Ian Talbot; Caroline Smith; Jeffrey Wickham; Josephine Tewson; Frank Williams; Johnny Worthy.

CC Number: 328103

Eligibility

Professional performers (under Equity or ITC contracts) with a minimum of ten years' experience as an adult (work performed below the age of 16 is not counted).

Types of grants

Grants to enable people to pursue a new career. They can be used towards books, equipment, instruments, fees, living expenses or childcare.

Annual grant total

In 2010/11 the fund had assets of £8.6 million and an income of £362,000. There were 44 grants for educational bursaries given to individuals with a total value of £117,000.

Exclusions

No grants to amateur performers, musicians or drama students.

Applications

On a form available from the correspondent or downloaded from the website. There are normally three meetings each year, with the first one taking place normally around about the middle of May.

Other information

The trust has an informative website.

Peggy Ramsay Foundation

£73,000

Correspondent: G Laurence Harbottle, Trustee, Hanover House, 14 Hanover Square, London W1S 1HP (020 7667 5000; fax: 020 7667 5100; email: laurence.harbottle@harbottle.com; website: www.peggyramsayfoundation.org)

Trustees: Laurence Harbottle; John Tydeman; Michael Codron; Simon Callow; David Hare; Rupert Rhymes; Harriet Walter; Neil Adleman; Tamara Harvey.

CC Number: 1015427

Eligibility

Writers for the stage who have been produced publicly, are 'of promise' and are in need of time to write which they cannot afford, or are in need of other assistance. Applicants must live in the British Isles (including Republic of Ireland and the Channel Islands).

Types of grants

One-off grants. Individual awards rarely exceed £5,000 for writing time or £1,000 for word processors.

Annual grant total

In 2011 the foundation had assets of £4.7 million and an income of £242,000. Grants to 70 individuals totalled £145,000.

Exclusions

No grants towards production costs or to writers who have not been produced. Drama students or other artists learning their trade are not supported, just experienced writers who could not otherwise follow their career. No grants are made for writing not intended for the theatre.

Applications

should also provide answers to the following questions:
- When and where was the first professional production of a play of yours
- Who produced the play which qualifies you for a grant
- When and where was your qualifying play produced, what was its run and approximate playing time and has it been revived
- For that production were the director and actors all professionals engaged with Equity contracts

▶ Did the audience pay to attend

Scripts and publicity material must not be included. Trustees meet quarterly although applications are dealt with between meetings. Applicants will usually receive a decision in six to eight weeks.

Other information

Grants to organisations totalled £18,000. Grants for welfare are also made.

TACT Education Fund

£13,000

Correspondent: Robert Ashby, 58 Bloomsbury Street, London WC1B 3QT (020 7636 7868; email: robert@tactactors.org; website: www. tactactors.org)

Trustees: Tim Denham; Lalla Ward; Geraldine James; Elizabeth Garvie.

CC Number: 802885

Eligibility

Dependents of members of the theatrical profession who are over the age of 18 and who wish to pursue higher education in the arts.

Types of grants

Maintenance grants of £1,200 per year to students in further and higher education, including mature students and postgraduates.

Annual grant total

In 2010/11 the trust had an income of £24,000 and an expenditure of £14,000.

Exclusions

Grants are not available for private drama school fees or study abroad.

Applications

On a form available from the correspondent. Applications are to be submitted directly by the individual and should include details of the theatrical parent's CV. Awards are decided in July each year.

Bankers

The Bank Workers Charity

£186,000

Correspondent: The Clerk, Pinners Hall, 105–108 Old Broad Street, London EC2N 1EX (0800 023 4834; email: info@bwcharity.org.uk; website: www. bwcharity.org.uk)

Trustees: David Turton; Linda Lawrence; M. Locke; Ian Keynes; Jacqueline Hopgood; Paul Haynes; Tony Ramos; Douglas Belmore; Paul

Szumilewicz; Christopher Beavan; Tariq Kazi; Lesley Davie; Lillian Boyle; Gary George; Shirley Hughes.

CC Number: 313080

Eligibility

Current and ex-employees of banks in the UK and their dependents.

Types of grants

One-off and recurrent grants for fees and other educational expenses.

Annual grant total

In 2010/11 the charity had assets of £45 million and an income of £1.5 million. Grants to 553 beneficiaries totalled £616,000, broken down as follows:

▶ Regular grants – £327,000
▶ School fees and expenses – £158,000
▶ Support in crisis – £103,000
▶ Grants to students – £28,000

Applications

Contact the charity in the first instance to discuss making an application.

Other information

The charity also provides support in three main areas: home, money and wellbeing. They have client advisors who offer information, advice and guidance covering a range of issue as well as offering independent and confidential counselling.

The Alfred Foster Settlement

£20,000

Correspondent: Stephen Yoxall, Barclays Bank Trust Co. Ltd, Executorship and Trustee Service, Osborne Court, Gadbrook Park, Rudheath, Northwich CW9 7UE (01606 313426)

Trustee: Barclays Bank Trust Company Ltd.

CC Number: 229576

Eligibility

Employees and former employees of banks and their dependents who are in need. Applicants must be students aged under 28 years.

Types of grants

One-off grants, for example, to help with university fees, books, travel costs and living expenses while in further education.

Annual grant total

In 2010/11 the trust had an income of £30,000 and a total expenditure of £51,000. Grants were given to 37 individuals totalling £41,000.

Applications

In writing to the correspondent. Applications can be submitted directly

by the individual or through the school/college or educational welfare agency.

Other information

The trust also makes grants to individuals for welfare purposes.

Barristers

The Barristers' Benevolent Association

£100,000

Correspondent: Susan Eldridge, Secretary, 14 Gray's Inn Square, London WC1R 5JP (020 7242 4761; fax: 020 7831 5366; email: enquiries@the-baa.com; website: www.the-bba.com)

Trustees: Terence Mowschenson; John Macdonald; David Phillips; Sara Hargreaves; Gillian Brasse; Mark Studer.

CC Number: 1106768

Eligibility

Past or present practising members of the Bar and their dependents, in England and Wales, who are in need.

Types of grants

Educational grants for dependents are only given in the most exceptional circumstances, for example where the death or disability of a barrister leaves his or her children stranded in mid-education. Grants or loans are given to schoolchildren towards books, educational outings, maintenance or school uniforms or clothing; students in further/higher education for help with books, fees and living expenses; mature students for books, travel, fees or childcare; and people starting work for books, equipment, clothing and travel. Loans are also available.

Annual grant total

In 2011 the charity had assets of £8.9 million and an income of £589,000. £239,000 was given in grants to individuals and £106,000 in loans.

Exclusions

School fees are only paid in exceptional circumstances such as if the student is facing imminent examinations.

Applications

On a form available from the website. Applications are considered throughout the year and should include the name and address of the chambers where they last practised as a barrister.

Other information

Grants are also made for welfare purposes.

Book retail

The Book Trade Charity

£5,500

Correspondent: David Hicks, Chief Executive, The Foyle Centre, The Retreat, Abbots Road, Kings Langley, Hertfordshire WD4 8LT (01329 848731; email: david@btbs.org; website: www.booktradecharity.org)

Trustees: Nigel Batt; Timothy Wright; Clare Harington; Marian Donne; Katie Fulford; Tony Mulliken; Lynette Owen; Timothy Lambert.

CC Number: 1128129

Eligibility

People in need who have worked in the book trade in the UK for at least one year (normally publishing/distribution/book-selling), and their dependents.

Types of grants

One-off grants of up to £1,000 are given to help retrain people from the book trade who have been made redundant. These grants are given to eligible mature students where a welfare need is evident.

The society is predominantly a relief-in-need charity and retraining is only a small part of their work. Therefore, general educational grants are not usually made.

Annual grant total

Education grants usually total around £5,500 each year.

Applications

On a form available from the correspondent. Applications can be submitted by the individual or through a recognised referral agency (social worker, Citizens Advice, doctor and so on). They are considered as they arrive.

Building trade

Scottish Building Federation Edinburgh and District Charitable Trust

See entry on page 86

Civic and public services

The Charity for Civil Servants

£4,000

Correspondent: The Help and Advisory Team, Fund House, 5 Anne Boleyn's Walk, Cheam, Sutton, Surrey SM3 8DY (0800 056 2424; fax: 020 8240 2401; email: info@foryoubyyou.org.uk; website: www.foryoubyyou.org.uk)

Trustees: Brian Fox; Graeme Henderson; Peter Connor; Richard Hatfield; Stephen Laws; Dr Catherine Bell; Anna Southall; Richard Corden; Tim Flesher; Hilary Douglas; Patrick Hughes; Siobhan Benita.

CC Number: 1136870

Eligibility

Serving, former and retired staff of the Civil Service and associated organisations, and their dependents, who are in need.

Types of grants

Grants, loans and allowances according to need. Grants are available for retraining, and to support people back into work. Grants are also available to support the education of dependents.

Annual grant total

In 2011 the charity had assets of £37 million and an income of £8.1 million. They supported 5,700 individuals totalling £4 million including £4,000 for education.

Exclusions

No grants for private education.

Applications

Either using the online application process, by downloading an application form or requesting one to be sent in the post. The charity runs a freephone help service providing advice and information and assistance with an application.

Other information

The fund also helps people by providing an information service on a range of community-based services and a confidential visiting service to aid and advice on funding opportunities.

Coalminers

The Miners' Welfare National Educational Fund

£62,000

Correspondent: V O S Jones, Secretary, The Old Rectory, Rectory Drive, Whiston, Rotherham, South Yorkshire S60 4JG (01709 728115; fax: 01709 839164; website: ciswo.org/index.php/education/)

Trustees: Richard Budge; Robert Young; C. D. Ambler; George Shearer; John Humble; Wayne Thomas; Christine Kaye; Ian Davies; Jon Hattersley; Terence Fox; J. Wood.

CC Number: 313246

Eligibility

People who are at least 17 years old and (i) employed in the coalmining industry of Great Britain (including any activity conducted by British Coal) or who have ceased to be so employed by reason of age or disability or who, having ceased to be so employed for any other reason, have not subsequently changed their occupation; or (ii) the dependant sons and daughters (and other dependents) of those described above.

Types of grants

Grants of not more than £500 a year to help with the costs of taking educational courses at degree or equivalent level. For applicants in category (i) above, all full-time courses and Open University courses are eligible. Otherwise the course must be one for which local education authority grants are mandatory. Grants are only considered for those taking postgraduate courses directly after and related to a first degree where it is essential for entry into a profession.

Annual grant total

In 2010/11 grants totalled £62,000, broken down by area in the trust accounts:
- North Yorkshire: 50 grants totalling £20,000
- Nottinghamshire: 32 grants totalling £15,000
- South Yorkshire: 22 grants totalling £8,000
- Central: 19 grants totalling £7,800
- South Wales: 11 grants totalling £4,400
- Scotland: 8 grants totalling £3,100
- HQ and others: 8 grants totalling £2,900
- North East: 2 grants totalling £700
- Western: 1 grant totalling £500
- Telegraph awards: 1 of £75

Applications

Application forms are available from the correspondent between March and August and must be submitted along with a cover letter and a reference from the applicant's school or college. The selection committee meet two or three times a year. Confirmation of A-level results and confirmation of award of student support must be included.

Other information

Applicants must reapply in each academic year of an eligible course.

Commerce

The George Drexler Foundation

£162,000

Correspondent: Jonathan Fountain, 35–43 Lincolns Inn Fields, London WC2A 3PE (020 7869 6080; email: georgedrexler@rcseng.ac.uk)

Trustees: Alastair Collett; Tina Dresher; Leela Kapila; Michael Edgar.

CC Number: 313278

Eligibility

People who have a direct link with commerce, i.e. who have owned and run their own commercial business. Applicants whose parents or grandparents have this link can also be supported. This does not include professional people such as doctors, lawyers, dentists, architects or accountants. No exceptions can be made. Preference is given to schoolchildren with serious family difficulties so that the child has to be educated away from home, and to people with special educational needs.

Types of grants

One-off and recurrent grants of £1,000 to £10,000. To enrich the educational experiences of younger people; assisting particularly gifted or talented students, undergraduates or postgraduates in developing their individual skills or supporting projects that develop new or enhance existing services or knowledge that benefit society, and particularly those students in medical education.

Annual grant total

In 2010/11 the foundation had assets of £5.7 million and an income of £222,000. Grants for educational purposes totalled £162,000.

Exclusions

No funding for medical electives, volunteering or gap year projects.

Applications

On a form available from the correspondent, submitted directly by the individual, enclosing an sae. Applications should be submitted in May for consideration in June/July.

Other information

The foundation also provides welfare grants to former employees of the Ofrex Group and their dependents.

The Ruby and Will George Trust

£30,000

Correspondent: Damien Slattery, 125 Cloverfield, West Allotment, Newcastle upon Tyne NE27 0BE (01912 664527; email: admin@rwgt.co.uk; website: www.rwgt.co.uk)

Trustees: David Waters; Jean Waters; Edward Ellis; Charles Ellis; William Ellis.

CC Number: 264042

Eligibility

The dependents of people in need who have been or who are employed in commerce. Preference is given to people who live in the north east of England.

Types of grants

One-off and recurrent grants of up to £2,000 towards maintenance and fees, mainly for those in secondary or further education. Grants relating to fees are usually paid directly to the educational establishment. Occasionally, assistance with maintenance, books and basic travel expenses will be awarded.

Annual grant total

In 2010/11 the trust had an income of £102,000 and a total expenditure of £57,000. Previously grants were given to individuals mainly for the advancement of education.

Exclusions

Expeditions, study visits and student exchanges are not funded.

Applications

The trust has an online application process, though those without access to the internet can still submit a paper-based application. Applicants will need to prove their commerce connection and their income and expenditure. Two references are required.

The trust considers applications four times a year, usually in January, May, July and October. Applications should be submitted two weeks in advance. Note: upcoming deadline dates can be found on the trust's website.

Other information

The trust also makes grants to institutions and to individuals for relief

in need purposes. Accounts were received by the Charity Commission but were unavailable to view.

Farming

The Dairy Crest and NFU Fund

£16,000

Correspondent: Catherine Booth, Higher Moorlake Cottage, Crediton, Devon EX17 5EL (01363 776623)

Trustees: Richard Kallaway; Steven Harris.

CC Number: 306598

Eligibility

Children of farmers, ex-farmers, smallholders and ex-smallholders, 16 years old or over, living in Cornwall, Devon, Dorset and Somerset. The applicant must be studying a dairy-related topic in further education, which will contribute to the future industry.

Types of grants

This fund aims to promote and encourage 'practical and scientific education in dairying and dairy farming'. Grants usually range from £200 up to £2,000 a year and can be for books, fees, equipment and maintenance/living expenses.

Annual grant total

In 2010/11 the trust had an income of £21,000 and an expenditure of £17,000. The trust usually distributes the majority of its income in grants to individuals.

Applications

On a form available from the correspondent; two references will be required. Applications should be submitted by the individual by August each year; for consideration in September.

Forestry/ timber

Forest Industries Education and Provident Fund

£7,000

Correspondent: Jane Karthaus, Woodland Place, Belford, Northumberland NE70 7QA (01668 213937; fax: 01668 213555; email: jane. karthaus@confor.org.uk; website: www. confor.org.uk)

Trustees: Jane Karthaus; Christopher Starr; Christopher Inglis; Michael Box.

CC Number: 1061322

Eligibility

Members of the Forestry and Timber Association (or ConFor) and their dependents who are in need. Members must have been involved with the association for at least one year.

Types of grants

One-off grants of up to £750 are made towards educational, training or professional development purposes in the field of forestry and for educational trips and activities.

Annual grant total

In 2011 the trust had an income of £4,600 and an expenditure of £7,500.

Other information

Anyone can join ConFor who has an interest in trees, woodlands or timber. Grants are also made for welfare purposes.

Furnishing trade

The City of London Linen and Furnishing Trades Benevolent Association

£750

Correspondent: Welfare Officer, Furniture Makers' Hall, 12 Austin Friars, London EC2N 2HE (020 7256 5954; fax: 020 7256 5155; email: welfare@furnituremakers.org.uk; website: www.ftba.co.uk)

Trustees: Earl Whitehead; Geoffrey Blake; Frederick Monger; Don Hanley; Ann Ashwin-Kean.

CC Number: 211522

Eligibility

Children whose parent (or guardian) are, or have been, employed in the UK furnishing industry for a minimum of two years, and are permanently or temporarily unable to maintain them.

Types of grants

One-off grants averaging £250 are given for uniforms, books, instruments, equipment and maintenance and living expenses. Preference is given to children with special needs.

Annual grant total

Grants usually total around £1,500 for education and welfare.

Applications

To request an application pack write, email or telephone the association giving a brief summary of your employment history and the reasons why you are applying for financial or medical assistance. Applications should be submitted through a third party such as a social worker, teacher, Citizens Advice or school.

Other information

The trust states that grants are mainly for the relief of need; education grants are of secondary importance.

Gardeners

Perennial

£16,000

Correspondent: Sheila Thomson, Director of Services, 115 – 117 Kingston Road, Leatherhead, Surrey KT22 7SU (0845 230 1839; fax: 01372 384055; email: info@perennial.org.uk; website: www.perennial.org.uk)

Trustees: Roger Singleton; Lisa Buckland; Jim Buttress; Christine Cohen; Ken Crowther; Geoff Dixon; Colin Ellis; Mike Fitt; Alan Kendall; Ian Maxwell-Scott; Charles Notcutt; Dougal Phillip; Lousie Robinson; Marie Seaton; Sue Tasker; Adrian Thompson.

SC Number: SC040180

Eligibility

Horticulturalists or those training to become one who are experiencing hardship. The dependent children of horticulturalists who are in full time education.

Types of grants

The charity runs a number of training bursaries with various criteria:

- Bursaries for placements for those who are undertaking a horticultural course at a UK training establishment to undertake the work based placement necessary to obtain the qualification
- Sons and daughters bursaries: Full time horticultural students under 40 who are themselves children of horticulturalists are eligible for bursaries of up to £3,000 (maximum of £1,500 per year)
- Hardship bursaries: Horticultural students experiencing exceptional, unforeseen hardship are eligible for one-off grants of £500 to £1,000
- Re-training for horticulturalists in hardship: Long-term career horticulturalists looking to regain satisfactory employment within the industry or elsewhere following

adverse circumstance such as an accident or ill health

- Training and public benefit: Ltd contributions towards horticulture-related training activities which fall outside the other funding streams
- Grants are also available for general education for the dependent children of horticulturalists. The regional Caseworker should be contacted in the first instance

Annual grant total

In 2011 £16,000 was awarded in training grants.

Applications

Applicants are advised to check the website for application advice relating to the separate schemes. For general casework phone numbers are available on the website or email the correspondent.

Other information

In 2010 this charity merged with the Royal Fund for Gardeners' Children.

The charity also provides free debt advice, available by contacting 0800 294 4244/debtadvice@perennial.org.uk.

Higher education

The Higher Education Academy

£315,000

Correspondent: Sean Mackney, Senior Deputy Chief Executive, Innovation Way, York Science Park, York YO10 5BR (01904 717500; fax: 01904 717505; email: enquiries@heacademy.ac.uk; website: www.heacademy.ac.uk)

Trustee: The Board of Directors.

Eligibility

Anyone who is responsible for the student learning experience, working in higher education institutions in the UK that subscribe to the Higher Education Academy, and students of those institutions.

Types of grants

Teaching development grants to a maximum of £7,000 for projects that aim to encourage innovations in learning and teaching. £28,000 of the £315,000 a year available for the teaching development grants is ring fenced for new academic staff (less than five years in a full time role). A further £28,000 is ring fenced for HEA Fellows who have never had a teaching development grant before.

The UK Travel Fund awards staff and students up to £300, three times a year to enable them to engage in events and meetings, to further good practice in learning, teaching and assessment within higher education.

Annual grant total

In 2010/11 the organisation had an income of £27 million and gave £315,000 in individual teaching grants.

Applications

Guidelines, terms and conditions and FAQs for the teaching development grants are available on the website, along with examples of recently funded projects. Applicants should note that this scheme is only open for applications for a limited amount of time each year, which is outlined on the website.

Application forms and guidelines for the travel fund, which is open throughout the year, are also available on the website.

Other information

This is not a charity, it is funded by UK HE bodies.

Horse-racing and breeding

National Trainers' Federation Charitable Trust

£3,000

Correspondent: Cedric Burton, 20b Park Lane, Newmarket, Suffolk CB8 8QD (01638 560763; email: info@ racingwelfare.co.uk; website: www. racingwelfare.co.uk)

Trustees: Peter Cundell; Toby Balding; Christian Wall; John Dunlop; Rupert Arnold.

CC Number: 1004308

Eligibility

People who have had an accident/been injured in the course of their employment in racing and as a result are unable to return to work in the same capacity and their dependents.

Types of grants

One-off and recurrent grants of £100 to £500 for retraining either in a different capacity within the racing industry or within a different industry.

Annual grant total

In 20210/11 the trust had an income and expenditure of £15,000. Previously about £3,000 has been given in grants to individuals.

Applications

On an application form available from the correspondent including a doctor's report. All applicants are invited to discuss their plans with a local welfare officer who can give guidance on the completion of the form.

Insurance

The Insurance Charities – The Orphans' Fund

£274,000

Correspondent: Mrs Annali-Joy Thornicroft, 20 Aldermanbury, London EC2V 7HY (020 7606 3763; fax: 020 7600 1170; email: info@ theinsurancecharities.org.uk; website: www.theinsurancecharities.org.uk)

Trustees: Kirsten Watson; Prof. David Bland; Graham Cave; Frank Smith; David Worsfold; Ralph Bradshaw; Anthony Alderman; Roger Carr; Julia Graham; John Greenaway; Peter Hutchinson; Andrew Miller; Ron Iles; Ray O'Doherty; Adrienne O'Sullivan; Allen Prior; Mary Rogerson; Nick Starling; Peter Staddon; Lindsay Williamson; Ian Templeton; Richard Wood.

CC Number: 206860

Eligibility

University students whose parents have been in the insurance industry for at least five years.

Types of grants

Help may be given to first degree students towards day-to-day expenses, particularly where there is family financial hardship.

Annual grant total

In 2010/11 the charities had assets of £26.6 million and an income of £1.6 million. Grants were made to 231 individuals totalling £674,000. This includes £66,000 that was contributed through the Paul Golmick Fund.

Applications

An initial form can be completed online or downloaded from the website.

Other information

The charities also make grants to past and present employees of the insurance industry and their dependents experiencing financial hardship.

The Paul Golmick Fund is administered by the charities and was set up to promote the maintenance and education of children and young people under the age of 24, but primarily under the age of 18, who reside in the UK or Republic of Ireland and who have at least one parent

or guardian with service to the insurance industry.

Management Accountant

The Chartered Institute of Management Accountants Benevolent Fund

£22,000

Correspondent: Caroline Aldred, Secretary, CIMA, 26 Chapter Street, London SW1P 4NP (020 8849 2221; email: benevolent.fund@cimaglobal.com; website: www.cimaglobal.com)

Trustee: The Chartered Institute of Management Accountants.

CC Number: 261114

Eligibility

Children of past and present CIMA members.

Types of grants

Educational grants for dependent children according to need.

Annual grant total

In 2011 the fund had assets of £1.8 million and an income of £92,000. Grants to 53 individuals totalled £97,000, 12 of these grants included funding for dependents of beneficiaries.

Applications

On a form available from the correspondent or to download from the website. Applications can be submitted directly by the individual or through a recognised referral agency (Citizens Advice, doctor, social worker and so on), or through a third party.

Other information

The charity can also signpost-people to relevant services and provide support from a welfare officer.

Meat Trade

The Worshipful Company of Butchers' Educational Charity

£1,800

Correspondent: The Clerk, Butchers' Hall, 87 Bartholomew Close, London EC1A 7EB (020 7600 4106; fax: 020 7606 4108; email: clerk@butchershall.com; website: www.butchershall.com)

Trustee: Master, Wardens and the Court of the Art or Mistery of Butchers of the City of London.

CC Number: 297603

Eligibility

People involved in the meat trade who are studying courses related to the trade.

Applicants for the Nuffield Farming Scholarship must be a UK resident between 22 and 45 years who have been in the industry for at least two years and intend to remain involved in the sector.

Types of grants

One-off grants towards further and higher education fees.

The company also provides one Nuffield Farming Scholarship each year to enable someone who is active in the meat and livestock industries to study a topic of their choice carrying out a tour anywhere in the world to further their knowledge and understanding.

Annual grant total

In 2010/11 the charity had assets of £767,000 and an income of £27,000. Grants to individuals totalled £1,800.

Applications

In writing to the correspondent. Applications should be submitted directly by the individual for consideration monthly.

To apply for the Nuffield Farming Scholarship contact Bob Bansback on bob@bansback.co.uk.

Other information

The trust also gives grants to organisations.

Media

The Chartered Institute of Journalists Orphan Fund

£14,000

Trustees: Harvey Thomas; Michael Moriarty; Charlie Harris; Cyril Bainbridge; Dominic Cooper; Doreen Grimwood; Ken Brookes; Mary Tomlinson; Norman Bartlett; Robin Morgan; Paul Leighton; Peter Brown; Barrie Welford; Joshua Aidoo; Jules Annan; Kenneth Russell; Daljit Sembai.

CC Number: 208176

Eligibility

Orphaned children of institute members who are in need, aged between 5 and 22 and in full-time education.

Types of grants

Grants are given to schoolchildren towards the cost of school clothing, books, instruments, educational outings and school fees. Grants are also given to students in further or higher education towards the cost of books, help with fees/living expenses and study or travel abroad.

Annual grant total

In 2011 the fund had assets of £1.8 million and an income of £86,000. Grants to individuals totalled £28,000, for welfare and education.

Applications

Applications should be submitted by the child's surviving parent or other third party. Applications are considered quarterly.

Other information

This fund also gives grants for relief-in-need purposes.

The Grace Wyndham Goldie (BBC) Trust Fund

£19,000 (15 grants)

Correspondent: The Trustees, BBC Pensions and Benefits Centre, Broadcasting House, Cardiff CF5 2YQ (02920 323772; fax: 02920 322408; website: www.bbc.co.uk/charityappeals/grant/gwg.shtml)

Trustees: Mark Scrimshaw; Sandra Phillips; Andy Baker; Liz Rylatt.

CC Number: 212146

Eligibility

Employees and ex-employees engaged in radio or television broadcasting or an associated activity, and their dependents.

Types of grants

One-off grants to help with educational costs such as school or college fees, travelling expenses, school uniforms, books and equipment, living expenses or to supplement existing educational awards.

Annual grant total

In 2011 the trust had assets of £1.1 million and an income of £49,000. They made 15 grants for education totalling £19,000, four of which are ongoing and one grant for hardship of £915.

Exclusions

Recurrent grants are not made.

Applications

On a form available from the correspondent. The deadline for applications is 31 July; they are considered in September. As the income of the fund is limited, and to ensure help can be given where it is most needed, applicants must be prepared to give full information about their circumstances.

The Journalists' Charity

£10,000

Correspondent: David Ilott, Director and Secretary, Dickens House, 35 Wathen Road, Dorking, Surrey RH4 1JY (01306 887511; fax: 01306 888212; email: enquiries@ journalistscharity.org.uk; website: www. journalistscharity.org.uk)

Trustees: Stephen Somerville; B. G. Ager; Ricky Marsh; Gillian James; Jean Morgan; Michael Watson; Nicholas Jones; Robert Gibson; Sydney Young; William Newman; William Hagerty; Laurie Upshon; Ramsay Smith; Chris Boffey; Raymond Massey; Keith Beabey; Anna Botting; Paul Jones; Susan Ryan; Stephen Dann.

CC Number: 208215

Eligibility

The dependents of journalists in need.

Types of grants

One-off and recurrent grants. This fund mainly supports welfare, not educational causes, although there is often some crossover.

Annual grant total

In 2011 the charity had assets of £12 million and an income of £1.7 million. Grants to 177 beneficiaries totalled £308,000, most of which was given for welfare purposes

Exclusions

Vocational support will only be made if the parent of the child is/was a journalist and there is evidence of need.

Applications

On a form available from the correspondent, to be submitted directly by the individual or a family member. Applications should include details of the career in journalism and are considered monthly.

Other information

The fund also runs residential homes in Dorking.

Medicine

The Dain Fund

£7,000

Correspondent: Marian Flint, Clerk to the Trustees, BMA Charities, BMA House, Tavistock Square, London WC1H 9JP (020 7383 6142; fax: 020 7554 6334; email: info.bmacharities@

bma.org.uk; website: bma.org.uk/about-the-bma/who-we-are/charities)

Trustees: Jane Richards; Aamir Syed; Connie Fozzard; Michael Downes; Michael Wilks; Andrew Mowat; Stephen Strange.

CC Number: 313108

Eligibility

Children of doctors or deceased doctors (not nurses or physiotherapists and so on) in state, private or higher education and whose families have experienced an unexpected change in financial circumstances following crises such as unemployment, family breakdown or serious illness of a parent or guardian. The trust has also undertaken outreach work to support the children of refugee doctors.

Types of grants

The principal objective and activity of the fund is to assist with the educational expenses of doctors' children when a family crisis threatens the continuity of that education.

The fund gives one-off and recurrent grants to:

- Children who are in private education already and approaching public examinations
- Children in state school towards the costs of school uniforms and field trips
- Originally the fund was intended only to help schoolchildren but, now that statutory grants have been withdrawn for students in higher education, a small number of awards are being made to support undergraduates. If students have been supported by the fund throughout their degree course, they may receive an interest-free loan for the final year instead of a grant

Normally support will be given to only one child in a family.

Annual grant total

In 2011 the fund had assets of £1.3 million and an income of £51,000. Grants were made totalling £7,000.

Applications

On a form available from the correspondent, to be submitted directly by the individual or a parent/guardian or through a social worker, Citizens Advice or other welfare agency for consideration throughout the year.

Other information

This fund is designed to help families in an emergency and is not a scholarship trust.

The Hume Kendall Educational Trust

£2,000

Correspondent: Keith Jeremiah, 30 Whyteleafe Road, Caterham, Surrey CR3 5EF

Trustees: Peter Rees; Cyril Chantler; Michael Maisey; Richard Hughes; P. Challacombe; Michael Gleeson; Tak Lee.

CC Number: 313208

Eligibility

Children of doctors or dentists whose fathers have died or are unable to work.

Types of grants

Contributions towards the cost of the education of beneficiaries up to and including first degree level.

Annual grant total

In 2010/11 the trust had an income of £6,200 and an expenditure of £2,000.

Applications

In writing to the correspondent. Applications can be made at any time.

The RCN Foundation
See entry on page 99

The Royal Medical Benevolent Fund

£360,000

Correspondent: The Senior Case Manager, 24 King's Road, Wimbledon, London SW19 8QN (020 8540 9194; email: enquiries@rmbf.org; website: www.rmbf.org)

Trustees: Robin Macleod; Dr Joan Trowell; Jackie Angel; Peter Bowen-Simpkins; Judith Bamber; Professor David Black; Mike Carter; John Farr; Dr Amit Malik; Dr Mary Pierce; Professor Bhupinder Sandhu; Andrew Robson; David Haldane; Dr Katie Petty-Saphon.

CC Number: 207275

Eligibility

Assists GMC-registered, UK resident doctors and their recognised dependents who, through illness or disability are in financial hardship, through the provision of grants, loans and advice services.

Types of grants

Schoolchildren may receive help towards school uniform and clothing, books and travel to school. People starting work can be awarded grants for books, equipment/instruments and clothing. In exceptional cases, the fund may assist with fees and expenses.

Annual grant total

In 2010/11 the fund had assets of £20 million and an income of £1.8 million. Grants were made to individuals totalling £725,000 for educational and welfare purposes.

Exclusions

The following are excluded:

- Private medical insurance/fees
- School fees
- Legal fees
- Inland revenue payments
- Debts to relatives or friends
- Private education

Applications

For general educational grants: on a form available from the correspondent, which can be submitted either directly by the individual or through a medical colleague or other medical and general charities. Two references are required (at least one of which should be from a medical practitioner). All applicants are visited before a report is submitted to the case committee. Income, capital and expenditure are fully investigated, with similar rules applying as for those receiving Income Support. Applications are considered bi-monthly.

Other information

Voluntary visitors liaise between beneficiaries and the office. The fund has an informative website.

The Royal Medical Foundation

£32,500

Correspondent: Helen Jones, RMF Office, Epsom College, College Road, Epsom, Surrey KT17 4JQ (01372 821010; email: rmf-caseworker@epsomcollege.org.uk; website: www.royalmedicalfoundation.org)

Trustees: Celia Berwick; Surgeon Vice-Admiral Tony Revell; Greg Andrews; Richard Bruce; Dr Hywel Bowen-Perkins; Michael Cook; Brigadier Alan Eastburn; Peter Hakim; Alan Hagdrup; Dr Alistaire Wells; Dr Andrew Vallance-Owen; Chris Titman; Helen Jones.

CC Number: 312046

Eligibility

Dependents, aged up to 18, of medical practitioners who are in need.

Types of grants

Grants of between £500 and £15,000 are given to schoolchildren and college students towards fees. Preference is given to pupils with family difficulties so that they have to be educated away from home, pupils with special educational needs and medical students.

Annual grant total

In 2010/11 the foundation gave grants to individuals totalling £77,000, which were broken down as follows:

Regular payments to medical practitioners and their widows/widowers	6	£18,600
Short-term or one-off grants for urgent assistance	18	£25,000
Financial assistance with educational expenses	8	£19,500
Financial assistance with educational expenses at Epsom College	1	£13,000
Other grants	2	£650

Applications

On a form available from the correspondent, for consideration throughout the year. Applications can be submitted either by the individual or a family member, through a third party such as a social worker or teacher, or through an organisation such as Citizens Advice or a school. The trust advises applicants to be honest about their needs. All applicants are means tested.

Other information

The Foundation has an informative website.

Metal trades

The Institute of Materials, Minerals and Mining

£46,000

Correspondent: Administrator, 1 Carlton House Terrace, London SW1Y 5DB (020 7451 7300; fax: 020 7839 1702; email: directorate@iom3.org)

Trustees: Ken Ridal; Charles Rhodes; Robert Siddall; Barry Douglas; Christopher Hallas; David Gooch; David Evetts; Martin Jarrett; Samuel Wood; Siobhan Matthews; Stannas Bellaby; Serena Best; Keith Forsdyke; Paul Withey; Jan Lewis; Stuart Patrick; Philip Bischler; Graham Hollox; Mick May; Mike Hicks; Keith Harrison; Steve Bedford; Chris Corti; Michael Forrest; Andrew Pitman; Keith Barnes; Colin Hindle; Jonathan Binner; Robert Pearce; Martin Cox; Rod Martin; John Wilcox; Richard Thackray; P. J. Foster; A. A. Haggie; A. D. Francis; Ileigo Akagwu; Michael Winstone.

CC Number: 269275

Eligibility

Members of the institution and former members and their dependents.

Types of grants

One-off and recurrent grants up to £5,000 and one-off grants in kind

towards educational needs. Travel grants for attending conferences in the UK and abroad. Various awards and prizes are also available

Annual grant total

In 2011 the institute had assets of £8.6 million and an income of £6.1 million. Grants, scholarships, awards and prizes totalled £46,000.

Applications

On forms available from the website or the correspondent. Note different grants and awards may have different deadlines, eligibility requirements and correspondents. See the Institute's website for further information.

Mining

Mining Institute of Scotland Trust

£12,500

Correspondent: The Secretary, 14/9 Burnbrae Drive, Edinburgh EH12 8AS

SC Number: SC024974

Eligibility

Members or former members of the Mining Institute of Scotland who are taking a university course with a mining element in it. The trust has a preference for supporting people from Fife in the first instance, and, secondly, those who are of Scottish origin, although other people can be considered. Applicants who are not already members of the institute will be invited to join. Members of the Mining Institute of Scotland, and their dependents, can also receive 'hardship grants'.

Types of grants

Educational grants are one-off or recurrent, normally of £1,500 a year. A recent grant was made, for example, towards an engineering course that had a mining element to it. Grants can be for the student's general upkeep, or for course fees, and so on.

Hardship grants are one-off or recurrent of up to £1,000 a year. A recent grant was made, for example, to the son of a member for travel to university.

Annual grant total

The trust has about £25,000 available to give in grants each year for both education and hardship.

Applications

In writing to the correspondent in the first instance, to request an application form.

Other information

Schools are also supported.

Motor industry

The BMTA Trust Ltd

See entry on page 24

Patent Agents

The Incorporated Benevolent Association of the Chartered Institute of Patent Attorneys

£0

Correspondent: Derek Chandler, 95 Chancery Lane, London WC2A 1DT

Trustees: T. W. Roberts; J. D. Brown; H. G. Hallybone; C. T. Eyles; H. M. Jones; M. A. Lynd; P. D. Eke; S. J. Mohun; D. R. Chandler.

CC Number: 219666

Eligibility

British members and former members of the institute, and their dependents.

Types of grants

One-off and recurrent grants or loans according to need.

Annual grant total

Previously £6,000. In 2010/11 the association had assets of £717,000 and an income of £47,000. Grants to individuals totalled £31,000, although no grants were given for educational assistance in this financial year.

Applications

In writing to the correspondent, marked 'Private and Confidential'. Applications can be submitted at any time. Where possible, grants are provided via a third party.

Other information

Grants are also made for welfare purposes.

Police

The Gurney Fund for Police Orphans

£94,000 (106 grants)

Correspondent: Christine McNicol, The Director, 9 Bath Road, Worthing, West

Sussex BN11 3NU (01903 237256; website: www.gurneyfund.org)

Trustees: Terry Spelman; Martin Richards; Paul Upham; Ian Davies; Tim Crux; Peter Land; John Apter; Nick Wilkinson; Steve Davenport; Julie Earle; Graham Riley; Peter Jones.

CC Number: 261319

Eligibility

Children under 18 of deceased or incapacitated police officers from 22 subscribing forces in southern and South Midland areas of England and South and Mid-Wales, excluding the Metropolitan and City of London Police Forces.

Types of grants

Grants are available for students up to 18 years old; applications from older students will be considered in certain circumstances at the discretion of the trustees. Grants can be for books, uniforms, equipment, educational travel, school trips, music lessons, sport and other extra-curricular activities. Grants can be both one-off cash grants for amounts of up to £1,800 each, or recurrent, ranging from between £10 and £60 per week.

Annual grant total

During 2010/11 the trust had assets of £6.7 million and an income of £515,000. Weekly allowances and grants for schoolchildren were made to 69 beneficiaries. Grants totalling £30,000 for fees and £13,000 for books and IT were awarded to 37 higher education students.

Exclusions

No grants for school fees or skiing holidays, but in the case of school fees exceptions can be made for children with special educational needs. The fund does not make grants to beneficiaries who go on to higher education. It may, however, consider assisting with the payment of annual tuition fees and, or, a grant towards the cost of books and ancillary equipment.

Applications

Applications can be made at any time and are considered in February, May, August and November. They must include a copy of the child's birth certificate and successful applicants will be asked to complete an income and expenditure form and provide receipts when assistance with specific expenditure is requested. A force welfare officer or local representative then assesses the application for a later decision by the trustees.

Other information

The trust also awards Christmas gifts and arranges holidays for beneficiaries.

The National Police Fund

£72,000 (72 grants)

Correspondent: Hannah Mueller, National Police Fund, 3 Mount Mews, High Street, Hampton TW12 2SH (020 8941 7661; fax: 020 8979 4323; email: office@nationalpolicefund.org.uk)

Trustees: Martin Richards; William Berry; Paul Barker; Ian Latimer; Les Gray; Stephen Gilligan; Sandie Wilde.

CC Number: 207608

Eligibility

Children of serving, retired or deceased members of police forces in England, Wales and Scotland who are aged over 18 years.

Types of grants

One-off and recurrent grants for general assistance to students in further or higher education of £1,000. Grants are sometimes, though rarely, given to mature students and younger children.

Annual grant total

In 2010 the fund had assets of £2.7 million and an income of £130,000. Grants to seventy two individuals totalled £72,000

Applications

Application forms can be obtained from the welfare officer of the police force where the officer is serving or has served. Applications must be returned by the individual in November for consideration in December. A reference from the student's college or university must be included.

Police Dependants' Trust

£1.4 million

Correspondent: David French, Chief Executive, 3 Mount Mews, High Street, Hampton, Middlesex TW12 2SH (020 8941 6907; fax: 020 8979 4323; email: office@pdtrust.org; website: www.pdtrust.org)

Trustees: Martin Richards; Sandie Wilde; Don Ratcliffe; Terry Spence; Pat Stayt; Paul Barker; Paul McKeever; Les Gray; Bill Berry; Marty Whittle; Rod Jarman; David Pellatt; Stephen Gilligan; Sue Akers; Graham Cassidy; Dr Ian Lattimer; Tony Harper.

CC Number: 251021

Eligibility

(i.) Dependents of current police officers or former police officers who have died from injuries received in the execution of duty.
(ii.) Police officers or former police officers incapacitated as a result of injury received in the execution of duty, or their dependents.

Types of grants

One-off grants ranging from £280 to £21,000, averaging about £2,300 each. Grants are available for retraining and to the children of police officers who are at school or university. Under the Children's grant scheme funding is given for the purchase of sports and computer equipment, musical instruments and other educational facilities. However, it is important to note that this is primarily a relief-in-need charity, so most of the grants are given for welfare rather than educational purposes.

Annual grant total

In 2010/11 the trust had assets of £25.2 million and an income of £1.2 million. Grants to individuals totalled £2.8 million and were distributed as follows:

Maintenance Grants	311
Children's grants	61
Special Purpose Grants	215
Holiday Grants	690
Funeral Grants	4

Applications

On a form available from the correspondent, to be submitted through one of the force's welfare officers. Applications are generally considered every two months although urgent cases can be addressed between meetings.

Precious metals

The Johnson Matthey Educational Trust

£60,000

Correspondent: Andrew Charman, Johnson Matthey plc, 25 Farringdon Street, London EC4A 4AB (020 7269 8124; email: group.hr@matthey.com)

Trustee: Johnson Matthey Ltd.

CC Number: 313576

Eligibility

People over the age of 16 with a parent or grandparent employed by Johnson Matthey or currently connected with the precious metals industry, and who are studying a scientific or technical subject.

Types of grants

Grants to college students and undergraduates for fees, books, equipment and maintenance/living expenses. Grants are usually for between £400 and £500.

Annual grant total

In 2010/11 the trust had an income of £19,000 and an expenditure of £72,000.

Exclusions

Grants are not made to students studying second degrees or mature students.

Applications

On a form available from the correspondent. Applications should be submitted by the relevant parent or grandparent, if possible, on behalf of the individual in October for consideration in December. Advertisements appear in the relevant trade journals.

Railway workers

The Railway Benefit Fund

£50,000

Correspondent: Margaret Skerratt, Grants Officer, Electra Way, Crewe, Cheshire CW1 6HS (01270 251316; fax: 01270 503966; email: info@ railwaybenefitfund.org.uk; website: www. railwaybenefitfund.org.uk)

Trustees: Simon Osborne; C. R. B. Goldson; David RedFern; Peter Trewin; Alan Marshall; Ken Watson; Richard Eccles; Dominic Booth; Deborah Gilshan; Steve Montgomery; Gregg Ryan.

CC Number: 206312

Eligibility

Active and retired members of the British Railway Board, its subsidiaries and related organisations, and their spouses and children.

Types of grants

One-off grants ranging from £100 to £1,500 to schoolchildren, college students, students entering higher education and those with special educational needs towards uniforms, clothing, books and equipment and maintenance/living expenses.

Annual grant total

In 2011 grants to individuals totalled £359,000, broken down as follows:

- 186 annuities (recurrent) – £87,000
- 339 single benevolent grants – £251,000
- 2 residential care grants – £5,000
- 29 Webb fund grants – £12,000
- 9 childcare grants – £3,200
- 45 other (Christmas presents) – £1,100

The 339 single benevolent grants were broken down again into various needs:

- 46 funeral expenses – £70,000
- 50 minor house repairs – £59,000
- 45 equipment for disability – £50,000
- 49 household equipment – £25,000
- 37 debts and arrears – £24,000
- 98 other – £20,000
- 14 convalescence – £7,800

Applications

On a form available from the correspondent. Applications can be submitted either directly by the individual or family member, or through a third party such as a social worker, teacher or Citizens Advice. Applicants must be able to provide verification of railway service.

Other information

This is primarily a welfare charity, and educational grants are part of its wider welfare work.

Religious workers

Children of the Clergy Trust

£2,000

Correspondent: Trustee, 4 Kierhill Gardens, Westhill, Aberdeenshire AB32 6AX

SC Number: SC001845

Eligibility

Children of deceased ministers of the Church of Scotland.

Types of grants

One-off or recurrent grants according to need. Previously grants have ranged from £500 to £1,000 for any educational need.

Annual grant total

About £2,000.

Applications

In writing to the correspondent. Applications should be submitted directly by the individual and should include information about the applicant's ministerial parent, general family circumstances and other relevant information.

The EAC Educational Trust

£32,000 (27 grants)

Correspondent: Michael Ross, Bramblings, 3 Bances Court, Gore End Road, Ball Hill, Newbury RG20 0PG (01635 253056; email: julian@bewick. org)

Trustees: Michael Ross; Julian Bewick; David Woodhead; Fergus Murison.

CC Number: 292391

Eligibility

Children of Church of England clergymen and of single parent families, aged 8 to 16. Preference is often given to the sons of clergymen.

Types of grants

Grants are almost exclusively for school fees including boarding. The trust has a close link with one particular school which specialises in educating the families of clergy. However, it accepts applications from other sources especially for the education of children in choir schools or other establishments with musical or dramatic emphasis. Individual grants almost never exceed one-third of the pupil's annual fees.

Annual grant total

In 2010/11 the trust had an income of £71,000 and made £32,000 in 27 grants to individuals.

Applications

In writing to the correspondent. Applications are considered in the spring.

The Silcock Trust

£10,000

Correspondent: A R T Hancock, Trustee, 4 Church Street, Old Isleworth, Middlesex TW7 6BH

Trustees: Christopher Turner; Richard Coombs; Alec Hancock; Peter Hancock; Brian Watkins.

CC Number: 272587

Eligibility

Children of clergy with learning and/or other difficulties.

Types of grants

Help with maintenance and fees for schoolchildren. Preference will be given to children with serious family difficulties and special educational needs. Grants range from £250 to £2,000.

Annual grant total

In 2010 the trust had both an income and a total expenditure of £12,000.

Applications

In writing to the correspondent.

The Sons and Friends of the Clergy

£524,000

Correspondent: Robert Welsford, Registrar, 1 Dean Trench Street, Westminster, London SW1P 3HB (020

7799 3696; fax: 020 7222 3468; email: enquiries@clergycharities.org.uk; website: www.clergycharities.org.uk)

Trustees: Tom Hoffman; Terry Knight; Graeme Knowles; Archbishop of Canterbury; David Brewer; Bishop of London; John Morrison; David Rossdale; David Lowman; Rodney Whiteman; Richard Askwith; Christopher Davies; Jill Sandham; John Chadwick; Charles Richardson; Colin Menzies; David Meynell; Fiona Daley; Ann Joyce; Alex Brougham; Patrick Walker; Lady Mawer; Roxanne Hunte.

CC Number: 207736

Eligibility

Dependent children (under 25 years of age) of Anglican clergy of the dioceses of the UK and Ireland and of the diocese in Europe or of the widows/widowers and separated or divorced spouses of such clergy. Grants are made only to the parent, not the child.

Types of grants

The corporation runs three different grant schemes; miscellaneous education grants, school fee grants for children attending independent schools and grants for children continuing in education after leaving school.

Miscellaneous education grant scheme

The corporation is able to consider help in the following areas:

- School uniforms
- Travel costs
- School trips
- Language exchanges
- Music lessons and musical instruments
- Arts and sports activities
- Computers (including related software)

Note: Children under the age of 11 are only eligible for grants towards school uniforms and school trips.

School fee grants for children attending independent schools

- Grants towards school fees can be considered where independent education is necessary for a clergy child
- Grants are paid in instalments three times a year just before the beginning of the school terms and can be considered towards both tuition fees and boarding fees
- The level of any grant is based upon the amount of fees the parents have to find after help from other sources, e.g. clergy bursary or scholarship, or other financial support. The normal grant is for a proportion of the net fees the applicant has to pay, up to a maximum limit which will be advised to applicants when the initial enquiry is made

- Grants are awarded up to GCSE level and will only be considered under special circumstances after this age
- Help is provided only where there is a demonstrable need for a child to be educated at the independent school in question, parental preference is not accepted

Note: Children aged under 11 can only receive a grant towards school fees if they are a chorister at a choir school (or have a probationary place).

Grants for children (under 25) continuing in education after leaving school

- The corporation is able to help with special outfits or equipment (but not books) required by a child who has left school and is undertaking vocational training
- Maintenance grants can be considered for children of the clergy who are undergraduates, but not postgraduates, at university
- Grants can also be considered for clergy children who are medical students, undertaking medical electives abroad, even if they have already graduated

Annual grant total

In 2011 the charity had assets of £27 million and an income of £1.7 million. Grants to individuals totalled £1.1 million, broken down as follows:

- General welfare: £296,000
- Resettlement and house expenses: £176,000
- School fees: £195,000
- University maintenance: £111,000
- School clothing: £59,000
- Other education expenses: £159,000
- Ordinand book grants: £30,000
- Christmas: £31,000
- Debt: £5,400
- Bereavement: £5,600

Exclusions

Grants are not awarded retrospectively and are generally based on one year's costs for any particular category.

Grants towards school fees are not normally available for those serving outside Great Britain and Ireland.

Applications

Before any grants are made, the corporation's educational advisor will usually contact the parents to discuss the application and needs of the child. Applicants will also be required to provide evidence of the need for independent education in support of their education, as parental preference is not accepted.

For school fee grants, a certificate from the principal of the school is also needed before any grant is awarded. This should state that the pupil is, or will be, in

attendance and not under notice of withdrawal, and that his or her progress is satisfactory. A copy of the relevant certificate will be issued with the application form.

Applications may be made during the year in which the child becomes 11 years of age and should ideally be submitted at least two clear terms before the grant is required. Initial enquiries may be made up to one year in advance of the proposed start date. When parents know they are likely to require help with school fees, they should approach the corporation before committing their child to a particular school. Failure to do so could result in disappointment, for both parents and child, if a grant is not awarded.

Grants are made for the school stated in the application only and are not transferable to any other school. Applicants are noted to advise the corporation at the earliest opportunity when a change of school is considered necessary.

Applications will need to be made each year for the renewal of any school fee grant.

Other information

The Sons of the Clergy and the Friends of the Clergy have traditionally worked in conjunction with each other in their grant work. Since January 2005 the two charities have been working even more closely together in their grant administration following the establishment of a single body of trustees common to both organisations and a combined staff. As a result, it no longer matters whether an applicant applies to the Sons or to the Friends as there is a common application form for both charities and all applications are automatically considered by both organisations. The charities also submit joint accounts.

Sons of the Clergy CC number: 207736

Friends of the Clergy CC number: 207736.

The Wells Clerical Charity

£3,800

Correspondent: Peter Thomas, The Rectory, Cat Street, Chiselborough, Stoke-Sub-Hamdon, Somerset TA14 6TT (01935 881202)

Trustees: Colin Alsbury; Peter Thomas; Tony Perris; Nicola Sullivan; Christopher Hare; Tim Hawkings; Richard Taylor; Rose Hoskins; David MacGeogh; Alexander Wheeler.

CC Number: 248436

Eligibility

People in need under 25 years old who are children of members of clergy of the Church of England serving (or who have retired or died and last served) in the former archdeaconry of Wells as constituted in 1738.

Types of grants

Grants are made to support eligible individuals in preparing for entering any profession or employment by paying travel fees, the costs of clothing/uniform or maintenance costs.

Annual grant total

In 2011 the charity had an income of £8,500 and an expenditure of £7,800.

Applications

In writing to the correspondent.

Women's Continuing Ministerial Education Trust

£50,000

Correspondent: The Director of Ministry, Ministry Division, Church House, Great Smith Street, London SW1P 3AZ (020 7898 1410 or 1396; email: grants@c-of-e.org.uk; website: www.cofe.anglican.org)

Eligibility

Any woman, ordained or not, who is licensed into a nationally recognised ministry in the Church of England or the Scottish Episcopal Church (with the exception of Readers). Religious Sisters and retired clergy who are involved in active ministry may also apply

Types of grants

Grants usually help with continuing education expenses including part-time degree course fees, conferences, sabbaticals and workshops, and also some welfare needs. Grants are intended to supplement funds available from the applicant's diocese.

Annual grant total

About £50,000 a year.

Applications

On a form available either as a download from the Church of England website, or via email on request which should be returned by post. Applications must be endorsed by the Diocesan CME Officer or Dean of the Women's Ministry. Applications will normally be considered in March, June, September and December; however applications for funding for research degrees will be considered at the March meeting and should therefore be submitted by 16 February.

Other information

Not a registered charity.

Sales representatives

The Royal Pinner School Foundation

£417,000 (176 grants)

Correspondent: David Newton, 110 Old Brompton Road, South Kensington, London SW7 3RB (020 7373 6168; email: admin@royalpinner.co.uk; website: www.royalpinner.co.uk)

Trustees: D. C. Bickerdike; Edward Mason; Gillian Brookes; Stephen Wilson; Yvonne Rowe; Jill Grant; Christopher Lane; Graham Paterson; Anita Farquharson; Anthony Fowler; Jane Pool; Annette Spencer; Duncan Cashmore; James Henry.

CC Number: 1128414

Eligibility

Children, preferably under 25, of travelling sales representatives and manufacturer's agents, where the family has experienced adversity or hardship.

Types of grants

Help is given in the following ways:

(i) Education: maintenance allowances or grants tenable at any school, college, university or other place of learning approved by the trustees. Most beneficiaries attend local state schools, or special schools in the case of disabled children, with parents awarded grants per term to cover books, equipment, travel and so on.

(ii) Careers: financial assistance, outfits, clothing, tools, instruments or books to help beneficiaries on leaving school, university or other educational establishment to prepare for or to assist their entry into a profession, trade or calling.

(iii) Travel: awards to assist beneficiaries to travel, whether in this country or abroad, in order to further their education and to participate in school-sponsored visits and field courses.

(iv) The arts: financial assistance to enable beneficiaries to study music or other arts.

(v) Continued education: in otherwise promoting the education (including social and physical training) of beneficiaries.

Annual grant total

In 2010/11 the foundation gave £417,000 in grants to 176 individuals, broken down as follows:

Assistance in the care, maintenance and education of children at day and boarding schools	101	£228,000
Supplementary assistance for students at universities and colleges of higher and further education	69	£120,000
Travel, the arts, outfitting grants and special educational needs	44	£69,000

Exclusions

No loans are given and no help for part-time education.

Applications

Application forms may be obtained from the correspondent, and should be submitted directly by the individual. The grants committee meets five times a year. Note that no applications can be considered except those applying for the sons and daughters of travelling sales representatives or manufacturer's agents.

Science

Royal Society of Chemistry Benevolent Fund

£19,000

Correspondent: Jennifer Tunbridge, Thomas Graham House, Science Park, Milton Road, Cambridge CB4 0WF (01223 432227; fax: 01223 426594; website: www.rsc.org)

Trustees: David Phillips; Keith Smith; Derek Stevenson; Peter Machin; Duncan Bruce; David Cole-Hamilton; Helen Fielding; Annie Powell; Annette Doherty; Emma Raven; Gillian Reid; Lesley Yellowlees; Tina Overton; Dominic Tildesley; Jannette Waterhouse.

CC Number: 207890

Eligibility

People who have been members of the society for the last three years, or ex-members who were in the society for at least ten years, and their dependents, who are in need.

Types of grants

This fund is essentially a relief-in-need charity which also makes grants for education. It offers regular allowances, one-off grants and loans towards needs such as school uniforms and educational trips.

Annual grant total

In 2011 the fund had assets of £10 million, an income of £551,000 and gave grants totalling £39,000.

Exclusions

Anything which should be provided by the government or local authority is ineligible for funding.

Applications

In writing or by telephone in the first instance, to the correspondent. Applicants will be requested to provide a financial statement (forms supplied by the secretary) and include a covering letter describing their application as fully as possible. Applications can be made either directly by the individual, or through a third party such as a social worker or Citizens Advice. They are considered every other month, although urgent appeals can be considered at any time.

Other information

The Society also provides advice and guidance services.

Seafarers

Royal Liverpool Seamen's Orphan Institution

£300,000

Correspondent: Linda Gidman, Secretary, 2nd Floor, Tower Building, 22 Water Street, Liverpool L3 1BA (01512 273417; fax: 01512 273417; email: enquiries@rlsoi-uk.org; website: www. rlsoi-uk.org)

Trustees: Ian Higby; Peter O. Copland; Trevor Hart; John Hulmes; Lynn Cook; David Barbour; Michael Finn.

CC Number: 526379

Eligibility

Children of deceased British merchant seafarers, who are of pre-school age or in full-time education (including further education). Help can also be given to seafarers who are at home caring for their family alone.

Types of grants

Monthly maintenance and annual clothing grants. Help may also be given for school fees.

Annual grant total

In 2011 the charity had assets of £2.8 million and an income of £246,000. Grants to 107 individuals totalled £324,000, primarily for educational purposes.

Applications

On a form available from the correspondent, to be considered at any time. Applications can be submitted either directly by the individual, or by the parent or guardian. They need to include confirmation of the seafarer's death, the child's birth certificate and proof of their educational status.

Other information

It was not possible to obtain a grant total for direct education purposes. However, all grants are given to children and young people who are in attendance at school and further or higher education institutions.

The Royal Merchant Navy School Foundation

£120,000 (108 grants)

Correspondent: The Secretary to the Trustees, Bearwood, Wokingham, Berkshire RG41 5BG (01189 977700; fax: 01189 775904; email: sec@merchantnavy. org.uk; website: www.merchantnavy. org. uk)

Trustees: Anthony Speed; Peter Lowndes; David Parsons; R. W. Dithfield; John Adey; Simon Devitt; Peter Hulse; Guiness Mahon Trust Corporation Ltd.

CC Number: 309047

Eligibility

Children in need who have a parent who has served or is serving as a seaman of any grade in the British Merchant Navy. This parent must either: have died whilst on duty; have left the sea because of illness (in which case the child must have been born before the parent left the sea); or be unable to provide fully for the education, maintenance and upbringing of the child.

Types of grants

One–off and recurrent grants are made towards school and university fees; educational extras; school uniform costs; some travel between home and school; educational equipment; educational visits; educational books; some university expenses. Career and personal development endeavours such as Outward Bound courses are also supported. Grants are tailored to meet the needs of each individual and are usually paid directly to institutions.

Annual grant total

In 2010/11 the foundation had assets of £17 million and an income of £1.1 million. Grants were made to support 108 beneficiaries totalling £120,000.

Applications

On a form available from the correspondent. Applications can be submitted at any time, either by the individual or their parent/guardian. Information about the parents' employment and financial situation is required. The application procedure normally includes a visit by the correspondent to the applicant's home.

The Sailors' Children's Society

£40,000

Correspondent: Ian Scott, Welfare Manager, Francis Reckitt House, Newland, Cottingham Road, Hull HU6 7RJ (01482 342331; fax: 01482 447868; email: info@sailorschildren.org. uk; website: www.sailorschildren.org.uk)

Trustees: Martin Needler; Neil Parkes; Com Geoff Noble; John Warburton; Christopher Towne; Greg Medici; Debbie Rosenberg; Richard Vernon.

CC Number: 224505

Eligibility

Seafarers children who are in full-time education and the families are in severe financial difficulties. Support may be given to two parent families where one of the parents is too ill or disabled to work and the other acts as the carer. Usually, the only source of income for the family is Income Support or Incapacity Benefit.

Types of grants

(i) School clothing grants payable per child twice a year, in January and August, to help children to start off the new school year and to buy a new winter coat. (ii) Educational holiday grants.

Annual grant total

In 2010/11 the society had assets of £1.7 million, an income of £429,000 and gave grants totalling £193,000.

Applications

On a form available from the correspondent, with details about children, income and expenditure, including copies of relevant certificates, for example, birth certificates and proof of seafaring service. Applications can be submitted directly by the individual or through a social worker, Citizens Advice, other welfare agency, or through seafaring organisations. Applications are considered every other month, beginning in February.

Other information

Previously known as Sailors' Families' Society.

The Society has an informative website.

Service/ex-service

ABF The Soldiers' Charity (also known as The Army Benevolent Fund)

£190,000

Correspondent: The Director of Grants and Welfare, Mountbarrow House, 6–20 Elizabeth Street, London SW1W 9RB (0845 241 4820; fax: 0845 241 4821; email: info@soldierscharity. org; website: www.soldierscharity.org)

Trustees: Maj. Gen. Peter Sheppard; Stephen Clark; Guy Davies; Alison Gallico; Maj. Gen. Richard Nugee; Damien Francis; Brig. Andrew Freemantle; Maj. Gen. George Kennedy; Maj. Sir Michael Parker; Maj. Gen. Malcolm Wood; Paul Hearn; Simon Martin; WO1 AcSM Andrew Stokes.

CC Number: 211645

Eligibility

Members and ex-members of the British Regular Army and the Reserve Army (TA) and their dependents who are in need. Serving TA soldiers must have completed at least one year satisfactory service, and former TA soldiers should have completed at least three years satisfactory service.

Types of grants

Mature student education/training grants for ex-soldiers who are unemployed and receiving training or education to enhance their prospect of gaining long-term employment. Such assistance is also available to soldiers who became disabled whilst with the army or after service and need to change their vocation.

Bursaries are also available in exceptional circumstances for the private education of dependents. Preference is given to orphans or children with only one parent, especially if the parent was killed in service. Other priorities include those where a parent is severely disabled or where the child has special needs, which may include where the home environment is such that the child has to be educated away from home.

Annual grant total

In 2010/11 the fund had assets of £45 million, an income of £16 million and a total expenditure of £15 million. Grants to individuals totalled £3.8 million with 3% given for employment and training and 2% for bursaries, totalling £190,000.

Applications

The fund does not deal directly with individual cases. Soldiers who are still serving should contact their regimental or corps association, who will then approach the fund on their behalf. Former soldiers should first contact SSAFA Forces Help or the Royal British Legion. Applications are considered at any time, but all are reviewed annually in July.

Enquiries may be made directly to the fund to determine the appropriate corps or regimental association.

Other information

The trust also gives grants to individuals for relief-in-need purposes and to organisations.

Greenwich Hospital

£4,000

Correspondent: Charity Administrator, Greenwich Hospital, 3 Creed Court, 5 Ludgate Hill, London EC4M 7AA (020 7396 0150; fax: 020 7396 0149; email: enquiries@grenhosp.org.uk; website: www.grenhosp.org.uk)

Eligibility

The children of serving or retired officers and ratings of the Royal Navy, Royal Marines and UK Merchant Navy. A minimum of three years qualifying seafaring service is usually required.

Types of grants

Bursaries are available to enable children or grandchildren of current or previous officers of the Royal Navy, Royal Marines, the UK Merchant Navy and also of certain other seafaring professions to attend the Royal Hospital School. In exceptional circumstances bursaries may be made to enable a child to attend a different school.

Three annual bursaries of £3,000 are available to students at Greenwich University studying courses related to engineering and architecture whose parents are serving, or served, in the Royal Navy or the Royal Marines.

Annual grant total

Educational grant total around £4,000.

Applications

Applicants should contact the admissions officer for an applications form which should be submitted before the closing date in December.

Lloyd's Patriotic Fund

£13,000

Correspondent: The Secretary, Lloyd's, One Lime Street, London EC3M 7HA (020 7327 5921; email: communityaffairs@lloyds.com; website: www.lloyds.com)

Trustees: Robert Finch; Fraser Newton; Max Taylor; John Nelson; Graham Findlay; Peter Levene; Chris Klein; Thomas Ashton; Michael Hardingham; Patrick Holcroft; Graham White; Tim Coles; James Kininmonth.

CC Number: 210173

Eligibility

Children of ex-servicemen and women. Preference is given to schoolchildren with serious family difficulties so that the child has to be educated away from home, and people with special educational needs.

Types of grants

Bursaries ranging from £800 to £1,500 per year for school fees at nominated schools.

Annual grant total

In 2010/11 the fund had assets of £1.8 million and an income of £477,000. Educational grants totalled £13,000.

Applications

Grants are awarded through the school and institutions listed below and all applications should be made through them.
- The Royal School, Haslemere
- The Royal Navy and Royal Marines Children's Fund
- The Royal Naval Scholarship Fund

Other information

Grants are also made for welfare purposes, and to organisations.

The Officers' Association

£200,000

Correspondent: Benevolence Department, 1st Floor, Mountbarrow House, 6–20 Elizabeth Street, London SW1W 9RB (020 7808 4175/0845 873 7150; email: k.wallis@officersassociation. org.uk; website: www.officersassociation. org.uk)

Trustees: Admiral the Lord Boyce; Lt Gen. Sir Alistair Irwin; Air Chief Marshal Sir Clive Loader; Vice Admiral Sir Richard Ibbotson; Lt Col Richard Marriott; Capt. Patrick Mitford-Slade; Dominic Fisher; Frank Froud; Jonathan Holdsworth; Air Commodore Peter Johnson; Maj. Jo Killip; Jocelyn Lynch; Capt. Giles Peel; David Scott; Alastair Singleton; Alex Spofforth; Capt. Ian Sutherland; Air Vice Marshall the Hon David Murray; Robert Robson; Maj. Gen. Martin Rutledge; Air Marshal Chris Nickols.

CC Number: 201321

Eligibility

The dependents of ex-officers who have held a commission in HM Forces.

Types of grants

Limited assistance for education and training needs will be given in only in exceptional circumstances. Help towards school fees will not normally be given unless the father has died, or become unemployed, at a stage in the children's education when it would seriously prejudice their future for them to be moved to non-fee-paying schools. In such cases, the applicant will be expected to apply first to the county education officer for a grant and to the school for reduced fees. Advice can be given about other charities specialising in educational assistance.

Annual grant total

In 2010/11 the association had assets of £12.2 million and an income of £3.6 million. Grants were made to 873 individuals totalling £1.4 million and were given mainly for relief-in-need purposes.

Exclusions

The association does not assist with the cost of further education.

Applications

On a form available from the Benevolence Secretary or downloaded from the website. Applications can be submitted either directly by the individual or via a third party. The association has a network of honorary representatives throughout the UK who will normally visit the applicant to discuss their problems and offer advice.

Other information

For applicants in Scotland: See entry for the Officers' Association Scotland.

The association has an informative website.

Royal Air Force Benevolent Fund

£265,000 (77 grants)

Correspondent: The Welfare Director, 67 Portland Place, London W1B 1AR (0800 169 2942; fax: 020 7636 7005; email: mail@rafbf.org.uk; website: www. rafbf.org)

Trustees: David Couzens; Simon Dougherty; Allan Vaughan; Lawrie Haynes; Victoria Raffe; Bridget Towle; Pamela Bagnall; Arabella Hastie; Anthony Lea; Nigel Beet.

CC Number: 1081009

Eligibility

The children (aged 8 to 18) of officers and airmen who have died or were severely disabled while serving in the Royal Air Force. Additionally, help may be considered in those circumstances where the parent dies or becomes severely disabled after leaving the Royal Air Force. Students studying for a first degree or equivalent qualification.

Types of grants

Grants to enable the education plans commenced or envisaged by the child's parents to be fulfilled. Help with the costs of boarding school fees may be given from the age of eight years up to the end of secondary phase only (i.e. up to A-level examinations). Educational assistance from the fund is subject to a parental contribution which is reviewed annually. Grants range from £250 to over £20,000. Where, at the time of the parent's death or disablement, the child has already commenced a 'critical stage' of education at a fee-paying school, education assistance may be provided to the end of the GCSE or A-level course; where the child is not at a 'critical stage', appropriate assistance may be provided only to the end of the current academic year. A 'critical stage' is the two-year course leading to GCSE examinations or A-level examinations. Those children eligible for help with education costs will also be eligible for a modest scholarship to assist with their studies towards a first degree or equivalent. Children are given priority at the Duke of Kent School in Surrey.

Student scholarships of £1,500.

Annual grant total

In 2011 the charity had assets of £144 million, an income of £18 million and gave 77 awards totalling £265,000 for school fees and university scholarships.

Exclusions

No grants for private medical costs or for legal fees.

Applications

On a form available directly from the correspondent or on their website via an online application form. Applications can be submitted by the individual or through an ex-service welfare agency such as RAFA or SSAFA. The fund runs a free helpline which potential applicants are welcome to call for advice and support on the application process. Applications are considered on a continual basis.

Other information

The charity provides advice and assistance on a range of issues including benefits and debt advice and relationships. The fund maintains a short-term care home in Sussex and a further three homes in Northumberland, Avon and Lancashire which are operated jointly with the RAFA. They may also be able to help with purchasing a house.

They also have two holiday homes available at reduced rates for beneficiaries.

Royal Artillery Charitable Fund

£55,000

Correspondent: The Welfare Officer, Royal Artillery Barracks, Larkill, Wiltshire SP4 8QT (01980 634309; fax: 01980 634020; email: artycen-rhqra-racf-WelfareAsst@mod.uk; website: www. theraa.co.uk/website)

Trustees: John Milne; Clive Fletcher-Wood; Alan Jolley; Anthony Richards; Andrew Dines; David Radcliffe.

CC Number: 210202

Eligibility

Dependents of members of the Royal Regiment of Artillery who are unable to work due to illness or death.

Types of grants

This is a relief-in-need charity, which as part of its welfare work supports the children of its members who have started private education before the family's 'breadwinner' became unable to earn – and therefore unable to help them continue their education. It also supports specialist clothing and fees for mature students and people starting work.

Annual grant total

In 2011 the fund gave grants to 1,672 individuals totalling £755,000. Most of which were probably made for welfare purposes.

Exclusions

No grants towards loans, credit card debts or telephone bills.

Applications

In writing to SSAFA Forces Help (details of local branches can be found in telephone directories or from Citizens Advice). Applications can also be made to the Royal British Legion in England and Wales or to Earl Haig Fund in Scotland (see Scotland section of this guide). Applications can be considered at any time.

Royal British Legion Women's Section President's Award Scheme

£25,000

Correspondent: Welfare Team, 199 Borough High Street, London SE1 1AA (020 3207 2183; email:

wswelfare@britishlegion.org.uk; website: www.rblws.org.uk)

Trustees: Eddie Dixon; Eddie Hefferman; John Farmer; Bill Parlin; Diana Henderson; Jim Drew; Keith Pritchard; Jenny Rowe; Terry Whittles; Mike Williams; Adrian Burn; John Crisford; Ken Draper; Cecilia Harper; Noel Duston; John Fisher; Dennis Compton; Ian Lindsey; Peter Twidle; Una Cleminson; Denise Edgar; Martyn Tighe; Anthony Macaulay; Wendy Bromwich.

CC Number: 219279

Eligibility

Ex-service personnel and their spouses and dependents (up to the age of 25), who are in need. This includes dependents of a couple including one ex-serving member where the couple may now be separated.

Types of grants

Scholarships of £1,500 per year for first degrees. One-off grants of up to £400 towards re-training programmes, books, travel costs and other specific needs relating to the course.

Annual grant total

Around £25,000 a year.

Applications

Initial enquiries by telephone or in writing requesting a visit by a welfare visitor who will submit an application form, which includes a financial statement. Applications are considered on a regular basis.

Other information

Grants are made through the Women's Section which is an autonomous organisation within the Royal British Legion, concentrating on the needs of widows and ex-servicewomen and dependent children of ex-service personnel. It works in close association with the Legion but has its own funds and its own local welfare visitors.

This scheme also helps with the costs of a welfare break. The Royal British Legion and the Women's section have many grants available for welfare purposes.

Royal Caledonian Asylum
See entry on page 124

Royal Naval Benevolent Trust

£16,000

Correspondent: The Grants Administrator, Castaway House, 311 Twyford Avenue, Portsmouth PO2 8RN (02392 690112; fax: 02392

660852; email: rnbt@rnbt.org.uk; website: www.rnbt.org.uk)

Trustees: Owen Shread; Philip Shuttleworth; Jacqueline McCafferty; Andrew Cameron; Jonathan Woodcock; Capt. Tim Martin; Carole Davis; Kenneth Lambert; Nicholas Gartside; Sarah Bryant; Ian Bailey; Steven Willett; Gary Harvey; Julian Holmes; Rear Admiral Anthony Rix.

CC Number: 206243

Eligibility

Serving and ex-serving men and women of the Royal Navy and Royal Marines (not officers) and their dependents.

Types of grants

Educational grants are available to schoolchildren and people wishing to change their careers. This is a welfare charity which makes these educational grants as part of its wider work.

Annual grant total

In 2010/11 the trust had assets of £31 million and an income of £4.6 million. Grants amounted to £1.2 million, with an additional £930,000 given in annuity payments. Grants made to individuals for educational purposes have previously totalled £16,000.

Applications

On a form available from the correspondent, to be submitted through a social worker, welfare agency, SSAFA Forces Help, Royal British Legion or any Royal Naval Association branch. Applications are considered twice a week.

Other information

The trust advises that: 'The very wide discretionary powers of the Grants Committee are such that there are but few cases of genuine distress to which the committee is unable to bring prompt relief. Once a need is known to exist and the applicant is deemed to be eligible to benefit and deserving of help, the trust's aim is to provide assistance at a sufficiently high level to enable the beneficiary to make a fresh start with a reasonable prospect of avoiding a further set-back... often, however, no such satisfactory solution is possible. [Many] face the prospect of long-term unemployment or low living standards and there is little that can be done to improve their lot. Occasional grants can be made to meet exceptional circumstances but frequently recurring applications have to be discouraged because... the trust's resources cannot be stretched to permit a regular supplementation of income.'

The trust has an informative website.

The Royal Naval Reserve (V) Benevolent Fund

£1,000

Correspondent: Commander J M D Curteis, Hon. Secretary and Treasurer, The Cottage, St Hilary, Cowbridge, Vale of Glamorgan CF71 7DP (01446 771108)

Trustee: Cdr John Curteis.

CC Number: 266380

Eligibility

The children of members or former members of the Royal Naval Volunteer Reserve, Women's Royal Naval Volunteer Reserve, Royal Naval Reserve and the Women's Royal Naval Reserve who are serving or who have served as non-commissioned rates.

Types of grants

One-off grants mainly for schoolchildren who, because of the poverty of their families, need help with clothes, books, equipment or necessary educational visits, and, secondly, for eligible children with aptitudes or disabilities which need special provision. Grants are normally limited to a maximum of £200 for any applicant.

Annual grant total

About £3,000.

Applications

In writing to the correspondent.

Other information

Grants are also made for welfare purposes.

The Royal Navy and Royal Marines Children's Fund

£800,000

Correspondent: Monique Bateman, Director, 311 Twyford Avenue, Stamshaw, Portsmouth PO2 8RN (02392 639534; fax: 02392 677574; email: rnchildren@btconnect.com; website: www.rnrmchildrensfund.org)

Trustees: Dr Miranda Whitehead; David Brazier; Sheila Owens-Cairns; Heather Rimmer; Dug Hickin; Lt Col Ian Grant; Com Malcolm Williams; Judge Anthony Thorpe; Com David Bridger; Paul Austin; Anne Binnie.

CC Number: 1075015

Eligibility

Young people under 25 who are in need and are the dependant of somebody who has served, or is serving, in the Royal Navy, Royal Marines, the Queen Alexandra's Royal Naval Nursing Service or the former Women's Royal Naval Service.

Types of grants

One-off and recurrent grants are made to schoolchildren, college students, undergraduates and vocational students where there is a special need. Grants given include those towards schools fees, uniforms, clothing, books, equipment, instruments, maintenance, living expenses and childcare.

Annual grant total

In 2010/11 the fund had assets of £8.3 million and an income of £1.1 million. The sum of £1.1 million was given in grants to individuals or families for educational and welfare purposes.

Applications

On a form available from the correspondent or to download from the website. Applications can be submitted directly by the individual or through the individual's school/college, an educational welfare agency, SSAFA or any other third party. They are considered on a monthly basis, though urgent cases can be dealt with between meetings.

The WRNS Benevolent Trust

£4,500

Correspondent: Sarah Ayton, General Secretary, Castaway House, 311 Twyford Avenue, Portsmouth, Hampshire PO2 8RN (02392 655301; fax: 02392 679040; email: generalsecretary@wrnsbt. org.uk; website: www.wrnsbt.org.uk)

Trustees: Janet Crabtree; Cdr Jackie Mulholland; Cdr Jane Walton; Cdr Maggie Robbins; Lt Cdr Jan Edwards; Lt Cdr Sally Prendergast; Mary Brittan; Commodore Annette Picton; Cdr A. Crook; J. Clink.

CC Number: 206529

Eligibility

Ex-Wrens and female serving members of the Royal Navy (officers and ratings) who joined the service between 3 September 1939 and 1 November 1993 who are in need. People who deserted from the service are not eligible.

Types of grants

This charity is essentially a relief-in-need charity which offers grants for educational purposes. These are usually given to schoolchildren for uniforms and other clothing and to students in further or higher education, including mature students, towards books, equipment, instruments, computers, fees and maintenance.

Annual grant total

In 2011 the trust had assets of £3.3 million and an income of £555,000. Educational grants totalled £4,500.

Applications

Applications can be made direct to the correspondent, or through SSAFA either by the individual, or a friend or relation.

Other information

Grants are mostly made in the form of pensions, or for relief in need.

Social work

The Social Workers' Educational Trust

£16,000

Correspondent: The Hon. Secretary, BASW, 16 Kent Street, Birmingham B5 6RD (email: secretary@ socialworkerseducationaltrust.org.uk; website: www.basw.co.uk/resources/ financial-support/social-workers-educational-trust)

Trustees: Elizabeth O'Dell; Catherine Poulter; Carolyn Holmes; Beverly Burke; Vivien Freeman; David Pitcher.

CC Number: 313789

Eligibility

Registered social workers, with at least two years' post-qualifying experience, involved with improving social work practice and undertaking post-qualifying training.

Types of grants

One-off and recurrent grants from £100 to £300 for fees, travel costs, childcare and books. Up to £1,500 is available for scholarships.

Annual grant total

In 2010/11 the trust had an income of £5,200 and an expenditure of £17,000.

Exclusions

The trust cannot assist those undertaking initial social work training or qualifications.

Applications

On a form available from the correspondent or the website along with guidelines. Applications are considered in February, June, September and November.

Other information

The trust also makes awards from specific bequests (one or two a year) following a competition; details are available in the Professional Social Worker journal and from the Hon. Secretary.

Solicitors

The Solicitors' Benevolent Association Ltd

£224,000

Correspondent: John Platt, 1 Jaggard Way, Wandsworth Common, London SW12 8SG (020 8675 6440; email: sec@ sba.org.uk; website: www.sba.org.uk)

Trustee: The Trustees.

CC Number: 1124512

Eligibility

Solicitors who are or have been on the Roll for England and Wales and have practised, and their dependents, who are in need.

Types of grants

One-off and recurrent grants and interest-free loans where applicable, towards university and other educational costs.

Annual grant total

In 2011 the charity had assets of £16 million and an income of £2.2 million. During the year grants and loans were made to 344 individuals. Grants totalled £1.1 million and loans advanced £612,000. Grants were broken down into:

- Cost of living allowances – £468,000
- Leisure, special and miscellaneous – £344,000
- Educational support – £224,000
- Nursing home fees – £15,000

Exclusions

Solicitors who have been considered to have brought the profession into disrepute are not eligible.

Applications

On a form available on the website or by contacting the fund. Applications are considered at board meetings held ten times a year.

Sport

Professional Footballers' Association Educational Fund

£101,000

Correspondent: Darren Wilson, Trustee, 20 Oxford Court, Bishopsgate, Manchester M2 3WQ (01612 360575; email: info@thepfa.co.uk)

Trustees: Garth Crooks; Darren Wilson; Gordon Taylor; David Weir; Brendon Batson; Christopher Powell; Paul Elliott; Gareth Griffiths.

CC Number: 306087

Eligibility

Current and former members of the Professional Footballers' Association who wish to retrain in order to continue employment once their football careers have ceased.

Types of grants

Grants for vocational training and educational courses.

Annual grant total

In 2010/11 the fund had assets of £22 million and an income of £17 million. Grants to individuals totalled £101,000.

Applications

In writing to the correspondent, applications are considered throughout the year.

Other information

The fund also gives grants to organisations to advance the public knowledge of the history and social significance of football, to promote good community and race relations at football events and towards medical initiatives that promote the health of beneficiaries.

The Rugby Football League Benevolent Fund

£11,000

Correspondent: Steve Ball, Red Hall, Red Hall Lane, Leeds, West Yorkshire LS17 8NB (0844 477 7113; email: info@ rflbenevolentfund.co.uk; website: www. rflbenevolentfund.co.uk)

Trustees: Philip Clarke; David Hinchliffe; Timothy Adams; Gary Hetherington; Emma Rosewarne; Geoffrey Burrow.

CC Number: 1109858

Eligibility

People who play or assist, or who have played or assisted, in the game of Rugby League in the UK or for a team affiliated to an association primarily based in the UK and their dependents. Beneficiaries should be in hardship or distress, in particular, as a result of injury through playing or training, or when travelling to or from a game or training session.

Types of grants

Grants are given towards educational courses.

Annual grant total

In 2011 the fund had assets of £398,000 and an income of £251,000. Grants to 99 beneficiaries totalled £87,000 including £11,000 for 'educational courses'.

Applications

In writing to the correspondent.

Other information

Grants are also made for welfare purposes, including those towards special vehicles and repairs, home improvements, furniture, wheelchairs, gym equipment, computers, hotel accommodation, travel, physiotherapy, home appliances and Christmas presents.

Stationers

The GPM Charitable Trust

£5,000

Correspondent: Keith Keys, 43 Spriggs Close, Clapham, Bedford MK41 6GD (07733 262991; email: gpmcharitabletrust@tiscali.co.uk; website: www.gpmtrust.org)

Trustees: Charles Cherrill; Glyn Beaver; Joe Smith; Rose Mooney; Brian Willoughby; Leslie Miller; Vernon Robson.

CC Number: 227177

Eligibility

Workers, former workers and their dependents in the printing, graphical, papermaking and media industries.

Types of grants

Grants for retraining, skills enhancement, educational requirement especially following redundancy or other reduction in income.

Annual grant total

In 2011/12 the trust had an income of £15,000 and an expenditure of £26,000.

Applications

On a form available to download from the website, or from the correspondent, to be returned by email or post.

Other information

The trust has also been funding a refurbishment project for people in sheltered housing with another charity. They also give grants for welfare purposes.

The Stationers' Foundation

£79,000 (26 grants)

Correspondent: Ian Larkham, Secretary of the Trustees, The Printing Charity, First Floor, Underwood House, 235 Three Bridges Road, Crawley, West Sussex RH10 1LS (01293 542820; fax: 01293 524826; email: ian@ theprintingcharity.org.uk; website: www. stationers.org)

Trustees: David Allan; Helen Esmonde; C. D. Jakes; Sue Pandit; Robert Flather; Hugh Sear; Robert Sanger; Robert Shepherd.

CC Number: 1120963

Eligibility

UK residents under the age of 25 who are studying printing, papermaking, publishing and distribution, journalism, librarianship, typography, book and graphic design, photography, conservation of books and manuscripts, packaging, advertising, website creation and all relevant electronic communication and publishing and the children of Liverymen or Freemen of the company.

Types of grants

The foundations runs two educational schemes, one offering around 20 scholarships and awards a year to those studying a trade of the guild, or the children of liverymen and freemen. These include general awards for fees/ living expenses, funds for projects, travel in the UK and abroad and musical education. The second scheme offers ten bursaries of £6,000 and mentoring for postgraduates studying trades of the guild.

Annual grant total

In 2010 the foundation had assets of £3.6 million and an income of £156,000. 26 grants were made to individuals totalling £79,000 for school and college fees, general awards and postgraduate bursaries.

Applications

On forms available from the website along with guidance notes, specific to each award. Applicants are advised to phone the correspondent in the first instance, to discuss an application. Applications are invited between September and December.

Other information

The foundation also supports schools, Shine School Media Awards, Saturday Supplementary Schools and a welfare fund.

Tailoring

The Merchant Taylors' Company

£13,000

Correspondent: The Charities Officer, Merchant Taylors' Hall, 30 Threadneedle Street, London EC2R 8AY (020 7450 4440; email: charities@merchant-taylors.co.uk)

Trustees: Hugh Oliver-Bellasis Frags; Andrew Moss; Peter Magill; Christopher Keville.

CC Number: 1069124

Eligibility

People who have attended one of the Merchant Taylors' family of schools: Merchant Taylors' School in Northwood; the Merchant Taylors' School in Crosby; the King's School, Macclesfield; Wallingford School; Wolverhampton Grammar School and Foyle and Londonderry College or who have some association with the Company.

Types of grants

Loans and grants to cover the direct educational costs of individuals in secondary, further and higher education.

Annual grant total

In 2011 the fund had assets of £601,000 and an income of £617,000. Education and training grants totalled £13,000.

Applications

Applications may be made to the correspondent at any time on the form available from the Correspondent or the website. Only one application is required for consideration by both charities.

Other information

The company owns two schools – Merchant Taylors' School, Sandy Lodge and St John's Preparatory School, Pinner. It is associated with six other schools by foundation – Merchant Taylors' School, Crosby; Merchant Taylors' School for Girls, Crosby; Wolverhampton Grammar School; Foyle and Londonderry College, Wallingford School and King's School, Macclesfield.

Tallow chandlers

Tallow Chandlers Benevolent Fund

£0

Correspondent: Susan Bunn, Tallow Chandlers Hall, 4 Dowgate Hill, London EC4R 2SH (020 7248 4726; fax: 020 7236 0844; email: clerk@tallowchandlers.org; website: www.tallowchandlers.org)

Trustees: Roger Newnham; John Zochonis; Michael Hollingsworth; Michael Snyder; John Kurkjian; Roy Wilde; Nicholas Bull; Ian McIntyre; Michael Webb; Tony Rogers; Christopher Tootal; Rupert Travis; Robert Nicolle; C. R. Lambourne; N. M. Wells; N. H. Thompson; Peter Purton; Phillip Edwards; R. B. Yates; Timothy Piper; David Simmonds; J. N. Harrington; Michael Sutcliffe; Peter Cazalet; Keith Prosser; Ian Bowden; Ronald Watts; Robert Pick; Christopher Pryke; Oliver Kirby-Johnson; Ian Robertson; Richard Fleck; Werner Pick; Robert Bexson.

CC Number: 246255

Eligibility

People in need who have a connection with the company in the City of London and adjoining boroughs.

Types of grants

Check the website for details of bursaries and scholarships, which change on a regular basis. In the latest annual report the trust stated it was considering setting up bursaries for higher education distance learning, one at St John's College Oxford and bursaries for engineering students at City University.

Annual grant total

In 2010/11 the trust had assets of £4.9 million, an income of £557,000 and made no grants to individuals. The trust mostly makes grants to schools and charities for educational purposes and only very rarely supports individuals, however the trust has been discussing setting up specific bursaries in their 2010/11 annual report.

Applications

In writing to the correspondent.

Teaching

IAPS Charitable Trust

See entry on page 26

NASUWT (The Teachers' Union) Benevolent Fund

£20,000

Correspondent: Legal and Casework Team, NASUWT, Hillscourt Education Centre, Rose Hill, Rednal, Birmingham B45 8RS (01214 536150; fax: 01214 576210; email: legalandcasework@mail.nasuwt.org.uk; website: www.nasuwt.org.uk)

Trustees: Michael Grant; Pamela Milner; Hopkin Thomas; Celia Foote; Andrew Curtis; Chris Holland.

CC Number: 285793

Eligibility

Members, former members and the dependents of members and former members and dependents of deceased members of NASUWT The Teachers' Union.

Types of grants

Grants of £125 for schoolchildren aged 16 and under and £150 for those 17 and over.

Annual grant total

In 2010 the fund had assets of £2.1 million and an income of £290,000. 787 grants were made to individuals totalling £202,000 for education and welfare purposes.

Exclusions

No support for private school fees, education courses, repayments of student loans or to assist students with general living expenses.

Applications

Contact the local association secretary or the legal and casework team at NASUWT headquarters. Arrangements may be made for a benevolence visitor to visit and complete the application form.

Other information

Help is also available from this fund for welfare purposes, and they also provide money advice.

Textile workers

The Fashion and Textile Children's Trust

£223,000

Correspondent: Anna Pangbourne, Director, Winchester House, 259- 269 Old Marylebone Road, London NW1 5RA (020 7170 4117; email: anna@ ftct.org.uk; website: www.ftct.org.uk)

Trustees: Kenneth Young; Colin Llewellyn Evans; David Carter-Johnson; Ian Thomson; Josephine Collins; Jill Butterworth; Anne Horton; Nikki Zamblera; David Shepherd; Jill Little; Nayna McIntosh; Sue Shipley; Jessica Brown; Amit Chowdhury; Mike Trotman.

CC Number: 257136

Eligibility

Children and young people under 18 years whose parents work or have worked in the UK fashion and textile retailing and manufacturing industry.

Types of grants

The trust concentrates its grant giving on 'the essential costs of education'; in practice this means particularly, but not exclusively, the payment of school fees. There is a preference for those with serious family difficulties so the child has to be educated away from home or at schools which offer vital pastoral care. The trust will also fund places at specialist schools for children with learning difficulties or for those who would benefit from attending a school that focuses on music or sport. Help is given with existing school fees where there has been a 'dramatic' change in family circumstances. Hardship grants are also available for clothing, books, computers, travel costs to attend school and educational trips.

Grants usually range from £200 to £300 for hardship awards and £3,600 spread over the academic year for educational support.

Annual grant total

In 2010/11 the trust had assets of £7.2 million and an income of £461,000. Grants were made to individuals totalling £268,000, broken down as follows:

- Ongoing school fee cases: 56 grants
- New school fee cases: 27 grants
- Welfare grants: 42 grants
- Bursaries: 6 grants

Educational grants totalled £223,000.

Exclusions

No grants are given towards child care, study/travel abroad; overseas students studying in Britain; student exchange; or people starting work. No grants are available for those in higher education.

Applications

On a form available from the correspondent or an initial enquiry form from the trust's website. Applications can be submitted at any time either directly by the individual or through a third party such as a social worker, teacher or Citizens Advice. Applicants are encouraged to call the trust in the first instance, to discuss an application.

National charities classified by subject

Actuary

Company of Actuaries Charitable Trust Fund

£22,000

Correspondent: David Johnson, Clerk, Cheapside House 138, Cheapside London EC2V 6BW (020 7776 3880; email: charity@actuariescompany.co.uk; website: www.actuariescompany.co.uk/en/charitabletrust)

Trustees: Fiona Morrison; Jeffrey Medlock; Michael Pomery; Nick Dumbreck; David Barford; Michael Turner.

CC Number: 280702

Eligibility
Further and higher education students progressing towards actuarial qualifications.

Types of grants
One-off grants of around £800 each to help students with course/exam fees so that they can complete their training for the profession.

Annual grant total
In 2010/11 the trust had assets of £333,000 and an income of £141,000. 25 bursaries were awarded totalling £22,000.

Applications
On a form available on the website. Applications are mainly considered in October, but also in January, April and July.

Other information
The trust also gives grants to organisations.

The Institute of Actuaries Research and Education Fund

£1,500

Correspondent: David Burch, Institute of Actuaries, Staple Inn Hall, 1–3 Staple Inn, London WC1V 7QJ (020 7632 2194; email: david.burch@actuaries.org.uk; website: www.actuaries.org.uk)

Trustee: Institute of Actuaries.

CC Number: 274717

Eligibility
Actuarial students at any educational establishment approved by the actuarial profession.

Types of grants
Awards, scholarships and grants for professional training and research in actuary.

Annual grant total
In 2010/11 the fund had an income of £4,600 and an expenditure of £1,500.

Applications
In writing to the correspondent.

Agriculture and related rural issues

The Dick Harrison Trust

£2,000

Correspondent: R Addison, Secretary, Hexham Auction Mart Co. Ltd, Tyne Green, Hexham NE46 3SG (01434 605444; website: www.dickharrisontrust.org.uk)

Trustees: David Goldie; Dawn Harrison; Lily Harrison; Nicholas Utting; Tim Atkinson.

CC Number: 702365

Eligibility
Further and higher education, mature and postgraduate students who are in need and are training in livestock auctioneering and/or rural estate management and who were born in Cumbria, Northumberland or Scotland, or who are (or whose parents or guardians are) at the time of the award living in any of these places.

Types of grants
One-off grants towards fees, books, equipment/instruments, maintenance/living expenses and study or travel abroad.

Annual grant total
About £2,000.

Applications
On a form available from the correspondent, or from the trust's website. Applications should be submitted directly by the individual and are considered at any time.

The Institute of Chartered Foresters Educational and Scientific Trust

£1,500

Correspondent: The Secretary, 59 George Street, Edinburgh EH2 2JG (01312 401425; email: icf@chateredforesters.org; website: www.charteredforesters.org)

SC Number: SCO08515

Eligibility
Students of forestry and related disciplines.

Types of grants

Grants are available for students and others at an early stage in their career in forestry. The trust offers three types of grant:

▶ EST travel bursary: one award of £500 made to one applicant for travel to benefit professional development

▶ EST professional development awards: a discretionary award of any amount made to one applicant

▶ EST Events awards: several awards of £100 made for attending the ICF National Conference or Study Tour

Annual grant total

The amount given in grants varies from year to year. Recent grants have totalled about £1,500.

Applications

On a form available from the website.

Applications for the Professional Development Awards are considered four times a year and should be received at the latest by 31 March, 30 June, 30 September or 31 December for consideration by Trustees. Applications for the Annual Travel Bursary should be received by 31 March. Events bursary awards are awarded annually.

The Elwyn Jones Memorial Fund

£1,000

Correspondent: Helen Edwards, Waled Young Farmers Clubs, Royal Welsh Showground, Llanelwedd, Builth Wells LD2 3NJ (01982 553502; email: information@yfc-wales.org.uk)

Trustees: Robert Lewis; Brian Jones; Ernie Beaumont; Gethin Havard.

CC Number: 260862

Eligibility

Individuals who want to travel abroad in order to study agriculture.

Types of grants

Grants for travel abroad to study agriculture.

Annual grant total

About £1,000.

Applications

In writing to the correspondent.

Nuffield Farming Scholarships Trust

£126,000 (19 grants)

Correspondent: John Stones, Blaston Lodge, Blaston, Market Harborough, Leicestershire LE16 8DB (01858 555544; email: nuffielddirector@aol.com; website: www.nuffieldscholar.org)

Trustees: Alison Blackburn; Anthony Evans; Stephen Watkins; Philip Hughes; Nigel Pulling; Wallace Hendrie; Joanna Franklin; Nick Chippendale; Robert Parker; Helen Woolley; Robert Darling; Ian Tremain.

CC Number: 1098519

Eligibility

UK residents aged 23 to 45 who have been working for at least two years in farming, growing, forestry, fish farming, and countryside management businesses and ancillary to these, and people in positions to influence them.

Types of grants

Around 20 awards of approximately £6,000 are given to study topics of interest to rural industry including agriculture, land management, horticulture and the food chain, which can be worldwide. The grants cover a period of eight weeks, and are for travel and subsistence costs.

Annual grant total

In 2010/11 nineteen awards were made totalling £126,000.

Exclusions

Full-time education and research projects will not be funded.

Applications

On a form available from the website. Awards are advertised in October each year and must be submitted by 31 July in the year before the applicant wishes to travel.

The John Oldacre Foundation

£211,000 (10 grants)

Correspondent: Stephen Charnock, 35 Broadwater Close, Hersham, Walton on Thames KT12 5DD

Trustees: Stephen Charnock; Henry Shouler; Ian Bonnet.

CC Number: 284960

Eligibility

Undergraduates and postgraduates who are carrying out research in the agricultural sciences which is meaningful to the UK agricultural industry. The research must be published.

Types of grants

One-off and recurrent grants according to need towards structured research in the UK and overseas. Previously funded research included projects on pig welfare, potato diseases and sustainable crops.

Annual grant total

In 2010/11 the foundation had assets of £8 million and an income of £158,000.

Ten awards were made totalling £211,000.

Applications

In writing to the correspondent through the individual's college/university. Applications are usually considered twice a year, in the autumn and spring.

The Royal Bath and West of England Society

£10,000

Correspondent: Dr Jane Guise, The Showground, Shepton Mallett, Somerset BA4 6QN (email: mary.holmes@bathandwest.co.uk; website: www.bathandwest.com)

Trustees: Edwin White; Robert Drewett; Richard Ash; Ewen Cameron; Anthony Gibson; Angela Yeoman; Alan Goode; Nell Matheson; John Alvis; Nicholas Hutchen; Annie Maw; Michael Felton; Richard Calver.

CC Number: 1039397

Eligibility

People studying any aspect of veterinary medicine, agriculture, horticulture, forestry, conservation or any form of food production or marketing. Other projects that have been supported include livestock photography, rural art and rural leadership.

Types of grants

Scholarships and grants.

Annual grant total

In 2010 the society had assets of £1.9 million and an income of £3.2 million. £10,000 was designated for scholarships and grants.

Applications

On a form available from the correspondent. Applications are considered twice a year, in spring and autumn.

The Studley College Trust

£67,000 (35 grants)

Correspondent: D J Brazier, Hill View, Chapel Lane, Ratley, Banbury OX15 6DS (01295 670397; email: studleyct@btinternet.com; website: www.studleytrust.co.uk)

Trustees: William Simpson; Margaret Herbert; Andrew McGreggor; Anthony Forsyth; Bryan Jarvis; Margaret Galloway; Richard Colwill; Adam Quinney; M. Pollock; M. Walker; R. Ogg; C. Flavell.

CC Number: 528787

Eligibility

British nationals aged 17 to 30 training at a public sector institution for a career in agriculture, horticulture, forestry and allied land-based industries whose progress is barred by insufficient financial resources. Pre-course practical experience is regarded as essential and students on industrial placements lasting over six weeks are not supported.

Courses in the following areas are supported: agriculture; horticulture; forestry; fish farming; agri-food technology; agricultural or horticultural marketing; arboriculture and agricultural engineering.

Types of grants

One-off and recurrent grants towards fees, books, travel, clothing, equipment, accommodation and living expenses. Grants can be for up to £2,000 according to circumstances. There is also an emergency fund to help eligible students for whom changed circumstances and a financial crisis threatens their continued studies.

Annual grant total

In 2010/11 the trust had assets of £9.4 million and an income of £94,000. Grants totalled £67,000.

Exclusions

No grants are available for hire purchase payments, support for dependents or long-term housing costs.

Applications

People at certain land-based colleges should apply through their institution (a list of these colleges is available on the website). In other cases application forms can be requested via the website or the correspondent. The trustees consider applications in May, July and September submitted by the first day of the previous month.

Archaeology/ antiquarian studies

Society of Antiquaries of London

£65,000

Correspondent: The General Secretary, Burlington House, Piccadilly, London W1J 0BE (020 7479 7080; fax: 020 7287 6967; email: admin@sal.org.uk; website: www.sal.org.uk)

Trustees: Margaret Richardson; Nathaniel Alcock; Philippa Glanville; Colin Haselgrove; Stephen Johnson; Sian Res; Maurice Howard; David Breeze; Graeme Barker; Anthony Emery; Leslie Webster; Aideen Ireland; Neil Cossons; Colin Renfrew; John Creighton; Brian Ayers; Gillian Andrews; David Adshead; Roger Bland; Alan Thacker.

CC Number: 207237

Eligibility

People in higher education, including postgraduates, early career researchers and scholars studying archaeological and antiquarian subjects.

Types of grants

Travel grants of up to £500 and research grants of up to £11,000 for projects and research in archaeology and antiquarian subjects. See the website for details of individual funds.

Annual grant total

The society allocates around £65,000 for research and travel grants each year.

Applications

On a form available from the website or the correspondent. Applications should be submitted by 15 January with references for consideration in March. Applicants will be notified of a decision by 31 March.

Arts

The Artistic Endeavours Trust

£10,000

Correspondent: Richard Midgley, Macintyre Hudson, 30–34 New Bridge Street, London EC4V 6BJ (020 7429 4100)

Trustees: Heather Gordon; Richard Midgley.

CC Number: 1044926

Eligibility

Students undertaking education in the arts or entering artistic professions.

Types of grants

Grants to graduates and undergraduates for fees, clothing equipment, books, travel and general subsistence.

Annual grant total

In 2010 the charity gave grants to organisations and individuals totalling £41,000 including five grants to students.

Applications

In writing to the correspondent.

Other information

The trust primarily gives grants to organisations.

The William Barry Trust

£10,000

Correspondent: W S Barry, 56 Avenue Close, London NW8 6DA (020 7722 3974)

Trustees: Keiko Iwaki; Teruko Iwanaga; Ahmad Amirahmadi; William Barry; Hisako Tomofuji; Kevin Daly.

CC Number: 272551

Eligibility

People engaged, or about to engage in technical, craft and artistic occupations.

Types of grants

One-off cash grants in the range of £600 and £1,000, including those for fees and maintenance/living expenses.

Annual grant total

In 2010/11 the trust had an income of £25,000 and an expenditure of £24,300.

Exclusions

No grants for career development or postgraduate degrees.

Applications

In writing to the correspondent. Applications should be submitted directly by the individual or a family member.

The Canada House Arts Trust

£15,000

Correspondent: Louise Spence, 8 Addison Bridge Place, London W14 8XP (email: alexiw@talktalk.net; website: www.canadahouseartstrust.org)

Trustees: Kat Kagan; Louise Spence; Rita Tushingham; Eve Gabereau; Kathleen Crook; Michina Ponzone-Pope.

CC Number: 1105941

Eligibility

Individuals and groups involved in projects in the visual and performing arts, music, literature, film, TV and media which have a Canadian focus or theme. Projects must take place in the UK.

Types of grants

The average grant is between £1,000 and £2,000.

Annual grant total

In 2010/11 the trust had an income of £60 and an expenditure of £16,000.

Exclusions

The trust does not support travel and accommodation expenses or costs for work in development.

Applications

In writing to the correspondent describing the nature of the project and the aspects, with costings, for which the application is being made. The trustees meet quarterly to decide allocation of funds.

Thomas Devlin Fund

See entry on page 115

Henry Dixon's Foundation for Apprenticing

£46,000

Correspondent: Charities Administrator, Drapers' Company, Drapers' Hall, Throgmorton Avenue, London EC2N 2DQ (020 7588 5001; fax: 020 7628 1988; email: charities@thedrapers. co.uk; website: www.thedrapers.co.uk)

Trustee: The Draper's Company.

CC Number: 314292

Eligibility

Apprentices or students under 25 studying in the fields of music, technical textiles and art.

Types of grants

One-off grants ranging from £100 to £2,000. Grants are made to four London music colleges, one London art college and any other institutions as the trustees see fit.

Annual grant total

In 2010/11 the trust had assets of £1.8 million and an income of £50,000. Grants were made totalling £46,000.

Applications

The trust makes block grants to educational institutions, who then administer the grants. Therefore grant recipients must apply to their educational institutions rather than the trust.

Other information

This trust was formerly called Drapers' Educational Foundation.

The Ann Driver Trust

£20,000

Correspondent: Penny Neary, Secretary to the Trustees, 10 Stratford Place, London W1C 1BA (07939 556574; email: secretary@anndrivertrust.org; website: www.anndrivertrust.org)

Trustees: Alan Traill; Robert Pritchett; Baroness Howe; Timothy Wakeley; Alasdair Tait; Kathleen Duncan,.

CC Number: 801898

Eligibility

Young people from the EU wishing to pursue an education in the arts, particularly music.

Types of grants

The trust makes awards to institutions on a rota basis which changes annually.

Annual grant total

£20,000 to £25,000 per year.

Applications

Application forms should be requested by the principle or head of department at place of study.

Other information

The trust selects different institutes for support in May of each year. A copy of the list of institutes can be obtained from the administrator by sending an sae.

The Exuberant Trust

£5,500

Correspondent: Megan Boyes, 42 Margaret Road, Oxford OX2 6RU (01865 751056; email: exuberant.trust@ntlworld.com; website: www.exuberant-trust.org.uk)

Trustees: Susanna Graham-Jones; Susan Cave; Jeremy Cunningham; Lyndsey Herford; Susie Crow; Steve Pratley.

CC Number: 1095911

Eligibility

People up to the age of 30 in Oxfordshire who are developing their interest in the arts: music drama, dance, arts and crafts, multimedia and so on who are in financial need.

Types of grants

One-off grants up to a maximum of £500 for a specific project or activity. Grants have previously been made for tools, training, music lessons, general costs and instruments.

Annual grant total

In 2011 the trust had an income of £15,000 and gave grants to 12 artists totalling £5,500. The artists included nine musicians, one designer, one jeweller and a theatre director.

Applications

Full guidelines are available from the trust's website, or by contacting the correspondent in writing. Trustees meet four times a year to consider applications.

Other information

Successful applicants are encouraged to take part in concerts and other activities in support of the trust.

The Fenton Arts Trust

£10,000

Correspondent: Shelley Baxter, Trust Manager and Administrator, PO Box 135, East Horsley, Surrey KT24 9AB (website: www.fentonartstrust.org.uk)

Trustees: David; Elyan; Sue Davies-Scourfield; Stephen Morris; Fiona Thompson; Tricia Friswell; Lisa Bryan.

CC Number: 294629

Eligibility

People who are making, or who aspire to make, a worthwhile contribution to the artistic and cultural life of the UK. Grants are made towards the creative arts, principally painting and drama. Students should have British nationality and be aged under 35.

Types of grants

Scholarships/bursaries are awarded for a one-year period to final year or postgraduate students undertaking arts courses. Grants are also made for individual works, activities, performances, exhibitions or prizes.

Annual grant total

In 2010/11 the trust had assets of £3.1 million and an income of £108,000. Grants made to organisations and individuals totalled £84,000. It is not possible to ascertain what proportion of this figure went to individuals as some grants to individuals were made through organisations.

Applications

Applications for The Fenton Arts Trust Scholarships/Bursaries may come from any institution which provides appropriate study opportunities and wishes to offer its students the scholarships/bursaries. (Individuals should only apply via their institution.)

Applications for other grants can be made in writing directly by the individual to the administrator at the address below. Requests should include a fully budgeted proposal with the amount requested and information regarding other sponsors to the project.

Applications should preferably be sent nine months to a year in advance.

The trustees meet to discuss applications four times a year.

Other information

The trust also provides grants to organisations.

The Gordon Foundation

£50,000

Correspondent: Gillian Hoyle, Administrator, PO Box 214, Cobham,

Surrey KT11 2WG (01483 579108; email: gordon.foundation@btinternet.com; website: www.gordon.foundation. btinternet.co.uk)

Trustees: Bruce Smith; Christopher Elliott; Claire Maynard.

CC Number: 1054934

Eligibility

Young people up to the age of 30. 'To support their education in the fine or performing arts, particularly music, drama or design, or to allow them to engage in educational travel which involves physical challenge and endeavour.'

Types of grants

One-off and recurrent grants according to need.

Annual grant total

Grants are made to organisations and individuals and in total usually amount to around £100,000.

Applications

Application forms are available by email or post. They can also be downloaded from the foundation's website.

Other information

The foundation also owns and maintains two long wheelbase Land Rovers which it loans without charge to groups of young people for expeditions or field trips.

The Haworth Charitable Trust

£3,000

Correspondent: Rooks Rider Solicitors, Rooks Rider Solicitors, Challoner House, London EC1R 0RR (020 7689 7000)

Trustees: Christopher Wright; Jeremy Haworth; Alison Godlee; Sarah Clark.

CC Number: 803239

Eligibility

Young musicians and painters in their final year of full-time study or the first year of their professional career. Preference is given to applicants from the north west of England, Herefordshire, Shropshire, The Wrekin and London.

Types of grants

Grants of £1,000 to £2,000 for one year only, paid in instalments over the year. Grants are for any purposes to further the establishment of a career in music, painting and the fine arts. Grants are not made for general welfare purposes.

Annual grant total

The trust usually gives about £3,000 a year in grants to individuals.

Exclusions

Loans are not made and mature students cannot be funded.

Applications

Applications should be made by letter, with a CV, to the correspondent, and must be supported by a recommendation of a tutor of a full-time course.

The Philip Bates Trust

£1,500

Correspondent: Rachel Bates, Secretary, 24 Elmfield Road, Castle Bromwich, Birmingham B36 0HL (01216 815663; email: info@philipbatestrust.org.uk)

Trustees: Karen Moulton; Margaret Maclachlan; Susan Bates; Alison Perrier-Burgess; Jill Robinson; John Saunders; Martin Bates; Rachel Bates.

CC Number: 1094937

Eligibility

People under 25 pursuing creative and artistic achievement. Preference is given to musicians and applicants in the West Midlands.

Types of grants

One off, and in exceptional circumstances recurrent, grants of £100 to £300 and musical instrument loans. There are also four prizes for composition awarded each year.

Annual grant total

In 2011 the trust had an income of £3,700 and an expenditure of £3,300.

Exclusions

Grants to individuals will not be made to more than one sibling per family.

Applications

Applications should be submitted in December or June for consideration in January and July. Where possible, trustees prefer to receive a personal request from the applicant rather than from a parent, guardian or other person on their behalf.

Other information

The trust also supports projects or workshops which aim to develop creative and artistic interests and skills in young people.

The Rhona Reid Charitable Trust

See entry on page 100

The Martin Smith Foundation

£0

Correspondent: The Trustees, Po Box 838, Oxford OX1 9LF

Trustees: E. Smith; M. Smith; Jeremy Smith; Katherine Wake; Elizabeth Buchanan; Bartholomew Peerless.

CC Number: 1072607

Eligibility

People undertaking further, higher or postgraduate training in ecology, environment and natural resources, music or performing arts.

Types of grants

One-off grants, of up to £2,500, towards books, equipment, fees, bursaries or fellowships.

Annual grant total

In 2010/11 the charity had assets of £21,000 and an income of £110,000. No grants to individuals were made during the year; previously around £30,000 has been given.

Exclusions

Travel expenses are not funded.

Applications

The trustees state that they do their own research and do not consider unsolicited applications.

The Society for Theatre Research

£6,600

Correspondent: Eileen Cottis, Hon. Secretary, c/o The Royal National Theatre Archive, 83–101 The Cut, London SE1 8LL (email: contact@str.org. uk; website: www.str.org.uk)

Trustees: Eileen Cottis; Francesca Franchi; Michael Ostler.

CC Number: 266186

Eligibility

People involved with research into the history, historiography, art and practice of the British theatre, including music-hall, opera, dance, and other associated performing arts. Applicants should be aged 18 or over. There are no restrictions on status, nationality, or the location of the research.

Applications are not restricted to those engaged in formal academic work and academic staff, postgraduate students, theatre professionals and private researchers are all equally eligible.

Types of grants

Annual theatre research awards ranging between £100 and £1,000. Grants can go towards research costs, study or travel overseas and foreign students studying in the UK. The society usually grants one or two awards of £1,000 then a number of smaller awards of £200 to £500.

Annual grant total

In 2010/11, fifteen research awards, one 'book prize' and one 'new scholars essay prize' were made, altogether totalling £6,600.

Exclusions

Exclusively literary topics are not eligible, nor are applications for course fees unless for specific professional training in research techniques and no grants for maintenance costs.

Applications

Application forms can be downloaded from the society's website. The Application period opens in October and completed forms should be returned by 1 February, with a detailed breakdown of costing and the names of two referees. Applications received later than this date, for whatever reason, will not be admitted.

The South Square Trust

£21,000

Correspondent: Nicola Chrimes, Clerk to the Trustees, PO Box 169, Lewes, East Sussex BN7 9FB (01825 872264; website: www.southsquaretrust.org.uk)

Trustees: Stephen Baldock; Christopher Grimwade; Brand Inglis; Paul Harriman; Andrew Blessley.

CC Number: 278960

Eligibility

Students aged 18 years and over studying full-time practical degree courses in the fine and applied arts, especially those related to gold, silver and metalwork, but also music, drama and dance.

Types of grants

The trustees assist individuals in two ways, firstly through direct scholarships to a number of schools and secondly by awarding grants to individuals who apply directly. Individual awards can be used to help with paying fees or for living expenses but no assistance is given for the purchase of equipment, private lessons or travel outside of the UK.

Annual grant total

In 2010/11 the trust had assets of £3.6 million and an income of £167,000. Grants were paid to 24 individuals totalling £21,000.

Exclusions

No grants for people under 18; part-time or short courses; expeditions, travel or shoes; courses outside the UK; or

courses not concerned with fine or applied arts.

No direct financial help is available to individuals wishing to study at schools and colleges already in receipt of a Bursary or Scholarship Award from the South Square Trust. A full list of these institutions is given on the trusts website. In these cases, the student would need to approach the school or college directly to enquire as to whether they can be considered.

Applications

On a form available from the correspondent, for submission from January to April for consideration in May for courses starting in September. Initial enquiries by telephone are welcomed. Two references and a photograph are required for submission with the application form (along with photographs of work if on an arts-related course).

Other information

Various bursaries have been set up with schools connected with the fine and applied arts. These are as follows: Byam Shaw School of Art; West Dean College (Metalwork); The Slade School of Fine Art; The Royal Academy Schools; London Metropolitan University (Silversmithing and Metalwork); Royal College of Music; Bristol Old Vic Theatre School; GSA Conservatoire; Royal Academy of Dramatic Art (RADA); School of Jewellery, Birmingham Institute of Art and Design; Guildhall School of Music and Drama; Royal Academy of Music; Royal College of Art; Textile Conservation Centre; and Royal Northern College of Music.

The Talbot House Trust

£10,000

Trustees: Joanne Lawrence-Hall; Andrew Sims.

CC Number: 1010214

Eligibility

Individuals undertaking courses in the performing arts, such as drama, dance and music. Only UK residents will be awarded grants, for study in the UK.

Types of grants

One-off grants to students in further/ higher education to help with the cost of fees. In exceptional circumstances a contribution towards equipment and instruments or maintenance and living costs will be considered.

Annual grant total

The trust has an annual grant giving total of around £5,000.

Exclusions

No grants to postgraduates.

Applications

Each year the trustees select a college or school to receive a larger grant to be distributed to individuals by them in accordance with the criteria of the Talbot House Trust. Therefore, potential applicants should enquire at the institution where they plan to study for details of any funding that is available there and **not** directly to the trust.

Other information

In 2012/13 the trust is supporting the Academy of live Recorded Arts and the Centre for Young Musicians.

The Wall Trust

£19,000 (15 grants)

Correspondent: Charles Wall, Chair, Flat 19 Waterside Point, 2 Anhalt Road, London SW11 4PD (020 7978 5838; email: charles@thewalltrust.org)

Trustees: Brian Carter; Charles Wall; Barbara Potts; Pen Stally.

CC Number: 291535

Eligibility

Students, including students from overseas who are studying in the UK, aged 16 and over and are nominated by an organisation with which the trust has a scholarship scheme (see Applications section). Individuals may be undertaking further, higher or postgraduate education or vocational training in the performing arts and be studying music, drama or dance.

Types of grants

Normally grants are paid for each year of a scholar's course – on average for three years. Grants normally range between £1,000 and £3,000 a year and are limited to training or tuition fees.

Annual grant total

In 2010/11 the trust had assets of £179,000 and an income of £37,000. 15 music, dance and drama scholarships were made totalling £19,000.

Applications

Applications should only be made via an organisation with which the trust has a scholarship scheme. These are the Royal Ballet School, London Studio Centre, RADA, Royal College of Music, Royal Academy of Music, Royal Northern College of Music and the Purcell School. The trust has previously stated that all its funds were allocated.

S. D. Whitehead's Charitable Trust

£31,000 (15 grants)

Correspondent: The Trustees, Moore Stephens, Chartered Accountants, 30 Gay Street, Bath BA1 2PA (01225 486100)

Trustees: Peter Whitehead Langley; Anne Prebensen; Jenny Clarke; Andrew Clarke.

CC Number: 207714

Eligibility

Children under 16 with special artistic talents, especially in music, dance or ballet.

Types of grants

Grants are available to help pay school fees or to help fund one-off purchases (for example musical instruments) for talented children, and range from £500 to £2,500.

Annual grant total

In 2010/11 the trust had assets of £987,000, an income of £37,000 and made 15 grants to individuals totalling £31,000.

Applications

On a form available from the correspondent, to be submitted directly by the individual for consideration in June.

Other information

Grants are also made to small local charities.

Crafts

Craft Pottery Charitable Trust

£3,800 (9 grants)

Correspondent: Elizabeth Gale, Trustee, Taplands Farm Cottage, Webbs Green, Soberton, Southampton SO32 3PY (02392 632686; email: lizgale@interalpha. co.uk)

Trustees: Elizabeth Gale; Emmanuel Cooper; Phil Rogers; Louise Taylor; Chris Keenan; Clare Twomey; Liz Aylieff; John Eccles.

CC Number: 1004767

Eligibility

People involved in the field of ceramics.

Types of grants

Grants and bursaries to assist with preparing books, conference papers and other projects relevant to the education of the public in craft pottery.

Annual grant total

Nine grants to individuals were made totalling £3,800

Applications

In writing to the correspondent.

Other information

Until 2010 income and expenditure had remained at around £7,000–£9,000 a year. In 2010 there was a dramatic increase in income to £62,000 due to a fundraising drive; however most of this was then given in one grant to The Craft Potters Association of Great Britain Ltd to fund the building of educational areas.

The Queen Elizabeth Scholarship Trust

£136,000 (16 grants)

Correspondent: The Secretary, 1 Buckingham Place, London SW1E 6HR (020 7828 2268; email: qest@rwha.co.uk; website: www.qest.org.uk)

CC Number: 802557

Eligibility

People involved in modern or traditional crafts who are reasonably well-established in the field, rather than those who are starting off. Applicants must be permanently resident in the UK.

Types of grants

One-off and staged grants, over a maximum of four years, of between £1,000 and £18,000 each for further education, such as work experience and training and can include related travel and research costs.

Annual grant total

In 2011 the trust had assets of £4.1 million, an income of £957,000 and awarded 16 scholarships totalling £136,000.

Exclusions

Grants are not made for tools, leasing studios/workshops, materials, staging exhibitions or for general educational courses.

Applications

On an application form available on written request with an A4 sae from the correspondent, or from the website. Scholarships are awarded twice a year, in spring and summer. See the website for application deadlines.

Dance

The Lionel Bart Foundation

£77,000

Correspondent: John Cohen, 55 Drury Lane, London WC2B 5SQ (020 7379 6080; email: jc@clintons.co.uk)

Trustees: John Cohen; Malcolm Webber; Michael Pruskin.

CC Number: 1086343

Eligibility

Prospective actors, composers, lyricists, bookwriters, playwrights, designers, choreographers, directors and anyone who wishes to make the theatre their career (undergraduate and postgraduate).

Types of grants

One-off grants towards fees are given in the range of £200 to £5,000.

Annual grant total

In 2010/11 the foundation's income increased substantially again to £104,000 (£39,000 in 2009/10). Bursary awards totalled £77,000.

Applications

In writing to the correspondent to be received by 15 May each year. Applications are considered in late May.

The Marie Duffy Foundation

Correspondent: Michael Pask, 4A Flaghead Road, Poole, Dorset BH13 7JL (01202 701173; email: mduffypask@ btinternet.com; website: www.marie-duffy-foundation.com/AboutUs.htm)

Trustees: Marie Duffy-Pask; Michael Pask; Leonard McLaughlin; James McCutcheon; Eben Foggitt.

CC Number: 1145892

Eligibility

People over 17 with proven excellence in Irish dance, composition or choreography.

Types of grants

Grants and awards for dancers, composers and choreographers to advance or support their education in Irish Dance.

Annual grant total

As the trust is newly registered, no financial information was available.

Applications

On the application form available to download from the trusts website. Forms should be submitted by 1 September at the latest.

Other information

Grants are also made for Irish Dance projects.

The Lisa Ullmann Travelling Scholarship Fund

£11,000 (19 grants)

Correspondent: The Secretary, Breach, Kilmington, Axminster, Devon EX13 7ST (01297 35159; email: jachapman@breachdevon.co.uk; website: www.lutsf.org.uk)

Trustees: Anna Carlisle; Judith Chapman; Barbara Lewis; Alysoun Tompkins.

CC Number: 297684

Eligibility

Individuals working in all areas of movement and dance who wish to travel abroad or in the UK.

Types of grants

Scholarships are awarded to fund the travel of individuals abroad or in the UK to attend conferences, to pursue a research project, or undertake a short course of study in the field of movement or dance.

Annual grant total

In 2010/11 the trust had an income of £4,300 and made 19 grants totalling £11,000.

Exclusions

The following are not supported: fees for courses or conferences are not paid; fees or travel for 'long' courses, e.g. courses extending over one, two or three years; these include, for example, most diploma, certificate, degree and postgraduate courses; individuals under the age of 18; projects which directly support the work of companies, institutions or organisations; set up costs of projects or festivals; those not resident in the UK for a minimum of two years continuously prior to the application; previous recipients of LUTSF scholarships are considered for a second award only after at least five years have passed and/or in exceptional circumstances.

Applications

On a form available from 1 September from the fund's website. Four signed copies of the form must be sent by post- to arrive no later than 25 January. Forms not received by this date cannot be considered. Forms sent by email or fax are not acceptable. Applicants are informed of the outcome of their application by the end of March, and scholarships winners may travel from April onward.

The Jeremy and Kim White Foundation

£2,000

Correspondent: Kim White, 65 Piccadilly Top Floor, London W1J 0DY (email: info@whitefoundation.com; website: www.whitefoundation.com)

Trustees: Jeremy White; Kim White; Nickolas Butler; Victoria Gillies.

CC Number: 1091332

Eligibility

Young people in the performing arts with a special emphasis on jazz and classical ballet.

Types of grants

One-off scholarships according to need.

Annual grant total

About £2,000.

Applications

Applications should be submitted by email including an explanation of the background of the applicant's financial hardship.

Other information

The charity also supports an orphanage in India and some organisations in the UK.

Music

The Tom Acton Memorial Trust

£3,200

Correspondent: A T Gage, Hamilton House, Cobblers Green, Felsted, Dunmow, Essex CM6 3LX (01371 820382; fax: 01371 821100; email: applications@tomacton.org)

Trustees: Alan Gage; Felicity Gage.

CC Number: 1088069

Eligibility

People up to the age of 30 who are resident in Essex.

Types of grants

Grants and loans according to need to a maximum of £750 for instruments, tuition and other expenses.

Annual grant total

In 2010/11 the trust had an income of £4,100 and a total expenditure of £3,400.

Applications

In writing to the correspondent. Applications should be supported by a teacher's recommendation.

The Alper Charitable Trust

£6,000

Correspondent: Simon Alper, Nelsons Loft, Creake Road, Burnham Thorpe, King's Lynn PE31 8HW (fax: 01223 895605; email: simonalper@yahoo.co.uk)

Trustees: Simon Alper; Joanne Alper; Andrew Muncey.

CC Number: 272104

Eligibility

Young musicians in full-time education.

Types of grants

The trust usually gives an interest-free loan (generally £200 to £500) to help buy a musical instrument.

Annual grant total

In 2009/10 the trust had an income of £10,000 and an expenditure of £6,400.

Applications

Write to the correspondent for an application form (enclosing an sae). Applications can be submitted directly by the individual at any time. Two references are essential.

Other information

It is not clear how active this trust is, accounts have been submitted very late and it was not possible to contact the trust.

The Amber Trust

See entry on page 21

The Australian Music Foundation in London

£15,000

Correspondent: Guy Parsons, 51 Musgrove Road, London SE14 5PP (020 7635 1680; fax: 01444 456192; website: www.amf-uk.com)

Trustees: John Tooley; Yvonne Kenny; William Cornish; John Emmott; Heather de Haes; Peter Carrington; Peter Tregear; James Pitman; Tim Hunter; Marcus Cox; Simon Thornton.

CC Number: 270784

Eligibility

Australian singers and instrumentalists under 30 years of age for study in Europe. Students should either be resident in Australia or the UK.

Types of grants

Grants are usually made towards the cost of musical equipment, study and development.

Annual grant total

In 2010 the foundation had an income of £7,000 and a total expenditure of £17,000.

Exclusions

Composers are not considered for grants.

Applications

In writing to the correspondent, applications should be submitted before the end of January each year.

Other information

There is a separate award jointly funded by the Australian Music Foundation and Sir Charles Mackerras, which is specifically for Australian conductors of merit. Potential applicants should request further information from The Australian Musical Foundation.

Awards for Young Musicians

£56,000 (110 grants)

Correspondent: Caroline Harvie, Administrator, PO Box 2754, Bristol BS4 9DA (01179 049906; fax: 01179 048957; email: enquires@a-y-m.org.uk; website: www.a-y-m.org.uk)

Trustees: Michael Lewin; Beverley Mason; Michael Littlechild; Philip Jones; Jerome Raphaely; Laurie Watt; Fiona Harvey; Susan Daniels; Catherine Hogel.

CC Number: 1070994

Eligibility

Musicians aged 5 to 18 who are in financial need and have musical potential.

Types of grants

£200 to £2,000 for instruments, music lessons, weekend music schools, music courses, orchestra fees and travel.

Annual grant total

In 2011 the charity had an income of £150,000. Ninety eight awards were made in Strand 1 and twelve in Strand 2, totalling £56,000.

Exclusions

No support for singers or students about to enter their first undergraduate year.

Applications

On a form available on the website, along with a music teachers reference, to be submitted by mid-March each year. Successful applicants will be informed by late May. All applications are means tested.

The applications panel recommends two strands of award beneficiaries: Strand 1, for those awarded funding up to £500, and Strand 2, for those awarded funding

of over £500. Applicants in Strand 2 will be invited to audition.

Other information

The organisation also provides advice, support and mentoring to young musicians.

The Josephine Baker Trust

£19,000

Correspondent: David Monro, Trustee, Grange Cottage, Frensham, Farnham, Surrey GU10 3DS (01252 792485; email: munrodj@aol.com)

SC Number: SC020311

Eligibility

People studying vocal music in the UK.

Types of grants

£125 or £250 to help to establish singers in their careers. Typically with their soloist fees at selected concerts.

Annual grant total

In 2010/11 the trust had assets of £34,000 and an income of £32,000. £19,000 was given in 47 grants to singers.

Applications

In writing to the correspondent. The trust has established links with the Royal Academy of Music and the Royal College of Music.

The BBC Performing Arts Fund

£150,000 (30 grants)

Correspondent: Miriam O'Keeffe, Room 4171, White City, 201 Wood Lane, London W12 7TS (020 8752 6511; email: performingartsfund@bbc.co.uk; website: www.bbc.co.uk/performingartsfund)

Trustees: Sarah Gee; Sally Stote; Alec McGivan; Susannah Simons; Roger Leathem; Dorothy Wilson; Kate Danielson; Jacqueline McKay.

CC Number: 1101276

Eligibility

Performing arts individuals. Eligibility differs for each individual scheme so it is recommended that applicants refer to the terms and conditions and other information on the fund's website.

Types of grants

Each year the fund's work focuses on a different art form: music, dance or theatre. Grants range from £500 to £10,000.

Annual grant total

In 2010/11 the fund had assets of £1.2 million and an income of £722,000.

£150,000 was awarded to over 60 students through the Training in Musical Theatre Scheme.

Applications

The fund has recently implemented a three year funding cycle with one art form being funded each year. This will be focused on theatre in 2013, dance in 2014 and music in 2015. Eligibility criteria, deadlines and online application forms are available for open schemes on the fund's website.

To keep up to date about the launch of new music schemes as they are announced, sign up to the Fund's newsletter online.

Other information

The charity is funded through the incidental revenue from the voting lines of BBC One entertainment programmes such as *Over the Rainbow*.

The fund also awards grants to performing arts community groups (£302,000 in 2010/11).

The R. and D. Burchett Charitable Foundation

£10,000

Correspondent: Rainer Burchett, Trustee, Watermillock House, Watermillock, Penrith CA11 0JH (01768 486191; email: rainer.burchett@talk21.com)

Trustees: Rainer Burchett; Doreen Burchett; Helen Burchett; Jude Burchett; Lutea (UK) Ltd.

CC Number: 1076739

Eligibility

People in education and those involved music and athletics.

Types of grants

Grants given according to need.

Annual grant total

In 2010/11 the charity had an income of £23,000 and an expenditure of £14,000.

Applications

In writing to the correspondent.

The Busenhart Morgan-Evans Foundation

£9,000

Correspondent: John F Bedford, Trustee, Brambletye, 455 Woodham Lane, Woodham, Surrey KT15 3QQ (01932 344806; fax: 01932 343908)

Trustees: Mrs Morgan Evans; Mr Morgan Evans; John Bedford.

CC Number: 1062453

Eligibility

Young musicians at the start of their professional career. The foundation is also able to assist organisations.

Types of grants

One-off and recurrent grants towards equipment, instrument and fees.

Annual grant total

In 2010/11 the foundation had an income of £12,000 and an expenditure of £18,000.

Applications

Through the individual's college, to be submitted to the Worshipful Company of Musicians, 6th Floor, 2 London Wall Buildings, London EC2M 5PP (020 7496 8980).

The Choir Schools' Association Bursary Trust Fund Ltd

£231,000 (117 grants)

Correspondent: The Administrator, 39 Grange Close, Winchester, Hants SO23 9RS (01962 890530; email: csamds@tiscali.co.uk; website: www. choirschools.org.uk)

Trustees: Nicholas Robinson; Claire Hickman; Timothy Cannell; Elizabeth Cairncross; Roger Overend; Robert Bacon; Alexander Donaldson.

CC Number: 1120639

Eligibility

Pupils or proposed pupils, aged 7 to 13, at a member school.

Types of grants

Grants are available to pay the fees of choristers attending CSA schools. Applications are means tested. Grants range from £300 to £2,400.

Annual grant total

In 2010/11 the trust had assets of £465,000 and an income of £393,000. Grants were made totalling £231,000 to 117 individuals, made possible by grants to the trust from the Department of Education, the School Fees Insurance Agency and the Welsh Assembly Government.

Applications

On an application form to the headmaster of the choir school concerned. Applications should be submitted by 15 March, 31 August and 15 December for consideration in May, October and February.

The Else and Leonard Cross Charitable Trust

£15,000

Correspondent: Helen Gillingwater, Trustee, The Wall House, 2 Lichfield Road, Richmond, Surrey TW9 3JR (020 8948 4950; email: helengillingwater@ hotmail.com)

Trustees: Helen Gillingwater; Brian Green; Paul Harris.

CC Number: 1008038

Eligibility

Students of music aged 11 to 27 years who have considerable potential as pianists and are in financial need.

Types of grants

The trust makes scholarships to musical institutes which are in turn passed on to individuals. Grants for fees, living costs and instruments.

Annual grant total

In 2010/11 the trust had an income of £7,000 and an expenditure of £22,000.

Applications

Applications must be made through the college the student is with, not directly to the trust.

Elizabeth Eagle-Bott Memorial Awards
See entry on page 22

The EMI Music Sound Foundation

£210,000

Correspondent: Janie Orr, 27 Wrights Lane, London W8 5SW (020 7795 7000; fax: 020 7795 7296; email: enquires@ emimusicsoundfoundation.com; website: www.emimusicsoundfoundation.com)

Trustees: John Deacon; Rupert Perry; D. Hughes; Leslie Hill; Tony Wadsworth; James Beach; Paul Gambaccini; Christine Walter; Charles Ashcroft; Jo Hibbitt; Richard Lyttelton; Leo Corbett.

CC Number: 1104027

Eligibility

Young people in the UK who are undertaking music education.

Types of grants

Grants of up to £2,000 for the purchase of musical instruments and equipment for children in full-time education and for courses and training opportunities for music teachers who work within schools.

The foundation also operates a bursary scheme of £5,000 for students at eight

musical colleges and institutes: International World Music Centre, Birmingham Conservatoire, Tech Music Schools, Royal Academy of Music, Royal Welsh College of Music and Drama, Royal Conservatoire of Scotland, National Children's Orchestra; Brighton Institute of Modern Music.

Annual grant total

In 2010/11 the trust had assets of £7.7 million and an income of £279,000. Grants to individuals totalled £170,000, plus £40,000 distributed in bursaries to individuals through institutions.

Exclusions

No grants are given to applications from outside the UK, or that relate to community projects or music therapy.

Applications

On a form available from the correspondent, or which can be downloaded from the website. Completed forms can be submitted either directly by the individual or through the individual's school. The trustees meet every six months, in March and September, and applications need to be received three weeks before the relevant meeting, with references and supplier's quotes. Applications for bursaries should be made directly to the individual's college.

Other information

The foundation also gives grants to non-specialist schools to fund music education.

The Gerald Finzi Charitable Trust

£16,000 (14 grants)

Correspondent: Elizabeth Pooley, Administrator, The Finzi Trust, PO Box 137, Shaftesbury SP7 0WX (email: admin@geraldfinzi.org; website: www. geraldfinzi.org)

Trustees: Robert Gower; Andrew Burn; Paul Spicer; Stuart Ritchie; Christian Alexander; Jean Finzi; Orlando Finzi; Judy Digney.

CC Number: 313047

Eligibility

Students of music aged between 25 and 70. Formal training or qualifications are not necessary.

Types of grants

The trust offers grants for the purchase of musical instruments and music scholarships for projects in the UK and overseas, lasting ideally between three to eight weeks. If a project involves travel then the trust can meet expenses along with the costs of accommodation, subsistence and equipment for the period involved.

Scholarships can be made for a variety of projects, such as gaining practical experience in performance, attending summer schools or education and research projects. Scholarships awarded in recent years have covered studies in Estonia, Finland, France, Germany, India, Ireland, Italy, South America, Sweden, the UK and the USA.

Grants to individuals in 2010/11 were between £200 and £500; scholarships were for between £400 and £3,600.

Annual grant total

In 2010/11 the trust made seven grants to individuals totalling £3,100 and seven scholarship awards totalling £13,000.

Exclusions

No grants are made for attendance at courses, for the support of academic degree courses, or for fees or living expenses. Applications from students of other art forms will not be supported and group applications are not considered.

Applications

Applications can be made on a form available by post-from the trust, using the online form or as a download from the trust's website. Applicants must include an outline of their proposal and an estimate of the cost. Applications are considered throughout the year.

The closing date for applications is November with interviews taking place the following January.

Other information

Grants are also made to organisations.

The Simon Fletcher Charitable Trust

£5,000

Correspondent: V Fletcher, 74 Hampstead Road, London NW1 2NT (020 7330 0982; email: info@ simonfletcher.org.uk; website: www. simonfletcher.org.uk)

Trustees: Brian Fletcher; Christopher Loake; Deborah Jones; Eliot Fletcher; Mary Fletcher; Alex Rumsey; Verity Fletcher.

CC Number: 1094808

Eligibility

People studying music, usually singers under 30, studying at a recognised music academy. Grants are made in the UK and Australia.

Types of grants

One-off grants of up to £1,000. Grants are made to schoolchildren for books and equipment/instruments and to

college students, undergraduates, vocational students, mature students and overseas students for fees, study/travel abroad and maintenance/living expenses.

The trust also administers the Simon Fletcher Award, an annual award given to one individual, usually of £1,000. This is awarded after a process of application, audition and interview, usually in June.

Annual grant total

Grants usually total around £5,000.

Applications

By emailing the correspondent in the first instance, with details of education, instrument being studied and reasons for requesting financial assistance.

Other information

Grants are also made to schools for the purchase of instruments, music and so on.

The Jean Ginsburg Memorial Foundation

£5,000

Correspondent: Ian Henry, The Garden Flat, Flat 1 3 Heath Drive, London NW3 7SY (077744 35130; email: info@ jeanginsburg.com; website: www. jeanginsburg.com)

Trustees: Andrew Henry; Judith Henry; Ian Henry.

CC Number: 1104077

Eligibility

People who wish to pursue a career in medicine or to train as a classical pianist.

Types of grants

Awards and scholarships.

Annual grant total

In 2010/11 the foundation had an income of £12 and an expenditure of £7,600. Previously about 70% of income had been dedicated to grants for individuals.

Applications

Initial contact can be made via email.

Other information

The trust also supports scholarships at The Royal Free Medical School, The Royal Academy of Music in London and Somerville College, Oxford University.

The Michael James Music Trust

£10,000

Correspondent: Edward Monds, Garden House, Cuthburga Road, Wimborne BH21 1LH (01202 887681)

Trustees: Raymond James; Edward Monds; Margaret James; Richard Hall.

CC Number: 283943

Eligibility

Individuals engaged in any musical education, particularly in a Christian context.

Types of grants

One-off and recurrent grants are given towards tuition fees and expenses. The present priority is to help organ scholars working to obtain ARCO/FRCO qualifications.

Annual grant total

In 2008/09 the trust had an income of £17,000 and a total expenditure of £15,000. Grants total about £10,000.

Exclusions

No grants for the purchase of instruments or equipment.

Applications

On an application form available from the correspondent. Applications should be received by 30 April each year.

Other information

Grants are also made to churches, universities and schools.

The Kathleen Trust

£20,000

Correspondent: Edward Perks, Secretary, Currey and Co., 21 Buckingham Gate, London SW1 6LS (020 7828 4091)

Trustees: Edward Perks; Oliver Scott; Phoebe Scott; Camilla Withington.

CC Number: 1064516

Eligibility

Young musicians of outstanding ability who are in need.

Types of grants

Loans in the form of musical instruments and sometimes bursaries to attend music courses, ranging between £500 and £2,500.

Annual grant total

In 2010/11 the trust had an income of £22,000 and a total expenditure of £84,000. Grants to individuals usually total around £30,000

Applications

In writing to the correspondent.

Other information

Grants are also made to organisations.

The Macfarlane Walker Trust

£2,000

Correspondent: Sophie Walker, 4 Shooters Hill Road, London SE3 7BD

(020 8858 4701; email: sophiewalker@ mac.com)

Trustees: David Walker; Nigel Walker; Catherine Walker.

CC Number: 227890

Eligibility

Music students over 18 who are in need, with a preference for those who live in Gloucestershire.

Types of grants

One-off grants ranging from £500 to £2,000, for the purchase of musical instruments for music students.

Annual grant total

Grants are mostly made to organisations, with about £2,000 a year given to individuals.

Applications

In writing to the correspondent, directly by the individual, giving the reason for the application and an outline of the project with a financial forecast. An sae and references from an academic referee must accompany the initial application.

The Music Libraries Trust

£5,000

Correspondent: Edith Speller, Secretary, c/o Jerwood Library of the Performing Arts Trinity Laban, King Charles Court, Old Royal Naval College, Greenwich, London SE10 9JF (020 8305 4422; email: e.speller@trinitylaban.ac.uk; website: www.musiclibrariestrust.org)

Trustees: Richard Chesser; Helen Mason; Nicholas Williams; Pam Thompson; Lewis Foreman; David Jones; Christopher Jackson; Katharine Ellis; Terri Anderson; Peter Baxter; Ann Wrigley.

CC Number: 284334

Eligibility

Music librarians involved in education or training, or people carrying out research into music librarianship and music bibliography.

Types of grants

The trust has a regular programme of allocating grants in support of projects, research and course attendance with a preference for supporting those who have been unable to receive financial support from elsewhere. Awards of between £100 and £5,000 have been given for initial funding, with second grants being considered in exceptional cases.

Annual grant total

About £5,000.

Applications

In writing to the correspondent. Applications can be submitted directly by the individual or through the school/ college or educational welfare agency.

The Ouseley Trust

£101,000 (27 grants)

Correspondent: Martin Williams, PO Box 281, Stamford, Lincolnshire PE9 9BU (01780 752266; email: ouseleytrust@btinternet.com; website: www.ouseleytrust.org.uk)

Trustees: Andrew Walters; Christopher Robinson; Richard White; Adam Ridley; Stephen Darlington; Martin Pickering; John Rutter; Gillian Perkins; Mark Boyling; Paul Mason; Timothy Byram-Wigfield.

CC Number: 527519

Eligibility

Children aged 9 to 16 who are choristers in recognised choral foundations in the Church of England, Church of Ireland or Church in Wales.

Types of grants

Grants towards choir school fees for up to three years. Grants usually range from £1,000 to £5,000. Grants can also be made for organ tuition.

Annual grant total

In 2011 the trust had assets of £3.7 million and an income of £146,000. Grants were made towards fees totalling £64,000. A further £37,000 was given in scholarships and bursaries belonging to specific endowments. Overall 27 children benefitted during the year.

Exclusions

No grants for music lessons. Help is unlikely to be available for choristers at Rochester, Ely or St Albans where the trust has donated funds to be used for scholarships. It does not usually award further grants to successful applicants within a two-year period.

Applications

On a form available from the correspondent by the school or choral foundation concerned, not by the chorister or his/her parents. A statement of financial resources by the child's parents or guardian will be required. Applications should be submitted by the end of February or June for consideration in March or October. The trust states that applicants are strongly advised to obtain and study the guidelines for applications.

The Geoffrey Parsons Memorial Trust

£7,000

Correspondent: B P Griffin, 50 Broadway, Westminster, London SW1H 0BL (020 7227 7000)

Trustees: Brian Griffin; Leslie Howard; Robert Rattray; William Lyne.

CC Number: 1049165

Eligibility

Concert pianists and people with the ability to become concert pianists, who have a particular interest in the accompaniment of song or in chamber music. There is a preference for people under 35.

Types of grants

One-off and recurrent grants, usually of sums up to £2,000, towards piano lessons with pre-eminent teachers and the purchase of music (i.e. sheet music and scores).

Annual grant total

In 2010/11 the trust had an income of £6,100 and an expenditure of £3,600.

Applications

Unsolicited applications will not be considered.

The Pratt Green Trust

£0

Correspondent: Brian Hoare, 5 Flaxdale Close, Knaresborough, North Yorkshire HG5 0NZ (01423 860750; email: brianhoare@sky.com; website: www. prattgreentrust.org.uk)

Trustees: Andrew Pratt; Brian Hoare; Judy Jarvis; Donald Pickard; Robert Canham; John Barnard; Bernadette Farrell.

CC Number: 290556

Eligibility

Hymn writers, church musicians and others involved in education, research, composition and performance in the area of church music and hymnody.

Types of grants

Scholarships, bursaries, prizes, research expenses, books and other grants.

Annual grant total

In 2010/11 the trust had assets of £61,000 and an income of £41,000. Grants to individuals usually total around £1,000 but none were made in 2010/11.

Exclusions

No grants towards course fees.

Applications

In writing to correspondent. All applications must be accompanied by a detailed budget covering the project/purpose for which the grant is requested, together with full details of any other grants or sponsorship applied for. Applications should be supported by a suitable second signatory, for example, college principal or other person with a connection to the purpose and by two references.

Other information

Grants are also made to organisations.

The Royal College of Organists

£12,000

Correspondent: The Registrar, PO Box 56357, London SE16 7XL (05600 767208; email: admin@rco.org.uk; website: www.rco.org.uk)

Trustees: Stephen Farr; David Saint; Gavin Barrett; Sarah Baldock; Graham Barber; Sarah MacDonald; Noel Flannery; Andrew Cantrill; James O'Donnell; Mark Brafield.

CC Number: 312847

Eligibility

Students of organ playing. Most awards are given to members or student members of the Royal College of Organists.

Types of grants

There are various scholarships and awards of £100 to £2,000 for travelling, course fees, specific musical pieces, and female organists. Consult the Royal College of Organists' website for further details.

Annual grant total

In 2008/09 the charity had assets of £1.3 million and an income of £495,000. From a direct charitable expenditure of £360,000, scholarships and prizes totalled £12,000.

Applications

On a form which can be downloaded from the charity's website.

The Rushworth Trust

£4,500

Correspondent: The Grants Team, Liverpool Charity and Voluntary Services, 151 Dale Street, Liverpool L2 2AH (01512 275177)

Trustees: David Rushworth; Michael Talbot; Phillip Duffy; Liverpool Charity and Voluntary Services.

CC Number: 1076702

Eligibility

People who are studying music who live within a 60-mile radius of Liverpool. Grants are awarded to composers, young conductors, young performers, student singers and instrumentalists, and choirs and choir singers, for assistance with publication, copying, training, promotion, equipment, instruments, music tours, apprenticeships, concerts and maintenance.

Types of grants

One-off grants of up to £300 to help with the cost of the study of music and to stimulate and encourage beneficiaries in their musical pursuits. Only single payments are made and can only be given if the individual is not eligible for grants from any other sources. Awards are not usually repeated.

Annual grant total

In 2010/11 the trust had both an income and expenditure of around £4,700.

Exclusions

No grants for course fees or maintenance costs of higher education.

Applications

By the individual on a form available from the correspondent, including all relevant information and documentary evidence. Applications are considered in March, June, September and December, and applications should be received before the start of the month. Applicants are advised of the outcome by the last day of the same month.

Other information

The trust has been formed by the merging of The William Rushworth Trust, The Thew Bequest and The A K Holland Memorial Award.

The Schools Music Association of Great Britain

£0

Correspondent: Carole Lindsay, Trustee, Brook House, 24 Royston Street, Potton, Bedfordshire SG19 2LP (01767 260815; email: secretary@schoolsmusic.org.uk; website: www.schoolsmusic.org.uk)

Trustees: Carole Lindsay-Douglas; David Bunkell; Gill Blazey; Hayley McDonagh; Reg Fletcher; Ann Sidney; Douglas Coombes; Steven Sammut; Liz Craik; Katherine Fear; Jean James; Jay Deeble; Ruth Adams; Karen Love; Richard Llewellyn.

CC Number: 313646

Eligibility

Musicians in full-time education up to the age of 18 who are in financial need.

Types of grants

Help towards buying musical instruments, summer schools, short courses and so on. Grants are one-off and usually range from £50 to £150.

Annual grant total

In 2010/11 there were no grants made, as the trust had little income due to low interest rates.

Exclusions

Ongoing courses cannot be funded.

Applications

On a form available from the correspondent. Applications must be supported in writing by a headteacher, principal, music teacher or music adviser/inspector, and by a member of the Schools Music Association. They should be submitted by the end of February or September.

Grants can be made upon receipt of written evidence of the expenditure having been made during the 12 months following the date of application, for example, a receipt for an instrument bought, or a summer school certificate of attendance. Grants are not normally made for expenditure before the date of application.

The Raphael Sommer Music Scholarship Trust

£3,000

Correspondent: Ian Ross, Trustee, 205 Crescent Road, Barnet EN4 8SB (020 8449 0011; email: genevieve.sommer@googlemail.com)

Trustees: Genevieve Sommer; David Sommer; Ian Ross; Nick Rollason; Yau Pascal Tortelier; Arts Noras.

CC Number: 1102269

Eligibility

Music students of the cello, in practice locally in London.

Types of grants

One-off and recurrent grants according to need.

Annual grant total

In 2010/11 the trust had an income of £1,300 and an expenditure of £3,400.

Applications

In writing to the correspondent.

The Stringwise Trust

£2,000

Correspondent: Cara Turtington, Lion House, Red Lion Street, London WC1R 4FP (020 7841 4000)

Trustees: Michael Max; Cecily Mendelssohn.

CC Number: 1048917

Eligibility

People who play stringed instruments.

Types of grants

Grants towards attendance at any training or experiential event.

Annual grant total

About £2,000.

Applications

In writing to the correspondent.

Other information

Grants are also made to organisations.

The Tillet Trust

£8,000

Correspondent: Katie Avey, PO Box 667, Dunsford, Exeter EX6 7WW (0845 070 4969; fax: 0845 070 4969; email: infor@thetillettrust.org.uk; website: www.thetillettrust.org.uk)

Trustees: Paul Strang; David Stiff; Paul Harris; Fiona Grant; Yvonne Minton; Harvey Chalmers.

CC Number: 257329

Eligibility

Young classical musicians at the start of their professional solo careers.

Types of grants

One-off grants of between £250 and £2,000 to assist young musicians undertake performance related projects designed to further their careers. Short performance courses, specialist coaching prior to performance of new repertoire; travel costs to participate in international competitions.

Annual grant total

In 2010 the trust held assets of £485,000. Income totalled £26,000 and £8,000 was given in grants to individuals.

Exclusions

No grants for new instruments, full time undergraduate courses, commissioning of new works or commercial readings.

Applications

In writing to the correspondent with full details of the project including an outline budget, together with details of their training and career to date, two written references, a recent demo tape/CD, any press cuttings and any other relevant material.

Other information

Also available each year are two to five postgraduate bursaries for an outstanding student about to enter their second/subsequent year of study.

Applicants must be nominated by a main British conservatoire.

The Society for Wessex Young Musicians Trust

£2,000

Correspondent: Sandrey Date, 7 Southbourne Coast Road, Bournemouth BH6 4BE (01202 423429)

Trustees: Sandrey Date; Sarah Richards; Colin Feltham; Stuart Rohr; Martin Outhwaite; Jean Harvey.

CC Number: 1100905

Eligibility

Young musicians who live in Dorset and Hampshire.

Types of grants

Grants towards equipment and facilities and loans.

Annual grant total

About £2,000 each year to individuals.

Applications

In writing to the correspondent.

Miss E. B. Wrightson's Trust

£12,000 (33 grants)

Correspondent: Trust Administrator, Swangles Farm, Cold Christmas, Hertfordshire SQ12 7SP (email: info@wrightsontrust.co.uk; website: wrightsontrust.co.uk)

Trustees: Tony Callard; Elizabeth Clarke; Patrick Dorking.

CC Number: 1002147

Eligibility

Musicians aged between 8 and 18 who are in financial need.

Types of grants

One-off and recurrent grants usually of £100 to £800 for instruments, lessons, choir/orchestra fees, Saturday conservatoires and travel costs.

Annual grant total

In 2010/11 the trust had assets of £1.2 million and an income of £27,000. Grants were made to 33 individuals totalling £12,000.

Applications

On a form available on the website along with supporting documentation evidencing financial hardship, a brief musical CV from those over 12, reasons for applying, details of other sources of funding applied to and two letters of support from music tutors/teachers. Trustees meet regularly to consider applications.

Performing arts

The Richard Carne Trust

£37,000 (14 grants)

Correspondent: Christopher Gilbert, Kleinwort Benson Trustees Ltd, 14 St George Street, London W1S 1FE

Trustees: Philip Carne; Marjorie Carne; Kleinwort Benson Trustees Ltd.

CC Number: 1115903

Eligibility

Young people in the performing arts who are in need. Preference is given to those studying music and theatre.

Types of grants

Grants given according to need.

Annual grant total

In 2011 the trust had assets of £903,000 and an income of £209,000. Grants totalling £37,000 were given to 14 individuals.

Applications

'The trustees' current policy is to consider all written appeals received, but only successful applications are notified of the trustees' decision.'

Other information

Grants are also given to organisations.

The Elizabeth Evans Trust

£5,000

Correspondent: Hazel Thorogoog, Trust Secretary, 4 Elder Grove, Llangunnor, Carmarthen SA31 2LQ (email: hazelthorogood@theelizabethevanstrust.co.uk; website: www.theelizabethevanstrust.co.uk)

Trustees: Wyn Davies; Huw Evans; Mark Evans; Wynne Evans; Anthony Jenkins; Paul Thomas; Hazel Thorogood.

CC Number: 210989

Eligibility

Young people between 16 and 26 who wish to pursue a professional career in the performing arts – as an actor, singer, instrumentalist or within stage management. Priority will be given to applicants who can demonstrate a close association, or connection with Carmarthenshire.

Types of grants

Funding may be applied for either a college or university course at both undergraduate and postgraduate level, or alternately for a short-term project such as a summer course or private study.

Annual grant total

Around £5,000. Fourteen individuals were supported in 2011.

Applications

Application forms and notes can be downloaded from the trust's website. Nearly all the trust's correspondence is done via email.

Applicants will not be means tested, but an applicant's personal circumstances may be a factor determining the amount and extent of any award.

Applications received by email or exceptionally by post-will be considered between 1 January and 30 April in any year. Consideration of applications received at other times will be deferred until 1 January following receipt of the application, unless sufficient reason can be established for expediting the application.

The Rebecca McNie Foundation

See entry on page 310

Theatre

The Actors' Charitable Trust (TACT)

£127,000

Correspondent: Robert Ashby, The Actors Charitable Trust, 58 Bloomsbury Street, London WC1B 3QT (020 7636 7868; email: robert@tactactors.org; website: www.tactactors.org)

Trustees: Tim Denham; Lalla Ward; Geraldine James; Elizabeth Garvie.

CC Number: 206809

Eligibility

Children (aged under 21) of professional actors who are in financial need with a particular focus on children with special needs, learning disabilities or long-term ill health and families who are living with cancer or other illness, or facing family crisis.

Types of grants

Grants for extracurricular activities, clothing, extra tuition to help with dyslexia or maths and additional therapy for children with disabilities. Grants are also made in the form of gift vouchers and payments to service providers.

Annual grant total

In 2010/11 the trust had assets of £4.8 million and an income of £536,000. Grants for educational and welfare purposes were made to 125 families, with 196 children between them, totalling £256,000.

Exclusions

No grants are made towards private school fees or other tuition fees.

Applications

On a form available from the correspondent or to download from the website. Applicants are strongly advised to contact the trust to discuss their situation before making an application. Applications can be submitted at any time either by the individual or a parent. Awards are decided in July each year.

Note: the trust has stated that it is currently over-subscribed and has a waiting list of potential beneficiaries.

Other information

The trust also administers the TACT Educational Fund for students who are children of professional actors, refer to the separate entry for this.

The Costume Society

£3,500

Correspondent: Jill Salen, Hon Secretary, 150 Aldersgate Street, London EC1A 4AB (email: awards@costumesociety.org.uk; website: www.costumesociety.org.uk)

Trustees: Chris Godfrey; Jill Salen; Sylvia Ayton; Judy Tregidden; Shaun Cole; Beatrice Behlen; Deirdre Murphy; Kerry Taylor; Linda Ballard; Lou Taylor; John Bright; Janet Wood.

CC Number: 262401

Eligibility

Students in history and theory of design (fashion and textiles) and theatre wardrobe and costume design. Support is given to students engaged in part-time study on further, higher and postgraduate courses.

Types of grants

Annual grants available: the Museum Placement Award – supports a placement offered jointly with a museum clothing/fashion/dress/costume collection (£1,000); the Patterns of Fashion Award – open to students in theatre wardrobe and costume design (£500); the Yarwood Award – restricted to students on a designated MA course (£500); the Student Bursary – offers full attendance and accommodation at the society's annual conference, *The Symposium* (about £400).

Annual grant total

In 2011 the society had assets of £123,000, an income of £45,000 and gave student grants and awards totalling £3,500.

Applications

Information is available on the society's website and is published in *Costume*, the annual journal of the society. Information can also be obtained by writing to the individual awards co-ordinators c/o the Costume Society. Applications are considered three times a year.

The John Thaw Foundation

£50,000

Correspondent: The Trustees, PO Box 477, Amyand Park Road, Twickenham TW1 9LF

Trustees: Helen Cotterill; Joanna Thaw; Sheila Hancock; Clare Vidal-Hall.

CC Number: 1090668

Eligibility

People wishing to pursue a career in the theatre and performing arts.

Types of grants

Funding for arts-based training courses.

Annual grant total

In 2010/11 the foundation had assets of £222,000 and an income of £133,000. Grants to individuals and organisations totalled £155,000.

Applications

In writing to the correspondent.

Other information

The charity works with a number of partner organisations to help achieve its objectives. Grants are also made to organisations and individuals.

Aviation

The Guild of Air Pilots Benevolent Fund

£45,000

Correspondent: Chris Ford, Almoner, Cobham House, 9 Warwick Court, Gray's Inn, London WC1R 5DJ (020 7404 4032; fax: 020 7404 4035; email: gapan@gapan.org; website: www.gapan.org)

Trustees: Capt. J. Robinson; Squadron Leader J. Davy; Capt. C. Spurrier; Squadron Leader C. Ford; R. Bridge; Group Capt. T. Eeles; Capt. R. Felix; Capt. O. Epton; Air Marshal C. Spink; P. Tacon; D. Howard-Budd; Air Commodore Hughesdon; Capt. R. Keegan.

CC Number: 212952

Eligibility

Young people who want to become pilots or wish to gain further qualifications in the aviation industry.

Types of grants

Scholarships and bursaries for young people.

Annual grant total

In 2010/11 the guild had assets of £551,000 and an income of £76,000. Scholarships totalling approximately £45,000 were made to seven individuals and a further £9,000 was given in welfare grants.

Applications

On a form available from the website. Details of individual criteria and dates relating to each scholarship are included in the application form. The fund works closely with the other aviation trusts for individuals (both military and civilian). If an applicant has approached another such trust, they should say so in their application to the fund.

Other information

The guild also gives grants for welfare purposes to members of the guild and those who have been engaged professionally as air pilots or air navigators in commercial aviation, and their dependents.

Built environment

Alan Baxter Foundation

£2,000

Correspondent: Nicholas Davies, 2A Farquharson Road, Croydon CR0 2UH (020 7250 1555; email: aba@alanbaxter. co.uk)

Trustees: Alan Baxter; Michael Coombs; John Thorne; William Filmer-Sankey.

CC Number: 1107996

Eligibility

People involved with the study of the built and natural environment.

Types of grants

Grants given according to need.

Annual grant total

In 2010/11 the foundation had an income of £7,500 and an expenditure of £30,000.

Applications

In writing to the correspondent.

Other information

Grants are mostly made to organisations and for research.

Carpentry and construction

The Carpenters Company Charitable Trust

£1,200 (1 grant)

Correspondent: Miss Mead, Charities Administrator, Carpenters Hall, 1 Throgmorton Avenue, London EC2N 2JJ (020 7588 7001; email: info@ carpentersco.com; website: www. carpentersco.com/pages/charities/ carpenters_company_charitable_trust1)

Trustees: Guy Morton-Smith; Michael Montague-Smith; Peter Luton; Michael Mathews.

CC Number: 276996

Eligibility

The trust is set up to 'support the craft' i.e. people wishing to set up in or to study carpentry.

Types of grants

Educational grants are awarded up to £2,400 to help with fees, maintenance, equipment and other necessities.

Annual grant total

In 2010/11 the charity had assets of £21 million and an income of £936,000. One grant of £1,200 was made to an individual but in previous years about eight individuals have been funded.

Applications

On a form available from the correspondent or from the website. Applications are considered in March, July and November.

Other information

Grants are also made to organisations.

Norton Folgate Trust

£197,000 (69 grants)

Correspondent: The Craft and Charities Administrator, Carpenter's Company, Carpenter's Hall, 1 Throgmorton Avenue, London EC2N 2JJ (020 7588 7001; email: info@carpentersco.com; website: www.carpentersco.com)

Trustee: The Worshipful Company of Carpenters.

CC Number: 230990

Eligibility

People in further or higher education at an institution in the UK who are studying the craft of carpentry or any branch of the building industry.

Types of grants

Grants are usually between £150 and £6,500 (a) for school pupils to help with the cost of books, equipment, clothing or travel and (b) to help with school, college or university fees or to supplement existing grants.

Annual grant total

In 2010/11 69 grants to individuals for education were made totalling £197,000.

Applications

On a form available on the website to be submitted before July for the academic year beginning in September. Applicants will be notified of a decision in August.

Students at the Building Crafts College should apply to the following address before May (applicants will be notified of a decision in June):

Head of Administration and Grants
BCC Grants and Bursaries Office
Building Crafts College
Kennard Road
Stratford
London E15 1AH.

Other information

Grants are also made for welfare purposes to liverymen, freemen, retirees and their dependents. In 2010/11 eight of these grants were made totalling £33,000.

Scottish Building Federation Edinburgh and District Charitable Trust

£21,000

Correspondent: The Trustees, Scott-Moncrieff, Exchange Place 3, Semple Street, Edinburgh EH3 8BL (01314 733500; email: charity@scott-moncrieff. com; website: www.scott-moncrieff.com/ charitable_trusts/page7.html)

Trustees: A. R. Watson; D. R. Brown; A. P. Goudie; J. F. Dundas; A. Dundas; L. Hughes; J. McMenamim; I. Robb; F. Spratt; D. Stephen; A. C. Walker; E. M. Walker.

SC Number: SCO29604

Eligibility

Students studying skills relating to the building industry at the following universities and colleges: Heriot-Watt University; Napier University; West Lothian College; Edinburgh's Telford College; Jewel and Esk Valley College. Dependents of persons who have been involved in the building trade in the Lothians, with a particular emphasis on owners and senior employees of companies.

Types of grants

Scholarships of up to £10,000 for study, research and travel associated with the construction industry and grants for course expenses such as books, equipment and travel.

Annual grant total

In 2011 the trust had assets of £1.1 million and an income of £41,000. Grants were made totalling £37,000, with £22,000 to 23 individuals for 'charitable aid', £10,000 in ten scholarships and £4,500 to institutions for prize money.

Applications

On forms available from the correspondent or the website which should be completed and forwarded to the appropriate department of the university or college for scholarships or to the trust for grants. Trustees meet four times a year to consider applications.

Other information

This trust also gives welfare grants to those who have been involved in the building trade in the Lothians.

Clockmaking

Clockmakers Museum and Educational Trust

£0

Correspondent: Joe Buxton, Clerk, Salter's Hall, Fore Street, London EC2Y 5DE (020 7638 5500; email: clerk@ clockmakers.org; website: www. clockmakers.org)

Trustees: Christopher Hurrion; Lawrence Hurst; Mark Levy; Janet Owen; Tina Millar; John Williams; Richard Stenning.

CC Number: 312876

Eligibility

Intending clockmakers from 18 to 22 years of age. Applicants must be British and intending to work in the horological industry in the UK.

Types of grants

One-off grants of between £400 and £1,200 are available to horology students in further/higher education for help with fees and living expenses, and grants to those researching the measurement of time.

Annual grant total

In 2010/11 the trust had assets of £1.3 million and an income of £62,000. No grants to individuals were made during the year but they usually total

around £2,000. The trust stated that they would like to increase the number and value of awards.

Applications

In writing to the correspondent. Applications can be submitted at any time by the individual and will be considered within three months; meetings are organised when there are sufficient applications to justify one.

Commerce

The Gustav Adolph and Ernest Koettgen Memorial Fund

£4,500

Correspondent: Ms Fiona Macgillivray, Family Welfare Association, 501–505 Kingsland Road, Dalston, London E8 4AU (020 7254 6251; fax: 020 7249 5443; email: grants.enquiry@ family-action.org.uk)

Trustee: Family Action.

CC Number: 313291

Eligibility

British-born subjects who wish to educate themselves or to obtain tuition for a higher commercial career but whose means are insufficient for them to obtain such education or tuition at their own expense.

Types of grants

Students and mature students of British nationality who are studying in this country and are in higher education can apply for financial help towards the costs of books, fees, living expenses and childcare. Applicants are only considered if they are in the final year of a course and if they have managed to raise almost the whole amount needed, or if they encounter unexpected difficulty, as these grants are only intended to be supplementary.

Annual grant total

In 2010/11 the fund had an income of £8,700 and a total expenditure of £4,900

Exclusions

Grants cannot be given for postgraduate study.

Applications

On a form available from the correspondent, submitted directly by the individual and supported by an academic reference. Trustees meet monthly.

Other information

Preference is given to employees of John Batt and Company (London) Ltd or members of their families.

The Worshipful Company of Chartered Secretaries and Administrators General Charitable Trust Fund

£4,300

Correspondent: Erica Lee, Saddlers Hall, 40 Gutter Lane, London EC2V 6BR (020 7726 2955; email: clerk@wccsa.org.uk)

Trustees: Julie Fox; Donald Kirkham; Jeffrey Greenwell; Philip Marcell; Ian Richardson; Stephen Gilbert; Christopher Hallam.

CC Number: 288487

Eligibility

Chartered secretaries and administrators who are undertaking studies connected with commerce. Apprentices of the Worshipful Company of Chartered Secretaries and Administrators.

Types of grants

Scholarships of £1,000 and prizes of between £50 and £500 for commercial education at various universities and apprentices with the company.

Annual grant total

In 2010/11 the trust had assets of £1.3 million and an income of £53,000. Grants to individuals for educational purposes totalled £4,300.

Applications

In writing to the correspondent. Grants are considered every three months, usually January, April, July and October.

Engineering

The Douglas Bomford Trust

£21,000

Correspondent: Paul Miller, 46 Howard Close, Haynes, Bedford MK45 3QH (01234 381342; email: enquiries@dbt.org. uk; website: www.dbt.org.uk)

Trustees: Jonathan Bomford; Peter Redman; Malcolm Crabtree; Raymond Clay; Richard Godwin; James Robinson; Anthony Burgess; Geoffrey Davies.

CC Number: 1121785

Eligibility

EU citizens who are or will be professional engineers or scientists applying their skills to mainly rural engineering problems.

Types of grants

Mainly grants for travel, language training and conference attendance.

Some discretionary awards in cases of hardship or for special projects, and some research projects.

Annual grant total

In 2010/11 the trust had assets of £3.7 million and an income of £107,000. Funding to individuals totalled £21,000 and was distributed as follows:

- Studentships- £7,800
- Travel grants- £7,200
- Other awards- £4,300
- Research Programme- £2,000

Applications

There are four grants schemes. Details of how to apply for each one are available on the trust's website.

Other information

The trust also gave grants totalling £83,000 to organisations.

The Bernard Butler Trust

£22,000

Correspondent: Bernard Butler, 37 Oasthouse Drive, Fleet, Hants GU15 2UL (01252 627748; fax: 01252 627748; email: info@bernardbutlertrust. org; website: www.bernardbutlertrust. org)

Trustees: Bernard Butler; Geoffrey Porter; David Comber; John Jameson.

CC Number: 1063735

Eligibility

Students in the field of engineering.

Types of grants

One-off and recurrent grants in the range of £700 and £2,000. About 12 grants are made each year. Grants are given to college students, undergraduates, vocational students and mature students for fees, study/travel abroad, books, equipment/instruments, childcare/costs of dependents and maintenance/living expenses.

Annual grant total

In 2010/11 the trust had an income of £12,000 and an expenditure of £24,000. Grants per year usually total about £22,000.

Applications

Application forms are available from the correspondent; alternatively they can be downloaded from the fund's website, or completed online. They should be submitted directly by the individual or a family member and are considered in May and November. The trust welcomes informal enquires to discuss applications.

Other information

Grants are also made to organisations.

The Coachmakers and Coach Harness Makers Charitable Trust 1977

£13,000 (11 grants)

Correspondent: The Clerk, 48 Aldernay Street, London SW1V 4EX (07505 089841; email: clerk@coachmakers.co.uk; website: www.coachmakers.co.uk)

Trustees: Roger Smith; Marcus Wills; Michael Davis.

CC Number: 286521

Eligibility

People studying/working in the aerospace, automotive, carriage building and associated trades.

Types of grants

Bursaries for college students and undergraduates for study/travel overseas and maintenance/living expenses and to mature students for awards for excellence.

Annual grant total

In 2010/11 the trust had assets of £991,000, an income of £307,000 and made 11 grants to individuals totalling £13,000.

Applications

In writing to the correspondent. Application deadlines are in December for consideration in January and October for consideration in November.

The Worshipful Company of Engineers Charitable Trust Fund

£17,000

Correspondent: A G Willenbruch, Clerk, The Worshipful Company of Engineers, Wax Chandlers Hall, 6 Gresham Street, London EC2V 7AD (020 7726 4830; email: clerk@engineerscompany.org.uk; website: www.engineerscompany.org.uk)

Trustees: Christopher Price; John Robinson; John Banyard; Peter Hartley; David Johnson; Malcolm Vincent; David Scahill.

CC Number: 298819

Eligibility

Final year undergraduates and postgraduate students who are in need and taking courses related to the science and technology of engineering; principally those who are in the UK.

Types of grants

One-off grants up to £1,000. Grants are given for one year only or as a top-up to people nearing the end of their course, towards fees, maintenance/living costs or awards for excellence.

Annual grant total

In 2010/11 the trust had assets of £564,000 and an income of £54,000. Grants totalled £14,000 with a further £3,000 being spent on medals, prizes and associated costs.

Applications

In writing to the correspondent at any time providing as much detail about your circumstances as possible. For hardship on completing a course, support from the Dean of Engineering is required. Applications are considered throughout the year and information on grant schemes and the range of awards are available on the company's website.

The Benevolent Fund of the Institution of Civil Engineers Ltd

£12,000

Correspondent: Kris Barnett, Chief Executive, 30 Mill Hill Close, Haywards Heath, West Sussex RH16 1NY (01444 417979; fax: 01444 453307; email: benfund@ice.org.uk; website: www.bfice. org.uk)

Trustees: Michael Chater; Edmund Brew; David Gallear; William Rogers; Ian Flower; David Orr; Andrew Scrimgeour; David Thomas; Brian Waters; Karen Dingley; Philip Hardy-Bishop; John Mouatt.

CC Number: 1126595

Eligibility

Student members of Institution of Civil Engineers (ICE), who are disabled or disadvantaged and are studying on an ICE accredited course at a UK university.

Types of grants

Grants of up to £1,000 per semester for living costs, travel, accommodation, equipment costs and course materials. They are not normally used to pay course fees.

Annual grant total

In 2011 the fund had assets of £13 million and an income of £904,000. Grants were made to 195 individuals totalling £532,000, including support for four students.

Exclusions

No grants for students who have not started their university course or have yet to be offered a university place; have mismanaged their finances and simply run out of money; or, are studying for a Civil Engineering degree not accredited by ICE. No support is given to postgraduates.

Funding may not be used to clear old debts, indulge in social activities, or to purchase non-essential equipment and materials.

Applications

On a form available from the correspondent. Applications must be accompanied by a reference or letter of support from the Head of Department, or their nominee. They can be made at any time. All applicants will be visited by one of the fund's volunteer visitors.

Other information

The fund operates a 24-hour helpline (0800 587 3428) which offers support and advice on a wide range of issues including, stress management, debt problems, childcare and substance abuse.

The Institution of Engineering and Technology (IET)

£393,000

Correspondent: Andrew Wilson, The Institution of Engineering and Technology, 2 Savoy Place, London WC2R 0BL (020 7344 5415; email: governance@theiet.org; website: www. theiet.org)

Trustees: Andrew Hopper; Michael Short; John Scott; William Webb; Stephen Williamson; Michael Carr; Alice Chan; Naomi Climber; Barry Jones; Hanna Sykulska-Lawrence; Barry Brooks; Jayne Bryant; Stephen Burgin; Simon Harrison; Jeremy McKendrick Watson.

CC Number: 211014

Eligibility

The following regulations apply as a general rule to all scholarships and prizes, however candidates should refer to the website for individual criteria:

(i) Students must be studying or about to study (in the next academic session) on an IEE-accredited degree course at a UK university.
(ii) Each candidate must be nominated by the head of the educational or training establishment, the course tutor, the university head of department or by a chartered member of the IEE.
(iii) A candidate who is shortlisted for an award may be required to attend an interview at the IEE.
(iv) During the tenure of an award, the professor or other person under whom the grant holder is studying will be asked to certify that the holder is making satisfactory progress.
(vi) The scholarship will be paid in instalments, as determined by the IEE. It will be withdrawn and any unpaid instalments withheld if the holder leaves the course.
(vii) Successful candidates must not hold

any other IEE scholarships or grants at the same time.

Types of grants

The IET offers a range of scholarships, prizes and travel awards ranging from £350 to £3,000. These include undergraduate scholarships and postgraduate scholarships and various awards for achievement and innovation.

Annual grant total

Previously, the institution has given £393,000 in undergraduate and postgraduate scholarships, travel awards and prizes.

Applications

Further details and application forms are available from the website. Applications are usually made by IEE members or people applying for membership.

Other information

The institution also administers a number of other funds:

Beauchamp Scholarship Fund; William Beedie Esson Scholarship: Scholarships for males training to become electrical engineers in the UK.

J R Beard Travelling Fund: To assist members with travel costs associated with engineering education and learning.

Will Geipel Scholarship; David Hughes Scholarship; M E A Scholarship fund; Sir Edward Manville Scholarship Fund; Sir Charles A Parsons Memorial Scholarship; Paul Scholarship; John S Robinson Memorial Fund; Salomons Scholarship; Swan Memorial Scholarship Fund; Thorrowgood Scholarship: Various scholarships in engineering and electrical engineering.

J D Knight and E D Knight; The Institution of Electrical Engineers Benefactors Trust Fund; O'Gorman Memorial Fund: Financial support for training and education in engineering and electrical engineering.

Applicants should contact the institute to discuss applications to these various funds.

The Benevolent Fund of the Institution of Mechanical Engineers (IMechE)

£44,000

Correspondent: Maureen Hayes, Casework and Support Officer, 3 Birdcage Walk, Westminster, London SW1H 9JJ (020 7304 6816; fax: 020 7973 1262; email: info@supportnetwork.org. uk; website: www.supportnetwork.org. uk)

Trustees: Michael Hannaway; Anne Woodbridge; John Atkins; Raymond

Buttifant; Dennis Wilcock; Fred Jacques; Bob Jeays; Scot Fisher; Roy Pressland; Michael Greenwood; David Mincher; Stephen Mullarkey; Muhammad Mohsin Iqbal.

CC Number: 209465

Eligibility

Disabled or financially disadvantaged students studying Mechanical Engineering on an IMechE accredited first degree course at a UK university who are IMechE Members. Preference is given to the following: disabled students; final year students; students with dependents, particularly lone parents; students aged 25 and over with extra financial commitments; local authority care leavers; students estranged from their parents; students with significant debts before commencing the course; students repeating a year due to causes outside their control and students with no access to other funds.

Types of grants

One-off grants of up to £1,000 for financially disadvantaged students for living costs, travel and accommodation. Grants for equipment costs and course materials such as software and books.

Annual grant total

In 2011 the fund had assets of £16 million and an income of £860,000. Grants to 224 individuals for both welfare and education totalled £394,000, including support for 21 students.

Exclusions

No grants for people who are studying outside the UK; have not been offered a university place or started their studies or those who have mismanaged their finances and run out of money.

Applications

Applicants should request the appropriate form from the correspondent. Three months are needed to process applications; this should be three months prior to when a decision is required, not necessarily the date of the activity. Closing dates are determined by the approximate dates of the committee meetings, which are held in March, June and September. Applicants requiring an interview will be notified.

Other information

The support network helps members of IMechE with many of life's challenges. It provides financial help as well as specialist advice and information. Visit the website to find out about the services on offer.

The Mott MacDonald Charitable Trust

£152,000

Correspondent: Steve Wise, Mott MacDonald House, 8–10 Sydenham Road, Croydon CR0 2EE (020 8774 2090; email: stephen.wise@mottmac. com)

Trustees: M. Hornsby; Guy Leonard; Richard Williams; Keith Howells.

CC Number: 275040

Eligibility

People undertaking higher education in the fields of civil, structural, mechanical, electrical and allied engineering.

Types of grants

Grants, bursaries, scholarships and awards. Generally bursaries are committed on an annual basis. Scholarships are usually committed for longer periods but are reviewed annually.

Annual grant total

During 2010 the trust had assets of £362,000 and an income of £188,000. Thirteen scholarships, two full time and eleven part time awards, and a number of bursaries were made during the year totalling £152,000.

Applications

In writing to the correspondent.

The Worshipful Company of Scientific Instrument Makers

£29,000

Correspondent: The Clerk, Glaziers Hall, 9 Montague Close, London SE1 9DD (020 7407 4832; email: theclerk@wcsim.co.uk; website: www. wcsim.co.uk)

Trustees: Guy Brocklebank; David Smith; Ken Reay; Derek Cornish; Harry Tee; David Kent; Keith Etherington.

CC Number: 221332

Eligibility

Schoolchildren, sixth formers, undergraduates and postgraduates with outstanding ability in science and mathematics and a creative and practical interest in branches of engineering connected with instrumentation and measurement.

Students must attend one of the following universities: Brunel, Cambridge, City, Glasgow Caledonian, Imperial, Oxford, Teesside, UCL, UMIST, Warwick.

Types of grants

Mentoring and grants of £500 per year for undergraduates. The Young Engineers Program supports people to attend national and international events, competitions, prizes and travel support plus apprenticeships. There are also scholarships of £300 for sixth formers. Postgraduate awards of £2,000 for 'exciting research and design and a postdoctoral award of £5,000 for up to three years.

Annual grant total

In 2010/11 the Company had assets of £1.4 million and an income of £71,000. Educational grants totalled £29,000, which were distributed under in the following categories:

- Scholarships – £21,000
- Beloe fellowships – £5,000
- Dining scholars – £1,200
- General grants – £1,300

Applications

See the company's website for details of how to apply to each separate scheme. Students must apply through the university and not directly to the company.

South Wales Institute Of Engineers Educational Trust

£9,500

Correspondent: Sandra Chapman, Administrative Officer, Suite 2 Bay Chambers, West Bute Street, Cardiff CF10 5BB (01792 879409/07594 551263; email: sandra.chapman@swieet2007.org. uk; website: www.swieet2007.org.uk)

Trustees: Daniel Brennan; Jarmila Davies; D. G. Griffiths; P. E. Hourahine; Denys Morgan; D. V. Morgan; Lewin Morgan.

CC Number: 1013538

Eligibility

Students, undergraduates and others involved with recognised engineering courses, apprentices and equivalents and graduates beginning engineering careers in Wales.

Types of grants

One-off and recurrent grants according to need, generally £200 to £1,000. The trust has funded engineering education from pre-GCSE level through to postgraduate/professional qualifications.

Annual grant total

In 2010/11 the trust had assets of £849,000 and an income of £35,000. Scholarships and bursaries totalled £9,500.

Applications

Contact the trust to discuss an application and obtain information about past awards.

Other information

Grants to organisations to support engineering education totalled £21,000 in 2010/11.

Environmental studies

Alan Baxter Foundation
See entry on page 86

The Alice McCosh Trust

£1,000

Correspondent: Grace Carswell, Trust Secretary, 49 Cluny Street, Lewes, Sussex BN7 1LN (email: info@ thealicemccoshtrust.org.uk; website: www.thealicemccoshtrust.org.uk)

Trustees: Eleanor Carswell; Rachel Lewis; Mungo McCosh.

SC Number: SC035938

Eligibility

People of any age undertaking work or study related to natural history and/or the environment. Preference will be given to individuals from (or work relating to) Scotland, England and Turkey.

Types of grants

One-off grants in the range of £300 to £1,000, for example, to cover the cost of a school field trip or project, an expedition as part of a research project or the development of new teaching materials for schools or institutes of higher education.

Annual grant total

Up to £1,000 each year.

Exclusions

Projects involving joining an existing commercial organisation on a pre-paid tour or expedition will not be considered.

Applications

On a form available from the website along with guidelines. Applications should be emailed to the correspondent between 1 October and 30 November each year. (Applications received at other times, or sent by post, will not be considered). Applications should be concise (no more than four typed pages) and include two referee statements.

The Martin Smith Foundation

See entry on page 75

The Water Conservation Trust

£19,000

Correspondent: The Secretary, HQS Wellington, Temple Stairs, Victoria Embankment, London WC2R 2PN (01189 833689; email: waterloo@aol.com)

Trustees: James Urquhart; Colin Bland; Jeffrey Rasbash; Ivor Richards; Peter Hall; Mike Williamson; Colin Drummond.

CC Number: 1007648

Eligibility

People who are working or intending to work in the water and environment industry and their dependents.

Types of grants

One-off grants for approved projects and courses of study.

Annual grant total

In 2010/11 the trust had assets of £454,000 and an income of £76,000. Individuals received £19,000 for educational purposes, broken down as follows:

- Grants to individuals: £1,900
- Bursary/dissertation support at Oxford, Sheffield and Brunel universities: £17,000
- Pupil prizes: £100

Exclusions

Unsolicited applications are not accepted.

Applications

When funds are available the trustees invite applications for scholarships through the water and environmental press.

Other information

Grants are also made towards research and to organisations.

Esperanto

Norwich Jubilee Esperanto Foundation

£6,000

Correspondent: David Kelso, c/o Esperanto-Asocio de Britio, Esperanto House, Station Road, Barlaston, Stoke-on-Trent ST12 9DE (website: www.esperanto-gb.org/nojef)

Trustees: Malcolm Jones; Hilary Chapman; Paul Gubbins; Michael Seaton.

CC Number: 313190

Eligibility

Students under 26 who are in need of financial help, who have a high level of Esperanto and are prepared to use it for travel abroad. Preference among non-Britons is normally given to those whose native language is not English, since contact with such is more useful to British students of Esperanto.

Types of grants

One-off grants are given to British students for travel to approved venues including insurance, conference fees and accommodation; and to overseas students for travel in the UK and simple accommodation where this is not provided by host groups. Grants to overseas students are only given towards the costs of travel to and from the UK in exceptional circumstances.

Research grants are given to teachers of Esperanto of any age on similar conditions.

Annual grant total

In 2010/11 the foundation had an income of £9,900 and an expenditure of £7,200.

Applications

Letters of applications should be in Esperanto, including if possible some details of travel plans, and preferably letters of support from one or two referees. Applications showing no knowledge of or interest in Esperanto are not normally acknowledged.

Other information

All grants are conditional on the recipient sending a written report in Esperanto on the visit. A proportion of the grant may be withheld until the report is received.

Fire-fighting, fire engineering, fire protection or fire research

Institution of Fire Engineers

£10,000

Correspondent: Professional Development Officer, London Road, Moreton-in-Marsh, Gloucestershire GL56 0RH (01608 812580; fax: 01608 812581; email: info@ife.org.uk; website: www.ife.org.uk)

SC Number: SC012694

Eligibility

All fire professionals, members of fire research organisations and the fire engineering profession or students of these areas in the UK.

Types of grants

Educational grants for assistance with fees, books or research associated with a project, degree or general course work, scholarships for major pieces of work and research grants.

Annual grant total

The income for the trust is donated by another charity (The Fire Service Research and Training Trust), and varies greatly. In 2010 it had an income of £920,000. Grants usually total around £10,000 each year.

Applications

Application forms and guidelines are available on the website.

Other information

The institute makes grants on behalf of the Fire Service Research and Training Trust.

Furniture

The Worshipful Company of Furniture Makers Company

£20,000

Correspondent: Jonny Westbrooke, The Clerk, Furniture Maker' Hall, 12 Austin Friars, London EC2N 2HE (020 7256

5558; fax: 020 7256 5155; email: welfare@furnituremakers.org.uk; website: www.furnituremakers.co.uk)

Trustees: Roger Richardson; David Burbidge; Martin Jourdan; Margaret Miller.

CC Number: 270483

Eligibility

Young people working or studying to work in the furniture industry. For student grants the course being studied must be at an accredited UK university.

Types of grants

There are awards for each branch of the industry, for example, design, manufacturing and retail. Students intending to enter the industry are eligible and there are awards for postgraduate studies. £300 towards materials for BA student's final year project, £5,000 for MA students.

Annual grant total

In 2010/11 the charity had assets of £1.1 million and an income of £258,000. Grants and scholarships totalled £20,000.

Exclusions

No grants are given for childcare.

Applications

On form available from the website to be submitted directly by an individual or a parent/guardian. Applications are considered throughout the year.

Other information

Grants are also made to institutions and for group college projects.

Game-keeping

The Gamekeepers Welfare Trust

£2,500

Correspondent: Helen M J Benson, Keepers Cottage, Tanfield Lodge, West Tanfield, Ripon, North Yorkshire HG4 5LE (01677 470180; email: gamekeeperwtrust@binternet.com; website: thegamekeeperswelfaretrust.com)

Trustees: Ken Butler; Earl of Aylesford; Dave Clark; Ian Grindy; Mike Swan; Walter Cole; Lady Scott; Raymond Holt.

CC Number: 1008924

Eligibility

Young people in need who wish to make gamekeeping their career. People over 24 will not be considered unless there are extenuating circumstances.

Types of grants

One-off and recurrent grants according to need.

Annual grant total

The latest accounts available were for 2010. During the year the trust had assets of £168,000, an income of £53,000 and gave educational grants totalling £2,500.

Applications

On a form available from the correspondent or through the website, along with guidelines. Applications can be made at any time.

Other information

The trust also makes grants for welfare purposes.

Gas engineering

The Institution of Gas Engineers Benevolent Fund

£1,500

Correspondent: Lesley Ecob, IGEM Secretariat, IGEM House, High Street, Kegworth, Derbyshire DE74 2DA (01509 678167; email: lesley@igem.org.uk; website: www.igem.org.uk)

Trustees: D. Morgan; G. Davies; E. Swindells; C. Taylor; G. Davies; S. Course; D. Cummings; N. Dalley; L. Ecob; R. Murray; R. Armstrong; G. Ng; M. Tonry; P. Brown; S. Mistry; G. Judge; E. Muriithi; D. Wasson; D. Anderson.

CC Number: 214010

Eligibility

UK and overseas students wishing to study gas engineering.

Types of grants

Grants are given according to need.

Annual grant total

In 2010 the trust had an income of £11,000 and a total expenditure of £6,000. Grants were made to individuals totalling £3,000.

Applications

In writing to the correspondent.

Geography

Royal Geographical Society (with the Institute of British Geographers)

£155,000

Correspondent: Grants Department, 1 Kensington Gore, London SW7 2AR (020 7591 3073; fax: 020 7591 3001; email: grants@rgs.org; website: www.rgs.org)

Trustees: Stephen Henwood; Mark Mulligan; Vanessa Lawrence; Paul Rose; Georgina Endfield; Michael Bradshaw; Michael Palin; Michael Asby; Jamie Buchanan-Dunlop; Benedict Allen; Anthony Parsons; David Thomas; Robin Ashcroft; Justin Marozzi; Peter Smith; Judith Rees; Paul Baker; Rebecca Stephens; Alison Blunt; Chris Philo; Barbara Hamnett; Sophie Yarker.

CC Number: 208791

Eligibility

Scientists, including non-academics, who are over 16 and are carrying out geographical research at any level in the UK and overseas.

The society states that its grants programme aims to promote geographical research and a wider understanding of the world and therefore applicants are not required to have a geography degree, work in a geography department or define themselves as a geographer, but must share the Society's interest in the world's people and environments.

Some grants are only open to Fellows of the Society.

Types of grants

The society administers a large numbers of grants, each with separate eligibility criteria and application processes. These are broken down into the following categories: Established Researchers; Early Career Researchers; Postgraduate; Undergraduate; Expeditions, Fieldwork and Independent Travel and Teaching.

Grants are for work in both the UK and overseas and range from £500 to £15,000. Refer to the Society's website for a full explanation of all the grants schemes.

Annual grant total

In 2011 the society had assets of £14 million, an income of £4.7 million and made grants totalling £155,000, broken down into the following categories:

- Research: £85,000
- Expeditions and fieldwork: £63,000

▶ Education and teaching: £7,000
Field projects in 49 countries across seven continents were supported.

Exclusions

No grants for fees or living costs associated with degrees.

Applications

All grant details, guidelines and forms can be obtained from the society's website. The application process lasts between three and four months.

Other information

The Society also provides information, advice and training to support anyone planning fieldwork.

Greece

The Hellenic Foundation

£7,000

Correspondent: George Lemos, Hon. Secretary, 150 Aldersgate Street, London EC1A 4AB (020 7251 5100)

Trustees: George Lemos; S. J. Fafalios; Pantelis Michelakis; Constantine Caroussis; Nicos Sideris; Leventis-Williamson; Mary Bromley; Joanna Caroussis; Nicki Chandris.

CC Number: 326301

Eligibility

Students studying the culture, tradition and heritage of Greece.

Types of grants

One-off and recurrent grants for projects involving education, research, music and dance, books and library facilities and university symposia.

Annual grant total

In 2010 the foundation had an income of £21,000 and an expenditure of £23,000.

Applications

In writing to the correspondent.

Other information

Grants are also made to organisations.

Historic conservation

Zibby Garnett Travelling Fellowship

£16,000

Correspondent: Robert Garnett, The Grange, Norwell, Newark,

Nottinghamshire NG23 6JN (01636 636288; fax: 01636 636760; email: info@zibbygarnett.org; website: www.zibbygarnett.org)

Trustees: Anne Coltman; Roger Peters; John Lord; David Garnett; Sally Machin; Emma Hulme; Michael Stock.

CC Number: 1081403

Eligibility

People working in one of the following conservation subjects: historic buildings, gardens and landscape; the traditional building trades; artefacts; historic and decorative crafts. Applicants can be at university or college, or within the formative years of their careers, trade apprentices, trainee architects or landscape architects.

Types of grants

Grants ranging from £300 to £3,000 for short study trips abroad. The awards are not restricted to British nationals, but overseas students should plan projects outside their country of origin.

Annual grant total

In 2010/11 the trust had an income of £19,000 and an expenditure of £17,000.

Exclusions

Generally grants are given for practical work in preference to pure study or research; they are intended for conservation, not new work. No grants for travel to conferences.

Applications

On a form available from the correspondent or the website to be submitted directly by the individual. The deadline for applications is 31 March for consideration that month. Awards are made in April/May.

Anna Plowden Trust

£34,000 (29 grants)

Correspondent: F J Plowden, Trustee, 4 Highbury Road, London SW19 7PR (020 8879 9841; email: info@annaplowdentrust.org.uk; website: www.annaplowdentrust.org.uk)

Trustees: Penelope Hoare; David Leigh; Francis Plowden; Penelope Martin; Susan Palmer; David Saunders; Jane McAusland; Frances Plowden.

CC Number: 1072236

Eligibility

Bursaries for studying qualifications in conservation and grants for short-mid-career skills improvement for conservators already working in the field. Courses must be on the conservation of the moveable heritage (paintings, textiles, archaeological objects and so on) rather than the non-moveable heritage (such as building conservation).

Types of grants

Bursaries and one-off grants towards full time training in conservation.

Annual grant total

In 2010/11 the trust had an income of £43,000 and made grants totalling £34,000. There were 13 awards made for conservation qualifications and a further 16 awards made for continuing professional development.

Applications

On a form available to download from the website. Applications should be submitted by June in each year.

Home economics

The British and Foreign School Society - Berridge Trust Fund

£700

Correspondent: Imogen Wilde, Director, Maybrook House, Godstone Road, Caterham, Surrey CR3 6RE (01883 331177; email: director@bfss.org.uk; website: www.bfss.org.uk)

Trustees: Graham Kingsley; Stephen Orchard; David Swain; Steve Hodkinson; Roger Howarth; David Tennant; Brian York; Stephen Ross; Emily Tomlinson; David Zahn; David Stephens; Shubhi Rao; Jaz Saggu; Ben Ramm; E. J. Weale.

CC Number: 314286

Eligibility

People training to become teachers of cookery or nutrition in England and Wales.

Types of grants

One-off grants according to need.

Annual grant total

Around £700.

Applications

Applicants should use the BFSS application form for individuals, which is available from the BFSS website.

Horticulture/ botany

The Merlin Trust

£10,000

Correspondent: Joanne Everson, Secretary, Royal Botanic Gardens, Kew Green, Richmond, Surrey TW9 3AB (020

8332 5585; email: info@merlin-trust.org.uk; website: www.merlin-trust.org.uk)

Trustees: Brent Elliot; Peter Cunnington; Sally Petitt; William Baker; Jim Jermyn; Fiona Crumley; Jonathan Miller.

CC Number: 803441

Eligibility

UK and Irish nationals, aged between 18 and 35, who are horticulturists or botanists or those in their first five years of a career in horticulture who wish to extend their knowledge of plants, gardens and gardening by travelling. Other nationalities are only eligible if they are studying full time at a UK horticultural establishment.

Types of grants

Grants towards visiting gardens in different parts of the country or abroad, or travelling to see wild plants in their native habitats. Both long- and short-term projects are supported. Previous support has been awarded for an expedition to southern Chile to observe the range of beautiful plants, a trip to New York's community gardens and a visit to Peru in search of orchids.

Annual grant total

In 2010/11 the trust had an income of £18,000 and an expenditure of £19,000. Grants usually total around £10,000.

Exclusions

Grants are not given towards postgraduate study or to fund highly technical laboratory-based research.

Applications

Application forms are available to download from the website. The form should be completed and emailed to the secretary along with a one page description of your project and a CV. A signed copy of the form should also be posted to the secretary. The trust welcomes telephone enquiries.

The Royal Horticultural Society

£67,000

Correspondent: The Secretary, RHS Bursaries Committee, Education Department, The RHS Garden, Wisley, Woking, Surrey GU23 6QB (01483 212380; fax: 01483 212382; email: bursaries@rhs.org.uk; website: www.rhs.org.uk/Learning/Education/bursaries.htm)

Trustees: Michael Balston; Prunella Scarlett; Rosie Atkins; Dougal Philip; Jekka McVicar; George Anderson; David Morrison; Sarah Joiner; Elizabeth Banks; Raymond Evison; Alastair Muirhead; Nicholas Bacon; Mark Fane; Christopher Blundell; Peter Gregory; David

Haselgrove; James Alexander-Sinclair; Dennis Espley.

CC Number: 22879

Eligibility

Priority is given to professional horticulturists and student gardeners, but applications are also considered from serious amateur gardeners, botanists and other related professions and institutions. Eligible proposals must be closely identified with horticulture.

Types of grants

Grants for horticultural projects including study visits or working placements in gardens, plant exploration and study, taxonomy and research, attendance at conferences and distinct projects of educational or historical value. More recently there has been the introduction of specific bursaries for exhibiting botanical art and botanical photography.

The Royal Horticultural Society administers a number of bursary funds, established and maintained through generous bequests and donations, to assist horticulturists and gardeners in financing specific horticultural projects, including overseas travel.

Annual grant total

In 2010/11 grants totalled £67,000.

Exclusions

Grants are not made for salary costs, tuition fees, exam fees or living costs for educational courses.

Applications

Full guidelines and forms can be downloaded from the Royal Horticultural Society website.

Hospitality trades

The Geoffrey Harrison Foundation

Correspondent: Richard Harrison, Oxford House, Oxford Road, Thame, Oxfordshire OX9 2AH

Trustees: Richard Harrison; Geoffrey Harrison; Claire Aylward; Gareth Harrison; Don Davenport; Lord Lingfield; Geoff Booth; David Foskett.

CC Number: 1142242

Eligibility

People in the hotel, restaurant and hospitality industries.

Types of grants

Grants to support education and training connected with the catering and hospitality industries.

Annual grant total

As the trust is newly registered no financial information is available.

Applications

In writing to the correspondent.

Other information

As the trust is newly registered it is currently developing its grants programmes and is not yet open to applications. The trust is developing a website which will provide more information.

The Savoy Educational Trust

£67,000 (35 grants)

Correspondent: Margaret Georgiou, Queens House, 55–56 Lincoln's Inn Fields, London WC2A 3BH (020 7269 9692; fax: 020 7269 9694; email: info@savoyeducationaltrust.org.uk; website: www.savoyeducationaltrust.org.uk)

Trustees: Robert Davis; Ramon Pajares; Dick Turpin; Stuart May; Mike Stapleton.

CC Number: 313763

Eligibility

Individuals undertaking a hospitality related course and those training for management within the hospitality industry.

Types of grants

Individuals can receive up to £500 for uniforms or other school clothing, books, equipment, instruments, fees, educational outings in the UK and study or travel abroad.

There is also a scholarship scheme run in partnership with the Worshipful Company of Innholders which gives around £3,000 per scholarship towards training for management in the hospitality sector.

Annual grant total

In 2010/11 the trust had assets of £42 million and an income of £1 million. It gave £60,000 in 19 scholarships and £6,500 in 16 small grants.

Applications

Initially in writing to the correspondent, who will then provide a form if the applicant is eligible. Meetings of the trustees are held in March, July, September and December, and applications can be submitted directly by the individual or through a third party such as the individual's school, college or educational welfare agency throughout the year.

Other information

Regular grants are made to educational institutions and associations connected with the hospitality industry.

International affairs

Gilbert Murray Trust: International Studies Committee

£5,000

Correspondent: David Faulkner, Trustee, 99 Blacketts Wood Drive, Chorleywood, Rickmansworth, Hertfordshire WD3 5PS (01923 283373; email: david.faulkner57@ntlworld.com)

Trustees: David Faulkner; Andrew Hurrell; Michael Trapp; Christopher Pelling; Peter Wilson; Edith Hall; Mike Edwards; Sam Daws; Fiona Macintosh; Leslie Vinjamuri; Matthew Fox; Christopher Stray.

CC Number: 212244

Eligibility

People who are studying, or have studied, international relations (or international law) at an institution of higher education in the UK. Applicants should be 25 years or younger on 1 April of the year they are applying, although other people can receive grants if they are able to put forward special reasons for their delayed education.

Types of grants

Awards are 'given to support a specific project (such as a research visit to the headquarters of an international organisation, to a particular country or a short course at an institution abroad) which will assist the applicant in his or her study of international affairs in relation to the purposes and work of the United Nations'.

Annual grant total

Around £5,000 each year.

Exclusions

No grants to assist with fees or maintenance costs for people studying international affairs.

Applications

In writing to the correspondent by 1 April. The letter should be supported by a short CV, a statement of career intentions and a description of the project for which the award is sought, with an estimate of its total cost and the sources of additional funding if required. (Preference will be given to applications where the award will cover all or the greater part of the project.) An assessment by a person in a position to judge the applicant in his or her suitability for the award is also necessary. All of this information should be submitted with four other copies, in typed form, only using one side of the paper.

Iraqi culture and history

The British Institute for the Study of Iraq
See entry on page 35

Italian culture

Il Circolo Italian Cultural Association Ltd

£23,000 (15 grants)

Correspondent: Colin Angwin, 32 Cristowe Road, London SW6 3QE (020 7603 2364; email: info@ilcircolo.org.uk; website: www.ilcircolo.org.uk)

Trustees: Rosanna de Hoghton; Elisa Walker; Luisella Strona; Ennio Falabella; Marina Fazzari; John Cullis.

CC Number: 1108894

Eligibility

Students who have been accepted onto a course at a British higher education institution, either at undergraduate or postgraduate level, pursuing studies, training or research relating to Italian culture (humanities, arts and crafts, sciences and performing arts).

Types of grants

Scholarships for students who wish to further their education in the field of Italian and related studies.

Annual grant total

In 2010 the trust had assets of £61,000 and an income of £57,000. Grants for 14 students studying courses relating to Italian culture totalled £18,000 and one Natuzzi scholarship of £4,700 was made for a scholarship in design.

Applications

In writing to the correspondent following the guidelines available from the website. Selected candidates will be interviewed in May.

Other information

Grants are also made to organisations.

Languages

John Speak Trust

£5,000

Correspondent: Sandy Needham, Bradford Chamber of Commerce, Devere House, Vicar Lane, Bradford, West Yorkshire BD1 5AH (01274 230090; email: accounts@bradfordchamber.co.uk)

Trustee: Bradford Chamber of Commerce.

CC Number: 529115

Eligibility

People who are over 18 and who have a sound basic knowledge (at least GCSE) of the foreign language they wish to study. Applicants must be British born and be prepared to live within the local community rather than with English speakers while abroad.

Types of grants

Grants to help with the cost of studying a foreign language abroad, normally for three to twelve months. They are aimed at people who are intending to follow a career connected with the export trade of the UK, so applicants should usually be (or should stand a reasonable chance of becoming) a representative who will travel abroad to secure business for the UK. The applicant is expected to obtain a post-as an unpaid volunteer with a respectable firm or to attend a school, college, university or be on another suitable training course. The average award is approximately £1,800 (to cover living and travel expenses) paid monthly.

Annual grant total

In 2010/11 the trust had an income of £16,000 and an expenditure of £6,300.

Applications

The scholarships are advertised in February, May and October each year. Applicants will be expected to read, translate and converse in their chosen language (at least to GCSE level) in their interview.

Leadership

The London Youth Trust (W. H. Smith Memorial)
See entry on page 340

Leather industry

The Leathersellers' Company

£177,000 (97 grants)

Correspondent: Lynne Smith, Charities and Education Administrator, 21 Garlick Hill, London EC4V 2AU (020 7330 1452; email: lsmith@leathersellers.co.uk; website: www.leathersellers.co.uk)

Trustees: David Santa-Olalla; The Leathersellers' Company.

CC Number: 278072

Eligibility

People who have an unconditional offer for, or are enrolled on a full time course at a UK university. Preference is given to people from Greater London and those studying engineering or subjects connected with the leather trade.

Types of grants

Up to £4,000 to support higher education.

Annual grant total

In 2010/11 the company had assets of £42 million, an income of £1.2 million and made 97 grants to individuals totalling £177,000.

Exclusions

No funding for one year professional conversion courses.

Applications

On the online form on the company's website by 1 June. References are taken up in June/July.

Other information

The company also gives grants to organisations.

Dr Dorothy Jordan Lloyd Memorial Trust

£4,000

Correspondent: Paul Pearson, Company Secretary, Leather Trade House, Kings Park Road, Moulton Park, Northampton NN3 6JD (01604 679917; email: paulpearson@uklf.org)

Trustees: Douglas Crack; Jonathan Muirhead; David Bailey; Mike Dodd; Paul Pearson; James Lang; Graham Lampard.

CC Number: 313933

Eligibility

People employed in the production of leather or research directly relevant to this sector. Non-UK students must be fluent in English and intend to return to their home country to work in the leather industry. The fellowship may not be offered to an applicant resident in, or a citizen of, a country which restricts free trade in hides, skins or leather. Applicants must be aged 20 to 40.

Types of grants

Grants ranging from £100 to £1,500 each are made towards travel and international exchange among young people involved in the leather industry. It does not aim to support students in following standard courses of education.

Annual grant total

Grants are made totalling about £4,000 each year to around ten individuals.

Applications

In writing to the correspondent, to be submitted by the individual for consideration at any time.

Levant

Council for British Research in the Levant

£65,000 (26 grants)

Correspondent: Penny McParlin, 10 Carlton House Terrace, London SW1Y 5AH (020 7969 5296; fax: 020 7969 5401; email: cbrl@britac.ac.uk; website: www.cbrl.org.uk)

Trustees: Graham Philip; Brennan Hiorns; Michael Robinson; Andrew Garrard; Lori Allen; Robert Bewley; Henry Hogger; Eleni Asouti; Philip Marfleet; Ted Kaizer; Adam Hanieh; Lindy Crewe; Michelle Obeid.

CC Number: 1073015

Eligibility

British citizens or those ordinarily resident in the UK, Isle of Man or the Channel Islands carrying out arts, humanities and social sciences research in connection with the countries of the Levant (Cyprus, Israel, Jordan, Lebanon, Palestine and Syria).

Types of grants

The foundation administers a range of support for scholars, currently:

- **CBRL BRISMES Research Network Award:** To support research networks exploring the impact of the Arab uprisings on politics, society and culture in the region. Up to £10,000
- **Visiting Research Fellowships and Scholarships:** For scholars in university posts, early career postdoctoral candidates and students conducting PhD/DPhil research to spend a period of time at CBRL's overseas institutes to conduct primary research, develop contacts, give lectures and write up project results/publications derived from a thesis/research. Applications by mid-January
- **Pilot Study Awards:** To enable postdoctoral scholars to undertake initial exploratory work or a feasibility study as a preliminary to making major funding applications to a Research Council, the British Academy or another body. Up to £7,500. Applications by the end of November
- **Travel Grants:** To cover costs of travel and subsistence of students, academics and researchers undertaking reconnaissance tours or smaller research projects in the countries of the Levant. Up to £800
- **Project Completion Awards:** To ensure the completion of research projects, including a number of projects inherited from the organisations predecessors

Annual grant total

In 2010/11 26 grants to individuals were made totalling £65,000 under the themes: research awards, pump-priming awards; visiting research fellowships, travel grants, scholarships and direct support.

Exclusions

No grants towards maintenance, fees, conferences, language courses, field schools/group tours, books or equipment.

Applications

Separate application forms for the awards together with guidance notes and conditions are available on the website. Also see the website for application deadlines as these vary.

Other information

This trust has an extremely comprehensive website which should be referred to by any interested applicants.

Littoral

The British Institute of Archaeology at Ankara

£55,000

Correspondent: The Administrator, 10 Carlton House Terrace, London SW1Y 5AH (020 7969 5204; fax: 020 7969 5401; email: biaa@britac.ac.uk; website: www.biaa.ac.uk)

Trustees: Nicholas Milner; David Ogan; Stephen Mitchell; Warren Eastwood; Alan Greaves; Philip Robins; Toby Wilkinson; Alexandra Fletcher; Richard Paniguian; Ulf Schoop; Sevket Pamuk; William Park; John Haldon.

CC Number: 313940

Eligibility

British undergraduates and postgraduates studying the Turkish and Black Sea littoral in all academic disciplines within the arts, humanities and social sciences. Scholars from Turkey and the countries surrounding the Black Sea who are studying in the UK can also be supported. Applicants for travel and conference grants must be based at a UK university or academic institution.

Types of grants

The trust gives grants for the following purposes:

- Travel grants – up to £500 to students in the fields of arts, humanities and social sciences for travel to and around Turkey and the region of the Black Sea littoral
- Study grants – comprising of an airfare (£300) and funding for basic subsistence and accommodation (£500 per month) for individuals carrying at doctoral or postdoctoral research in the arts, humanities and social sciences relating to Turkey and the Black Sea littoral
- Fieldwork grants – up to £400 to enable an undergraduate or postgraduate fieldwork project that relates to Hellenic studies in its widest sense
- Conference grants – up to £500 to support conferences, day-schools, workshops and seminars in the fields of the arts, humanities and social sciences relating to Turkey and the Black Sea littoral. Grants are mainly intended to be used to pay the travel expenses of speakers

The trust offers funding for an annual postdoctoral research fellowship and a research scholarship based at the Institute in Ankara, and also provides scholarships to enable students from Turkey and the Black Sea region to travel to the UK.

Annual grant total

In 2010/11 the organisation had assets of £397,000 and an income of £659,000. Grants to individuals were made totalling £55,000.

Applications

Application forms are available from the correspondent or on the website.

Other information

The institute also runs a number of schemes solely for postgraduates as well as overseeing a number of other funds. See the institute's website for further details.

Marxism, socialism and working class history

The Barry Amiel and Norman Melburn Trust

£120,000

Correspondent: Willow Grylls, Administrative Officer, 8 Wilton Way, London E8 3EE (07921 280378; fax: 020 7254 1561; email: apply@ amielandmelburn.org.uk; website: www. amielandmelburn.org.uk)

Trustees: Rodney Bickerstaffe; Michael Rustin; Robin Blackburn; Bilkis Malek; Rebecca Amiel; Martin McIvor; Kate Hudson; Tariq Ali; Victoria Brittain; Alan Finlayson; Majorie Mayo.

CC Number: 281239

Eligibility

Groups and individuals working to advance public education in the philosophy of Marxism, the history of socialism, and the working class movement.

Types of grants

Grants to individuals and organisations range from £200 to £7,000, and are paid for a range of archiving, research, printing, publishing and conference costs.

Previously funded projects have included the organisation of lectures, discussions, seminars and workshops; the carrying out of research, written work and publications; and the maintenance of libraries and archive material.

Annual grant total

In 2010/11 the trust had assets of £2.3 million and an income of £31,000. Grants were made totalling £157,000 (mostly to individuals) and included the following activities:

- Research and archiving – £80,000
- Conferences and seminars – £17,000
- Website project – £20,000
- Publications and pamphlets – £40,000

Exclusions

The trust does not award funds to subsidise the continuation or running of university/college courses, or subsidise fees/maintenance for undergraduate/postgraduate students.

Applications

On a form available with guidelines from the correspondent which must be returned in hard copy. The trustees meet twice a year to consider applications, usually in January and June.

The General Federation of Trade Unions Educational Trust

See entry on page 5

Media

George Viner Memorial Fund

£21,000

Correspondent: Gayle Baldwin, Administrator, Headland House, 308–312 Gray's Inn Road, London WC1X 8DP (020 7843 3700; email: georgeviner@nuj.org.uk; website: www. georgeviner.org.uk)

Trustees: Lionel Morrison; Carole Plaster; Jim Boumelha; Michelle Stanistreet; Cara Simpson.

CC Number: 328142

Eligibility

British Black and Asian students wishing to gain employment in radio, print and photo journalism who have gained a place on an industry recognised course relating to these fields, but not yet commenced.

Types of grants

Grants of up to £8,000 for course fees, books, equipment or travel payments.

Annual grant total

In 2010/11 the charity had an income of £19,000 and an expenditure of £23,000.

Applications

On a form available from the website, along with guidance notes. Applications can be made from April, with the deadline in August.

Other information

The trust also provides mentoring, course and careers guidance.

The Welsh Broadcasting Trust

£12,000

Correspondent: Mali Parry-Jones, Islwyn, Lôn Terfyn, Morfa Nefyn, Pwllheli, Gwynedd LL53 6AP (01758 720132; email: info@wbt.org.uk; website: www.ydg.org.uk)

Trustees: Euryn Williams; Kathryn Morris; Mari Owen; Peter Edwards; Gwenda Griffith; Wil Stephens; Sian Gale.

CC Number: 700780

Eligibility

People who wish to expand and improve their knowledge of and skills in television, film, radio and new media. Applicants must have been fully resident in Wales for at least two years prior to making the application, have been born in Wales, or be Welsh speakers.

Types of grants

Participation in appropriate training or career development courses, full or part-time, for example writing workshops/ specialist technical skills/business development; attendance of educational courses at higher degree level; travel grants to accredited festivals/markets; projects which enrich the cultural experience through the medium of television, film, radio and new media.

Annual grant total

About £12,000 each year to individuals.

Exclusions

The trust does not fund undergraduate entry to courses.

Applications

Application forms are available from trust's website, or contact the trust for a printed application form. There are two deadlines for applications each year, 1 March and 1 August.

Other information

Grants are also made to training bodies or companies which offer specific training/educational programmes.

Medicine, including medical research, nursing and veterinary studies

The Ted Adams Trust Ltd

£34,000

Correspondent: The Trustees, 208 High Street, Guildford, Surrey GU1 3JB (email: tedadamstrust@live.co.uk; website: www.tedadamstrust.org.uk)

Trustees: Barbara Stokes; Rosemary Bryant; Jeffrey Saunders; Georgina Saunders.

CC Number: 1104538

Eligibility

Students of nursing/midwifery, whether pre- or post-registration, working or on courses in the Guildford area.

Types of grants

Grants of £300 to £5,000 for course fees or other costs, to enable nurses and midwives to further their professional education and development. The trust is particularly keen to fund individuals where the outcomes of their course/study will enhance patient care in the local area.

Annual grant total

In 2010/11 the trust had an income of £130,000 and made grants to individuals totalling £34,000. The directors are aiming for an annual grant distribution level of £40,000.

Exclusions

The trust cannot help with debts or living expenses.

Applications

An application form can be downloaded from the trust's website, or is available by email.

Other information

The trust also maintains Ted Adams House for the use of pre-registration students of nursing and midwifery.

The Worshipful Society of Apothecaries General Charity Ltd

£38,000 (45 grants)

Correspondent: Andrew Wallington Smith, Apothecaries Hall, Black Friars Lane, London EC4V 6EJ (020 7236 1189; email: clerk@apothecaries.org)

Trustee: The Worshipful Society of Apothecaries- governors of the committee of management.

CC Number: 284450

Eligibility

Penultimate and final year medical and pharmaceutical students who are in need.

Types of grants

One-off and recurrent grants of about £1,000 a year.

Annual grant total

In 2010/11 the charity had assets of £1.2 million and an income of £78,000. Grants to individuals for educational purposes totalled £38,000.

Grants were made to 30 undergraduate medical students, six students studying history of medicine, six students

studying ethics and philosophy of healthcare and one Guildhall student.

The Colman Kenton fund which is also managed by the society provided bursaries to two undergraduate medical students.

Applications

Every year the trustees write to the dean of every medical school in the country requesting nominations of eligible students, to be submitted by 30 June. The committee considers the recommendations in July, and the grants are disbursed in August.

Other information

Organisations are also supported.

British Society for Antimicrobial Chemotherapy

£16,000

Correspondent: Tracey Guise, Griffin House, 53 Regent Place, Birmingham B1 3NJ (01212 361988; fax: 01212 129822; email: tguise@bsac.org.uk; website: www.bsac.org.uk)

Trustees: Matthew Dryden; Alasdair MacGowan; Ian Morrissey; Laura Piddock; Nicholas Brown; Peter Davey; Michael Cooper; Conor Jamieson; Andrew Stacey; Jayshree Dave; Mandy Wootton; Michael Allen; Barbara Isalska; Alex O'Neill; Frances Burke; Keith Miller; Wendy Lawson.

CC Number: 1093118

Eligibility

Postgraduate and undergraduate students and members of the society involved in research and training in antimicrobial chemotherapy.

Types of grants

The trust offers the following grants:

- Project grants – up to £10,000 for projects of up to one year duration
- Research grants – up to £50,000 for projects of up to one year duration
- Overseas scholarships – up to £1,000 per calendar month, to enable workers from other countries the opportunity to work in UK departments for up to six months
- Vacation scholarships – £180 per week for up to ten weeks, designed to give undergraduate experience in research. Candidates should be on a full-time first degree course in the sciences, medicine, veterinary medicine or dentistry
- Travel grants – up to £1,500, restricted to BSAC members, to enable individuals to attend the annual meetings of ECCMID and ICAAC

▶ Education grants – up to £50,000 for research projects and initiatives of benefit to the field

Annual grant total

In 2011 the society had assets of £5.5 million and an income of £2 million. During the year the society gave £16,000 in vacation and travel grants directly to individuals and £138,000 through institutions for research and education projects.

Applications

Each programme has specific application forms, guidance notes and deadlines. See the society's website for full details for each programme.

Other information

The society also makes large grants to institutions to fund research.

The Jean Ginsburg Memorial Foundation

See entry on page 81

The Dr Robert Malcolm Trust

£500

Correspondent: Ian Brash, Trustee, Fa'side Castle, Tranent, East Lothian EH33 2LE (01316 657654)

Eligibility

Students studying for a medicine degree. Grants are only given for first degrees. Applicants do not have to be in Scotland.

Types of grants

Grants towards the cost of medical education.

Annual grant total

The trustees state that this is a 'small family trust with limited assets'.

Applications

In writing to the correspondent. Recently the trustees have found it more successful to directly target potential applicants through referral from school headteachers. The headteachers must give details of the students' potential, ability and their funding needs.

The Nightingale Fund

£14,000 (10 grants)

Correspondent: Jennifer Chambers, Honorary Secretary, 55 Recreation Road, Shortlands, Bromley, Kent BR2 0DY (020 8464 7354; email: jachambers28@ btinternet.com; website: www. thenightingalefund.org.uk)

Trustees: Edmund Verney; Margaret Rudland; Paul Beard; Robina Talbot-Ponsonby; Elizabeth Redpath; O'Dowd; Edward Bonham-Carter; Marion Richardson; Natalie Tiddy; Rosemary Burch.

CC Number: 205911

Eligibility

Nurses, midwives and community public health nurses who are registered with the Nursing and Midwifery Council and healthcare assistants in the UK.

Types of grants

One-off and recurrent grants of £300 to £3,000 for further or higher education and training to enhance nursing practice.

Annual grant total

In 2010/11 the fund had an income of £20,000 and an expenditure of £19,000. Grants to ten people totalled £14,000 and were for between £500 and £2,300.

Applications

On a form available on the website to be submitted with a current CV via email. All applicants are interviewed either by telephone or in person. Applications are considered in March, July and November and applications should be submitted six weeks before the meeting.

The Nurses Association of Jamaica (NAJ) (UK)

£4,000

Correspondent: Bernice Woode, Executive Secretary, PO Box 1270, Croydon, Surrey CR9 3DA (01216 810952; email: info@najuk.org; website: www.naj.org.uk)

Trustees: Lyrell McNish; Charmaine Case; Dorothy Turner; Paulette Lewis; Lorna Grant.

CC Number: 1063008

Eligibility

Primarily people from black and ethnic minority groups, especially African-Caribbean groups, who are aged 18 or over. The trust will consider any studies to promote the practice of nursing, midwifery and health visiting. This may range from students undertaking studies in health education, nursing courses at degree, diploma, certificate and attendance levels, sociology, psychology, nursing and other health and health science related programmes, in particular where the course of study will impact positively on the health and health care of ethnic minority groups. The trust also considers the following funding priorities: business schools and pre-school education; IT training; special needs education; and training for community development. Preference is given to people living in Birmingham,

London, Nottingham and internationally.

Types of grants

One-off grants ranging between £50 and £300 towards books, fees, educational outings in the UK, study or travel abroad and student exchanges.

Priority is given to part-funding for one year or less, although a period of up to two years may be considered.

Annual grant total

In 2010 donations totalled £8,000. Grants are made to organisations and individuals.

Applications

Application forms are available from the association's website. Application forms can be submitted directly by the individual, through a school/college or educational welfare agency, or through another third party. All applications should be supported with a reference. The completed form can be returned in February or August, with supporting statements to justify the purpose of the application, costings and how the money will be used, and specific details about the study/projects supported. They are considered in September and March.

The May Price SRN Award

See entry on page 139

The RCN Foundation

£41,000 (80 grants)

Correspondent: Jane Clarke, Welfare Service, 20 Cavendish Square, London W1G 0RN (0345 408 4391; email: jane. clarke@rcn.org.uk; website: www. rcnfoundation.org.uk)

Trustees: John Colyer; Carol Evans; Susan Fern; Robert Sowney; Gordon Peterkin; Helen Carter; Sarah Coward; Tony Butterworth; Jane Miles; Nicholas Pearson; Claire Hicks; Christopher Piercy; Ian Norris.

CC Number: 1134606

Eligibility

Registered nurses, midwives, health practitioners, health care assistants and people training for these professions. Some bursaries are available for specific areas of medicine, such as orthopaedic and trauma care or palliative care and pain.

Types of grants

Various bursaries of up to £5,000 for learning and development including degrees, training, conference attendance and projects and research.

Annual grant total

In 2010/11 the foundation funded 80 awards totalling £41,000.

Applications

The bursaries have different opening and closing dates, potential applicants should check the website for the most recent information. There are also application forms available to download for the separate bursaries.

Other information

Previously known as The Royal College of Nursing Benevolent Fund.

The Rhona Reid Charitable Trust

£10,000

Correspondent: Miss K Clayton, c/o Rathbone Taxation Services, Port of Liverpool Buildings, Pier Head, Liverpool L3 1NW (01512 366666; email: karen.owen-jones@rathbones.com)

Trustees: Phillip Taylor; Alan Keer; Elizabeth Mitchell; Andrew Jervis.

CC Number: 1047380

Eligibility

People involved in the study and advancement of opthalmology, music and the arts.

Types of grants

One-off and recurrent grants according to need.

Annual grant total

In 2010/11 the trust had an income of £13,000 and an expenditure of £17,000.

Applications

In writing to the correspondent. Applications are considered in March and September.

Other information

Grants are also made to organisations.

Sandra Charitable Trust

£75,000 (134 grants)

Correspondent: Keith Lawrence, Secretary to the Trustees, Moore Stephens, St Paul's House, Warwick Lane, London EC4M 7BP (020 7334 9191; email: keith.lawrence@ moorestephens.com)

Trustees: Richard Moore; Michael Macfadyen.

CC Number: 327492

Eligibility

People pursuing a career in nursing.

Types of grants

One-off and recurrent grants according to need.

Annual grant total

In 2010/11 the trust had assets of £18 million and an income of £644,000. Grants to 134 individuals totalled £75,000.

Applications

In writing to the correspondent, although the trust's funds are largely committed. The trustees meet on a frequent basis to consider applications.

Other information

Grants are also made to organisations.

The Society for Relief of Widows and Orphans of Medical Men

£23,000

Correspondent: Lotte Farrar, Secretary, Medical Society of London, Lettsom House, 11 Chandos Street, Cavendish Square, London W1G 9EB (01837 83022; email: info@widowsandorphans.org.uk; website: www.widowsandorphans.org.uk)

Trustees: Gordon Hickish; Priya Singh; Celia Palmer; Cyril Nemeth; Anthony Richards; Christopher Hutter; Frank Schweitzer; Geoffrey Rose; Patrick England; John Barker; Roy Palmer; Simon Payne; Stewart Kilpatrick; Emily MacDonald; Stephanie Brown; Rohit Malliwal.

CC Number: 207473

Eligibility

Medical students who have at least one parent who is a doctor, and whose family is in financial need.

Types of grants

One-off and recurrent grants of £500 to £3,000 to college students, undergraduates, vocational and mature students for fees, books, maintenance/ living expenses, instruments/equipment and clothing (not to mature students), and to schoolchildren and people starting work for maintenance/living expenses.

Annual grant total

In 2011 the society had assets of £4.8 million and an income of £136,000. Grants to 75 individuals totalled £46,000

Exclusions

Grants are not normally given for second degrees.

Applications

On a form available from the correspondent or to download from the website. Applications should be submitted directly by the individual and are considered in February, May, August and November.

Sir John Sumner's Trust

£0

Correspondent: Ian Henderson, Secretary to the Trustees, 1 Colmore Square, Birmingham B4 6AA (0870 763 1490)

Trustees: J. Sumner; J. Fea; Lady J. Wellesley; Mrs V. McKie; A. Robson.

CC Number: 218620

Eligibility

People studying nursing or medicine, including veterinary studies, who are in need and living in the UK, although there is a strong preference for the Midlands.

Types of grants

Grants towards equipment, instruments, fees or living expenses.

Annual grant total

In 2010/11 the trust had assets of £765,000 and an income of £33,000. Grants made to institutions totalled £32,000; it appears that no grants were made to individuals during the year.

Exclusions

No grants towards religious or political causes.

Applications

In writing to the correspondent, through the individual's college or a welfare agency. Two referees should be provided, one of whom must be from the relevant educational establishment. Applications can be considered at any time.

Metal work and metal jewellery

The Goldsmiths Arts Trust Fund

£38,000

Correspondent: The Clerk, The Goldsmiths' Company, Goldsmiths' Hall, Foster Lane, London EC2V 6BN (020 7606 7010; fax: 020 7606 1511; email: charity@thegoldsmiths.co.uk; website: www.thegoldsmiths.co.uk)

Trustee: The Goldsmiths' Company Trustee.

CC Number: 313329

Eligibility

Apprentices and students (including postgraduate) studying silversmithing and precious metal jewellery at art colleges.

Types of grants

Bursaries for specific projects of £100 to £500. Previous donations have been made for financing exhibitions, assistance with educating apprentices, bursaries, masterclasses and courses.

Annual grant total

The latest accounts available were for 2009/10 when the trust had assets of £85,000 and an income of £1 million. Bursaries and grants awarded to 66 individuals totalled £38,000.

Exclusions

Grants are not normally made for fees or subsistence on standard courses at further or higher education institutions. Grants are not made to overseas students studying in the UK.

Applications

In writing to the correspondent, through an organisation such as a college or university. Applications are considered quarterly.

Other information

Grants are also given to organisations.

The South Square Trust

See entry on page 76

Nautical or maritime courses

Reardon Smith Nautical Trust

£117,000

Correspondent: John Cory, Cob Cottage, Garth Hill, Pentyrch, Cardiff CF15 9NS (email: cory@cobcottage. fsworld.co.uk)

CC Number: 1104019

Eligibility

Residents of Wales up to the age of 25 studying recognised nautical or maritime courses. These should relate to shipping, maritime law and commerce, navigation, sailing, oceanography and marine related environmental issues, in particular those which give the individual first-hand, practical experience of being at sea. Preference is given to residents of Cardiff.

Types of grants

Grants, scholarships, exhibitions and bursaries.

Annual grant total

In 2011/12 the trust had assets of £3 million and an income of £65,000. Grants totalled £117,000.

Applications

Applications should be made via a relevant educational establishment or sail training provider.

Sailors' Society

£3,900

Correspondent: Welfare Fund Manager, 350 Shirley Road, Southampton SO15 3HY (02380 515950; fax: 02380 515951; email: welfare@sailors-society. org)

Trustees: Jake Watson; William Ward; Ross Sinclair; Peter Goldberg; Michael Burridge; Jonathan Stoneley; Shyam Sharma; Natalie Shaw; Norman Jones; Michael Drayton; Peter Swift.

CC Number: 237778

Eligibility

Students or nautical cadets preparing for a career at sea in the merchant navy (of any country) and enrolled at a recognised college or academy of nautical education. Seafarers who have already entered the profession and have been accepted on a course of study by an accredited institution to further their qualifications.

Applicants must be able to demonstrate that they have no other source of funds to pursue their nautical education.

Types of grants

One-off and recurrent grants towards course study fees, related books and necessary course materials.

Annual grant total

In 2009 the society had assets of £13 million and an income of £3 million. Grants were made totalling £23,000, of which £13,000 was given in welfare grants and £10,000 in educational awards.

In 2011 the society had assets of £13 million and an income of £3.5 million. Educational grants totalled £3,900.

Applications

On a form available on request to nauticalgrant@sailors-society.org. Any application must be fully supported by the respective course tutor.

Note: beneficiaries who do not complete the full course of study may be required to repay all or any part of the grant.

Other information

The society maintains a network of Chaplains at the various key ports around the world, who carry out ship visiting routines and minister to

seafarers. It also provides centres and clubs for seafarers and associated maritime workers at strategic seaports.

The society administers the Leith Aged Mariners' Fund and the Dundee Seaman's Friend Society.

Physics

Institute of Physics Undergraduate Research Bursary

£75,000

Correspondent: Institute of Physics (email: supportandgrants@iop.org)

Eligibility

Undergraduate physics students studying a degree accredited by the Institute of Physics who are in the middle year of their course. Bursaries are aimed at students who may be considering a research career, to give some hands-on experience in a real-life research environment.

Types of grants

£180 per week (£190 in London) for up to eight weeks to undertake a research placement within a university department.

Annual grant total

Up to 70 bursaries are offered every year.

Applications

Applications for summer bursaries open at the end of the preceding year. Applications must be submitted by the supervisor.

Physio- therapy

The Chartered Society of Physiotherapy Charitable Trust

£61,000 (90 grants)

Correspondent: Susan Williams, Awards Administrator, 14 Bedford Row, London WC1R 4ED (020 7306 6666; email: edawards@csp.org.uk; website: www.csp. org.uk/charitabletrust)

Trustees: Susan England; Jeryl Stone; Suzanne McDonough; Catherine McLouglin; Sue Rees; Alison Avil; Elizabeth Cavan.

CC Number: 279882

Eligibility

Qualified, associate and students members of the society.

Types of grants

Grants for qualified and associate members for UK and international presentations, overseas travel and study, projects for educational or research purposes, and for international education and development projects. Grants for student members for overseas elective placements. Grants are for £150 to £3,000.

Funding is also available for postgraduate accredited courses in physiotherapy.

Annual grant total

In 2011 the society had assets of £2.1 million and an income of £663,000. Educational awards made to 90 individuals totalled £61,000.

Applications

On a form available to download from the website, or from the administrator. Applications should be submitted to the appropriate panel: Scientific Panel, Education Awards Panel and the Joe Jeans Scholarship Award Panel. Applications for electives should be submitted by 15 February for spring/summer electives and 1 October for autumn/winter.

Polish history, literature or art

The Broncel Trust

£5,000

Correspondent: Anna Marianska, Secretary, 371 Uxbridge Road, London W3 9RH (020 8992 9997)

Trustees: Irma Pietron; Anna Marianska; Andrej Blonski.

CC Number: 1103737

Eligibility

People working in the fields of Polish history, literature or art.

Types of grants

Scholarships, research and grants for publishing Polish works of literature.

Annual grant total

Income and expenditure have fluctuated over the past few years. In 2010/11 the trust had an income of £11,000 and an expenditure of £16,000. Previously

around £5,000 has been given in grants to individuals.

Applications

In writing to the correspondent.

Other information

Grants are made to organisations with occasional financial support for libraries, museums and exhibitions.

Postal history

The Stuart Rossiter Trust Fund

£21,000

Correspondent: Ray Dixon, 39 Braybank, Bray, Maidenhead, Berkshire SL6 2BH (email: nhrossitertrust@hotmail.co.uk; website: www.rossitertrust.com)

Trustees: Robin Pizer; David Tett; Gavin Fryer; Susan McEwan; Richard Wheatley; Rex Dixon.

CC Number: 292076

Eligibility

Anyone of any nationality undertaking original research into postal history with a view to publication. English language is preferred in published or electronic form to promote accessibility.

Types of grants

Grants towards: translations; cost of hire of researchers; publication costs; and costs of research. Part or the entire grant may be recovered from sales of the publication.

Annual grant total

In 2011 the trust had assets of £381,000, an income of £36,000 and gave grants for research and publication totalling £21,000.

Exclusions

The trust only gives grants for research into postal history with a view to publication.

Applications

Application forms are available from the correspondent, or from the trust's website.

Other information

Grants are also made to organisations.

Religion/ ministry

The Andrew Anderson Trust

£19,000

Correspondent: Andrew Anderson, Trustee, 1 Cote House Lane, Bristol BS9 3UW (01179 621588)

Trustees: Anne Anderson; Margaret Anderson; Andrew Anderson.

CC Number: 212170

Eligibility

People studying theology.

Types of grants

One-off and recurrent grants according to need.

Annual grant total

In 2010/11 the trust had assets of £10 million and an income of £247,000. Grants to individuals for welfare and education totalled £39,000.

Applications

The trust states that it rarely gives to people who are not known to the trustees or who have been personally recommended by people known to the trustees. Unsolicited applications are therefore unlikely to be successful.

The Aria (Portsmouth) Trust

£400

Correspondent: Joanna Benarroch, Office of the Chief Rabbi, 305 Ballards Lane, London N12 8GB (020 8343 6301; fax: 020 8343 6310; email: joanna@ chiefrabbi.org; website: www.chiefrabbi.org)

Trustees: Alan Placey; Jonathan Sacks; Conrad Morris; Reuben Turner; Stephen Forman; Irving Jacobs.

CC Number: 307249

Eligibility

Men under 35 in Great Britain who intend to enter the Anglo-Jewish ministry and attend a recognised educational establishment. Preference is given to those residing in the County of Southampton.

Types of grants

One-off grants according to need.

Annual grant total

In 2010/11 the trust had an income of £8,700 and an expenditure of £400. Expenditure over the past two years has been significantly lower than previously.

Applications

In writing to the correspondent, directly by the individual.

The Barnabas Trust

£38,000 (13 grants)

Correspondent: Mrs Doris Edwards, Secretary, Lawn Farm, Pillows Green Road, Corse, Gloucester GL19 3NX (01452 840371; email: richard@padfield. me.uk)

Trustees: Julie Jarman; Richard Padfield; Stephen Burden.

CC Number: 900487

Eligibility

People embarking on Christian mission activities and people on religious education courses.

Types of grants

One-off grants according to need.

Annual grant total

In 2010/11 the trust had assets of £17,000 and an income of £49,000. Grants were made to 13 individuals totalling £38,000.

Applications

In writing to the correspondent. Applications should be submitted by the end of February. Trustees meet quarterly.

Other information

The trust also makes some grants to organisations.

The CPAS Ministers in Training Fund

£10,000

Correspondent: Mrs Pauline Walden, CPAS, Athena Drive, Tachbrook Park, Warwick CV34 6NG (01926 458458; email: mail@cpas.org.uk; website: www. cpas.org.uk)

Trustees: Alan Hawker; Paul Williams; Richard Owen; Andrea Irvine; Helen Simpson; Gordon Kuhrt; Nicholas Burt; Anthony Wells; Richard Moy; Jeremy Clack; Andrew Porter; Tim Crook.

CC Number: 1007820

Eligibility

Evangelical Anglican ordinands who are in financial need during their training. Applicants must be contemplating parochial or ordained pioneer ministry in the UK or Ireland for at least three years after ordination. Those in Church Army training may also be eligible for a grant.

Types of grants

Recurrent grants, one per academic year, to help with maintenance and personal

expenses. They range between £50 and £500.

Annual grant total

In 2010/11 the society had assets of £6.5 million and an income of £4 million. Grants through the Ministers in Training Fund totalled £10,000.

Exclusions

No grants for books or fees.

Applications

Application forms, budget forms and an information sheet are available from the website. Applications should be submitted by the end of September, January or, (for students not in their final year) April. Applicants are asked for two referees and a completed budget form to detail income and expenditure including figures from LEA/CFMT/ diocese. Time should be allowed for references to be taken up.

Other information

The fund gives most of its income to other ecumenical causes such as parish support, publications, training events and children and youth projects.

The Elland Society

£4,500

Correspondent: Colin Judd, 57 Grosvenor Road, Shipley, West Yorkshire BD18 4RB (01274 584775; email: thejudds@saltsvillage.wanadoo.co. uk; website: www.ellandsocietygrants.co. uk)

Trustees: Colin Judd; Susan Penfold; Peter Jeffrey; Paul Deo; Richard Radley; Jim Dearden; Helen Hodgson; John Hallat; Anne Young; Bryan Short; David Mann.

CC Number: 243053

Eligibility

Men and women in training for the ordained ministry of the Church of England who are evangelical in conviction and outlook. Priority for grants is given to ordinands from dioceses in the province of York or who will serve their title in that province.

Types of grants

Grants are given to those who have already started training at theological college, be it residential or non-residential, and who have financial needs outside their anticipated agreed budget relating to actual items of expenditure. Recent grants given were towards, for example, family educational expenses, postgraduate study, car expenses where it was needed for training or a spouse's job, replacement of fridge and dental treatment. Grants to individuals seldom exceed £500 per person.

Annual grant total

In 2010/11 the trust had an income of £6,200 and an expenditure of £5,300.

Applications

Download an application form from the website or request one from the correspondent.

The Lady Hewley Trust

£54,000

Correspondent: Neil Blake, Clerk, Military House, 24 Castle Street, Chester CH1 2DS (01244 400315)

Trustees: Gordon Simmonds; Stephen Gorton; John Lumsden; Phillip Thake; Dr David Robinson; Sarah Dodds; Neil Mackenzie.

CC Number: 230043

Eligibility

Young men or women preparing for United Reformed and Baptist Church ministries. Preference will be given to students who were born in the north of England.

Types of grants

Exhibitions are given to students who are approved by the relevant church authorities and attend one of the following colleges: Northern Baptist College, Manchester; Northern College, Manchester; Mansfield College, Oxford; Westminster College, Cambridge; or The Queen's Foundation, Birmingham. The size of grants given is related to other income, although the usual maximum is £300 to £400.

Annual grant total

In 2010/11 the trust had assets of £13.8 million and an income of £357,000. Grants to individuals totalled £129,000, of which £54,000 was given in student grants.

Exclusions

No grants will be given when local authority funds are available.

Applications

On a form available from the college concerned. Applications should be submitted via the college by 15 July for the meeting of the trustees in November.

Lady Peel Legacy Trust

£2,500

Correspondent: Mrs Chris Ruge-Cope, 21 Chace Avenue, Potters Bar, Hertfordshire EN6 5LX

Trustees: Charles Pickstone; C. Ruge-Cope; Richard Chamberlin; Christopher Irvine; Andrew Davison.

CC Number: 204815

Eligibility

Men and women, who are in training at a theological college or on a recognised course.

Types of grants

One-off grants generally for the provision of books or, for especially needy candidates, a small cash sum. Grants are occasionally made to clergy undertaking further academic work. Application for book grants should be for books of lasting value to assist in the building up of a priest's working library.

Annual grant total

About £5,000 a year for educational and welfare purposes.

Applications

On a form available on written request from the correspondent. The closing dates for applications are 1 April and 1 November each year. Telephone contact is not invited.

Powis Exhibition Fund

£6,000

Correspondent: John Richfield, 39 Cathedral Road, Cardiff CF11 9XF (02920 348200; fax: 02920 387835; email: louisedavies@churchinwales.org.uk)

Trustees: Dominic Walker; Barry Morgan; John Davies; Andrew Griffith; John Powis; Wyn Evans; Gregory Cameron.

CC Number: 525770

Eligibility

People who are training as ordinands in the Church in Wales. Applicants must have an adequate knowledge of the Welsh language; and have been born, or be resident, in Wales.

Types of grants

Grants of up to £700 annually, for no longer than the period of study.

Annual grant total

About £6,000.

Applications

Application forms are available from the correspondent or from individual dioceses.

Sola Trust

£197,000 (58 grants)

Correspondent: Simon Pilcher, Trustee, Green End Barn, Wood End Green, Henham, Bishop's Stortford CM22 6AY (01279 850819; email: simon@pilchers.org)

Trustees: G. J. Mote; Rachel Pilcher; Simon Pilcher.

CC Number: 1062739

Eligibility

Individuals training for full-time Christian work (especially while at theological college), as well as to those already involved in full-time ministry.

Types of grants

One-off grants to enable people to buy books, attend conferences, retreats and so on, as well as training courses. Additionally the charity aims to relieve the financial hardship that those involved in Christian ministry can face.

Annual grant total

In 2010/11 the trust had assets of £101,000 and an income of £460,000, mostly from donations. Grants to individuals for theological and ministry training totalled £197,000.

Applications

In writing to the correspondent. Where appropriate grants may be routed through a church or equivalent body that is providing training to individuals. Trustees meet around ten times a year to consider applications.

Other information

A small number of grants are also made to individuals for relief and missionary work. Grants to organisations in 2010/11 totalled £163,000.

The Spalding Trust

£65,000

Correspondent: Tessa Rodgers, Secretary, PO Box 85, Wetherden, Stowmarket, Suffolk IP14 3NY (website: www.spaldingtrust.org.uk)

Trustees: Kevin Ward; Anne Spalding; Oliver Davies; Edmund Bosworth; John Emerton; Julius Lipner; Michael Loewe.

CC Number: 209066

Eligibility

To enable students to study a religion other than their own or to study religion from a comparative perspective at academic institutions. Projects must have a primarily religious concern, rather than sociological or anthropological.

Types of grants

Up to £2,000 for the comparative study of the major religions. Grants for direct and indirect educational costs including for travel to conferences or to study a religion in the country where it is practiced.

Annual grant total

In 2010 the trust had assets of £1.7 million, an income of £76,000 and made grants totalling £65,000.

Exclusions

No retrospective grants.

Applications

In writing to the correspondent detailing:

- An outline of the proposal
- A copy of the applicant's curriculum vitae, with their own religious commitment, if any
- Details of the budget and of other possible sources of funding that have been applied for. This should be done using a copy of the financial statement available on the website
- Preferably two academic references
- Daytime and evening phone numbers and email address

Applications guidelines are available on the trusts website. They are considered monthly and it takes trustees around three months to make a decision on an application.

In special circumstances trustees will consider applications for recurrent grants that may extend over one year; applicants will usually be expected to make an application on each occasion that a grant is requested.

Other information

The trust also makes grants to institutions. A subsidiary of the trust, the Ellen Rebe Spalding Memorial Fund, makes grants to individuals for welfare.

St Christopher's College Educational Trust

£5,700 (7 grants)

Correspondent: Lindsey Anderson-Gear, 55 Manston Close, Bicester, Oxfordshire OX26 4FA (email: stchristopherstrust@hotmail.co.uk)

Trustees: Janina Ainsworth; Leslie Francis; David Isaac; Paul Wheatley.

CC Number: 313864

Eligibility

People studying religious education connected with promoting the objects of the Church of England/Wales.

Types of grants

One-off and recurrent grants in the range of £250 and £2,000 to enable individuals to take advantage of educational or research facilities or attend courses designed to promote religious education.

Annual grant total

In 2011 the trust had an income of £108,000 and gave grants to seven individuals totalling £5,700.

Exclusions

No grants to students studying overseas.

Applications

In writing to the correspondent.

The Foundation of St Matthias

£17,000

Correspondent: Lynette Cox, Clerk to the Trustees, Hillside House First Floor, 1500 Parkway North, Newbrick Road, Stoke Gifford, Bristol BS34 8YU (01179 060100; email: stmatthiastrust@ bristoldiocese.org; website: www. stmatthiastrust.org.uk)

Trustees: Lesley Farrall; Robert Springett; Nick Denison; Beryl Downe; Katie Jones; Paul Smith; Andy Piggott; Benjamin Smith; Rosemary Harrott; Colin McArthur; Philip Perks; Helena Arnold; Theresa Gale; Douglas Holt; John Swainston.

CC Number: 311696

Eligibility

Further and higher education students, including mature students and occasionally postgraduates, who are studying in accordance with the doctrine of the Church of England. Preference is given to people studying teaching or religious education who are living in the dioceses of Bristol, Bath and Wells and Gloucester. In practice funding is absorbed by people who meet these preferences.

Types of grants

One-off grants usually ranging from £100 to £750. Grants can be for books, fees, maintenance/living expenses, childcare and for some study or travel abroad. Foreign students studying in the UK may also be supported (but not at postgraduate level) and overseas courses may be supported if the visit is integral to the course or research.

Annual grant total

In 2011 the foundation made 27 grants to individuals of less than £1,000 and four of more than £1,000, altogether totalling £17,000.

Applications

Applicants should telephone in the first instance to discuss the nature of study and so on. Applications must be made on a form available from the foundation's website. They should be submitted by 31 May for consideration in July or 30 September for consideration in November.

Other information

Grants can also be given to educational organisations and schools with a Christian focus.

The Thornton Fund

£7,500

Correspondent: Dr Jane Williams, 93 Fitzjohn Avenue, Barnet, Hertfordshire EN5 2HR (020 8440 2211)

Trustees: Dr David Wykes; Dr Doreen Williams; Jeffrey Teagle; Prof. Richard Booth; Revd Clifford Reed.

CC Number: 226803

Eligibility

Students at Unitarian colleges or training for Unitarian ministry.

Types of grants

Grants between £250 and £1,500 to help with books, equipment, instruments, living expenses, study exchange and study or travel abroad.

Annual grant total

Grants usually total around £15,000 per year.

Applications

In writing to the correspondent through a third party such as a minister, including the total and annual estimated costs of study. They are considered on an ongoing basis.

Other information

The fund occasionally makes grants to the general assembly of Unitarian and Free Christian Churches for special projects and also to Unitarian ministers for welfare needs.

Torchbearer Trust Fund

£24,000

Correspondent: The Secretary, Capernwray Hall, Carnforth, Lancashire LA6 1AG (01524 733908; fax: 01524 736681; email: info@capernwray.org.uk; website: www.capernwray.org.uk)

Trustees: Alexander Thomas; Eveline Thomas; Susan Gilmore.

CC Number: 253607

Eligibility

People engaged in full-time Christian instruction or training. Preference is given to students and former students of Torchbearer Bible schools.

Types of grants

One-off grants and bursaries according to need.

Annual grant total

In 2010/11 the fund had assets of £168,000 and an income of £45,000. Grants totalled £53,000.

Applications

In writing to the correspondent.

Other information

Grants are also available for missionary work.

Turath Scholarship Fund

£1,700

Correspondent: Imran Satia, 4 West Park Road, Blackburn BB2 6DG (07825 346320; email: scholarship@turath.co.uk; website: www.turath.co.uk/front/turath-scholarship-fund)

Trustees: Imran Satia; Yahya Batha; Bilal Anwar; Assiya Satia.

CC Number: 1138153

Eligibility

UK citizens between 18 and 24 studying for a skill or doing vocational training that will benefit their community in some way. Preference is given to people studying any aspect of Islamic Science including for example, learning Arabic.

Types of grants

Grants to pay for training or tuition including fees, travel and equipment/tools.

Annual grant total

In 2010/11 the fund had an income of £2,000 and an expenditure of £1,700.

Applications

On a form available on the website to be returned by email.

Seafaring

The Corporation of Trinity House, London

£7,000

Correspondent: Graham Hockley, Secretary, Trinity House, Tower Hill, London EC3N 4DH (020 7481 6914; email: graham.hockley@thls.org; website: www.trinityhouse.co.uk)

Trustees: Rear Admiral Sir Jeremy de Halpert; Capt. Duncan Glass; Simon Sherrard; The Viscount; Cobham; Capt. Nigel Pryke; Commodore David Squire; Capt. Richard Woodman; Commodore James Scorer; Capt. Roger Barker; Capt. Ian McNaught.

CC Number: 211869

Eligibility

Candidates must be between 16 and 18½ years old with five GCSE at grade C or better and must also have passed the Department of Transport medical examination. Applicants must also be British and permanently resident in the British Isles. Applicants must be applying to become an officer in the Merchant Navy.

Types of grants

The Trinity House Merchant Navy Scholarship Scheme provides financial support for young people seeking careers as officers in the Merchant Navy.

Cadets undertake a three or four year programme split between nautical college and time at sea in a variety of British-managed vessels. Cadets can train as either Deck or Engineer Officers or pursue a Marine Cadetship encompassing both disciplines. Full scholarships are available for this programme of £7,000, under the Trinity House Cadet Training Scheme.

Annual grant total

In 2010/11 the corporation had assets of £138 million and an income of £7.1 million. Grants to individuals totalled £14,000. Most of the corporation's funds are reserved for welfare purposes, namely almshouse accommodation.

Applications

Details of the scholarship scheme are available upon application in writing to the correspondent.

The Honourable Company of Master Mariners

£27,000

Correspondent: The Clerk, HQS Wellington, Temple Stairs, Victoria Embankment, London WC2R 2PN (020 7836 8179; email: info@hcmm.org.uk; website: www.hcmm.org.uk)

CC Number: 1127213

Eligibility

People who are serving in the Merchant navy and their dependents, and those intending to serve.

Types of grants

Grants to encourage the education, instruction and training of applicants.

Annual grant total

In 2011 the charity had assets of £2.9 million and an income of £106,000. Grants to individuals totalled £54,000.

Applications

In writing to the correspondent. Applications can be submitted directly by the individual, through a social worker, Citizens Advice, or other welfare agency, or by a friend or relative. They are considered quarterly.

Other information

This trust is an amalgamation of four separate funds: the Education Fund, the Benevolent Fund, the London Maritime Institution and the Howard Leopold Davis Fund.

The Marine Society and Sea Cadets

£500,000

Correspondent: Claire E Barnett, 202 Lambeth Road, London SE1 7JW (020 7654 7011; fax: 020 7928 8914; email: info@ms-sc.org; website: www.ms-sc.org)

Trustees: Capt. Nigel Palmer; Mr A. F. Given; Dr Louise Bennett; Rear Admiral K. J. Borley; Mr M. J. Gladwyn; Dr Sheila Fitzpatrick; David Jeffcoat; Alan Marsh; Alex Marsh; Chris Ledger; Dame Mary Richardson; Colin Wilcox; Richard J. Sayer; Robin Woods; David Snelson; Sir Alan Massey; Commodore W. M (BILL) Walworth; Rear Admiral Chris Hockley.

CC Number: 313013

Eligibility

Professional seafarers, active or retired, members of the Sea Cadet Corps and any other young persons considering a maritime career.

Types of grants

It is the society's policy to help where financial hardship is evident. If the applicant is likely to be employed or re-employed then interest-free loans may be given rather than grants. The award of a loan or grant is usually made to an applicant who is attempting to improve his career prospects, or who has to change his career due to unforeseen circumstances. In addition, the society offers a scholarship scheme for seafarers or prospective seafarers.

Annual grant total

In 2010/11 the trust had assets of £17.2 million and an income of £12.8 million. Grants to individuals totalled £1 million, although the trust states that 'individual grants given are small and not material within the overall total.'

Exclusions

Recurrent grants are not made.

Applications

On a form obtainable from the correspondent. Applications are considered as they arrive.

Other information

Grants are also made to sea cadet units.

Shipbuilding

The Worshipful Company of Shipwrights' Educational Trust

£12,000 (12,000 grants)

Correspondent: The Clerk, Worshipful Company of Shipwrights, Ironmongers' Hall, Shaftesbury Place, Barbican, London EC2Y 8AA (020 7606 2376; email: clerk@shipwrights.co.uk; website: www.shipwrights.co.uk)

Trustees: Simon Sherrard; Jock Slater; Archie Smith; William Everard; Simon Robinson; Graham Clarke; Worshipful Company of Shipwrights.

CC Number: 313249

Eligibility

UK citizens, preferably under 25, who are involved in any craft or discipline connected with ship and boatbuilding, design or research.

Types of grants

Grants range from £250 to £1,500 to help with fees, living expenses, uniforms and tools/equipment. They are made under the 'Billmeir Award Scheme' to support individuals training at a school teaching modern and traditional timber ship and boat building, naval architecture and marine engineering.

Annual grant total

In 2010/11 the trust had assets of £863,000 and an income of £53,000. Grants were given totalling £12,000 to 12 individuals.

Exclusions

No grants to non-UK citizens.

Applications

Application forms can be downloaded from the trust's website and are considered three times a year in January, May and October.

Other information

Other educational grants are given to universities and organisations.

Sport

Athletics for the Young

£23,000

Correspondent: Alan Barlow, 12 Redcar Close, Hazel Grove, Stockport SK7 4SQ (01614 839330)

Trustees: Richard Float; Geoffrey Clarke; Eric Nash; Norma Blaine; David

Cropper; John Lofts; Rodney Walker; Alan Barlow; Richard Carter; Val Rutter; Walter Nicholls.

CC Number: 1004448

Eligibility

Young people under the age of 25 who are in full time education and not receiving any other funding.

Types of grants

One-off educational grants towards athletic pursuits.

Annual grant total

In 2010 the charity had an income of £2,000 and a total expenditure of £23,000, mostly in grants.

Applications

In writing to the correspondent using the application form available on the Northern Athletics website, the closing date is mid-February.

Other information

The charity has also made grants to athletics clubs in previous years.

The Dickie Bird Foundation

£10,000

Correspondent: Les Smith, 47 Ripon Road, Earlsheaton, Dewsbury, West Yorkshire WF12 7LG (01924 430593; email: info@thedickiebirdfoundation.org; website: www.thedickiebirdfoundation.org)

Trustees: Dickie Bird; Les Smith; Keith Dibb; Eric Stephens; Stephen Mowbray; Warren Cowley.

CC Number: 1104646

Eligibility

Disadvantaged young people under the age of 18 who are participating in sport.

Types of grants

One-off grants usually ranging from £100 to £1,000, according to need. Grants are usually given for items of sports clothing such as shirts, shorts and footwear, and for equipment and travel within the UK.

Annual grant total

In 2010/11 the foundation had an income of £16,000 and a total expenditure of £12,300.

Exclusions

Grants cannot be given for:

- Professional fees of any kind, including club membership, or club fees
- Travel outside the UK
- Scholarships, summer/winter/training camps

- Equipment that is available for use elsewhere
- Overnight accommodation

Applications

Application forms can be downloaded from the foundation's website along with guidelines. Applicants need to show that they are unable to raise the finance necessary through any other means. Applications also need to be supported by two independent referees. The trustees meet every two months in February, April, June, August, October and December to consider applications which should be submitted one month before a meeting.

The R. and D. Burchett Charitable Foundation
See entry on page 79

The Monica Elwes Shipway Sporting Foundation

£2,000

Correspondent: S Goldring, RadcliffesLeBrasseur, 5 Great College Street, Westminster, London SW1P 3SJ (020 7227 7290)

Trustees: Simon Goldring; Gillian Williams.

CC Number: 1054362

Eligibility

Schoolchildren and university students engaged in sporting activities who live in England and Wales and have limited resources.

Types of grants

One-off grants ranging from £100 to £250 to schoolchildren and students towards school clothing, equipment and fees.

Annual grant total

In 2010/11 the trust had an income of £1,600 and an expenditure of £2,900.

Applications

In writing to the correspondent, for consideration throughout the year.

The Brian Johnston Memorial Trust

£12,000 (16 grants)

Correspondent: Tim Berg, c/o The Lord's Taverners, 10 Buckingham Place, London SW1E 6HX (020 7821 2828; email: tim.berg@lordstaverners.org; website: www.lordstaverners.org)

Trustees: Jonathan Rice; Christopher Jenkins; Nigel Seale; The Lords Taverners.

CC Number: 1045946

Eligibility

Young 'promising' cricketers between the ages of 11 and 19 who are in need of financial assistance to further their personal and cricketing development.

Types of grants

Scholarships of £500 for young cricketers.

Annual grant total

In 2010/11 the trust had assets of £33,000 and an income of £70,000. Scholarships totalling £12,000 were given to 16 individuals.

Applications

In writing to the correspondent. Scholarships are awarded on the recommendation of the ECB Performance Department.

Other information

The trust also makes grants to cricket associations to support visually impaired and blind cricketers.

The John Taylor Foundation for Young Athletes

£1,000

Correspondent: Kirstin Bailey, 1 Smithy Fold, Rushton Spencer, Macclesfield, Cheshire SK11 0SD (01260 226694; email: enquiries@johntaylorfoundation.org.uk; website: www.johntaylorfoundation.org.uk)

Trustees: Timothy Williams; Kirstin Bailey; Christopher Cariss; David Hodgson.

CC Number: 1101008

Eligibility

Young amateur athletes based within the UK, with a preference for fell runners.

Types of grants

Grants given include those towards equipment and travel costs.

Annual grant total

In 2010/11 the foundation had an income of £200 and an expenditure of £1,000.

Applications

On a form which can be downloaded from the trust's website. Applications are considered twice a year.

Other information

The other aim of this foundation is to promote awareness of cardiomyopathy.

The Torch Trophy Trust

£12,000

Correspondent: Angela Sasso, 4th Floor, Burwood House, 14–16 Caxton Street, London SW1H 0QT (020 7976 3900; fax: 020 7976 3901; email: angela.sasso@ torchtrophytrust.org; website: www. torchtrophytrust.org)

Trustees: Mark Day; Sir Richard Buckley; Dame Mary Peters; Christopher Baillieu; Christine Janes; Patricia Day; Roger Uttley; Nicholas Adamson; Ian Peacock; Jimmy Hill; John James; Mike Denness; Barry Newcombe; Derek Ufton; Paul Dimond; Sallie Barker; Ray Kiddell.

CC Number: 306115

Eligibility

Volunteers for sports organisations who want to improve their skills and whose governing body is keen to help out but is unable to provide the necessary funding.

Types of grants

In most cases, the minimum bursary would be £100 and the maximum £1,000, and it would not be for more than 50% of the total costs involved. Exceptional applications may be considered for grants outside these guidelines. Grants are mostly made for courses to qualify as coaches, officials or administrators.

Annual grant total

Bursaries and awards are made each year totalling around £12,000.

Applications

On an application form available from the correspondent, or from the trust's website. A supporting letter from the relevant Governing Body must be included.

Stationery

The Stationers' Foundation
See entry on page 68

Surveying

Company of Chartered Surveyors 1991 Trust

£16,000

Correspondent: Amanda Jackson, 75 Meadway Drive, Horsell, Woking, Surrey GU21 4TF (01483 727113; fax: 01483 720098; email: wccsurveyors@ btinternet.com; website: www. surveyorslivery.org.uk)

Trustee: The Worshipful Company of Chartered Surveyors.

CC Number: 1012227

Eligibility

Further and higher education students of the surveying profession who live in the UK.

Types of grants

One-off grants ranging from £100 to £500 for books, fees and maintenance/ living expenses.

Annual grant total

In 2011 there were bursaries awarded totalling £16,000.

Applications

In writing to the correspondent. Applications can be submitted at any time in the year directly by the individual or through the individual's college, university or educational establishment. Letters of support from the individual's tutor or head of department must be provided. Applications are considered quarterly, in January, March, June and September.

Other information

This trust also gives grants to universities to be given to students as prizes.

Teaching

All Saints Educational Trust

£317,000

Correspondent: Stephen Harrow, Clerk, Suite 8C, First Floor, VSC Charity Centre, Royal London House, 22–25 Finsbury Square, London EC2A 1DX (020 7920 6465; fax: 020 7261 9758; email: aset@aset.org.uk; website: www.aset.org.uk)

Trustees: Diane McCrea; Peter Hartley; Keith Riglin; David Trillo; Clive Wright; Barbara Harvey; Augur Pearce; Antony Leeds; Stephan Welch; Stephanie Valentine; Joanna Moriarty; Robert Gwynne; Frances Smith; Anna Cumbers; Michael Jacob; Stephen Brooker.

CC Number: 312934

Eligibility

People aged 18 or over who are training to be teachers, or are connected with education, in home economics or related subjects, and in religious subjects including multi-cultural and inter-faith matters. Applicants must be UK or EU citizens at UK institutions. Serving teachers who are seeking further relevant qualifications are also supported.

Types of grants

One-off and recurrent grants are given to help with fees, maintenance, books and travel costs. The trust only gives partial funding. Students on part-time or one-year courses take preference over people on longer courses. Grants usually range from £300 to £10,000.

Annual grant total

In 2010/11 the trust had assets of £9.7 million and an income of £382,000. Grants were made totalling £317,000.

Exclusions

No grants are made people who are: classified as an overseas student (grants to overseas students who are Commonwealth citizens, engaged in one-year courses at postgraduate level, enrolled in a UK higher education institution can be assisted); under 18 years of age; hoping to have a career in business/management, engineering, law, medicine, nursery nursing, social or welfare care; intending to train for ordination; requesting a Sabbatical period; or eligible for government assistance, such as an NHS bursary.

Applications

On an initial form available from the website, or by sending an A4 sae to the correspondent. Once it has been verified that the candidate is eligible, a full application form will be sent. The closing date for this completed form is 31 March. Applicants are advised to complete the initial form as early as possible as extensions to the final deadline are only made at the clerk's discretion.

The Bell Educational Trust Ltd

£6,000

Correspondent: Chief Executive, Hillscross, Red Cross Lane, Cambridge CB2 3QX (01223 275520; email: lynda. connon@bell-centres.com; website: www. bell-centres.com)

Trustees: Peter Smith; Ellen Fleming; John Robinson; Andrew Fellowes; Robert Baird; Nicholas Tellwright; Eileen Milner.

CC Number: 311585

Eligibility

Funds are used for providing opportunities for the English language learning and teacher training to students and teachers from overseas who would not otherwise have the chance to benefit from this educational opportunity. Providing scholarships is only a small part of the trust's activities.

Types of grants

Attendance at a relevant Bell course.

Annual grant total

Educational grants to individuals tend to be small, with around £6,000 available each year.

Applications

In writing to the correspondent or via the ESU or British Council.

The Hockerill Educational Foundation
See entry on page 14

Textiles

The British Cotton Growing Association: Work People's Collection Fund

£32,000

Correspondent: Steven Delderfield, Research Office, Christies Building, University of Manchester, Oxford Road, Manchester M13 9PL (01612 758204; email: steven.delderfield@manchester.ac.uk; website: www.campus.manchester.ac.uk/researchoffice/finding/cotton)

Trustees: Alan Bond; Keith Burdett; David Colman; Roger Green.

CC Number: 509075

Eligibility

Anyone, including postgraduates, undertaking approved study and/or research of a medical, nursing or social nature beneficial to workers in the UK textile industry.

Types of grants

Research grants, of up to £30,000 per year, for approved study or research of a medical, nursing or social nature which will benefit the industry, including PhD studentships. The association also considers fees, maintenance costs and foreign students living and studying in the UK.

Annual grant total

In 2010/11 the trust had assets of £1.7 million and an income of £42,000. Grants made to individuals to support research totalled £32,000.

Applications

In writing to the correspondent. Applications (one to two pages) should include full details of the proposed research, background, relevant publications, costings and the names of two referees. Applications should be submitted by mid-April for consideration in May.

Coats Foundation Trust

£25,000

Correspondent: Mrs S MacNicol, Secretary, Coats Pensions Office, Pension Office, Pacific House, 70 Wellington Street, Glasgow G2 6UB (01412 076820; email: andrea.mccutcheon@coats.com)

Trustee: The Coats Trustee Company Ltd.

CC Number: 268735

Eligibility

University students living in the UK who are studying textile and thread-related subjects. Those with long-term futures in the UK and without a previous degree are prioritised by the trust.

Types of grants

One-off grants according to need. Grants are made to college students, undergraduates and mature students for fees, books and equipment/instruments. Schoolchildren may also receive grants for books and equipment/instruments.

Annual grant total

In 2010/11 the trust had an income of £21.000 and an expenditure of £48,000.

Applications

In writing to the correspondent enclosing a CV, an sae, details of circumstances (e.g. student status, name of college), the nature and amount of funding required and referee names and addresses. There is no formal application form. Only applicants enclosing an sae will receive a reply. Applications are considered four times a year.

Other information

Grants are also made to organisations and to individuals for welfare purposes.

Henry Dixon's Foundation for Apprenticing
See entry on page 74

The Weavers' Company Textile Education Fund

£30,000

Correspondent: The Clerk, The Worshipful Company of Weavers, Saddlers' House, Gutter Lane, London EC2V 6BR, The Worshipful Company of Weavers, Saddlers' House, Gutter Lane, London EC2V 6BR (email: clerk@weavers.org.uk; website: www.weavers.org.uk)

Trustee: Bailiffs Wardens and Assistants of the Worshipful Company of Weavers.

CC Number: 266189

Eligibility

Students of weaving technology or design attending six specified centres of excellence: Central St Martins College of Art and Design, Chelsea College of Art and Design, Glasgow School of Art, Loughborough University, Royal College of Art and University of Manchester. Students of weaving technology or design. Applications are invited from undergraduates who have completed at least one year of study and from postgraduate students. Applicants must be British.

Types of grants

Scholarships usually of £1,000 to £4,000.

Annual grant total

Around £30,000 is allocated for scholarships each year.

Applications

Applications must be supported by a reference from the course tutor and be submitted to the student's head of department for approval, counter signature and submission. The company will not accept direct applications. Applicants will be informed of a decision in December.

Other information

Grants are also made to educational establishments in the UK to encourage the quality of textile teaching.

Wine making

The Wine Guild Charitable Trust

£1,000

Correspondent: Jane Grey-Edwards, Council Secretary, Christmas Cottage, North Street, Petworth, West Sussex GU28 0DF (01798 345262; email: jgrey-edwards@tiscali.co.uk)

Trustee: Wine Guild Trustees Ltd.

CC Number: 1105374

Eligibility

Individuals wishing to further their studies in the wine making industry.

Types of grants

Grants, loans or bursaries.

Annual grant total

About £1,000.

Applications

In writing to the correspondent.

Work/study overseas

The English Speaking Union

£957,000 (144 grants)

Correspondent: The Clerk, Dartmouth House, 37 Charles Street, London W1J 5ED (020 7529 1550; email: esu@esu.org)

Trustee: The Board of Governors.

CC Number: 273136

Eligibility

People involved in teaching the English language overseas and other education-related or cross-cultural projects. There are scholarships relating to the clergy, library professionals and scientists, teachers and students of various subjects.

Types of grants

The union administers a number of grant and scholarship awards for young people, often in the form of travel scholarships. For details of individual funds, applicants are advised to refer to the website and approach the union.

Annual grant total

In 2010/11 expenditure on scholarships and other educational programmes totalled £957,000.

Applications

Applications vary for the different scholarships; applicants should refer to the website and contact the union for information on how to apply.

Other information

Applicants will be invited to interview.

Go Make it Happen

See entry on page 10

Local charities

This section lists local charities that give grants to individuals for educational purposes within a specific area. The information in each entry applies only to educational grants and not to other work that the charity may do for relief in need or with organisations; however, it will state in the entry if grants are given for other purposes. The information is concentrated on what a charity actually does rather than what its trust deed allows it to do, as this is a more realistic picture of how charities fund.

All of the entries give at least £500 a year to individuals for educational purposes, most considerably more than this.

Regional classification

We have divided the UK into nine geographical areas, as numbered on the map on page 112. Scotland, Wales and England have been separated into areas and counties in a similar way to previous editions of this guide. On page 113 we have included a list under each such area or county of the unitary and local authorities they include.

The Northern Ireland section has not been subdivided into smaller areas as there are a limited number of trusts in that section. Within the other sections, the trusts are ordered as follows.

Scotland
- Firstly, the charities which apply to the whole of Scotland, or to at least two areas in Scotland.
- Secondly, Scotland is sub-divided into five areas. The entries which apply to the whole area, or to at least two unitary authorities within, appear first.
- The rest of the charities in the area are listed in alphabetical order of unitary authority.

Wales
- Firstly, the charities which apply to the whole of Wales, or to at least two areas in Wales.
- Secondly, Wales is sub-divided into three areas. The entries which apply to the whole area, or to at least two unitary authorities within, appear first.
- The rest of the charities in the area are listed in alphabetical order of unitary authority.

England
- Firstly, the charities which apply to the whole area, or to at least two counties in the area.
- Secondly, each area is sub-divided into counties. The entries which apply to the whole county, or to at least two towns within it, appear first.
- The rest of the charities in the county are listed in alphabetical order of parish, town or city.

Please note, in the North East section, we have included a section called Teesside incorporating Hartlepool, Stockton-on-Tees, Middlesbrough and Redcar & Cleveland.

London
- Firstly, the charities which apply to the whole of Greater London, or to at least two boroughs.
- Secondly, London is sub-divided into the boroughs. The entries are listed in alphabetical order within each borough.

In summary, within each county or area section, the trusts in Scotland and Wales are arranged alphabetically by the unitary or local authority which they benefit, while in England they are listed by the city, town or parish, and in London, by borough.

To ensure you identify every relevant local charity, look first at the entries under the heading for your:
- Unitary authority, for people in Scotland and Wales
- City, town or parish under the relevant regional chapter heading, for people living in England
- Borough, for people living in London

People in London should then go straight to the start of the London chapter, where trusts which give to individuals in more than one borough in London are listed.

Other individuals should look at the sections for trusts which give to more than one unitary authority or town before finally considering those trusts at the start of the chapter that make grants across different areas or counties in your country or region.

Having found the trusts in your area, ensure that you read any other eligibility requirements – most trusts have other criteria that applicants must meet.

Geographical areas

Northern Ireland

General

Aisling Bursaries

£30,000

Correspondent: Tina McCann, West Belfast Partnership Board, 218–226 Falls Road, Belfast BT12 6AH (02890 809202; email: info@wbpb.org; website: aislingbursaries.com)

Eligibility

Students aged over 18 who live in the West Belfast Westminster Parliamentary Electoral Constituency. Applicants must be preparing to study or be currently studying on a full-time or part-time further education, higher education or vocational training course. Special consideration is given to candidates who have significant barriers preventing them from realising their full potential, for example economic or family circumstances.

Types of grants

Grants of £1,000 for a full time bursary and £500 for a part time bursary are available.

Annual grant total

In 2011/12 there were 38 bursaries of £1,000 or £500 given to individuals.

Exclusions

Grants are not available to current students who are repeating part or all of an academic year unless this has been formally agreed on the basis of medical or personal circumstances. Previous recipients of a full time bursary cannot re-apply but previous applicants are welcome to.

Applications

On a form available from the correspondent or the West Belfast Partnership Board website. Deadlines are usually in June/July and are advertised in the Andersonstown News and on the West Belfast Partnership website.

Other information

Local businesses in West Belfast contribute the funds that make these bursaries.

The Belfast Association for the Blind

£16,000

Correspondent: R Gillespie, Hon. Secretary, 30 Glenwell Crescent, Newtownabbey, County Antrim BT36 7TF (02890 836407)

IR Number: XN45086

Eligibility

People who are registered blind in Northern Ireland. Consideration may also be given to those registered as partially sighted.

Types of grants

One-off grants for educational needs such as computers, course fees and so on. Grants are also given for welfare purposes.

Annual grant total

Previously around £16,000 was given in grants to individuals.

Applications

In writing to the correspondent through a social worker. Applications are considered throughout the year.

Other information

Grants are also made to organisations.

Thomas Devlin Fund

£6,600 (8 grants)

Correspondent: Community Foundation for Northern Ireland, Community House, Citylink Business Park, Albert Street, Belfast BT12 4HQ (02890 245927; email: info@communityfoundationni. org; website: www. communityfoundationni.org)

Trustees: Tony McCusker; Les Allamby; Barbary Cook; Mike Bamber; Maurna Crozier; Geraldine Donaghy; Brian Dougherty; Sammy Douglas.

Eligibility

Young people aged 15 to 19 residing in Northern Ireland who wish to pursue specific arts programmes.

Types of grants

Bursary awards of £500 to £1,500 to enable young people to develop their career in the arts field.

Annual grant total

In 2011 the fund made eight grants to individuals totalling £6,600.

Applications

Information will be available on the Community Foundation for Northern Ireland's website when the fund is open to applications, usually end of April until end of June in each year.

Other information

This fund was set up in memory of Belfast teenager Thomas Devlin and has its own website www.thomasdevlin.com. The fund is administered by the Community Foundation for Northern Ireland which also administers a number of funds for organisations.

Educational Trust

£1,000

Correspondent: Heather Reid, Amelia House, 4 Amelia Street, Belfast BT2 7GS (02890 320157; fax: 0870 432 1415; email: heather@niacro.co.uk; website: www.niacro.co.uk)

Trustee: Executive Committee of NIACRO.

IR Number: XN48280

Eligibility

Ex-prisoners, ex-offenders and their immediate relatives from Ireland who are seeking access to education and/or training and for whom no other sources of funding are available.

Types of grants

The Educational Trust is a North/South charitable Trust which helps ex-offenders and ex-prisoners in Ireland to access education and training. The trust helps ex-offenders to complete academic qualifications and vocational training upon leaving prison. One-off and recurrent grants are offered towards degrees, postgraduate qualifications, NVQs and HGV driving licenses. The client group has also been extended to include all offenders and ex-prisoners and their families, and the coverage includes the whole of Ireland.

Annual grant total

About £1,000 is given in grants each year.

Exclusions

No grants are made towards computer hardware, capital equipment or setting-up costs of small business initiatives.

Applications

On a form available from the correspondent. They are considered every four to six weeks.

Other information

The foundation's main activities are supporting ex-offenders and their relatives.

EMMS International

£9,500 (28 grants)

Correspondent: Joe Cooney, Office Manager, 7 Washington Lane, Edinburgh EH11 2HA (01313 133828; fax: 01313 134662; email: info@emms.org; website: www.emms.org)

Trustees: John Andrew; Philip Brookes; Peter Brown; Carol Finlay; Manish Joshi; Crispin Longden; Angus McLeod; Christopher Mackay; Joan McDowell; Helen Paxton.

SC Number: SC032327

Eligibility

Medical, nursing, dental and therapy (i.e. physiotherapy, occupational therapy) students at universities in Scotland, Northern Ireland or developing countries who are undertaking a placement abroad for their elective period in a mission hospital in a developing country. Preference is given to those with an 'active Christian testimony' and who are involved in a college, university or hospital Christian fellowship.

Types of grants

Bursaries usually range from £200 to £300; however more may be awarded to applicants working in one of the trusts partnership hospitals in India, Israel, Malawi or Nepal.

Annual grant total

In 2011 the trust had an income of £818,000 and made grants totalling £9,500 to 28 students.

Exclusions

Students studying at universities in England and Wales are not eligible. The trust cannot be held responsible for assessing the suitability of any proposed elective, nor organise electives or provide elective training.

Applications

Application forms can be obtained through the website and can be submitted at any time of the year. Applications should be made at least three months prior to the start of the elective and typically take six to eight weeks to be processed. Successful applicants will receive their bursaries four weeks prior to an elective starting.

References are required from two referees, with one preferably as a contact from the local church such as a minister or an elder.

Other information

The trust states that 'Grants are not awarded solely on the basis of academic merit, but rather on your desire to experience healthcare in a mission context'.

The trust also funds mission hospitals and schools, community health projects, primary health care and staff and volunteer training and education in developing countries.

Grants are also given from this trust to enable individuals suffering, or recovering from a serious illness, to have a recuperative holiday.

Fermanagh Recreational Trust

Correspondent: Charlene Black, Executive Secretary, The Fermanagh Trust, Fermanagh House, Broadmeadow Place, Enniskillen BT74 7HR (02866 320210; fax: 02866 320230; email: charlene@fermanaghtrust.org; website: www.fermanaghtrust.org)

Trustees: Joanna McVey; Kathleen Richey; Jim Ledwith; Frank McManus; Aideen McGinley; David Bolton; Ernie Fisher.

CC Number: XR 22580

Eligibility

Individuals based in County Fermanagh.

Types of grants

Grants for equipment, training and other costs associated with assisting individuals to develop their potential, particularly through recreation and sport.

Annual grant total

No grants total was available.

Applications

On a form available to download from the website which should be submitted by 28 February or 31 August. Two independent references should also be included.

Other information

This fund is administered by the Fermanagh Trust which also administers funds for organisations for a variety of purposes in Fermanagh.

The Presbyterian Orphan and Children's Society

£250,000

Correspondent: Dr Paul Gray, Glengall Exchange, 3 Glengall Street, Belfast BT12 5AB (02890 323737; fax: 02890 434352; email: paul-gray@presbyterianorphanandchildrens society.org; website: www.presbyterianorphanandchildrens society.org)

Trustees: His Honour J. McKee; Revd P. P. Campbell; Dr G. D. B. Harkness; Mr B. Corry; Revd T. R. Graham; Very Revd Dr S. Hutchinson; Mrs V. McGuffin; Revd P. A. McBride; Mr N. W. Todd; Judge J. A. H. Martin; Mrs L. Yates; Mrs W. R. Wilson; Mr R. Orr; Revd Dr J. I. Thompson; Mrs H. Morrow.

IR Number: XN45522

Eligibility

Children aged 23 or under who are in full or part-time education, living in Northern Ireland and Republic of Ireland, usually in single parent families. One parent must be a Presbyterian.

Types of grants

Regular grants paid each quarter. Depending on financial resources, a summer grant and Christmas grant is paid to each family. Exceptional grants of up to £300 (very occasionally up to £500) are also available.

Annual grant total

Around £500,000 per year.

Applications

Applications are made by Presbyterian clergy; forms are available from the correspondent or to download from the website. They are considered in April and October. As recurrent grants are means tested, applications should be submitted with details of the applicant's income and expenditure. Any application for an exceptional grant must be made on the 'Exceptional Grant' application form.

The Royal Ulster Constabulary Benevolent Fund

£800,000

Correspondent: The Secretary, Police Federation for Northern Ireland, 77–79 Garnerville Road, Belfast BT4 2NX (02890 764215; email: info@ rucbenevolentfund.org; website: www. rucgc-psnibenevolentfund.com)

IR Number: XN 48380

Eligibility

Ex-members of the Royal Ulster Constabulary and their dependents who are experiencing financial hardship. The main objectives being to look after widows and their dependents, injured and disabled officers, pensioners, parents of deceased officers and serving PSNI officers experiencing financial hardship or difficulty.

Types of grants

Support is given to schoolchildren, college students, undergraduates, mature students, people with special educational needs and overseas students towards uniforms, fees, study/travel overseas, books and equipment.

Annual grant total

About £800,000.

Applications

Initial contact should be made with the central point of contact who will advise the applicant on which of the police organisations is most appropriate to offer support in their circumstances. Contact may be made by calling 02890 768686 or emailing office@northernirelandpolicefamilyassist-ance.org.uk with a brief outline of your circumstances. All applicants will be visited by a fund representative in order to prepare a case to present to the committee at their monthly meeting.

The Society for the Orphans and Children of Ministers and Missionaries of the Presbyterian Church in Ireland

£15,000

Correspondent: Paul Gray, Church House, Fisherwick Place, Belfast BT1 6TW (02890 323737)

Eligibility

Children and young people aged under 26 who are orphaned and whose parents were ministers, missionaries or deaconesses of the Presbyterian Church in Ireland.

Types of grants

One-off grants of £300 to £2,000 for general educational purposes.

Annual grant total

Grants to individuals for educational and welfare purposes total about £30,000.

Applications

On a form available from the correspondent. Applications should be submitted directly by the individual in March for consideration in April.

Other information

The trust also gives welfare grants to the children of deceased ministers, missionaries and deaconesses.

Scotland

General

The Arrol Trust

See entry on page 16

The Avenel Trust

£5,000

Correspondent: Administrator, 23 West Ferryfield, Edinburgh EH5 2PT

SC Number: SC014280

Eligibility

Children in need under 18 and students of nursery nursing living in Scotland.

Types of grants

One-off grants of £10 to £500 are given for safety items such as fireguards and safety gates, shoes, clothing, bedding, cots and pushchairs, money for bus passes, recreational activities for young carers and washing machines.

Annual grant total

In 2010 the trust had an income of £11,000.

Exclusions

Grants are not given for holidays or household furnishings.

Applications

Applications are considered every two months and should be submitted through a tutor or third party such as a social worker, health visitor or teacher. Applicants are encouraged to provide as much information about their family or individual circumstances and needs as possible in their applications. Applications can only be accepted from people currently residing in Scotland.

The June Baker Trust

£19,000 (47 grants)

Correspondent: Priscilla Ramsey, 9 Kirk Wynd, Cupar, Fife KY15 5AW (email: ramseyph@tiscali.co.uk)

Trustees: John Cotterill; Antony Ramsden; David Munro; J. Reader; Leon Lovett; Robert Porter.

CC Number: 1086222

Eligibility

Individuals working in the conservation of historic and artistic artifacts in Scotland, or those training to do so.

Types of grants

Awards of £200 to £500 each will be available for travel, training, fees, purchase of equipment, short courses and other suitable projects to students, mature and vocational students and people starting work.

Annual grant total

In 2010 the trust had an income of £1,200.

Exclusions

Fees for long, full-time courses are not given.

Applications

On a form available from the correspondent. Applicants may have to attend an interview. A CV and two referees should also be provided. Applications are considered in June, and should be submitted directly by the individual.

The Black Watch Association

£75,000

Correspondent: Maj. A R McKinnell, Balhousie Castle, Hay Street, Perth PH1 5HR (01738 623214; fax: 01738 643245; email: bwassociation@btconnect. com; website: www.theblackwatch.co.uk)

SC Number: SC016423

Eligibility

Serving and retired Black Watch soldiers, their wives, widows and children.

Types of grants

One-off grants ranging from £250 to £500. Grants can be made to schoolchildren, people starting work and students in further/higher education for equipment/instruments, fees, books and maintenance/living expenses.

Annual grant total

In 2010 the trust had an income of £158,000.

Exclusions

No grants towards council tax arrears, loans or large debts.

Applications

On an application form to be completed by a caseworker from SSAFA Forces Help (19 Queen Elizabeth Street, London SE1 2LP. Tel: 020 7403 8783; Fax: 020 7403 8815; Website: www.ssafa. org.uk). Applications are considered on a monthly basis.

The Buchanan Society

£25,000

Correspondent: The Secretary, 1F Pollockshields Square, Glencairn Drive, Pollockshields, Glasgow G41 4QT

SC Number: SC013679

Eligibility

People with any of the following surnames: Buchanan, McAuslan (any spelling), McWattie or Risk.

Types of grants

Bursaries for students in severe financial difficulties of about £1,000. One-off grants can also be given for general educational purposes.

Annual grant total

In 2010 the society had an income of £51,000. Around 70 people are supported each year. Grants are also made for welfare purposes.

Applications

On a form available from the correspondent, to be submitted either directly by the individual or a family member, or through a third party such as a social worker or teacher. Applications are considered throughout the year.

Other information

The Buchanan Society is the oldest Clan Society in Scotland having been founded in 1725. Grantmaking is its sole function.

The Carnegie Trust for the Universities of Scotland

£1.7 million

Correspondent: The Secretary, Andrew Carnegie House, Pittencrief Street, Dunfermline, Fife KY12 8AW (01383 724990; fax: 01383 749799; email: jgray@carnegie-trust.org; website: www.carnegie-trust.org)

Trustees: David Edward; Louise Adams; Janet Morgan; Richard Burns; Kenneth Cameron; John Kerr; Janet Lowe; Eileen Mackay; Iain McMillan; Charles Robertson; Judith Sischy; David Smith; Ian Sword; David Wilson.

SC Number: SC015600

Eligibility

For fee assistance: undergraduates taking a first degree at a Scottish university who were born in Scotland, or had a parent born in Scotland, or have had at least two years of secondary education in Scotland.

For university expeditions: the expedition must have a coherent programme of research and must not comprise a number of unrelated individual research projects. To qualify for a grant, an expedition must be sponsored by, and given the name of, the appropriate Scottish university or combination of universities, and must receive some material support in money or equipment. The trust will give preference to expeditions that are multi-disciplinary; but this is not a requirement.

Scholarships: graduates of a Scottish university holding a degree with first-class honours in any subject and intending to pursue three years of postgraduate research for a PhD degree at a UK university.

Small research grants: members of staff or, on a discretionary basis, retired members of staff of a Scottish university for personal research, personally conducted.

Types of grants

Fee assistance: help with tuition fees for a first degree course at a Scottish university.

University expeditions: expeditions which are approved and supported by a Scottish university.

Scholarships: the value of the scholarship/stipend for the 2010/11 academic year was £15,000; this figure is expected to rise in future academic years in line with awards funded by the Research Councils.

Small research grants: up to £2,200 can be awarded for travel and accommodation, for up to three months, incurred while undertaking the project. Assistance can also be given with the publication of scholarly books.

Postgraduate schemes are also available, see the website for details.

Annual grant total

In 2010/11 the trust had assets of £52 million and an income of £2.5 million. Awards through all schemes totalled £1.7 million.

Applications

Directly by the individual, on a form available from the correspondent or the website. A preliminary telephone call may be helpful. Applications are considered as follows:

Fee assistance: applications are considered from 1 April to 1 October for assistance with fees for the following academic year.

University expeditions: applications must be received by 15 January.

Scholarships: applications must be received by 15 March.

Small research grants: the closing dates for applications are 15 January, 15 May and 15 October.

Other information

Large grants for research are also given to Scottish universities for collaborative projects (£158,000 in 2010/11).

Churchill University Scholarships Trust for Scotland
See entry on page 17

Creative Scotland – Professional Development Fund

£134,000 (37 grants)

Correspondent: Laura MacKenzie-Stuart, Portfolio Manager, Waverley Gate, 2–4 Waterloo Place, Edinburgh EH1 3EG (0845 603 6000; email: professionaldevelopment@creativescotland.com; website: www.creativescotland.com)

Eligibility

People working at professional level in the arts, screen and creative industries based in Scotland.

Types of grants

Awards of £500 to £15,000 for personal professional development, to accelerate individual talent and release potential.

Annual grant total

From April to December 2011 the trust gave awards to 37 individuals totalling £134,000.

Exclusions

No awards for individuals in permanent employment within foundation organisations, flexibly funded organisations or national companies and collections. Applications from students, architects/designers, academics amateur companies will not be accepted.

Applications

On a form available from the website along with full guidelines, including a CV and any supporting material such as audio or video. Applications should only be submitted by email in word format. The fund is open to applications all year round.

The Cross Trust

£129,000 (98 grants)

Correspondent: Kathleen Carnegie, 25 South Methven Street, Perth PH1 5ES (01738 620451; fax: 01738 631155; email: kathleencarnegie@mccash.co.uk; website: www.thecrosstrust.org.uk)

SC Number: SC008620

Eligibility

Young people aged 16 to 30 who are of Scottish birth or parentage proposing 'a study or project that will extend the boundaries of their knowledge of human life.'

Applicants must be in genuine financial need.

Types of grants

Grants of £200 to £2,800 for university or college costs (some courses are subject to restrictions), grants for travel and study abroad in respect of approved projects, and support for vacation projects and study visits. The trustees will consider proposals from university students for study at an overseas institution. Attendance at conferences, symposia and extra-curricular courses can be considered. Voluntary work performed through a recognised charity, such as gap year activities, can also be funded.

Annual grant total

In 2010 91 grants were awarded to individuals totalling £129,000.

Applications

On a form including a passport photo available from the correspondent or the website, with guidelines. Trustees meet four times a year in March, February, June and November. It can take up to three months for a final decision to be made.

Other information

Grants totalling £16,000 were awarded to six organisations.

EMMS International
See entry on page 116

The Esdaile Trust

£28,000

Correspondent: R Graeme Thom, Exchange Place 3, Semple Street, Edinburgh EH3 8BL (email: graeme. thom@scott-moncrieff.com; website: www.scott-moncrieff.com/charitable_trusts/page2.html)

SC Number: SC006938

Eligibility

Ministers of the Church of Scotland or Deaconesses of the Church of Scotland who are widows and missionaries appointed or nominated by the Overseas Council of the Church of Scotland with daughters at secondary school and university.

Daughters should normally be between 12 and 25 years of age and preference is given to families with a low income.

Types of grants

Annual grants towards the cost of education, ranging between £100 and £800.

Annual grant total

In 2010/11 the trust had an income of £23,000 and an expenditure of £33,000. Approximately £28,000 is available to distribute each year.

Applications

Application forms can be obtained from the website and should be completed and returned to the correspondent.

Applications should be submitted by no later than 31 May each year and grants are distributed by early September.

The Ferguson Bequest

£1,500

Correspondent: Ronald D Oakes, Secretary, 182 Bath Street, Glasgow G2 4HG

SC Number: SC009305

Eligibility

Ministers, or people intending to become ministers, who live in south west Scotland.

Types of grants

Scholarships are given.

Annual grant total

In 2010/11 the trust had an income of £156,000. Previously only a small proportion of grants have been given to individuals.

Applications

On a form available by writing to the correspondent, to be considered at any time.

The Caroline Fitzmaurice Trust

£2,300

Correspondent: The Secretaries, Pagan Osborne Solicitors, 12 St Catherine Street, Cupar, Fife KY15 4HN (01334 653777; fax: 01334 655063; email: enquiries@pagan.co.uk)

SC Number: SC00518

Eligibility

Young women under the age of 23 who live in the diocese of St Andrews, Dunkeld and Dunblane. Broadly speaking, the diocese covers the whole of Perthshire and Fife, part of Stirlingshire and a small part of Angus, including Forfar and the towns to the west of Forfar, but excluding Dundee.

The trust states that applicants must show both financial need and a good academic background.

Types of grants

Grants of between £200 and £5,000 are given if there is a specific need. The trust aims 'to assist applicants who show promise of future excellence in their educational, cultural or social fields; applicants are expected to show the intention, in their turn, to contribute to the community wherever they may settle; and are endeavouring to raise funds through their own personal efforts'.

Annual grant total

In 2010/11 the trust had an income of £15,000. Previously grants have totalled around £2,300.

Applications

On a form available from the correspondent. Written references and details of parents' financial situation are required. The trustees meet once a year. The closing date for full, complete applications (including referees' reports and reports on parents' means) is 30 April.

James Gillan's Trust

£2,000

Correspondent: Stewart Michael Murray, Solicitor, c/o R and R Urquhart, 121 High Street, Forres, Moray IV36 1AB (01309 672216)

SC Number: SC016739

Eligibility

People training for the ordained ministry in the Church of Scotland who have lived in, or whose parents have lived in, Moray or Nairn for at least three years. There is a preference for those native to the parishes of Forres and Dyke, Kinloss, Rafford, Edinkillie and Dallas.

Types of grants

Grants of up to £1,000.

Annual grant total

In 2010/11 the trust had an income of £47,000. The trust normally gives approximately £2,000 in grants to individuals each year.

Applications

In writing to the correspondent.

The Glasgow Highland Society

£9,000

Correspondent: The Secretaries, Alexander Sloan C A, 38 Cadogan Street, Glasgow G2 7HF (01413 540354; email: kt@alexandersloan.co.uk; website: www. alexandersloan.co.uk/ghs)

SC Number: SC015479

Eligibility

Students who have a connection with the Highlands (for example, lived or went to school there) and who are now studying in Glasgow. Grants are normally given for first degrees only, unless postgraduate studies are a natural progression of the degree.

Types of grants

Grants of around £75 help with fees for people at college or university or who are in vocational training (including mature students). Grants may also be given for Gaelic research projects and apprenticeships.

Annual grant total

In 2011 the trust had an income of £5,400 and an expenditure of £9,100.

Applications

On a form available from the correspondent. Applications should be submitted directly by the individual by 2 November and are considered in December.

Other information

The correspondent has informed us that the trust may be winding down; however a decision has not been made yet. Applications are still being accepted.

The Glasgow Society of the Sons and Daughters of Ministers of the Church of Scotland

£27,000

Correspondent: Janice Couper, Exchange Place, 3 Semple Street, Edinburgh EH3 8BL (website: www. scott-moncrieff.com/charitable_trusts)

SC Number: SC010281

Eligibility

Children of ministers of the Church of Scotland who are in need, particularly students and the children of deceased ministers.

Types of grants

One-off and recurrent grants according to need.

Annual grant total

About £55,000 per year is given in educational and welfare grants to individuals.

Applications

On a form available from the correspondent or downloaded from the website. Applications should be sent in no later than 31 May each year and grants are distributed by early September.

Other information

In 2011 forty grants were made in connection with university students ranging from £400 to £800 per annum.

The Grand Lodge of Ancient, Free and Accepted Masons of Scotland

£25,000

Correspondent: D M Begg, Grand Secretary, Freemasons Hall, 96 George Street, Edinburgh EH2 3DH (01312 255304; website: www. grandlodgescotland.com)

SC Number: SC001996

Eligibility

Children of members and deceased members.

Types of grants

Grants for people entering further education.

Annual grant total

In 2010/11 the trust had an income of £1.9 million. About £155,000 is given in welfare grants each year and £25,000 in educational grants.

Applications

On a form available from the correspondent, or by direct approach to the local lodge. They are considered three times a year, although urgent requests can be dealt with between meetings.

Other information

The trust also runs care homes for older people.

The Highlands and Islands Educational Trust Scheme

£7,000

Correspondent: The Trustees, c/o Tods Murray LLP, Edinburgh Quay, 133 Fountainbridge, Edinburgh EH3 9AG

SC Number: SC014655

Eligibility

Students living in the counties of Argyll, Bute, Caithness, Inverness, Orkney, Ross and Cromarty, Sutherland or Shetland and be of the Protestant faith. Applicants should be in the fifth or sixth form at school and about to leave to go on to university or other institution of further education. Preference is given to Gaelic speakers.

Types of grants

Grants of £120 to £160 a year are given to students about to study for a first degree at college/university, towards their university/college books and maintenance. Bursaries are awarded at

the discretion of the governors on merit, based on the results of the 'Higher' grade examinations. In determining the award, parental means are taken into account.

Annual grant total

In 2010/11 the trust had an income of £11,000. About £7,000 is given annually in grants to individuals.

Applications

In writing to the correspondent. Applications should be submitted through the individual's school between March and June inclusive and include: confirmation that the applicant is of the Protestant faith; details of the occupation and gross income of parent/ guardian; ability at Gaelic, if any; university/college course to be undertaken; and intended career of the applicant. Decisions are made in September.

Jewish Care Scotland

£18,000

Correspondent: Irene Black, Office Manager, The Walton Community Care Centre, May Terrace, Giffnock, Glasgow G46 6LD (01416 201800; fax: 01416 202409; email: admin@jcarescot.org.uk; website: www.jcarescot.org.uk)

Trustees: Maureen Solomons; David Bishop; George Hecht; Trevor Schuster-Davis; Lesley Roles; Natalie Cahif; Sylvia Cohen; Angela Hecht; Paul Morron; Oli Norman; Vivian Strang; Albert Tankel.

SC Number: SC005267

Eligibility

Schoolchildren, people starting work and students in further or higher education, including mature students, who are Jewish and live in Scotland.

Types of grants

One-off grants are given towards uniforms, other school clothing, equipment, instruments, fees, maintenance and living expenses. There is a preference for schoolchildren with serious family difficulties so that the child has to be educated away from home.

Annual grant total

Educational grants to individuals usually total around £18,000.

Exclusions

No grants are given to postgraduates.

Applications

In writing to the correspondent.

Other information

The board also helps with friendship clubs, housing requirements, clothing, meals-on-wheels, counselling and so on.

The Lethendy Trust

£3,000 (9 grants)

Correspondent: George Hay, Henderson Loggie, Chartered Accountants, Royal Exchange, Panmure Street, Dundee DD1 1DZ (01382 201234; fax: 01382 221240; email: ghay@hendersonloggie.co.uk)

Trustees: N. M. Sharp; W. Alexander; D. L. Laird; I. B. Rae; A. F. Thomson.

SC Number: SC003428

Eligibility

Young people with a strong connection to the Tayside or North Fife areas.

Types of grants

Grants of £150 to £400 for young people travelling abroad with charitable organisations to carry out charitable activities.

Annual grant total

In 2010/11 the trust gave £3,000 in nine grants to individuals.

Exclusions

No support to individuals for school fees or for purely academic based funding requests.

Applications

In writing to the correspondent. The trusts states that there are regular meetings throughout the year to consider applications.

Other information

£72,000 was given in grants to organisations during the year.

The Dr Thomas Lyon Bequest

£3,500 (3 grants)

Correspondent: The Secretary, The Merchant Company, The Merchants' Hall, 22 Hanover Street, Edinburgh EH2 2EP

Trustee: The Master's Court of the Company of Merchants of the City of Edinburgh.

SC Number: SC010284

Eligibility

Scottish orphans, aged 5 to 18, of members of Her Majesty's Forces and those of the Mercantile Marine, who are in need.

Types of grants

Grants are given towards primary and secondary education for school uniforms, other school clothing, books, educational outings and school fees. They range from £500 to £1,500.

Annual grant total

In 2010/11 the fund had assets of £226,000 and an income of £4,500 and made three awards totalling £3,500.

Applications

In writing to the correspondent. Applicants must state their total income, the regiment/service of their parent and the cause and date of their death.

The Catherine Mackichan Trust

£2,000

Correspondent: The Administrator, 2 Hutton Avenue, Houston, Renfrewshire PA6 7JS (website: www.mackichantrust.co.uk)

Trustees: Helen Brodley; David Breeze; M. Cook; D. Ferguson; Doreen Grove.

SC Number: SC020459

Eligibility

People who are researching various aspects of Scottish history, including archaeology, genealogy and language studies. Those attending a recognised academic conference on historical, genealogical, archaeological or related topics.

Types of grants

Grants of £200 to £500, more in exceptional circumstances, are given to: schoolchildren for books and educational outings; and students in further or higher education, including mature and overseas students, towards books and study or travel overseas. Grants are also given to postgraduate students, individuals without formal attachment to any institute of education and amateur historians.

Annual grant total

About £2,000.

Exclusions

No grants are given to people whose education or research should be funded by statutory sources. No grants for undergraduate or postgraduate fees or living expenses.

Applications

On a form available by submitting contact details on the website or by post-from the correspondent to be submitted between 1 January and 16 April. Grants will be awarded in June.

Other information

Grants are also given to schools and local history societies for local history and archaeological purposes.

Mathew Trust

£10,000

Correspondent: Fiona Bullions, Henderson Loggie, Chartered Accountants, Royal Exchange, Panmure Street, Dundee DD1 1DZ (email: fiona.bullions@hendersonloggie.co.uk)

SC Number: SC016284

Eligibility

Adults in need who live in the local government areas of the City of Dundee, Angus, Perth and Kinross and Fife.

Types of grants

One-off grants of up to £400 for study/travel abroad are given to college students, undergraduates, vocational students, mature students, people starting work, overseas students and people with special educational needs.

Annual grant total

About £10,000 to individuals.

Applications

In writing to the correspondent. Applications can be submitted directly by the individual for consideration every two months.

Other information

Grants are also made to organisations.

Maxton Bequest

Correspondent: Susan Raw, Admin Support Co-ordinator, Education Service 5th Floor, Fife Council, Rothesay House, Rothesay Place, Glenrothes KY7 5PQ (email: susan.raw@fife.gov.uk)

Eligibility

People ordinarily resident, or who have parents resident in Crieff or Kirkcaldy.

Types of grants

Grants of around £100 for clothing, books, equipment, educational outings in the UK, fees or living expenses for secondary school, further education, university, training or apprentices.

Applications

On a form available from the correspondent. The application deadline varies each year around end October/early November.

Other information

Not a registered charity.

The McGlashan Charitable Trust

£36,000

Correspondent: The Administrator, 11 Melrose Gardens, Glasgow G20 6RB

SC Number: SC020930

Eligibility

Students of music, other arts studies, medicine, veterinary science, architecture, law, together with science and technology, aged 16 to 30 with a preference for those who were born in, or are studying or working in, Scotland.

Types of grants

One-off and recurrent grants in the range of £250 and £1,000 are given to people in further or higher education, including mature, vocational and overseas students and undergraduates, towards fees, books, equipment, instruments and living expenses.

Annual grant total

In 2010/11 the trust had an income of £75,000. Previously around £36,000 has been given in grants to individuals.

Exclusions

No grants are given towards sports.

Applications

Initially, in writing to the correspondent directly by the individual. Initial applications must be comprehensive enough for trustees to decide on issuing a formal application form or not. Applications are considered at irregular times during the year.

Other information

Grants are also made to organisations.

The Muirhead Trust

£6,000

Correspondent: Franci Law LLP, 24 St Enoch Square, Glasgow G1 4DB (email: ann@franchilaw.co.uk; website: www.themuirheadtrust.org.uk)

SC Number: SC016524

Eligibility

Female students of Scottish origin, studying one of the following subjects at an institution in Scotland: medicine, veterinary science; pharmacy; nursing, dentistry, science or engineering.

Types of grants

Grants are for two years, after which the student is eligible for a statutory grant for the further three years.

Annual grant total

The trust has an annual income of around £6,000.

Exclusions

No grants for students studying biomedical or forensic science.

Applications

On a form available to download from the website which should be posted with a CV to the correspondent by 31 August.

North of Scotland Quaker Trust

£4,000

Correspondent: Marion Strachan, Treasurer, Quaker Meeting House, 98 Crown Street, Aberdeen AB11 6HJ

SC Number: SC000784

Eligibility

People who are associated with the Religious Society of Friends in the North of Scotland Monthly Meeting area and their dependents.

Types of grants

Grants are given to schoolchildren and to people studying in further or higher education for books, equipment, instruments and educational outings. Grants for travel and conferences are also available.

Annual grant total

In 2011 the trust had an income of £15,000 and an expenditure of £9,500.

Exclusions

No grants are given to people studying above first degree level.

Applications

In writing to the correspondent.

Other information

Grants are also given for welfare purposes.

Poppyscotland (The Earl Haig Fund Scotland)

£30,000

Correspondent: Charitable Services Department, New Haig House, Logie Green Road, Edinburgh EH7 4HR (01315 501557; email: GetHelp@ poppyscotland.org.uk; website: www. poppyscotland.org.uk)

SC Number: SC014096

Eligibility

People in Scotland of working-age who have served in the UK Armed Forces (regular or reserve) and are now unemployed, low-skilled or in low-paid employment.

Types of grants

One-off grants of up to £2,000 for training to improve employment prospects.

Annual grant total

In 2010/11 the fund had an income of £4.2 million. Grants were made to 1,360 individuals totalling £799,000, mostly for welfare purposes.

Applications

Application packs can be downloaded from the 'civvy street' website: www. civvystreet.org. Alternatively, contact Poppyscotland on 01315 501586 or email d.pringle@poppyscotland.org.uk for further information.

Other information

Poppyscotland is in many respects the Scottish equivalent of the benevolence department of the Royal British Legion in the rest of Britain. Like the legion, it runs the Poppy Appeal, which is a major source of income to help those in need. There is, however, a Royal British Legion Scotland, which has a separate entry in this guide. The two organisations share the same premises and work together.

In 2006 the Earl Haig Fund Scotland launched a new identity – 'Poppyscotland' – and is now generally known by this name.

Royal Caledonian Asylum

£112,000

Correspondent: James MacBain, Chief Executive, Unit 75 Wenta Business Park, Colne Way, Watford, Hertfordshire WD24 7ND (01923 215350; email: admin@rcst.org.uk; website: www.rcst. org.uk)

Trustees: Catriona Butler; David Cullens; Keith Robertson; Hugh Cowan; Ian Hunter; Dottie Strickland; James Robertson; Malcolm Noble.

CC Number: 310952

Eligibility

Dependents of Scottish people who have served or are serving in the Armed Forces. Preference is given to children and those in full time education including those returning to education. Support is also given to the children of Scottish people in financial need living in London

Types of grants

Grants for school clothing and uniforms, clothing and equipment for extracurricular activities, living expenses for further and higher education, books and equipment, after school clubs and activities, school trips, music and art training, gap year projects and in exceptional circumstances school fees.

The trust states that it views education in its widest sense and welcomes enquires from applicants who are unsure as to whether they can be helped.

Annual grant total

In 2010/11 the trust had assets of £4.3 million and an income of £298,000. Grants awarded totalled £112,000.

Applications

On a form available from the correspondent or to download from the trust's website. Applications are considered quarterly.

Other information

The trust is also involved in a number of initiatives connected with the education of Scottish service children, namely, the Education Programme (email Carolyn MacLeod at Edprogramme@rcst.org.uk).

Scotscare

£50,000

Correspondent: Isabel Dunlop, Team Leader- Caseworkers, 22 City Road, London EC1Y 2AJ (020 7240 3718; fax: 020 7256 6527; email: info@scotscare. com; website: www.scotscare.com)

Trustees: John Clemence; Stuart Steele; P. Scott; Peter Hay; Wylie Crawford White; Angus Gilroy; Fred Gray; Jock Meikle; Brian Griffin; David Couchtrie; Eben Hamilton; Etienne Duval; James Chestnut; Joyce Harvie; Graeme Wilson; Amanda Brock.

CC Number: 207326

Eligibility

Scottish people, their children and widows, who are in need and have lived within a 35-mile radius of Charing Cross for at least two years.

Types of grants

Training grants for fees, books and computers to enable people to secure qualifications with a view to gaining employment. Student grants for fees, books/equipment and maintenance. Grants are also given for school uniforms and trips.

Annual grant total

In 2010/11 the organisation had assets of £45 million and an income of £2.1 million. Grants to 1,346 individuals totalled £388,000, most of which was given for welfare purposes.

Exclusions

No grants are made for debts or for items that have already been purchased.

Applications

On a form available by contacting the organisation. After receiving the

completed form, which should include copies of the birth/wedding certificates, the corporation decides whether to submit the application for consideration at the trustees' monthly meeting. They may also decide to visit or ask the applicant to visit the corporation's office to discuss their case.

Other information

The organisation runs a dedicated helpline: 0800 652 2989.

The Scottish Chartered Accountants' Benevolent Association

£60,000

Correspondent: Robert Linton, Secretary, Robert Linton and Co., Suite 30, 2nd Floor, 53 Bothwell Street, Glasgow G2 6TS (01415 728465; fax: 01412 487456; email: mail@robertlinton. co.uk)

SC Number: SC008365

Eligibility

The dependents of members of the Institute of Chartered Accountants of Scotland who are in financial need.

Types of grants

One-off grants for a variety of needs. Recent grants have been given for school fees, maintenance expenses and retraining.

Annual grant total

Grants usually total about £120,000 each year.

Applications

An initial letter or telephone call should be made to the correspondent. A member of the fund will then make contact and arrange a visit if appropriate. Following this, an application, report and recommendation will be made to the fund's council for approval.

Other information

Grants are also made for welfare purposes.

Scottish International Education Trust

£20,000 (12 grants)

Correspondent: Gavin McEwan, Turcan Connell, Princes Exchange, 1 Earl Grey Street, Edinburgh EH3 9EE (email: siet@ turcanconnell.com; website: www. scotinted.org.uk)

Trustees: Andrew Irvine; Joseph Campbell; Menzies Campbell; Sean Connery; Lady Gibson; David Michie; Alexander Salmond; Gerda Stevenson;

Jackie Stewart; Stewart Sutherland; William Sweeney; Edward Davison; Ginnie Atkinson; George Donald.

SC Number: SC009207

Eligibility

Scottish people who wish to take their studies or training further in order to start a career. Preference is given to postgraduates.

Types of grants

One-off and recurrent grants of up to £2,000 for educational expenses such as fees, books/equipment or travel.

The trust has informed us that 'awards for travel are currently suspended due to pressure on trust funds'.

Annual grant total

In 2010/11 the trust had assets of £959,000 and an income of £44,000. Grants to 12 individuals totalled £20,000, distributed in the following areas:

- International Affairs: £5,000
- History: £4,300
- Drama, Dance and Ballet: £4,000
- Music: £2,200
- Law: £2,000
- Film making, Cinematography and so on: £2,000
- Scientific, Engineering and Technology: £300

Exclusions

No grants are normally made for courses leading to qualifications required for entry into a profession (such as teaching or legal practice) or purchase of musical instruments.

Applications

In writing via post-or email to the correspondent including CV; details of the course; a statement of aims and two references (further details of information required are available on the website). Applications may be submitted at any time and will be assessed when received. Grants may be awarded at this stage or may be submitted to the board of trustees for a second assessment, therefore if timings are crucial, applications should be submitted by mid-February or mid-July in time for the twice yearly trustee meetings.

Other information

The trust also supports youth organisations and schools, making two grants totalling £4,500 during the year.

The Society for the Benefit of Sons and Daughters of the Clergy of the Church of Scotland

£25,000

Correspondent: The Secretary, Scott-Moncrieff, Exchange Place 3, Semple Street, Edinburgh EH3 8BL (website: www.scott-moncrieff.com/charitable_trusts/page4.html)

SC Number: SC008760

Eligibility
Children of ministers of the Church of Scotland aged between 12 and 25, unmarried and widowed daughters of ministers and unmarried sisters over 40 of ministers.

Types of grants
Grants of £100 to £1,000 towards the cost of education.

Annual grant total
About £25,000.

Applications
An application form can be downloaded from the Scott-Moncrieff website. Applications should be sent in no later than 31 May each year and grants are distributed by early September.

John Suttie Memorial Fund

£500

Correspondent: Will Cowie, Solicitor, R and R Urquhart Solicitors, 117–121 High Street, Forres, Moray IV36 1AB (01309 672216)

SC Number: SC007345

Eligibility
People who live in Moray and Nairn, with preference for people under 30 who are starting on an agricultural or veterinary career.

Types of grants
Grants towards further or higher education.

Annual grant total
About £500.

Applications
Information regarding awards is circulated annually to schools and through agricultural and veterinary organisations. Applications should be made in writing to the correspondent.

John Watson's Trust

£50,000

Correspondent: Elaine Young, Administrator, Signet Library, Parliament Square, Edinburgh EH1 1RF (01312 201640; fax: 01312 204016; email: johnwatsons@wssociety.co.uk; website: www.johnwatsons.com)

SC Number: SC014004

Eligibility
People under 21 who have a physical or learning disability or are socially disadvantaged and who live in Scotland. There is a preference for people who live in or are connected with the Lothian region.

Types of grants
Help in connection with special tuition, educational trips, computers for people with special educational needs, books, tools or expenses for further training and education, and equipment, travel and other activities contributing to education and advancement in life. Grants range from £30 to £2,000.

The trust also gives grants of £300 to £1,000 towards the cost of a boarding education for children normally resident in Scotland who are experiencing serious family difficulties and who would benefit from an education away from home.

Annual grant total
The grants committee has an annual budget of approximately £150,000 to disburse in grants.

Exclusions
No grants for day school fees or university costs. Applications for school trips to outdoor residential centres must be made by the school, not the individual.

Applications
On a form available from the correspondent or from the trust's website along with guidance notes. Applications can be submitted directly by the individual, or through a social worker, Citizens Advice, other welfare agency or through another third party on behalf of an individual. Applications must include full details and dates and locations of any trips being undertaken. The grants committee meets approximately six times a year and the dates for their next meeting plus application deadlines can also be found on the website.

Other information
Grants are also made to organisations and groups.

Aberdeen and Perthshire

The Aberdeen Endowments Trust

£13,000

Correspondent: William Russell, Clerk, 19 Albert Street, Aberdeen AB25 1QF (01224 640194; fax: 01224 643918; email: info@aet.demon.co.uk)

SC Number: SC010507

Eligibility
People of any age who were born and brought up in Aberdeen, as constituted in 1967. This area does not include Denestone.

Types of grants
The Trust awards a number of free places to Robert Gordon's Secondary College, also school bursaries, postgraduate scholarships, travel scholarships, grants for special equipment, sports facilities, promoting education in the arts and adult education. Grants tend to be around £200 each.

Annual grant total
In 2011 the trust had an income of £993,000 and an expenditure of £1 million. The majority of the funds go to supporting 60 children to attend Robert Gordon's College. The remainder totals around £13,000 and is spent 40% on educational travel grants and the rest on small grants for students at university.

Applications
On a form available from the correspondent. Applications are considered nine or ten times a year.

Other information
Grants are also occasionally made to organisations.

Dr John Calder Trust

£8,000

Correspondent: Clive Phillips, 21 Ferryhill Place, Aberdeen AB11 7SE

SC Number: SC004299

Eligibility
People in need who live in the parish of Machar, or within the city of Aberdeen, including people only resident for their education and people from the area studying elsewhere.

Types of grants

Grants for educational needs.

Annual grant total

Around £8,000 is available for educational grants.

Applications

The trust stated in January 2006 that funds were fully committed and that this situation was likely to remain so for the medium to long-term.

The Anne Herd Memorial Trust

£12,000

Correspondent: The Trustees, Bowman Solicitors, 27 Bank Street, Dundee DD1 1RP (01382 322267; fax: 01382 225000)

SC Number: SC014198

Eligibility

People who are blind or partially sighted who live in Broughty Ferry (applicants from the city of Dundee, region of Tayside or those who have connections with these areas and reside in Scotland will also be considered).

Types of grants

Grants are given for educational equipment such as computers and books. Grants are usually at least £50.

Annual grant total

In 2010/11 the trust had an income of £29,000. The trust gives approximately £25,000 a year in grants for education and welfare.

Applications

In writing to the correspondent, to be submitted directly by the individual in March/April for consideration in June.

The Morgan Trust

£11,000

Correspondent: The Clerk, Miller Hendry, 13 Ward Road, Dundee DD1 1LU

SC Number: SC010527

Eligibility

Children of people who: (i) were born or educated in the former royal burghs of Dundee, Forfar, Arbroath and Montrose; or (ii) have been resident in one or more these burghs for five years immediately before applying for an award or immediately before his/her death.

Types of grants

One-off and recurrent grants of up to £200, usually for maintenance/living expenses. Grants are reviewed each year. Emergency grants are available to allow pupils to continue their education following some family crisis.

Annual grant total

In 2010/11 the trust had an income and an expenditure of £12,000.

Exclusions

Grants are not given to people with an income of more than £10,000, unless there are exceptional circumstances.

Applications

On a form available from the correspondent, for completion on behalf of the applicant with full details of their financial situation. Applications are usually considered at May and November meetings.

The Gertrude Muriel Pattullo Advancement Award Scheme

£1,500

Correspondent: The Clerk, Blackadders Solicitors, 30–34 Reform Street, Dundee DD1 1RJ (01382 229222; fax: 01382 342220; email: toni.mcnicoll@ blackadders.co.uk)

SC Number: SC000811

Eligibility

Young people aged 16 to 25 who are physically disabled and live in the city of Dundee or the county of Angus.

Types of grants

One-off and recurrent grants of £100 to £500 to schoolchildren and students in further or higher education towards books, equipment, instruments, fees, living expenses and educational outings in the UK.

Annual grant total

The trust has an income of around £4,500 per year. Grants are made to organisations and individuals.

Exclusions

No grants are given towards the repayment of debts.

Applications

On a form available from the correspondent at any time. Applications can be submitted directly by the individual or through any third party.

Aberdeen and Aberdeenshire

Aberdeenshire Educational Trust

£10,000

Correspondent: The Administrator, Trust Section, Aberdeenshire Council, St Leonards, Sandyhill Road, Banff AB45 1BH (01261 813336; email: maureen.adamson@aberdeenshire.gov. uk)

SC Number: SC028382

Eligibility

Residents of the former county of Aberdeen and schoolchildren and students whose parents reside there.

Types of grants

Grants of approximately £200 are available to individuals going on to study further education for travel, fees, books, equipment and so on. Support is also given towards school trips and annual school prizes. There is a preference for education in the visual arts, music and drama. Support is given to people starting work or apprenticeships. Grants may be awarded for postgraduate research or special study.

Annual grant total

In 2010/11 the trust had assets of £1.9 million and an income of £63,000. Grants were made totalling £45,000, most of which was given to schools, clubs and other educational establishments.

Applications

On a form available from the correspondent, to be considered throughout the year. All applications are means tested so applicants must provide documentary evidence of income from the last tax year.

Huntly Educational Trust 1997

£4,000

Correspondent: Clerk, 3 The Square, Huntly, Aberdeenshire AB54 8AE

SC Number: SC026920

Eligibility

People living in the district of Huntly.

Types of grants

Grants are given for the education and training of individuals and average £200.

Annual grant total

In 2010/11 the trust had both an income and expenditure of £8,200.

Applications

In writing to the correspondent for consideration at a monthly meeting.

Other information

The trust also makes grants to local schools, colleges and other educational establishments.

Kincardineshire Educational Trust

£1,800

Correspondent: Grant Administrator, Trust Section, Aberdeenshire Council, St Leonard's, Sandyhill Road, Banff AB45 1BH (01261 813336; email: maureen.adamson@aberdeenshire.gov. uk)

SC Number: SC028381

Eligibility

People who permanently reside or are educated in the former county of Kincardine and schoolchildren whose parents live there.

Types of grants

Grants of up to £100 are given to: schoolchildren towards books, equipment, instruments and educational outings; and people in further or higher education, including mature students and postgraduates, towards books, equipment, instruments, fees, living expenses, student exchanges and educational outings and trips in the UK and overseas. Support is also given to people staring work or apprenticeships and adult education.

Annual grant total

In 2010/11 the trust had an income of £2,900 and grants totalled £1,800.

Applications

On a form available from the correspondent, to be received by 30 November for consideration in March. Applications are means tested so documentary evidence of income should be included.

Other information

Grants are also made to clubs, schools and other educational establishments.

Angus

Angus Educational Trust

£20,000

Correspondent: The Secretary, Education Department, Angus House, Orchardbank Business Park, Forfar DD8 1AE (01307 476339; fax: 01307 461848; website: www.angus.gov.uk/ services/view_service_detail. cfm?serviceid=1362)

SC Number: SC015826

Eligibility

Residents of the Angus Council area who have been offered a place on, or are attending, any full-time or part-time courses at university (excluding postgraduate courses). Note: any student entitled to apply for a loan under the Student Loans Scheme must have taken up this option before an application to the trust will be considered.

Types of grants

The trust provides financial assistance in the following areas:

- Travel expenses for those studying higher educational courses outside of Scotland
- Residents of the Angus Council area for undergraduate university courses
- Young people travelling abroad for educational purposes
- Clubs and groups working to improve educational opportunities and learning in the Angus Council area
- Rural primary schools, for excursions of an educational nature

Grants are given to supplement existing grants. Household income is taken into account in determining whether or not a grant is awarded.

Annual grant total

In 2010 the trust had an income of £22,000.

Applications

Application forms can be requested from the correspondent or downloaded from the website. The governors meet twice a year in March and September to consider applications and can take three to four months to come to a decision.

Other information

Grants for pre-university gap years are also considered and are provided specifically for the purpose of improving educational outcomes either for the individual or for the group that they are visiting. Individuals applying for such a grant must state the specific outcomes expected from their visit, how long they intend to stay and the costs and support that are envisaged.

The David Barnet Christie Trust

£3,000

Correspondent: Graham McNicol, Thorntons WS, Brothockbank House, Arbroath DD11 1NJ (01241 872683; fax: 01241 871541)

SC Number: SC004618

Eligibility

Men or women aged up to 40, preferably living in or originating from the Arbroath area (or failing this Angus), who are about to enter into an engineering apprenticeship, have already taken up such or similar training, or wish to progress by taking further engineering qualifications.

Types of grants

One-off grants of up to £500 to people starting work or students in further or higher education, including mature students and postgraduates, towards books, study or travel abroad, equipment, instruments, maintenance and living expenses.

Annual grant total

In 2010/11 the trust had an income of £4,000. No further information was available.

Exclusions

Students from any other area in the UK, EU or overseas are not eligible for funding.

Applications

On a form available from the correspondent. Applications should be submitted directly by the individual by the end of September each year.

The Duncan Trust

£5,000

Correspondent: G J M Dunlop, Solicitor, Thorntons W S, Brothockbank House, Arbroath, Angus DD11 1NE (01241 872683)

SC Number: SC015311

Eligibility

Candidates for the Ministry of the Church of Scotland, especially those who have a connection with the former Presbytery of Arbroath.

Types of grants

Cash grants to student applicants studying for their first degree.

Annual grant total

In 2010/11 the trust had an income of £21,000. The trust typically gives around £5,000 a year in grants.

Exclusions

Postgraduate studies.

Applications

In writing to the correspondent to request an application form, to be returned by 31 October each year.

Dundee Masonic Temple Trust

£2,000

Correspondent: The Trustees, 2 India Buildings, 86 Bell Street, Dundee DD1 1JQ

SC Number: SC005364

Eligibility
Children of Freemasons who are or were members of Lodges in Angus.

Types of grants
Recurrent grants of £200 to £500 to students in further or higher education, including mature students, for living expenses.

Annual grant total
The trust has an annual income of around £2,500.

Applications
On a form available from the correspondent. Forms should be returned directly by the individual in October for consideration in November/December.

Dundee

City of Dundee Educational Trust

£12,000

Correspondent: J Hope, Miller Hendry, 13 Ward Road, Dundee DD1 1LU (01382 200000)

SC Number: SC015820

Eligibility
Students in further or higher education who have a strong connection with Dundee. Priority is given to students who do not receive a mandatory award.

Types of grants
Grants of around £300 each.

Annual grant total
In 2011 the trust had an income of £66,000 and an expenditure of £16,000, with roughly £12,000 given in grants to individuals annually.

Applications
On a form available from the correspondent, along with a full CV. Applications should be submitted at least two weeks before the quarterly meetings in March, June, September and December.

The Polack Travelling Scholarship Fund

£1,500

Correspondent: The Clerk, Henderson Loggie, Royal Exchange, Panmure Street, Dundee DD1 1DZ (01382 200055; email: feb@hendersonloggie.co.uk)

Eligibility
People over 17 attending an educational institution within Dundee or the surrounding area who wish to undertake study or research abroad.

Types of grants
To enable attendance on courses or conferences abroad to study foreign languages, international law, management studies or aspects of company and commercial education. Grants are one-off and range from £250 to £400.

Annual grant total
About £1,500.

Applications
In writing to the correspondent directly by the individual. Applications are to be submitted by 31 March for consideration in May.

Moray

The Banffshire Educational Trust

£10,000

Correspondent: Jean-Anne Goodbrand, Admin Officer, Educational Services, Moray Council Headquarters, High Street, Elgin, Moray IV30 1LL (01343 551374; fax: 01343 563478; email: jeananne.goodbrand@moray.gov.uk; website: www.moray.gov.uk)

Trustee: Moray Council.

Eligibility
Residents of the former county of Banffshire, people who attend schools or further education centres in the former county, and school pupils whose parents live in the former county of Banffshire. Grants are means tested to those earning £34,000 a year or less.

Types of grants
One-off grants of between £15 and £200 are given towards postgraduate scholarships, higher education bursaries, mature students, apprentices and trainees, travel scholarships for people studying outside Scotland, and travel and educational excursions for schoolchildren and people in adult education.

Annual grant total
Grants totalling around £10,000 are made annually, usually to around 50 individuals.

Applications
Application forms are available from the correspondent or the Moray Council website and should be submitted by 30 September for consideration in November/December.

Moray and Nairn Educational Trust

£6,000

Correspondent: Administrative Officer, Education and Social Care, Moray Council, High Street, Elgin, Moray IV30 1BX (01343 551374; fax: 01343 563478; email: educationalservices@moray.gov.uk; website: www.moray.gov.uk)

Eligibility
People who have lived, or whose parents live in the former counties of Moray and Nairn for at least five years and children/young people attending school or further education establishments in the area. No grants are given to people whose household earnings are over £20,000 a year (plus an allowance for dependent children).

Types of grants
One-off grants, ranging from £50 to £200, are available to schoolchildren for educational outings in the UK and study or travel abroad and to students in further or higher education, including mature students and postgraduates, for any purpose. Grants are available for the organisation of events that promote adult education in the area.

Annual grant total
About £6,000 to individuals.

Applications
On a form available from the website, along with application guidelines, to be submitted by 30 September each year.

Other information
Grants are also made to organisations.

Ian Wilson Ski Fund

£10,000

Correspondent: Ian Hamilton, Hon. Secretary and Treasurer, Slack Villa, King Edward Terrace, Portknockie, Moray AB56 4NX

SC Number: SC026750

Eligibility
Young people aged under 21 who are in full time education in a school run by

Moray council. Preference is given to families with a restricted income.

Types of grants
One-off grants are given to advance education by promoting outdoor activities, including sport and related studies.

Annual grant total
In 2010/11 the fund had an income of £11,000.

Applications
On a form available from the correspondent. Applicants are encouraged to apply in plenty of time, by the end of the school holidays in October for consideration by the trustees later that month, as there are a limited number of grants available. Applications can be submitted either directly by the individual or through his or her school, college, educational welfare agency, or another third party.

Perth and Kinross

The Guildry Incorporation of Perth

£20,000

Correspondent: Lorna Peacock, Secretary, 42 George Street, Perth PH1 5JL (01738 623195)

SC Number: SC008072

Eligibility
Young people aged 17 to 25 who are in need, living in Perth or Guildtown and following a course of further or higher education in the UK. The guild also supports young people taking part in Raleigh International, Link Overseas Exchange Projects and similar activities.

Types of grants
Grants up to £800.

Annual grant total
In 2010/11 the guild had an income of £206,000. Previously grants to individuals have totalled around £80,000, with approximately £20,000 given for educational purposes.

Applications
Application forms can be requested from the correspondent. They are considered at the trustees' meetings on the last Tuesday of every month. Applicants are required to write a short covering letter of around 250 words explaining why they require funding and how the grant they receive could help their local community.

Perth and Kinross Educational Trust

£8,000

Correspondent: The Trust Administrator, Perth and Kinross Council, Chief Executive's Service, 2 High Street, Perth PH1 5PH (01738 476767)

SC Number: SC012378

Eligibility
Students in further or higher education, including mature students and postgraduates, who were born or attended school in Perth and Kinross.

Types of grants
Grants of up to £150 towards books, fees, living expenses and study or travel abroad.

Annual grant total
Previously about £8,000 to individuals.

Applications
On a form available from the correspondent. Applications should be received by mid-May for consideration in June. The exact closing date can be found on the application form. Late applications cannot be considered.

Central Scotland

Clackmannanshire

Clackmannanshire Educational Trust

£450

Trustee: Clackmannanshire Council.

SC Number: SC008282

Eligibility
People resident in the county of Clackmannanshire.

Types of grants
Grants of £50 to £100 towards educational travel (in the UK or overseas) and adult education.

Annual grant total
In 2011/12 the trust made grants to individuals totalling £450.

Applications
Directly by the individual on a form available from the education services team, or the website, including two references. Applications are considered on the first Thursday of January, April, July and October.

Paton Educational Trust

£400

Correspondent: William Jarvis, Solicitor, 27 Mar Street, Alloa FK10 1HX (01259 723408)

SC Number: SC005800

Eligibility
People (usually aged 16 to 26) who live in the burgh of Alloa or Clackmannanshire or whose parent was employed by Patons and Baldwins Ltd – Alloa or who are members or adherents of West Church of Scotland – Alloa or Moncrieff U F Church – Alloa.

Types of grants
Supplementary grants of £50 to £100 per year for students in further and higher education. Grants can go towards books and fees/living expenses. Grants can also sometimes be given for study or travel abroad or for student exchanges.

Applications
On a form available from the correspondent. Applications are usually considered in September/October.

Other information
The trust has not submitted any accounts to the Scottish Charity Regulator since 2009.

Fife

Fife Educational Trust

£1,200

Correspondent: Education Services, Fife Council, Rothesay House, Rothesay Place, Glenrothes KY7 5PQ

SC Number: SC004325

Eligibility
People who have a permanent address within the Fife council area and who attended a secondary or primary school there.

Types of grants
Support for individuals below postgraduate level is usually restricted to travel grants where this is an integral part of the course of study, but can also be given for music, drama and visual arts. Grants range from £50 to about £75.

Annual grant total
Grants to individuals usually total about £1,200 a year.

Applications

In writing to the correspondent. Applicants must give their permanent address, details of schools they attended within Fife with dates of attendance, and details of other money available. Applications are considered in March.

New St Andrews Japan Golf Trust

£3,000

Correspondent: J Phillip, Trustee, 7 Pilmour Links, St Andrews, Fife KY16 9JG

SC Number: SC005668

Eligibility

Children and young people in need living in the county of Fife who are undertaking sports and recreational activities with a preference for golf.

Types of grants

One-off and recurrent grants ranging from £200 to £1,500, for sports equipment, travel, accommodation and coaching assistance to individuals, and university fees for sports scholarships.

Annual grant total

The trust gives around £6,000 a year in grants to organisations and individuals.

Applications

In writing to the correspondent, providing the contact details of two referees.

Stirling

The Stirlingshire Educational Trust

£85,000

Correspondent: The Clerk/Treasurer, 68 Port Street, Stirling FK8 2LJ (01786 474956; fax: 01786 474956; website: www.stirlingeducationaltrust.org.uk)

SC Number: SC007528

Eligibility

People who were born in, or have lived for six years in, Stirlingshire and are in need.

Types of grants

Grants are made to schoolchildren for study/travel abroad and excursions and to college students, undergraduates, vocational students and mature students, and those entering a trade or profession or apprenticeship, including those for clothing/uniforms, fees, study/travel abroad, books, equipment/instruments and excursions. Grants are also available for postgraduate research, advanced or

special study. Grants range from £150 to £500.

Annual grant total

In 2010/11 the trust had an income of £2.4 million. About £85,000 a year is usually distributed in educational grants.

Applications

On a form available from the correspondent. Applications must be received by February, May, August and November for consideration on the first Wednesday of the following month.

Edinburgh, the Lothians and Scottish Borders

City of Edinburgh

The Colin O'Riordan Trust

£4,000

Correspondent: Rory O'Riordan, Chair, 23 Glencairn Crescent, Edinburgh EH12 5BT (website: www. thecolinoriordantrust.org.uk)

SC Number: SC033062

Eligibility

Children and young people under the age of 20 who are involved in music and live in Edinburgh (EH postcode).

Types of grants

Grants given according need to help young people develop their musical abilities by playing individually and in groups.

Annual grant total

About £2,000 per year.

Exclusions

No grants are made outside the EH postcode area.

Applications

In writing to the correspondent before the annual closing date of 31 May each year stating the reason the award is needed, family circumstances and the contact details of a referee which should be the headteacher or head of music at the applicants' school.

Other information

The trust also supports groups of young musicians studying all forms of music including classical orchestral, solo performers, jazz, and folk and wind bands.

The James Scott Law Charitable Fund

£3,500

Correspondent: Alistair Beattie, Secretary and Chamberlain, Merchants' Hall, 22 Hanover Street, Edinburgh EH2 2EP (01312 257202; fax: 01312 204842; email: alistair.beattie@mcoe.org. uk)

Trustee: The Master's Court of the Company of Merchants of the City of Edinburgh.

SC Number: SC008878

Eligibility

Young people, aged between 5 and 18 years who attend primary or secondary Edinburgh Merchant Company Schools.

Types of grants

Grants are given for school fees, clothing, books and allowances. The maximum award is about £2,000.

Annual grant total

In 2010/11 the fund had assets of £106,000 and an income of £3,600. Nine awards were made totalling £3,500.

Applications

On a form available from the correspondent for consideration in August, a bursar at their school usually interviews applicants.

East Lothian

East Lothian Educational Trust

£25,000

Correspondent: Kim Brand, Clerk, John Muir House, Haddington, East Lothian EH41 3HA (01620 827436; email: eleducationaltrust@eastlothian.gov.uk; website: www.eastlothian.gov.uk/info/ 563/student_awards/756/east_lothian_ educational_trust)

SC Number: SC010587

Eligibility

People in education who live in the former county of East Lothian.

Types of grants

One-off grants in the range of £100 and £700 are given to: schoolchildren, college students, undergraduates, vocational students, mature students and people with special educational needs, including those towards uniforms/clothing, fees, study/travel abroad, books, equipment/ instruments, maintenance/living expenses, research, accommodation and excursions.

Annual grant total

In 2010/11 the trust had an income of £105,000. Previously it has given around half its income in educational grants to individuals.

Applications

On a form available from the correspondent or the website. Applications can be submitted directly by the individual or a parent/guardian, through a third party such as a teacher, or through an organisation such as a school or an educational welfare agency. Trustees meet four times a year in February, May, August and November.

Other information

Grants are also available to clubs and organisations for a variety of educational purposes, such as equipment, travel costs or specific trips and projects.

The Red House Home Trust

£10,000

Correspondent: Fiona Watson, Scott-Moncrieff, 17 Melville Street, Edinburgh EH3 7PH (01314 733500; fax: 01314 733500; email: graeme.thom@scott-moncrieff.com; website: www.scott-moncrieff.com/charitable_trusts/page8.html)

SC Number: SC015748

Eligibility

Young people under the age of 22 who are in need and live in East Lothian.

Types of grants

Grants in the range of £250 to £1,000 for education and training.

Annual grant total

In 2011 the trust had an income of £19,000 and an expenditure of £26,000. About £10,000 is available for distribution each year.

Applications

On a form available from the trust's website, or from the correspondent. The trustees normally meet three times a year to review applications and to agree grants.

Scottish Borders

The Elizabeth Hume Trust

£500

Correspondent: Revd D Murray, The Manse, The Glebe, Chirnside, Duns, Berwickshire TD11 3XL

SC Number: SC005995

Eligibility

People in need who live in the parish of Chirnside.

Types of grants

Grants are made to schoolchildren for uniforms/clothing and equipment/instruments and to undergraduates for fees and books.

Annual grant total

In 2011 the trust had an expenditure of £10,000. Income and expenditure have been erratic in recent years.

Applications

Applications can be made either directly by an individual or family member, through a third party such as a social worker or teacher, through an organisation such as a Citizens Advice or school or through a church elder.

Charities Administered by Scottish Borders Council

£10,000

Correspondent: The Clerk, Community Services Council, Newtown St Boswells, Melrose, Roxburghshire TD6 0SA (01835 825020)

Eligibility

Within the Scottish Borders there are four educational trusts corresponding to the four former counties of Berwickshire, Peeblesshire, Roxburghshire and Selkirkshire. Grants may be awarded for a variety of educational purposes to people who are ordinarily living in the above areas.

Types of grants

One-off and recurrent grants are made under the following headings: (i) educational excursions; (ii) special grants; (iii) travel grants; (iv) adult education; and (v) drama, visual arts and music.

Annual grant total

The annual grants budget is about £10,000.

Applications

On a form available from the correspondent or the Scottish Borders Council website. Applications are considered all year round and funds are administered on a first come first served basis.

Other information

Grants are also given to schools.

West Lothian

The West Lothian Educational Trust

£6,000 (32 grants)

Correspondent: Fiona Watson, Scott-Moncrieff, Exchange Place 3, Semple Street, Edinburgh EH3 8BL (01314 733500; website: www.scott-moncrieff.com/charitable_trusts/page9.html)

Eligibility

People who were born in West Lothian or have lived there for at least the last three years.

Types of grants

One-off and recurring grants of £100 to £300 are given for travel within and outside Scotland, trips, equipment, sports, music, drama, research, adult education, undergraduate and postgraduate scholarships, apprenticeships and other practical experience of trades.

Annual grant total

After various prize monies and bursaries have been paid, about £6,000 is available for distribution each year. In 2010/11 32 grants of £100 to £300 were made.

Applications

Application forms are available from the correspondent or the website. Applications must be received by 1 February, 1 May and 1 September each year.

Glasgow and West of Scotland

The Ayrshire Educational Trust

£5,000

Correspondent: Community Learning and Development, East Ayrshire Council, Rennie Street Office, Rennie Street, Kilmarnock KA1 3AR (01563 578101; fax: 01563 578102; email: CLDenquires@ east-ayrshire.gov.uk)

SC Number: SC018195

Eligibility

People who live in the former county of Ayrshire.

Types of grants

Grants are given to students in further/higher education for travel in either the UK or abroad for educational purposes, and are given to schoolchildren for educational outings or for Scottish Youth Theatre or Scottish Youth Choir. Grants can also be made to buy special equipment for mentally or physically disabled students. Equipment for pilot projects or of an experimental nature will be considered. Grants are also given to support the formation, maintenance and encouragement of clubs, societies and organisation that provide educational benefit to young people and children in Ayrshire.

Annual grant total

In 2010/11 the trust had an income of £5,400 and an expenditure of £6,100.

Exclusions

Assistance cannot be given towards personal equipment or to help with student's course fees when following full-time or part-time courses of education.

Applications

On a form available from the correspondent. Applications are usually considered four times a year. They should be submitted directly by the individual.

Dunbartonshire Educational Trust

£3,000

Correspondent: The Trustees, West Dunbartonshire Council, Council Offices, Garshake Road, Dumbarton G82 3PU

Eligibility

People who live in the old county area of Dumbarton district aged 16 and over. There is a preference for people from deprived areas and a policy of positive discrimination (for instance, people with disabilities or children of single parents).

Types of grants

Grants of £50 to £100 towards fees, maintenance, travel and equipment for students in further or higher education and to obtain practical experience of trades, for example the cost of books during an apprenticeship.

Annual grant total

About £2,000 is available each year.

Applications

On a form available from the correspondent. Applications can be considered at any time, but students usually apply before the start of the course.

The Glasgow Society for the Education of the Deaf and Dumb

£30,000

Correspondent: Nancy Ward, Administrator, c/o Alexander Sloan, Chartered Accountants, 38 Cadogan Street, Glasgow G2 7HF (01412 048989; fax: 01412 489931; email: nancy.ward@ alexandersloan.co.uk; website: www. gsedd.org.uk)

Trustees: Mark Mulholland; Alex Harrison; Alastair Cook; Sandy Mowat; John Boyle; Stewart MacKay.

SC Number: SC003804

Eligibility

Children over school age who are deaf and/or speech impaired and live in the west of Scotland.

Types of grants

Grants to help with the cost of providing tutors to support deaf people, courses (for example, sign language, lip reading), holidays, radio aids, computers and so on.

Annual grant total

Around £30,000.

Exclusions

No grants for taster or introductory courses.

Applications

On a form available from the correspondent, or from the society's website. Applications can be submitted at any time directly by the individual or through a social worker. Applications usually take between three and eight weeks to be processed, giving time for the possible need for additional information.

Other information

The society also gives grants to organisations and schools.

The Logan and Johnstone School Scheme

£5,000

Correspondent: Deputy Director of Education, Education Services, Wheatley House, 25 Cochrane Street, Merchant City, Glasgow G1 1HL

Eligibility

Students in further/higher education, including mature students, people starting work and postgraduates, who live in the former Strathclyde region.

Types of grants

One-off grants for books, equipment, instruments and fees.

Annual grant total

About £5,000.

Exclusions

Grants are not made towards living or travel expenses.

Applications

On a form available from the correspondent. Applications should be submitted directly by the individual between April and June for consideration in August.

Colonel MacLean Trust Scheme

£1,000

Correspondent: Deputy Director of Education, Customer and Business Services, Trust Applications, Glasgow City Council, Nye Bevan House, 20 India Street, Glasgow G2 4PF (01412 769918)

Eligibility

Students in further/higher education, including mature students and postgraduates and those undergoing training and apprenticeships who live in the former Strathclyde region.

Types of grants

One-off grants for books, equipment, instruments and fees.

Annual grant total

About £1,000.

Applications

On a form available from Glasgow City Council. Applications should be submitted directly by the individual between April and June for consideration in August.

Renfrewshire Educational Trust

£10,000

Correspondent: Sarah White, Renfrewshire Council, Cotton Street, Paisley PA1 1JB (01418 403147; email: ret.cs@renfrewshire.gov.uk; website: www.renfrewshire.gov.uk/ilwwcm/publishing.nsf/Content/Navigation-cs-RenfrewshireEducationalTrust)

SC Number: SC008876

Eligibility

People who have lived within either the Renfrewshire, East Renfrewshire or Inverclyde areas for the last three years or have come from one of the aforementioned areas but currently live elsewhere in order to undertake their course of studies. Student's family income must not exceed £34,000 per annum. For children's excursions the minimum criteria is receiving free school meals.

Types of grants

Grants of typically £200 to £400 for fees, maintenance or travel costs associated with further or higher education including the performing arts. Schoolchildren can receive help with the costs of educational outings.

One award of £3,400 is made each year to a student on a one-year taught master's degree course.

Annual grant total

About £10,000 is distributed annually in educational grants to individuals, with the remainder being given in grants for music, drama and sport.

Exclusions

No grants for individuals whose household income is £30,000 or over.

Applications

On a form available from the correspondent or the website. (Separate application forms are available for general grants and travel grants.) Details of household income are requested. Applications can be submitted either directly by the individual or via their school. Applications are considered every six weeks.

The Spiers Trust

£2,000

Correspondent: Corporate Director, Education and Skills, North Ayrshire Council, Cunninghame House, Irvine KA12 8EE (01294 324428)

Trustee: North Ayrshire Council.

Eligibility

People in need who live in the parishes of Beith, Dalry, Dunlop, Kilbirnie, Lochwinnoch and Neilston. Preference is given to students from families with restricted income.

Types of grants

Awards known as Spier Grants to help secondary school pupils and students in further/higher education to meet the cost of attending a course or obtaining special tuition in any academic, artistic, scientific or technological subject or subjects, in or outside of Scotland. Grants may also be given to help with travelling costs.

Annual grant total

About £2,000.

Applications

Applications can be submitted directly by the individual on an application form available by phoning the correspondent. Evidence of need will have to be shown. Each year applications are considered regularly until all the funds have been spent.

Argyll and Bute

Charles and Barbara Tyre Trust

£35,000

Correspondent: Christine Heads, The Clerk, Loch Awe House, Barmore Road, Tarbet, Argyll PA29 6TW (01880 820227; email: christine@williamduncantarbert.co.uk)

SC Number: SC031378

Eligibility

People aged 18 to 25 who live in the former county of Argyll and are of the Protestant faith.

Types of grants

Grants are given to obtain qualifications, train in a trade or profession, undertake Open University courses, undertake training in leadership and initiative and for respite holidays for people with physical or mental disabilities.

Annual grant total

In 2010/11 the trust had an income of £30,000 and an expenditure of £39,000.

Applications

On a form available to download from the website which must be submitted by 31 May each year. Decisions are usually made by the end of August.

City of Glasgow

Glasgow Educational and Marshall Trust

£50,000 (65 grants)

Correspondent: Avril Sloane, Secretary and Treasurer, 21 Beaton Road, Glasgow G41 4NW (01414 232169; fax: 01414 241731; email: enquiries@gemt.org.uk; website: www.gemt.org.uk)

SC Number: SC012582

Eligibility

People over 18 years old who are in need and who have lived in the city of Glasgow (as at the re-organisation in 1975) for a minimum of five years (excluding time spent studying in the city with a home address elsewhere).

The trust states that only in exceptional circumstances will awards be made to undergraduate students.

Types of grants

Grants range from £100 to £1,000, although in exceptional cases higher awards have been made. They are given towards: books, course fees/living expenses, study/travel abroad for people in further/higher education; and course fees, travel, books, equipment/instruments for people wishing to undertake vocational training. Mature students can also qualify for assistance with childcare costs, books, travel and fees.

Grants can be one-off or recurrent and are normally given for courses where a Students Awards Agency for Scotland grant is not available, or where such grants do not cover the total costs.

Annual grant total

In 2010/11 the trust had an income of £94,000, a total expenditure of £91,000 and made 65 awards totalling £50,000.

Exclusions

No grants are given retrospectively or for courses run by privately owned institutions.

Applications

Directly by the individual on a form available from the website along with guidance notes, together with two written references. Applicants should show evidence of savings and other fundraising activity and are expected to apply for any loans available through the Student Loans Company. The main meetings of governors are held on the first Wednesday of March, June, September and December. Interim meetings may be held if required as a result of the number of applications received.

Other information

The trust also makes grants to organisations.

The JTH Charitable Trust

£11,000

Correspondent: Lynne Faulkner, Biggart Baillie, Dalmore House, 310 St Vincent Street, Glasgow G2 5QR (01412 288000)

SC Number: SC000201

Eligibility

People in need who live in Glasgow and are undertaking education which enhances the cultural and social fabric of society with a view to meeting unmet local needs which are not municipal, governmental or religious.

Types of grants

One-off grants ranging from £100 to £1,000 to schoolchildren for study/travel overseas, books, equipment/instruments and maintenance/living expenses, to college students, undergraduates, vocational students and mature students for fees, study/travel overseas, books, equipment/instruments, maintenance/ living expenses and childcare, to overseas students for fees, books, equipment/ instruments and maintenance/living expenses and to individuals with special educational needs for excursions.

Annual grant total

In 2010/11 the trust had an income of £167,000. Previously grants to individuals totalled £11,000, with the majority of grant-giving focused towards organisations.

Exclusions

Grants are unlikely to be made to people at Glasgow or Strathclyde Universities or Royal Scottish Academy of Music and Dance as the trust makes block payments to the hardship funds of these institutions. Grants are also not normally awarded towards medical electives, second or further qualifications, payments of school fees or costs incurred at tertiary educational establishments.

Applications

An application form to be submitted together with a summary in the applicant's own words, extending to no more than a single A4 sheet, of the purpose and need of the grant. The possible costs and financial need should also be broken down.

The trustees meet four times a year normally in March, June, September and December, but this can vary. All applications should be submitted one month prior to the meeting.

It is a condition that with any grant given, a report should be made as to how the funds have been used. Grants not used for the purposes stated must be returned. Applicants receiving help one year may expect to be refused in the next.

The Trades House of Glasgow

£15,000

Correspondent: The Clerk, Administration Centre, North Gallery – Trades Hall, 85 Glassford Street, Glasgow G1 1UH (01415 531605; website: www. tradeshouse.org.uk)

SC Number: SCO40548

Eligibility

People in need who live in Glasgow.

Types of grants

Grants to encourage promising young people in university or colleges.

Annual grant total

About £15,000 in educational grants to individuals.

Applications

In writing to the correspondent.

Other information

The Trades House also operates the Drapers Fund which distributes £50,000 annually to children-in-need who are under the age of seventeen. To apply write supplying as much detail as possible highlighting the circumstances of the individual/organisation concerned to: The Manager, The Drapers Fund, The Trades House of Glasgow, Trades Hall, 85 Glassford Street, Glasgow G1 1UH.

Dumfries and Galloway

The Dumfriesshire Educational Trust

£18,000

Correspondent: School Services Department, Dumfries and Galloway Council, Municipal Chambers, Buccleuch Street, Dumfries DG1 2AD (01387 722164)

SC Number: SC003411

Eligibility

People normally living in Dumfriesshire who have had at least five years of education in Dumfriesshire.

Types of grants

Grants of up to £60, usually recurrent, are given to: schoolchildren towards educational outings; students in further/

higher education for books, fees/living expenses, study/travel abroad and student exchanges; and mature students towards books and travel.

Annual grant total

In 2011 the trust had an income of £48,000 and an expenditure of £47,000. Grants to individuals total around £18,000 a year.

Exclusions

Grants are not available for childcare for mature students or foreign students studying in the UK.

Applications

On a form available from the correspondent, for consideration in March, June, September or December. Applications should be submitted in the preceding month directly by the individual or through the relevant school/college/educational welfare agency or through another third party and signed by the applicant. For recurrent grants, applicants must reapply each academic year.

The Holywood Trust

£75,000

Correspondent: Richard Lye, Trust Administrator, Mount St Michael, Craigs Road, Dumfries DG1 4UT (01387 269176; fax: 01387 269175; email: funds@holywood-trust.org.uk; website: www.holywood-trust.org.uk)

Trustees: Clara Weatherall; Charles Jencks; Louise Jencks; Ben Weatherall; Valerie McElroy.

SC Number: SC009942

Eligibility

Young people aged 15 to 25 living in the Dumfries and Galloway region, with a preference for people who are mentally, physically or socially disadvantaged.

Types of grants

One-off and recurrent grants of £50 to £500 to schoolchildren, people in further or higher education, vocational students, people with special educational needs and people starting work for books, equipment, instruments, fees, living expenses, childcare, educational outings and study or travel overseas. Applications which contribute to their personal development are more likely to receive support. This could include financial or material assistance to participate in education or training, access employment, establish a home or involve themselves in a project or activity which will help them or their community.

Annual grant total

Grants to individuals total around £150,000 annually.

Exclusions

No grants are given towards carpets or accommodation deposits.

Applications

On a form available from the correspondent, or which can be downloaded from the trust's website. Applications are considered at least four times a year. The trust encourages applicants to provide additional information about any disadvantage which affects them where their application form has not given them an opportunity to do so. It also welcomes any supporting information from third party workers.

Other information

The trust also supports individuals with welfare needs and groups and project applications which benefit young people.

John Primrose Trust

£7,000

Correspondent: The Trustees, 1 Newall Terrace, Dumfries DG1 1LN

SC Number: SC009173

Eligibility

Young people in need with a connection to Dumfries and Maxwelltown by parentage or by living there.

Types of grants

Grants to students to help with educational needs or help for people starting work.

Annual grant total

About £14,000, half of which is given to individuals for relief-in-need and educational purposes.

Applications

On an application form available from the correspondent, to be considered in June and December.

The Stewartry Educational Trust

£2,000

Correspondent: The Clerk, Corselet College, Buittle, Castle Douglas DG7 1NJ

SC Number: SC017079

Eligibility

Persons belonging to the Stewartry of Kirkcudbright (i.e. the area of the Stewartry of Kirkcudbright prior to local government re-organisation in 1975).

Types of grants

One-off grants are given to schoolchildren for educational outings in Scotland and for general study costs to people starting work and students in

further or higher education, including mature students and postgraduates.

Annual grant total

In 2010/11 the trust had an income of £6,200. Grants usually total around £2,000 a year.

Applications

On a form available from the correspondent with details of any grants available from other sources. Applications can be submitted directly by the individual or through a parent/ guardian, social worker, Citizens Advice, other welfare agency or other third party. They should be submitted in February, May or August for consideration in the following month.

John Wallace Trust Scheme

£6,000

Correspondent: The Department for Finance And Corporate Services, Dumfries And Galloway Council, Carruthers House, English Street, Dumfries DG1 2HP (website: www. dgcommunity.net/dgcommunity/services. aspx?id=498)

SC Number: SC011640

Eligibility

Young people who live in the following areas: the electoral wards of Kirkland, Kello, Crichton, Douglas, Cairn, Morton and that part of Dalswinton Ward lying outside the parish of Dumfries and all in the local government area of Nithsdale District.

Types of grants

Bursaries for educational costs and travel grants for visits of an educational nature.

Annual grant total

About £6,000 a year.

Applications

Application forms are available from the correspondent or the website. The closing date is 31 December each year.

Wigtownshire Educational Trust

£1,500

Correspondent: Council Secretariat, Dumfries and Galloway Council, Department Of Corporate Finance, Carruthers House, English Street, Dumfries DG1 2HP

SC Number: SC019526

Eligibility

People who live in the former county of Wigtownshire who can demonstrate

personal hardship and that no other source of funding is available.

Types of grants

Grants ranging from £50 to £300 to schoolchildren, college students, undergraduates, vocational students, mature students, people with special educational needs and people starting work. Grants given include those towards, clothing/uniforms, fees, study/ travel abroad, books, equipment/ instruments and excursions. Assistance is also given towards gaining practical experience of trades and promoting education in the visual arts, music and drama.

Annual grant total

About £1,500.

Applications

On a form available from the above address. Applications are considered throughout the year. If the applicant is a child/young person, details of parental income are required.

East, North and South Ayrshire

The John Longwill Education Trust

£0

Correspondent: James McCosh, Clydesdale Bank Chambers, Dalry, Ayrshire KA24 5AB

SC Number: SC005483

Eligibility

Scholars or students who are attending higher grade school or university in Scotland and who are native to Dalry and of Scottish descent.

Types of grants

Payments of about £100 each.

Annual grant total

In 2010 the trust had an income of £520. There has been no expenditure for the past five years. The trustees state that it is active, they are open to applications and the lack of expenditure is due to the very narrow eligibility criteria, which they are looking to widen in the future.

Applications

In writing to the correspondent at any time.

The C. K. Marr Educational Trust

£200,000

Correspondent: David Stewart, Clerk, 1 Howard Street, Kilmarnock KA1 2BW (01563 572727)

SC Number: SC016730

Eligibility

People who currently live in Troon or the Troon electoral wards.

Types of grants

Mainly bursaries, scholarships and educational travel grants for those at college or university.

Annual grant total

Over £200,000 a year.

Applications

On a form available from the correspondent to be submitted either directly by the individual, or through an organisation such as a school or an educational welfare agency.

North and South Lanarkshire

Loaningdale School Company

£1,500

Correspondent: Fiona Watson, Exchange Place 3, Semple Street, Edinburgh EH3 8BL (01314 733500)

SC Number: SC001065

Eligibility

Children and young people aged 12 to 20 who are in need and live within the Clydesdale local area of South Lanarkshire, especially former pupils of Loaningdale School.

Types of grants

One-off grants ranging from £100 to £1,000 towards furthering the individual's education or employment prospects. Priority is given to creative or outdoor pursuits for young people, young unemployed people and post-school education and training of young people.

Annual grant total

In 2010/11 the trust had an income of £21,000, a considerable increase on previous years. Previously, grants to individuals have totalled around £1,500.

Applications

On a form available from the correspondent or the website, with guidelines for applicants. Applications are considered in March, June, September and December, and should be submitted in the previous month.

Other information

Grants are primarily made to organisations.

Highlands and Islands

The Fresson Trust

£500

Correspondent: The Secretary, The Pilk, 18 Academy Street, Fortrose, Ross-shire IV10 8TW (email: info@fressontrust.org.uk; website: www.fressontrust.org.uk)

Trustees: R. A. Fresson; T. Whittome; B. Spence; George Chesworth; J. P. Dacre; Hugh Halcro-Johnston; Duncan MacDonald; David Morgan; D. Ratter; C. Birks; D. Lockett; J. Hamilton; W. F. F. Hamilton; John Harris; John Young; P. Clegg.

SC Number: SC020054

Eligibility

People wishing to further their career in aviation who are living in, or visiting, the Highlands and Islands.

Types of grants

Grants in the past have been given to assist in the payment of flying lessons and in the form of a scholarship bursary. One-off grants can be given to help people starting work to buy books, equipment and clothing and help with their travel expenses. Students in further or higher education may be provided with money for books, fees or living expenses. Mature students can receive grants for books, travel, fees and childcare.

Annual grant total

About £500.

Applications

In writing to the correspondent at any time. Applicants should state how they can assist in the development of aviation in the Highlands and Islands.

Highland

The Highland Children's Trust

£10,000

Correspondent: The Administrator, 105 Castle Street, Inverness IV2 3EA (01463 243872; fax: 01463 243872; email: info@hctrust.co.uk; website: www.hctrust.co.uk)

SC Number: SC006008

Eligibility

Children and young people in need who are under 25 and live in the Highlands.

Types of grants

One-off grants of £50 to £500 are available for the following purposes:
- Student hardship funding
- School or educational trips
- Family holidays
- Educational items for children with special educational needs

Annual grant total

Around £20,000 for both education and welfare.

Exclusions

Grants are not given for postgraduate study, to pay off debts, nor to purchase clothing, footwear, food, furniture or cars and so on.

Applications

On a form available from the correspondent or downloaded from the website, where criteria and guidelines are also posted. They can be submitted at any time either directly by the individual or through a social worker, Citizens Advice or other welfare agency. Applications must include details of income and savings and are considered at board meetings held on a regular basis.

Other information

No funding is given to organisations.

Isle of Lewis

Ross and Cromarty Educational Trust

£5,000

Correspondent: The Director of Education, Comhairle nan Eilean, Sandwick Road, Stornoway, Isle of Lewis HS1 2BW (01851 709546; email: catriona-maciver@cne-siar.gov.uk; website: www.cne-siar.gov.uk/education)

Eligibility

People who live on the Isle of Lewis.

Types of grants

Grants range from £30 to £200 for: (a) books, fees and living expenses and study or travel abroad for students in further and higher education; (b) books, equipment, instruments and clothing for people starting work; (c) books, travel and fees for mature students; and (d) books and educational outings for schoolchildren. Grants are sometimes considered for various social, cultural and recreational purposes for individuals.

Annual grant total

The trust has an income of about £10,000 each year, all of which is available in grants to individuals and organisations.

Applications

On a form available from the Comhairle nan Eilean Siar website.

Orkney Islands

Orkney Educational Trust Scheme 1961

£2,500

Correspondent: The Director of Education, Orkney Islands Council, Education Department, Council Offices, School Place, Kirkwall, Orkney KW15 1NY (01856 873535)

Eligibility

People on postgraduate courses, in further education or on apprenticeships who live in the former county of Orkney.

Types of grants

Subsidiary grants of £8 to £50 to help with travel, material costs and fees/living expenses for further education students. Grants are also made to people starting work to help with books, equipment/ instruments, clothing and travel costs, and to schoolchildren to help with books and educational outings. Grants may also be given for the promotion of education in the community.

Annual grant total

Grants totalling about £2,500 are made to around 50 individuals each year.

Applications

In writing to the correspondent. Applications are considered in October.

Wales

General

The Cambrian Educational Foundation for Deaf Children

£17,000 (57 grants)

Correspondent: Pamela Brown, Clerk to the Trustees, Montreux, 30 Lon Cedwyn, Sketty, Swansea SA2 0TH (01792 207628)

Trustees: Margaret Hughes; John Jeremy; Edward Jenkins; Roger Meredith; Norman Moore; June Talbot; Christopher Elmore.

CC Number: 515848

Eligibility

People who are deaf or have partial hearing aged under 25 who live or whose parents live in Wales. Beneficiaries can be in special classes (units) in ordinary and special schools in Wales; students in further education; and people entering employment.

Types of grants

One-off and occasionally annual grants of £100 to £500. Grants have been provided for computers, software, school uniforms, tools/equipment, instruments, books, occasionally for educational outings in the UK and for study or travel abroad, to people starting work and to further and higher education students for books.

Annual grant total

In 2011 the foundation made grants to 57 individuals, four of them aged under 18 and the rest over 18. Grants totalled £17,000.

Exclusions

Grants are not given for leisure trips.

Applications

Applications, on a form available from the correspondent, can be submitted directly by the individual, or through their school/college/educational welfare agency or other third party. They are considered throughout the year.

Other information

Grants are also given to organisations.

The Cambrian Educational Trust Fund

£2,000

Correspondent: Owen Williams, Wales Council for the Blind, Hallinans House, 2nd Floor, 22 Newport Road, Cardiff CF24 0TD (02920 473954; fax: 02920 433920; email: owen@wcb-ccd.org.uk; website: www.wcb-ccd.org.uk)

Trustees: Peter Curtis; Brian Mawby.

CC Number: 525768

Eligibility

People under the age of 21 who are blind or partially-sighted and were born in, or live in, Wales.

Types of grants

One-off grants to promote education, such as towards care and maintenance costs.

Annual grant total

Grants usually total around £2,000 each year.

Applications

On a form available from the correspondent. Applications are considered quarterly. The trust welcomes telephone enquiries from potential applications to discuss suitability and how to apply.

The James Pantyfedwen Foundation

£87,000 (30 grants)

Correspondent: Richard H Morgan, Executive Secretary, Pantyfedwen, 9 Market Street, Aberystwyth SY23 1DL (01970 612806; email: pantyfedwen@btinternet.com)

Trustees: Ifan Hughes; William Phillips; Ken Richards; Emrys Jones; Roy Sharp; Rhidian Griffiths; Geraint Jones; Alun Evans; Enid Morgan; Derec Morgan; David Lewis; Eryn White.

CC Number: 1069598

Eligibility

Candidates for Christian ministry from Wales and Welsh postgraduate students.

Types of grants

One-off and recurrent grants according to need. Most grants are for fees and in exceptional circumstances, living costs.

Annual grant total

In 2010 the trust gave grants to twenty eight postgraduate students for the cost of their tuition fees and two Undeb Cymru Fydd scholarships of £1,000 each totalling £87,000.

Exclusions

Undergraduate, accountancy, PGCEs, social work, master's degrees of more than one year's duration or those courses which have not been approved by the department of education.

Applications

On a form available to download from the website, which should be returned by post. The closing date is 30 June preceding the academic year for which the application is being made. Applications are considered in July.

Other information

This trust also supports organisations and churches.

The May Price SRN Award

£500

Correspondent: Roger Jones, Director of Resources, Carmarthenshire County Council, County Hall, Carmarthen SA31 1JP (01267 234567)

Trustees: Hei Williams; G. H. Wooldridge; R. Sully.

CC Number: 514578

Eligibility

People who have lived in Cardiganshire, Carmarthenshire or Pembrokeshire for at least two years and who are pursuing a course in medical or medically related studies.

Types of grants
Grants to help with the cost of books or equipment or to supplement existing grants.

Annual grant total
In 2010/11 the fund had both an income and expenditure of £500.

Applications
On a form available from the correspondent, to be returned by 31 October each year.

Reardon Smith Nautical Trust
See entry on page 101

The Michael Sobell Welsh People's Charitable Trust

£1,500

Correspondent: S E Davies, Dolenog Old Hall, Llanidloes, Powys SY18 6PP

Trustees: Prudence Williams; Shan Davies; Jeremy Bird; Colin Wilkes; Leyson Howell.

CC Number: 255437

Eligibility
People in need who live in Wales.

Types of grants
One-off and recurrent grants ranging from £40 to £500.

Annual grant total
In 2010/11 the trust had an income of £3,600 and a total expenditure of £3,300.

Applications
In writing to the correspondent.

Other information
This trust makes grants to both individuals and organisations.

The Welsh Broadcasting Trust
See entry on page 97

Mid-Wales

Ceredigion

The Cardiganshire Intermediate and Technical Educational Fund

£3,000

Correspondent: Mr Alun Morgan, Ceredigion County Council, Canolfan Rheidol, Rhodfa Padarn, Aberystwyth SY23 2DE (01970 633691; email: decsdata@ceredigion.gov.uk)

Trustee: Ceredigion County Council.

CC Number: 514597

Eligibility
Individuals who have, at any time, been in attendance for at least two years at a maintained secondary school in the Ceredigion area (the former county of Cardiganshire).

Types of grants
Grants of £100 to £150 a year, to help with secondary school, college or university expenses and fees or to supplement existing grants.

Annual grant total
In the two financial years to 2011 the trust had an income of £0 and an expenditure of £3,000.

Applications
Application forms are available from the correspondent from August, to be submitted by 30 November.

Powys

The Thomas John Jones Memorial Fund for Scholarships and Exhibitions

£44,000

Correspondent: David Meredith, Clerk to the Trustees, Cilmery, The Avenue, Brecon, Powys LD3 9BG (01874 623373)

Trustees: Gillian Benyon; Patricia Clarke; Liam Fitzpatrick; Gillian Thomas; William Powell; Emma Metcalfe.

CC Number: 525281

Eligibility
People under the age of 26 whom, for a period of at least two years, have both lived and attended a secondary school in the former county of Brecknockshire. Preference is given to applicants

undertaking courses of study or training in civil engineering at universities or colleges. Postgraduate applicants must have gained an upper second class degree or above except in exceptional circumstances.

Types of grants
Grants of up to £1,500 a year for those studying technical studies at a further or higher education level and up to £2,800 a year for postgraduates. After this grants for non-technical studies may be made and postgraduate grants of up to £2,300 for one year only.

Annual grant total
In 2010/11 the trust had assets of £1.4 million and an income of £51,000. Educational grants totalled £44,000.

Applications
In writing to the correspondent.

Edmund Jones' Charity

£21,000

Correspondent: Ruth Jefferies, Steeple House, Brecon, Powys LD3 7DJ (01874 638024; email: edmundjonescharity@gmail.com)

Trustees: Ieuan Williams; Bryan Williams; M. J. Jenkins; R. Evans; Geoffrey Marshall; Mark Morgan.

CC Number: 525315

Eligibility
People under the age of 25 who live or work within the town of Brecon.

Types of grants
Help towards the cost of education, training, apprenticeship or equipment for those starting work and grants tenable at any Brecon town secondary school, training college for teachers, university or other institution of further education approved by the trustees. Grants range from £50 to £300.

Annual grant total
The latest accounts available were for 2010. During the year the charity had assets of £443,000, an income of £34,000 and made grants totalling £21,000.

Applications
On a form available from the correspondent giving details of the college/course/apprenticeship and the anticipated cost, together with details of any other grants received or applied for. Applications may be submitted by the individual, parent or college. They are considered at any time, but mainly in October.

The Llanidloes Relief-in-Need Charity

£700

Correspondent: Mrs S J Jarman, Clerk, Llwynderw, Old Hall, Llanidloes, Powys SY18 6PW (01686 412636)

Trustees: Gwenda Trow; John Williams; Lynne Evans; Ann Hughes; Revd Michael Starkey.

CC Number: 259955

Eligibility

Students who live in the communities of Llanidloes and Llanidloes Without. No support to students not living within three miles of the town, or to foreign students studying in the area.

Types of grants

Grants to help with the cost of books, living expenses and other essential items for those at college or university.

Annual grant total

About £1,500.

Applications

In writing to the correspondent.

The Powys Welsh Church Acts Fund

£300

Correspondent: The Chief Financial Officer, Powys County Council, County Hall, Llandrindod Wells, Powys LD1 5LG (01597 826337)

Trustee: Powys County Council.

CC Number: 507967

Eligibility

People under 25 years living in Powys.

Types of grants

Grants, ranging from £50 to £250 for those wishing to follow a course of study at college or university for uniforms/clothing, fees, study/travel abroad, equipment/instruments and books. Help may also be available for those preparing for, or entering a trade, profession or calling.

Annual grant total

In 2010/11 the fund had assets of £2.1 million and an income of £56,000. Grants to individuals totalled £300.

Applications

On a form available from the correspondent to be submitted directly by the individual.

Other information

Grants are also made to organisations.

Ceredigion

Visual Impairment Breconshire

£2,000

Correspondent: Edward Vince, Ken Dy Gwair, Aber Farm, Talybont-on-Usk, Brecon LD3 7YS (01874 676202)

Trustees: Michael Knee; Edward Vince; Terrence Ottewell; Eileen Bufton; Margaret James; Margaret Seaman; John King; John Lloyd; Derek Stephens.

CC Number: 217377

Eligibility

Blind and partially-sighted people living in Brecknock.

Types of grants

One-off grants at Christmas and for special equipment/special needs, such as talking books and college fees.

Annual grant total

In 2010/11 the charity had an income of £4,600 and an expenditure of £4,500.

Applications

In writing to the correspondent, to be considered when received.

Other information

The charity also organises audio newsletters and social activities.

North Wales

Doctor William Lewis' Charity

£40

Correspondent: Michelle Freeman, The Diocesan Centre, Cathedral Close, Bangor, Gwynedd LL57 1RL (01248 354999)

Trustee: Susan Jones.

CC Number: 216361

Eligibility

Students under the age of 25 who live in the former counties of Anglesey, Caernarvon, Merioneth, Montgomery, Flint and Denbigh.

Types of grants

A portion of the foundation's income is used to make awards for students at Oxford, Cambridge or the University of Wales and St David's University College, Lampeter. Grants are also given to applicants who are in training for a profession or trade.

Annual grant total

In 2010/11 the charity had an income of £1,700 and an expenditure of £40.

Expenditure in previous years has been around £500.

Applications

On a form available from the correspondent, to be submitted directly by the individual by the beginning of October.

The Wrexham (Parochial) Educational Foundation

£12,000 (24 grants)

Correspondent: Frieda Leech, Clerk, Holly Chase, Pen Y Palmant Road, Minera, Wrexham LL11 3YW (01978 754152; email: clerk@wpef@gmail.com)

Trustees: John Partington; Ida Turley; Mike West; Roger Berry; Carol Jones; Noel Carter; John Kenworthy; Joan Lowe; James Harris; Shirley Griffiths.

CC Number: 525414

Eligibility

People under 25 who live in the county borough of Wrexham and who attended for at least two years one of the following: Minera and Brymbo Aided Primary School or St Giles Voluntary Controlled Infant and/or Junior Schools, Wrexham.

Types of grants

Grants for costs such as clothing/uniform, travel, books and equipment to help students in secondary and further education, and those starting an apprenticeship or training. Grants have included supporting a student with disabilities who was living at home and unable to receive a statutory grant.

Annual grant total

In 2011 the foundation had assets of £10.6 million and an income of £393,000. Grants to 24 individuals totalled £12,000.

Applications

In writing to the correspondent. Applications must be submitted directly by the individual for consideration in September.

Other information

Grants are also made to schools within the area of benefit.

Anglesey

The Owen Lloyd Educational Foundation

£5,000

Correspondent: Emlyn Evans, Nant Bychan Farm, Moelfre, Gwynedd LL72 8HF (01248 410269)

Trustees: Geraint Edwards; Thomas Jones; Owen Hughes; Thomas Evans; Derlwyn Hughes; Andrew John; John Jones.

CC Number: 525253

Eligibility

People between 16 and 25 who live in the parishes of Penrhosligwy, Moelfre or the neighbouring civil or ecclesiastical parishes studying at a further or higher education establishment. Preference is given (larger grants) to residents of Penrhosligwy, as this was the original area covered by the trust's deed.

Types of grants

Grants are given to help with: books, fees/living expenses, travel costs (but not for study/travel abroad) and tools and equipment for students in further/higher education; and apprenticeship costs such as books, equipment, clothing and travel.

Annual grant total

About £5,000 is awarded annually.

Applications

On a form available from the correspondent, including details of income and expenditure. Applications are considered in October. Grants are given in June.

Conwy

The Sir John Henry Morris-Jones Trust Fund

£2,500

Correspondent: C Earley, Clerk to the Trustees, Town Hall, 7 Rhiw Road, Colwyn Bay LL29 7TG (01492 532248; email: colwyncouncil@freenetname.co.uk)

Trustees: Alice Robinson; Glyn Jones; Jim Barry; Brian Cossey; Hazel Meredith.

CC Number: 504313

Eligibility

People living in the former municipal borough of Colwyn Bay, as existing on 31 March 1974 (that is, prior to the reorganisation of local government in 1974). Applicants must be under the age of 19 on 31 March.

Types of grants

Applicants have to satisfy the trustees, at a personal interview, of their degree of excellence in one of the following activities: arts and crafts; sport; academic and research; science and technology; industry and commerce; and any other field of activity that applicants may feel would meet the requirements of the trustees. Grants are one-off.

Annual grant total

Each year around £2,500 is distributed.

Applications

On a form available from the correspondent. Applications are considered in April/May.

Richard Owen Scholarships

£500

Correspondent: Tessa Wildermoth, Llandudno Town Council, Town Hall, Lloyd Street, Llandudno, Gwynedd LL30 2UD (01492879130)

Trustees: Philip Evans; Carys Roberts; Terence Davies.

CC Number: 525286

Eligibility

People aged under 25 who live in Llandudno. Preference is given to undergraduates at the University of Bangor, but not exclusively so.

Types of grants

Grants, ranging from £70 to £100 are given towards clothing, tools, instruments or books for people leaving education and preparing for work. Student bursaries are also available as are grants towards educational travel abroad.

Annual grant total

About £500.

Applications

On a form available from the correspondent, to be submitted in September for consideration in August.

Denbighshire

The Freeman Evans St David's Day Denbigh Charity

£1,000

Correspondent: Medwyn Jones, Denbigh Town Council, Town Hall, Crown Square, Denbigh, Clwyd LL16 3TB (01745 815984; email: townclerk@denbightowncouncil.gov.uk)

Trustees: Revd Jonathan Smith; Revd Wayne Roberts; Medwyn Jones; Ann Larson; Gwyrfai; Dr Chris Madoc-Jones; Alan Davies.

CC Number: 518033

Eligibility

People in need who live in Denbigh and Henllan.

Types of grants

One-off grants towards the cost of volunteer programmes overseas, educational equipment and so on.

Annual grant total

In 2010/11 the charity had an income of £112,000 and made four grants to individuals totalling £6,000. The charity also gave grants totalling £30,000 to organisations.

Applications

In writing to the correspondent. Applications can be made either directly by the individual or through a third party such as a social worker, Citizens Advice or other welfare agency. The trustees meet regularly throughout the year to consider applications.

Other information

Grants are also given for welfare purposes.

The Robert David Hughes Scholarship Foundation

£18,000

Correspondent: Peter Bowler, Trustee, McLintocks Blease Lloyd, Hamilton House, 56 Hamilton Street, Birkenhead Wirral CH41 5HZ (01516 479581)

Trustees: Peter Bowler; Robert Roberts; Janie Smith; Nia Lyon.

CC Number: 525404

Eligibility

University students who were either born in the community of Denbigh, or had a parent or parents resident in the area at the time of his or her birth, or at the date of the award have a parent or parents resident in the area who have lived there for at least ten years. Full documentary evidence is required.

Types of grants

Grants are made according to need to university students.

Annual grant total

In 2010/11 the foundation had both an income and expenditure of £19,000. Previously the foundation has spent the majority of its income on grants to individuals.

Exclusions

Individuals attending colleges of further education do not qualify for a grant.

Applications

On a form available from the correspondent, to be submitted not later than 30 September. Applications are considered in November each year. Grants are made each term on receipt of completed certificates of attendance, signed by the principal or registrar of the university. After the first year, applicants are automatically sent forms for subsequent years.

The Llanynys Educational Foundation

£600

Correspondent: Robert Kinnier, Rhewl Post-Office, Ruthin, Denbighshire LL15 1TH (01824 702730)

Trustees: Robert Kinnier; Clwyd Thomas; Elizabeth Hughes; Marion Bates; Meirion Roberts.

CC Number: 507513

Eligibility

People under 25 who live in the community of Llanynys Rural, and that part of the community of Ruthin which was formerly the parish of Llanynys Urban.

Types of grants

One-off and recurrent grants up to £100 for students in further and higher education to assist with books, fees/living expenses, and study/travel abroad.

Annual grant total

About £600 is available each year.

Applications

The charity places advertisements in the local press shortly after A-level results are published. Applications are considered in September. If a large number of requests are received in relation to the funds available, preference is given to first time applicants.

Applicants should include in their application their age; place of residence; course to be followed; qualification pursued; institution attended; and the purpose to which the grant will be put.

John Matthews Educational Charity

£9,000

Correspondent: P B Smith, Lyndhurst, 6 Vernon Avenue, Hooton, South Wirral, Cheshire CH66 6AL (01513 276103; email: pbsberlian@aol.com; website: www.johnmatthewscharity.co.uk)

Trustees: Judge Swift; Eryl Williams; Catrin Penge; Andrew Sully; Anthony Rees; Philip Bowd.

CC Number: 525553

Eligibility

People under 25 resident in the North Wales areas comprising of Chirk, Llanarmon-Yn-Lal, Llandegla, Llangollen Rural, Llantysilio, Glyndwr, the Borough of Wrexham Maelor, the County of Clwyd and the Borough of Oswestry in the County of Shropshire

Types of grants

Grants of £250 to £2,000 for equipment or course fees. Grants have been given to assist musicians, actors, journalists, tree surgeons and medical students.

The charity favours postgraduate or second degree students with a vocational element who are not getting other financial support, although undergraduates can be supported.

Annual grant total

In 2011 the charity had an income of £16,000 and an expenditure of £9,300.

Applications

On a form available from the website along with a covering letter giving as much information as possible and proof of identity including proof of residence within the area of benefit. Trustees usually meet twice a year in May and November.

Flintshire

The Owen Jones Charity

£1,500

Correspondent: Dr Jack Wolstenholme, Secretary, 18 St Peter's Park, Northop, Mold, Clwyd CH7 6DP (01352 840739)

Trustees: Revd Ray Billingsley; Dr Jack Wolstenholme; Muriel Patterson.

CC Number: 525453

Eligibility

College and university students and apprentices from Northop who are in need.

Types of grants

One-off and recurrent grants according to need. Recent grants have been given to students with inadequate grants to allow them to buy basic food and to apprentices entering a trade for tools and equipment.

Annual grant total

In 2010/11 the charity had an income of £4,500, a total expenditure of £7,300 and made grants to individuals totalling £3,000.

Applications

In writing to the correspondent. An application form for students to use is currently being drafted and should be used when available.

Other information

The charity also makes grants to local schools.

Gwynedd

The Morgan Scholarship Fund

£1,000

Correspondent: Strategic Director, Cyngor Gwynedd Council, Shirehall Street, Caernarfon, Gwynedd LL55 ISH (01286 679273; email: davidroberts@gwynedd.gov.uk)

Trustee: Resources Directorate.

CC Number: 525297

Eligibility

People born or living in the civil parish of Llanengan who are under the age of 25. When funds permit, the area of benefit may be extended to include other parishes in the rural district of Lleyn.

Types of grants

Preference is given to undergraduates of the University College of North Wales. However, grants are also given for the following purposes: for those at college or university; for those going abroad to pursue their education; financial assistance, clothing, tools, instruments or books to help those leaving school, college or university to prepare for, or enter, a profession, trade or calling.

Annual grant total

About £1,000 is given a year.

Applications

On a form available from the correspondent. Applications are considered in September.

The R. H. Owen Memorial Fund (Cronfa Goffa R. H Owen)

£500

Correspondent: John Hughes, Trustee, Tan-y-Clogwyn, Llanberis, Caernarfon, Gwynedd LL55 4LF (01286 871562)

Trustees: Brian Jones; David Pritchard; John Hughes; H. Williams; Ralph Jones; Robin Parry; Trefor Edwards; Barry Thomas; Robert Townsend.

CC Number: 532326

Eligibility

People in secondary, further or higher education who were born in, or whose parents have lived for at least five years in, the parish of Llanberis and Brynrefail Comprehensive School catchment area.

Types of grants

Recurrent grants are given to schoolchildren, undergraduates, vocational students and people starting work for any academic or vocational need.

Annual grant total

Grants total around £500 each year.

Applications

On a form available from the correspondent which should be submitted directly by the individual. The closing date for applications is 31 August.

The Peter Saunders Trust

£2,500

Correspondent: Peter Saunders, Trustee, PO Box 67, Tywyn LL36 6AH (01654 713939; email: enquiries@ petersaunderstrust.co.uk; website: www. petersaunderstrust.co.uk)

Trustees: Peter Saunders; Ifor Williams; Theresa Hartland; Keith Bartlett; Richard Saunders.

CC Number: 1108153

Eligibility

People who live within Tywyn and the surrounding villages. 'The trust favours projects which show endeavour, a measure of self-reliance and spirit of enterprise.'

Types of grants

Grants towards providing opportunities and learning experiences.

Annual grant total

In 2010/11 the trust had an income of £2,400 and an expenditure of £51,000, including grants to organisations and individuals. Previously grants to individuals have totalled £2,500.

Applications

In writing to the correspondent. Full guidelines are available from the trust's website.

Dr Daniel William's Educational Fund

£33,000 (160 grants)

Correspondent: Dwyryd Williams, Bryn Golau, Pencefn, Dolgellau, Gwynedd LL40 2YP (email: dwyryd@pencefn. freeserve.co.uk)

Trustees: Anne Roberts; Gwyneth Roberts; Gerallt Hughes; Gwenan Williams; Tecwyn Owen; Tegwen Humphreys; Wyn Meredith; Ann Lloyd-Jones; Rona Lewis.

CC Number: 525756

Eligibility

People under 25 attending college or university, particularly schoolchildren

with serious family difficulties and people with special educational needs. Preference for (i) former pupils or close relatives of former pupils of Dr William's School, Dolgellau and (ii) people who live, or who have a parent who lives, in the district of Meirionnydd. This preference is strictly applied in view of the demands on the trust's income.

Types of grants

Recurrent grants towards the cost of books, equipment, fees/living expenses and study or travel abroad for students who are part of or linked to an educational course. Awards are usually of a maximum of £500.

Annual grant total

160 grants were made totalling £33,000 during 2010/11, distributed in the following categories:

- Course fees: 33 grants
- Travelling: 31 grants
- Music tuition: 28 grants
- Books: 20 grants
- Clothing and equipment: 16 grants
- Computer equipment: 13 grants
- Music equipment: five grants

Applications

In writing, directly by the individual to the correspondent, requesting an application form. The grants committee meets on a monthly basis.

Wrexham

Dame Dorothy Jeffreys Educational Foundation

£1,500

Correspondent: Frieda Leech, Holly Chase, Pen Y Palmant Road, Minera, Wrexham LL11 3YW (01978 754152; email: clerk.wpef@gmail.com)

Trustees: Mike West; Roger Berry; Carol Jones; Ida Turley; Noel Carter; Peter Blore; John Kenworthy; Joan Lowe; James Harris; Shirley Griffiths; Nicola Hulley.

CC Number: 525430

Eligibility

People in need aged between 16 and 25 who live or have attended school in the former borough of Wrexham or the communities of Abenbury, Bersham, Broughton, Bieston, Brymbo, Esclusham Above, Esclusham Below, Gresford, Gwersyllt and Minera.

Types of grants

Grants of £50 minimum. Grants for general education purposes are given to schoolchildren, further/higher education students, people starting work and vocational students. Mature students up to the age of 25 can also receive grants.

Annual grant total

In 2011 the trust had an income of £1,400 and an expenditure of £1,900.

Applications

On a form available from the correspondent to be submitted directly by the individual. Applications are considered in November/December and should be submitted by 1 October.

The Ruabon and District Relief-in-Need Charity

£700

Correspondent: J R Fenner, Secretary, 65 Albert Grove, Ruabon, Wrexham LL14 6AF (01978 820102; email: jamesrfenner@tiscali.co.uk)

Trustees: Mrs Mair Mates; Vera Wainwright; John Griffiths; Joan Lowe; Jean Speare; Michael Edwards.

CC Number: 212817

Eligibility

People in need who live in the county borough of Wrexham, which covers the community council districts of Cefn Mawr, Penycae, Rhosllanerchrugog (including Johnstown) and Ruabon.

Types of grants

One-off and occasionally recurrent grants of up to £200. Grants are given to schoolchildren towards uniforms/ clothing, equipment/instruments and educational visits/excursions.

Annual grant total

About £1,400 in educational and relief-in-need grants.

Exclusions

Loans are not given, nor are grants given to investigate bankruptcy proceedings.

Applications

In writing to the correspondent either directly by the individual or a family member, through a third party such as a social worker or teacher, or through an organisation such as Citizens Advice or a school. Applications are considered on an ongoing basis.

South Wales

The David Davies Memorial Trusts

£10,000

Correspondent: Andrew Morse, Coal Industry Social Welfare Organisation, Woodland Terrace, Maesycoed, Pontypridd, Mid-Glamorgan CF37 1DZ

(01443 485233; fax: 01443 486226; email: andrew.morse@ciswo.org.uk)

Trustees: Tyrone O'Sullivan; Wayne Thomas.

CC Number: 307363

Eligibility

South Wales mineworkers or their (unemployed) dependents, or redundant or retired mineworkers who have not taken up employment since leaving the coalmining industry.

Types of grants

Grants ranging from £200 to £500, to enable people to pursue educational courses or other approved studies at university which they otherwise could not afford.

Annual grant total

In 2010 the trust had an income of £9,000 and an expenditure of £15,000

Applications

On a form available from the correspondent. Applications can be made directly by the individual and are considered throughout the year.

The Roger Edwards Educational Trust (formerly the Monmouthshire Further Education Trust Fund)

£1,000

Correspondent: Jonathan Stephens, Ty Cornel, 11 Castle Parade, USK NP15 1AA (01291 673344)

Trustees: Geoffrey Hughes; Jonathan Stephens; Anthony John Kear; Martyn Llewillin; Christopher Cowburn; Brian Strong; Elizabeth Baker.

CC Number: 525638

Eligibility

Further or higher education students who have attended a local comprehensive/secondary school and have lived in the Greater Gwent area, except Newport, that is, the council areas of Caerphilly (part), Torfaen, Blaenau Gwent and Monmouthshire.

Types of grants

One-off grants, although students can reapply in subsequent years, towards books, fees, living costs, travel and equipment. Grants range between £60 and £360, depending on student's circumstances. Full-time students receiving funding from another source are not funded.

Annual grant total

In 2010/11 the trust made grants totalling £1,000 to individuals for educational purposes.

Applications

Application forms are available from the correspondent, for consideration throughout the year.

Other information

Two thirds of the income of the trust is dedicated to the Monmouthshire Farm School Trust and the remainder is distributed between individuals and local schools.

The Gane Charitable Trust

£10,000

Correspondent: Ken Stradling, c/o Bristol Guild of Applied Art, 68–70 Park Street, Bristol BS1 5JY (01179 265548)

Trustees: Kenneth Stradling; Ben Barman; Byron Thomas; Cleo Witt; Jeremy Cornwell; Peter Metcalfe; Shekar Bheenuck.

CC Number: 211515

Eligibility

Students of arts and crafts, or design and social welfare. There is a preference for applicants from Bristol and south Wales and those in further education.

Types of grants

Grants are available to help meet the educational costs of college students, vocational students and mature students and their children. Grants are given towards fees, books and equipment/instruments and range from £200 to £500 and are normally one-off.

Annual grant total

In 2011 the trust had assets of £703,000 and an income of £29,000. Grants, gifts and donations to organisations and individuals totalled £20,000.

Applications

On a form available from the correspondent. Applications are considered in January, May and September.

The Glamorgan Further Education Trust Fund

£48,000

Correspondent: Naomi Davies, 1st Floor Aberafan House, Educational Finance, Port Talbot Civic Centre, Port Talbot, West Glamorgan SA13 1PJ (01639 763553)

Trustee: Neath Port Talbot County Borough Council.

CC Number: 525509

Eligibility

Pupils who attend a county secondary school in Glamorgan and female pupils who attend a maintained primary schools in the parishes of Llantrisant, Pontypridd, Pentyrch, Llanfabon, Llantwit Fardre, Eglwysilan and that part of the parish of Llanwonno comprising the former Ynysybwl ward of the former Mountain Ash urban district.

Types of grants

Cash grants tenable at any teacher training college, university or other institution of further education (including professional and technical) approved by the council and governed by rules made by the council. Financial assistance, outfits, clothing, tools, instruments or books to assist those leaving school, university or other educational establishments to prepare for or enter a profession, trade or calling.

Annual grant total

The latest accounts available were for 2009/10. During the year the trust had an income of £62,000 and gave grants totalling £48,000.

Exclusions

Applicants are not eligible for assistance if they are in receipt of a central government bursary or a mandatory or discretionary award, or are exempt from the payment of the tuition fee.

Applications

On a form available from the correspondent. Applications should be submitted before 31 May each year for consideration in July/August.

The Gwent Further Education Trust Fund

£10,000

Correspondent: The Trustees, c/o Pupil and Student Services Section, Monmouthshire County Council, Education Department, County Hall, Cwmbran, Gwent NP44 2XH (01633 644507/644664; email: jemmacleverly@monmouthshire.gov.uk)

CC Number: 525638

Eligibility

People over 16 studying part-time who are resident in the former Gwent area (excluding Newport) and went to a Gwent secondary school.

Types of grants

Grants to help with school, college or university fees, books and equipment. Students on Income Support or Job Seekers Allowance can receive grants of about £360; employed students receive grants of around £60.

Annual grant total

About £10,000 each year is available for grants to individuals.

Applications

On a form available from the correspondent. The trust welcomes informal contact prior to applications being formally made.

The Geoffrey Jones (Penreithin) Scholarship Fund

£2,500

Correspondent: Keith Butler, 17–19 Cardiff Street, Aberdare, Rhondda Cynon Taff CF44 7DP (01685 885500)

Trustees: Keith Butler; Colin Howells; Menna Davies; Teifwen George.

CC Number: 501964

Eligibility

People who have lived in the following parishes or districts for at least 12 months: Penderyn, Ystradfellte Vaynor and Taff Fechan Valley, Merthyr Tydfil.

Types of grants

Grants to students in further or higher education (no upper age limit) to help with the cost of books, fees/living expenses and study or travel abroad.

Annual grant total

In 2010/11 the fund had an income of £3,500 and an expenditure of £4,200. About 25 grants are made each year totalling £2,000 to £3,000.

Applications

In writing to the correspondent, including details of any educational grant received. Applications are considered in September/October each year.

Caerphilly

The Rhymney Trust

£2,000

Correspondent: David Brannan, 11 Forge Crescent, Rhymney, Tredegar NP22 5PR (01685 843094)

Trustees: Ann Dykes; David Brannan; Leonard Dykes; Thomas Perry; David Marsh; David Protheroe; Michael James; Percy Hall; Richard Pugh.

CC Number: 517118

Eligibility

People in need who live in Rhymney.

Types of grants

One-off grants ranging from £30 to £100 to schoolchildren and college students.

Annual grant total

Around £2,000 is given each year.

Applications

In writing to the correspondent directly by the individual. Applications should be submitted in June for consideration in August.

Carmarthenshire

The Dorothy May Edwards Charity

£1,000

Correspondent: Roger Jones, Director of Resources, Carmarthenshire County Council, County Hall, Carmarthen, Dyfed SA31 1JP (01267 234567)

Trustees: I. J. Jackson; N. W. Jones; Julie Griffiths.

CC Number: 1070293

Eligibility

Former pupils of Ysgol Pantycelyn School, Llandovery who are under 25 and are pursuing a course of higher education.

Types of grants

Grants of £15 to £125 to provide outfits, clothing, tools, instruments or books on leaving school, university or other educational establishment to prepare for and to enter a profession, trade or calling; travel in this country or abroad to pursue education; study music or other art; continue education at college or university or at any approved place of learning.

The Elizabeth Evans Trust

See entry on page 84

The Minnie Morgans Scholarship

£13,000

Correspondent: Roger Jones, Carmarthenshire County Council, County Hall, Carmarthen, Dyfed SA31 1JP (01267 234567)

Trustees: Roger Jones; Ieuan Jones; Gwynne Wooldridge; Patricia Jones; Roger Price.

CC Number: 504980

Eligibility

People under the age of 25 who have attended any of the secondary schools in Llanelli and who are studying drama and dramatic art at the University of Wales or any school of dramatic art approved by the trustees.

Types of grants

One-off grants usually of £1,000.

Annual grant total

In 2010/11 the trust had an income of £13,000 and an expenditure of £14,000.

Applications

Application forms are available from the correspondent and should be returned by 31 October.

The Mary Elizabeth Morris Charity

£1,000

Correspondent: Roger Jones, Director of Resources, Carmarthenshire County Council, County Hall, Carmarthen, Dyfed SA31 1JP (01267 234567)

Trustees: Elizabeth Thomas; N. W. Jones; Enid Gealy; Julie Griffiths.

CC Number: 514297

Eligibility

Past and present pupils of Ysgol Rhys Prichard School and Ysgol Pantycelyn School, who are under 25.

Types of grants

Grants to: pupils transferring from Ysgol Rhys Pritchard; supplement existing grants of beneficiaries in further or higher education; help towards the cost of education, training, apprenticeships or education for those starting work; and help with the cost of educational travel at home or abroad.

Annual grant total

About £1,000.

Applications

Application forms are available from the correspondent and should be returned in either June (for primary school pupils) or by 31 October (for secondary school pupils).

Other information

The trust also provides a Christmas tree and dinner for pupils at a local school.

The Robert Peel/ Taliaris School Charity

£400

Correspondent: Roger Jones, Director of Resources, Carmarthenshire County Council, County Hall, Carmarthen SA31 1JP (01267 234567)

Trustees: Alun Evans; John Davies; Russell Prytherch; Michael Sadler; Peter Jones.

CC Number: 525382

Eligibility

People under the age of 25 years who at the time of application live in the ancient parish of Llandeilo Fawr and have done so for a minimum of two years. Preference is given to applicants who are members of or are connected with the Church in Wales. The ancient parish of Llandeilo Fawr was a very large parish extending from Capel Isaac and Taliaris in the north west down to the outskirts of Brynamman in the south east and including the township of Llandeilo.

Types of grants
Awards to promote the educational interests of individuals transferring to a recognised course of further or higher education and also to assist school pupils in need.

Annual grant total
Around £400 a year.

Applications
On a form available from the correspondent to be returned by 31 October.

City of Cardiff
The Cardiff Caledonian Society

£3,500

Correspondent: Cathy Rogers, 2 Llandinam Crescent, Cardiff CF14 2RB (02920 623680)

Trustees: Iain Breckenridge; Len Richards; Douglas Gowans.

CC Number: 257665

Eligibility
People of Scottish nationality and their families, who live in Cardiff or the surrounding district and are in need.

Types of grants
Grants are made to college students, undergraduates, vocational students and mature students, including those towards fees, books and instruments and equipment. Grants are also made to people starting work.

Annual grant total
Grants usually total around £7,000 each year, for both educational and welfare purposes.

Applications
In writing to the correspondent. Applications can be submitted directly by the individual or through a social worker, Citizens Advice or other welfare agency at any time. Applications are considered on a regular basis.

The Cardiff Further Education Trust Fund

£90,000

Correspondent: N Griffiths, Cardiff City Council, City Hall, King Edward VII Avenue, Cardiff CF10 3ND

Trustees: The county council of the city and county of Cardiff; The Community Foundation in Wales.

CC Number: 525512

Eligibility
Young people who are resident in Cardiff and who attended a primary or secondary school in the city and are in need.

Types of grants
Grants in connection with the costs of further education.

Annual grant total
In 2010/11 the trust had assets of £2.6 million and an income of £132,000. Charitable activities amounted to £353,000. Previously grants to individuals totalled around £90,000.

Applications
In writing to the correspondent.

The Howardian Educational Trust

£0

Correspondent: N Griffiths, Cardiff City Council, City Hall, King Edward VII Avenue, Cardiff CF10 3ND (02920 872324)

Trustees: David Salter; James Philips; John Evans; Julie Crowley; Gerald Nowell; Andrew Doe.

CC Number: 1019801

Eligibility
Young people who are resident in Cardiff and who attended a primary or secondary school in the city and are in need.

Types of grants
Grants in connection with the costs of further education.

Annual grant total
The trust always has an annual income of around £1,000. In 2010/11 there was no expenditure.

Applications
In writing to the correspondent.

Monmouthshire
Llandenny Charities

£500

Correspondent: Dr Graham Russell, Forge Cottage, Llandenny, Usk, Monmouthshire NP15 1DL (01633 432536; email: gsrussell@btinternet.com)

Trustees: Dr Graham Russell; Noel Porter; Revd Joan Wakeling; Richard Moorby; Sue Russell.

CC Number: 223311

Eligibility
Students in full-time higher education who live in the parish of Llandenny and have lived there for more than one year.

Types of grants
Recurrent.

Annual grant total
About £1,000 for educational and welfare purposes.

Applications
In writing to the correspondent, to be submitted directly by the individual. Applications should be submitted by 15 January for consideration in February.

Monmouth Charity

£5,000

Correspondent: Andrew Pirie, Pen-y-Bryn, Oakfield Road, Monmouth NP25 3JJ (01600 716202)

Trustees: Andrew Pirie; George Griffiths; Heather Colls; Stephen Clarke.

CC Number: 700759

Eligibility
Further education students who live within a ten-mile radius of Monmouth.

Types of grants
One-off grants usually up to a maximum of £500.

Annual grant total
In 2010/11 the charity had an income of £12,000 and an expenditure of £11,000. Grants are made for both educational and welfare purposes.

Applications
The trust advertises in the local press each September/October and applications should be made in response to this advertisement for consideration in November. Emergency grants can be considered at any time. There is no application form. Applications can be submitted directly by the individual or through a social worker, Citizens Advice or other welfare agency.

The Monmouthshire Farm School Endowment

£20,000

Correspondent: Monmouthshire County Council, Education Finance Dept-LLL, Monmouthshire County Council, County Hall, Cwmbran, Gwent NP44 2XH (01633 644495)

Trustees: Ruth Edwards; Bob Greenland; Bryan Jones; Douglas Edwards; W. Symondson; J. D. Hayes; Keith Backhouse; Christine Walby; Andrew James; Steve Kent; Mary Barnett; Mark Edwards; J. J. Hopkins.

CC Number: 525649

Eligibility

Further and higher education agriculture students (and those studying related subjects) living in the former county of Monmouthshire (as constituted in 1956). Preference is given to students who are under the age of 25.

Types of grants

Grants of between £500 and £1,000 to help with the costs of study at the Usk College of Agriculture or any other farm institute, school, university or department of agricultural education approved by the governors. Grants can be for books, equipment/instruments, fees, living expenses and educational outings in the UK.

Annual grant total

Between £10,000 and £20,000 a year.

Applications

On a form available from the correspondent which can be submitted at any time directly by the individual including an estimate of costs. Applications are considered in October and January.

Other information

The trust has previously stated that owing to a shortage of applications, the trust deed is in the process of being revised in an attempt to widen the field of applications. However, the endowment remains open for applications.

The Monmouthshire Welsh Church Acts Fund

£90,000

Correspondent: David Jarrett, Central Finance, Monmouthshire County Council, County Hall, Cwmbran, Monmouthshire NP44 2XH (01633 644657; website: www.monmouthshire. gov.uk)

Trustee: Monmouthshire County Council.

CC Number: 507094

Eligibility

People of any age studying at school, university or any other place of study, who live in the boundaries of Monmouthshire County Council and their dependents. Grants are also made to people starting work.

Types of grants

Scholarships, bursaries, loans and maintenance allowances ranging from £50 to £500 for uniforms, other clothing, books, equipment, fees, childcare and travel in the UK and overseas for educational purposes. Grants include those for music or arts courses.

Annual grant total

In 2010/11 the fund had assets of £4.8 million and an income of £69,000. Grants totalled £186,000. The grants were made to the following administering Local Authorities for them to make to individuals on behalf of the fund: Monmouthshire County Council, Torfaen County Borough Council, Newport City Council, Blaenau Gwent County Borough Council and Caerphilly County Borough Council.

Applications

On a form available from the correspondent or downloaded from the website, which can be submitted at any time, and must be signed by a county councillor. Applications can be made either directly by the individual, or through his or her school, and are usually considered in June, September, December and March.

James Powell's Education Foundation

£3,500

Correspondent: D T Hayhurst, Rose Cottage Chapel, Llanvetherine, Abergavenny, Gwent NP7 8PY (01873 821449)

Trustees: Christopher Lewis; Ceinwen Davies; Lyndon Trumper; Ann Couldwell; Tony Watkins; David Osborn.

CC Number: 525640

Eligibility

People who live in the ancient parish of Llantilio Crossenny and who are 16 years old and over.

Types of grants

Grants are given for books, equipment and other essentials for people starting work, and for students and pupils for maintenance and living expenses.

Annual grant total

In 2011 the foundation had an income of £3,800 and an expenditure of £3,100.

Applications

In writing to the correspondent, by a parent or guardian of the applicant. Applications should be made by August for consideration in September.

Neath Port Talbot

Elizabeth Jones' Charities

£5,000

Correspondent: David Scott, 28 Wildbrook, Part Talbot SA13 2UN (01639 887953; email: scott-david11@ sky.com)

Trustees: David Scott; Ken Tucker; David Lewis.

CC Number: 525517

Eligibility

People under the age of 25 in further/ higher education who live in the old borough of Port Talbot and are in need.

Types of grants

One-off grants ranging from £50 to £400, towards books and study abroad.

Annual grant total

In 2010/11 the fund had an income of £2,500 and an expenditure of £7,100.

Applications

On a form available from the correspondent. Applications can be submitted directly by the individual.

Pembrokeshire

The Charity of Doctor Jones

£12,000

Correspondent: Dai Rees, 33 Whitehall Drive, Pembroke SA71 4QS (01646 687158)

Trustees: Thomas Rees; David Ollyott; Malcolm Crossman; John Lavender.

CC Number: 241351

Eligibility

People between 16 and 25 who live in Pembroke.

Types of grants

Help towards the cost of education, training, apprenticeship or equipment for students, schoolchildren and those starting work.

Annual grant total

In 2011 the charity made grants to students totalling £12,000.

Applications

Application forms are available from the correspondent.

Other information

The charity advertises locally when grants are available, usually twice each year.

Milford Haven Port Authority Scholarships

£6,000 (4 grants)

Correspondent: Sara Andrew, Communications and Marketing Assistant, Gorsewood Drive, Milford Haven, Pembrokeshire SA73 3ER (01646 696158; fax: 01646 696125; email: sara. andrew@mhpa.co.uk; website: www. mhpa.co.uk)

Eligibility

Undergraduates at British universities. Applicants must have resided at some time in Pembrokeshire and have spent the majority of their secondary education in a Pembrokeshire school. Students who have lived in Pembrokeshire but attended secondary schools in nearby counties are also eligible.

Types of grants

Scholarships of £1,500 for undergraduates.

Annual grant total

Each year the scheme provides four awards of £1,500 each to undergraduates.

Applications

Application forms are available from the correspondent. All communication should be marked 'Scholarship Scheme'.

Other information

One placement is also available each year at Milford Haven Port Authority during the summer. This is not a registered charity.

Narberth Educational Charity

£1,500

Correspondent: M R Lewis, Education Offices, Pembrokeshire County Council, County Hall, Haverfordwest, Pembrokeshire SA61 1TP (01437 764551)

Trustees: W. E. Evans; H. George; A. Morse; D. Simpson; Pembrokeshire County Council.

CC Number: 1013669

Eligibility

People who have lived in the community council areas of Narberth, Llawhaden, Llanddewi Velfrey, Lampeter Velfrey (including Tavernspite and Ludchurch), Templeton, Martletwy (including Lawrenny), Begelly, part of Jeffreyston, Minwere and Reynalton. Applicants must have lived there for at least two years and be aged under 25.

Types of grants

Grants ranging from £100 to £150 to help those at school and those transferring to a recognised course or further or higher education.

Annual grant total

About £1,500.

Applications

Application forms are available from the correspondent. They must be returned directly by the individual by August for consideration in November.

Other information

The charity also provides financial assistance for local organisations engaged in youth activities and the promotion of education for young people/children living in the catchment area.

The Tasker Milward and Picton Charity

£2,400

Correspondent: Anne Evans, 11 Albert Street, Haverfordwest SA61 1TA (01437 764073)

Trustees: Margaret Thomas; Helen Curtlin; Georgina Bryan; Cyril Hughes; Stanley Hudson; Patricia Barker; Nicola Howells; John Morris.

CC Number: 525678

Eligibility

Former pupils of the Sir Thomas Picton School or the Tasker Milward School in Haverfordwest, Pembrokeshire, who are under the age of 25 and are experiencing financial hardship or other circumstances which could affect their studies.

Types of grants

One-off and recurrent grants ranging from £100 to £1,000. Students in further or higher education can receive grants towards books, living expenses and study or travel abroad.

Annual grant total

In 2010/11 the trust had assets of £902,000 and an income of £44,000. Grants to individuals totalled £2,400.

Applications

On a form available from the correspondent. Applications should be made directly by the individual or

through a school/college/educational welfare agency and should be received by 1 September although individual applications are accepted throughout the year. Applications are considered twice in the autumn term and once in the spring and summer terms.

Swansea

The Swansea Foundation

£9,000

Correspondent: Tracey Meredith, Legal Department, City and County of Swansea Council, Civic Centre, Oystermouth Road, Swansea SA1 3SN (01792 636040)

Trustee: The City and County of Swansea.

CC Number: 1086884

Eligibility

People in education who live in Swansea and are under 25. Preference is given to people who have attended one of the following schools or colleges: Bishop Gore Comprehensive School, Dynevor Comprehensive School, Swansea College and Swansea Institute of Higher Education.

Types of grants

One-off and recurrent grants according to need.

Annual grant total

In 2010/11 the foundation had an income of £3,100 and an expenditure of £9,700.

Applications

In writing to the correspondent.

Torfaen

The Cwmbran Trust

£10,000

Correspondent: Kenneth Maddox, Arvinheritor HVBS (UK) Ltd, Grange Road, Cwmbran, Gwent NP44 3XU (01633 834040; email: cwmbrantrust@ arvinmeritor.com)

Trustees: Ken Maddox; John Cunningham; Anthony Rippon; David Bassett; Anna Price; C. Thomas.

CC Number: 505855

Eligibility

People in need who live in the former urban area of Cwmbran, Gwent.

Types of grants

The trust gives one-off and recurrent grants and loans for a wide variety of purposes. Previous grants of an educational nature have included funding for home-study courses and IT equipment. Grants usually range between £125 and £2,500.

Annual grant total

In 2011 the trust had assets of £1.9 million and an income of £80,000. Grants were made to 34 individuals totalling £21,000 for educational and welfare purposes. One loan of £2,000 was also provided

Applications

In writing to the correspondent. Applications can be submitted directly by the individual or through a social worker, Citizens Advice, welfare agency or other third party. Applications are usually considered in March, May, July, October and December.

Vale of Glamorgan

The Cowbridge with Llanblethian United Charities

£1,300

Correspondent: Clerk to the Trustees, 66 Broadway, Llanblethian, Cowbridge, Vale of Glamorgan CF71 7EW (01446 773287; email: unitedcharities@aol.com)

Trustee: Jacqueline Thomas.

CC Number: 1014580

Eligibility

People in need who live in the town of Cowbridge with Llanblethian.

Types of grants

Grants are towards clothing, fees, travel and maintenance for people preparing, entering or engaging in any profession, trade, occupation or service.

Annual grant total

In 2010/11 the charities had an income of £20,000 and a total expenditure of £25,000. Previously grants to individuals for educational purposes came to £1,300 which was given in student grants.

Applications

In writing to the correspondent. Applications can be submitted directly by the individual or through a school/college or educational welfare agency.

North East

General

The Christina Aitchison Trust

£600

Correspondent: Revd Massingberd-Mundy, c/o The Old Post-Office, The Street, West Raynham, Fakenham, Norfolk NR21 7AD

Trustees: Allen Carding; Paul Mundy; Revd Roger Massingberd-Mundy.

CC Number: 1041578

Eligibility

Young people under the age of 25 years from north east or south west England.

Types of grants

One-off or recurrent grants for up to £300 to support young people in educational music, riding or sailing activities and other educational purposes. Donations are made in the form of books, equipment, fees, bursaries and fellowships.

Annual grant total

In 2010/11 the trust had an income of £1,800 and a total expenditure of £2,400.

Applications

On a form available from the correspondent, to be submitted in March or September for consideration in April or November.

Other information

Grants are also given to assist people who have an ophthalmic disease or who are terminally ill and to organisations.

M. R. Cannon 1998 Charitable Trust

See entry on page 253

Lord Crewe's Charity

£174,000

Correspondent: Philip Davies, Clerk, The Cathedral Office, The College, Durham DH1 3EH (01913 751226; email: philip.davies@durhamcathedral.co.uk)

Trustees: Harry Vane; Paul Langford; Ian Jagger; John Anderson; Stuart Bain; Geoffrey Miller; John Blackett-Ord.

CC Number: 230347

Eligibility

Necessitous clergy, their widows and dependents, who live in the dioceses of Durham and Newcastle. Grants may also be given more generally to people in need who live in the area.

Types of grants

The trust can give grants for a whole range of education needs up to and including first degrees.

Annual grant total

The latest accounts available were for 2010, when educational grants made to clergy dependents totalled £174,000.

Applications

On a form available from the correspondent.

Hylton House Fund

£4,000

Correspondent: Brenda Dye, Grants Manager, County Durham Community Foundation, Victoria House, St John's Road, Meadowfield Industrial Estate, Durham DH7 8XL (01917 806344; fax: 01917806344; email: brenda@cdcf.org.uk; website: www.cdcf.org.uk)

Trustee: County Durham Community Foundation.

CC Number: 1047625–2

Eligibility

People in the North East (County Durham, Darlington, Gateshead, South Shields, Sunderland and Cleveland) with cerebral palsy and related disabilities, and their families and carers. Applicants (or their family members, if aged under 18) must be on income support or a low income or have a degree of disability in the family, which creates a heavy financial demand.

Types of grants

Grants of up to £500 towards: education, training and therapy, such as sound and light therapy for people with cerebral palsy to improve quality of life or funding towards further education courses; training and support for carers and self-help groups where no statutory support or provision is available); provision of aids and equipment, particularly specialist clothing, communication and mobility aids; travel costs, such as taxi and rail fares to attend a specific activity if no alternative transport is available; and respite support for an individual when the needs of the person requires them to either be accompanied by an employed carer or by visiting a specialist centre where full-time extensive care is provided.

Annual grant total

Grants usually total around £4,000.

Exclusions

No grants for: legal costs; ongoing education; medical treatment; decorating and/or refurbishment costs (unless the work is due to the nature of the applicant's disability); motor vehicle adaptations; motor insurance, deposits or running costs; televisions or DVD players; assessments, such as the costs involved in the Scope Living Options Schemes; or retrospective funding. Only one grant can be held in each financial year starting in April.

Applications

On a form available from the correspondent or to download from the website. All applications must include a reference from a social worker or professional adviser in a related field, with a telephone number and the individual's permission for them to be contacted about an application. A full breakdown of costs should also be included. For specialist equipment and therapy, confirmation from an occupational therapist/doctor/physiotherapist or other professional advisor that the equipment is suitable, is also required.

Appeals are considered in January, April, July and October and should be received before the start of the month. They can be considered between these dates within a month of application if the need is urgent, but the applicant will need to request this and provide a reason why an exception to the usual policy needs to be made.

The Northern Counties Children's Benevolent Society

£50,000 (21 grants)

Correspondent: Glynis Mackie, 29a Princes Road, Gosforth, Newcastle upon Tyne NE3 5TT (01912 365308; email: info@gmmlegal.co.uk)

Trustees: Elizabeth Gray; William Rainbow; Adam Waugh; David Holloway; Joyce Doherty; Suzanne Record; Frances Jones.

CC Number: 219696

Eligibility

Children in need through sickness, disability or other causes with a preference for those who live in the counties of Cheshire, Cleveland, Cumbria, Durham, Greater Manchester, Humberside, Lancashire, Merseyside, Northumberland, North Yorkshire, South Yorkshire, Tyne and Wear and West Yorkshire.

Types of grants

Both one-off and recurrent grants for education and clothing. The trust has previously stated that assistance takes the form of grants towards school fees, the cost of school clothing and equipment and, in a limited number of cases, the provision of special equipment of an educational or physical nature for disabled children. In almost every case, the need for assistance arises through the premature death of the major wage earner, or the break-up of the family unit. Applications are treated in strict confidence and the financial circumstances of each applicant are fully and carefully considered by the trustees before an award is made.

Annual grant total

In 2010 the trust had assets of £1.3 million and an income of £62,000. Grants were made totalling £50,000.

Applications

On a form available from the correspondent, for consideration in January, April, July or October. Reports from third parties such as doctors or teachers should be included if relevant.

The Northumberland Village Homes Trust

£0

Correspondent: Eileen Savage, Trustee, Robson House, 4 Middle Street, Corbridge, Northumberland NE45 5AT (01434 632505)

Trustees: Eileen Savage; Diana Barkes; Richard Long; Richard Savage; Claire Macalpine.

CC Number: 225429

Eligibility

Young people under the age of 21 who live in Tyne and Wear, Durham, Cleveland or Northumberland.

Types of grants

One-off and recurrent grants according to need. Grants are given to promote the education and training of young people. Grants are available for a wide range of needs. In the past help has been given towards the costs of books, clothing and other essentials.

Annual grant total

In 2010/11 the trust had assets of £1.3 million and an income of £45,000. 16 grants to organisations were made during the year totalling £25,000 but no grants were made to individuals.

Exclusions

Grants are not given for gap year projects.

Applications

In writing to the correspondent. The trustees meet in November and applications should be submitted in September. No personal applications will be considered unless supported by an accompanying letter from the headteacher or an official from the local authority or other such body.

The Sir John Priestman Charity Trust

£18,000

Correspondent: McKenzie Bell, 19 John Street, Sunderland, Tyne and Wear SR1 1JG (01915 674857)

Trustees: Peter Taylor; Richard Farr; Timothy Norton; Anthony Coates; Thomas Greenwell.

CC Number: 209397

Eligibility

People in need who live in the historic counties of Durham and York (especially the county borough of Sunderland).

Types of grants

Grants to help towards the cost of school fees and for gap year activities including Christian mission.

Annual grant total

In 2011 the charity gave £11,000 for young people to attend outward bound courses and one Christmas gift of £400.

Applications

In writing to the correspondent. Applications are considered quarterly.

Other information

The trust also assists charities serving County Durham (especially the Sunderland area) and helps maintain Church of England churches and buildings in the above area.

The Provincial Grand Charity

£200

Correspondent: Michael de-Villamar Roberts, Ingham and Co., George Stanley House, 2 West Parade Road, Scarborough, North Yorkshire YO12 5ED (01723 500209)

Trustees: David Burnett; Derek Broderick; Gordon Gildener; John Woolway.

CC Number: 517923

Eligibility

Children (including adopted and step-children) of present and deceased masons who live or lived in North Yorkshire and Humberside.

Types of grants

Grants for those at school, college or university towards school clothing, books, school fees and living expenses depending on the parental circumstances. Grants range from £100 to £3,000.

Annual grant total

In 2011 the charity had assets of £890,000 and an income of £90,000. Grants to individuals totalled £200.

Applications

In writing to the correspondent, to be considered at quarterly meetings. Applications must be supported by the relative who is a member of the masons.

Prowde's Educational Foundation

£15,000

Correspondent: Richard Lytle, 39 Stanley Street, Southsea PO5 2DS (02392 799142)

Trustees: Guy Powell; Doreen Engall; Christopher Wolverson; James Dugdale; William Goring; Lady Stirling.

CC Number: 310255

Eligibility

Boys and young men between the ages of 9 and 25 who live in Somerset or the North or East Ridings of Yorkshire. There is a preference for those who are descendants of the named persons in the will of the founder. There is also a preference for boys with serious family difficulties such that the child has to be educated away from home and for those with special education needs.

Types of grants

One-off grants to boys and men in further or higher education, including postgraduates, for fees, uniforms, other school clothing, books, equipment, instruments, fees and study or travel abroad. The average grant to an individual is £450.

Annual grant total

In 2010/11 the foundation had an income of £17,000 and an expenditure of £18,000.

Applications

Applications can be submitted directly by the individual, parents or occasionally social workers, and should include a birth certificate and evidence of acceptance for a course. They should be submitted in May/June for consideration in July.

The Sherburn House Educational Foundation

£1,500

Correspondent: Stephen Hallett, Ramsey House, Sherburn Hospital, Durham DH1 2SE (01913 722551; email: peter.pybus@sherburnhouse.org; website: www.sherburnhouse.org)

Trustees: Ray Pye; Mary Hawgood; Tony Garland; Harold Perks; Ian Stewart; Margaret Bozic; Margaret Rushford; William Brooks; Mac Williams; Susan Davey; Michael Laing; Susan Martin.

CC Number: 527325

Eligibility

People aged between 16 and 21 who live in the civil parish of Sherburn House and other parishes within County Durham.

Types of grants

Grants to assist pupils to attend schools, universities or other educational institutions and courses. Grants of between £50 and £450 are available to students towards books, equipment, instruments and fees.

Annual grant total

About £1,500.

Exclusions

Individuals who have been awarded a grant or refused a grant within the last 24 months cannot be funded.

Applications

Applications should be made through the individual's school/college, educational welfare agency or a third party such as social services or Citizens Advice. They are considered throughout the year.

Other information

Grants are also made for welfare purposes. Refer to the Sherburn House Charity entry for details.

The Yorkshire Training Fund for Women

£2,000

Correspondent: Ann Taylor, 1 High Ash Close, Notton, Wakefield, West Yorkshire WF4 2PF (01226 722155)

Trustees: Nancy Donner; Carole Pullan.

CC Number: 529586

Eligibility

British women aged 16 and over who live in, or have connections to, Yorkshire and are in higher or further education.

Types of grants

One-off grants of up to £400, for women undertaking courses of study that should enable them to become self-sufficient financially. Grants are given towards books, equipment and instruments.

Annual grant total

In 2011 the fund had both an income and expenditure of £2,500.

Exclusions

People on access courses are not eligible and grants are not given for fees.

Applications

On a form available from the correspondent, to be submitted either by the individual or through a social worker, Citizens Advice or other welfare agency. Applicants should provide details of two referees and detailed information of their financial position. Completed forms should be returned by 1 May for the June meeting or by 1 November for the December meeting.

Other information

The trust states that 'there is a great deal of competition for the grants'.

County Durham

County Durham Community Foundation

£143,000

Correspondent: Barbara Gubbins, Chief Executive, Victoria House, Whitfield Court, St John's Road, Meadowfield Industrial Estate, Durham DH7 8XL (01913 786340; email: info@cdcf.org.uk; website: www.cdcf.org.uk)

Trustees: Mark I'Anson; David Watson; Michele Armstrong; Ada Burns; George Garlick; Christopher Lendrum; Andrew Martell; David Martin; Lady Sarah Nicholson; Gerry Osborne; Kate Welch; Ruth Thompson.

CC Number: 1047625

Eligibility

Young people who live in the County Durham area.

Types of grants

Grants are made towards the cost of course fees, tuition fees, books, educational, sporting and musical equipment and travel costs. Bursaries are also awarded.

Annual grant total

In 2010/11 the foundation held assets of £8.5 million and had an income of £2 million. Grants for education and training purposes totalled £143,000.

Applications

Visit the foundation's website for full details of grant schemes. Application forms are also available to download from the foundation's website.

Other information

Grants are also made to organisations.

The Lady Dale Scholarship

£800 (4 grants)

Correspondent: Elaine Sayers, Clerk to the Trustees, Children's Services, Town Hall, Darlington DL1 5QT (01325388814)

Trustees: M. Senior; D. Judson; K. Cotgrave; P. Howarth; D. Smith; P. Armstrong; A. Appleyard; T. Fisher.

CC Number: 507231

Eligibility

Girls and young women from poorer families going from school to further and higher education and who have attended Branksome, Eastbourne,

Haughton, Hummersknott, Hurworth or Longfield comprehensive schools – Darlington.

Types of grants
£200 scholarships for those going on to colleges of further education.

Annual grant total
In 2010/11 the trust had an income of £1,200 and an expenditure of £800.

Applications
In writing to the correspondent, to be submitted through the individual's school by early August, although preferably earlier.

The Darlington Education Fund

£10,000

Correspondent: Elaine Sayers, Clerk to the Trustees, Children's Services, Town Hall, Darlington DL1 5QT (01325 388814)

Trustees: M. Senior; D. Judson; K. Cotgrave; P. Howarth; D. Smith; P. Armstrong; A. Appleyard; T. Fisher.

CC Number: 514784

Eligibility
Persons under the age of 25 who attend or have attended Branksome, Eastbourne, Haughton, Hummersknott, Hurworth or Longfield comprehensive schools, or the Queen Elizabeth Sixth Form College – Darlington.

Types of grants
Grants are made for the following purposes:
- People at school/college/university
- People leaving any educational establishment to prepare for and enter a profession, trade or calling
- Educational travel in this country and abroad and for people to study music or other arts
- Financial assistance for clothing, training, travel, equipment, books and the like

With the approval of the managing trustees, the award of exhibitions tenable at any secondary school, college of education, university or other institution of further education (including professional and technical) can also be made.

Students currently attending the Darlington College of Technology and who previously attended one of the above mentioned schools are also eligible to apply for grants. Except in exceptional circumstances, assistance will not be given towards the cost of travel expenses within the Darlington area. Awards are made on a quarterly basis.

Annual grant total
In 2010/11 the trust had an income of £22,000 and an expenditure of £18,000.

Applications
Further information and an application form are available from the correspondent. Pupils still in attendance at any of the schools/college listed may discuss the matter with the headteacher in the first instance. Full details of the purpose for which the award is required and some indication of the cost involved should be given. The trustees meet once each term to consider applications.

The Sedgefield District Relief-in-Need Charity

£2,500

Correspondent: John Hannon, Clerk, East House, Mordon, Sedgefield, County Durham TS21 2EY (01740 622512; email: east.house@btinternet.com)

Trustees: Christine Hearmon; Edwin Lofthouse; John Robinson; Robert Elders; Shirli Traynor; Peter Brookes; Kenneth Threlfall; Susan Cook; Alan Thompson; Peter Terry; Patricia Little; Christine Luke; Michael Gobbett; Allan Blakemore.

CC Number: 230395

Eligibility
College, university, vocational and mature students who live in the parishes of Bishop Middleham, Bradbury, Cornforth, Fishburn, Mordon, Sedgefield and Trimdon in County Durham.

Types of grants
One-off grants are made to undergraduates and mature students for books and maintenance/living expenses. Support may also be given towards training fees.

Annual grant total
About £5,000 to individuals for welfare and educational purposes.

Applications
On a form available from the correspondent, to be submitted by 30 September each year.

Other information
This trust also makes grants to local organisations.

The Sedgefield Educational Foundation

£3,000

Correspondent: John Hannon, East House, Mordon, Stockton-on-Tees TS21 2EY (01740 622512; email: east.house@btinternet.com)

Trustees: Christine Hearmon; Edwin Lofthouse; Trevor Terry; Gloria Wills; Kenneth Threlfall; David Brown; Susan Hannan; Christine Luke.

CC Number: 527317

Eligibility
People who normally live in the civil parishes of Sedgefield, Fishburn, Bradbury and Morden in County Durham and are aged between 18 and 25.

Types of grants
Recurrent grants during period of study. Grants to help with college, university or technical college courses or other vocational courses towards the cost of books and to help with fees/living expenses. The trustees normally only help with education higher than A-level and current policy is to limit aid to courses not available at schools. Grants range from £140 to £300 (depending on the applicant's circumstances).

Students seeking funds for study or travel abroad and mature students over 25 may be referred to the Sedgefield District Relief-in-Need Charities, to which welfare applications are also referred (see separate entry).

Annual grant total
About £3,000.

Applications
On a form available from the correspondent. Applications must be submitted by 30 September for consideration in October.

Durham
The Johnston Educational Foundation

£4,000

Correspondent: Cathy Mallam, CYPS Finance Team Room G67, Durham County Council, County Hall, Durham DH1 5UJ (01913 834724; fax: 01913 834597; email: jo.barker@durham.gov.uk)

Trustees: Dennis Morgan; Carolyn Roberts; Nigel Martin; Arthur Raymond.

CC Number: 527394

Eligibility
People under 25 who live or whose parents live in the city of Durham and who have attended one of the city's comprehensive schools for at least two years.

Types of grants
One-off and recurrent grants ranging from £50 to £1,000. Grants are made to students in further/higher education to help with the cost of books, equipment/

instruments, fees, living expenses and study or travel abroad and to people starting work, entering a trade or undertaking voluntary work.

Annual grant total

In 2010/11 the trust had an income of £3,100 and an expenditure of £4,400.

Applications

On a form available from the correspondent. Applications are considered in February, June and October and should be submitted directly by the individual.

Frosterley

The Frosterley Exhibition Foundation

£2,000

Correspondent: Judith Bainbridge, 6 Osborne Terrace, Frosterley, Bishop Auckland, County Durham DL13 2RD (01388 527668)

Trustees: Audrey Ward; Judith Bainbridge; Jessie Percival; Paul Nelson; Ronald Tanner; William Wilthew.

CC Number: 527338

Eligibility

People in full-time education, from secondary school age upwards, whose parents live in the parish of Frosterley. Preference is given to college and university students.

Types of grants

Grants are given towards books, uniforms and any other educational requirement deemed necessary.

Annual grant total

In 2010/11 the trust had an income of £4,000 and an expenditure of £2,400.

Applications

In writing to the correspondent, to be submitted by the applicant's parent, to whom the cheque will be made. Applications should be submitted in August for consideration in September.

Stanhope

The Hartwell Educational Foundation

£1,900

Correspondent: Dorothy Foster, Sowen Burn Farm, Stanhope, County Durham DL13 2PP (01388 528577)

Trustees: Edward Rowell; John Thirlwell; Angela Bolam; Peter Bowes; Betty Pickard; John Anstee; Ian Shuttleworth; Susan Kent; Malcolm Skipp; Anita Savory.

CC Number: 527368

Eligibility

People aged between 11 and 21 who live in the civil parish of Stanhope. Eligibility is dependent on parental income.

Types of grants

Grants are primarily awarded on a recurrent basis to students going to college or university for help with fees/ living expenses and books. Students from low-income families receive larger grants and one-off grants can also be given to younger pupils attending secondary school towards the cost of uniforms, other clothing, books, and so on.

Annual grant total

In 2008/09 the foundation had an income of £1,200 and a total expenditure of £1,900.

Applications

Applications should be made by the last Saturday in August, on a form available from the correspondent, for consideration in September/October. Applications can be made either directly by the individual or by a parent/ guardian.

East Yorkshire

Joseph Boaz Charity

£2,000

Correspondent: Philip Evans, Graham and Rosen Solicitors, 8 Parliament Street, Hull HU1 2BB (01482 323123; email: pre@graham-rosen.co.uk)

Trustees: Michael Mitchell; Richard Palmer; Philip Evans.

CC Number: 1011882

Eligibility

People from Hull and East Yorkshire who are in further or higher education, including mature students and postgraduates.

Types of grants

One-off grants of £250 to £500 are given towards books, equipment and instruments.

Annual grant total

In 2010/11 the trust had an income of £12,000 and an expenditure of £13,000. In previous years the trust has concentrated its giving to organisations, although applications are welcomed from individuals.

Exclusions

Grants are not given for course fees or living expenses.

Applications

In writing to the correspondent to be submitted either directly by the individual or a parent/guardian, through a third party such as a teacher, or through an organisation such as a school or an educational welfare agency. Applications are considered in June and December.

The Joseph and Annie Cattle Trust

£12,500

Correspondent: Roger Waudby, Administrator, PO Box 23, Hull HU12 10WF (01964 671742; fax: 01482 211198)

Trustees: Michael Gyte; Joan Collier; Stephen Jowers; Paul Edwards.

CC Number: 262011

Eligibility

Schoolchildren who have dyslexia and live in Hull or the East Riding of Yorkshire area.

Types of grants

One-off grants of £200 to £500.

Annual grant total

In 2010/11 the trust had assets of £7.5 million and an income of £269,000. Grants for educational and welfare purposes were made to 41 individuals totalling £25,000.

Applications

In writing to the correspondent, only via a welfare organisation, for consideration on the third Monday of every month. Note, if applicants approach the trust directly they will be referred to an organisation, such as Disability Rights Advisory Service or social services.

Other information

Grants are also made to organisations (£251,000 – 2010/11).

The Leonard Chamberlain Trust

£8,800

Correspondent: Avril Russell, Fieldside House, Hooks Lane, Thorngumbald, Hull HU12 9QA (07961 034643)

Trustees: Mavis Lake; Michael Tracey; John Williams; Barry Cundill.

CC Number: 1091018

Eligibility

People who live in Selby or the East Riding of Yorkshire and are in further or higher education.

Types of grants

Grants of £50–£1,000 are given for items such as books.

Annual grant total

In 2010 the trust had assets of £5.7 million and an income of £139,000. Grants to individuals for education totalled £8,800.

Applications

On a form available from the correspondent. They should be returned in August for consideration in September.

Other information

This trust also provides accommodation and relief in need.

The East Riding Director's Charity Fund

£1,000

Correspondent: Caroline White, Finance Manager, East Riding of Yorkshire Council, County Hall, Cross Street, Beverley, North Humberside HU17 9BA (01482 394263; email: caroline.white@ eastriding.gov.uk)

Trustees: Nigel Pearson; Stephen Button.

CC Number: 1102990

Eligibility

People who live in the East Riding of Yorkshire.

Types of grants

Grants for educational purposes including social and physical training. Assistance for clothing, tools, instruments, books and travel in the UK or abroad.

Annual grant total

Grants usually range between £500 and £1,500 each year.

Applications

In writing to the correspondent.

Other information

Grants are also made to organisations.

The Hesslewood Children's Trust (Hull Seamen's and General Orphanage)

£18,000

Correspondent: Mr Rex Booth, 1 Canada Drive, Cherry Burton, East Yorkshire HU17 7RQ

Trustees: Mr R. Allenby; Mr D. Moore; Mr C. Andrews; Mr P. Evans; Revd T. Boyns; Mrs Lidgett; Mr M. Mitchell; Mrs G. Munn; Dr D. Nicholas; Mr D. Turner; Capt. P. Watts; Dr C. Woodyatt.

CC Number: 529804

Eligibility

Young people under 25 who live or have firm family connections with the former county of Humberside and North Lincolnshire. The trust also gives to former Hesslewood Scholars.

'Applicants must be in need, but must show their resolve to part fund themselves.'

Types of grants

One-off grants, typically up to £1,000, are given towards: books, school uniforms, educational outings and maintenance for schoolchildren; books for students in higher and further education; and equipment and instruments and clothing for people starting work.

Annual grant total

In 2010/11 the trust had assets of £2.5 million and an income of £82,500. Grants made to or on behalf of individuals totalled £34,500.

Exclusions

Loans are not made.

Applications

On a form available from the correspondent, accompanied by a letter from the tutor or an educational welfare organisation (or from medical and social services for a disability grant). Applications can be submitted by the individual, through their school, college or educational welfare agency, or by another third party such as the Citizens Advice or health centre. Details of the applicant's and parental income must be included, along with an indication of the amount the applicant will contribute and a contact telephone number. Applications are considered in February, June and September.

Other information

Grants are also made to organisations (£39,000 in 2010/11).

The Hook and Goole Charity

£10,000

Correspondent: K G Barclay, 3–15 Gladstone Terrace, Goole, East Yorkshire DN14 5AH (01405 765661; email: ken.barclay@heptonstalls.co.uk)

Trustees: Michael Collier; Robin Houlston; Simon Jarrold; Mrs Moore; Mary Pepper; Alan Osborne; Revd Ball.

CC Number: 513948

Eligibility

People aged 16 to 25 who are in further or higher education or apprentices and have lived or attended school in the parish of Hook and the area of the former borough of Goole as constituted on 31 March 1974 for at least two years.

Types of grants

Grants of between £150 and £400 are given towards books, tools/equipment, living expenses, educational outings and study or travel overseas.

Annual grant total

In 2011 the charity had an income of £13,000 and an expenditure of £11,000.

Applications

On a form available from the correspondent. Applications should be submitted directly by the individual in July/August for consideration in September.

The Nancie Reckitt Charity

£5,000

Correspondent: M Stansfield, Clerk, Heath House, 19 Northside, Patrington, East Yorkshire HU12 0PA (01964 630960)

Trustees: J. Cockin; Nick Hildyard; T. Heap.

CC Number: 509380

Eligibility

People under 25 who have, or whose parents have, been resident for at least five years in the civil parishes of Patrington, Winestead and Rimswell in East Yorkshire.

Types of grants

Recurrent grants of £100 to £600 are given to people starting work for clothing and equipment and to students in further or higher education for equipment, books and fees.

Annual grant total

In 2010/11 the charity had an income of £5,900 and an expenditure of £5,700.

Applications

On a form available from the correspondent to be submitted directly by the individual. Applications from people starting work should be submitted in April for consideration in May. University and college students should apply in August for consideration in September. Claims for books, materials, tools and so on should have the cost substantiated by forwarding receipts.

The Sir Philip Reckitt Educational Trust Fund

See entry on page 19

Sir Henry Samman's Hull Chamber of Commerce Endowment Fund

£5,000

Correspondent: Ian Kelly, Hull and Humber, Chamber of Commerce, Industry and Shipping, 34–38 Beverley Road, Hull HU3 1YE (01482 324976)

Trustees: Carol Thomsett; John Clugston; David Garbutt.

CC Number: 228837

Eligibility

Preference to young people of Hull and the former East Riding. Applicants should normally have reached the age of 18, and be studying, or planning to study, at degree level, although consideration will be given to those slightly under this age limit.

Types of grants

The fund provides scholarships to assist young people who wish to spend a period overseas to further their study of 'business methods or a foreign language' with a view to taking up a career in commerce or industry.

Annual grant total

In 2010/11 the fund had an income of £14,000 and an expenditure of £5,400.

Applications

In writing to the correspondent.

Other information

The fund was set up in 1917 originally to encourage the study of Russian in a commercial context, but has since been extended.

The Sydney Smith Trust

£0

Correspondent: D Kedzior, Trust Manager, HSBC Trust Company (UK) Ltd, 10th Floor Norwich House, Commercial Road, Southampton SO15 1GX (02380 722739)

Trustees: HSBC. Trust Company (UK) Ltd; A. Cheesewright; D. J. Coke; B. A. Cook; H. Docherty; J. A. W. Doyle; D. J. Nibloe; P. K. Stanley; V. Wales; D. L. Wells.

CC Number: 252112

Eligibility

Long-term residents of Kingston upon Hull and its immediate vicinity who are

undertaking further, higher or vocational training or re-training, and are in need. Applicants must be under 35 and have attended secondary school in Hull.

Types of grants

One-off grants to people starting work and students in further/higher education, including mature students under 35, towards equipment and instruments.

Annual grant total

No grants to individuals were made during 2010/11, grants to organisations totalled £30,000.

Applications

In writing to the correspondent at any time. Details of schools attended, qualifications obtained and future plans are required.

Other information

Grants are made to local schools and youth organisations.

Robert Towries Charity

£3,000

Correspondent: Mrs Debbie Ulliot, The Cottage, Carlton Lane, Aldbrough, Hull HU11 4RA (01964 527255; email: roberttowerytrust@googlemail.com)

Trustees: Donald Fields; John Hart; John Clayton; Peter Greaves; Timothy Maltas; Geoffrey North; John Porter.

CC Number: 222568

Eligibility

People under 25 years old who live in Aldbrough and Burton Constable or who have parents living in the area.

Types of grants

One-off grants for educational needs.

Annual grant total

In 2010/11 the charity had an income of £10,000 and a total expenditure of £6,000.

Applications

In writing to the correspondent directly by the individual.

Other information

Grants are also made for welfare purposes.

Ann Watson's Trust

£55,000

Correspondent: Karen Palmer, Flat 4, The College, 14 College Street, Sutton-on-Hull, Hull HU7 4UP (01482 709626; email: awatson@awatson.karoo.co.uk)

Trustees: Anthony Dunn; June Dunk; Keith Stevenson; David Butterfield; Peter Overoode; David Clune; Kathryn Lawrie; Neal Barnes.

CC Number: 226675

Eligibility

People in need under the age of 25 who live in the former borough of Kingston upon Hull and the East Riding of Yorkshire.

Types of grants

One-off and recurrent grants according to educational need.

Annual grant total

In 2011 the trust had assets of £1.3 million and an income of £337,000. Educational grants totalled £55,000.

Applications

In writing to the correspondent at any time during the year. The trustees meet quarterly.

Other information

Grants are also given to local organisations, churches and to individuals for welfare purposes.

The Christopher Wharton Educational Foundation

£2,000

Correspondent: Evelyn Catterick, Trustee, 25 High Catton Road, Stamford Bridge, York YO41 1DL (01759 373544)

Trustees: Clare Wood; Barbara Tate; Evelyn Catterick; Michael Harran; Fran Wakefield; Paul Hammond.

CC Number: 506958

Eligibility

People under 25 who live in the former parish of Stamford Bridge with Scoreby or the parish of Gate Helmsley and Kexby.

Types of grants

Grants of about £100 to help with further education, tools, instruments or apprenticeships not normally provided by the local education authorities.

Annual grant total

About £2,000.

Applications

In writing to the correspondent by 31 October.

Barmby on the Marsh

The Blanchard's Educational Foundation

£1,400

Correspondent: John Burman, Clerk, Heptonstalls Solicitors, 7–15 Gladstone

Terrace, Goole, East Yorkshire
DN14 5AH (01405 765661; fax: 01405
764201)

Trustees: Dorothy Houlder; Joan Giles;
John Shaw; Peter Bassindale; David
Pridmore; James Little.

CC Number: 529857

Eligibility

People under the age of 25 living in
Barmby on the Marsh.

Types of grants

Grants are available for (a)
schoolchildren, including help with the
cost of clothing, books and educational
outings but not school fees or
maintenance; (b) students in further or
higher education including help with the
cost of books and study or travel abroad,
but not for fees/living expenses; (c)
people starting work for books and
equipment, but not clothing or travel;
and (d) mature students (under 25) for
books and travel, but not for fees or
childcare expenses.

Annual grant total

In 2010/11 the foundation had an
income of £1,900 and an expenditure of
£1,400.

Applications

In writing to the correspondent.
Meetings are held in July and December.

Beverley

The Christopher Eden Educational Foundation

£10,000

Correspondent: Mrs Judy Dickinson,
85 East Street, Leven, Beverley
HU17 5NG (01964 542593; email:
judydickinson@mac.com)

Trustees: Nev Holgate; Judy Dickinson;
Wendy Cross; Janet Davis; Tony Knight.

CC Number: 529794

Eligibility

People under the age of 25 who live in
the town of Beverley and the villages in
Beverley Rural Ward or have been to
schools in that area. People with special
educational needs are given preference.

Types of grants

One-off grants of £50 to £400 are given
to: (a) schoolchildren and students in
higher education to help with books,
equipment, clothing, travel, field trips,
sports equipment and training and for
studying music and the arts, but not for
school fees or school uniforms; (b)
people in further or higher education
towards fees or to supplement existing
grants, including grants to travel in
connection with education and books;

and (c) people starting work to help
with the cost of books, equipment,
clothing and travel.

Recurrent grants are occasionally given
for the duration of the course, but no
loans are available.

Annual grant total

In 2010/11 the trust had both an income
and expenditure of £11,000.

Applications

On a form available from the
correspondent. Applications for
assistance with university or college costs
should be submitted in September for
consideration in October. Applications
for any other purposes are considered in
January, April, July and October. A
parent/guardian should complete the
application for those under 16.
Applications must also include course
details, education details, parents'
income, applicant's income and
outgoings and the reason why help is
needed. Incomplete or incorrectly
completed applications will not be
considered and are not returned.

Other information

The charity has endowed a berth on a
sail training schooner and selects a
deserving young person for the berth
each year.

The James Graves Educational Foundation

£1,500

Correspondent: Ian Merryweather,
10 West Close, Beverley, North
Humberside HU17 7JJ (01482 867958)

Trustees: Roger Shaw; Dorothy
Hailstone; Matthew Snowden; Geoffrey
Stephenson; Liz Munro; Jeremy Fletcher.

CC Number: 529796

Eligibility

Students preferably under the age of 18
who live in the parish of St Martin,
Beverley.

Types of grants

Grants to help towards the costs of
books and other essentials for
schoolchildren, particularly those with a
church connection and with a specific
emphasis on religious education. The
maximum grant is £500.

Annual grant total

The trust has both an income and a total
expenditure of around £2,000
consistently. About £1,500 is usually
given in grants per annum.

Applications

In writing to the correspondent.
According to the trust not many suitable

applications are received each year.
Applications are considered twice yearly.

The Wray Educational Trust

£5,000

Correspondent: Judy Dickinson, 85 East
Street, Leven Beverley, North
Humberside HU17 5NG (01964 542593;
email: judydickinson@mac.com)

Trustees: Judy Dickinson; Lucy Mayo;
Robert Richardson; Graham McDonald;
Anne Tennison; Patricia Ablett; James
Grainger-Smith.

CC Number: 508468

Eligibility

People aged 25 or under who have lived
in the parish of Leven in Beverley for at
least three years.

Types of grants

One-off grants are given to
schoolchildren, people starting work and
students in further or higher education
towards books, equipment, instruments,
fees, educational outings and study or
travel abroad.

Annual grant total

About £5,000.

Applications

On a form available from the
correspondent, who knows many of the
people in the village and is always willing
to discuss needs. Applications are
considered in January, April, July and
October.

Other information

Grants are also given to organisations.

Hedon

The Hedon Haven Trust

£1,500

Correspondent: Ian North, Secretary,
Burnham House, Souttergate, Hedon,
Hull HU12 8JS (01482 897105; fax:
01482 897023; email: iannorth@
iannorth.karoo.co.uk)

Trustees: Ian North; John Ledger; Cliff
Everingham; Geoff Norrison; Peter
Norrison; Stephen Green; John Groome.

CC Number: 500259

Eligibility

People at any stage or level of their
education, undertaking study of any
subject, who live in Hedon near Hull.
Preference is given to children with
special educational needs.

Types of grants

One-off grants ranging from £50 to £500 are given to: schoolchildren for educational outings in the UK and abroad; students in further or higher education towards study or travel abroad and maintenance/living expenses; and mature students for living expenses.

Annual grant total

In 2011 the trust had an income of £3,500 and an expenditure of £2,400.

Applications

In writing to the correspondent at any time, enclosing an sae. Applications can be submitted directly by the individual or through the school/college or educational welfare agency.

Other information

Grants are also made to organisations.

Horbury

The Daniel Gaskell and John Wray Foundation

£2,000

Correspondent: Martin Milner, Meadow View, Haigh Moor Road, Tingley, Wakefield WF3 1EJ (07947 611100)

Trustees: Christine Cudworth; Susan Bedford; Christine Hudson; Keith Lister; Nancy Denison; Cate Taylor; William Ingham; David Watts; Alyson Ripley.

CC Number: 529262

Eligibility

People under 25 in full-time education who live in the former urban district council of Horbury.

Types of grants

Grants towards books, equipment, field trips, travel, course expenses for those at school, college or university. Grants tend to range from £50 to £200 depending on the number of suitable applications.

Annual grant total

About £2,000 is given annually in grants to individuals.

Applications

Applications should be made after advertisements are placed in the local press. The trustees meet annually in September, so applications should be received by the end of August.

Humbleton

Heron Educational Foundation

£11,000

Correspondent: Brenda Frear, Trustee, 2 The Bungalows, Humbleton Road, Lelley HU12 8SP (01964 670788; email: fay@cold-harbour-farm.freeserve.co.uk)

Trustees: Brenda Frear; Diana Hoskins; Francis Caley; Jane Hart; Fay Crawforth; John Sawyer; John Burton.

CC Number: 529841

Eligibility

People living in the parish of Humbleton, under the age of 25.

Types of grants

Grants for clothing and books given on entering primary and secondary school, further education or university.

Annual grant total

In 2010/11 the foundation had an income of £14,000 and a total expenditure of £11,000.

Applications

In writing to the correspondent.

Kingston upon Hull

Alderman Ferries Charity

£11,000

Correspondent: Victoria Fisher, Trust Manager, Hull United Charities, Northumberland Court, Northumberland Avenue, Hull HU2 0LR (01482 324135; fax: 01482 322965; email: office@hulluc.karoo.co.uk)

Trustees: John Broughton; Alderman Castleton; Jim Dunlop; Jean Moore; Mike Craughan; David Whellan; R. Walker; L. Labrom; A. Chaikin; Helen Smith; David Morgan; J. F. Abbott; J. Hornby; O'Mullane.

CC Number: 529821

Eligibility

People aged under 25 who have lived in the city of Kingston upon Hull for at least two years.

Types of grants

One-off grants ranging from around £300 to £500 each. Grants are given to students undertaking secondary education, further education and apprenticeships for fees, books, equipment, clothing, travel costs and maintenance expenses.

Annual grant total

In 2011 the charity had both an income and expenditure of £12,000.

Applications

On a form available from the correspondent. Applications are available in September and should be submitted directly by the individual or a parent/guardian by the end of October for consideration at the beginning of December.

The Doctor A. E. Hart Trust

£20,000

Correspondent: John Bullock, Williamsons Solicitors, Lowgate, Kingston upon Hull HU1 1EN (01482 323697; fax: 01482 328132; email: admin@williamsons-solicitors.co.uk)

Trustees: C. Radcliffe; Chris Collinson; John Bullock; Stewart Scargill; Michael Rogerson; Damien Walmsley; Graham Nettleton.

CC Number: 529780

Eligibility

People who live within the city boundary of Kingston upon Hull (this does not include students who only live in Hull while at college). Applications are not encouraged from students under 18.

Types of grants

The trust was established for 'the promotion and encouragement of education for needy students'. Assistance may be given towards course fees, maintenance, study or travel overseas, text books, equipment and other essentials for schoolchildren, students, mature students and people starting work. Grants for childcare can also be given to mature students. One-off and recurrent grants are made ranging from £200 to £300, but not loans.

Annual grant total

In 2010/11 the trust had an income of £16,000 and an expenditure of £30,000. Previously grants to individuals have totalled around £20,000.

Exclusions

No grants to overseas students studying in Britain or for student exchanges.

Applications

On an application form (seven pages long which must be photocopied four times by the applicant and stapled together) available from the correspondent from June onwards. One academic and one character reference must accompany the form. Applications for awards must be submitted in October each year and are usually considered in December or January.

Only in the most exceptional circumstances (e.g. for a course starting in January and of which the applicant had no knowledge the previous June) can applications outside these dates be considered, provided they explain why they are applying at that time.

The grants available from this trust are relatively modest, and are most unlikely to have any significant bearing on an applicant's decision to embark on any given course. In any event, the amount of the award (if any) will not be known until January/February, by which time most courses will have already started. Grants are paid in cheques and applicants must have their own bank accounts.

Kingston upon Hull Education Foundation

£2,000

Correspondent: Brice McDermid, Corporate Finance, City Treasury, Hull City Council, Guildhall Road, Kingston upon Hull HU1 2AB (01482 615010)

Trustees: Sheila Waudby; Leonard Bird; Charles Cracknell; Helene O'Mullane; Alan Gardiner; Mary Glew.

CC Number: 514427

Eligibility

People over 13 who live, or whose parents live, in the city of Kingston upon Hull and either attend, or have attended, a school in the city.

Types of grants

Grants of £80 to £250 towards: (i) scholarships, bursaries or grants tenable at any school, university or other educational establishment approved by the trustees or (ii) financial assistance towards the cost of outfits, clothing, tools, instruments or books to assist such persons to pursue their education or to prepare for and enter a profession, trade, occupation or service on leaving school, university or other educational establishment.

Annual grant total

In 2010/11 the foundation had an income of £4,700 and an expenditure of £2,500.

Applications

On a form available from August from the correspondent. Applications are considered in November (closing date mid-October) and February (closing date mid-January). A letter of support from the applicant's class or course tutor, plus evidence of their progress and attendance on the course is needed before a grant is made.

Newton on Derwent

Newton on Derwent Charity

£5,000

Correspondent: The Clerk to the Charity, FAO, Grays Solicitors, Duncombe Place, York YO1 7DY (01904 634771)

CC Number: 529830

Eligibility

Students in higher education who live in the parish of Newton on Derwent.

Types of grants

One-off grants towards fees, usually paid directly to the relevant institution.

Annual grant total

Educational grants usually total around £5,000 per annum.

Applications

In writing to the correspondent, for consideration throughout the year.

Other information

This charity has been given a dispensation by the Charity Commission from publishing the names of its trustees.

Ottringham

The Ottringham Church Lands Charity

£3,000

Correspondent: Luisa Hopkinson, Jasmine House, Station Road, Ottringham, East Yorkshire HU12 0BJ (01964 626323; email: luisahopkinson@ btinternet.com)

Trustees: John Hinchcliffe; Revd Ronald Howard; Mary Fairweather; Patricia Taylor; Sylvia Sugden; Ernie Oldfield; Cathryn Brown; Julia Billaney; Graham Houston.

CC Number: 237183

Eligibility

People in need who live in the parish of Ottringham.

Types of grants

Grants are made according to need.

Annual grant total

About £6,000 for education and welfare.

Exclusions

No grants are given which would affect the applicant's state benefits.

Applications

In writing to the correspondent at any time. Applications can be submitted

either directly by the individual, through a third party such as a social worker or teacher, or through an organisation such as Citizens Advice or a school.

Rawcliffe

The Rawcliffe Educational Foundation

£12,000

Correspondent: Julie Parrott, 26 Station Road, Rawcliffe, Goole, North Humberside DN14 8QR (01405 839637)

Trustee: Hilary Leach.

CC Number: 509656

Eligibility

People who live or whose parents live in the parish of Rawcliffe, who were educated at one of the local schools, and are aged between 16 and 25.

Types of grants

One-off and recurrent grants of up to £600 to assist young people remaining in full-time education beyond normal school leaving age. This includes help with the cost of books and fees/living expenses for students. Apprentices and people starting work are also eligible for grants to help with the costs of books, equipment, clothing and travel.

Annual grant total

In 2010/11 the charity had assets of £181,000, an income of £30,000 and made grants totalling £12,000.

Exclusions

It does not include school fees or study or travel overseas.

Applications

Applications should be made in writing, including the type and duration of the course to be studied. Students must affirm that they are not in receipt of any salary. They are considered in September.

Riston

The Peter Nevill Charity

£1,000

Correspondent: Julie Rhodes, Marleigh, Arnold Lane West, Arnold, Hull HU11 5HP (01964 562872)

Trustees: Audrey Ashcroft; Julie Rhodes; Chris Simmons; Tina Hammond; Julie Richardson.

CC Number: 506325

Eligibility

Young people under 25 who live, or who have a parent who lives, in the parish of Long Riston and Arnold.

Types of grants

Grants of £50 to £200 are given towards books, clothing and other essentials for school-leavers taking up employment and for students in further or higher education.

Annual grant total

Grants to individuals usually total around £1,000.

Applications

In writing to the correspondent.

Other information

Grants also made to Riston Church of England Primary School and village organisations serving young people.

North Yorkshire

The Beckwith Bequest

£6,000

Correspondent: Peter Hannam, Solicitor, Hileys Solicitors, Market Place, Easingwold, York YO61 3AB (01347 821234; email: peter.hannam@ harrowells.co.uk)

Trustees: Richard Tanner-Smith; Irene Marwood; Jane Harrison; Rebecca Bainbridge; Carol Fenwick; Kevin Hollinrake; Nathan Harrison.

CC Number: 532360

Eligibility

People living or educated in the parishes of Easingwold and Husthwaite who are in need of financial assistance.

Types of grants

Cash grants of £100 to £150 for beneficiaries to help with books, equipment, clothing and travel. (Grants are also made towards the provision of facilities not normally provided by the local education authority for recreation, education, and social and physical training for those receiving education.)

Annual grant total

In 2010/11 the fund had an income of £9,300 and an expenditure of £6,700.

Applications

In writing to the correspondent. Applications are considered at quarterly trustees' meetings.

Bedale Educational Foundation

£500

Correspondent: P J Hirst, 25 Burrill Road, Bedale DL8 1ET (01677 424306;

email: johnwinkle@awinkle.freeserve.co.uk)

Trustees: Robert Dunning; Neil Pocklington; Robert Pocklington; Adrienne Reynolds; Harry Lillystone; Herbert Smith; Malcolm Young; Mary Megson; Richard Vasey; Susan Nattrass; John Weighell; Mike Barningham; Alan Johnson; Brian Hall; Eileen Cockburn; John Thompson; Stephen Wilkinson; Sue Inglis Trevor Johnson; Malcolm Gill; Jonathan Neale; Ian Watkins; Simon Rudkin.

CC Number: 529517

Eligibility

People aged between 5 and 25 who live in the parishes of Aiskew, Bedale, Burrill, Cowling, Crakehall, Firby and Leeming Bar. Preference is given to people with special educational needs.

Types of grants

One-off grants in the range of £200 and £600 are given to schoolchildren and college students, including those towards books, fees maintenance/living expenses and excursions.

Annual grant total

In 2010/11 the charity had an income of £550 and an expenditure of £500.

Applications

On a form available from the correspondent, to be submitted at any time either directly by the individual or a parent.

Bedale Welfare Charity

£1,000

Correspondent: John Winkle, 25 Burrill Road, Bedale, North Yorkshire DL8 1ET (01677 424306; email: johnwinkle@ awinkle.freeserve.co.uk)

Trustees: Robert Dunning; Robert Pocklington; Adrienne Reynolds; Denis O'Neil; Harry Lillystone; Herbert Smith; Malcolm Young; Mary Megson; Richard Vasey; Susan Nattrass; John Weighell; Mike Barningham; Alan Johnson; Brian Hall; Eileen Cockburn; John Thompson; Dr Stephen Wilkinson; Sue Inglis; Malcolm Gill; Trevor Johnson; Neil Pocklington; Jonathan Neale; Ian Watkins; Revd Simon Rudkin.

CC Number: 224035

Eligibility

People who live in Bedale and the immediate surrounding area.

Types of grants

One-off grants usually ranging from £50 to £5,000.

Annual grant total

In 2010/11 the charity had an income of £14,000 and a total expenditure of

£7,000, most of which is distributed in relief-in-need grants and to organisations, although this does not exclude applications for educational purposes.

Applications

On a form available from the correspondent, to be submitted at any time either directly by the individual or through a third party such as a social worker or teacher.

Other information

Grants are also made to organisations.

The Gargrave Poor's Land Charity

£2,800

Correspondent: The Trustees, Kirk Syke, High Street, Gargrave, Skipton, North Yorkshire BD23 3RA

Trustees: Hugh Turner; Valerie Cutter; Geoffrey Gardner; Philip Ellis; Graham Thomson; Lynn Cuthbert.

CC Number: 225067

Eligibility

People in need who live in Gargrave, Banknewton, Coniston Cold, Flasby, Eshton or Winterburn.

Types of grants

One-off and recurrent grants and loans are given to: schoolchildren for uniforms, clothing and outings; and students in further or higher education towards maintenance, fees and textbooks. Help is also available to students taking vocational further education courses and other vocational training.

Annual grant total

In 2010/11 the trust had assets of £386,000 and an income of £42,000. Educational grants totalled £2,800.

Applications

On a form available from the correspondent. Applications can be submitted at any time.

Other information

The charity also gives grants for welfare purposes.

Reverend Matthew Hutchinson Trust (Gilling and Richmond)

£5,000

Correspondent: Mrs C Wiper Gentry, 3 Smithson Close, Moulton, Richmond, North Yorkshire DL10 6QP (01325 377328)

Trustees: Gilling: Anthony Warton; Marian Lewis; Richard Watts; Shiona Robotham; Jennifer Ross; Revd Alan Gledhill; Revd Stan Haworth. Richmond: Jean Robertson; Revd Stan Haworth; Margaret Clayson; Alison Metcalf; Revd Alan Gledhill; Elisabeth Grant.

CC Number: 220870/220779

Eligibility

People who live in the parishes of Gilling and Richmond in North Yorkshire.

Types of grants

Grants are given to schoolchildren for fees, equipment and excursions. Undergraduates, including mature students, can receive help towards books whilst vocational students can be supported for study/travel overseas.

Annual grant total

This charity has branches in both Gilling and Richmond, which are administered jointly, but have separate funding. In 2010 the combined income of the charities was £20,500 and their combined expenditure was £13,000. The combined grant total is usually about £10,000 a year.

Applications

In writing to the correspondent. Applications can be submitted directly by the individual or through a trustee, social worker, Citizens Advice or other welfare agency.

Other information

Grants are also made to local schools and hospitals.

The Kirkby-in-Malhamdale Educational Foundation

£500

Correspondent: Robin Bolland, 2 Cove Road, Malham, Skipton BD23 4DH (01729 830501; email: brussell@emeraldinsight.com)

Trustees: Robin Bolland; William Russell; Elizabeth Hesleden; Michael Holden; Jenny Cawthorne; Sheila Blackshaw.

CC Number: 1003640

Eligibility

People under 25 who have a parent or guardian living in one of the following parishes in the county of North Yorkshire: Airton, Calton, Hanlith, Kirkby Malham, Malham, Malham Moor, Otterburn and Scosthrop.

Types of grants

One-off grants of £100 to £200 to: schoolchildren for uniforms/clothing, study/travel overseas, books, equipment/instruments and excursions; college students, undergraduates and children with special educational needs for uniforms/clothing, fees, study/travel overseas, books, equipment/living expenses and excursions; and to people starting work for work clothes, fees, books and equipment/instruments.

Annual grant total

About £500.

Applications

In writing to the correspondent. Applications can be submitted either directly by the individual or through the individual's school/college or an educational welfare agency. Applications are considered three times per year.

The Nafferton Feoffee Charity Trust

£4,700

Correspondent: Margaret Buckton, South Cattleholmes, Wansford, Driffield, East Yorkshire YO25 8NW (01377 254293)

Trustees: Margaret Buckton; David Wigglesworth; Winifred Cooper; Jean Artley; Fiona Trewartha; Jean Towers; Andrew Oliver; Hugo Glover; Caroline Harrison.

CC Number: 232796

Eligibility

People in need who live in the parish of All Saints Nafferton with St Mary's Wansford.

Types of grants

Bursaries are available to local students for things such as educational overseas trips.

Annual grant total

In 2011 the trust had assets of £1.5 million and an income of £48,000. Scholarships and awards totalled £4,700.

Exclusions

The trust stated that the parish only consists of 3,000 people and every household receives a copy of a leaflet outlining the trust's work. People from outside this area are not eligible to apply.

Applications

In writing to the correspondent at any time, directly by the individual.

Other information

Grants are also made to organisations and to individuals for welfare purposes.

The Rowlandson and Eggleston Relief-in-Need Charity

£1,000

Correspondent: Peter Vaux, Chair, Brettanby Manor, Barton, Richmond, North Yorkshire DL10 6HD (01325 377233; fax: 01325 377647)

Trustees: Allan Flowers; Colin Tennick; Gwendoline Cook; Peter Vaux; Dr Mark Hodgson; Patricia Walsh; Clifford Howe; Barry McQueen.

CC Number: 515647

Eligibility

People with a disability who are in education in the parishes of Barton and Newton Morrell.

Types of grants

One-off grants of £100 to £500 for educational expenses in cases of need. Expenses can include those towards uniforms/clothing, fees, study/travel abroad, books, equipment/instruments and maintenance/living expenses.

Annual grant total

In 2010/11 the charity had an income of £3,600 and a total expenditure of £2,300.

Applications

In writing to the correspondent including details of circumstances and specific need(s), for consideration throughout the year. Applications may be submitted directly by the individual, through a social worker, Citizens Advice or other welfare agency or any third party.

Other information

This charity also provides other facilities and make grants to individuals for relief-in-need purposes.

York Children's Trust

£21,000

Correspondent: Margaret Brien, 29 Whinney Lane, Harrogate, North Yorkshire HG2 9LS (01423 504765)

Trustees: Colin Stroud; Mark Sessions; Lenore Hill; Keith Hayton; Peter Watson; William Miers; Lynn Wagstaff; Alan Ward; Anne Kelly; Percy Roberts; Rosalind Fitter; Julie Simpson; Dawn Moores; Kathy Pickard; Kitty Lamb.

CC Number: 222279

Eligibility

Children and young people under 25 who live within 20 miles of York.

Types of grants

One-off grants of between £100 to £300 are awarded to schoolchildren for uniforms/clothing, equipment/ instruments and excursions, college students for study/travel overseas, equipment/instruments, maintenance/ living expenses and childcare, undergraduates for study/travel overseas, excursions and childcare, vocational students for uniforms/clothing, fees, study/travel overseas, excursions and childcare, mature students for childcare, and to people starting work and those with special educational needs for uniforms/clothing.

Preference is given to schoolchildren with serious family difficulties so that the child has to be educated away from home and to people with special educational needs who have been referred by a paediatrician or educational psychiatrist.

Annual grant total

In 2010 the trust had assets of £2 million and an income of £79,000. £8,700 was given for educational purposes and £12,000 for 'travel and fostering talents'.

Exclusions

Grants are not available for private education or postgraduate studies.

Applications

Application forms are available from the correspondent and can be submitted directly by the individual or by the individual's school, college or educational welfare agency, or a third party such as a health visitor or social worker. Applications are considered in January, April, July and October, and should be received one month earlier.

Acaster

The Knowles Educational Foundation

£3,500

Correspondent: J Jenkinson-Smith, The Granary, Mill Lane, Acaster Malbis, York YO23 2UL (01904 706153)

Trustees: Edwin Gray; Roger Raimes; Christine Burt; James Hall; Olivia Blacker; Nichola Stephenson-Barr; Kitty Lamb; Murray Addison.

CC Number: 529183

Eligibility

People who live in the ancient parish of Acaster Malbis which includes part of the village of Naburn.

Types of grants

In the past grants have been given towards swimming lessons for small children, field trips and visits abroad for schoolchildren and students at college and university. Grants have also been given towards books, materials and cost

of transport from place of study to residence.

Annual grant total

In 2011 the foundation had an income of £2,400 and an expenditure of £3,700.

Applications

In writing to the correspondent, including invoices for expenses. As each case is considered on its own merit, applicants are asked to supply as much information as possible. Applications are considered in March, June and October.

Harrogate

The Haywra Crescent Educational Trust Fund

£1,700

Correspondent: The Student Support Manager, North Yorkshire County Council Room 69, County Hall, Northallerton, North Yorkshire DL7 8AL (01609 780780)

Trustee: North Yorkshire County Council.

CC Number: 1042141

Eligibility

People who live in the Harrogate Borough Council area and are in any form of post-16 education.

Types of grants

One-off grants towards books, equipment or travel.

Annual grant total

In 2010/11 the trust had an income of £11,000 and an expenditure of £10,000. The trust gives about 17% of its annual income to individuals and about 68% to organisations with the balance being used for further investment.

Applications

On a form available from the correspondent. Students in post-16 educational courses at secondary schools in Harrogate or at Harrogate College are expected to make their application through their institution. The deadline for applications is 30 November; they are considered in December.

Kirkbymoorside

The John Stockton Educational Foundation

£800

Correspondent: Elizabeth Kendall, Clerk, Park Garth, School Lane, Nawton, York YO62 7SF (01439 771575)

Trustees: Bernard Simpson; Elizabeth Capstick; Norma Tueart; Peter Simpson;

Jane Poole; Karen Scaling; Martin Dickinson; Richard Metcalfe; D. Mead; J. Worrall; J. Lovering; Geoff Acombe; Munro Donald; Robin Colley; William Blizzard; Julia Bretman.

CC Number: 529642

Eligibility

Students and apprentices aged 16 to 25 who live in certain parishes in the Kirkbymoorside area and have done so for at least two years.

Types of grants

Grants range from £30 to £60. Apprentices can receive help towards the cost of tools. Vocational students and students at university can receive grants towards books, fees, living expenses and study or travel abroad. Students may apply for three years.

Annual grant total

In 2010/11 the foundation had an income of £900 and an expenditure of £800.

Exclusions

Sixth form students do not qualify for grants.

Applications

On a form available from the correspondent, to be submitted by the first week of June or December. Applications can be made directly by the applicant or parent.

Lothersdale

Raygill Trust

£5,000

Correspondent: Roger Armstrong, Armstrong Wood and Bridgman, 12–16 North Street, Keighley, West Yorkshire BD21 3SE (01535 613660; email: mail@awbclaw.co.uk)

Trustees: Patricia Wilson; Robert Davis; Jennifer Smith; Harry Liversedge; Revd Gill Hall; Geoffrey Carr.

CC Number: 249199

Eligibility

Full-time students on a first degree or equivalent course at a university or college who live in the ecclesiastical parish of Lothersdale.

Types of grants

Grants to students in the first three years of their further education.

Annual grant total

In 2010/11 the trust had an income of £11,000 and a total expenditure of £10,500.

Applications

In writing to the correspondent. Applicants who do not send thank you letters will not be considered for future grants.

Newton upon Rawcliffe

Poad's Educational Foundation

£1,500

Correspondent: P J Lawrence, Secretary to the Trustees, 23 Larchfield, Stockton Lane, York YO31 1JS (01904 415526)

Trustees: Jill Jacklin; Angela Hemingway; Derick Pickering; Rosemary McWhirter; William Garrett.

CC Number: 529639

Eligibility

People from a low income background who are under 25 and live in the ancient town of Newton upon Rawcliffe.

Types of grants

Grants towards course fees, travel, books, incidental expenses and maintenance costs. Grants are towards a broad range of educational needs including support for courses that are not formal and after-school swimming classes.

Annual grant total

Grants total about £1,500.

Applications

In writing to the correspondent by 25 March.

Scarborough

The Scarborough Municipal Charities

£9,000

Correspondent: Elaine Greening, 42 Green Lane, Scarborough YO12 6HT (01723 371063; email: scar.municipalcharity@yahoo.co.uk)

Trustees: Ken Dale; Dorothy Clegg; Janette Wilby; D. C. Jeffels; Janet Jefferson; W. Chatt; Bernard Pearson; Eileen Vickers; Geoffrey Evans.

CC Number: 217793

Eligibility

People who live in the borough of Scarborough.

Types of grants

Support is given to college, vocational, mature student and undergraduates, including those for books, fees, uniforms, travel, equipment, maintenance/living expenses and excursions.

Annual grant total

In 2011 the charity had assets of £1.6 million and an income of £160,000. Grants to individuals for welfare and education totalled £18,000.

Applications

On a form available from the correspondent. Applications are considered quarterly. A subcommittee of three trustees interview each applicant.

The Scarborough United Scholarships Foundation

£8,000

Correspondent: Anne Morley, 169 Scalby Road, Scarborough, North Yorkshire YO12 6TB (01723 375908)

Trustees: Tom Potter; William Chatt; David Sutcliffe; Trish Kinsella; John Hunter; Steph Brown; Jane McCaulay; Michael Ward; Marianne Harvey; Janet Jefferson.

CC Number: 529678

Eligibility

People under 25 who live in the former borough of Scarborough and have attended a school in the area for at least three years.

Types of grants

Grants range from £100 to £500 a year. Grants are usually given to those at Scarborough Sixth Form College, Yorkshire Coast College or a college of further education 'where a student is following a course which is a non-advanced course'.

Grants are also given to schoolchildren, college students, undergraduates, vocational students, mature students and to people starting work for uniforms/clothing, study/travel overseas, books, equipment/instruments and excursions.

Grants are occasionally given to second-degree students, and loans are sometimes obtainable.

Annual grant total

In 2010/11 the trust had an income of £8,700 and an expenditure of £9,100

Exclusions

No grants for fees.

Applications

The foundation mostly deals with the local colleges to ensure potential applicants are made aware of when and how to apply.

Swaledale

Muker Educational Trust

£2,000

Correspondent: Michael B McGarry, Secretary, 21 Galgate, Barnard Castle, North Yorkshire DL12 8EQ (01388 603073; email: office@mbmcgarry.co.uk)

Trustees: K. Guy; T. Metcalfe; John Kilburn; Caroline Hewitt; Maurice Guy; Raymond Hunter; John Rukin.

CC Number: 1002488

Eligibility

People who live in the ecclesiastical parish of Swaledale.

Types of grants

The trust gives one-off and recurrent grants of £15 to £400 to schoolchildren for books, equipment/instruments and travel/study overseas and to college students, undergraduates, vocational students and mature students for fees, study/travel overseas, books and equipment/instruments.

Annual grant total

Grants usually total around £2,000.

Exclusions

Grants are not given for maintenance, clothing or living expenses.

Applications

On a form available from the correspondent. Replies are only given if an sae is enclosed. Applications are considered in November and should be submitted in October either directly by the individual or through an organisation such as a school or educational welfare agency.

Wensleydale

Yorebridge Educational Foundation

£3,000

Correspondent: Robert Tunstall, Treasurer, Kiln Hill, Hawes, North Yorkshire DL8 3RA (01969 667428)

Trustees: David Hodgson; Peter Annison; Robert Tunstall; Allen Kirkbridge; Anne Middleton; Laurence Alderson; Joanne Hammond; John Blackie; Yvonne Brown.

CC Number: 518826

Eligibility

Students under 25 years of age undertaking full-time courses of further education. Students or parents must live in Wensleydale, North Yorkshire.

Preference is given to those with parents resident in the parishes of Askrigg, Bainbridge, Hawes, High Abbotside or Low Abbotside.

Types of grants
One-off grants, typically of £200 a year, towards books, fees and living expenses.

Annual grant total
Grants to individuals total around £3,000.

Applications
Applications are considered in September/October each year and should be submitted in writing directly by the individual.

Other information
Grants are also made to organisations.

York

The Merchant Taylors of York Charity

£13,000

Correspondent: Richard Taylor, Clerk, Taylors Hall, Aldwark, York YO1 7BX (01904 557570; email: clerk@merchant-taylors-york.org; website: www. merchant-taylors-york.org)

Trustee: The Company of Merchant Taylors of the City of York.

CC Number: 229067

Eligibility
Young people involved in education/training in arts, crafts and music who live in Yorkshire, particularly in York and the surrounding area.

Types of grants
Bursaries, prizes and maintenance grants of up to £1,000.

Annual grant total
In 2010/11 the charity had assets of £414,000 and an income of £65,000. Grants to individuals were made totalling £13,000 with £1,000 of that being given in prizes and the remainder in bursaries and scholarships.

Applications
On a form available from the correspondent or to download from the website. Applications are considered throughout the year.

The Micklegate Strays Charity

£100

Correspondent: Roger Lee, 29 Albemarle Road, York YO23 1EW (01904 653698)

Trustees: Roger Lee; Alec Stephenson; Beryl Stephenson; Geoffrey Barraclough; Gerald Downs.

CC Number: 237179

Eligibility
Freemen or dependents of freemen, under 25, of the city of York and who are now living in the Micklegate Strays ward. (This is now defined as the whole of the part of the city of York to the west of the River Ouse.) The applicant's parents must be living in the above area.

Types of grants
Grants of £30 a year are given to schoolchildren and people starting work for uniforms, clothing, books, equipment, instruments, fees, maintenance and living expenses. Grants are also given to students in further or higher education towards study or travel abroad.

Annual grant total
In 2010/11 the charity had an income of £300 and a total expenditure of £100. Grants are for educational and welfare purposes.

Applications
Applications can be submitted directly by the individual or by a parent. They must include the date at which the parent became a freeman of the city and the address of the parent. Applications are considered twice a year.

Other information
The trust was created by the 1907 Micklegate Strays Act. The city of York agreed to pay the freemen £1,000 a year in perpetuity for extinguishing their rights over Micklegate Stray. This sum has been reduced due to the forced divestment of the trust government stock, following the Charities Act of 1992.

York City Charities

£500

Correspondent: M Richard Watson, Clerk, Crombie Wilkinson, 17–19 Clifford Street, York YO1 9RJ (01904 624185; email: r.watson@ crombiewilkinson.co.uk)

Trustees: Ian Carstairs; M. Browne; Anne Hamilton; Keith Scott; Elizabeth Fieldsend; G. Ball; Neil Barnes.

CC Number: 224227

Eligibility
People in need who live within the pre-1996 York city boundaries (the area within the city walls).

Types of grants
This trust has three funds. Lady Hewley's Fund gives grants to mature students aged 21 or over for general purposes.

The Advancement Branch gives grants to young people aged under 21 for general educational purposes, except school trips. There is also The Poor's Branch which has relief-in-need purposes.

Annual grant total
In 2011 the charities had assets of £1.1 million and an income of £226,000. Grants made to individuals totalled £1,000.

Applications
In writing to the correspondent.

Northumber-land

Coates Educational Foundation

£14,000

Correspondent: A Morgan, 14 Bell Villas, Ponteland, Newcastle upon Tyne NE20 9BE (01661 871012; email: amorgan@nicholsonmorgan.co.uk)

Trustees: Christopher Matthew; Mary Bailey; Beryl Simpson; Ian Suttie; Clive Rongrose; Peter Barham.

CC Number: 505906

Eligibility
People up to the age of 25 who live in the parishes of Ponteland, Stannington, Heddon-on-the-Wall, and the former district of Newburn. Pupils and former pupils of Coates Endowed Middle School are also supported.

Types of grants
One-off grants to help with the cost of books, clothing, educational outings, maintenance and fees for schoolchildren and students at college or university. People starting work can be helped with books, equipment/instruments, clothing or travel.

Annual grant total
In 2010 the charity had an income of £!9,000 and an expenditure of £18,000.

Applications
On a form available from the correspondent, to be submitted directly by the individual. Applications are considered in February and June.

Giles Heron Trust

£2,000

Correspondent: George Benson, Trustee, Brunton House, Wall, Hexham, Northumberland NE46 4EJ (01434 681203)

CC Number: 224157

Eligibility

People in need who live in the ancient parish of Simonburn.

Types of grants

One-off grants according to need towards the cost of education, training, apprenticeship and equipment for those starting work and for educational visits abroad.

Annual grant total

In 2010/11 the charity had both an income and a total expenditure of £12,000. Previously grants were made totalling around £8,000, of which about £4,000 was given in individual awards, with the rest being donated to local organisations.

Applications

In writing to the correspondent directly by the individual.

Other information

Individual grants are also made for welfare purposes.

The Rothbury Educational Trust

£5,000

Correspondent: Susan Rogerson, 1 Gallow Law, Alwinton, Morpeth, Northumberland NE65 7BQ (01669 650390)

CC Number: 505713

Eligibility

People aged 18 to 25 who live in the parishes of Cartington, Hepple, Hesleyhurst, Rothbury, Snitter, Thropton and Tosson and the parts of the parishes of Brinkburn, Hollinghill and Netherton that lie within the ancient parish of Rothbury. Applicants must be pursuing a full-time further education course at a technical college, university or similar establishment approved by the trustees.

Types of grants

Cash grants, usually of about £100.

Annual grant total

In 2010/11 the trust had an income of £6,100 and an expenditure of £5,600.

Applications

In writing to the correspondent for consideration in late August/early September. Grants are advertised in the local newspapers.

Allendale

Allendale Exhibition Endowment

£6,000

Correspondent: G Ostler, 51 Hackwood Park, Hexham NE46 1AZ (01434 600498)

CC Number: 505515

Eligibility

People under 25 (on 31 September in year of application) who live in the parishes of East and West Allendale.

Types of grants

Grants of £50 to £150 are available to: schoolchildren for educational outings in the UK or overseas; people starting work for books, equipment, instruments, maintenance, living expenses, educational outings in the UK and study or travel abroad; and students in further or higher education for all of the above as well as student exchanges.

Annual grant total

In 2010/11 the trust had an income of £7,400 and a total expenditure of £6,500.

Applications

On a form available from the correspondent. Applications should be submitted directly by the individual and the deadline is usually at the end of October. An advert is placed in the local paper, library and shops in mid-August.

Blyth

The Blyth Valley Trust for Youth

£4,000

Correspondent: Nathan Rogerson, Blyth Valley Arts and Leisure, Concordia Leisure Centre, Forum Way, Cramlington NE23 6YB (01670 542222; email: nrogerson@bval.co.uk)

CC Number: 514145

Eligibility

People who live in the borough of Blyth Valley and are under 21.

Types of grants

Grants to assist people active in the fields of arts, music and physical recreation. Support can be given for uniforms/clothing, fees, books, equipment, instruments and awards for excellence. Applicants should be of amateur status and support may only be given to those who are able to identify specific 'Centres of Excellence' which they will be attending. Grants usually range from £50 to £250 and are one-off.

Annual grant total

From 2008 to 2010 no grants were made, however during 2010/11 it seems that the trust has become active again, with an expenditure of £4,000.

Applications

Application forms are available from the correspondent and can be submitted directly by the individual. Full details of the activity and references must be included on the form. The trust advises applicants to apply early (preferably before February each year) in time for the trustees' meeting, usually held in April.

Haydon Bridge

Shaftoe Educational Foundation

£15,000 (38 grants)

Correspondent: Richard Snowdon, Clerk, The Office, Shaftoe Terrace, Haydon Bridge, Hexham NE47 6BW (01434 688871; email: shaftoe@fsmail.net)

CC Number: 528101

Eligibility

Individuals in need who live, or have a parent who lives, in the parish of Haydon Bridge.

Types of grants

One-off and recurrent grants of at least £400. Grants are made to schoolchildren for fees and study or travel abroad, people starting work for equipment or instruments, and further and higher education and mature students for fees.

Annual grant total

In 2010/11 the foundation had assets of £5.8 million and an income of £191,000. Grants were made to 38 individuals totalling £15,000.

Applications

In writing to the correspondent, for consideration in March, July and November. Initial telephone calls are welcomed. Applications can be made either directly by the individual or through the individual's school, college or educational welfare agency.

Other information

Grants are also made to organisations and schools.

Kirkwhelpington

The Kirkwhelpington Educational Charity

£1,000

Correspondent: Helen Cowan, 11 Meadowlands, Kirkwhelpington, Newcastle upon Tyne NE19 2RX (01830 540374)

Trustees: Isaac Elliott; Anne Palmer; Susan Hofmann; Alf Robson; Robert Fairbairn.

CC Number: 506869

Eligibility

People who live or whose parents live in the civil parish of Kirkwhelpington who are under the age of 25, to promote education including social and physical training. (Grants are also given to schools and voluntary organisations in the parish who provide facilities for people under the age of 25.)

Types of grants

Individuals who have gone on to some form of training or further education after school have received help with items such as equipment, books, cost of transport and extra courses where these are not covered by Local Education Authority grants. Schoolchildren have received help with the cost of educational outings and special tuition. Grants are usually one-off and in the range of £50 and £300.

Annual grant total

In 2011 the trust had an income of £5,000 and an expenditure of £1,200. About £1,000 is given annually in grants to individuals.

Applications

In writing to the correspondent including details of how the money is to be spent, other possible sources of grants and receipts of money spent where possible. Applications are usually considered in February, May and October.

Other information

Grants are also given to schools and voluntary organisations in the parish

who provide facilities for people under the age of 25.

South Yorkshire

The Aston-cum-Aughton Educational Foundation

£10,000

Correspondent: James Nuttall, 3 Rosegarth Avenue, Aston, Sheffield S26 2DB (01142 876047)

Trustees: James Nuttall; Hilda Jack; Mildred Nuttall; Ossie Eyre; Terry Drury; Bob Okeeffe; Ian Jennings; Geoff Boulton; Bernadette Bartholomew.

CC Number: 529424

Eligibility

Pupils in the area of Aston-cum-Aughton and Swallownest with Fence, where needs cannot be met from official sources.

Types of grants

One-off and recurrent grants towards items the LEA cannot provide, such as books and other equipment.

Annual grant total

In 2010 the trust had an income of £7,800 and a total expenditure of £10,100.

Applications

In writing to the correspondent or to any trustee either by the individual or their headmaster. Applications are considered in March and September, but special cases will be considered throughout the year. Applications should include some details of what the grant is to be spent on and the total cost.

The Bolsterstone Educational Charity

£4,000

Correspondent: Cliff North, 5 Pennine View, Stocksbridge, Sheffield S36 1ER (01142 882757; fax: 01142 887404; email: cliff.north@virgin.net)

Trustees: Joan Teale; Graham Helliwell; Kevin Barnard; David Rogers; Barbara Raynor; Martin Brelsford; Kate Cottyn-Williams.

CC Number: 529371

Eligibility

People aged between 16 and 25 who live in the parishes of St Mary's,

Bolsterstone, St Matthias' and Stocksbridge.

Types of grants

Grants of between £50 and £200 are given towards books, equipment/instruments and study or travel abroad.

Annual grant total

In 2010/11 the charity had an income of £9,800 and an expenditure of £9,600

Exclusions

No grants are given to mature students or people starting work.

Applications

On a form available from the correspondent. They should be submitted directly by the individual for consideration at the start of March, July or November.

Other information

The charity gives grants to schools as well as individuals.

The Elmhirst Trust

£8,000

Correspondent: John Butt, 2 Paddock Close, Staincross, Barnsley S75 6LH

Trustees: Tony Green; Michael Dower; Paul Elmhirst; John Wain; Pamela Gibson; Terry Connolly.

CC Number: 701369

Eligibility

People who live in Barnsley, Doncaster and Rotherham, normally over the age of 30, seeking to develop their life in new directions and who are prevented from doing so by low income. Particular emphasis is given to those whose proposals benefit the community as a whole. Applicants may be undertaking vocational training or retraining in any subject, and must be in need of financial assistance to support them in their training. The trust strongly prefers to support people who have had little or no post-16 education and are involved in the voluntary sector to offer them a second chance of personal or vocational development.

Types of grants

One-off grants range from £100 to £850 which has previously been spent predominantly on fees but also on travel, books, equipment and childcare.

Annual grant total

In 2010/11 the trust had an income of £6,000 and an expenditure of £9,000.

Applications

On a form available from the correspondent. 'A response, by telephone or post, is made to all applicants and where applications are considered an assessor visits the applicant. The trust attempts to maintain contact with beneficiaries during their course/activity and thereafter.'

The Robert Woods Exhibition Foundation

£1,000

Correspondent: Dave Telford, 15 Woodford Road, Barnby Dun, Doncaster DN3 1BN (01302 883496)

Trustees: Roy Hirst; David Sykes; John Howard.

CC Number: 529415

Eligibility

Students in higher education who live in the ecclesiastical parish of Kirk Sandall or Edenthorpe. Applicants must be resident in either parish at the date of application.

Types of grants

Grants of £20 to £50 a year to help with the cost of books for first degree students.

Annual grant total

The foundation has an annual income and expenditure of about £1,000.

Applications

On a form available from local secondary schools or the correspondent. Applications must be submitted by 30 August, for consideration in September.

The Sheffield Bluecoat and Mount Pleasant Educational Foundation

£23,000 (46 grants)

Correspondent: G J Smallman, c/o Wrigleys, Fountain Precinct, Balm Green, Sheffield S1 1JA (01142 675588; fax: 01142 763176)

Trustees: Jonathan Hunt; Maureen Neill; R. G. Grayson; Anne Hunter; Patrick Toomey; Maureen Roberts; Heather Morris.

CC Number: 529351

Eligibility

People up to the age of 25 who live within a 20-mile radius of Sheffield Town Hall and have done so for at least three years.

Types of grants

One-off and recurrent grants towards artistic and sporting activities, educational travel, clothing, equipment and private school fees. Grants can range between £250 and £3,500.

Annual grant total

In 2010/11 the foundation had assets of £1.4 million and an income of £60,000. Grants were made to 46 individuals totalling £23,000.

Applications

In writing to the correspondent or through the school/college or educational welfare agency. Applications are considered in April and September and should be submitted by March and August.

Other information

The foundation also gives to organisations.

The Sheffield West Riding Charitable Society Trust

£2,500

Correspondent: Malcolm Fair, Diocesan Secretary, Diocesan Church House, 95–99 Effingham Street, Rotherham S65 1BL (01709 309100; email: malcolm.fair@sheffield.anglican.org; website: www.sheffield.anglican.org)

Trustee: Sheffield Diocesan Board of Finance.

CC Number: 1002026

Eligibility

Clergy children at school and in further education in the diocese of Sheffield.

Types of grants

Only a small proportion of the grants are educational and are to help with the cost of books, clothing and other essentials.

Annual grant total

In 2010 the trust had an income of £11,000 and a total expenditure of £5,500. Around 20 grants are made each year.

Applications

On a form available from the correspondent.

Other information

Welfare grants are also made to the clergy, house-keepers and disadvantaged families in the diocese.

The Swann-Morton Foundation

£8,000

Correspondent: M I Hirst, Swann-Morton Ltd, Owlerton Green, Sheffield S6 2BJ (01142 344231)

Trustees: Judith Gilmour; Michael McGinley; George Rodgers.

CC Number: 271925

Eligibility

Students who live in South Yorkshire with a preference for those who are studying in the fields of surgery and medicine.

Types of grants

One-off and recurrent grants according to need.

Annual grant total

In 2010/11 the trust had an income of £51,000 and gave £8,000 in student grants and electives.

Applications

In writing to the correspondent. Previously the trust has stated that applications have exceeded available funding.

Armthorpe

Armthorpe Poors Estate Charity

£4,000

Correspondent: Frank Pratt, 32 Gurth Avenue, Edenthorpe, Doncaster DN3 2LW (01302 882806)

Trustees: Revd Richard Landall; Frederick Arthur; John Lowndes; Pat Grant; Lyn George.

CC Number: 226123

Eligibility

People who are in need and live in Armthorpe.

Types of grants

One-off and recurrent grants of £50 minimum to schoolchildren who are in need for educational outings and to undergraduates for books.

Annual grant total

In 2010/11 the charity had both an income and total expenditure of £10,000.

Applications

Contact the clerk by telephone who will advise if a letter of application is needed. Applicants outside of Armthorpe will be declined. Undergraduates are required to complete an application form, available from the correspondent, and return it by 31 August.

Other information

The trust gives to both individuals and organisations.

Barnsley
The Shaw Lands Trust

£13,000 (23 grants)

Correspondent: Jill Leece, 35 Church Street, Barnsley, South Yorkshire S70 2AP (01226 213434)

Trustees: John Bostwick; Linda Burgess; Elizabeth Norris; Barry Eldred; J. Foster; A. Fletcher; Malcolm Price; Brian Swaine; Malcolm Bird; Steve Hernshaw.

CC Number: 224590

Eligibility
People under 25 who live within the former county borough of Barnsley (as defined pre-1974) or are, or have for at least two years at any time been, in attendance at any county or voluntary aided school in the borough.

Types of grants
To provide scholarships/grants for university, school or other place of learning; assistance for purchase of clothing, tools, books and so on to help beneficiaries enter a profession, trade or calling; travel overseas to enable beneficiaries to further their education; assistance for provision of facilities of any kind not normally provided by the local education authority for recreation and social and physical training for beneficiaries who are receiving primary, secondary and further education; to assist in the study of music and other arts. Grants range from £100 to £750 and may be paid in three instalments.

Annual grant total
In 2010/11 the trust had assets of £1.2 million and an income of £39,000. 23 grants to individuals for education totalled £13,000.

Applications
In writing to the correspondent. Applications are considered in September.

Other information
Grants are also made to organisations.

Beighton
Beighton Relief-in-Need Charity

£3,500

Correspondent: Diane Rodgers, 41 Collingbourne Avenue, Sothall, Sheffield S20 2QR (01142 692875; email: beightonrelief@hotmail.co.uk)

Trustees: Ian Saunders; Sheila Dootson; Norman Dunn; Ruth Hodson; Mike Healey; Diane Rodgers.

CC Number: 225416

Eligibility
Students who live in the former parish of Beighton and are in need.

Types of grants
One-off grants according to need.

Annual grant total
Grants usually total around £7,000 per year.

Applications
In writing to the correspondent. Applications can be submitted directly by the individual or through a social worker, Citizens Advice, other welfare agency or a third party such as a relative, neighbour or trustee.

Other information
Grants are also made for relief in need purposes.

Bramley
The Bramley Poor's Allotment Trust

£1,500

Correspondent: Mrs Marian Houseman, 9 Horton Rise, Rodley, Leeds LS13 1PH (01132 360115)

Trustees: Margaret Charnley; John Stocks; Revd Ian Rodley; Jeffrey Houseman; Margaret Seaman.

CC Number: 224522

Eligibility
People in need who live in the ancient township of Bramley, especially people who are elderly, poor and sick.

Types of grants
One-off grants between £40 and £120.

Annual grant total
In 2010 the trust had both an income and total expenditure of £3,000.

Applications
In writing to the correspondent. The trust likes applications to be submitted through a recognised referral agency (social worker, Citizens Advice, doctor, headmaster or minister). They are considered monthly.

Epworth
Epworth Charities

£500

Correspondent: Mrs Margaret Draper, 16 Fern Croft, Epworth, Doncaster, South Yorkshire DN9 1GE (01427 873234; email: margaret.draper1@tiscali.co.uk)

Trustees: John Lambert; Stephen Selby; Jayne Oliver; Susan Astle; Ian Walker; Eileen Tatton.

CC Number: 219744

Eligibility
People in need who live in Epworth.

Types of grants
One-off and recurrent grants in the range of £50 and £250. Grants are made to schoolchildren for equipment/instruments and college students, undergraduates, vocational students and mature students for books.

Annual grant total
Grants usually total between £400 and £1,000 per year.

Applications
In writing to the correspondent to be submitted directly by the individual. Applications are considered on an ongoing basis.

Other information
Grants are also made for welfare purposes.

Sheffield
The Church Burgesses Educational Foundation

£129,000

Correspondent: G J Smallman, The Law Clerk, 3rd Floor Fountain Precinct, Balm Green, Sheffield S1 2JA (01142 675594; fax: 01142 673176; email: sheffieldchurchburgesses@wrigleys.co.uk)

Trustees: G. D. Sims; D. Stanley; J. F. W. Peters; S. A. P. Hunter; D. I. Heslop; B. R. Hickman; Heather Morris.

CC Number: 529357

Eligibility
People up to the age of 25 who live or whose parents have lived in Sheffield for the last three years.

Types of grants
Grants are given towards books, clothing and other essentials for schoolchildren. Grants are occasionally available for those at college or university, although no grants are made where a LEA grant is available. Postgraduates can only receive funding if there is a special need for retraining or education in a different subject. School fees are only paid where there is a sudden, unexpected hardship.

Special grants can also be made to individuals for gap year projects and overseas expeditions, helping churches and missions in the UK and abroad, attending summer schools and festivals, artistic, musical and athletic activities and so on.

Annual grant total

In 2010 the foundation awarded a total of £84,000 in individual educational grants and £45,000 in 'special individual grants' which cover such things as gap year projects, expeditions, summer schools and so on.

Applications

On a form available from the website. Trustees meet four times a year however grants can be made outside these times.

Other information

Recent accounts were overdue; the latest available were for 2010.

Sir Samuel Osborn's Deed of Gift Relief Fund

£2,700

Correspondent: Sue Wragg, South Yorkshire Community Foundation, Unit 3 – G1 Building, 6 Leeds Road, Attercliffe, Sheffield S9 3TY (01142 424294; fax: 01142 424605; email: grants@sycf.org.uk; website: sycf.org.uk)

Trustees: Alan Sheriff; Lady Ruby Sykes; Frank Carter; Galen Ives; Timothy Greenacre; Dr Robert John Giles Bloomer; Jonathan Hunt; Maureen Shah; Jane Marshall; Jane Kemp; Jackie Drayton; Allan Jackson; Sue Scholey; Timothy Henry Reed; Peter John Hollis; Charles William Hugh Warrack; Earl of Scarborough Richard Scarborough.

CC Number: 1140947

Eligibility

Residents of Sheffield, with some preference for those with a connection to the Samuel Osborn Company.

Types of grants

Grants of up to £1,000 for costs associated with any training or education, for example, books, equipment and living costs.

Annual grant total

In 2010/11 grants totalled around £2,700.

Applications

On a form available to download from the website. The community foundation welcomes informal approaches about applications prior to submitting. Applicants with a connection to the Osborn company should include written evidence. Decisions should be made within 12 weeks.

Only one grant per applicant per year.

Other information

The fund is now administered by the South Yorkshire Community Foundation. Grants are also made for social welfare purposes.

The Sheffield Grammar School Exhibition Foundation

£99,000 (88 grants)

Correspondent: G J Smallman, Clerk, 3rd Floor, Fountain Precinct, Balm Green, Sheffield S1 2JA (01142 675594)

Trustees: J. Binfield; D. Booker; Joy Peters; J. Stephenson; P. Foster; M. Cousins; P. Bradley; J. Boulton; M. Bateman; J. Brayshaw.

CC Number: 529372

Eligibility

People who live in the city of Sheffield and have done so for at least three years (this excludes residency for educational purposes).

Types of grants

Grants can be given to people starting work for fees, living expenses, books, equipment, childcare, clothing or travel. The trust will occasionally give towards schoolchildren's educational outings. Funds are also available for medical electives, field trips, gap year activities, sports and musical training.

There is a preference for people who are attending or have attended King Edward VII School. Grants are also given for the benefit of the school.

Annual grant total

In 2010/11 the foundation had assets of £2.7 million and an income of £173,000. Grants to individuals totalled £99,000.

Applications

In writing to the correspondent. Applications are considered in March, July, October and December and should be submitted either directly by the individual or through their school, college or educational welfare agency.

Teesside

The Hill Bursary

Correspondent: Tees Valley Community Foundation, Tees Valley Community Foundation, Wallace House, Falcon Court, Preston Farm Industrial Estate, Stockton-on-Tees TS18 3TX (01642 260860; email: info@ teesvalleyfoundation.org; website: www. teesvalleyfoundation.org/grants/the-hill-bursary)

Trustees: Peter Rowley; Alan Kitching; Christopher Hope; Pamela Taylor; Rosemary Young;.

CC Number: 1111222–2

Eligibility

People residing in Teesside including Hartlepool, Middlesbrough, Redcar and Cleveland and Stockton on Tees who are intending to study Business Economics or Accounts at a UK university.

Types of grants

£6,000 over three years.

Annual grant total

Successful applicants receive £1,000 a term for the three years of their degree.

Applications

On a form available from the website, to be submitted by 29 June.

Other information

This fund is administered by the Tees Valley Community Foundation.

The Teesside Power Fund Educational Bursary

Correspondent: Paul Atkinson, Tees Valley Community Foundation, Wallace House, Falcon Court, Preston Farm, Stockton-on-Tees TS18 3TX (01642 440440; email: info@ teesvalleyfoundation.org)

Trustees: Peter Rowley; Alan Kitching; Christopher Hope; Pamela Taylor; Rosemary Young; John Irwin; Marjory Houseman; Keith Robinson; Neil Kenley; Wendy Shepherd; Brian Beaumont; Tracey Stonehouse.

CC Number: 1111222–1

Eligibility

Students who live in Eston, Dormanstown, Kirkleatham, Teesville, Newcomen, Coatham, Grangetown, South Bank or Normanby who wish to follow courses at university in disciplines relevant to energy generation. Courses which qualify for this scheme must incorporate some elements of the following disciplines: engineering; chemistry; physics or mathematics.

Types of grants

Up to £4,500 over three years.

Annual grant total

This fund is managed by Tees Valley Community Foundation. Grants are paid as £500 a term for three years.

Applications

On a form available from the community foundation's website, to be submitted by the end of June.

Other information

Recipients of this bursary are also encouraged to undertake temporary employment at the power station in Teesside in the summer holidays to get some more experience of the energy generation industry.

The Captain John Vivian Nancarrow Fund

£5,000

Correspondent: Mark Taylor, Accounts, Po Box 340, Middlesbrough, Cleveland TS1 2XP (01642 727337)

Trustee: Middlesbrough Council.

CC Number: 506937

Eligibility

People under the age of 25 who live or work in Middlesbrough and who are or have at any time been in attendance at the following schools or colleges: Acklam Grange, Brackenhow/Kings Academy, Hall Garth, Kings Manor, Langbaurgh/Keldholme/Unity City Academy, Middlesbrough College and Teesside Tertiary College.

Types of grants

Grants are given for the following: attendance at any approved place of learning; clothing, equipment, and so on needed to prepare for, or enter, a trade or profession; educational travel scholarships; study of music and other arts; educational research; recreational and social and physical training; assistance in the event of sickness, disability and so on to enable full benefit from educational facilities.

Annual grant total

In 2010/11 the trust had an income of £500 and an expenditure of £700.

Exclusions

No grants where statutory funding is available or to people who have received a grant from Middlesbrough Council in the current financial year.

Applications

Applications to this fund may be made directly by the individual or by recommendation, where appropriate, from a headteacher. Application forms are available from the correspondent.

Other information

In the case of educational research, assistance may also be provided to people over 25.

Guisborough

The Hutton Lowcross Educational Foundation

£0

Correspondent: Sally Clark, Redcar and Cleveland Borough Council, Kirkleatham Street, Redcar TS10 1RT (01642 774774)

Trustees: Graham Jeffery; David Williams; Joe Keenan.

CC Number: 508537

Eligibility

People under the age of 25 who live, or whose parents live, in the parish of Guisborough.

Types of grants

One-off and recurrent grants in the range of £50 to £500. Grants are given for the following: (i) attendance at any approved place of learning; (ii) clothing, equipment, etc. needed to prepare for, or enter, a career; (iii) educational travel at home or abroad; (iv) the study of music or the other arts; (v) educational research; and (vi) recreational, social and physical training.

Annual grant total

In 2010/11 the trust had an income of £200 and an expenditure of £0. Previously grants have totalled around £1,500.

Applications

On a form available from the correspondent to be submitted directly by the individual or a parent/guardian. Applications are considered in October each year.

Hartlepool

The Preston Simpson Scholarship in Music

£6,000

Correspondent: Alan McNab, Hartlepool Borough Council, Civic Centre, Victoria Road, Hartlepool TS24 8AY (01429 284085; email: alan.macnab@hartlepool.gov.uk)

Trustees: Frank Rogers; Jane Shaw; Raymond Waller; Sophia Hanson; Mick Donnelly; Bill Iseley.

CC Number: 512606

Eligibility

People aged 15 to 25 who were either born in Hartlepool or who have had at least one parent living in Hartlepool for the last five years.

Types of grants

Cash grants to help with the cost of the study of music at any school or college or towards instruments.

Annual grant total

In 2010/11 the trust had an expenditure of £7,600.

Applications

On a form which is available from local schools and on request from the civic centre (see below). Grants are considered

once a year, usually just before the start of the school summer holidays.

Middlesbrough

Middlesbrough Educational Trust Fund

£2,500

Correspondent: The Voluntary Sector Liaison Team, Middlesbrough Council, PO Box 500, Middlesbrough TS1 9FT (01642 729041)

Trustee: Middlesbrough Council.

CC Number: 532293

Eligibility

People under 25 who live in Middlesbrough.

Types of grants

Grants of up to £250 for the following: attendance at any approved place of learning (minimum period one year); the purchase of clothing, equipment or books to prepare for, or enter, a trade or profession; educational travel scholarships; assistance with the provision of facilities for recreation, sport and social and physical training for pupils and students; the study of music and other arts; educational research.

Annual grant total

Around £2,500.

Exclusions

No grants where statutory funding is available or to people who have received a grant from Middlesbrough Council in the current financial year.

Applications

On a form available from the correspondent. Applicants should have an endorsement from an educational establishment or tutor. Applications are normally considered on a bi-monthly basis.

Other information

Following a new funding agreement, the trust expects its grantmaking level to increase again.

Yarm

The Yarm Grammar School Trust

£1,000

Correspondent: Student Support, Stockton Borough Council, PO Box 228, Municipal Buildings, Church Road, Stockton-on-Tees TS18 1XE (01642 526608; email: schooladmissions@stockton.gov.uk; website: www.stockton.gov.uk/citizenservices/learning/

financialsupport/
yarmgrammerschooltrust)

Trustees: Marjorie Simpson; David Rigg; Katherine Simpson; Peter Monck; Vicky Parker; Simon Trantor.

CC Number: 514301

Eligibility

People under 25 years of age who live, or have a parent who lives, in the parish of Yarm.

Types of grants

Grants of around £100 are given to schoolchildren for uniforms and other school clothing, books, educational outings and study or travel abroad and to students in further or higher education for books, equipment, instruments, fees, living expenses, educational outings and study or travel abroad.

Annual grant total

About £1,000.

Applications

On a form available from the website. Applications should be submitted directly by the individual by the end of May for consideration in July, or by the end of November for consideration in January.

Tyne and Wear

The Cullercoats Educational Trust

£2,500

Correspondent: Helen Lawlan, 20 The Uplands, Newcastle upon Tyne NE3 4LH (01912 858511; email: helenlawlan@sky.com)

Trustees: Shirley Mortimer; Lawrence Goveas; Gavin Gilchrist; Gordon Wightman; Gerald Lang.

CC Number: 506817

Eligibility

People who live in the ecclesiastical parishes of St Paul – Whitley Bay and St George – Cullercoats.

Types of grants

Grants are made towards religious instruction in accordance with the doctrines of the Church of England and to promote the education, including social and physical training, of beneficiaries.

Annual grant total

Grants are made to individuals and organisations usually totalling about £5,000 each year.

Applications

By letter to the correspondent in February or August for consideration in March or September.

Charity of John McKie Elliott Deceased

£500

Correspondent: Robert Walker, 6 Manor House Road, Newcastle upon Tyne NE2 2LU (01912 814657; email: bobwalker9@aol.com)

Trustees: Ronald Eager; David Napier; Bob Walker.

CC Number: 235075

Eligibility

People who are blind in Gateshead or Newcastle upon Tyne.

Types of grants

One-off and recurrent grants according to need.

Annual grant total

Annual income usually ranges between £200 and £2,500.

Applications

In writing to the correspondent.

Other information

The trust gives educational grants and grants to individuals in need.

The Sunderland Orphanage and Educational Foundation

£11,000

Correspondent: Peter Taylor, McKenzie Bell, 19 John Street, Sunderland SR1 1JG (01915 674857)

Trustees: Denys Briggs; Mary Smith; Mrs W. Lundgren; John Mann; John Knight; Carole Pattison; Paul Madison; Michael Mordey.

CC Number: 527202

Eligibility

Young people under 25 who are resident in or around Sunderland who have a parent who is disabled or has died, or whose parents are divorced or legally separated.

Types of grants

(i) Maintenance payments and clothing for schoolchildren.
(ii) Help towards the cost of education, training, apprenticeship or equipment for those starting work.
(iii) Help with travel to pursue education, for the provision of athletic coaching and for the study of music and other arts.

Annual grant total

In 2010/11 the trust had an income of £22,000 and a total expenditure of £25,000.

Applications

Applications should be made in writing to the correspondent. They are considered every other month.

Community Foundation – Tyne and Wear and Northumberland

£109,000

Correspondent: Fund Development Managers, Cale Cross House, 156 Pilgrim Street, Newcastle upon Tyne NE1 6SU (01912 220945; fax: 01912 300689; email: general@communityfoundation.org.uk; website: www.communityfoundation.org.uk)

Trustees: Prof. Christopher Drinkwater; Susan Winfield; Ashley Winter; Alastair Conn; Jamie Martin; Colin Seccombe; Dean Huggins; Prof. Charles Harvey; John Clough; Betty Weallans; Gev Pringle; Fiona Cruickshank; Kate Roe; Jane Robinson; Jo Curry.

CC Number: 700510

Eligibility

People in need who live in Northumberland or Tyne and Wear.

Types of grants

The Community Foundation is essentially a local umbrella organisation of grantmaking trusts, which pools together money from various sources to maximise the interest levels on the investments. There are over 100 smaller funds administered by the foundation and only a handful support individuals. Information on funds is available from the foundation, or on its website.

Annual grant total

In 2010/11 there were over 214 grants made to individuals totalling £109,000.

Applications

On a form available from the correspondent. The foundation is responsible for managing many different funds and will forward any application to the one most suitable, though it is important to note that several funds do have a separate application form and it is worth contacting the foundation prior to completing any submission. Applications can be made at any time and the foundation will generally reply within three months of receipt.

Other information

More detailed information on this foundation can be found in DSC's *A Guide to the Major Trusts Volume 1*. Also see the foundation's website for more information on the application process and the different grantmaking funds.

Newcastle upon Tyne

The Newcastle upon Tyne Education Fund

£300 (3 grants)

Correspondent: Aidan Jackson, Room 505, Civic Centre, Barras Bridge, Newcastle upon Tyne NE1 9PU (01912 777510)

Trustee: Newcastle upon Tyne City Council.

CC Number: 518115

Eligibility

People under 25 who live in Newcastle upon Tyne and received a secondary school education in the city are eligible for mandatory or discretionary awards from Newcastle upon Tyne LEA.

Types of grants

Grants of between £100 for equipment/ instruments, books, extracurricular activities, educational outings, study or travel abroad. Successful claimants will receive a cheque made payable to their school or a specific project organiser, not directly to the claimant.

Annual grant total

In 2010/11 the fund made three awards of £100.

Exclusions

No grants for fees, living expenses, childcare costs or any other non educational needs.

Applications

In writing to the correspondent, to be considered at any time. Applications should include details of date of birth, secondary school attended and home address in the city.

South Tyneside

Westoe Educational Charity

£6,000

Correspondent: Debra Baxter, South Tyneside MBC, Town Hall and Civic Offices, Westoe Road, South Shields, Tyne and Wear NE33 2RL (01914 247041)

Trustees: Helen Watson; Borough of South Tyneside.

CC Number: 1074869

Eligibility

People under 25, resident in the Metropolitan Borough Council of South Tyneside (or have a parent resident) and are in financial need.

Types of grants

One-off and recurrent grants for schoolchildren, people with special educational needs, further/higher education students, vocational students, and people starting work towards uniforms/clothing, fees, study or travel abroad, books, equipment/instruments, maintenance/living expenses and excursions.

Annual grant total

In 2010/11 the trust had an income of £4,800 and an expenditure of £7,000.

Exclusions

Grants are not made for musical instrument tuition.

Applications

In writing to the correspondent at any time.

Sunderland

The Mayor's Fund for Necessitous Children

£500

Correspondent: Children's Services Financial Manager, Children's Services, Sandhill Centre, Grindon Lane, Sunderland SR3 4EN (01915 531826)

Trustees: I. W. Kay; Paul Maddison; Patricia Smith; J. Kelly.

CC Number: 229349

Eligibility

Children in need (under 16, occasionally under 19) who are in full-time education, live in the city of Sunderland and whose family are on a low income.

Types of grants

Grants of about £25 for the provision of school footwear, paid every six months.

Annual grant total

About £500.

Exclusions

No grants are made to asylum seekers.

Applications

Applicants must visit the civic centre and fill in a form with a member of staff. The decision is then posted at a later date. Proof of low income is necessary.

West Yorkshire

The Boston Spa Educational Charitable Trust

£500

Correspondent: Christopher Walsh, Boston Spa Comprehensive School, Clifford, Moor Road, Boston Spa, Wetherby, West Yorkshire LS23 6RW

Trustees: Christopher Walsh; Stephen Hall.

CC Number: 702676

Eligibility

People in need who live in Boston Spa, Collingham, Harewood, Alwoodley, Shadwell, Crossgates, Scholes, Barwichin Elmet, Bardsey, East Keswick, Whinmoor, Aberford, Thomer, Bramham, Clifford, Walton and Thorp Arch in the north east area of West Yorkshire.

Types of grants

One-off grants are usually given for expeditions and explorations or to students on higher education courses where no grants are available, such as postgraduate courses.

Annual grant total

Expenditure has been sporadic over the last few years. From 2009 to 2011 the trust had no income, however spent £2,800 in 2010.

Applications

In writing to the correspondent, to be considered in March, June and November.

Lady Elizabeth Hasting's Educational Foundation

£148,000 (195 grants)

Correspondent: E F V Waterson, Clerk, Carter Jonas, 82 Micklegate, York YO1 1LF (01904 558201)

Trustees: Mark Granger; Peter Bristow; Christopher Wilton; Michael Fox; Andrew Robinson.

CC Number: 224098

Eligibility

Individuals in need who live in the parishes of Burton Salmon, Thorp Arch, Collingham with Harewood, Bardsey with East Keswick, Shadwell and Ledsham with Fairburn.

Types of grants

One-off and recurrent grants according to need, usually averaging between £500 and £700.

Annual grant total

In 2010/11 the foundation made 195 grants to individuals totalling £148,000.

Exclusions

Applicants must reside in one of the above parishes to qualify for a grant.

Applications

In writing to the correspondent. The trustees meet four times a year, although grants can be made between the meetings, on the agreement of two trustees.

Other information

The trust is managed by, and derives its income from, Lady Elizabeth Hastings Estate Charity. The trust also gives yearly grants of £3,000 to designated local schools.

The North Yorkshire Fund Educational Travel Award

£2,000 (2 grants)

Correspondent: The Student Support Officer, Two Ridings Community Foundation, Primrose Hill, Buttercrambe Road, Stamford Bridge, York YO41 1AW (01759 377400; email: office@trcf.org.uk; website: www.trcf.org.uk)

Trustee: Two Ridings Community Foundation.

CC Number: 1084043

Eligibility

Students in full-time attendance on a first degree course at a British university but who have not yet taken their final first degree examination at the date any awards are payable. Applicants must be ordinarily living in the former West Riding of Yorkshire as constituted on 31 March 1974. Individuals must be able to demonstrate need and/or lasting community benefit.

Types of grants

Two grants of about £1,000 each are given towards travelling abroad to further education in a field of study which is the subject of the individual's full-time university course or a directly related field of study. Awards are tenable until 30 June of the year following the year of application.

Annual grant total

About £2,000.

Exclusions

No grants to students in the last year of their course.

Applications

On a form available from the website. Applications are considered in May and should be submitted by March, including a reference from a university tutor.

Other information

This award was previously called the Charity of Lady Mabel Florence Harriet Smith.

The Frank Wallis Scholarships

£5,000

Correspondent: Deborah Beaumont, Bradford M D C Dept 24, Britannia House, Hall Ings, Bradford BD1 1HX (01274 434956)

Trustees: David Horrocks; Irene Sutcliffe; David Delaney; City of Bradford MDC.

CC Number: 529080

Eligibility

Students who have lived within the area of the former Clayton urban district council for at least three years.

Types of grants

Grants range from £50 to £100 and are given for any course of higher education to assist with the purchase of books and equipment.

Annual grant total

About £500 a year.

Applications

In writing to the correspondent.

Calderdale

The Bearder Charity

£18,000

Correspondent: Richard Smithies, Secretary, 5 King Street, Brighouse, West Yorkshire HD6 1NX (01484 710571; email: bearders@btinternet.com; website: www.bearder-charity.org.uk)

Trustees: Leyland Smith; Peter Townend; Trevor Simpson; Richard Smithies; Brendan Mowforth; Derek Sharpe.

CC Number: 1010529

Eligibility

People resident in Calderdale.

Types of grants

Grants for educational needs such as instruments/equipment/tools, travel, clothing and the arts.

Annual grant total

In 2010/11 the trust had assets of £4.4 million and an income of £107,000. Grants to individuals for educational purposes totalled £18,000.

Applications

In writing to the correspondent detailing requirements and costings. Trustees meet six times a year to assess applications. Applications can also be made via organisations such as Citizens Advice or social services.

Other information

Grants are also made to individuals for welfare purposes and to local charities.

The Community Foundation for Calderdale

£5,000

Correspondent: Grants Department, The 1855 Building (first floor), Discovery Road, Halifax, West Yorkshire HX1 2NG (01422 438738; fax: 01422 350017; email: grants@cffc.co.uk; website: www.cffc.co.uk)

Trustees: Leigh-Anne Stradeski; Rod Hodgson; Russell Earnshaw; John Beacroft-Mitchell; Juliet Chambers; Roger Moore; Claire Townley; Susannah Hammond; Wim Batist; Stuart Rumney; Andy Banks; Spencer Lord; Trevor Lodge; Nick Worsnop.

CC Number: 1002722

Eligibility

Children and young people up to 18 who are living, studying or working in Halifax.

Types of grants

Grants from the 'Noel John Greenwood Halifax Children's Trust' of up to £130 for the costs of school trips, clothing, books or equipment and so on.

Annual grant total

£5,000 in 2010/11.

Applications

Individuals should apply through a referring agency, such as Citizens Advice, on an application form available from the website. Grants will only be awarded to individuals in the form of a cheque; cash is not given.

Other information

The foundation also gives to organisations and to individuals for relief-in-need purposes.

Elland

The Brooksbank Educational Charity

£6,000

Correspondent: Alan Blackburn, Ryburn, 106 Victoria Road, Elland, Calderdale HX5 0QF (01422 372014)

Trustees: David Mitchell; John Batchelor; Kathryn Shickell; Margaret Sykes; Michael Bailey; Norman Kemp; Ronald Hannah; Alan Blackburn; Dilys Longbottom; Caroline Garsed.

CC Number: 529146

Eligibility

People under the age of 25 who live in the former urban district of Elland (as constituted on 31 March 1974).

Types of grants

Grants for people who are moving from junior to secondary schools and to students going on to higher education. Grants are usually £30 per student.

Annual grant total

In 2010/11 the charity had an unusually high income and expenditure of £7,250.

Applications

Application forms are issued through the local junior schools; other students should apply direct to the correspondent. Juniors should apply in May, seniors in September. Trustees meet twice yearly, but can act rapidly in an emergency.

Haworth

The Haworth Exhibition Endowment Trust

£700

Correspondent: Andrew Collinson, 38 Gledhow Drive, Oxenhope, Keighley, West Yorkshire BD22 9SA (01535 644447)

Trustees: Isobel Scarborough; Andrew Collinson; Dorothy Hindley; Sue Green; Rosemary Key; Ian Palmer; John Prestage; Tony Maw; Rebecca Poulson.

CC Number: 507050

Eligibility

People who live, or whose parents lived, in the ancient township of Haworth. Candidates must have attended one of the schools (including Oakbank) in the district of Haworth (including Oxenhope and Stanbury, but excluding Lees and Crossroads) for at least three years.

Types of grants

One-off grants ranging from £25 to £75 to people following A-levels and taking up further education, for books and equipment.

Annual grant total

In 2010/11 the trust had an income of £800 and an expenditure of £700.

Applications

On an application form available from the town hall information desk following an advertisement in the local newspaper. The closing date for applications is 31 August. The trustees meet once a year in October.

Keighley

Bowcocks Trust Fund for Keighley

£6,000

Correspondent: Alistair Docherty, 17 Farndale Road, Wilsden, Bradford BD15 0LW (01535 272657)

Trustees: Richard Wilkinson; Samuel Stell; David Binns; Richard Marriott; Roy Feather; Jason Scott; Philip Vaux.

CC Number: 223290

Eligibility

People in need who live in the municipal borough of Keighley as constituted on 31 March 1974.

Types of grants

One-off grants according to need.

Annual grant total

In 2010/11 the trust had an income of £8,000 and a total expenditure of £6,000. In previous years a majority of the grant total has gone towards educational grants. Grants do not exceed £350.

Applications

Initial telephone calls are welcomed. Applications should be made in writing to the correspondent by a third party.

Kirklees

The Huddersfield Education Trust

£1,200

Correspondent: Carole Hardern, Kirklees Metropolitan Council, Civic Centre 1, Floor 3 South, High Street, Huddersfield HD1 2NF (01484 225226)

Trustees: G. A. Rolfe; Norman Eales; Linda Wilkinson; Alun Jones; Alan John; Stephen Day.

CC Number: 529228

Eligibility

Children under 16 who live in the former county borough of Huddersfield.

Types of grants

The trustees do not normally like to be the sole funders of the proposal. The trust stated that it is currently fully subscribed and any new beneficiaries would result in all beneficiaries receiving slightly less, although this is not something which would necessarily mean applications would be declined.

Annual grant total

Grants to both individuals and organisations total around £2,500 each year.

Applications

In writing to the correspondent, preferably through a school, educational welfare agency or a social worker. Applications are considered in April/May.

Leeds

The Community Shop Trust

£100

Correspondent: Lynn Higo, Administrator, Unit 4, Clayton Wood Bank, West Park Ring Road, Leeds LS16 6QZ (01132 745551; fax: 01132 783184; email: info@leedscommunitytrust.org; website: www.leedscommunitytrust.org)

Trustees: Teresa Felton; John Felton; Marjory Stephens; Sheila Goodall; Norman Jones; John Crawley.

CC Number: 701375

Eligibility

Children and young people in need who live in Leeds.

Types of grants

Small one-off grants towards the costs associated with education, music and sports are available under the 'Keen Kids' programme. Recent grants have been made towards a computer, learning aids, playgroup fees, a drum kit, DJ mixing decks and sports clothes.

Annual grant total

In 2011 the trust made 417 grants to 351 families totalling £35,000, broken down as follows:
- 213 emergency grants – £22,000
- 183 Christmas grants – £8,300
- 17 holidays – £3,400
- 3 'Kosy Kids' grants – £250
- 1 'Keen Kids' grant – £100

Applications

In writing to the correspondent through a social worker, Citizens Advice or other welfare agency. Potential applicants are then sent an application form to complete. For this reason the initial letter must give full details of the personal circumstances.

Other information

The trust is also known as the Leeds Community Trust. It runs two shops and distributes the profits to local charities, groups and individuals in need, particularly people in vulnerable situations.

Kirke Charity

£2,500

Correspondent: J A B Buchan, 8 St Helens Croft, Leeds LS16 8JY (01924 465860)

Trustees: John Hamilton; Selwyn Pennington; David Breton; Bruce Buchan; Norman Green; Ian White; Stuart Lewis.

CC Number: 246102

Eligibility

People in need who live in the ancient parishes of Adel, Arthington or Cookridge.

Types of grants

One-off grants of around £100.

Annual grant total

In 2010/11 the charity had an income of £8,600 and an expenditure of £5,300. Grants usually total around £5,000 for education and welfare purposes.

Applications

Applications can be submitted directly by the individual or through a social worker, Citizens Advice or other welfare agency.

Leeds Community Foundation – Looked after Children's Fund

£10,000

Correspondent: Grants Department, 51a St Paul's Street, Leeds LS1 2TE (01132 422426; email: info@leedscf.org.uk; website: www.leedscf.org.uk)

Trustees: Andrew Wriglesworth; Kevin O'Connor; Steve Rogers; Helen Thomson; Julie Meakin; Nicholas Burr; Stephen Smith; Catherine Mahoney.

CC Number: 1096892

Eligibility

Looked after children in Leeds.

Types of grants

Grants of up to £500 for extra educational costs not covered by the statutory allowance such as school trips including residential trips.

Applications

On a form available on request from social workers to be submitted by a social worker or carer.

Mirfield

The Mirfield Educational Charity

£5,600 (9 grants)

Correspondent: Malcolm Parkinson, 7 Kings Street, Mirfield, West Yorkshire WF14 8AW (01924 499251; email: malcolm.parkinson@ramsdens.co.uk)

Trustees: David Brook; Edward Speight; Howard Grason; Paul Morton; Vivien Lees-Hamilton; Christopher Oldfield; Geoffrey Jones; Martyn Bolt; Brian Nicholson.

CC Number: 529334

Eligibility

People under the age of 25 who live (or whose parents live) in the former urban district of Mirfield.

Types of grants

Grants of £200 to £1,500 are made for a wide range of educational purposes such as trips abroad, training, fees, travel and living expenses.

Annual grant total

In 2010/11 the charity had assets of £1.4 million and an income of £46,000. Nine grants to individuals totalling £5,600 were made.

Applications

In writing to the correspondent. The trustees meet three times a year, in February, May and October.

Rawdon

The Rawdon and Laneshaw Bridge School Trust (Rawdon Endowment)

£1,000

Correspondent: Anthea Hargreaves, Park Dale, Layton Drive, Rawdon, Leeds LS19 6QY (01132 504061)

Trustees: David Havenhand; Stanley Waddington; Esme Cottle; Anthea Hargreaves; Brian Cleasby; David Longley; Cayte Norman; John Peebles.

CC Number: 529197

Eligibility

People under the age of 21 and living in the former urban district of Rawdon.

Types of grants

Grants for people at college or university (typically for books or equipment) and to needy students pursuing education at lower levels, and changing to higher levels of education.

Annual grant total

About £1,000 a year.

Applications

In writing to the correspondent. Grants are awarded annually in October after applications have been invited in the local press during September.

Other information

The correspondent also administers the Charity of Francis Layton. This is for the advancement in life of deserving and necessitous Rawdon residents under the age of 21. It was formerly to assist with apprentice fees, but now tends to support other educational purposes. It gives one or two grants a year totalling £100.

Wakefield

Lady Bolles Foundation

£6,000

Correspondent: Stephen Lawrence, 6 Lynwood Drive, Wakefield WF2 7EF (01924 250473)

Trustees: Ian Ridgway; Geoffrey Townend; Stephen Skellern; Jonathan Greener; M. M. Fieldhouse.

CC Number: 529344

Eligibility

People under 21 who live in the county borough of Wakefield, and who are in full-time education.

Types of grants

Grants are given to schoolchildren towards uniforms, other school clothing, fees and educational outings. Students in further and higher education can receive help towards books and fees. Apprentices and people starting work are also eligible for support.

Annual grant total

Grants total about £6,000 per year.

Applications

In writing to the correspondent, for consideration in February and October.

Feiweles Trust

£10,000

Correspondent: Paul Rogers, c/o Yorkshire Sculpture Park, Bretton Hall, Bretton, Wakefield, West Yorkshire WF4 4LG (01924 832519; email: patricia.jorgensen-ghous@ysp.co.uk; website: www.ysp.co.uk)

CC Number: 1094383

Eligibility

Young artists at the beginning of their career.

Types of grants

One bursary is awarded per year to an artist near the beginning of their career, to allow them to work in short residencies in a variety of school contexts.

Annual grant total

In 2008/09 the trust had an income of £15,000 and a total expenditure of £12,000.

Applications

In writing to the correspondent, to be submitted directly by the individual. The deadline is January; applications are considered in February/March.

North West

General

The Bowland Charitable Trust

£385 (1 grant)

Correspondent: Carole Fahy, Activhouse, Philips Road, Blackburn, Lancashire BB1 5TH (01254 290433)

Trustees: Ruth Cann; Tony Cann; Hugh Turner; Carole Fahy.

CC Number: 292027

Eligibility

Young people in need for educational purposes in the north west of England.

Types of grants

One-off and recurrent grants towards educational character-forming activities for young people.

Annual grant total

In 2010 just one grant of £385 was made to an individual.

Applications

In writing to the correspondent, to be considered at any time.

Other information

During 2010 the trust made grants to organisations totalling £1 million.

Cockshot Foundation

£3,000

Correspondent: The Trustees, Belle Isle, Windermere, Cumbria LA23 1BG (01539 447087; email: cockshotfoundation@ belleisle.net)

Trustees: Peter Cassidy; Michelle Lefton; Roger Coleman.

CC Number: 1104085

Eligibility

Children attending any institution in the counties of Cumbria, Lancashire and Greater Manchester.

Types of grants

Grants towards the furtherance of education (including social and physical training).

Annual grant total

In 2010/11 the foundation had an income of £2,000 and a total expenditure of £9,000.

Applications

In writing to the correspondent.

Crabtree North West Charitable Trust

£7,500

Correspondent: Ian Currie, 3 Ralli Courts, West Riverside, Manchester M3 5FT (01618 311512)

Trustees: Janet Currie; Joan Ingram; Gavin Steele; Ian Currie.

CC Number: 1086405

Eligibility

Young people up to the age of 18 in education in the North West.

Types of grants

One-off according to need.

Annual grant total

Grants to individuals usually total between £5,000 to £10,000 each year.

Applications

In writing to the correspondent.

Herbert Norcross Scholarship Fund

£6,200

Correspondent: Michael Garraway, Legal and Democratic Services, Committee Services Section, Legal and Democratic Services, Town Hall, Rochdale OL16 1AB (01706 864716; email: michael-garraway@rochdale.gov.uk)

Trustees: Irene Davidson; Miles Parkinson; Ciaran Wells; Karen Burke; Stephanie Mills.

CC Number: 526666

Eligibility

People under 30 who have a permanent residence within the borough of Rochdale or the former administrative County of Lancaster. Applicants must already have completed course of study at any university, college or other institution approved by Rochdale Council and be undertaking a second or further qualification. Preference is given to residents of the former Borough of Middleton.

Types of grants

Grants of £250 to £1,000 for course fees, travel, books/equipment and other expenses incurred during studies.

Annual grant total

In 2010/11 the trust had an income of £8,500 and gave grants totalling £6,200.

Applications

On a form available from the website or the correspondent.

Manchester Publicity Association Educational Trust

£1,000

Correspondent: Gordon Jones, Secretary, 38 Larkfield Close, Greenmount, Bury, Lancashire BL8 4QJ (01204 886037)

Trustees: Ian Tinker; Gordon Jones; Rupert Smith; Eamonn Gallagher.

CC Number: 1001134

Eligibility

People aged 16 or over, living in Greater Manchester and the surrounding area, who are already working in or hoping to enter marketing or related occupations or who are studying marketing communications.

Types of grants

Grants ranging between £200 and £500 towards the cost of books or fees for education or training, usually to cover the second half of the year.

Annual grant total

Grants average around £1,000 each year.

Applications

On a form available from the correspondent. Applications must be supported by a tutor and are considered on demand.

The Northern Counties Children's Benevolent Society

See entry on page 152

The Shepherd Street Trust

£28,000 (103 grants)

Correspondent: Judith Turner, PO Box 658, Longridge, Preston PR3 2WJ (01995 678236; email: enquiries@ shepherdstreettrust.co.uk; website: www. shepherdstreettrust.co.uk)

Trustees: John Smith; Brenda Smales; John Brandwood; Timothy Scott; Catherine Penny; Stuart Shorthouse; Jeremy Lamburn; Wendy Evans.

CC Number: 222922

Eligibility

People under the age of 21 residing within a radius of 50 miles around Preston Town Hall.

Types of grants

Grants are given to: (i) support educational, social and physical training needs; (ii) provide funds for outfits, clothing, tools, instruments, equipment which will help to further education or entry into a profession, trade or calling; or (iii) assist towards facilities for recreation or other leisure occupations in the interests of social welfare.

Annual grant total

In 2010/11 the trust had assets of £1.3 million and an income of £58,000. Grants to individuals totalled £28,000.

Applications

Application forms can be downloaded from the trust's website. Applications for grants exceeding £500 will be discussed at the trustee meetings held every two months unless there is a pressing need for funds, in which case, earlier consideration will be made. Applications for grants of less than £500 will be decided on by the trustees within four weeks of receipt.

Other information

The trust also donates funds to charitable institutions and organisations which help such persons, and to the children's ward at Preston Royal Infirmary.

The Bishop David Sheppard Anniversary Trust

£7,000

Correspondent: Jen Stratford, St James House, 20 St James Road, Liverpool L1 7BY (01517 099722)

Trustees: Peter Bradley; Ruth Christie; Ricky Panter; Brian Denton; Monica Weld-Richards; Helen Blackburn.

CC Number: 517368

Eligibility

People between the ages of 21 and 49 who live in the Anglican diocese of Liverpool (which includes Southport, Kirkby, Ormskirk, Skelmersdale, Wigan, St Helens, Warrington and Widnes) and who are doing second-chance learning at a college or training centre.

Types of grants

Grants are one-off, about £100 and are made to people in second-chance learning such as access courses and training. Priority is given to those who are unemployed or who have difficulty in finding the money for books, equipment, uniforms. Grants cannot be given for fees, travel or childcare. Grants can be for training purposes to enable applicants to get a job, for example, in order to obtain a HGV licence.

Annual grant total

In 2010 the charity had both an income and expenditure of £8,000.

Exclusions

No grants to students who have had no break from their education (or schoolchildren), to people with good vocational qualifications or on degree courses, or to organisations.

Applications

On a form available from the administrator to be submitted directly by the individual at any time. Applications are usually considered in March, May, September and December.

Winwick Educational Foundation

£2,500

Correspondent: Alastair Brown, Forshaws Davies Ridgway, 17–21 Palmyra Square South, Warrington WA1 1BW (01925 230000; email: alastair.brown@fdrlaw.co.uk)

Trustees: Suzanne Knight; June Steventon; Edith Smith; Geoffrey Maines; Keith Deakin; Charles Banks; Sandra Dyer; Joan Matthews.

CC Number: 526499

Eligibility

Children and young people under the age of 25 who live in the parishes of Winwick, Newton St Peter's, Newton All Saints, Emmanuel Wargrave, St John's Earlestown, Lowton St Mary's and Lowton St Luke's.

Types of grants

One-off or recurrent grants for books, equipment and fees. Grants range from £75 to £100.

Annual grant total

In 2010/11 the foundation had an income of £3,600 and an expenditure of £5,000.

Applications

On a form available from the correspondent. Applications should be submitted in February and March for consideration in April. They can be made directly by the individual or through a third party such as the individual's school, college or educational welfare agency.

Other information

Grants are also given to local schools.

World Friendship

£16,000

Correspondent: The Applications Secretary, 15 Dudlow Lane, Liverpool L18 0HH (01517 229700; email: su05@ liv.ac.uk; website: www.worldfriendship. merseyside.org)

Trustees: R. H. Arden; Jim Huthwaite; J. Steen; M. Jones; Bob Lewis; Anne Gray; F. J. Rayner; P. M. James E. J. Rayner; Joan Grieve; Philip Anderson.

CC Number: 513643

Eligibility

International students studying at universities in the diocese of Liverpool. Preference is given to people in the final year of their course.

Types of grants

One-off grants of about £500 towards relieving unexpected hardships which have arisen since the start of the course.

Annual grant total

In 2011 the trust had an income of £10,000 and an expenditure of £18,000.

Exclusions

Grants are not given to those whose place of study is outside the diocese of Liverpool. Students from an EU country, or who are intending to stay in the UK at the end of their course, are not usually supported.

Applications
On a form available from the individual's institution. For details of the relevant contact, or to download a form, applicants should view the trust's website.

Cheshire

The Sir Thomas Moulson Trust

£500

Correspondent: Julie Turner, Meadow Barn, Cow Lane, Hargrave, Chester CH3 7RU

Trustees: Edward Thornton-Firkin; Betty Manford; Christopher Houlbrooke; Michael Whittingham; Paul Barrow; John Simpson; Paul Ellams; Michael Gilbertson; Mike Jones.

CC Number: 214342

Eligibility
Students under 25 who live in the villages of Huxley, Hargrave, Tarvin, Kelsall and Ashton in Cheshire. Preference is given to those resident in the parish of Foulk Stapleford.

Types of grants
One-off grants ranging from £100 to £500 to students in further/higher education towards books, fees/living expenses and study or travel abroad.

Annual grant total
About £500 to individuals with further monies distributed to organisations.

Applications
In writing to the correspondent. Applications should be submitted directly by the individual and are usually considered in September.

The Thornton-Le-Moors Education Foundation

£500

Correspondent: Roy Edwards, Trustee, Jesmin, 4 School Lane, Elton, Chester CH2 4LN (01928 725188)

Trustees: Roy Edwards; Ellen Nesbitt; Margaret Williams; Zora Davey; Edith Webster; Jennifer Pilling; Margaret Fletcher.

CC Number: 525829

Eligibility
People under 25 in full-time education who live in the ancient parish of Thornton-Le-Moors which includes the following villages: Dunham Hill, Elton, Hapsford, Ince and Thornton-Le-Moors.

Types of grants
The trust gives grants mostly to students going to university for books and also to the local youth groups, mainly the guides, brownies, scouts and cubs.

Annual grant total
About £500.

Applications
In writing to the correspondent. Trustees meet twice a year, usually in April and November.

The Verdin Trust Fund

£2,000

Correspondent: John Richards, Rose Cottage, 2 Vale Royal Drive, Whitegate, Northwich, Cheshire CW8 2BA (01606 889281; email: johnrichards78@live.co.uk)

Trustees: Nicholas Marsh; Richard Verdin; Clive Steggel; Janice Birdsey; Trevor Caldecott.

CC Number: 221295

Eligibility
People who live in Northwich and surrounding districts.

Types of grants
Most of the trust's funds are given in the form of prizes to local schools, Young Farmers' Associations and courses, gap years and so on.

Annual grant total
This trust has about £2,000 a year to distribute in grants.

Applications
In writing to the correspondent.

Other information
Grants are also made to organisations.

The Wrenbury Consolidated Charities

£1,000

Correspondent: Helen Smith, Eagle Hall Cottage, Smeatonwood, Wrenbury, North Nantwich CW5 8HD (01270 780262)

Trustees: Bruce Edwards; George Bebbington; Helen Smith; Peter Bebbington; Roger Blake; Roger King; Ronald Benbow; Ruth Harrison; William Wright; Donald Mason; Paul Griffiths; Revd David Walton.

CC Number: 241778

Eligibility
People in need who live in the parishes of Chorley, Sound, Broomhall, Newhall, Wrenbury and Dodcott-cum-Wilkesley.

Types of grants
Payments on St Marks' (25 April) and St Thomas' (21 December) days to pensioners and students. Grants are also given for one-off necessities.

Annual grant total
About £1,000.

Applications
In writing to the correspondent either directly by the individual or through another third party on behalf of the individual. The Vicar of Wrenbury and the parish council can give details of the six nominated trustees who can help with applications. Applications are considered in December and March.

Other information
Grants are also given to churches, the village hall and for welfare purposes.

Alsager

The Alsager Educational Foundation

£5,000

Correspondent: Catherine Lovatt, Secretary, 6 Pikemere Road, Alsager, Stoke-on-Trent ST7 2SB (01270 873680)

Trustees: Andrew Smith; Ronald Tyson; Charles Bennion; Derek Bould; Janet Evans; Michael Elkin; Christine Richards; Shirley Jones; Toby May; Saeed Ashtiany; Lena Isherwood; Matthew Sutton; Francis Williams.

CC Number: 525834

Eligibility
People who live in the urban district of Alsager.

Types of grants
One-off and recurrent grants of £200 to £1,000 are given to schoolchildren, college students, undergraduates, vocational students and to individuals with special educational needs for fees, study/travel overseas, books, instruments/equipment and excursions, and also to schoolchildren for uniforms and clothing.

Annual grant total
In 2010/11 the trust had an income of £15,000 and an expenditure of £20,000. Previously around £5,000 has been given in grants to individuals.

Exclusions
Postgraduates and people who do not have a permanent home address in Alsager will not be supported.

Applications
In writing to the correspondent directly by the individual. Applications are considered four times per year.

Audlem

Audlem Educational Foundation

£3,000

Correspondent: Louisa Ingham, People's Finance Department, Cheshire East Council, Delamere House, Delamere Street, Crewe CW1 2JZ (01270 686223; email: louisa.ingham@cheshireeast.gov.uk)

Trustee: Chris Mann.

CC Number: 525810

Eligibility

Young persons under 25 years of age who are resident in the Ancient Parish of Audlem and who are in need of financial assistance to support educational development.

Applicants can submit an application to the Audlem Board of Trustees who assess whether the candidate is suitable.

Types of grants

One-off and recurrent grants according to need.

Annual grant total

In 2010/11 the foundation had an income of £13,000 and an expenditure of £6,400.

Applications

In writing to the correspondent.

Chester

Chester Municipal Charities

£25,000

Correspondent: Grants Administrator, PO Box 360, Tarporley CW6 6AZ (01829 759416; fax: 01829 759010; email: info@chestermunicipalcharities.org)

Trustees: Jeanne Storrar; Elizabeth Bolton; Peter Catherall; Denis Ainsworth; Mark Fearnall; Peter Lowe; Peter Dutton; Philip Hebson; Kevin Hassett; Christine Russell; David Challen; John Ebo; Clive Pointon.

CC Number: 107806

Eligibility

The foundation provides grants to individual young people under the age of 25 years who are attending or have attended a school in Chester and who are Chester residents, in order to help with their education. Some preference is given to beneficiaries whose fathers are freemen of the city.

Types of grants

Grants may come in the form of bursaries/grants paid directly to schools/colleges/universities. Help is also available to meet the cost of travel expenses or the purchase of equipment and uniforms.

Annual grant total

About £25,000.

Applications

On a form available from the correspondent. Applications should be submitted directly by the individual for consideration in September and October.

Congleton

The Congleton Town Trust

£5,000

Correspondent: Ms J Money, Clerk, c/o Congleton Town Hall, High Street, Congleton CW12 1BN (01260 291156; email: info@congletontowntrust.co.uk; website: www.congletontowntrust.co.uk)

Trustees: Gordon Baxendale; Louise Beard; Robert Boston; Alex Hurst; David Daniel; James Morris; Dennis Murphy; Douglas Parker; Arthur Smart; Jeanne Whitehurst; Margaret Williamson.

CC Number: 1051122

Eligibility

People in need who live in the town of Congleton (this does not include the other two towns which have constituted the borough of Congleton since 1975).

Types of grants

The principal aim of the trust is to give grants to individuals in need or to organisations which provide relief, services or facilities to those in need. The trustees will, however, consider a grant towards education or training if the applicant is in need. Support can be given in the form of books, tools or in cash towards tuition fees or maintenance.

Annual grant total

In 2010 the trust had an income of £24,000 and a total expenditure of £20,000.

Applications

On a form available from the correspondent or downloaded from the trust's website, to be submitted directly by the individual or a family member. Applications are considered quarterly, on the second Monday in March, June, September and December.

Other information

The trust also administers several smaller trusts.

Wilmslow

The Lindow Workhouse Trust

£2,500

Correspondent: Jacquie Bilsborough, 15 Westward Road, Wilmslow SK9 5JY

Trustees: Stanley Horner; William Warburton; Barbara Briggs; Pat Burrow; Grahame Harris; Pat Breen; Richard Briggs; Ken Mackay; James Montgomery; Jackie Watts; Richard Lowson; Magdalen Smith; Myra Clarke; Jenny Lloyd.

CC Number: 226023

Eligibility

Children with special educational needs who live in the ancient parish of Wilmslow.

Types of grants

One-off grants of up to £500.

Annual grant total

About £5,000 for welfare and educational purposes.

Applications

In writing to the correspondent at any time. Applications can be submitted either directly by the individual or a family member, through a third party such as a social worker or teacher, or through an organisation such as Citizens Advice or a school.

Warrington

The Police-Aided Children's Relief-in-Need Fund

£0

Correspondent: Stephanie Saxon, Warrington Council For Voluntary Services, The Gateway, 89 Sankey St, Warrington WA1 1SR (01925 444263)

Trustees: Diana Terris; Brian Maher; Lynton Green.

CC Number: 223937

Eligibility

Children of pre-school or primary school age living in the borough of Warrington and whose families are in financial or physical need. Applications from students of secondary school age and over will be considered in exceptional circumstances.

Types of grants

Vouchers to help with the cost of clothing and footwear. Vouchers are only redeemable at selected retailers in the borough.

Annual grant total

No accounts have been submitted since 2008/09 when the fund had an income of £5,000 and an expenditure of £0.

Applications

The trust states that grantmaking is currently suspended whilst various structural issues are sorted out.

Widnes

The Widnes Educational Foundation

£1,000

Correspondent: Miss Wendy Jefferies, Halton Borough Council, Municipal Buildings, Kingsway, Widnes, Cheshire WA8 7QF

Trustee: Anthony McDermott.

CC Number: 526510

Eligibility

People under 25 who attend school or college in Widnes.

Types of grants

The foundation mainly focuses on giving grants to help with educational trips and visits. Cash grants can also be given for books and educational outings for those at school. Very occasionally small grants are given to help with school/college fees or to supplement existing grants. There is no set grant amount; applications are considered on a case by case basis.

Annual grant total

About £1,000.

Applications

Applications should be made through the school or college and must be supported by a third party, such as a teacher.

Cumbria

The Barton Educational Foundation

£1,000

Correspondent: A Wright, 15 Church Croft, Pooley Bridge, Penrith, Cumbria CA10 2NL (01768 486312)

Trustees: Harold Threlkeld; M. Tweddell; Elizabeth Stewart; Gillian Mackey; Alan Wright; David Wood; Joan Lowis; Joyce Robinson.

CC Number: 526927

Eligibility

People who live in Barton, Yanwath, Pooley Bridge, Martindale or Patterdale.

Types of grants

Recurrent grants ranging between £25 and £100 to students at colleges and universities for help with books, fees and living expenses. Help with the costs of books for schoolchildren is also occasionally provided. People starting work and apprentices can also be supported.

Annual grant total

About £1,000.

Applications

Directly by the individual on a form available from the correspondent. Applications are considered in October.

The Brow Edge Foundation

£2,000

Correspondent: Robert William Hutton, 20 Ainslie Street, Ulverston, Cumbria LA12 7JE (01229 585888; email: gordon@421.co.uk)

Trustees: Doreen Fell; Gordon Egglestone; Christina Watkinson; Ian Nicol; Susan Sanderson.

CC Number: 526716

Eligibility

People in need who live in the area of Haverthwaite and Backbarrow, aged between 16 and 25.

Types of grants

Small grants to assist pupils attending schools, institutions or classes for post-16 education. Preference is given to young people from disadvantaged backgrounds.

Annual grant total

About £2,000.

Applications

In writing to the correspondent, directly by the individual. Applicants must state the type of course of study or apprenticeship they are about to undertake. Applications are usually considered in September.

The Burton-in-Kendal Educational Foundation

£2,000

Correspondent: Elizabeth Falkingham, 7 Hollowrayne, Burton-in-Kendal, Cumbria LA6 1NS (01524 782302; email: liz.falk21@tiscali.co.uk)

Trustees: Peter Cummings; Terence Long.

CC Number: 526953

Eligibility

People aged between 16 and 25 years who live in the parishes of Burton, Beetham, Arnside, Storth and Meathop, Ulpha, Holme, Preston and Patrick and are in need of financial assistance. Applicants must have attended a county or voluntary primary school for no less than two years.

Types of grants

Grants ranging between about £10 and £60 a year are made to schoolchildren, college students, undergraduates and vocational students towards fees, study/travel abroad, books, equipment/instruments and maintenance/living expenses. Grants are also made to people with special educational needs.

Annual grant total

In 2010/11 the foundation had an income of £2,700 and an expenditure of £2,300.

Applications

On a form available from the correspondent, which should be submitted directly by the individual. Applications are considered in May and October/November and should be received by April and September respectively.

The Cartmel Old Grammar School Foundation

£10,000

Correspondent: Anthony William Coles, Clerk, 2 Rowan Side, Grange-over-Sands, Cumbria LA11 7EQ (01539 534348; email: tony@tonycoles.myzen.co.uk)

Trustees: Paul Bond; David Huggett; Frederick Hampson; Sheila Phizacklea; Howard Martin; Ann Boardman; John Addison; Kathryn Strawbridge; Jennifer Weir; Anthea Wilson.

CC Number: 526467

Eligibility

People between the ages of 18 and 25 who live in the parishes of Cartmel Fell, Broughton East, Grange-over-Sands, Lower Holker, Staveley, Lower Allithwaite, Upper Allithwaite and that part of the parish of Haverthwaite east of the River Leven.

Types of grants

Cash grants of about £85, usually for up to three years, for students in higher education to help with books, fees/living expenses or study or travel abroad. Help is also given for those studying music and the arts in special cases.

Annual grant total

In 2010/11 the foundation had both an income and expenditure of £11,000.

Applications

On a form available from the correspondent, including schools attended, qualifications and place of higher education. Applications are considered in October/November.

Edmond Castle Educational Trust

£3,000

Correspondent: The Administrator, Cumbria Community Foundation, Dovenby Hall, Dovenby, Cockermouth CA13 0PN (01900 825760; email: enquiries@cumbriafoundation.org; website: www.cumbriafoundation.org)

Trustees: G. H. Mounsey-Heysham; A. I. Bullough; S. R. Brown.

CC Number: 1027991

Eligibility

Children and young people under the age of 21 who are or have been in the care of, or provided with accommodation, by Cumbria County Council and, also children and young people who are in need who have experienced mental health problems.

Types of grants

Grants of up to £500 given according to need for equipment, course fees, computers, childcare costs and other activities which extend opportunities.

Annual grant total

In 2010/11 the trust had an income of £1,100 and an expenditure of £4,000. Grants to individuals totalled about £3,000.

Applications

On the *Under 18s or full time education* or *Over 18s and vocational training* application forms available on the Cumbria Community Foundation's website along with guidelines specific to the trust.

Other information

In 2010/11 the trust made one grant of £1,000 to an organisation.

Cumbria Community Foundation

£32,000

Correspondent: The Grants Team, Cumbria Community Foundation, Dovenby Hall, Cockermouth, Cumbria CA13 0PN (01900 825760; fax: 01900 826527; email: enquiries@ cumbriafoundation.org; website: www. cumbriafoundation.org)

Trustees: J. R. Carr; D. L. Brown; J. F. Whittle; I. W. Brown; Robin Burgess; S. F. Young; A. Naylor; J. Chapman; R. J. Cairns; C. A. Alexander; M. Casson; W. Slavin; S. E. Snyder; J. E. Humphries; J. B. Donnelly; C. Tomlinson; T. Foster; T. J. Knowles; C. A. Giel; T. Jones.

CC Number: 1075120

Eligibility

People resident in Cumbria. Other restrictions including geographical and age related pertain depending upon the fund being applied to.

Types of grants

One-off and recurrent grants for various amounts for a wide range of needs including travel abroad and in the UK, educational or training activities or preparations to enter a trade or profession, writing and publishing, the arts

Annual grant total

In 2010/11 the foundation made 1,070 grants to individuals totalling £735,000, including £671,000 from various flood recovery funds to relieve hardship arising from the floods of November 2009. The remaining £64,000 was given for both welfare and educational needs. Flood grab bags distributed to households cost an additional £153,000.

Applications

The foundation administers numerous funds that give grants to individuals, and they have differing eligibility criteria and application forms. Applicants should check the website for full details of each scheme, and how to apply.

Other information

The trust administers funds for both individuals and organisations, some of which may open and close regularly.

The Mary Grave Trust

£68,000

Correspondent: Jane Allen, Cumbria Community Foundation, Dovenby Hall, Dovenby, Cockermouth CA13 0PN (01900 825760; email: enquiries@ cumbriafoundation.org; website: www. cumbriafoundation.org)

Trustee: Cumbria Community Foundation.

CC Number: 1075120

Eligibility

People in need aged between 11 and 21 who were born in the former county of Cumberland (excluding those whose parents were resident in Carlisle).

Applicants must live, study or have studied (for at least two years, in secondary/further education) in one of the following areas, listed in order of priority: (i) the former boroughs of Workington or Maryport, or (ii) the former borough of Whitehaven, (iii) elsewhere in the former county of Cumberland.

Students in sixth forms, further education colleges, universities and higher education colleges or in the gaps between these stages can all be considered as can those at work, in training or involved through youth organisation activities.

Activities should usually be based abroad but can take place within the UK, providing that they involve a residential element away from home and are beyond the boundaries of Cumbria.

Types of grants

Grants up to £1,000 to assist in travel overseas which is of educational value.

The trust offers bursaries in two principal areas:

- Activities organised by a school or college, whereupon students/pupils can apply for funding through a teacher or lecturer. The trust states that a major venture in this field is the Educational Cruise which takes place every two years (October 2008, 2010 etc.), and can usually take up a large proportion of funding
- The trust is also keen to encourage applications from post-GCSE students for activities such as field-work trips, work-experience visits and specialist study bursaries for art and music schools, and from further and higher education students for gap year activities and outward bound courses such as Raleigh International

Annual grant total

In 2010/11 the trust had assets of £1.4 million and an income of £55,000. Grants to individuals totalled £68,000. The trust states that it will use the reserves to maintain this level of grantmaking.

Exclusions

Funding cannot be given to employees of British Steel or the National Coal Board.

Applications

On a form available from the correspondent, submitted through the individual's school or college or directly by the individual. The trustees require a copy of the applicant's birth certificate and information about his/her financial circumstances. Applications should be received by 2 April, 1 October and 31 December.

The Greysouthen Educational Charity

£2,500

Correspondent: John Chipps, Brunlea, Greysouthen, Cockermouth, Cumbria CA13 0UA (01900 825235)

Trustees: Edward Sewell; John Chipps; David King; Christine Caddy; Margaret Allison.

CC Number: 512662

Eligibility
People under 25 who live in Greysouthen or Eaglesfield.

Types of grants
Help with the cost of books, clothing, educational outings, fees and other essentials for schoolchildren. Grants are also available for those at college or university towards books, fees/living expenses, childcare costs and study or travel abroad. Grants for people starting work will be made for books, equipment/instruments, clothing and travel.

Annual grant total
In 2010/11 the trust had an income of £2,500 and an expenditure of £3,000.

Applications
In writing to the correspondent either directly by the individual or through his/ her school, college or an educational welfare agency. Applications are considered in July/August.

Kelsick's Educational Foundation

£104,000

Correspondent: Peter Frost, Clerk, Kelsick Centre, St Mary's Lane, Ambleside, Cumbria LA22 9DG (01539 431289; fax: 01539 431292; email: john@ kelsick.plus.com; website: www.kelsick. org.uk)

Trustees: Peter Jackson; Linda Dixon; Leslie Johnson; Nigel Hutchinson; John Halstead; Angela Renouf; Helen Fuller; Norman Tyson; Reginald Curphey; William Coke; Nicholas Martin; Dr Twiselton.

CC Number: 526956

Eligibility
Young people, under the age of 25, who were born or who have lived in Ambleside, Grasmere, Langdale or part of Troutbeck (the Lakes Parish) for at least four years. There is a preference for children/students with special needs.

Types of grants
Grants are given for: extra help at school for pupils with special needs; music

lessons; extracurricular activities such as performing arts and sports; hire of musical instruments; travel costs for certain educational trips; tools, equipment and extra training for apprentices or working trainees; subsistence grants for college students; computers for first year university students; and books for A-level, college and university courses. Grants are one-off and recurrent and range from £25 to £3,000.

Annual grant total
In 2010/11 the trust had assets of £6.7 million and an income of £67,000. Grants to individuals totalled £104,000 and were broken down as follows:
- Primary £5,800
- Secondary and further £20,000
- Higher £66,000

Applications
On a form available from the correspondent or to download from the website. Applications are considered in February, May, August and November – deadline dates for submission at these meetings are 31 January, 30 April, 31 July, 31 October, respectively. Applicants must list detailed costs (with receipts) of the items required. Forms should be submitted directly by the individual or by a parent/guardian if the applicant is under 18.

Other information
Grants totalling £127,000 were awarded to voluntary schools and organisations.

Lamonby Educational Trust

£1,500

Correspondent: Lynne Miller, Arbour House, Lamonby, Penrith, Cumbria CA11 9SS (01768 484385)

Trustees: Elizabeth Smith; Jean Parker; Jim Mills; Stella Jackson.

CC Number: 517966

Eligibility
People who live in the Lamonby area who are under the age of 25.

Types of grants
One-off grants in the range of £20 and £200 to schoolchildren, college students, undergraduates, vocational students including those for clothing/uniforms, study/travel abroad, books, equipment/ instruments and excursion. Grants are also made to people starting work and people with special educational needs.

Annual grant total
In 2010/11 the trust had an income of £2,000 and an expenditure of £3,000.

Applications
On a form available from the correspondent. Applications are considered in October and May.

Other information
Grants are also given to local schools.

Silecroft School Educational Charity

£1,000

Correspondent: Catherine Jopson, Hestham Hall Farm, Millom LA18 5LJ (01229 772525)

Trustees: Richard Rushton; David Griffiths; Janet Harris; Sarah Wilson; Joan Hobbs.

CC Number: 509580

Eligibility
People under 25 who were born in the parishes of Whicham, Millom, Millom Without and Ulpha.

Types of grants
Recurrent grants are given for a wide range of educational needs for people at university or college, from books, clothing, equipment and other supplementary awards to foreign travel and other educational visits. However, the trust does not give grants for travel to and from the applicant's place of residence.

Annual grant total
About £1,000.

Exclusions
Grants are not given for schoolchildren, people starting work or to students who have not moved away from home to continue their education.

Applications
On a form available from the correspondent, to be submitted in September for consideration in November. Applications can be made either directly by the individual, or through their school, college or educational welfare agency.

The Wiggonby School Trust

£24,000

Correspondent: M Fleming, Flemsyam, Aikton, Wigton, Cumbria CA7 0JA (01697 342829)

Trustees: Amy Bragg; Ian Langley; James Thomlinson; John Hewson; Margaret Hodgson; Richard Graham; Robert Blamire; Thomas Graham; Gordon Thomlinson; Wendy Betts.

CC Number: 526850

Eligibility

People who have left school, are under 25 and live in the parishes of Aikton, Beaumont and Burgh-by-Sands, or are former pupils of Wiggonby School.

Types of grants

Grants, usually of around £200, for people engaged in further education or training, including help with fees/living expenses, books, equipment and so on. People starting work may also receive help.

Annual grant total

In 2010/11 the trust had assets of £614,000 and an income of £26,000. Grants totalled £24,000, which were distributed under the following categories:

- School prizes – £400
- Grants to children – £7,100
- Wiggonby School fund – £17,000

Applications

Applications are invited annually in answer to an advertisement placed in the Cumberland News in August. They can be made on a form available from the correspondent and are considered in September. Information required includes place of further study and qualification aimed for.

Barrow-in-Furness

The Billincoat Charity

£2,000

Correspondent: Kenneth Fisher, Glenside House, Springfield Road, Ulverston, Cumbria LA12 0EJ (01229 583437)

Trustees: John Wharton; John Wood; Alan Mitchell; Dorothy James; Edward Stanley; Lynne Slavin; Frank Murray; Wendy Maddox; Katherine Unwin; Lynn Murray; Jillian Heath.

CC Number: 233409

Eligibility

People under 21 who live in the borough of Barrow-in-Furness.

Types of grants

One-off grants towards the cost of education, training, apprenticeship or equipment for those starting work; and books, equipment/instruments, fees, educational outings in the UK and study or travel abroad for schoolchildren and people in further and higher education. Schoolchildren can also be supported for uniforms or other school clothing.

Annual grant total

In 2010/11 the trust had an income of £3,300 and an expenditure of £2,600.

Applications

On an application form available from the correspondent to be submitted in December and June for consideration in January and July. Applications can be submitted by the individual or through their school, college, social services or probation service and so on.

Carlisle

The Carlisle Educational Charity

£9,400 (44 grants)

Correspondent: Peter Mason, The Civic Centre, Carlisle CA3 8QG (01228 817039; fax: 01228 817072; email: peterm@carlisle.gov.uk; website: www.carlisle.gov.uk)

Trustees: Mark Boyling; Brian McConnell; David Jenkins; Margaret Boumphrey; James Bainbridge; Joe Hendrie; Elizabeth Mallinson; James Tootle; Christopher Southward; Richard Hunt.

CC Number: 509357

Eligibility

People (or whose parents) who live in the area of Carlisle city (i.e. north and north east Cumbria), aged under 25. Applicants should be due to attend a full time course at a university or institute of further education, a graduate wishing to undertake higher studies or professional qualifications or a student who has to travel in this country or abroad as part of their course.

Types of grants

Grants of £50 to £400 are given to: (i) students due to attend full time courses at a university or institution of further education; (ii) graduates undertaking, or wishing to undertake higher studies or obtaining professional qualifications; (iii) students who have to travel in the UK or abroad as part of their course.

Grants are for general educational costs, such as books and equipment.

Annual grant total

In 2010/11 the charity had an income of £9,900 and gave £9,400 in 44 grants.

Applications

On a form available from the correspondent or from the website. Applications are considered in March and October and should be submitted by February and September respectively.

Crosby Ravensworth

The Crosby Ravensworth Relief-in-Need Charities

£1,200

Correspondent: G Bowness, Ravenseat, Crosby Ravensworth, Penrith, Cumbria CA10 3JB (01931 715382; email: gordonbowness@aol.com)

Trustees: George Bowness; John Hall; Frank Jackson; James Relph; Joyce Raine; Thomas Harris; Hazel Blenkinship; Betsy Bell; Jill Winder; Revd S. Fyfe.

CC Number: 232598

Eligibility

People in need who have lived in the ancient parish of Crosby Ravensworth for at least 12 months.

Types of grants

One-off and recurrent grants. As well as relief-in-need grants, funds can also be given to local students entering university if they have been educated in the parish.

Annual grant total

In 2010 the trust had an income of £12,000 and a total expenditure of £3,400.

Applications

In writing to the correspondent submitted directly by the individual including details of the applicant's financial situation. Applications are considered in February, May and October.

Egton-cum-Newland

Egton Parish Lands Trust

£1,000

Correspondent: Joyce Ireland, Threeways, Pennybridge, Ulverston, Cumbria LA12 7RX (01229 861405)

Trustees: Jerit Hockenhull; Geoffrey Moore; James Newby; John Bell; John Dover; Mark Southern; Jane Carson.

CC Number: 221424

Eligibility

Children and young people in need living in the parish of Egton-cum-Newland. Particular favour is given to parents on low incomes whose children wish to go on educational trips.

Types of grants

One-off and recurrent grants of £100 to £1,000 to schoolchildren for equipment/ instruments and excursions and to college and university students for books.

Annual grant total

In 2010/11 the charity had an income of £10,000 and an expenditure of £12,000. Most of the expenditure usually goes in grants to organisations.

Applications

In writing to the correspondent. Applications should be submitted in April and October for consideration in May and November. They can be made either by the individual or through his/ her school, college or welfare agency, or other third party.

Sedbergh

Robinson's Educational Foundation

£10,000

Correspondent: Ian Jenkinson, Milne Moser Solicitors, 100 Highgate, Kendal, Cumbria LA9 4HE (01539 729786; email: solicitors@milnemoser.co.uk)

Trustees: Arthur Capstick; John Booth; George Capstick; Thomas Postlethwaite; Alistair Mackie; Ronald Luffman.

CC Number: 529897

Eligibility

People below the age of 25 who live in the parish of Sedbergh, with a preference for people who live in Howgill.

Types of grants

One-off grants from £15 to £1,000 are given for a wide range of educational needs not covered by the local education authority. Grants can be given to schoolchildren towards music lessons. Students in further/higher education can receive help for books, fees/living expenses or study or travel abroad.

Annual grant total

In 2010/11 the foundation had an income of £12,000 and an expenditure of £13,000.

Applications

In writing to the correspondent, either directly by the individual or through a social worker, Citizens Advice, other welfare agency or other third party. Applications are considered in September.

Greater Manchester

The Barrack Hill Educational Charity

£3,500

Correspondent: J H Asquith, 24 Links Road, Romiley, Stockport, Cheshire SK6 4HU (01614 303583; email: cllr. mikewilson@stockport.gov.uk)

Trustees: John Alletson; M. Wilson; John Asquith; Mary Nuttall; Hazel Lees; Pamela Jeffery; Phillip Clarke; Julie Green.

CC Number: 525836

Eligibility

People under the age of 21 who live or whose parents live in Bredbury and Romiley.

Types of grants

One-off grants to assist towards educational expenses. Students in full-time and part-time education can receive grants towards books, study or travel abroad and equipment; people in vocational training can be helped with tools, uniform, equipment and so on; and schoolchildren can be given grants towards school uniforms, other school clothing and equipment or instruments.

Annual grant total

In 2011 the charity had an income of £8,200 and an expenditure of £9,000.

Applications

On a form available from the correspondent, usually made available from local libraries towards the end of the school year. Applications are considered in September and October.

Other information

The charity also gives grants to schools in the area.

The Dorothy Bulkeley and Cheadle Lads' Charity

£1,000

Correspondent: Peter Dooley, Secretary, 48 Chorlton Drive, Cheadle, Cheshire SK8 2BG (01614 911816; email: p.m. dooley@salford.ac.uk)

Trustees: Mark Tomlinson; Helen Livingston; Andrew Taylor; Dave Clark; Jillian Wilkinson.

CC Number: 525895

Eligibility

People under the age of 25 living in the former district of Cheadle and Gatley (as constituted on 30 April 1974) or people who are or who have attended school in the above district.

Types of grants

Grants are given for general educational purposes to schoolchildren, students in further/higher education, vocational and mature students and people starting work. This can include assistance for professional training, apprenticeships and schooling costs. Grants usually range from £500 to £1,000 and are usually given to two or three individuals each year.

Annual grant total

About £1,000.

Applications

On a form available from the correspondent. Applications are considered in November.

The Ann Butterworth and Daniel Bayley Charity

£800

Correspondent: The Trust Administrator, Gaddum Centre, Gaddum House, 6 Great Jackson Street, Manchester M15 4AX (01618 346069; fax: 01618 398573; email: gaddumcentre@hotmail.com; website: www.gaddumcentre.co.uk)

Trustee: Michael Braid.

CC Number: 526055

Eligibility

Children and young people aged 25 and under who are of the Protestant religion and live in Manchester.

Types of grants

Grants towards the cost of education, training apprenticeships and so on, including for books, equipment, clothing, uniforms and travel. School and university/college fees are not met.

Annual grant total

Grants usually total around £800 each year.

Applications

On a form available from the correspondent which must be submitted with support from a sponsor such as a social worker, health visitor or teacher. The charity stated that it receives more applications than it can possibly support.

The Darbishire House Trust

£700

Correspondent: Anne Hosker, Gaddum Centre, Gaddum House, 6 Great Jackson Street, Manchester M15 4AX (01618 346069)

Trustees: Irene Walton; Robert Payne; David Carmichael; David Tattersall; Michael Arundel; Janet Hennessey.

CC Number: 234651

Eligibility

Women teachers and ex-teachers who were born in, reside in or work(ed) in Greater Manchester and are now retraining.

Types of grants

Grants towards the costs of education and retraining, including for books, equipment, clothing, uniforms and travel. A one-off contribution to fees may be considered.

Annual grant total

Expenditure averages around £700 each year.

Applications

On a form available from the correspondent which must be completed by a sponsor from an educational establishment.

Forever Manchester

£44,000

Correspondent: The Grants Team, 5th Floor, Speakers House, 39 Deansgate, Manchester M3 2BA (01612 140953 (grants hotline: 01612 140951); fax: 01612 140941; email: enquiries@ communityfoundation.co.uk; website: forevermanchester.com)

Trustees: A. Burns; J. Farrell; C. Hurst; P. Hogben; Han-Son Lee; S. Lindsay; N. Qureshi; J. Sandford; S. Webber.

CC Number: 1017504

Eligibility

People in need who live in Greater Manchester.

Types of grants

Grants are usually one-off. Funds for individuals have included those from the Greater Manchester Sports Fund and the Joshua Short Foundation, for parents of pre-school children who have autism and live in the borough of Stockport.

Annual grant total

£89,000 in 2010/11 to individuals for welfare and education.

Applications

Visit the foundation's website or contact the foundation for details of grant funds that are appropriate for individuals to apply for.

Other information

The Community Foundation for Greater Manchester manages a portfolio of grants for a variety of purposes which are mostly for organisations, but there are a select few which are for individuals. Funds tend to open and close throughout the year as well as new ones being added, and others being spent out. Check the website for information on current schemes.

Mynshull's Educational Foundation

£15,000

Correspondent: Ann Hosker, Gaddum Centre, Gaddum House, 6 Great Jackson Street, Manchester M15 4AX (01618 346069; email: amh@gaddumcentre.co. uk)

Trustees: Michael Colin; Shirley Adams; A. J. Burden; William Egerton; Mark Ashcroft; Jenny Curtis.

CC Number: 532334

Eligibility

Children and young people aged 25 and under who are at school, university or college, on an apprenticeship or attending another educational/training course, except postgraduates. Applicants must be resident or have been born in the city of Manchester and the following adjoining districts: Reddish, Audenshaw, Failsworth, Chadderton, Middleton, Prestwich, Old City of Salford, Stretford, Sale, Cheadle, Heaton Moor, Heaton Mersey and Heaton Chapel.

Types of grants

Grants towards the costs of education, training, apprenticeship and for items such as books, equipment, clothing, uniforms and travel costs.

Annual grant total

In 2010/11 the foundation had an income of £11,000 and an expenditure of £17,000.

Exclusions

No grants for course fees, rent or any other ongoing expenditure.

Applications

On a form available from the correspondent which must be completed by a sponsor from the educational establishment.

The Pratt Charity

£1,000

Correspondent: Anne Hosker, Gaddum Centre, Gaddum House, 6 Great Jackson Street, Manchester M15 4AX (01618 346069; email: info@gaddumcentre.co. uk)

Trustees: The Revd Canon Michael Arundel; John Miller; Janet Hennessey; Robert Payne; Barbara Schofield; Irene Walton; David Tattersall.

CC Number: 507162–1

Eligibility

Women over 60 who live in or near Manchester and have done so for a period of not less than five years.

Types of grants

Grants are given towards education, health and relief of poverty, distress and sickness.

Annual grant total

About £1,000 per year.

Applications

In writing to the correspondent via a social worker.

Other information

The charity is administered by the Gaddum Charity.

The Rochdale Ancient Parish Educational Trust

£4,200 (31 grants)

Correspondent: Jim Murphy, Legal and Democratic Services, Committee Services Section, Town Hall, Rochdale OL16 1AB (01706 927474; website: www.rochdale. gov.uk/grants__trusts/charitable_trusts. aspx)

Trustees: Robert Clegg; Thomas Hobson; Pat Swanston; Jane Gartside; Alan Shackleton; Corrine Ogden; Dorothy Brierley; Martin Coupe; Donna Martin; Pat Flyn; Maureen Jones.

CC Number: 526318

Eligibility

People, preferably but not exclusively under 25, who live in Rochdale, Littleborough, Milnrow, Wardle, Todmorden, Saddleworth, Newhey, Bacup and Whitworth and who attend or have attended a school in the area of the ancient parish. Preference is given to schoolchildren with serious family difficulties who have to be educated away from home, and people with special educational needs.

Types of grants

One-off grants to schoolchildren and further and higher education students, including mature students and postgraduates, towards the cost of uniforms or other school clothing, books, equipment/instruments, fees, educational outings in the UK, study or travel abroad and student exchanges. Further and higher education students can also receive help with maintenance/living expenses and childcare costs. People starting work can receive financial assistance. Grants range between £50 and £330

Annual grant total

In 2010/11 the trust had assets of £566,000, an income of £38,000 and made grants totalling £4,200.

Exclusions

No grants to students studying at a level they already hold a qualification in (such as a second degree course) or to people who have received assistance from either the Hopwood Hall College Access Fund or the Rochdale Educational Trust.

Applications

On a form available from the correspondent or the website; applications can be submitted directly by the individual or through the school/college or educational welfare agency, and are considered in January, March, July and September.

Other information

The trust also owns and maintains several cottages.

Seamon's Moss Educational Foundation

£400

Correspondent: R Drake, Secretary, 32 Riddings Court, Timperley, Altrincham, Cheshire WA15 6BG (01619 697772)

Trustees: Kenneth Williams; Michael Duckworth; Roger Drake; Ronald Hutchinson; Christine Drake.

CC Number: 525823

Eligibility

People aged under 25 who live in the ancient townships of Dunham Massey, Bowden and Altrincham.

Types of grants

One-off grants up to a maximum of £250 each.

Annual grant total

The foundation has an annual expenditure of £840.

Exclusions

People must reside in the ancient townships of Dunham Massey, Bowden and Altrincham.

Applications

In writing to the correspondent. Applications should be submitted directly by the individual and are considered in August. Ineligible applications will not be responded to.

Other information

Grants are also given to schools in the area of benefit.

Billinge

John Eddleston's Charity

£500

Correspondent: Graham Bartlett, Parkinson Commercial Property Consultants, 10 Bridgeman Terrace, Wigan, Lancashire WN1 1SX (01942 740 180)

Trustees: James Heyes; Raymond Hutchinson; Cliff Stockley; William Tyrer; Charles Mather; William Bradbury; Gillian Sainsbury.

CC Number: 503695

Eligibility

Persons under the age of 25 years in need of financial assistance who live in, or whose parents live in, the parish of Billinge.

Types of grants

One-off grants for educational purposes including social and physical training.

Annual grant total

Grants to individuals usually total around £1,000 for both education and welfare purposes.

Applications

In writing to the correspondent by the end of March. The annual meeting of the trustees takes place after the end of March.

Other information

The trust gives to both individuals and organisations.

Bolton

The Chadwick Educational Foundation

£6,300

Correspondent: Diane Abbott, Secretary, 71 Chorley Old Road, Bolton, Lancashire BL1 3JA (01204 534421)

Trustees: Ebrahim Adia; Peter Liptrott; Michael Williams; Stan Wilson; Pamela Taylor; M. Smith; Amy Liptrott; Matt Thompson.

CC Number: 526373

Eligibility

People under 25 years of age, living in Bolton and, who are in need.

Types of grants

One-off grants of £100 to £250 for text books, uniforms, equipment/instruments, educational outings in the UK and study or travel abroad. Grants are available for schoolchildren, students, apprentices and people starting work and for music or arts education. The foundation prefers to support the promotion of education in the principles of the Church of England.

Annual grant total

In 2011 the trust made grants to four individuals totalling £6,300.

Applications

Application forms available from the correspondent, to be submitted by the individual or through a headteacher in July for consideration in September. Proof of parental income is essential.

Other information

The Marsden and Popperwell Educational Charity is administered by the same correspondent and has the same eligibility.

Fifteen grants to local schools were made totalling £117,000.

The James Eden Foundation

£10,000

Correspondent: The Trustees, R P Smith and Co., 71 Chorley Old Road, Bolton BL1 3AJ (01204 534421; fax: 01204 535475; email: info@rpsmithbolton.co.uk)

Trustees: Brian Leigh-Bramwell; Andrew Taylor; Ebrahim Adia; Eve Walker; Pamela Senior; David Arkwright; Leilia Price.

CC Number: 526265

Eligibility

Students in or entering full-time further education at universities or colleges, aged under 25, who are residents of the metropolitan borough of Bolton. Preference is given to people who have lost either or both parents, or whose parents are separated or divorced.

Types of grants

Cash grants of between £400 and £1,500 are given to assist college students and undergraduates with fees, books, equipment/instruments, maintenance/

living expenses, educational outings in the UK and study or travel overseas. Parental income is taken into account in awarding grants.

Annual grant total

In 2010/11 the trust had an income of £17,000 and an expenditure of £21,000.

Applications

On a form available from the correspondent, to be returned by the individual before September for consideration in October. If an individual has applied previously the trustees are particularly interested to know about his or her progress.

Other information

Grants are also given to organisations.

Golborne

The Golborne Charities

£1,000

Correspondent: Paul Gleave, 56 Nook Lane, Golborne, Warrington WA3 3JQ (01942 727627)

Trustees: Alan Tootell; Jeanette Ashurst; Pauline Lawrence; Rita Williams; Sheila Ince; Linda Owen; Beryl O'Hare; John Reed; Julie Jameson.

CC Number: 221088

Eligibility

People in need who live in the parish of Golborne as it was in 1892.

Types of grants

One-off grants for equipment such as books, school uniforms and instruments, or for excursions. Grants are usually of between £50 and £80, but occasionally of up to £250. They are usually cash payments, but are occasionally in kind.

Annual grant total

The charities have an average expenditure of £5,000 per year.

Exclusions

Loans or grants for the payments of rates are not made. Grants are not repeated in less than two years.

Applications

In writing to the correspondent through a third party such as a social worker or a teacher, or via a trustee. Applications are considered at three-monthly intervals. Grant recipients tend to be known by at least one trustee.

Other information

Grants are also given to charitable organisations in the area of benefit, and for relief-of-need purposes.

Leigh

The Leigh Educational Endowment

£8,000

Correspondent: The Director of Education, Children and Young People's Services, Progress House, Westwood Park Drive, Wigan WN3 4HH (01942 486053; email: education@wigan.gov.uk)

Trustees: George Bent; Frank Rothwell; D. A. Boardman; Guest.

CC Number: 526469

Eligibility

People under the age of 25 who live in the former borough of Leigh, are going on to higher education and have achieved high A-level results.

Types of grants

Grants for students attaining good examination results and proceeding with further training to help with fees and living expenses, books and equipment. Grants are between £250 and £500 per year per student.

Annual grant total

In 2010/11 the trust had an income of £3,100 and an expenditure of £9,800. About 20 individuals are supported each year.

Applications

Applications should be submitted in September after A-level results are released for consideration in October. Applications must be submitted through the individual's college, which submits a list of suitable applicants for the trustees to choose from.

Rochdale

The Emerson Educational Trust for Middleton

£6,900

Correspondent: Michael Garraway, Committee Services Section, Legal and Democratic Services, Town Hall, Rochdale OL16 1AB (01706 924716; email: michael.garraway@rochdale.gov. uk; website: www.rochdale.gov.uk/ grants__trusts/charitable_trusts.aspx)

Trustees: John Robinson; Peter Burton; Jim Russell; John Durcan; Peter Brown; Lynn Wellens; Donna Martin; Alan Godson.

CC Number: 510495

Eligibility

People who live or attend or have attended a school in the area of the former borough of Middleton, Rochdale.

Types of grants

One-off grants of £250 to £500 for schoolchildren with books, equipment/ instruments, uniforms and other school clothing, educational outings in the UK, study or travel abroad and student exchanges. Grants to students in further and higher education, including mature students, postgraduates and foreign students, also include assistance for fees, maintenance/living expenses and childcare. People starting work can also receive financial assistance.

Annual grant total

In 2010/11 the trust gave grants totalling £6,900.

Applications

On a form available from the website or the correspondent. Applications can be submitted directly by the individual or through the individual's school/college/ educational welfare agency and they are considered twice yearly in April and September.

The Heywood Educational Trust

£1,100

Correspondent: Michael Garraway, Heywood Phoenix Trusts, Heywood Township Office, The Phoenix Centre, Church Street, Heywood, Lancashire OL10 1LR (01706 924716; email: michael.garraway@rochdale.gov.uk)

Trustees: Brian Davies; Linda Robinson; James Crossley; Michael Peers; Brian Bennion; Terry Carpenter.

CC Number: 526690

Eligibility

People of any age who live in the Heywood area or the village of Birch or those attending or who have previously attended a school in the area.

Types of grants

One-off grants for schoolchildren and further and higher education students, including mature students, to help with uniforms or other school clothing, books, equipment/instruments, fees, educational outings in the UK, study or travel abroad and student exchanges.

Annual grant total

In 2010/11 the trust had an income of £1,900 and made grants totalling £1,100.

Applications

By the individual on a form available from the website or the correspondent for consideration in February and

September. Applications should include confirmation that the student is on the course, and details of academic record, family income, previous awards, LEA awards and student loans.

Salford

The Salford Foundation Trust

£23,000 (82 grants)

Correspondent: Helen Fenton, Grants Administrator, Foundation House, 3 Jo Street, Manchester M5 4BD (01617 873834; fax: 01617 878555; email: mail@ salfordfoundationtrust.org.uk; website: www.salfordfoundationtrust.org.uk)

Trustees: Ian Townley; Anthony Bannister; Sally Cockshaw; Kenneth Palmer; Nick Abbott; Stewart Almond; Peter Openshaw; Michael Dulhanty; Siobhan Almond.

CC Number: 1105303

Eligibility

People aged 5 to 25 who are resident in Salford. Preference is given to applicants under 21 and those who have lived in Salford for a minimum of three years.

Types of grants

Grants of up to £500 to fund opportunities that will enable a young person to learn and/or develop new skills or take part in a character building experience or activity. Examples of this could be an item of equipment, an activity or a training course. The trust is keen to hear about the impact the opportunity will have on the applicant and what they hope to achieve from it.

Annual grant total

In 2010/11 the trust had an income of £46,000 and made 82 grants totalling £23,000, broken down into the following categories:

- Performing arts: £7,000
- Sport and recreation: £6,600
- Skills and talent for self-employment: £1,100
- Academic/vocational: £1,000

Exclusions

Funding will not be considered for the following: driving lessons, childcare costs, higher education course fees, living expenses, remedial intervention i.e. therapies (speech/language/ occupational etc.), retrospective funding. No consideration will be made on opportunities that have a political or religious focus or should be financed by statutory services.

Applications

Application forms are available from the trust or to download from the website and can be submitted directly by the individual, a family member, a third party such as a teacher or social worker or through an organisation such as a Citizens Advice or school. Applications should include two references and be submitted via post. If an applicant experiences difficulties completing the form, alternative methods of application may be submitted, such as a tape recording of responses to the questions. There are a number of funding rounds each year, usually lasting for six weeks, check the website for the most recent information.

Other information

One of the trust's patrons is Peter Hook, of Joy Division and New Order fame.

Stockport

The Ephraim Hallam Charity

£2,000

Correspondent: Gordon Pickering, 48 South Street, Alderley Edge SK9 7ES (01625 586300)

Trustees: Charles Hamilton; Dennis Robinson; Philip Kershaw; Alistair Lockhart; Roger Yates; John Whitfield; Anne Mack; Philip Davies; Jean Dooley.

CC Number: 525975

Eligibility

People under 25 resident in Stockport.

Types of grants

Grants to support people at any institution of further or higher education, including the study of music and arts, travel costs, vocational training and people starting work

Annual grant total

In 2010/11 the charity had an income of £5,800 and an expenditure of £5,200.

Applications

In writing to the correspondent.

Other information

Grants are also made to local youth organisations.

Sir Ralph Pendlebury's Charity for Orphans

£1,400

Correspondent: S M Tattersall, Carlyle House, 107–109 Wellington Road South, Stockport SK1 3TL

Trustees: Nigel Neary; Philip Cuddy; Peter Robinson; Stephen Jones; David Kerr.

CC Number: 213927

Eligibility

People who have been orphaned and live, or whose parents lived, in the borough of Stockport for at least two years.

Types of grants

Grants for schoolchildren towards the cost of clothing, holidays and books. Grants can be for £5 or £6 a week and recipients also receive a clothing allowance twice a year. The main priority is for relief-in-need.

Annual grant total

Previously about £1,400 a year for educational purposes.

Applications

In writing to the correspondent.

Other information

Grants are also made for welfare purposes.

Tameside

The Ashton-under-Lyne United Scholarship Fund (The Heginbottom and Tetlow and William Kelsall Grants)

£3,500

Correspondent: Scott Littlewood, Finance Officer, Tameside Metropolitan Borough Council, Education and Cultural Services, Council Offices, Wellington Road, Ashton under Lyne OL6 6DL (01613 422878)

Trustee: Tameside MBC.

CC Number: 526478

Eligibility

People under the age of 25 who have attended a secondary school in the former borough of Ashton under Lyne or who live, or whose parents live, in the former borough and who will not have any award or grant other than a local education authority or state grant. Applications from residents in Audenshaw, Denton and the area of the former Limehurst Rural District Council will also be considered.

Types of grants

Grants for those who will be attending university, teacher training college or an institution of full-time technical education.

Annual grant total

In 2010/11 the trust had an income of £5,400 and a total expenditure of £3,700.

Applications

On a form available from the correspondent to be submitted directly by the individual by 30 September for consideration in October.

Other information

Various grants are administered under this fund. The above refers to The Heginbottom and Tetlow Grants and William Kelsall Grants. There are also two smaller trusts: Thomas Taylor Grant to those studying full-time for a degree or diploma in electrical engineering; and J B Reyner Grants to those attending approved colleges of music.

The Dowson Trust and Peter Green Endowment Trust Fund

£300

Correspondent: Scott Littlewood, Finance Officer, Education and Cultural Services, Council Offices, Wellington Road, Ashton Under Lyne OL6 6DL (01613 422878)

Trustee: Tameside MBC.

CC Number: 525974

Eligibility

People aged under 25 who live in the former borough of Hyde.

Types of grants

Grants to those undertaking approved courses at universities or teacher training colleges.

Annual grant total

The trust has an income and expenditure of around £300.

Applications

In writing to the correspondent. Applications should be submitted by the individual by 30 September for consideration in October.

Timperley

The Timperley Educational Foundation

£900

Correspondent: Philip Turner, Clerk to the Trustees, 103 Sylvan Avenue, Timperley, Altrincham, Cheshire WA15 6AD (01619 693919)

Trustees: John Sutton; Stephen Taylor; Philip Turner; Cliff Carr; Judith Woolley.

CC Number: 1018845

Eligibility

Pupils, students or apprentices under the age of 21 and in need, who have a parent resident in the parish of Timperley. Assistance is also given to educational establishments and youth organisations within the parish.

Types of grants

One-off and recurrent grants to meet general expenses for students in further/ higher education, including those being instructed in the doctrines of the Church of England. Schoolchildren may receive assistance on the recommendation of the headteacher only.

Annual grant total

In 2011 the foundation had an income of £1,300 and an expenditure of £1,800. Grants are made to individuals and organisations.

Applications

On a form available from the correspondent, either directly by the individual or, more usually, through the individual's parent/guardian, school, college or educational welfare agency. Applications are usually considered in August prior to the academic year for which support is needed, although this is not always essential. Application forms for new university entrants, however, must be received by 31 August.

Tottington

The Margaret Ann Smith Charity

£1,500

Correspondent: The Clerk, Woodcock and Sons, West View, Princess Street, Haslingden, Rossendale, Lancashire BB4 6NW (01706 213356)

Trustees: Neville Kenyon; Bill Johnson; Marian Price.

CC Number: 526138

Eligibility

People who live in the urban district of Tottington, Bury as defined on 23 June 1964.

Types of grants

Grants of about £200 to help towards the cost of overseas exchange visits. There is an emphasis on Commonwealth countries.

Annual grant total

About £1,500.

Applications

In writing to the correspondent. Applications should be submitted directly by the individual or through the individual's school/college or an educational welfare agency.

Isle of Man

The Manx Marine Society

£5,000

Correspondent: Capt. R K Cringle, 10 Carrick Bay View, Ballagawne Road, Colby, Isle of Man IM9 4DD (01624 838233)

Eligibility

Young Manx people under 18 who wish to attend sea school or become a cadet.

Types of grants

One-off grants for people about to start a career at sea towards uniforms, books, equipment/instruments and fees.

Annual grant total

About £5,000.

Applications

In writing to the correspondent. Applications are considered at any time and can be submitted by the individual or through the school/college or educational welfare agency.

Lancashire

The Baines Charity

£7,500

Correspondent: Duncan Waddilove, 2 The Chase, Normoss Road, Blackpool, Lancashire FY3 0BF (01253 893459)

Trustees: Graham Cocker; James Hargreaves; Capt. John Caley; Patricia Catlow; Julie Newsham; Lyne Bowen; David Bannister; Susan Hawley.

CC Number: 224135

Eligibility

People in need who live in the ancient townships of Carleton, Hardhorn-cum-Newton, Marton, Poulton and Thornton.

Types of grants

One-off grants ranging from £100 to £250. 'Each case is discussed in its merits.'

Annual grant total

In 2011 the charity had an income of £12,000 and a total expenditure of £20,000. Grants are made for both welfare and educational purposes.

Applications

On a form available from the correspondent, either directly by the individual, or through a social worker, Citizens Advice or other welfare agency. Applications are considered upon receipt.

The Educational Foundation of John Farrington

£3,500

Correspondent: Dennis Johnson, 35 Ribblesdale Drive, Grimsargh, Preston PR2 5RJ (01772 703050; email: dvicj@talktalk.net)

Trustees: Dennis Johnson; J. Chessell; Michael Dolan; Nigel Stimpson; Carole Kelly.

CC Number: 526488

Eligibility

People under the age of 25 who live, or have a parent who has lived for at least two years, in any of the following areas: the parish of Ribbleton in the borough of Preston, the parishes of Goosnargh, Grimsargh, Haighton, Longridge, Whittingham and part of Fulwood. Residents in the Ribbleton area will be given preference over the residents in other areas. There is a preference for people with special educational needs.

Types of grants

Help with the cost of books and educational outings for people at school. People starting work can receive grants towards equipment/instruments, fees, childcare and educational outings in the UK. Students in further or higher education may be given help towards books and equipment or instruments. Grants range from £25 to £250.

Grants are also made to help people to develop leadership qualities and social awareness, towards, for instance, leadership courses, community development activities, camping expeditions or any other 'suitable' activity.

Annual grant total

In 2010/11 the foundation had an income of £2,700 and an expenditure of £3,800.

Exclusions

Grants are not given where the applicant is already in receipt of a local authority grant. Nor are they intended to cover night-school fees for courses which do not lead to some form of educational progression in a young person's career.

Applications

In writing to the correspondent for consideration in March and October. The foundation has a leaflet outlining the format and contents of any application letter. Applications can be either made by the individual or through a school, college, educational welfare agency or other third party.

Fort Foundation

£0

Correspondent: E S Fort, Trustee, Fort Vale Engineering Ltd, Calder Vale Park, Simonstone Lane, Simonstone, Burnley BB12 7ND (01282 440000)

Trustees: Edward Fort; Ian Wilson; Susan Friedlander.

CC Number: 1028639

Eligibility

Young people in Pendle Borough and district, especially those undertaking courses in engineering.

Types of grants

One-off grants of £50 to £1,000 to schoolchildren, college students, undergraduates and vocational students for uniforms/clothing, study/travel overseas, books and equipment/instruments and excursions.

Annual grant total

In 2010/11 the trust had assets of £221,000 and an income of £103,000. No grants to individuals for educational purposes were made.

Exclusions

Grants are not made for fees.

Applications

In writing to the correspondent, directly by the individual. Applications are considered at any time.

Other information

Grants are also made to organisations and small groups.

The Harris Charity

£3,800

Correspondent: P R Metcalf, Richard House, 9 Winckley Square, Preston PR1 3HP (01772 821021; fax: 01772 259441; email: harrischarity@mooreandsmalley.co.uk; website: theharrischarity.co.uk)

Trustees: W. Huck; E. Booth; B. Banks; T. Scott; S. Smith; S. Huck; R. Jolly; K. Mellalieu; A. Scott; N. Fielden.

CC Number: 526206

Eligibility

People in need under 25 who live in Lancashire, with a preference for the Preston district, who are in further or higher education.

Types of grants

One-off grants of £250 to £1,000 for equipment/instruments, tools, materials and so on.

Annual grant total

In 2010/11 the charity had assets of £3.1 million, an income of £97,000 and a total expenditure of £92,000, of which £7,400 was given in grants to individuals. Organisations received grants totalling £59,000.

Exclusions

No grants are available to cover the cost of course fees or living expenses.

Applications

On an application form downloaded from the website, where guidance and criteria can also be found. Applications are considered during the three months after 31 March and 30 September and can be submitted directly by the individual or through a school/college or educational welfare agency.

Other information

The charity also supports charitable institutions that benefit individuals, recreation and leisure and the training and education of individuals.

The Khaleque and Sarifun Memorial Trust

£1,000

Correspondent: Ahmed Zaman, 8 Cobden Villas, Oldfield Avenue, Darwen BB3 1QY (01254 777403)

Trustee: Ahmed Zaman.

CC Number: 518794

Eligibility

People who live in Lancashire (including overseas students studying there).

Types of grants

Grants are made to schoolchildren, further and higher education students and postgraduates towards the cost of uniforms or other school clothing, books, equipment/instruments and maintenance/living expenses. Foreign students in further and higher education in the UK can also be supported. Grants range from £50 to £1,100.

Annual grant total

The trust gives grants totalling around £1,000.

Applications

In writing to the correspondent directly by the individual with a supporting letter from the individual's school or college. Applications should be submitted in October for consideration in November.

Other information

Grants are also available for educational projects in Bangladesh and India.

Peter Lathom's Charity

£3,000

Correspondent: Christine Aitken, 13 Mallard Close, Aughton, Ormskirk, Lancashire L39 5QJ (01515 202717)

Trustees: William Waterworth; Peter Godfrey; Lynda Tither; Anthony Lewis; Ellis Draper; Owen Taylor; Philip Scarisbrick; Robert Brunswick; John McKie; William Cropper; John Snape; Geoffrey Monk; Kenneth Mather; Kenneth Vincent; Hilary Rosbotham; James Halsall; Henry Butler; A. Owens; Christopher Byron; David Lawrenson; Jim Hill; John Stanley; Peter Harrison; Terence Aldridge; Terry Kershaw; Beatrice Fairclough; Eileen Doran; Elizabeth Sharrock; Jennifer Rushton; Edward Hey; Ian Tinsley; Sheila Braithwaite.

CC Number: 228828

Eligibility

People under 25 resident in West Lancashire.

Types of grants

Cash grants according to need for education and training.

Annual grant total

In 2011 the charity had assets of £1.2 million and an income of £40,000. Educational grants to seven individuals totalled £3,000.

Applications

On a form available from the correspondent, to be submitted by 30 September. Awards in all cases are based on financial need as applications always exceed distributable income. Grants are awarded in November/December of each year.

John Parkinson Charity

£4,000

Correspondent: John Bretherton, Clerk to the Trustees, Lower Stanlea Farm, Stanlea Lane, Goosnargh, Preston PR3 2EQ (01995 640224)

Trustees: Norman Coulthurst; Tom Kirby; Trevor Tomlinson; Bill Watson; Stan Hunter; John Bretherton; John Pearson; John Singleton; Stephen Cooper.

CC Number: 526060

Eligibility

People under 25 who live in the parishes of Goosnargh, Whittingham and part of Barton.

Types of grants

One-off grants of up to £150 for tools, books, outfits or payment of fees towards entering a profession, trade,

occupation or service. People who have to travel outside Lancashire to attend an interview for a further education course or a job interview can receive grants towards travel expenses and living expenses. Students in further or higher education can be given help towards books.

Annual grant total

In 2011 the charity had an income and expenditure of £4,000.

Applications

On a form available from the correspondent, to be submitted by the individual's parent or guardian. Applications are considered in May and November.

The Peel Foundation Scholarship Fund

£2,500

Correspondent: Catherine Oldroyd, Barnfield, Billinge End Road, Blackburn BB2 6QB (01254 56573)

Trustees: Frank Robinson; Lillian Croston; Christopher Armstrong; David Hempsall; Anthony Hedley; Brian Lloyd.

CC Number: 526101

Eligibility

People in need aged 18 to 25 who live in and around Blackburn. This area is defined as: the borough of Blackburn, the whole borough except the civil parish of North Turton; the borough of Hyndburn, those parts of the former urban districts of Rishton and Oswaldtwistle which are close to the boundary with Blackburn; and the Ribble Valley borough, the civil parishes of Balderstone, Billington, Clayton-le-Dale, Dinckley, Mellor, Osbaldeston, Ramsgreave, Salesbury and Wilpshire.

Types of grants

Awards of £500 to students entering university or other institutions of higher education for first or second degree courses. Candidates must begin their course in the term following the award of scholarships (usually in September), unless excused by the trustees for sufficient cause. Grants are for general student expenses.

Annual grant total

About £2,500.

Applications

On a form available from the correspondent. Candidates must be nominated by the headteacher or principal of the school or college and applicants are called for an interview. Applications are considered in July and August and should be submitted in April and May.

Superintendent Gerald Richardson Memorial Youth Trust

£4,000

Correspondent: David Williamson, Northdene, Stoney Lane, Hambleton, Poulton-Le-Fylde FY6 9AF (01253 590510)

Trustees: Douglas Leatham; Christopher Holden; Bernard Booth; Maureen Richardson; David Williamson; Jacqueline Longdon; Jeff Meadows; Peter Noblett; Roderic Norton.

CC Number: 504413

Eligibility

People under 25 who live within 15 miles of Blackpool Town Hall. There is a preference for people with physical or mental disabilities.

Types of grants

One-off and recurrent grants, typically in the range of £50 to £250. Grants can be made to schoolchildren and further and higher education students to attend character-building courses or training courses in the arts or sports. Grants can also be made to cover the cost of equipment for outdoor courses.

Annual grant total

In 2010/11 the trust had an income of £14,000 and an expenditure of £15,000. Grants are made to schools, youth organisations and individuals.

Applications

In writing to the correspondent, giving details of the individual's age, the cost of the course and so on. Applications should be submitted at least two months before the amount being requested is required. They are considered bimonthly from September and can be submitted either directly by the individual, or via a third party such as a school/college welfare agency or carer.

The Shaw Charities

£1,000

Correspondent: Mrs E Woodrow, 99 Rawlinson Lane, Heath Charnock, Chorley, Lancashire PR7 4DE (01257 480515; email: woodrows@tinyworld.co.uk)

Trustees: Colin Nelson; Alison South; Harold Howard; Dr Frank Yates; James Ashworth; Prof. John Baldwin; Ann Tomlinson; Pamela Smith; Lynn Wilcox; Robert Davison; Lyn Berry; John Appleyard.

CC Number: 214318

Eligibility

People in need who live in Rivington, Anglezarke, Heath Charnock and Anderton.

Types of grants

Grants to students on first degree courses for books.

Annual grant total

In 2010/11 the charities had an income of £2,700 and a total expenditure of £2,200.

Applications

On a form available from the correspondent to be submitted for consideration in March and November.

Other information

Educational funding from The Shaw Charities is given through the subsidiary charity The Shaw Educational Endowments. The charities also make grants for relief of need.

Tunstall Educational Trust

£3,500

Correspondent: Joyce Crackles, Mill Farm, Burrow, Carnforth, Lancashire LA6 2RJ (01524 274239)

Trustees: Joyce Crackles; Lynn Glaves; Peter Wood; David Bury; Joe Towers; Julia Taylor; Robert Hannaford; Gill Stevenson; Sue Brennand; Jane Greenhalgh.

CC Number: 526250

Eligibility

Young people under 25 living in Burrow, Tunstall and Cansfield.

Types of grants

One-off and recurrent grants according to need. The trust mainly makes travel grants.

Annual grant total

In 2011 the charity had an income of £5,000 and an expenditure of £3,800. The trust makes grants to individuals and organisations.

Applications

In writing to the correspondent. Trustees meet in June and November to consider applications.

Bickerstaffe

Bickerstaffe Education Trust

£3,000

Correspondent: M W Rimmer, Trustee, Primrose Cottage, Hall Lane, Bickerstaffe, Ormskirk, Lancashire

L39 0EH (01695 727848; email: hilaryrosbotham@hotmail.co.uk)

Trustees: Hilary Rosbotham; Merrick Rimmer; Anne Rosbotham-Williams; Elizabeth Hall; Josephine O'Neill.

CC Number: 1108104

Eligibility

Mainly children and young people resident in the parish of Bickerstaffe or attending Bickerstaffe Voluntary Controlled School.

Types of grants

Grants given according to need.

Annual grant total

In 2010 the trust had an income of £20,000 and an expenditure of £21,000.

Applications

In writing to the correspondent.

Other information

Grants are also made to organisations.

Blackburn with Darwen

The John Bury Trust

£15,000

Correspondent: The Secretary, 2 Eckersley Close, Blackburn, Lancashire BB2 4FA (email: applications@ thejohnburytrust.co.uk; website: www. thejohnburytrust.co.uk)

Trustees: Julie Wareing; Pamela Rodgers; Shirley Watson; Gladys Rhodes; Andrea Sturgess; Kath Warner-Bond; Steven Parker.

CC Number: 1108181

Eligibility

Young people between the ages of 10 and 25 years within the administrative area of Blackburn with Darwen borough council.

Types of grants

Grants to 'promote the mental, spiritual, moral and physical development and improvement of young people'.

Annual grant total

In 2010/11 the trust had an income and expenditure of £21,000.

Applications

An application form can be downloaded from the trust's website with terms and conditions.

Penine Lancashire Youth Enterprise Fund

£3,000

Correspondent: Programmes Team, Kent Community Foundation, Suite 22, The Globe Centre, St James Square, Accrington, Lancashire BB5 0RE (01512 322444; fax: 01512 322445; email: programmes@lancsfoundation; website: www.lancsfoundation.org.uk)

Trustees: Elizabeth Hall; Peter Robinson; Arthur Roberts; Terence Hephrun; Pamela Barker; Peter Butterfield; Wendy Swift; Joanne Turton.

CC Number: 1123229

Eligibility

Young people aged 14–25 in Blackburn with Darwen, Burnley, Hyndburn, Pendle and Rossendale.

Types of grants

Grants of £1,000 for 14 to 17 year olds or £2,000 for 18 to 25 year olds to support entrepreneurial and enterprising behaviour and help to support and develop business ideas. Grants can be for items such as training courses; residential courses; qualifications; educational visits; computer equipment/ software; research; business start-up costs (equipment/tools, promotional/ marketing materials, business insurance, professional subscriptions, stationery, uniforms) and specialist services such as speakers, mentors or consultants.

Annual grant total

£3,000 in 2011/12

Applications

On a form available to download from the website along with guidelines.

Other information

This fund is administered by Lancashire Community Foundation, which also administers a number of funds for organisations.

Blackpool

The Blackpool Children's Clothing Fund

£4,000 (200 grants)

Correspondent: Alan Rydeheard, 96 West Park Drive, Blackpool FY3 9HU (01253 736812)

Trustees: Alan Rydeheard; Joseph Harris; George Jeffrey; Christine Atkins; Lorraine Lane.

CC Number: 215133

Eligibility

Children aged 4 to 16 who live in the Blackpool area and attend an educational establishment there.

Types of grants

Help with providing school clothing for children whose parents cannot afford it. The fund does not give cash grants but vouchers which can be exchanged at designated retailers.

Annual grant total

In 2010/11 the fund had an income of £1,700 and a total expenditure of £4,000.

Applications

In writing to the correspondent, by an education social work service on behalf of the applicant. Individuals in need identified by the local education authority are also considered.

The Swallowdale Children's Trust

£0

Correspondent: The Secretary, 23 Abingdon Street, Blackpool FY1 1DG (01253 712937)

Trustees: Dr D. Haworth; J. Leeson; J. Baggaley; Dr C. Taylor; N. Law; J. Barlow; S. Marshall; Dr H. Miller.

CC Number: 526205

Eligibility

People who live in the Blackpool area who are under the age of 25. Orphans are given preference.

Types of grants

One-off grants are given to: schoolchildren, college students, undergraduates, vocational students and people starting work, including those for clothes/uniforms, fees, study/travel abroad and equipment/instruments.

Annual grant total

In 2010/11 the trust had assets of £968,000 and an income of £39,000. There were 193 relief-in-need grants made during the year totalling £26,000. No grants were made for educational purposes.

Applications

On a form available from the correspondent, with the financial details of the individual or family. Applications must be made through a social worker or teacher. They are considered six times per year.

Burnley

The Edward Stocks Massey Bequest Fund

£7,100

Correspondent: Saima Afzaal, Burnley Borough Council, Town Hall, Manchester Road, Burnley BB11 1JA (01282 425011)

Trustees: David Knagg; Neil Beecham.

CC Number: 526516

Eligibility

People who live in the borough of Burnley.

Types of grants

Whilst consideration will be given to applications for financial assistance with education courses, this is not seen as the primary purpose of the fund which is to assist individuals and voluntary organisations to promote education and projects in the arts, sciences and general cultural activities.

Annual grant total

In 2010/11 the fund had assets of £925,000 and an income of £33,000. Grants and scholarships to individuals totalled £7,100.

Exclusions

No assistance will be given to applicants in receipt of a mandatory award from their LEA. Other sources of funding must have been explored.

Applications

On a form available from the correspondent, either directly by the individual or by the secretary or treasurer of an organisation. Applications are considered in April/May.

Other information

Grants are mostly given to organisations and groups.

Darwen

The W. M and B. W. Lloyd Trust

£10,000

Correspondent: John Jacklin, Trustee, Gorse Barn, Rock Lane, Tockholes, Darwen, Lancashire BB3 0LX (01254 771367)

Trustees: Mrs D. E. Parsons; Mr J. N. Jacklin; Mr D. G. Watson.

CC Number: 503384

Eligibility

People in need who live in the old borough of Darwen in Lancashire. Preference is given to single parents.

Types of grants

One-off and recurrent grants according to need. Grants are made to schoolchildren, college students, undergraduates, vocational students and mature students, including those for uniforms/clothing, books, study/travel abroad, equipment/instruments, excursions and awards for excellence.

Annual grant total

In 2010/11 the trust had an income of £76,000 and made grants totalling £70,000 to organisations and individuals.

Applications

In writing to the correspondent to be submitted either directly by the individual or through a relevant third party. Applications are considered quarterly in March, June, September and December.

Leyland

The Balshaw's Educational Foundation

£1,500

Correspondent: J G Demack, 10 Pendlebury Close, Longton, Preston PR4 5YT (01772 612556)

Trustees: David Gibb; Geoffrey Demack; Ann Hanson; Carol Powell; Gina Lewis; Josephine Venn; May Griffiths; Michael Otter; John Davies; Tim Callaghan; Linda Williams; Philip Banks; Philip Hamman; Thomas Brown; Michael Heaton.

CC Number: 526595

Eligibility

People living in the parish of Leyland.

Types of grants

Help with educational needs including the cost of books, clothing and other essentials for schoolchildren. Grants may also be available for those at college or university.

Annual grant total

This trust has an annual income and expenditure of around £1,750.

Applications

In writing to the correspondent.

Lowton

The Lowton United Charity

£2,000

Correspondent: J Naughton, Secretary, 51 Kenilworth Road, Lowton, Warrington WA3 2AZ (01942 741583)

Trustees: Alan McLeod; Norman Holt; Alan Baldwin; Gillian Dickinson; Jeremy Dean; Joseph Newson; Pamela Hampson; Revd William Stalker; Avis Freeman; Linda Graham.

CC Number: 226569

Eligibility

People in need who live in the parishes of St Luke's and St Mary's in Lowton.

Types of grants

Help with the cost of books, clothing and other essentials for schoolchildren. Grants are also available for those at college or university.

Annual grant total

Grants total about £4,000 each year. About half of grants are given at Christmas for relief-in-need purposes and the rest throughout the year.

Exclusions

Grants are not given to postgraduates.

Applications

Usually through the rectors of the parishes or other trustees.

Over Kellett

Thomas Wither's Charity

£3,000

Correspondent: David Mills, Clerk, 51 Greenways, Over Kellett, Carnforth, Lancashire LA6 1DE (01524 732194)

Trustees: Vera Assiak; Patricia Lawson; Vivienne Avery; Alistair Angus.

CC Number: 526079

Eligibility

People under 25 who live in the parish of Over Kellett.

Types of grants

Grants are given to people starting work and apprentices.

Annual grant total

In 2011 the charity had an income of £5,400 and an expenditure of £3,800.

Applications

On a form available from the correspondent, which should be submitted on or before 1 May or 1 November each year.

Preston

The Roper Educational Foundation

£5,300

Correspondent: Mark Belderbos, Blackhurst, Swainson, Goodier, 3 and 4 Aalborg Square, Lancaster LA1 1GG (01524 386500; fax: 01772 201713; email: mwb@bsglaw.co.uk)

Trustees: Peter Williams; Michael O'Halloran; Thomas Burns; John Whittle; Martin Hothersall; Carl Crompton.

CC Number: 526428

Eligibility

People aged 11 to 25, who live in St Wilfrid's Parish, Preston or who have attended a school in the parish for at least two years.

Types of grants

The trust will consider supporting any educational need, at any educational level.

Annual grant total

Income for the foundation tends to average around £63,000 each year, with grants usually totalling about £1,500.

In 2011 the foundation had assets of £778,000 and an income of £62,000. Bursaries to three individuals totalled £5,300.

Applications

On a form available from the correspondent. Applications should be submitted directly by the individual. They are considered in February, July and October.

Other information

Grants are also made to voluntary aided Roman Catholic schools in the county borough of Preston.

Rishton

The George Lawes Memorial Fund

£500

Correspondent: The Trustees, Scaithcliff House, Ormerod Street, Accrington, Lancashire BB5 0PF (01254 388111)

Trustee: Hyndburn Borough Council.

CC Number: 224118

Eligibility

People under the age of 21 who live in the township of Rishton and are in financial need.

Types of grants

One-off grants to help schoolchildren and further and higher education students, including mature students, with books, equipment, clothing/uniforms, fees, maintenance/living expenses, educational outings in the UK and study or travel abroad.

Annual grant total

About £500 a year.

Applications

In writing to the correspondent directly by the individual. Applications should be submitted around November/December for consideration in December.

Merseyside

The Girls' Welfare Fund

£4,500

Correspondent: S M O'Leary, West Hey, Dawstone Road, Heswall, Wirral CH60 4RP (email: gwf_charity@hotmail.com)

Trustees: S. O'Leary; M. Von Zweighbergk; P. D. Milne.

CC Number: 220347

Eligibility

Girls and young women, usually those aged between 15 and 25 years, who were born in Merseyside. Applications from outside this area will not be acknowledged. Preference will be given to those who are pursuing vocational or further education courses rather than other academic courses.

Types of grants

Both one-off and recurrent grants of £100 to £1,000 for leisure and creative activities, sports, welfare and the relief of poverty. Grants may be given to schoolchildren and students for uniforms/clothing, college students and undergraduates for uniforms/clothing, study/travel overseas and books, vocational students for uniforms/clothing, books and equipment/instruments and to people starting work for clothing and equipment/instruments. The fund is particularly interested in helping individual girls and young women of poor or deferred education to establish themselves and gain independence.

Annual grant total

In 2011 the fund had an income of £9,400 and a total expenditure of £9,300.

Exclusions

Grants are not made to charities that request funds to pass on and give to individuals.

Applications

In writing to the correspondent or by email. Applications can be submitted directly by the individual or through a social worker, Citizens Advice, other welfare agency or college/educational establishment. Applications are considered quarterly in March, June, September and December, and should include full information about the college, course and particular circumstances.

Other information

The trust also gives grants to individuals in need and organisations helping girls and young women in Merseyside.

The Holt Education Trust

£5,000

Correspondent: Roger Morris, Secretary, Room 607, India Buildings, Water Street, Liverpool L2 0RB (01514 734693)

Trustees: Martin Cooke; Nikki Eastwood; Ken Ravenscroft; Tilly Boyce; Neil Kemsley; Pauge Earlam; Anthony Hannay.

CC Number: 1113708

Eligibility

People in need who are studying on a course of higher education and have lived for most of their life on Merseyside and still have a home there.

The trust concentrates on first degree level courses; academic subjects are given preference. Some grants are given to students reading medicine who have already obtained another first degree.

Most awards are given for full-time study, although applicants who can only study part-time because of family circumstances will be considered.

Types of grants

Grants are single payments ranging from £50 to £300 to help with college or university fees, books, equipment, study trips and, increasingly, with childcare, accommodation and travel.

Annual grant total

About £5,000.

Applications

On a form available from the correspondent. Applications should be made by those who have already started the relevant course and must be accompanied by a reference from the tutor. They should be submitted before the meetings held in February, July and November. Applications must include details of previous education, family circumstances, funding for the present course and the reason for seeking help.

Other information

An explanatory leaflet available from the trust describes current policy in detail as the criteria for applications can vary from year to year. These can be obtained from the correspondent.

This trust is part of the P H Holt Foundation.

The Sheila Kay Fund

£52,000

Correspondent: Victoria Symes, 18 Seel Street, Liverpool L1 4BE (01517 025545; fax: 01517 074305; email: gill.gargen@ skffund.org.uk; website: www. sheilakayfund.org.uk/site)

Trustees: John Lansley; Julie Ledger; Shelagh Bradley; David Bingham; Lilias Ward; Rosemary Kay.

CC Number: 1021378

Eligibility

People in need living in Merseyside who have a background in social/community work/the voluntary sector. Priority is given to those who have left school with few, if any, qualifications, and people from minority communities who have experienced difficulties in entering education.

Types of grants

One-off and recurrent grants are made ranging between £50 to £300 for people engaged in social, youth and community work (paid or voluntary) who cannot afford the relevant education or training. Any of the costs of education, including fees, childcare, travel expenses and books, can be considered.

The trust helps people at a wide variety of educational stages, including Higher Education in social work and youth work, Access courses, GNVQs, GCSEs, counselling qualifications, introductory courses to Maths, English and IT, and Community courses such as Credit Union, Playwork and Capacity Building.

Annual grant total

In 2010/11 the fund had an income of £57,000 and made grants to individuals totalling £52,000.

Exclusions

No grants for postgraduates.

Applications

On forms available on the website which can be returned by email or post.

Other information

The aim of the trust is to support individuals and community groups across Merseyside to increase their knowledge and skills in the field of social and community work for the wider benefit of those within their community. To this end it also provides: guidance, information and support materials; support to community and voluntary groups seeking training; advocacy services to other funding agencies for students; positive action for black, ethnic and disabled applicants; and networking contacts throughout the voluntary sector on Merseyside.

The organisation can also refer applicants to other funds, to obtain further grant support.

Community Foundation for Merseyside

£15,000

Correspondent: Sue Langfeld, Stanley Building, Liverpool, Merseyside L1 3DN (01512 322444; email: info@ cfmerseyside.org.uk; website: www. cfmerseysde.org.uk)

Trustees: Michael Eastwood; Abi Pointing; Andrew Wallis; Robert Towers; William Bowley; Sally Yeoman; David McDonnell; Jayne Pugh.

CC Number: 1068887

Eligibility

People in need who live in Merseyside.

Types of grants

The foundation currently administers three funds which provide grants to individuals for education:

The John Goore Fund: Up to £350 for the advancement of higher education and training, particularly adults who need to retrain after a period of unemployment or redundancy.

The Joseph Harley Bequest Fund: Education and training of residents of Formby.

Sefton Education and Learning Fund: Up to £250 for educational materials and courses for residents of Sefton.

Annual grant total

In 2010/11 the foundation awarded £31,000 in 65 grants to individuals for both education and welfare.

Applications

Visit the foundation's website or contact the foundation directly for full guidelines on how to apply to the separate funds.

Other information

The foundation administers funds for a variety of purposes, which are mostly for organisations; however there are a few which give to individuals but they tend to open and close regularly, therefore potential applicants should contact the foundation directly for the most recent updates.

The John James Rowe Foundation

£15,000

Correspondent: G Gargan, 18–28 Seel Street, Liverpool L1 4BE (01517 025555)

Trustees: I. M. Chapman; John Kershaw; Alan McClelland; Angela Shute; Jude Wild; Anne Venables; Roger Hoyle; Sinead Martin.

CC Number: 526166

Eligibility

Girls aged 10 to 24 who live in Merseyside and: (i) have lost one or both parents; (ii) whose parents are separated; or (iii) whose home life is especially difficult.

Types of grants

Assistance is given for those at secondary school, college, university or other institutions of higher education. Grants are made for equipment, clothing, tools, instruments and books to help prepare for, or assist entry into, a profession, trade or calling. Maximum grant is £200. Single payment grants only are given.

Annual grant total

Grants total about £15,000 per year.

Applications

In writing to the correspondent for consideration at any time.

The Rushworth Trust

See entry on page 83

Great Crosby

The Halsall Educational Foundation

£1,000

Correspondent: Hugh Hollinghurst, 37 St Michaels Road, Crosby, Merseyside L23 7UJ (01519 247889)

Trustees: Paula Parry; Jane Murrow; Peter Spiers; Hugh Hollinghurst; Amy Causley.

CC Number: 526236

Eligibility

Girls who are leaving sixth form education and entering higher education and live or whose parents live in the ancient township of Great Crosby.

Types of grants

One-off towards books, stethoscopes and so on.

Annual grant total

Small grants to individuals and an annual grant to Halsall School total about £1,000 each year.

Exclusions

Grants are made only to girls living in the ancient township of Great Crosby.

Applications

In writing to the correspondent. Applications should be submitted between March and 31 May, including an sae, for consideration in August and September.

Liverpool

The Liverpool Council of Education

£8,000

Correspondent: Roger Morris, P H Holt Foundation, Room 607, India Buildings, Water Street, Liverpool L2 0RA (01514 734693)

Trustees: Roger Morris; John Phillips; Courteney Owen; John Bell; Paul Clein; Elizabeth Kelly; Jeffery Dunn; Stephen Tiffany.

CC Number: 526714

Eligibility

Sixth form pupils of Liverpool schools studying for A-levels.

Types of grants

Grants of £50 to £350 for pupils to study overseas or advance their education in other ways.

Annual grant total

In 2010/11 the charity had both an income and expenditure of £17,000.

Applications

The correspondent writes to the headteachers of every school with a sixth form in Liverpool at the beginning of each school year, giving details of the trust. Applications should be made in writing and must be supported by a letter of recommendation from the headteacher. The closing date for applications is the last week in January.

Other information

Grants are also made to schools in Liverpool.

Lydiate

John Goore's Charity

£4,500

Correspondent: E R Bostock, Stanley Building, 43 Hanover Street, Liverpool, Merseyside L1 3DN (01772 642387;

email: info@cfmerseyside.org.uk; website: www.cfmerseyside.org.uk)

Trustees: Keith Moakes; Michael Formby; Thomas Adamson; Kathleen Jones; Robbie Fenton; Edith Pope.

CC Number: 238355

Eligibility

People who live in the Lydiate area and are entering or continuing with higher education or training.

Types of grants

Grants of up to £250 towards books/ equipment, travel costs and clothing required for courses or interviews. Support is also given for short courses, relevant accreditations and items or activities which advance education or training.

Annual grant total

In 2010/11 the charity had an income of £6,700 and an expenditure of £9,700.

Applications

Applications should be made through the Community Foundation for Merseyside. Forms are available on request either by post, telephone or email, or to download directly from the Foundation's website.

Applications should include written proof of residence in Lydiate and a letter of acceptance from the university/higher education establishment.

Other information

The charity also makes grants to organisations and to individuals for welfare purposes.

St Helens

The Rainford Trust

£125 (1 grant)

Correspondent: William H Simm, Executive Officer, c/o Pilkington Group Ltd, Prescot Road, St Helens, Merseyside WA10 3TT (01744 20574; email: rainfordtrust@btconnect.com)

Trustees: Kirsty Pilkington; Frances Graham; Annabel Moseley; Hector Pilkington; David Pilkington; Simon Pilkington; Louisa Walker.

CC Number: 266157

Eligibility

People in need who are normally resident in the borough of St Helens.

Types of grants

One-off and recurrent grants ranging from £100 to £750 are paid directly to the college or other third party organisation. Grants can be for schoolchildren for equipment/ instruments, fees, maintenance/living expenses and educational outings in the

UK. Further and higher education students and mature students can receive grants for books, equipment/instruments, fees, childcare and educational outings in the UK.

Annual grant total

In 2010/11 the trust had assets of £7.3 million and an income of £173,000. During the year only one grant of £125 was made to an individual for educational purposes.

Applications

In writing to the correspondent, for consideration throughout the year. Applications can be made directly by the individual, or through his or her school, college or educational welfare agency. The trust sends out a questionnaire, if appropriate, after the application has been made.

Other information

Grants are mostly made to organisations.

Wirral

The Lower Bebington School Lands Foundation

£4,000

Correspondent: S R Green, Poulton Hall, Bebington, Wirral, Cheshire CH63 9LN (01513 343000)

Trustees: Hugo; Charteris; S. R. Green; Alan Jennings; Christina Muspratt; Jackie Hall; Philip Venables; Ben Morris.

CC Number: 525849

Eligibility

People over 18 who live in Lower Bebington; other candidates cannot be considered.

Types of grants

Recurrent grants ranging from £200 to £300 for students in higher/further education to help with the cost of books and fees/living expenses, and for mature students towards books, travel and fees.

Annual grant total

In 2010/11 the trust had an income of £3,000 and an expenditure of £4,000.

Applications

By August each year, on a form available from the correspondent. Applications may be considered at other times if funds are available. Each application is considered on its merit.

The Thomas Robinson Charity

£1,000

Correspondent: Charles F Van Ingen, 1 Blakeley Brow, Wirral, Merseyside CH63 0PS

Trustees: Canon Anne Samuels; Diane Shaw; David Evans.

CC Number: 233412

Eligibility

People in need who live in Higher Bebington.

Types of grants

One-off grants in the range of £50 to £500.

Annual grant total

About £2,000 for welfare and education.

Applications

In writing to: The Vicar, Christ Church Vicarage, King's Road, Higher Bebington, Wirral CH43 8LX. Applications can be submitted directly by the individual or a family member, through a social worker, or a relevant third party such as Citizens Advice or a school. They are considered at any time.

Midlands

General

The Beacon Centre for the Blind

£10,000

Correspondent: Chief Executive, Beacon Centre for the Blind, Wolverhampton Road East, Wolverhampton WV4 6AZ (01902 886781; fax: 01902 886795; email: enquiries@beacon4blind.co.uk; website: www.beacon4blind.co.uk)

Trustees: Michael Beardsmore; Dr John Wright; George Bullock; Joan Quirke; Colin Banks; Richard Ennis; John Throneycroft; Simon Biggs; Sue Rawlings; Pauline Heffernan; Nick Price; Joe Ledwidge; James Fernihough.

CC Number: 216092

Eligibility

People who are registered blind or partially sighted and live in the metropolitan boroughs of Dudley (except Halesowen and Stourbridge), Sandwell and Wolverhampton, and part of the South Staffordshire District Council area.

Types of grants

One-off grants up to a maximum of £250 for specific items or improvements to the home.

Annual grant total

In 2010/11 the charity had assets of £8.9 million, an income of £2.1 million and a total expenditure of £2.3 million. In previous years a small number of grants have been made to individuals.

Applications

In writing to the correspondent stating the degree of vision and age of the applicant, and their monthly income and expenditure. Applications can be submitted through a social worker or a school, and are considered throughout the year.

The Birmingham and Three Counties Trust for Nurses

£2,000

Correspondent: David Airston, 16 Haddon Croft, Halesowen B63 1JQ (01216 020389; email: ruthmadams_45@msn.com)

Trustees: Ann Hirons; Clare Norton; Joy Hey; Joan McManus; Paul Hyde; Joan Smith; Joyce Mellors; Margaret Standly; Margaret Humpherson; Mary Nobles; Norah Warnaby; Margaret Emes; Jenny Edwards; Jeanette Griffiths.

CC Number: 217991

Eligibility

Nurses on any statutory register, who have practiced or practice in the city of Birmingham and the counties of Staffordshire, Warwickshire and Worcestershire.

Types of grants

One-off grants up to £300 per annum to nurses taking post-registration courses (post-basic nurse training or back-to-nursing course). Grants are made towards books, travel and/or fees.

Annual grant total

In 2010/11 the trust had an income of £8,000 and a total expenditure of £17,000. Previous grants have mostly been made for welfare purposes.

Applications

On a form available from the correspondent to be submitted directly by the individual. Applications are considered at any time.

The Francis Bernard Caunt Education Trust

£40,000

Correspondent: J D Kitchen, Larken and Co., 10 Lombard Street, Newark, Nottinghamshire NG24 1XE (01636 703333; website: www.larken.co.uk)

Trustees: James Kitchen; Clive Rossin; Alan Hudson; Nicholas Newsum; Martin Purser; Raymond Fisher; Joanna Parlby.

CC Number: 1108858

Eligibility

People aged between 16 and 25 who are, or whose parents or guardians are, resident within a 12 mile radius of Newark on Trent Parish Church. Applicants should have attended or attend Newark schools or colleges or Southwell or Tuxford schools in the previous eight years for at least two years and be intending to study part-time or full-time for at least one year on a recognised academic or vocational course.

Types of grants

Grants and loans of £500–£2,000.

Annual grant total

In 2010/11 the trust had assets of £1.3 million, an income of £42,000 and made grants totalling £40,000.

Applications

On the application form available from the website with a letter of reference from a headteacher, employer or other appropriate person such as a career adviser.

The Charities of Susanna Cole and Others

£3,500

Correspondent: Peter Gallimore, Trustee, 19 Oak Tree House, 153 Oak Tree Lane, Bournville, Birmingham B30 1TU (01214 714064)

Trustees: Anne Ullathorne; Peter Gallimore; Michael Andrews; Stella Roberts; Betty Haglund; Tony Pegler; Elizabeth MacGregor; Anna Baker.

CC Number: 204531

Eligibility

Quakers in need who live in parts of Worcestershire and most of Warwickshire and are 'a member or attendee of one of the constituent meetings of the Warwickshire Monthly Meeting of the Society of Friends'. Preference is given to younger children (for education).

Types of grants
One-off and recurrent grants for education or re-training.

Annual grant total
In 2010 the charity had an income of £18,000 and a total expenditure of £7,000. Grants are made for welfare and educational purposes.

Applications
In writing to the correspondent via the overseer of the applicant's Quaker meeting. Applications should be received by early March and October for consideration later in the same months.

Thomas Monke's Charity

£750

Correspondent: C P Kitto, Steward, 5/7 Breadmarket Street, Lichfield, Staffordshire WS13 6LQ (01543 267995)

Trustees: Charles Wollaston; Dawn Roach; Josephine Beniston; Jean Angus; Sally Wollaston.

CC Number: 214783

Eligibility
Young individuals between the ages of 17 and 21 who live in Austrey in Warwickshire and Mersham, Shenton and Whitwick in Leicestershire.

Types of grants
One-off and recurrent grants in the range of £100 to £500 to college students, undergraduates, vocational students and people starting work for books and equipment/instruments. Vocational students and people starting work can receive grants for fees.

Annual grant total
About £1,500 to individuals for educational and welfare purposes.

Exclusions
Expeditions, scholarships and university course fees are not funded.

Applications
Application forms are available from the correspondent and should be submitted directly by the individual before 31 March, in time for the trustees' yearly meeting held in April.

The Newfield Charitable Trust

£11,200

Correspondent: D J Dumbleton, Clerk, Rotherham and Co. Solicitors, 8–9 The Quadrant, Coventry CV1 2EG (02476 227331; fax: 02476 221293; email: d. dumbleton@rotherham-solicitors.co.uk)

Trustees: E. Bresnen; R. Stanley; A. Parsons; Mrs H. Jones; Revd Canon J. Eardley; Mrs R. Bott; Mrs S. Walden.

CC Number: 221440

Eligibility
Girls and women (under 30) who are in need of care and assistance and live in Coventry or Leamington Spa.

Types of grants
Grants towards school uniforms and other school clothing, educational trips, books and childcare costs. Most grants are under £500.

Annual grant total
In 2010/11 the trust had assets of £1.5 million and an income of £45,000. During the year, the trustees received a total of 155 applications, from which 154 applicants were awarded. Grants totalled just over £36,500 and were distributed as follows:

Educational	8	£3,200
Clothing	43	£8,000
General	103	£25,400

Exclusions
No grants for postgraduate education.

Applications
Write to the correspondent for an application form. Applications are accepted from individuals or third parties e.g. schools, social services, Citizens Advice etc. A letter of support/reference from someone not a friend or relative of the applicant (i.e. school, social services etc.) may be required. Details of income/expenditure and personal circumstances should also be given.

Applications are considered eight times a year.

The Norton Foundation

£3,600 (25 grants)

Correspondent: Clerk to the Trustees, PO Box 10282, Redditch, Worcestershire B97 9ZA (01527 544446; email: correspondent@nortonfoundation.org; website: www.nortonfoundation.org)

Trustees: Graham Suggett; Michael Bailey; Alan Bailey; Jane Gaynor; Parminder Singh Birdi; Richard Hurley; Sarah Henderson; Brian Lewis; Robert Meacham; Richard Perkins; Louise Sewell.

CC Number: 702638

Eligibility
Young people under 25 who live in Birmingham, Coventry or Warwickshire and are in need of care, rehabilitation or aid of any kind, 'particularly as a result of delinquency, maltreatment or neglect or who are in danger of lapsing or relapsing into delinquency'.

Types of grants
One-off grants of up to £500 are available to schoolchildren and further and higher education students for school clothing, books, equipment, instruments, fees, maintenance and living expenses and educational outings in the UK.

Annual grant total
In 2010/11 the trust had assets of £4.2 million and an income of £137,000. Grants were made totalling £105,000, of which £14,000 was given in individual grants, £26,000 was awarded in discretionary grants and the remaining £65,000 was given to institutions. Grants to individuals were distributed as follows:

Clothing	15	£1,600
Education and training	25	£3,600
Household	72	£8,600

Applications
By letter which should contain all the information required as detailed in the guidance notes for applicants. Guidance notes are available from the correspondent or the website. Applications must be submitted through a social worker, Citizens Advice, probation service, school or other welfare agency. They are considered quarterly.

Sir John Sumner's Trust
See entry on page 100

The Anthony and Gwendoline Wylde Memorial Charity

£2,000

Correspondent: D J Nightingale, Clerk, 3 Waterfront Business Park, Dudley Road, Brierley Hill, West Midlands DY5 1LX (0845 111 5050)

Trustees: Geoffrey Hill; Brian Edwards; Martyn Morgan; David Johnson; Dianna Jeffries; Olive Dukes; Ian Lowe; Patricia Gardener; Michael Evers.

CC Number: 700239

Eligibility

People in need with a preference for residents of Stourbridge (West Midlands) and Kinver (Staffordshire).

Types of grants

One-off grants in the range of £50 and £500 are given to college students and undergraduates for clothing, fees, books, equipment/instruments, maintenance/living expenses, voluntary work overseas and excursions.

Annual grant total

In 2010/11 the charity had assets of £882,000 and an income of £43,000. Grants were made totalling £37,500, of which £4,000 was given to individuals for educational and relief-in-need purposes. The remainder was given to organisations.

Exclusions

No grants towards bills or debts.

Applications

In writing to the correspondent. Applications can be submitted directly by the individual or a family member and are considered on an ongoing basis.

Derbyshire

Coke's Educational Charity

£2,000

Correspondent: Amanda Ayre, Bentley Top, Leapley Lane, Alkmonton; Ashbourne; Derbyshire DE6 3DJ (01335 330528)

Trustees: Desmond Hislop; Freda Sills; Jeremy Dunn; John Ayre; Michael Bishop; Thomas Turner; Virginia Leedham; Michael Monk.

CC Number: 527028

Eligibility

People under 25 who live in the parishes of Alkmonton, Hollington, Hungry Bently, Longford and Rodsley.

Types of grants

One-off and recurrent grants for educational purposes.

Annual grant total

In 2011 the charity had an income of £3,900 and an expenditure of £2,700. Grants in previous years have totalled about £2,000.

Applications

In writing to the correspondent.

The Dronfield Relief-in-Need Charity

£1,000

Correspondent: Dr A N Bethell, Ramshaw Lodge, Crow Lane, Unstone, Dronfield, Derbyshire S18 4AL (01246 413276)

Trustees: Christine Smith; Frances Robinson; Dr Anthony Bethell; Jane Shute; Doug Oxspring; Sue O'Donnell; Angela Talford.

CC Number: 219888

Eligibility

People under 25 who live in the ecclesiastical parishes of Dronfield, Holmesfield, Unstone and West Handley.

Types of grants

One-off grants up to a value of £100 are given, including those for social and physical training.

Annual grant total

This charity gives around £1,000 in grants each year.

Applications

In writing to the correspondent though a social worker, doctor, member of the clergy of any denomination, a local councillor, Citizens Advice or other welfare agency. The applicants should ensure they are receiving all practical/financial assistance they are entitled to from statutory sources.

Other information

Grants are also given to local organisations.

Hilton Educational Foundation

£3,700

Correspondent: Sue Cornish, 6 Willow Brook Close, Hilton, Derby DE65 5JE (01283 734110)

Trustees: Carole Curry; Christine Helliwell; Kenneth Tunnicliffe.

CC Number: 527091

Eligibility

Young people aged under 25 in further or higher education who live, or whose parents live, in Hilton and Marston on Dove.

Types of grants

One-off grants, usually £100 to £150, towards travel, books and/or equipment needed for studies.

Annual grant total

In 2011 the foundation had an income of £11,000 and an expenditure of £4,600. Previously grants have been divided as

follows: £1,000 to schools, £350 to a playgroup and £3,700 to individuals.

Applications

In writing to the correspondent directly by the individual. Applications should be submitted in March and October, for consideration in the same month.

The Risley Educational Foundation

£8,400 (39 grants)

Correspondent: Margaret Giller, The Clerk to the Trustees, 27 The Chase, Little Eaton, Derby DE21 5AS (01332 883361)

Trustees: Joyce Brown; Ernest Tryner; Annette Noskwith; John Astle-Flether; Christopher Smedley; Frank Jones; Gilbert Skelston; Margaret Stocks; Ann Wallace; Derek Orchard; Mark O'Neill.

CC Number: 702720

Eligibility

People under 25 who live in the parishes of Breaston, Church Wilne, Dale Abbey, Draycott, Hopwell, Risley, Sandiacre or Stanton-by-Dale.

Types of grants

Grants of £150 for books, equipment, educational travel and promoting the instruction of Church of England doctrines. People on music and arts courses can be supported.

Annual grant total

In 2010/11 the foundation had an income of £44,000 and made thirty nine grants to individuals totalling £8,400.

Applications

On a form available from the correspondent. Applications are considered on a quarterly basis.

Scargill's Educational Foundation

£9,000

Correspondent: Stephen Marshall, Clerk, 10–11 St James Court, Friar Gate, Derby DE1 1BT (01332 254105; email: stephen.marshall@robinsons-solicitors.co.uk)

Trustees: Carol Hart; I. E. Gooding; Alan Cooper; Norma Futers; Simon White; Elizabeth Campbell; Alison Ingram; Bridget Pugh; Francis Farmer.

CC Number: 527012

Eligibility

People under the age of 25 who live in the parishes of West Hallam, Dale Abbey, Mapperley and Stanley (including Stanley Common).

Types of grants

The main beneficiary of the charity is Scargill Church of England Primary School. Priority is also given to three other schools in the area. After that, help is available for groups and also for individuals for the following purposes:

(i) Grants, usually up to about £45, for sixth form pupils to help with books, equipment, clothing or travel.

(ii) Grants, usually up to about £175, to help with school, college or university fees or to supplement existing grants.

(iii) Grants to help with the cost of books and educational outings for schoolchildren.

(iv) For the study of music and other arts and for educational travel.

Annual grant total

Around £8,000 to £10,000 is given in educational grants to individuals each year.

Applications

On a form available from the correspondent. The foundation places advertisements in August, and the formal closing date is 29 September, although applications after this date will be considered if funds permit.

The Stanton Charitable Trust

£500

Correspondent: Clive Turner, Saint-Gobain PAM plc, Lows Lane, Stanton-by-Dale, Ilkeston DE7 4QU (01159 898012)

Trustees: Geoffrey Norton; Clive Turner; Phillip Burrows; Stewart Nicholas; George Bennett.

CC Number: 328727

Eligibility

People at any stage or level of their education, undertaking study of any subject who are in need and live near Staveley Works in Chesterfield, Derbyshire, namely Staveley, Brimington, Barrowhill, Hollingwold and Inkersall.

Types of grants

Grants can be given towards, maintenance/living expenses, equipment/instruments and excursions.

Annual grant total

This trust has an annual income of around £2,000.

Applications

In writing either directly by the individual or a family member, or through an organisation such as Citizens Advice or a school. Applications should state the specific amount for a specific item.

Other information

Grants are also made to schools, churches, scouts, guides and local fundraising events.

Limited information is available as documents have never been filed with the Charity Commission.

Ault Hucknall

The Hardwick Educational Charity

£1,000

Correspondent: C E Hitch, Stainsby Mill Farm, Heath, Chesterfield, Derbyshire S44 5RW (01246 850288)

Trustees: Tony Bell; Ann Syrett; David Wilson; Elizabeth Adsetts; Judith Ottewell.

CC Number: 526995

Eligibility

People aged between 16 and 24, inclusive, whose parent(s) live in the civil parish of Ault Hucknall.

Types of grants

Help with the cost of books for students in further/higher education and with the cost of books, equipment and instruments for people starting work.

Annual grant total

About £1,000.

Exclusions

Grants are not available for student exchanges, maintenance, fees or mature students.

Applications

In writing to the correspondent. Applications are considered in April and October.

Buxton

The Bingham Trust

£4,400

Correspondent: Roger Horne, Trustee, Blinder House, Flagg, Buxton, Derbyshire SK17 9QG (01298 83328; email: binghamtrust@aol.com; website: www.binghamtrust.org.uk)

Trustees: Dr Geoffrey Willis; Roger Horne; Alexandra Hurst.

CC Number: 287636

Eligibility

People in need, primarily those who live in Buxton. Most applicants from outside Buxton are rejected unless there is a Buxton connection.

Types of grants

One-off grants ranging from £200 to £1,500. Grants are made to individuals for a wide variety of needs, including further education.

Annual grant total

In 2010/11 the trust had assets of £2.4 million and an income of £91,000. Grants to individuals for welfare and education totalled £8,800.

Exclusions

No grants are made for debts or higher education study. In exceptional circumstances the trust may support people in higher education if they are suffering from disabilities and require specialised equipment for them.

Applications

On a form available from the correspondent or to download from the website. Applications should include a supporting letter from a third party such as a social worker, Citizens Advice, doctor or minister. They are considered during the first two weeks of January, April, July and October and should be received before the end of the previous month.

Other information

The trust gives primarily to organisations.

Derby

The Derby City Charity

£500

Correspondent: Jacquelynne Dominiczak, Derby City Council, Constitutional Services, 5th Floor, Saxon House, Friary Street, Derby DE1 1AN (01332 643654)

CC Number: 214902

Eligibility

People under 25 who live in the city of Derby and are in need.

Types of grants

Grants for education, training, apprenticeships, and for equipment for those starting work.

Annual grant total

In 2010/11 the charity had an income of £3,500 and an expenditure of £1,000. Grants are given for education and welfare.

Exclusions

Assistance is not given where other funds are available or towards books or fees for pupils and students if the LEA already has a scheme covering such items.

Applications
On a form available from the correspondent, on written request.

Holmesfield
The Holmesfield Educational Foundation

£6,000

Correspondent: Geraldine Austen, Greenways, Holmesfield, Dronfield, Derbyshire S18 7WB (01142 890686)

Trustees: Robert Burrell; Roger Webb; William Eardley; Carol Huckerby; Godfrey Smythe; Charles Morton.

CC Number: 515723

Eligibility
People living in the parish of Holmesfield, under the age of 25.

Types of grants
The cost of books, clothing and other essentials for schoolchildren. Grants may also be available for those at college or university.

Annual grant total
In 2010 the foundation had an income of £4,600 and an expenditure of £6,500.

Applications
In writing to the correspondent.

Matlock
The Ernest Bailey Charity

£1,500

Correspondent: Brian Evans, Derbyshire Dales District Council, Town Hall, Bank Road, Matlock, Derbyshire DE4 3NN (01629 761100; email: brian.evans@ derbyshiredales.gov.uk)

Trustee: Derbyshire Dales District Council.

CC Number: 518884

Eligibility
People in need who live in Matlock (this includes Bonsall, Darley Dale, South Darley, Tansley, Matlock Bath and Cromford).

Types of grants
Most applications have been from local groups, but individuals in need and those with educational needs are also supported. Educational grants are one-off and generally of around £100 to £200. Grants are given to students in further/higher education towards books, fees, living expenses and study or travel abroad. Mature students can apply towards books, travel, fees or childcare.

People with special educational needs are considered. Each application is considered on its merits.

Annual grant total
In 2009/10 the trust had an income £16,000. A total of £3,000 was given in grants.

Applications
On a form available from the correspondent. Applications can be submitted directly by the individual and/ or can be supported by a relevant professional. They should be returned by the end of September for consideration and award in October. Applications should include costings (total amount required, funds raised and funds promised). Previous beneficiaries may apply again, with account being taken of assistance given in the past.

Spondon
The Spondon Relief-in-Need Charity

£3,600

Correspondent: Richard J Pooles, Secretary and Treasurer, PO Box 5073, Spondon, Derby DE21 7ZJ (01332 669879; email: info@ spondonreliefinneedcharity.org; website: www.spondonreliefinneedcharity.org)

Trustees: Malcolm Stevens; Pauline Jennings; Peter Berry; Adrian Martin; Margaret Bools; Rosemary Archer; Susan Bown; Teresa Kokiet; Chris Poulter; Julian Hollywell; Catherine Leatherbarrow.

CC Number: 211317

Eligibility
People in education who live in the ancient parish of Spondon within the city of Derby.

Types of grants
Grants of amounts up to £500 are made to schoolchildren, college students, undergraduates and mature students, including those towards uniforms/ clothing, study/travel abroad, books, equipment/instruments, excursions, awards for excellence and childcare.

Annual grant total
In 2009 the trust had an income of £25,000 and a total expenditure of £26,000. Grants are made for educational and welfare purposes.

In 2011 educational grants totalled £3,600 consisting of 15 school uniform grants totalling £2,000 and four student grants totalling £2,500.

Exclusions
This grant is not intended to supplement an LEA grant.

Applications
On a form available from the correspondent to be submitted either directly by the individual or a family member, through a third party such as a social worker or through an organisations such as Citizens Advice or a school. Each form must be accompanied by a letter of support from a sponsor such as a doctor, health authority official, social worker, city councillor, clergyman, headteacher, school liaison officer, youth leader or probation officer. The sponsor must justify the applicant's need. The latter is particularly important. The applicant should provide as much information on the form as possible. It is better to ask for a visit by a trustee if possible. The trustees meet quarterly.

West Hallam
The Foundation of Ann Powtrell

£10,000

Correspondent: Peter Briggs, 12 High Lane East, West Hallam, Ilkeston, Derbyshire DE7 6HW (01159 328274)

Trustees: Bruce Broughton; Carol Hart; Robert Lee; Helena Chapman; Alan Edwards; Linda Webster; Janet Hayes; Richard Hartshorn.

CC Number: 506638

Eligibility
Students under the age of 25 who live, or whose parents live, in the parish of West Hallam.

Types of grants
Grants of up to £250 have been given for apprentices and educational trips, such as Duke of Edinburgh Awards and a trip to a world scout jamboree in Chile.

Annual grant total
In 2010/11 the foundation had an income of £7,800 and an expenditure of £21,000. Grants are made to organisations and individuals.

Applications
In writing to the correspondent.

Hereford-shire

The Hereford Society for Aiding the Industrious

£4,500

Correspondent: Sally Robertson, Secretary, 18 Venns Close, Bath Street, Hereford HR1 2HH (01432 274014 – Thursdays only; email: hsaialms@ talktalkbusiness.net)

Trustees: C. George; G. Kent; M. Bricknell; Mrs J. O'Donnell; Mrs M. E. Phillips; M. Jones; R. Miller; R. Weston; T. Nellist.

CC Number: 212220

Eligibility

People in need who live in Herefordshire, with preference for Hereford City and its immediate environs. Applicants may be undertaking primary, secondary, further or higher education, non-vocational training or vocational training or re-training, in most subjects.

Types of grants

Normally one-off grants ranging between £50 and £1,000 and occasionally interest-free loans. Grants can be made towards: schoolchildren for educational outings; people starting work towards books and equipment/instruments; students in further/higher education towards books, fees and living expenses; and mature students towards books, travel, fees and childcare.

Annual grant total

In 2010/11 the trust had assets of £949,000 and an income of £96,000. Grants to individuals totalled £5,500, the majority of which was given as educational grants ranging from £170 to £1,000.

Exclusions

Grants are rarely given towards gap year expeditions.

Applications

In writing to the correspondent. If eligible, an application form will be sent and the applicant will probably be asked to attend an interview (between 2.00pm and 4.00pm on Thursday). Grants are rarely given directly to the applicant; instead they are given to the bookseller, college and so on. The trust has stated that applications should be 'precise' and 'honest'. Applications are considered every month.

Other information

The trust also makes grants to organisations.

The Herefordshire Community Foundation

£2,500

Correspondent: The Secretary, The Fred Bulmer Centre, Wall Street, Hereford, Herefordshire HR4 9HP (01432 272550; email: info@ herefordshirecommunityfoundation.org)

Trustees: Miss S. Evans; Mrs C. Forrester; Ms W. Gilmour; Mr R. Hunter; Mr N. Hone; Mr W. Lindesay; Ms B. Parkinson.

CC Number: 1094935

Eligibility

People in need who live in Herefordshire.

Types of grants

One-off and recurrent grants according to need.

Annual grant total

In 2010/11 the foundation had assets of £1.2 million and an income of £334,000. Approximately £5,000 is given each year to individuals.

Applications

In writing to the correspondent including standard information such as contact details, what the grant is to be used for and why it is needed.

Other information

Grants are also made to organisations.

Jarvis Educational Foundation

£3,000

Correspondent: Betty Maura-Cooper, 4 Church Street, Hay-on-Wye, Hereford HR3 5DQ (01497 821023; email: bettymchay@googlemail.com)

Trustees: John Hope; Angela Pearson-Gregory; Bryan Powles; Roy Jenkins; David King; Martin Powell; Richard Skyrme; Bob King; Sheila Stone; Mike Saunders; William Sewell; Annelisa Foster.

CC Number: 526881

Eligibility

People who live the parishes of Staunton-on-Wye, Bredwardine and Letton in Herefordshire.

Types of grants

One-off grants can be given: to individuals at secondary school, university or college where education authority support is not available, to provide outfits, clothing, tools, instruments or books to help people enter a trade, profession or calling on leaving education; and to enable such people to travel to pursue their education. Grants can range from £100 to £1,000.

Annual grant total

In 2011 the foundation had an income of £23,000 and an expenditure of £69,000. Previously grants to individuals have totalled around £3,000.

Applications

In writing to the correspondent for consideration at any time.

The Emma Russell Educational Foundation

£700

Correspondent: Charles Masefield, The Cloisters, Worcester Road, Ledbury, Herefordshire HR8 1PL (01531 632638)

Trustees: William Masefield; Hilary Jones; Paul Winter.

CC Number: 527246

Eligibility

People under 25 who live in the parishes of Ledbury Rural and Wellington Heath.

Types of grants

Grants to help people with expenses at university and those undertaking apprenticeships and training generally.

Annual grant total

About £700 is distributed each year.

Applications

On a form available from the correspondent. Awards are made in October.

Bosbury

Bosbury Educational Foundation

£9,000

Correspondent: Jane Bulson, willow End, Southfield Lane, Bosbury, Ledbury HR8 1PZ

Trustees: William Rees; Peter Thomas; Sven Bosley; Shirley Eyles; Harold Powles.

CC Number: 527140

Eligibility

Young people leaving school who live in the parish of Bosbury and have done so for at least three years.

Types of grants

Grants of up to £250 towards books are given to young people 'on leaving school' going on to further education. Students undertaking university courses of three years or longer are invited to apply for a further grant in their final year. Grants may also be given towards school uniform for children in need.

Annual grant total

In 2011 the trust had an income of £20,000 and an expenditure of £9,400.

Applications

In writing to the correspondent, including details of the course. Applications should be submitted directly by the individual and are considered at any time.

Other information

The parish of Bosbury consists of around 500 people. In previous years the trust has stated that it is being inundated by applications from outside the parish which cannot be considered due to the deeds of the trust, and these applications will not be acknowledged.

Hereford

The Hereford Municipal Charities

£1,800

Correspondent: The Trustees, 147 St Owen Street, Hereford HR1 2JR (01432 354002; email: herefordmunicipal@btconnect.com)

Trustees: Derek Duffett; Polly Andrews; Aubrey Oliver; Alan Blake; John Lewis-Davies; Kenneth Rayner; Elizabeth Evans; Jennifer Davies; Jennifer Holmes; Jim Kenyon.

CC Number: 218738

Eligibility

People in need who live in the city of Hereford.

Types of grants

One-off grants of up to £200. Grants are given to help with the cost of education and starting work.

Annual grant total

In 2011 the charity had assets of £3.7 million and an income of £257,000. Grants to individuals for education totalled £1,800.

Exclusions

No grants towards debts or nursery fees.

Applications

On a form available from the correspondent to be submitted directly by the individual or through a relevant third party. Applications are considered five times a year but can be authorised within meetings if they are very urgent.

Other information

Most of the charity's expenditure is allocated to the running of its almshouses.

Middleton

The Middleton-on-the-Hill Parish Charity

£1,000

Correspondent: Clare Halls, Secretary, Highlands, Leysters, Leominster, Herefordshire HR6 0HP (01568 750257; email: leystershalls@aol.com)

Trustees: Clare Halls; Glyn Morgan; James Turner; Philip Reynolds; Robin Moseley; Thomas Merrick; William Price; Pamela Moseley.

CC Number: 527146

Eligibility

People living in the parish of Middleton-on-the-Hill.

Types of grants

One-off and recurrent grants for both welfare and educational purposes.

Annual grant total

About £2,000 each year is given in grants.

Applications

In writing to the correspondent.

Norton Canon

The Norton Canon Parochial Charities

£5,000

Correspondent: Mary Gittins, Ivy Cottage, Norton Canon, Hereford HR4 7BQ (01544 318984)

Trustees: David Palliser; Howard Jones; Nigel Lewis; Robert Loxston; Mairion Jones; Robert King.

CC Number: 218560

Eligibility

Young people who live in the parish of Norton Canon.

Types of grants

Grants have been given towards books and educational outings for schoolchildren, books, fees/living expenses and study or travel abroad for students in further or higher education and equipment/instruments, books, clothing and travel for people starting work.

Annual grant total

Grants total around £10,000 per year and are given for educational and welfare purposes.

Applications

In writing to the correspondent at any time.

Ross

The Ross Educational Foundation

£4,000

Correspondent: Margaret Bickerton, 3 Silver Birches, Ross-on-Wye, Herefordshire HR9 7UX (01989 563260)

Trustees: Derek Bedford; Peggy Luker; Neil Pascoe; Paul Deneen; William Hazleton; Melanie Mellor; Sarah Jones; Colin Gray.

CC Number: 527229

Eligibility

People under 25 who live (or whose parents live) in the urban district of Ross and the civil parish of Ross Rural only.

Types of grants

One-off and recurrent grants for those at school to help with equipment/ instruments, excursions and study or travel abroad and to vocational students and further and higher education students for books, excursions equipment/instruments and study or travel abroad. People starting work and apprenticeships and those studying music and other arts may also apply. Grants range from £25 to £120.

Annual grant total

In 2011 the trust had an income of £3,500 and an expenditure of £4,500.

Exclusions

Accommodation costs and day-to-day travel expenses will not be considered.

Applications

On a form available from the correspondent to be submitted directly by the individual. Grants should be submitted in February and August for consideration in April and October respectively.

Leicester-shire and Rutland

The Dixie Educational Foundation

£13,000

Correspondent: P Dungworth, Clerk to the Trustees, 31 Oakmeadow Way, Groby, Leicestershire LE6 OYN (01162 913683; email: pdungworth@hotmail.co.uk.)

Trustees: Reginald Ward; Andrew Goodwin; Elea; Jane Glennon; John Plant; Michael Preston; Philip Owen; Robert Furniss; Pamela Ryley; David Grewcock; Victoria Willetts; Edward Goold; Brian Sutton; Tina Chastney.

CC Number: 527837

Eligibility

People under 25 who live or whose parents/guardians live, or have at any time lived, in the area of the former district of Market Bosworth Rural District Council for a period of not less than two years.

Types of grants

One-off grants in the range of £75 and £150 for clothing, books, equipment, instruments, educational outings in the UK or study or travel abroad.

Annual grant total

In 2010/11 the charity had assets of £88,000 and an income of £36,000. Grants to individuals totalled £13,000.

Applications

In writing to the correspondent. Applications can be submitted directly by the individual, through the individual's school, college or educational welfare agency, or through a parent or guardian. Applicants must give their date of birth, residential qualification and brief details of educational background and present course of study or apprenticeship together with details and costs of items against which a grant is sought. Applications must be received at least two weeks before each of the termly meetings which are held on the first Friday of March, June and November.

Other information

The foundation also supports local schools and organisations.

The Leicestershire Coal Industry Welfare Trust Fund

£6,000

Correspondent: Peter Smith, Trustee, Miners Offices Unit 12, Springboard Centre, 18 Mantle Lane, Coalville, Leicestershire LE67 3DW (01530 832085; email: leicesternum@ukinbox.com)

Trustees: Mr Howe; Peter Smith; Mrs Smith; George Dixon.

CC Number: 1006985

Eligibility

Redundant or retired mineworkers (and their dependents) from the British coal mining industry in Leicestershire, who have not taken up other full-time work.

Types of grants

Grants are given for education, relief-in-need, health and to organisations linked with the mining industry.

Annual grant total

In 2011 the trust had assets of £365,000 and gave grants to individuals totalling £13,000.

Applications

In writing to the correspondent, including details of mining connections, residence in Leicestershire and dependence on the mineworker (in the case of children).

The Thomas Rawlins Educational Foundation

£2,000

Correspondent: Geoffrey Gibson, 2 Wallis Close, Thurcaston, Leicestershire LE7 7JS (01162 350946)

Trustees: Anne Horton; David Bowler; David Slater; D. C. Cawdell; A. L. Siddons; C. Orr; B. P. Tyler; J. E. Siddons; M. E. Slater; Dorothy Holt.

CC Number: 527858

Eligibility

People under 25 years of age living in Quorn, Woodhouse, Woodhouse Eaves and Barrow upon Soar only (preference is given to the first three villages).

Types of grants

(i) Grants, usually between £50 to £250, for school pupils, to help with books, equipment, school uniform, maintenance or fees, but not other school clothing or educational outings. (ii) Grants, up to about £250, for students in further and higher education, to help with books, equipment, instruments, study or travel abroad or fees, but not for student exchange or for foreign students

studying in the UK. (iii) Help towards the cost of books, equipment and instruments, travel and clothing for people starting work.

Annual grant total

About £2,000.

Applications

On a form available from the correspondent, including details of the parent/guardian's financial position. Applications can be submitted through a parent or guardian at any time.

The Harry James Riddleston Charity of Leicester

£18,000

Correspondent: Elizabeth Bass, 44 High Street, Market Harborough, Leicestershire LE16 8ST (01858 463322; website: www.harryriddleston.org.uk)

Trustees: M. G. Hearth; Geoffrey Simpson; Gill Jameson; Philip Dodd; S. Duxbury; William Richmond; S. Longhill; Clive Smith; David Brooks; Sheila Berridge; M. J. Page.

CC Number: 262787

Eligibility

People aged 21 to 34 (exceptionally those over 18) who live in Leicestershire or Rutland.

Types of grants

Interest free loans of up to £10,000 for between five and ten years to start or expand a business, or for vocational or educational advancement.

Annual grant total

In 2010/11 the charity had an income of £21,000 and an expenditure of £22,000.

Applications

On a form available from the correspondent, to be submitted directly by the individual. Applications are considered in February, May, August and November. Applicants will need two guarantors for a loan of up to £6,000 and three for a loan of between £6,000 and £10,000.

The Rutland Trust

£4,000

Correspondent: Richard Adams, Clerk, 35 Trent Road, Oakham, Rutland LE15 6HE (01572 756706; email: adams@apair.wanadoo.co.uk)

Trustees: Alistair Haywood; Frank Hinch; Elizabeth Bingley; Colonel James Weir.

CC Number: 517175

Eligibility

People, usually under 35, in need who live in Rutland and are at any level or stage of their education.

Types of grants

One-off grants ranging between £50 and £400. There are no restrictions on how the grants may be spent. In the past, grants have been made towards music and school trips for needy young people, for European exchange trips, and for young people to take part in educational, missionary and life-experience programmes overseas. Grants may also be spent on books, equipment, fees, bursaries, fellowships and study visits.

Annual grant total

In 2011 the trust had an income of £17,000 and a total expenditure of £14,000. Grants are also made for welfare purposes and to organisations.

Applications

An initial telephone call is recommended.

The Sir John Sedley Educational Foundation

£4,000

Correspondent: Trevor Forrester-Coles, Sir John Sedley Educational, 13 Carlton Crescent, East Leake, Loughborough LE12 6JF (01509 852581)

Trustees: Jennifer Gretton; David Hatton; Hester Bonham; Lorraine Watkins; Philip Gaskell; Malise Graham; Richard Tollemache; Dorothy Tittensor.

CC Number: 527884

Eligibility

Anyone attending an educational course including sixth form college, institutes of further or higher education, NVQ and TEC courses who is under 25 years old living in the civil Parish of Wymondham.

Types of grants

Scholarships, bursaries, equipment, clothes and books.

Annual grant total

In 2010/11 the foundation had an income of £6,900 and an expenditure of £53,000.

Applications

In writing to the correspondent. The trust prefers if a supplier's quotation for the requested item is included.

Other information

The foundation also maintains a hall for the benefit of the local area.

The Marc Smith Educational Charity

£5,000

Correspondent: Diana Jones, Secretary, 21 Highcroft, Husbands Bosworth, Lutterworth, Leicestershire LE17 6LF (01858 880741)

Trustees: Trevor Dawes; William Howard; Peter Smith; Zoe Ridley; Simon Smith.

CC Number: 1045965

Eligibility

Students (usually under 25) living or attending school in the ancient parishes of Claybrook Magna, Claybrook Parva, Wibtoft and Ullesthorpe.

Types of grants

Help towards the cost of education, training, apprenticeship or equipment for those starting work. A clothing grant is given to pupils moving from the village schools to the high school. Grants are also given to students in further or higher education.

Annual grant total

In 2011 the trust had an income of £7,300 and an expenditure of £11,000.

Applications

Applications for clothing grants should be in writing and they are considered in May. Further education applications are considered in September, and should be submitted at a meeting which applicants are invited to through local advertisements near to the time of the meeting.

Other information

Grants are also made to local schools.

The Wyvernian Foundation

£2,500

Correspondent: Andrew York, 6 Magnolia Close, Leicester, Leicester LE2 8PS (01162 835345; email: andrew_york@sky.com)

Trustees: Frank Whitelam; Maurice Cattermole; Bob Evatt; Philip Cattermole; Steve Hunt.

CC Number: 509225

Eligibility

People who live in the city or county of Leicester (i.e. those who have been permanently or ordinarily resident in the city or county for at least three years, excluding those temporarily resident whilst undertaking a period of study).

Types of grants

One-off and recurrent grants, generally for those in further and higher education (including mature students), towards the cost of fees/living expenses, study or travel overseas, and possibly books and equipment where they are an integral part of the course. Childcare expenses may be given. Grants range from £50 to £300. Loans for individuals may also be given.

Annual grant total

About £2,500.

Exclusions

Grants are not given to those in private education.

Applications

An application form must be obtained by sending an sae to the correspondent. Applications should be completed by the applicant and supported by the sponsor. An sae and CV should also be submitted. They should be submitted by early February, May, August and December each year for consideration in the following months.

Ashby-de-la-Zouch

The Mary Smith Scholarship Fund

£2,500

Correspondent: R Wright, Education Finance, Leicestershire County Council, County Hall, Glenfield, Leicester LE3 8RF (01163 057643; fax: 01530 560645; email: edfinance@leics.gov.uk; website: www.ashbyschool.org.uk)

Trustee: Leicestershire County Council.

CC Number: 527890

Eligibility

People under 25 who live in Ashby-de-la-Zouch.

Types of grants

Maintenance allowances and bursaries for any place of learning that is approved by the governors. Help is given towards the cost of books; educational outings; maintenance; study/travel broad; student exchange; equipment/instruments; protective clothing; and childcare (mature students only). Grants are also given to enable people to prepare for, or to assist entry into, a profession, trade or calling. Grants can be given to study music or the arts, or to travel abroad to pursue education.

Annual grant total

About £2,500 a year.

Applications

On a form available from the correspondent to be considered in April.

Cossington

Babington's Charity

£7,000

Correspondent: The Trustees, 14 Main Street, Cossington, Leicester, Leicestershire LE7 4UU (01509 812271)

Trustees: John Gregory; Helen McCague; Rachel Cutts; Gary Drew; Dean Hopkinson; Louise Turnbull.

CC Number: 220069

Eligibility

People in need in the parish of Cossington.

Types of grants

One-off and recurrent grants according to need.

Annual grant total

In 2010 the trust had assets of £452,000, an income of £34,000 and a total expenditure of £31,000. Grants totalled £19,000, of which £15,000 was given to students and individuals.

Applications

In writing to the correspondent.

Great Glen

Great Glen Town Charity

£500

Correspondent: Gerald Hincks, Trustee, 19 Naseby Way, Great Glen, Leicester LE8 9GS (01162 593155)

Trustees: Gerald Hincks; Mary Ireland; Alan Selway; Frazer Gilbert; Andrew Duerden.

CC Number: 701901

Eligibility

People who live in the parish of Great Glen who are in need.

Types of grants

One-off and recurrent grants, for example, to people going to university, people starting work and people undertaking voluntary work in their gap year. The charity also has a welfare branch which distributes grants at Christmas to older residents at a rate of £15 per individual and £30 per couple.

Annual grant total

Grants total around £500 each year.

Applications

In writing to the correspondent. Applications from outside the beneficial area will not be acknowledged.

Groby

Thomas Herbert Smith's Trust Fund

£1,000

Correspondent: A R York, 6 Magnolia Close, Leicester LE2 8PS (01162 835345; email: andrew_york@sky.com)

Trustees: Jamie Craig; Martyn Allison; Peter Griffin; Martin Cartwright; Ken Rushby.

CC Number: 701694

Eligibility

People who live in the parish of Groby in Leicestershire.

Types of grants

One-off and recurrent grants ranging from £100 to £500.

Annual grant total

In 2010/11 the fund had an income of £14,000 and a total expenditure of £28,000. Grants are made to organisations and individuals.

Applications

On a form available from the correspondent, for consideration throughout the year. Applications can be submitted either directly by the individual, or through a social worker, Citizens Advice or other third party.

Harborough

Market Harborough and The Bowdens Charity

£23,000 (10 grants)

Correspondent: James G Jacobs, Steward, Godfrey Payton and Co., 149 St Mary's Road, Market Harborough, Leicester LE16 7DZ (01858 462467; fax: 01858 431898; email: admin@mhbcharity.co.uk; website: www.mhbcharity.co.uk)

Trustees: Janice Hefford; Ian Wells; Mark Stamp; Adrian Trotter; George Stamp; John Clare; Tim Banks; Joan Williams; Paul Edward Beardsmore; Alan Walker; Janet Roberts; David Battersby; Julie Jones; Lennie Rhodes; Guy R. D. Hartopp.

CC Number: 1041958

Eligibility

Apprentices aged 19 to 30, undergraduates and vocational students resident within Market Harborough including Little Bowden and Great Bowden.

Types of grants

Grants of up to £3,000 for fees and general maintenance.

Annual grant total

In 2011 the trust had assets of £15 million and an income of £584,000. Grants totalling £23,000 were awarded to ten individuals for education.

Applications

On forms available from the correspondent or the website. Applications must be supported by two suitable referees such as an employers, teachers and tutors. Applications for vocational and undergraduate support should be submitted by mid-April with interviews taking place in June.

Keyham

Keyham Educational Foundation

£5,000

Correspondent: David Whitcomb, Chair, Tanglewood, Snows Lane, Leicester, Leicestershire LE7 9JS (01162 595663)

Trustees: Brian Atkin; Richard Windle; David Witcomb; Margaret Hughes; Carole Johnson; John Stanfield.

CC Number: 527965

Eligibility

People up to 25 who live in the parish of Keyham, Leicestershire, who are in need. People who have strong family connections with the parish can also be considered.

Types of grants

One-off grants ranging between £100 and £1,000 for books/equipment, travel, the arts and other educational expenses.

Annual grant total

In 2011 the foundation had an income of £0 and an expenditure of £8,800.

Applications

In writing to the correspondent, to be submitted directly by the individual, for consideration in March and October. Urgent applications can be considered at other times. If the applicant does not live in Keyham, information about their connection with residents should be provided with the application.

Other information

Parish groups are also supported.

Leicester

Alderman Newton's Educational Foundation

£20,000

Correspondent: Jim Munton, Clerk to the Governors, Leicester Charity Link, 20a Millstone Lane, Leicester LE1 5JN (01162 222200; website: www.charity-link.org/alderman-newton)

Trustees: Michael Chamberlin; Cheryl Pharoah; Derek Goodman; Donald Moore; Patricia Mounfield; Pater Taylor; Vivienne Faull; Lynn Moore.

CC Number: 527881

Eligibility

People under 25 years of age who live (or people who have one parent who lives) in the city of Leicester.

Types of grants

Grants are given for educational activities, including social and physical training, to students in need of financial assistance. Grants are also given to assist those preparing to enter a profession or trade. Recent grants have been made towards the cost of school uniforms, other school clothing, books, equipment, instruments, fees and study or travel overseas.

Annual grant total

In 2010/11 the foundation had assets of £3.6 million and an income of £146,000. Grants to individuals and organisations totalled £88,000. Note, the amount given in grants varies each year.

Applications

On an application form, available from the correspondent and from the Leicester Charity Link website. Applications can be submitted directly by the individual and are considered regularly throughout the year.

Other information

The foundation also makes grants to Church of England and other maintained schools in Leicester.

The W. P B. Pearson Bequest

£150

Correspondent: Jason Rollinson, Education Department, Leicester City Council, Malborough House, 38 Welford Road, Leicester LE2 7AA (01162 527753)

Trustee: Leicester City Council.

CC Number: 532263

Eligibility

Pupils who have received their early education at council or denominational schools in the city of Leicester and who proceed to a training college for teachers or to any university or college of higher education.

Types of grants

A non-recurrent award of £30 to £50 to each eligible student to help with college or university fees, to supplement existing grants, or to help those on teacher training courses.

Annual grant total

In 2010/11 the charity had an income of £3,000 and an expenditure of £150.

Applications

Any secondary school in the city of Leicester may write to the correspondent with the names and addresses of recommended students whom they consider meet the criteria. Applications can also be made directly in writing to the correspondent.

Loughborough

The Dawson and Fowler Foundation

£16,000

Correspondent: Lesley Cutler, Clerk to the Trustees, Po Box 73, Loughborough, Leicestershire LE11 0GA (07765 934117; email: dawsonfowler@fsmail.net)

Trustees: Adrian Lungenmuss; Jane Hunt; Albert Dodd; Keiron Shaw; Elliot Harris; Margaret Tomlinson; Ann Maddocks; Ron Jukes; Joanne Wright; Clive Williams; Christine Scoggins; Ayesha Shahid.

CC Number: 527867

Eligibility

People who have lived in the borough of Loughborough (including Hathern) for at least three years and are aged between 11 and 25 years.

Types of grants

School uniform grants – £50 once a year for pupils in years 7, 8, 9, 10 and 11

School grants – Lump sums are given to local senior schools for grants of up to £200 to help with books, equipment/instruments, trips, conferences and interview expenses. The following schools are supported: Loughborough Grammar School; Loughborough High School; Burleigh Community College; Garendon High School; Limehurst High School; Woodbrook Vale High School; De Lisle Catholic Science College; Rawlins Community College and Our Lady's Convent School.

Other grants – Grants for students in higher education; apprentices, young people involved in Scouts or Guiding, sports activities, Duke of Edinburgh Awards and other volunteering that requires a uniform.

Annual grant total

In 2011 grantmaking totalled £16,000, broken down as follows:

- Scholarships and grants: endowed schools: £3,500
- Grants to state schools: £5,200
- Other grants for course: £550
- Uniform grants: £6,800

Exclusions

No grants are given for accommodation, subsistence, day to day travelling costs, tuition, examination fees or crèche costs. Applications from groups of students or classes of pupils cannot be considered.

Applications

On a form available from the correspondent or a school office. The trustees meet quarterly so applications should be made well in advance to avoid disappointment. The school uniform subcommittee considers uniform application in July or August prior to the start of the academic year.

Other information

The trustees have stated that they would like to encourage independent applications.

Market Overton

Market Overton Charity

£0

Correspondent: M Crowther, Trustee, 6 The Limes, Market Overton, Oakham LE15 7PX (01572 767779)

Trustees: Michael Crowther; Alan Lane.

CC Number: 242932

Eligibility

People in need who live in the parish of Market Overton.

Types of grants

One-off grants of up to £250 for those in need, typically for help towards replacement domestic appliances, but also help towards education needs e.g. school educational visits.

Annual grant total

In 2010 the charity had an income of about £400. Since 2008 the total expenditure has been zero.

Applications

In writing to the correspondent. Applications can be submitted directly by the individual or through a social worker, Citizens Advice, Church or other welfare agency. They are considered at any time.

Mountsorrel

Mountsorrel Educational Fund

£98,000 (148 grants)

Correspondent: Paul Blakemore, Clerk to the Trustees, c/o KDB Bookkeeping Ltd, 21 Hollytree Close, Hoton, Loughborough LE12 7SE (01509 889369; website: mountsorrelunitedcharities.co.uk)

Trustees: David Allard; Linda Tyman; Joan Valerie; Peter Hodson; Peter Osborne; Frederick Newitt; Geoffrey Whitaker; K. C. Emmett; Nina Ladner; Sandra Utteridge; Trevor Wright.

CC Number: 527912

Eligibility

People under 25 who have been, or have a parent who has been, resident in the parish of Mountsorrel for at least a year. Preference is given to pupils and former pupils of Christ Church and St Peter's Church of England School.

Types of grants

One-off and recurring grants of £100 to £1,000.

Annual grant total

In 2010/11 the fund had assets of £94,000 and an income of £78,000 (the fund's income is provided by Mountsorrel United Charities). Grants to individuals totalled £98,000, broken down as follows:

- Higher education and training: 77 grants totalling £84,000
- A-level college students: 38 grants totalling £6,000
- Music education: 15 grants totalling £3,400
- Other grants: 18 grants totalling £4,200

Applications

In writing to the correspondent, or via the website. The trustees meet twice a year in November and April.

Other information

Grants to a local school totalled £14,000 in 2010.

Oadby

The Oadby Educational Foundation

£16,000

Correspondent: Rodney Waterfield, 2 Silverton Road, Oadby, Leicester LE2 4NN (01162 714507)

Trustees: Mrs Gore; Robert Borthwick; Gillian Austen; Kay Relf; Michael Rusk; Michael Thornton; Paul Webster; Donald Smith; Rodeny Waterfield.

CC Number: 528000

Eligibility

People with a home address within the former urban district of Oadby and were educated in Oadby.

Types of grants

One-off grants in the range of £50 and £200 are made to schoolchildren, college students and undergraduates, including those towards uniforms/clothing, study/travel abroad and equipment/instruments.

(ii) People of any age can receive one-off grants towards expeditions and voluntary work such as Operation Raleigh or Voluntary Service Overseas.

Grants are in the range of £50 and £200.

Annual grant total

In 2011 the foundation had assets of £1 million and an income of £46,000. £16,000 was given in educational grants and no grants for welfare were made during the year.

Applications

On a form available from the correspondent. They should be submitted either through the individual's school, college or educational welfare agency, or directly by the individual. They are considered on the second Friday in March, June and October (the deadline for grants to undergraduates is 1 October). Applicants must have a home address in the parish of Oadby.

Other information

Grants are also made to organisations.

Peatling Parva

Richard Bradgate's Charity

£1,000

Correspondent: Brian Higginson, The Old Rectory, Main Street, Peatling Parva, Leicester LE17 5QA (01162 478240)

Trustees: Alan Tacy; Brian Higginson; Raymond Hanson.

CC Number: 217379

Eligibility

People living in the parish of Peatling Parva.

Types of grants

Help for students in further and higher education towards books or help with fees/living expenses or for people starting work for books and equipment/instruments.

Annual grant total

Grants total about £1,000 each year.

Applications

In writing to the correspondent. Applications are usually considered in October/November.

Smisby

The Smisby Parochial Charity

£500

Correspondent: Mrs S Heap, Clerk, Cedar Lawns, Forties Lane, Smisby, Ashby-De-La-Zouch, Leicestershire LE65 2SN (01530 414179)

Trustees: Barbara Ball; Jeffrey Barnes; Peter Heap; Andrew Parnham.

CC Number: 515251

Eligibility

People in need who live in Smisby.

Types of grants

Grants are given to schoolchildren, people starting work, further and higher education students, mature students and postgraduates towards books and equipment. Grants are in the range of £10 and £500.

Annual grant total

About £1,500 to individuals, mostly for welfare purposes.

Applications

In writing to the correspondent.

Wigston

The Norton, Salisbury and Brailsford Educational Foundation

£1,300

Correspondent: Debbie Watson, Oadby and Wigston Borough Council, Station Road, Wigston, Leicester LE18 2DR (01162 572680)

Trustees: Orson Lucas; Garth Boulter; Layton Curtis; Marion Daetwyler; Patrick Thacker; Shirley Spence; Michael Charlesworth; Joy Heskins.

CC Number: 527930

Eligibility

People under the age of 25 who live in Wigston.

Types of grants

One-off grants towards the cost of books, tools, equipment and travel, including travel abroad.

Annual grant total

About £1,000.

Applications

On a form available from the correspondent. Applications are considered three times a year, usually in March, September and November.

Wymeswold

The Wymeswold Parochial Charities

£2,000

Correspondent: The Trustees, 94 Brook Street, Wymeswold, Loughborough LE12 6TU (01509 880538)

Trustees: Sandra Brown; Nicholas Shaw; Mr C. Collington; Mr J. Mills.

CC Number: 213241

Eligibility

People in need who have lived in Wymeswold for the last two years.

Types of grants

One-off grants are given for educational and relief-in-need purposes.

Annual grant total

Grants total about £4,000 per year.

Applications

In writing to the correspondent at any time.

Lincolnshire

The Alenson and Erskine Educational Foundation

£4,000

Correspondent: Grants Secretary, Crooks Cottage, Wrangle Bank, Wrangle, Boston PE22 9DL (01205 270352; email: wranglepc@aol.com)

Trustees: Betty Parker; Christine Bowles; Frank Pickett; George Danby; Jenny Hampstead; John Edwards; Rose Tulpin; Peter Featherstone; Susan Jaques; Christine Lockey; Geoff Barnett.

CC Number: 527671

Eligibility

People who live in the parishes of Wrangle, Old Leake and New Leake and are under 25. Applications are only considered from local people who have resided for at least five years in the parish.

Types of grants

Grants vary and are given to: (i) school leavers to help with books, equipment, clothing or travel; (ii) college or university students to help with fees or

to supplement existing grants, but not to travel or study abroad.

Schoolchildren, other than those with special education needs, are only considered if family difficulties are serious.

Annual grant total

In 2010 the trust had an income of £3,400 and an expenditure of £4,300. The trust has previously stated that the grant total varies from year to year.

Applications

In writing to the correspondent. Applicants can only claim for what they have bought and not what they would like to buy and so must submit receipts with the application, which are usually considered in October/November.

Allen's Charity (Apprenticing Branch)

£4,500

Correspondent: Keith Savage, Lenton Lodge, 94 Wignals Gate, Holbeach, Spalding PE12 7HR (01406 490157)

Trustees: John Clarey; David Dewsberry; Diana Tavner; Ruth Barber; Charles Neaverson; Ivor Peacock; Revd Sibley; June Baker; Theresa Watts.

CC Number: 527627

Eligibility

Young people who live in Long Sutton and Sutton Bridge.

Types of grants

Grants for apprentices.

Annual grant total

In 2010 the charity had both an income and expenditure of £5,000.

Applications

On a form available from the correspondent. The scheme is advertised in the local press and is promoted by local employers.

Cowell and Porrill

£7,000

Correspondent: Roger Hooton, 33 Glen Drive, Boston, Lincolnshire PE21 7QB (01205 310088)

Trustees: Jane Moore; Bernard Bell; Robert Bell; Neil Sharpe; Rona Wright; Andrew Higginson.

CC Number: 240438

Eligibility

People under 25 who live or whose parent(s) live in the parishes of Benington and Leverton, at any level or stage of their education and undertaking the study of any subject.

Types of grants

Grants of £250 to £600 for general educational needs.

Annual grant total

In 2011 the trust had an income of £12,000 and an expenditure of £13,000. Grants have previously totalled £7,000 a year.

Applications

On a form available from the correspondent, to be submitted by the end of July for consideration in September each year. Applications should be submitted directly by the individual.

Gainsborough Educational Charity

£7,000

Correspondent: Maria Bradley, Clerk to the Trustees, Burton and Dyson Solicitors, 22 Market Place, Gainsborough, Lincolnshire DN21 2BZ (01427 610761; fax: 01427 616866; email: law@burtondyson.co.uk)

Trustees: Bernard Stonehouse; Patricia Greatorex; William Parry; Alistair Heppenstall; Judith Rainsforth; Susan Ritchie; David Tinsley.

CC Number: 527299

Eligibility

People of at least secondary school age and under 25 who live, or whose parents live, in the former urban district council area of Gainsborough or the parishes of Thonock, Morton and Lea and are in need.

Types of grants

Grants are given to schoolchildren, further and higher education students, postgraduates and people starting work, including those for uniforms/other school clothing, books, equipment/ instruments, fees, educational outings in the UK and study or travel abroad. Grants can also be made for the study of music or other arts.

Annual grant total

In 2010/11 the charity had an income of £5,600 and a total expenditure of £7,800.

Applications

On a form available from the correspondent for consideration in March and November; applications can be submitted directly by the individual up to three weeks prior to this. References are required.

The Hesslewood Children's Trust (Hull Seamen's and General Orphanage)

See entry on page 156

The Kirton-in-Lindsey Exhibition Endowment

£2,500

Correspondent: Penelope Hoey, Woodbine Cottage, 6 Queen Street, Kirton-in-Lindsey, Gainsborough, Lincolnshire DN21 4NS (01652 640075)

Trustees: Hazel Robinson; Ian Fowler; Joan Lacey; Victoria Halmshaw; Roger Warwick; Paul Metheringham.

CC Number: 529749

Eligibility

People who live in Kirton-in-Lindsey, Hibaldstow, Redbourne or Manton, Messingham, Blyborough or Waddingham, Grayingham, Northorpe or Scotter and Scotton and have attended one of the following primary schools for at least two years: Kirton-in-Lindsey, Scotter, Messingham, Waddingham or Hibaldstow.

Types of grants

Grants to help with the cost of books and other essentials for schoolchildren/ mature students going on to college, university or teacher training.

Annual grant total

In 2010/11 the foundation had an income of £2,900 and an expenditure of £3,600. Grants to individuals usually total about £2,500 each year.

Applications

On a form available from the correspondent to be submitted before 1 September.

Kitchings Educational Charity

£4,000

Correspondent: M Sankey, 50 Station Road, Bardney, Lincolnshire LN3 5UD (01526 398555)

Trustees: M. Sankey; Barry Percival; B. Taylor; Peter Butcher; Jane Hornsby; K. Hutchinson.

CC Number: 527707

Eligibility

People under 25 who live in Bardney, Bucknall, Southrey or Tupholme.

Types of grants

Grants to further and higher education students to assist with books, equipment/instruments, fees and other educational expenses.

Annual grant total

In 2010/11 the charity had both an income and expenditure of £8,700.

Exclusions

No support is given to students who choose to take A-levels (or equivalent) at college when they could take the same course at their school.

Applications

In writing to the correspondent. Applications can be submitted either through the individual's school, college, educational welfare agency or directly by the individual. They are considered in October and should be received by the end of September.

Other information

The charity also gives grants to two local primary schools.

The Kitchings General Charity

£4,000

Correspondent: J Smith, Secretary, 42 Abbey Road, Bardney, Lincoln LN3 5XA (01526 398505)

Trustees: M. Sankey; Maurice Bellwood; Barry Percival; Geoffrey Pacey; Richard Muxlow; Robert Armstrong; Marjorie Cash; Elizabeth Franklin.

CC Number: 219957

Eligibility

Students, especially mature (over 25 years of age), part-time, and vocational students, living in the parish of Bardney (covers Stainfield, Apley, Southrey, Tupholme and Bucknall).

Types of grants

Grants are given for playgroup fees, books, excursions, uniforms and sports equipment. Grants are in the range of £200 and £500 but can be up to £1,000.

Annual grant total

In 2011 the trust had an income of £4,000 and made educational grants totalling £4,000.

Applications

In writing to the correspondent giving details of age, course name, college and brief description of education to date. Applications are considered in May, October and January.

Other information

Grants are also given to local schools and organisations, and to individuals for welfare purposes.

The Kochan Trust

£14,900

Correspondent: Revd Roger Massingberd-Mundy, Secretary to the Trustees, The Old Post-Office, West Raynham, Fakenham, Norfolk NR21 7AD (01328 838611)

Trustees: Robert Blake; Roger Massingberd-Mundy; Sarah Bruce-Gardyne; James Hoff.

CC Number: 1052976

Eligibility

People living in Lincolnshire who are in need of financial assistance for their study of the creative arts, music or veterinary medicine.

Types of grants

One-off grants according to need, e.g. towards concerts or instruments for students of the creative arts and music, or towards research projects or general course expenses for veterinary students.

Annual grant total

In 2010/11 the trust made grants to four veterinary students totalling £6,000 with a further £8,900 being paid in grants for music tuition and instruments

Applications

In writing to the correspondent initially, either directly by the individual or through the individual's school/college/ educational welfare agency, with brief details about who you are and what you would like the grant for. An application form is then sent out. Applications are considered January, April, July and November.

Lincolnshire Community Foundation

£12,000

Correspondent: Sue Fortune, Grants Manager, 4 Mill House, Moneys Yard, Carre Street, Sleaford, Lincolnshire NG34 7TW (01529 305825; email: lincolnshirecf@btconnect.com; website: www.lincolnshirecf.co.uk)

Trustees: Charles Richard Ferens; Stephen Cousins; David Close; Jean Burton; Margaret Serna; Bernadette Jones, Dr Cheryl Berry; Jane Hiles; Paul Scott; Lizzie Milligan-Manby.

CC Number: 1092328

Eligibility

People in need in Lincolnshire although eligibility differs depending on the scheme applied for, see the types of grants section.

Types of grants

Funds currently administered by the foundation include:

- Make A Start (MAST) – grants of up to £250 for people aged 16 and over in receipt of benefits or working no more than 16 hours a week to assist with re-entry into employment, education or training
- Thonock Trust – grants of up to £200 to help with costs associated with work or training, for example, course materials, uniforms, transport and training costs. Applicants must be resident in Gainsborough, Corringham, Blyton, Springthorpe or Lea

Annual grant total

Grants from the MAST Fund totalled £12,000. No figures were available for the Thonock Trust.

Exclusions

Grants cannot be awarded retrospectively.

Applications

For the MAST scheme applications are usually made by registering interest with the correspondent who will then organise an assessment.

Application forms are available to download from the website for the Thonock Trust. Applications are considered twice a year and the deadlines are 1 June and 15 November.

Be aware that like other community foundations schemes can open and close at very short notice. Check the website before applying.

The Mapletoft Scholarship Foundation

£3,000

Correspondent: Patrick Purves, The Old Vicarage, Church Street, Louth, Lincolnshire LN11 9DE (01507 605883; email: pmp@bmcf.co.uk)

Trustees: Jean Johnson; Jean Robinson; Joseph Gibson; Trevor Smith; Peter Pettifer; Karen Smith; Alan McKinnell.

CC Number: 527649

Eligibility

People who have attended primary school in the parishes of North Thoresby, Grainsby and Waite, for not less than two years.

Types of grants

Grants up to about £150 to help with further/higher education books and fees/living expenses or to supplement existing grants. Travel grants are also available. Grants are recurrent.

Annual grant total

In 2010/11 the foundation had an income of £2,800 and an expenditure of £3,900.

Applications

Applications should be received no later than 30 September for consideration in November.

Sir Thomas Middlecott's Exhibition Foundation

£20,000

Correspondent: Frank Wilson, Clerk to the Board of Governors, 57a Bourne Road, Spalding, Lincolnshire PE11 1JR (01775 766117; email: info@ middlecotttrust.org.uk; website: www. middlecotttrust.org.uk)

Trustees: Cyril Baker; David Chester; David May; Margaret Welberry; Michael Priestley; Peter Ullyatt; Trevor Blackamore; Carol Lidgett; Ann Yates; Gary Morgan; Stephen Johnson.

CC Number: 527283

Eligibility

Students who live in the parishes of Algarkirk, Fosdyke, Frampton, Kirton, Sutterton and Wyberton in Lincolnshire, who are in further/higher education and are aged under 25. Applicants must have attended a maintained primary school in the area for at least two years.

Types of grants

Grants are given to students in further/higher education towards books, clothing and equipment/instruments.

Annual grant total

In 2010/11 the trust had assets of £726,000 and an income of £33,000. Grants were made totalling £20,000.

Applications

On a form available from the correspondent, or from the foundation's website, to be submitted directly by the individual via post. Applications are considered in October and should be submitted by the end of September.

Mary Parnham's Lenton Charity

£0

Correspondent: F P J Grenfell, Lenton House, Ingoldsby Road, Lenton, Grantham, Lincolnshire NG33 4HB

Trustees: Francis Grenfell; Betty Richardson; Priscilla Allen; Richard Ireson.

CC Number: 512303

Eligibility

People under 23 who live in the parishes of Lenton, Keisby and Osgodby.

Types of grants

Help with the cost of books, clothing and other essentials for schoolchildren. Help may also be available for those at college or university and those undertaking apprenticeships or other professional training. Preference is given to people with special educational needs and to schoolchildren with serious family difficulties so the child has to be educated away from home.

Annual grant total

The charity has an income of around £500 a year. The correspondent has informed us that no grants have been made in recent years as the charity is trying to build up its assets.

Applications

The charity has previously stated that it is trying to build up its asset fund so that it 'will continue to survive'.

Phillips Charity

£2,500

Correspondent: Keith Savage, Clerk, Lenton Lodge, 94 Wignals Gate, Holbeach, Spalding, Lincolnshire PE12 7HR (01406 490157)

Trustees: Ivor Peacock; Revd Sibley; Teresa Watts.

CC Number: 213843

Eligibility

People living in the parishes of Long Sutton, Little Sutton and Sutton Bridge, aged between 11 and 20.

Types of grants

Grants of up to £200 are given: (i) to schoolchildren for books, equipment, clothing or travel; (ii) to students in further/higher education towards the cost of books and travel or study overseas; and (iii) for help with the study of music and the other arts, as well as for overseas study.

Annual grant total

In 2011 the charity had an income of £4,500 and an expenditure of £4,100. Around £2,500 a year is given in grants to individuals.

Exclusions

Grants are not given for school fees or maintenance, student fees/living expenses or for people starting work.

Applications

On a form available from the correspondent. They are considered at trustees' meetings usually held in July and September.

The Pike and Eure Educational Foundation

£2,500

Correspondent: Susan Smith, Clerk to the Trustees, Susan Smith, 18 Oxford Close, Washingborough, Lincoln LN4 1DT (01522 792406)

Trustees: Stephen Jones-Crabtree; Elizabeth Bland; Terry Gibbon; Philip Hyde; Elaine Hutton; Peter Trevelyan; Jane Dunning; Gilbert Griffin; Ron Oxby; Robert Dowlman.

CC Number: 527725

Eligibility

Young people between the ages of 16 and 25 who are in need and live in the parishes of Washingborough and Heighington in Lincolnshire.

Types of grants

One-off grants for students in further or higher education or apprenticeships towards books, equipment/instruments, scholarships. The foundation also makes grants to young people who need assistance to participate in sport and other outdoor related activities.

Annual grant total

In 2011 the trust had an income of £4,500 and an expenditure of £2,700.

Exclusions

People starting work are not eligible.

Applications

On a form available from the correspondent, submitted directly by the individual, with information about the nature of the course, location, and the occupation of the parent(s). Applications should be submitted in early August for consideration in October.

The Educational Foundation of Philip and Sarah Stanford

£3,000

Correspondent: Eleanor Hine, Clerk, 86 Brigsley Road, Waltham, Grimsby, South Humberside DN37 0LA (01472 827883)

Trustees: Dennis Read; Brian Lingard; Ray Mawer; Michael Hodgins; Patrick Anderson; Peter Mills; Philip Bray; Melanie Dickerson; Nigel Morrison; Andrew Poppleton; Ray Sutton; Margaret Cracknell.

CC Number: 529755

Eligibility

People under 25 who live in the ancient parishes of Aylesby, Barnoldby-le-Beck, Bradley, Irby-upon-Humber and Laceby.

Types of grants

Grants of £60 to £100 towards books, clothing or equipment/instruments for college students and undergraduates.

Annual grant total

In 2011 the foundation had an income of £15,000 and an expenditure of £7,000.

Exclusions

Grants are not given for subjects and courses available in schools, nor for help with student fees, travel or living expenses.

Applications

On a form available from the correspondent, submitted directly by the individual, including reasons for the application and plans for the future. The closing date is 1 October each year. Applications must be in the applicant's own handwriting.

Other information

Grants are also made to organisations and the foundation provides bibles and food vouchers.

The Sutton St James United Charities

£8,000

Correspondent: Keith Savage, Clerk, Lenton Lodge, 94 Wignals Gate, Holbeach, Spalding, Lincolnshire PE12 7HR (01406 490157; email: keithsavage@btinternet.com)

Trustees: Brian Sadd; Alison Campling; Elaine Harrison; Christopher Gaff; Mathew Ellis; John Garner; Philip Newton.

CC Number: 527757

Eligibility

People under 25 who are in need and live in the parish of Sutton St James and the surrounding area.

Types of grants

(i) Grants, of up to £100, to all pupils living in the village at age 11 when transferring to secondary schools, to help with books, equipment, clothing etc. (ii) Grants, of up to £100, to help students aged 16 who are taking A-levels and further education courses. (iii) Grants, of up to £600 a year, to students entering university to help with general expenses and to supplement existing grants.

Help is also given to people entering a trade or profession.

Annual grant total

In 2010/11 the charities had an income of £17,000 and a total expenditure of £16,000. Grants are made for educational and welfare purposes.

Applications

On a form available from the correspondent. Applications are considered in April/May for primary schoolchildren and December/January for A-level and university students.

Dame Margaret Thorold's Apprenticing Charity

£1,500

Correspondent: Jackie Watts, Clerk, Tallents Solicitors, 2 Westgate, Southwell NG25 0JJ (01636 813411)

Trustees: Diana Thorold; G. Wade; Terry Jones; Andrew Watson; Kayleigh Moor.

CC Number: 527628

Eligibility

People aged 18 to 25, who live in the ancient parishes of Sedgebrook, Marston and Cranwell.

Types of grants

Small cash grants to assist students in further or higher education, especially vocational training. Grants may be recurrent or one-off and are towards books, fees/living expenses or study/travel abroad.

Annual grant total

About £1,500 per year.

Applications

Applications should be submitted in writing by the individual or parent/guardian or through the school/college/educational welfare agency, by mid-January for consideration in February. If appropriate, a letter of support from the employer or place of training should be included with the application.

Barkston

The Barkston Educational Foundation

£4,000

Correspondent: T S Kelway, Clerk, Tallents, 2 Westgate, Southwell, Nottinghamshire NG25 0JJ (01636 813411; email: tim.kelway@tallents.co.uk)

Trustees: Herbert Wheat; Celia Salwey; Richard Watson; N. Reynolds; Andrew Lane.

CC Number: 527724

Eligibility

People under 25 who live or whose parents live in the parish of Barkston.

Types of grants

One-off and recurrent grants for educational purposes, according to need.

Annual grant total

In 2010/11 the trust had an income of £6,700 and an expenditure of £4,800.

Applications

In writing to the correspondent.

Boston

The Sutterton Education Trust

£2,500

Correspondent: Deirdre McCumiskey, 6 Hillside Gardens, Wittering, Peterborough PE8 6DX (01780 782668)

Trustees: Joy Gadd; Cyril Baker; Richard Leggott; John Thorpe; Elizabeth Thorpe; Rachel Hunn; David de Varny; Aaron Spencer.

CC Number: 527771

Eligibility

People in need who live in parishes of Sutterton or Ambellhill in Boston.

Types of grants

Grants of between £50 and £200 are available for: (i) uniforms, school clothing, books and educational outings for schoolchildren; (ii) books, fees, living expenses, study or travel abroad for students in further/higher education, but not overseas students or student exchange; and (iii) books, travel and fees for mature students, but not childcare. Each case is considered individually.

Annual grant total

About £2,500.

Applications

In writing to the correspondent.

Corby Glenn

The Willoughby Memorial Trust

£0

Correspondent: Timothy Paul Clarke, Estate Office, Grimsthorpe, Bourne, Lincolnshire PE10 0LY (01778 591205)

Trustees: John Kirkman; Nancy Willoughby de Eresby.

CC Number: 527647

Eligibility

People who live in the Corby Glen area of Lincolnshire.

Types of grants

Grants to promote the study, education and knowledge of people in the Corby Glen area.

Annual grant total

In 2011 the fund had assets of £719,000, an income of £37,000 and made no grants to individuals.

Applications

On a form available from the correspondent, to be submitted by the individual's headteacher.

Other information

This trust mainly gives grants to schools and organisations, although it budgets a small amount each year for grants to individuals.

Deeping

The Deeping St James United Charities

£7,300

Correspondent: Julie Banks, Clerk, The Institute, 38 Church Street, Deeping St James, Lincolnshire PE6 8HD (01778 344707 (Tues/Thurs 9am-12pm); email: dsjunitedcharities@btconnect.com; website: www.dsjunitedcharities.org.uk)

Trustees: Kate Shinkins; Phil Dilks; Ray Auger; Revd Janet Donaldson; Carol Precey; Judy Stevens; Trevor Harwood; Peter Francis Ward; Graham Thompson; Les Bullock.

CC Number: 248848

Eligibility

School, college and university students from the parish of St James, Deeping.

Types of grants

All young university (or equivalent) students are given an annual grant towards the cost of their studies for three years. The grant may be used for books or equipment needed for study towards a degree or vocational qualification, such as scissors for hairdressing or knives for a chef, for example.

In order to qualify, applicants should normally be aged 18 to 25 years, be studying for their first degree or college qualification and be resident in Deeping St James (including Frognall).

Grants are also made to schoolchildren in the three local schools to enable them to take part in activities which they may not otherwise experience, including school trips, as well as the expense of school uniforms.

Annual grant total

In 2011 the charities had assets of £2.5 million and an income of £75,000. Educational grants totalled £7,300.

Applications

Application forms for third-level grants may be downloaded from the website and returned to the Institute. For those entering higher education in the autumn applications should be submitted as soon your place and qualifications have been confirmed.

Applications for schoolchildren should be directed to the school and not the Institute.

Other information

This trust also gives grants to individuals for relief-in-need purposes and local organisations.

Dorrington

Dorrington Welfare Charity

£500

Correspondent: Mrs Susan Tong, Penneshaw Farm, Sleaford Road, Dorrington, Lincoln LN4 3PU (01526 833395; email: susantong@btinternet.com)

Trustees: John Fox; Frank Cheffings; Ruth Blackbourn; Peter Eastwood; Susan Tong.

CC Number: 216927

Eligibility

People under the age of 25 who have lived in the village of Dorrington for at least a year.

Types of grants

Traditionally one-off grants have been made in amounts of up to £200.

Annual grant total

Grants usually total around £1,000 per year.

Applications

In writing to the correspondent or any trustee directly by the individual. Applications are considered at any time.

Fleet

The Deacon and Fairfax Educational Foundation

£1,500

Correspondent: Jill Harrington, 11 West End, Holbeam, Lincolnshire PE12 7LW (01406 426739)

Trustees: Donald Waltham; Jane King.

CC Number: 527639

Eligibility

People who live in the parish of Fleet (Lincolnshire), aged between 16 and 25 and attending further education.

Types of grants

Grants are given to further and higher education students, including those for clothing, books, equipment/instruments and fees.

Annual grant total

In 2010 the foundation had an income of £3,200 and an expenditure of £3,000.

Applications

In writing to the correspondent directly by the individual. Applications are considered in October and should be received in August or September.

Other information

Grants are also made to schools in the area.

Frampton

The Frampton Educational Foundation

£3,000

Correspondent: Mark Hildred, Moore Thompson, Bank House, Broad Street, Spalding, Lincolnshire PE11 1TB (01775 711333)

Trustees: Wendy Cope; Peter Udy; Myra Scott; Ted King; John Cooper; Colin Semmelroth.

CC Number: 527784

Eligibility

People who have lived in the ancient parish of Frampton for at least five years.

Types of grants

One-off and recurrent grants according to need.

Annual grant total

In 2010/11 the foundation had an income of £5,500 and an expenditure of £3,600.

Applications

In writing to the correspondent. Applications are considered in early October and students must reapply each year.

Other information

Grants are also given to local schools.

Gainsborough

The Tyler Educational Foundation

£5,000

Correspondent: Mrs E M Bradley, 22 Market Place, Gainsborough, Lincolnshire DN21 2BZ (01427 010761)

Trustees: Peter Blagg; Derrick Hill; Hilary Churchman; Matthew Gleadell; Alan Clapham.

CC Number: 527691

Eligibility

People under 21 who live in Morton and Thornock and are in financial need, with a preference for Church of England Christians.

Types of grants

Grants for educational purposes.

Annual grant total

In 2010/11 the foundation had an income of £8,600 and an expenditure of £5,700.

Applications

In writing to the correspondent.

Holbeach

The Farmer Educational Foundation

£10,000

Correspondent: M J H Griffin, Hurdletree Farm, Hurdletree Bank, Whaplode, Spalding, Lincolnshire PE12 6SS (01406 540424; email: griff@hurdletree.orangehome.co.uk)

Trustees: Martin Howard; Samuel Mossop; Terence Harrington; J. C. Woolley; B. Dobbs; Elizabeth Bailey; John Wickstead; Stephen Baragwanath; Christopher Penney; Jenny Worth; Paul Brighton.

CC Number: 527636

Eligibility

People who live in the parish of Holbeach, South Lincolnshire, and are above the statutory school-leaving age.

Types of grants

Grants, to a usual maximum of about £100, to help students in higher/further education and to assist schools serving Holbeach with projects.

Annual grant total

In 2010/11 the trust had an income of £25,000 and an expenditure of £27,000. Grants to individuals usually total around £20,000 per annum.

Applications

On a form available from Holbeach Library, to be submitted by the individual at the end of August. Applications are considered in September.

Horncastle

George Jobson's Trust

£7,500

Correspondent: Sarah Steel, Chattertons, 5 South Street, Horncastle LN9 6DS (01507 522456)

Trustees: Monica Smith; Bill Emerson; Jack Simpson; Nigel Bartle; Ian Bye.

CC Number: 213875

Eligibility

Young people in need who attend or have attended schools in Horncastle or live in the parish of Horncastle.

Types of grants

Recurrent grants between £50 and £500 for general education costs.

Annual grant total

In 2010/11 the trust had assets of £1 million and an income of £61,000. Grants to individuals totalled £7,500.

Exclusions

No grants are given to postgraduate students.

Applications

On a form available from the correspondent. Applications can be submitted directly by the individual or through a social worker, Citizens Advice or other welfare agency.

Other information

Grants are also made to organisations.

Kesteven

The Kesteven Children in Need

£500

Correspondent: Mrs Alexandra Howard, Ram Farm, Bloxholm Lane, Nocton Heath, Lincoln LN4 2AH (01522 722701; email: enquiries@kcin.org; website: www.kcin.org)

Trustees: Lucy Lee; Sarah Robertson; Sue Knott; Tracey Bridges-Webb; Alexandra Howard; Erica Spurrier; Katherine Robertson; Stephanie Thorne.

CC Number: 700008

Eligibility

Children/young people up to the age of 16 who live in Kesteven.

Types of grants

Grants of up to £500 towards books, clothing and educational outings.

Annual grant total

In 2010 the charity had an income of £21,000 and a total expenditure of £17,500. Previously the majority of grants were made for welfare purposes (about £19,000), with an additional £500 given for educational purposes.

Applications

Generally through local social workers, health visitors, teachers and education officers. Information should include the family situation, the age of the child and his/her special needs. Applications are considered throughout the year.

Lincoln

The Leeke Church Schools and Educational Foundation

£59,000

Correspondent: Carolyn Goddard, Clerk and Grants Officer, 5 Woburn Avenue, Lincoln LN1 3HJ (01522 522058; email: leeke@idnet.co.uk)

Trustees: Jeanette Davies; Derek James; David Edgar; Kate McLean-Mair; Pippa Duce; Christine-Anne Talbot; Clive Young; James Hillyer; John Davies; Patricia Cowie; Margaret Campion; Steve Rudman; Jayne Arnold; Michael Marsden.

CC Number: 527654

Eligibility

People under 25 years old who live, or whose parents live, in the city of Lincoln. People studying in Lincoln with a home address elsewhere are ineligible.

Types of grants

One-off and recurrent grants in the range of £150 to £500 each term. Grants are given to: schoolchildren for educational outings in the UK, study or travel abroad and student exchanges; and further and higher education students for uniforms, books, equipment/ instruments, fees, educational outings in the UK, study or travel abroad and student exchanges. Grants are not given for private education – there must be a financial need.

Annual grant total

In 2008/09 the foundation had assets of £432,000 and an income of £53,000. Grants made to individuals totalled £59,000.

Applications

On a form available from the correspondent to be submitted by the individual for consideration at any time. Educational costs should be listed, and either the real amount given, or a fair estimate.

Other information

The foundation also made four grants to schools totalling £10,000 in 2010/11.

Lindsey

The Joseph Nickerson Charitable Foundation

£8,000

Correspondent: Eric White, Villa Office, Rothwell, Market Rasen, Lincolnshire LN7 6BJ (01472 371216; email: j.n. farms@farmingline.com)

Trustees: M. S. Edmundson; Peter Braithwaite; William Emms; Eugenie Nickerson.

CC Number: 276429

Eligibility

Young people in further education in the old county of Lindsey. Beneficiaries are usually aged 18 or over and are studying at university.

Types of grants

Recurrent grants of about £900 a year, donated in three tranches.

Annual grant total

The trust had a total expenditure of £21,000 in 2010/11. About £8,000 is usually given to individuals for educational purposes.

Applications

In writing to the correspondent. Applications for grants starting in September should be made by 30 June for consideration in July.

Moulton

The Moulton Poors' Lands Charity

£1,000

Correspondent: Richard Lewis, Clerk, Maples and Son Solicitors, 23 New Road, Spalding, Lincolnshire PE11 1DH (01775 722261)

Trustees: John Grimwood; Tom Charlton; David Buck; Derek Thorpe; John Biggadike; Peter Dean; Robert Oldershaw; Pamela Pates; John Barnett.

CC Number: 216630

Eligibility

People in need, generally older people, who live in the civil parish of Moulton.

Types of grants

Mainly relief-in-need grants, very occasional education grants are available.

Annual grant total

In 2011 the trust had an income of £24,000 and an expenditure of £31,000. Previously grants to individuals have totalled £9,000.

Applications

In writing to the correspondent, usually through a trustee. Applications are considered in April and December.

Navenby

The Navenby Towns Farm Trust

£5,000

Correspondent: Mr Leonard Coffey, Secretary, 17 North Lane, Navenby, Lincoln LN5 0EH (01522 810273)

Trustees: Leonard Coffey; Jennifer Playford; Peter Welbourne; Brian Henderson; Ruth Sharp.

CC Number: 245233

Eligibility

University students and young people doing their A-levels who are in need and live in the village of Navenby.

Types of grants

Recurrent grants while at university, but only following reapplication every year.

Annual grant total

About £11,000 to individuals and organisations.

Exclusions

No grants can be given outside the village.

Applications

On a form available from the correspondent, the post-office, or Smith and Willows the newsagents. Applications are considered in September. Unsolicited applications are not responded to.

Other information

Grants are also made for welfare purposes.

North Lincolnshire

The Withington Education Trust

£1,000

Correspondent: Stephen Piper, Education Office, North Lincolnshire Council, PO Box 35, Brigg, South Humberside DN20 8XJ (01724 297200)

Trustees: James Wheat; John Fitzgerald; Ben Lawrence; Judith Gray; Michelle Travers; Stephen Piper.

CC Number: 507975

Eligibility

People under the age of 21 who live in the area of the new North Lincolnshire Council (comprising Scunthorpe, Glanford and Boothferry).

Types of grants

Grants to help with fees/living expenses, travel and other education needs, but not normally books or equipment. Grants to assist with non-formal education such as music and ballet are also given. Grants range from £50 to £300.

Annual grant total

About £1,000.

Exclusions

Grants towards fees for private schooling are not given.

Applications

In writing at any time, preferably supported by the school or college. Applications are considered once per term.

Potterhanworth

The Christ's Hospital Endowment at Potterhanworth

£13,000 (168 grants)

Correspondent: Yvonne Woodcock, The Conifers, Barff Road, Potterhanworth, Lincoln LN4 2DU (01522 790942)

Trustees: Peter Gaskell; Ralph Wilford; Martin Parry; Gordon Lindsay; Geoffrey Mountain; Margaret Pocklington; Marianne Overton.

CC Number: 527669

Eligibility

People under the age of 25 who live, or whose parent(s) live, in the parish of Potterhanworth, Lincolnshire.

Types of grants

Grants are available for the cost of educational visits for schoolchildren and towards fees for extra-curricular activities such as music, the arts and social and physical training. A block grant only is given to further education students.

Annual grant total

In 2010 the trust had assets of £296,000 and an income of £30,000. Grants to individuals totalled £13,000

During the year, 19 grants of £94 were made to further education students and

£180 was used to purchase books for primary school leavers. 149 grants totalling £11,000 were made to individuals for music and dance lessons, sports coaching and lessons and for school trips and playgroup fees.

Exclusions

Grants are not given for other costs for schoolchildren such as books or for school fees, nor for people starting work, other than for equipment.

Applications

In writing to the correspondent, either by the individual, his/her parents, or through the individual's school, college or university. Applications are considered once a year in November and must include valid receipts where applicable. Applications must be received before 31 October.

Other information

The trust also gave some grants to schools and nurseries.

Quadring

The Cowley and Brown School Foundation

£1,000

Correspondent: K J Watts, Clerk, 99 Hawthorne Bank, Spalding, Lincolnshire PE11 1JQ (01775 760911)

Trustees: Ian Walters; Amanda Puttick; Ann Spridgen; Keith Casswell; Thomas Mews; Wendy Simpson.

CC Number: 217099

Eligibility

People under 25 who live in the ancient parish of Quadring.

Types of grants

Grants towards the cost of books, clothing and other essentials for schoolchildren. Help may also be available for students at college or university.

Annual grant total

In 2011 the foundation had an income of £2,200 and an expenditure of £1,900.

Applications

In writing to the correspondent. Applications are considered in July and November.

Scunthorpe

The James R. Heslam Settlement

£2,000

Correspondent: Donald V Johnson, 2 Park Square, Laneham Street, Scunthorpe DN15 6JH (01724 281616; email: don.johnson@sbblaw.com)

Trustees: Donald Johnson; Andrew Horwich.

CC Number: 256464

Eligibility

People in need who live in Scunthorpe.

Types of grants

One-off grants of up to £1,000 towards books, computers, laptops and fees for further education.

Annual grant total

In 2010/11 the trust had an income of £2,300 and an expenditure of £2,000.

Applications

In writing to the correspondent by post or email. Applications must include a CV and details of the applicant's financial situation.

South Holland

The Moulton Harrox Educational Foundation

£500

Correspondent: Richard Lewis, Clerk to the Trustees, Maples and Son Solicitors, 23 New Road, Spalding, Lincolnshire PE11 1DH (01775 722261)

Trustees: William Webb; John Grimwood; Anthony Casson; Paul Winn; Robert Oldershaw; Robin Buck; Thomas Charlton; Ann Willingham; David Mawby; Rosamund Seal; Bob Merchant.

CC Number: 527635

Eligibility

People up to 25 who live in the South Holland district council area.

Types of grants

Grants for school pupils and college students, including mature students, to help with books, equipment, fees, clothing, educational outings and study or travel abroad. Preference is given to schoolchildren with serious family difficulties so the child has to educated away from home, and to people with special education needs.

One-off and recurrent grants according to need. Individuals must reapply in order to receive the grant in the following year.

Annual grant total

Most of the income goes to organisations and schools, with about £500 to individuals.

Applications

On a form available from the correspondent. Applications should be submitted before 31 August for consideration in September.

The Spalding Relief-in-Need Charity

£13,000

Correspondent: R A Knipe, Clerk and Solicitor, Dembleby House, 12 Broad Street, Spalding, Lincolnshire PE11 1ES (01775 768774; email: patrick.skells@ chattertons.com)

Trustees: S. R. Coltman; George Hastings; Cllr Angela Newton; Alexander Walton; Pat Sykes; George Hay; Christopher Longstaff; John Lister; Petronella Keeling; Revd John Bennett; Diane Clay; Elizabeth Sneath.

CC Number: 229268

Eligibility

People in need who live in the area covered by South Holland District Council with priority to residents of the parishes of Spalding, Cowbit, Deeping St Nicholas, Pinchbeck and Weston.

Types of grants

One-off grants in the range of £100 to £400. Normally payments are made directly to suppliers.

Annual grant total

In 2011 the charity had an income of £43,000 and gave grants totalling £31,000, broken down as follows:
- Individuals: £27,000
- Individuals TV licences: £2,400
- Individuals annual grants: £1,500

Applications

On a form available from the charity. Applications can be submitted directly by the individual or assisted if appropriate by a social worker, teacher, school, Citizens Advice, other welfare agency or third party. Grants are considered fortnightly.

Other information

Grants can also be made to organisations and to individuals for welfare purposes.

Stickford

The Stickford Relief-in-Need Charity

£7,500

Correspondent: Katherine Bunting, Clerk, The Old Vicarage, Church Road, Stickford, Boston, Lincolnshire PE22 8EP (01205 480455)

Trustees: Geoffrey Hattersley; Pamela Bryant; Michael Bursnell; Wendy Morely.

CC Number: 247423

Eligibility

Schoolchildren in need who live in the parish of Stickford.

Types of grants

School clothing grants. Grants are also made for welfare purposes.

Annual grant total

About £15,000.

Applications

In writing to the correspondent. Applications should be submitted directly by the individual and are considered all year.

Sutton St Edmund

The Sutton St Edmund Charities United Educational Foundation

£1,000

Correspondent: Jane Ripley, 231 Broadgate, Sutton St Edmund, Spalding, Lincolnshire PE12 0LT (01945 700268)

Trustees: William Webb; Willa Howe; Simon Coates; Margaret Norman; Deborah Rogers; Stamford Matthews; Cynthia Pate.

CC Number: 527706

Eligibility

Children or young people who live in the ancient parish of Sutton St Edmund.

Types of grants

Recurrent grants are given to further and higher education students for books, equipment/instruments, fees and maintenance/living expenses. The amount given in individual grants is dependent on the number of applicants and the amount of available income.

Annual grant total

About £1,000.

Applications

In writing to the correspondent either directly by the individual, or through a parent or guardian including details of the course attended i.e. A-level, NVQ, degree, and so on. Applications should be submitted by mid-February each year and grants are paid in April.

Waddingham

James Thompson's Educational Charity

£3,000

Correspondent: Brian Milton, Trustee, South View, Moor Road, Snitterby, Gainsborough, Lincolnshire DN21 4TT (01673 818314)

Trustees: Brian Milton; Colin Bell; Jackie Burton; David Waite; Dennis Churchill; Andrew Dunsmore.

CC Number: 1039838

Eligibility

People under 25 who live in the parish of Waddingham and are in need.

Types of grants

One-off and recurrent grants ranging from £50 to £250. Grants are given to: schoolchildren towards school uniform, other school clothing, books, equipment/ instruments and educational outings; and vocational students and students in further and higher education towards clothing, books, other equipment, fees/ living expenses and study/travel overseas or in the UK.

Annual grant total

In 2010/11 the trust had both an income and expenditure of £3,200.

Exclusions

No grants to children below primary school age.

Applications

In writing to the correspondent, either directly by the individual or by their parent or guardian, stating who requires the grant and why, the educational establishment attended and the course being studied. Applications are usually considered in September and should be received in August.

Other information

Grants are also given to schools which serve the parish.

Northamp-tonshire

Arnold's Education Foundation

£8,000

Correspondent: Jane Forsyth, 4 Grange Park Court, Roman Way, Grange Park, Northampton NN4 5EA (01604 876697)

Trustees: Ross Northing; Peter White; Ann Slater; Margaret Hooper; Joanna Dickson; Nicholas Hugh Adams; Joan Kirkbridge; Adrian Peter; John Stuart; Ian Brodie.

CC Number: 310590

Eligibility

People in need who are under 25 and live in the parishes of Stony Stratford, Buckinghamshire; Nether Heyford, Upper Heyford, Stowe-Nine-Churches, Weedon Bec, Northamptonshire; and the ancient parish of St Giles, Northampton. Preference for members of the Church of England.

Types of grants

One-off and recurrent grants for educational purposes (including social and physical training). Grants are made: for schoolchildren towards the cost of clothing, books, educational outings, maintenance and school fees; towards the cost of books, fees/living expenses, travel exchange and study or travel abroad for students in further or higher education; and towards books, equipment/instruments, clothing and travel for people starting work. Grants range from £200 to £500.

Annual grant total

The trust has an annual income and expenditure of £10,000

Applications

On a form available by writing to the correspondent. Applications are considered in April and October.

The Hervey and Elizabeth Ekins Educational Charity

£10,000

Correspondent: Richard Pestell, 41 Thorburn Road, Northampton NN3 3DA (01604 408712; email: richard@rpestell.freeserve.co.uk)

Trustees: Cyril Steward; David Kirby; Richard Pestell; Camilla Fazackerley; John White; Julia Richardson; Phillip Ball; M. R. Greenwell; M. Johnson.

CC Number: 309858

Eligibility

People who (i) have lived in the borough of Northampton or the parish of Great Doddington for not less than three years; (ii) attended a maintained school in Northampton for not less than one year and (iii) attended an Anglican church on a regular basis. Applicants should be under 25 (or in exceptional cases under 30). No grants to non-Anglicans.

Types of grants

Grants are given to schoolchildren, students in further or higher education and to people starting work towards books, equipment and educational outings in the UK and overseas. Grants are also given for music tuition fees.

Grants average around £200, but in exceptional circumstances can be for as much as £500. Other grants are given to a school for larger projects.

There is a preference for those entering the ministry of the Church of England.

Annual grant total

In 2010/11 the trust had an income of £24,000 and an expenditure of £23,000. Previously around half the expenditure has gone in grants to individuals.

Exclusions

Grants are not given for school fees.

Applications

In writing to the correspondent directly by the individual, including details of school and church attended. Applications are considered in January, March, May, September and November.

The Horne Foundation

£163,000 (82 grants)

Correspondent: R M Harwood, PO Box 6165, Newbury RG14 9FY (email: hornefoundation@googlemail.com)

Trustees: Julie Davenport; Tina Horne; Ros Harwood.

CC Number: 283751

Eligibility

Schoolchildren and students in need who live in Northamptonshire.

Types of grants

Bursaries are made towards living expenses, course fees and so on, to a maximum of £5,000.

Annual grant total

In 2010/11 the trust had assets of £6.8 million and an income of £175,000. Grants were made to 82 individuals totalling £163,000.

Applications

The bursary scheme is run in conjunction with the local council, and bursaries to schoolchildren are made on the recommendation of schools. If the applicant is at school, he or she should therefore apply through the headteacher of the school. Students can apply to the trust directly, in writing. Applications are considered twice a year.

Other information

£14,000 was given in three grants to national appeals and £44,000 in grants to local youth organisations.

The Isham Educational Foundation

£1,000

Correspondent: Jenny Sturt, 16 North Street, Rothersthorpe, Northampton NN7 3JB (01604 830591)

Trustees: I. Kennedy; J. Farr; Jan Fossey; Christopher Millar; David Ward; Tim Short.

CC Number: 309839

Eligibility

People under 25 who live in the ancient parish of Lamport and Hanging Houghton.

Types of grants

One-off and recurrent grants of between £50 and £1,000 are given to: (i) school pupils, to help with books, equipment, clothing, travel or school fees but not for maintenance; (ii) students in further/higher education towards fees or to supplement existing grants; and (iii) those leaving school, college or university to prepare for or enter a trade, profession or calling.

Preference is given to schoolchildren with serious family difficulties so the child has to be educated away from home.

'In the allocation of all benefits the trustees shall have regard to the principles of the Church of England.'

Annual grant total

About £1,000 is given in grants each year.

Applications

In writing to the correspondent. Applications can be submitted by the individual or by parents and are considered in July and November.

The Dorothy Johnson Charitable Trust

£20,000

Correspondent: Z B Silins, Clerk, Hybank, Old Road, Walgrave, Northampton NN6 9QW (01604 780662 email: zinaida@zinaidasilins.com)

Trustees: Gillian Hood; Jane Wilson; Jonathan; Williams; Ian Dove.

CC Number: 298499

Eligibility

People under 25 who were born and are living, have lived or were educated at some time in Northamptonshire.

Types of grants

One-off and recurrent grants in the range of £100 and £500. Grants are made to schoolchildren, college students, undergraduates, vocational students and people with special educational needs, towards clothing/uniforms, fees, study/travel abroad, books, equipment/instruments, maintenance/living expenses and excursions.

Annual grant total

In 2010/11 the trust had an income of £19,000 and an expenditure of £21,000.

Applications

In writing to the correspondent. Applications are considered three times a year.

The Kettering Charities (Apprenticing)

£9,000

Correspondent: Anne Ireson, Kettering Borough Council, Council Offices, Bowling Green Road, Kettering NN15 7QX (01536 534398; email: anneireson@kettering.gov.uk)

Trustees: Ian Watts; Bryn Morgan; Shirley Lynch; Duncan Bain; Lloyd Bunday; Stephen Bellamy; Jennifer Henson; Cliff Moreton.

CC Number: 207698

Eligibility

People over 16 who live in the town of Kettering or Barton Seagrave and are in training or further education.

Types of grants

One-off grants for general educational needs such as books and equipment. They are given towards students in further and higher education, vocational and mature students, people starting work and people with special educational needs.

Annual grant total

In 2009/10 the charity had an income of £14,000 and an expenditure of £28,000.

Applications

Applications should be made by the individual, their parent or guardian or through the individual's school, college or educational welfare agency for consideration in November and February. Details of the applicant's financial situation must be included. Grants are subject to the parents' income

if the applicant is under 21, otherwise they are subject to the applicant's income.

Other information

'The Trustees are keen to encourage applications from mature students, as well as school leavers and students in higher education, to reflect the national trend for more mature students entering higher education.'

The charities also make grants for welfare purposes and to the local church.

Parson Latham's Educational Foundation

£3,000

Correspondent: Graham Sands, Magnolia Cottage, 1 Main Street, Cotterstock, Peterborough PE8 5HD (01832 226025; email: grahamsands@btconnect.com; website: www.parsonlathamscharity.org.uk)

CC Number: 309843

Eligibility

Children 12 aged years and upwards who have lived in the urban district of Oundle and Ashton since birth or have been resident for at least five years and have attended a local school. The foundation will consider giving grants to mature students, although prefers to support people under 25.

Types of grants

One-off and recurrent grants of £100 to £250 are given to: (i) Schoolchildren for uniforms/other school clothing, books, equipment/instruments, fees and educational outings in the UK; (ii) People starting apprenticeships for equipment/instruments; (iii) Further education students for clothing, books, equipment/instruments, fees and maintenance/living expenses; (iv) Higher education students for fees, books and maintenance/living expenses; (v) Mature and vocational students for books and fees.

Annual grant total

In 2010/11 the charity had an income of £23,000 and an expenditure of £4,400. Grants to individuals usually total around £3,000.

Exclusions

No grants are given to overseas students studying in the UK or for student exchange.

Applications

On a form available from the correspondent, the local tourist information centre or the website. Applications to be submitted directly by the individual before 20 August for consideration in September.

Other information

The foundation also makes grants to organisations and its related charity runs almshouses.

Northamptonshire Community Foundation

£7,200 (31 grants)

Correspondent: Rachel McGrath, Grants Director, Within Royal and Derngate, 19 Guildhall Road, Northampton NN1 1DP (01604 230033; fax: 01604 636303; email: enquiries@ncf.uk.com; website: www.ncf.uk.com)

Trustees: Sandra Bell; Alan Maskell; John Bruce; David Laing; Wendi Buchanan; Linda Davis; Ian Leather; Brian Lehane; Robert Tomkinson; Christopher Houghton; Anne Burnett.

CC Number: 1094646

Eligibility

- Northamptonshire Champions Fund: people up to the age of 25, or 35 if you have a disability, competing at a regional level, and ideally at national level. Applicants must live, train, coach or officiate in Northamptonshire. For athletes with disabilities over the age of 35 you can still apply if you can demonstrate that you have, within the last three years, taken up the sport for which you are applying. There are approved list of priority and non-priority sports published on the foundation's website. Successful applicants may only apply once per year
- Arts and Music Fund: young people taking part in the theatre

Types of grants

- Northamptonshire Champions Fund: grants of up to £400 per year to assist with sports based activities, for example travel expenses to training grounds, personal sports equipment, attendance at competition or specialist coaching. Grants can be used to support applicants in education in order to allow them to remain in education if they are experiencing financial difficulties; to athletes on a low income generally or to athletes with disabilities who require an assistor or carer in order to compete
- Arts and Music Fund: bursaries of up to £55 per term for young people taking part in Royal and Derngate Youth Theatre

Annual grant total

In 2011/12 16 individuals received grants totalling £4,300 from the Champions Fund and 15 individuals and one group received grants totalling £3,100 from the Arts and Music Fund.

Applications

On an application form available to download from the website. Applications must be supported by an independent referee with knowledge of your ability in the case of the Champions Fund and from a school teacher for the Arts and Music Fund. They are considered monthly. The foundation staff are willing to offer informal advice and feedback on applications prior to final submission.

As with all community foundations, funds may open and close at short notice. Check the website before applying.

Other information

Funds available from the foundation are predominantly for the benefit of organisations.

The Foundation of Thomas Roe

£1,000

Correspondent: Ursula Morris, Highfield Grange, Highfield Park, Creaton, Northampton NN6 8NT (01604 505554; email: ursula@ursulamorris.co.uk)

Trustees: Richard Turney; Gabriel Leeming; Margaret Vinton; Pam Long; Rod King; Steve Pointer; Chris Millar; Richard Monk.

CC Number: 309801

Eligibility

People in need who are under 25 and live in the parishes of Scaldwell and Brixworth, Northamptonshire.

Types of grants

One-off grants of £50 to £150 to schoolchildren, students in further or higher education and people starting work for school uniform, school clothing, books, educational outings in the UK, study or travel abroad, maintenance, fees, living expenses and equipment/instruments.

Annual grant total

About £1,000.

Applications

On a form available from the correspondent to be considered in March and September each year.

Sir Thomas White's Northampton Charity

£161,000

Correspondent: Angela Moon, Hewitsons, 7 Spencer Parade, Northampton NN1 5AB (01604 233233; email: angelamoon@hewitsons.com)

Trustees: Tim Hadland; Ulric Gravesande; David Wiseman; Donald Edwards; Frank Lilley; Paul Morris; Wendy Howes; Frances Wire; Garry Simmons; Trevor Bailey; John Nightingale; Philip Ager; Jean Bulteel; Jenny Conroy; Michael O'Leary; Andrew Simpson; Matthew Golby; Janet March.

CC Number: 201486

Eligibility

People who live within the extended borough of Northampton.

Types of grants

(i) Nine-year interest-free loans to people aged between 21 and 34 for education and new businesses (and home improvements). (ii) Grants to young people aged between 16 and 25 attending school, college or university.

The fund was originally set up for the provision of tools for people setting up in a trade or profession.

Annual grant total

In 2011 the trust had assets of £3.2 million and an income of £247,000. 70 loans totalling £175,000 and £74,000 in student grants were made.

Applications

Apply in writing for a form in November, following a public notice advertising the grants.

Other information

Previously called Sir Thomas White's Loan Fund.

The Wilson Foundation

£19,000 (38 grants)

Correspondent: The Trustees, The Maltings, Tithe Farm, Moulton Road, Holcot, Northamptonshire NN6 9SH (01604 782240; email: polly@tithefarm.com; website: www.thewilsonfoundation.co.uk)

Trustees: Anthony Hewitt; Giles Wilson; Nicholas Wilson; Fiona Wilson; Adam Welch; Pollyanna Wilson.

CC Number: 1074414

Eligibility

Young people in who have lived in Northamptonshire for at least a year, or were born there, with a particular emphasis on the underprivileged or disadvantaged.

Types of grants

Scholarships and 'character building' trips/expeditions. Grants have also been made for uniforms/equipment/books.

Annual grant total

In 2011 the foundation had assets of £4.5 million and an income of £53,000. There were 38 grants to individuals totalling £19,000.

Applications

An application form can be downloaded from the foundation's website. A reference must be supplied.

Other information

Grants are also made to organisations.

Blakesley

The Blakesley Parochial Charities

£3,000

Correspondent: Derek Lucas, Bradworthy, Main Street, Woodend, Towcester NN12 8RX (01327 860517)

Trustees: B. Bird; John Hall; A. Bell; J. Weekley; N. Manners; P. Osborne; Christine Hill; Ian Spiby; Michael Adams.

CC Number: 202949

Eligibility

People who are in need and live in Blakesley.

Types of grants

One-off and recurrent grants according to need for post-16 education and apprentices.

Annual grant total

In 2011 the charity had both an income and expenditure of £6,500.

Applications

In writing to the correspondent. Applications are considered in September.

Other information

The charities also make grants for welfare purposes.

Brackley

The Brackley United Feoffee Charity

£7,000

Correspondent: Rosemary Hedges, 7 Easthill Close, Brackley, Northamptonshire NN13 7BS (01280 702420; email: caryl.billingham@tesco.net)

Trustees: Caryl Billingham; Geoffrey Wilkins; George Britchfield; Keith Bunker; Nicholas Gandy; Philip Stevens; Trevor Gregory; Blake Stimpson; Peter Jeskins; Gwenllian Rhys.

CC Number: 238067

Eligibility

People under the age of 25 who live in the parish of Brackley.

Types of grants

One-off grants in the range of £100 and £1,000 to:

- Schoolchildren for uniforms/clothing, study/travel abroad, books, equipment/instruments, excursions and childcare
- College students and undergraduates for study/travel abroad, books and excursions
- People with special educational needs for excursions and childcare

Previous educational grants (2006/07) have included funding for educational trips to developing countries, music lessons, purchasing of musical instrument and contributions towards fees to attend a musical college.

Annual grant total

In 2010/11 the trust had an income of £30,000 and gave grants to individuals for educational purposes totalling £7,000.

Applications

In writing to the correspondent either directly by the individual or through the individual's school, college or educational welfare agency. Trustees meet every three to four months.

Brington

The Chauntry Estate

£5,000

Correspondent: Rita Tank, Walnut Tree Cottage, Main Street, Great Brington, Northampton NN7 4JA (01604 770809)

Trustees: Robert Billingsby; Dr Elizabeth Gardner; John Lawrence; Martin Wright; Robert Spokes; Derek Bull; Jenny Cooch; Donna Ibbott; Revd Sue Kipling.

CC Number: 200795

Eligibility

People who live in the parish of Brington. Applicants must have lived in the parish for at least five years.

Types of grants

One-off grants for payment of uniforms for children transferring to secondary schools, books and equipment for students in further/higher education or apprentices, and assistance towards items of school equipment not provided by LEA. Grants are also available for mature students.

Annual grant total

In 2010/11 the trust had both an income and total expenditure of £10,000.

Applications

In writing to the correspondent. Ineligible applications are not acknowledged.

Burton Latimer

The Burton Latimer United Educational Foundation

£2,500

Correspondent: Rebecca Hall, 23 Spring Gardens, Burton Latimer, Kettering NN15 5NS (01536 722113)

Trustees: Janet Kirton; Peter Hartley; Ruth Groome; Christopher Groome; Caroline Finn; Gwyneth Mellors; Derek Zanger; Jez Safford; Carol Sharman.

CC Number: 309818

Eligibility

People who live in Burton Latimer (people who live in other parts, or outside, the borough of Kettering are not eligible).

Types of grants

A general grant is made to students in further or higher education, usually to be used for books; grants to people undertaking training with low earnings to be used at their discretion; and a few grants to schoolchildren towards the cost of field study courses for GCSE work.

Grants are also made to mature students undertaking full or part-time training, in the latter case dependent on their income.

Annual grant total

Around £2,500 a year.

Applications

Application forms are available and must be submitted directly by the individual. Applications are usually considered in October. Applications unrelated to educational needs will not be considered.

Other information

Grants are also given to the three primary schools in the town.

Byfield

The Byfield Poors Allotment

£400

Correspondent: Ms Delith Jones, 15 Banbury Lane, Byfield, Daventry, Northamptonshire NN11 6UX (01327 261405)

Trustees: Angela Weller; Rosemary Johnson; Jean Hicks; Joyce Goddard; Mark Challice; Delith Jones; Christopher Buck; Chris Cross.

CC Number: 220321

Eligibility

People in need who live in the parish of Byfield.

Types of grants

Grants are given to undergraduates for books and study/travel overseas.

Annual grant total

In 2010 the allotment had both an income and total expenditure of £800.

Applications

On a form available from the correspondent. Applications can be made directly by the individual or a relevant third party. They can be submitted at any time for consideration in March, June, September and December.

Other information

The charity also makes grants for welfare purposes.

Chipping Warden

Relief in Need Charity of Reverend William Smart

£1,500

Correspondent: Mr N J Galletly, 3 Allens Orchard, Chipping Warden, Banbury, Oxfordshire OX17 1LX (01295 660365)

Trustees: Revd Chris Whiteman; Mr N. J. Galletly; David Cross; Val Woodford.

CC Number: 239658

Eligibility

People in need who live in the parish of Chipping Warden, Northamptonshire. Preference is given to elderly people and young people in education.

Types of grants

One-off grants according to need.

Annual grant total

About £3,000 each year.

Applications

In writing to the correspondent either directly by the individual or by another third party such as a social worker. Applications are considered at any time.

East Farndon

The United Charities of East Farndon

£1,500

Correspondent: C L Fraser, Linden Lea, Main Street, Market Harborough, Northamptonshire LE16 9SJ (01858

464218; email: fraser-cameron@hotmail.com)

Trustees: Cameron Fraser; Shirley Biggin; Nigel Haynes; Adrian Hill.

CC Number: 200778

Eligibility

Students in need who live in East Farndon.

Types of grants

One-off grants of up to £50 for people starting work, schoolchildren and college students. Grants given include those for books, equipment and instruments, as well as to schoolchildren for excursions.

Annual grant total

In 2011 the charity had an income of £6,300 and an expenditure of £3,400.

Applications

In writing to the correspondent directly by the individual or a family member for consideration as they are received.

Other information

Grants are also made for welfare purposes.

Harringworth

The Harringworth Parochial Charities

£2,000

Correspondent: Paul Manning, Vale House, Gretton Road, Harringworth, Corby NN17 3AD

Trustees: Janet Gledhill; Nigel Lugg; Jane Baxter; Ian Saunders; Pamela Cooper; Irene Houghton; Alan Wordie; Joanne Jones; Helen Harrison; Paul Manning.

CC Number: 241784

Eligibility

Students under 25 who live in Harringworth.

Types of grants

One-off grants of between £50 and £300 are given to schoolchildren, students in further/higher education and vocational students for books and equipment/instruments.

Annual grant total

In 2010/11 the charity had an income of £3,600 and an expenditure of £2,300.

Exclusions

No grants for school fees or clothing.

Applications

In writing to the correspondent, either directly by the individual or through the individual's school/college/educational welfare agency. Applications should be submitted in February for consideration in March.

Isham

The Isham Apprenticing and Educational Charity

£500

Correspondent: A S Turner, 36b South Street, Isham, Kettering, Northamptonshire NN14 1HP (01536 722500)

Trustees: A. S. Turner; Alan Jenkinson; Geoffrey Timms.

CC Number: 309885

Eligibility

Young people under the age of 25 who live in the parish of Isham, Northamptonshire.

Types of grants

Help with (a) the cost of books, clothing, educational outings, maintenance and school fees for schoolchildren and (b) books, equipment/instruments, clothing and travel for people starting work.

Annual grant total

About £500.

Applications

Directly by the individual or their parent/guardian in writing to the correspondent. Applications are considered regularly.

Litchborough

Litchborough Parochial Charities

£2,000

Correspondent: Maureen Pickford, 18 Banbury Road, Litchborough, Towcester, Northamptonshire NN12 8JF (01327 830110)

CC Number: 201062

Eligibility

Young people resident in or connected to the ancient parish of Litchborough following a formal programme of study.

Types of grants

One-off and recurring grants to help with course fees.

Annual grant total

In 2010/11 the charities had an income of £5,600 and an expenditure of £5,300.

Applications

In writing to the correspondent.

Other information

Grants are also given for widows pensions and to assist with the costs of heating bills.

Middleton Cheney

Middleton Cheney United Charities

£1,000

Correspondent: Linda Harvey, 1 The Avenue, Middleton Cheney, Banbury, Oxfordshire OX17 2PE (01295 712650)

Trustees: Roger Solesbury; Nigel Watts; William Woolland; E. Hutchinson; Philip Aris.

CC Number: 202511

Eligibility

People who live in Middleton Cheney.

Types of grants

One-off grants are available to schoolchildren for equipment/instruments, and to students in higher and further education, including mature students, for books and study or travel abroad. Grants are in the range of £100 to £200.

Annual grant total

About £1,000 in educational grants.

Applications

In writing to the correspondent. Applications should be submitted directly by the individual and are considered four times a year.

Northampton

The Beckett's and Sergeant's Educational Foundation

£85,000 (123 grants)

Correspondent: Anglea Moon, Hewitsons, 7 Spencer Parade, Northampton NN1 5AB (01604 233233; email: angelamoon@hewitsons.com)

Trustees: Philip Saunderson; Richard Pestell; Eileen Beeby; L. A. Mayne; Christine Allsop; David Smith; Hilary Spenceley; Margaret Pickard; Christopher Davidge; Andrew Cowling.

CC Number: 309766

Eligibility

People under 25 who either live in the borough of Northampton and are attending or have attended a school or further education institution in the borough for at least two years; or are attending or have attended for at least two years All Saints Middle School or Becketts and Sergeants School.

Types of grants

Grants of up to £1,000 can be given for a wide range of educational purposes, including: educational trips;

supplementing existing grants; purchasing books and equipment and studying music or the arts.

Annual grant total

In 2011 the trust had assets of £3 million and an income of £216,000. Grants to 123 individuals totalled £85,000.

Applications

A written request should be made to obtain an application form. Applications are considered four times a year.

Other information

Grants may also be given to other Church of England schools and organisations that are connected with the Church of England.

The Blue Coat Educational Charity

£4,000

Correspondent: R L Pestell, 41 Thorburn Road, Northampton NN3 3DA (01604 401237)

Trustees: Agnes Goodman; Anne Jones; Monica Bull; Richard Pestell; Gill Walton; Terry Wire; Carol Fordyce.

CC Number: 309764

Eligibility

People in need who are under 25 years old and live in the borough of Northampton.

Types of grants

One-off and recurrent grants to schoolchildren and students for a wide range of educational purposes, including the costs of school clothing, educational outings, books, school fees and study/travel abroad or student exchange. People starting work may also receive help towards equipment/instruments. Grants range from £100 to £400.

Annual grant total

In 2010/11 the charity had an income of £7,400 and an expenditure of £8,200.

Exclusions

No support for mature students or for overseas students studying in Britain.

Applications

Application forms are available by writing to the correspondent, they are usually considered in February, July and November.

Other information

Grants are also made to Church of England schools in Northampton.

Old

The Old Parish Charities

£0

Correspondent: Mrs J Willis, Clerk to the trustees, 5 Townson Close, Old, Northampton NN6 9RR (01604 781252)

Trustees: Revd Karen Jongman; Joan Barrett; William Beers; Mohammed Jalil Akhter Asif; Sarah Hampden Smith; Andrew John Hamson; Catherine Elizabeth Beckett.

CC Number: 252168

Eligibility

People who live in the parish of Old.

Types of grants

Help with the cost of books, clothing and other essentials for schoolchildren. Help is also available for students at college or university.

Annual grant total

In 2010 the trust held assets of £1.1 million and had an income of £64,000. No grants (2009: £3,000) were made to individuals during the year.

Applications

In writing to the correspondent.

Other information

The charities state their objectives as follows: 'The first obligation of the trustees is to meet the outgoings and repair and maintain the homes. Up to one third of any remaining income may be distributed as grants for the advancement of education. The balance may be applied for relief of those in need among the residents. Any residue may be used for the general benefit of parish inhabitants'.

Ringstead

The Ringstead Gift

£500

Correspondent: Mrs D Pentelow, 20 Carlow Street, Ringstead, Kettering, Northamptonshire NN14 4DN (01933 626894)

Trustees: Andrew Sharman; Revd Shena Bell; Geoffrey Goodchild; Clifford Harris; Philip Surridge.

CC Number: 239517

Eligibility

People up to the age of 25 whose parents live in the parish of Ringstead.

Types of grants

One-off grants in kind to schoolchildren, college students, undergraduates and vocational students, including those for uniforms/clothing, study/travel abroad, books and equipment/instruments.

Annual grant total

About £1,000 each year for educational and welfare purposes.

Applications

In writing to the correspondent, to be submitted either directly by the individual or a family member, through a third party such as a social worker or teacher or through an organisation such as Citizens Advice or a school. Applications are considered in June and November and should be submitted at least two weeks prior to this.

Scaldwell

The Scaldwell Charity

£1,500

Correspondent: James Kearns, Clerk to the Trustees, Wilson Browne Solicitors, Manor House, 12 Market Street, Higham Ferrers, Rushden, Northamptonshire NN10 8BT (01933 410000; email: jkearns@qswblaw.com)

Trustees: Colin Telling; Harry Darby; Julie Barfoot; Chris Millar; Hayley May; Susan Dodds-Smith.

CC Number: 277208

Eligibility

People in need who live in the parish of Scaldwell.

Types of grants

Help with the cost of books, clothing and other essentials for schoolchildren; books, fees and travel expenses for students in further or higher education; books, equipment and clothing for people starting work; and books, travel and fees for mature students.

Annual grant total

In 2011 the trust had an income of £3,000 and an expenditure of £3,400.

Applications

In writing to the correspondent, including details of financial circumstances. Applications are considered in March, July and November.

Towcester

The Sponne and Bickerstaffe Charity

£1,150

Correspondent: T Richardson, Clerk to the Trustees, Moorfield, Buckingham Way, Towcester, Northamptonshire

NN12 6PE (01327 351206; email: sponneandbickerstaffe@btconnect.com)

Trustees: S. J. Burnley; Jacqueline Hart; Penelope Bennett; Peter Allen; Tony Bryer; E. Nunn; Dennis Dale; Carole Tyrrell; Brian Giggins; Julie Godwin; Karen Wheeler; Alan Maycock; James Rawbone; Dominique Yates.

CC Number: 204117

Eligibility

People in need who live in the civil parish of Towcester.

Types of grants

Grants of £50 to £250 are given to schoolchildren for uniforms, clothing and excursions, to college students for books and to mature students for childcare.

Annual grant total

The latest accounts available were far 2010 when the charity gave £2,300 for welfare and educational purposes.

Applications

In writing to the correspondent, through a social worker, Citizens Advice or other welfare agency. Applications are considered monthly.

Welton

Welton Village Hall (formerly The Welton Town Lands Trust)

£700

Correspondent: Mr Gary Holmes, c/o Kingsford Solutions Ltd, 37 Churchill Road, Welton, Daventry NN11 2JH (01327 312055)

Trustees: Robert Somerville; Caroline Maxwell; Peter O'Mahoney; Carole Bertozzi; Michael Taylor; Clive Younger; Lee Henstridge; Gary Holmes; Revd Chris Tremththanmor.

CC Number: 304449

Eligibility

Students in higher education who are in need and have lived in the village of Welton for at least two years.

Types of grants

One-off grants of up to £75 to assist students in higher education for the cost of books, equipment and so on.

Annual grant total

In 2010/11 the charity had an income of £6,500 and a total expenditure of £5,500. Previously, grants were made to individuals totalling £2,000, of which £700 was given in educational grants and £1,300 was distributed in welfare awards.

Exclusions

Grants are not made to school-aged children unless they have a mental or physical disability or to individuals pursuing a hobby.

Applications

In writing to the correspondent. Applications are considered on 1 March and distributed in the same month. Only one application is allowed per financial year. The details of the trust are usually well publicised within the village.

Other information

The trust also makes grants to local schools and churches.

Nottingham-shire

The John and Nellie Brown Farnsfield Trust

£12,000

Correspondent: Alan Dodd, Roan House, Crabnook Lane, Farnsfield, Newark NG22 8JY

Trustees: Alan Dodd; Frank Reynolds; Dr Elisabeth Hiller; John Brown; Peter Teather; Heather Johnston; David Harvey.

CC Number: 1078367

Eligibility

People in need who live in the Farnsfield, Edingley Halam and Southwell area of Nottinghamshire.

Types of grants

Grants given according to need.

Annual grant total

In 2010/11 the trust had an income of £5,300 and a total expenditure of £21,000.

Applications

In writing to the correspondent.

Other information

Grants are also made to organisations and for welfare purposes.

Nottingham Gordon Memorial Trust for Boys and Girls

£6,600

Correspondent: Anna Chandler, Cumberland Court, 80 Mount Street, Nottingham NG1 6HH (01159015562; fax: 01159 015500; email: anna. chandler@freethcartwright.co.uk)

Trustees: John Foxon; Nigel Solicitor; Paul Watts; Jean Ramsden; John Tordoff; Peter Hill; Anthony King; Ian Wiseman; Bill Hammond.

CC Number: 212536

Eligibility

Children and young people aged up to 25 who are in need and live in Nottingham and the area immediately around the city.

Types of grants

Grants are given to schoolchildren and further and higher education students including those for books, equipment, maintenance/living expenses, educational outings in the UK and study or travel abroad. Grants are also given for school uniforms/other school clothing.

Annual grant total

In 2011 the trust had assets of £1.1 million and an income of £46,000. There was £47,000 awarded to individuals including £6,600 in educational grants.

- Bed and bed linens – £7,200
- Educational grants – £6,600
- Electrical goods – £6,500
- Holidays/trips – £6,100
- Baby items and equipment – £3,500

Applications

On a form available from the correspondent to be submitted through the individual's school, college, educational welfare agency, health visitor, social worker or probation officer. Individuals, supported by a reference from their school/college, can also apply directly. Applications are considered all year round.

Other information

The trust also supports organisations in the Nottingham area.

The Nottingham Roosevelt Memorial Travelling Scholarship

£14,000

Correspondent: The Hon. Secretary, 8 Mornington Crescent, Nuthall, Nottingham NG16 1QE (01159 755669; website: www.rooseveltscholarship.org)

Trustees: Paul Balen; Joan Taylor; Andrew Buchanan; David Sadler; Martin Rudge; Paul Ashdown; Russell Blenkinsop; John France; Keith Taylor; John Brewington; Gordon Waine; Cassie Muir; Louise Darby; Ellen Burns; Sarah McNicol; John Town; Nottinghamshire County Council; Nottinghamshire City Council.

CC Number: 512941

Eligibility

People between the ages of 20 and 30 who are engaged in industry, commerce or 'the professions' and live or work in Nottingham and Nottinghamshire.

Types of grants

Grants to help with the cost of visiting the USA for between three and six months to investigate a topic of the applicant's and/or employer's choice. The value of each scholarship can be up to about £3,000, plus return flight tickets to New York. 'Scholars are expected to travel widely throughout the USA and learn about the American way of life – an ambassadorial role.'

Annual grant total

In 2011 the fund had an income of £17,000 and an expenditure of £15,000.

Exclusions

Grants are not given to students.

Applications

Detailed guidelines and application forms can be downloaded from the trust's website.

The Puri Foundation

£30,000

Correspondent: Nathu Ram Puri, Environment House, 6 Union Road, Nottingham NG3 1FH (01159 013000)

Trustees: Nathu Ram Puri; Mary McGowan; Mr A. Puri.

CC Number: 327854

Eligibility

Individuals in need living in Nottinghamshire who are from India (particularly the towns of Mullan Pur near Chandigarh and Ambala). Employees/past employees of Melton Medes Group LTD, Blugilt Holdings or Melham Inc. and their dependents, who are in need, are also eligible.

The trust wants to support people who have exhausted state support and other avenues, in other words to be a 'last resort'. Eligible people can receive help at any stage of their education, including postgraduates and mature students.

Types of grants

One-off and recurrent grants according to need. The maximum donation is usually between £150 and £200.

Annual grant total

In 2010/11 the foundation had assets of £3.4 million and an income of £922,000. Grants mostly to organisations totalled approximately £526,000.

Applications

In writing to the correspondent, either directly by the individual or through a social worker.

Arnold

The Arnold Educational Foundation

£15,000

Correspondent: Brian West, 73 Arnot Hill Road, Arnold, Nottingham NG5 6LN (01159 206656)

Trustees: Peter Hill; Gordon Asher; Ken Shill; Jen Cole; Alan Langton; Bob Lockyer; Stella Lane; Gillian Allcock; Graham Bennett.

CC Number: 528191

Eligibility

People under the age of 25 who live, or whose parents live, in the ancient parish of Arnold, Nottinghamshire.

Types of grants

Primarily help for those at college or university, for example, for equipment or books. Help with the cost of books, clothing and other essentials for schoolchildren is given, but only in special circumstances.

Annual grant total

In 2010/11 the foundation had an income of £19,000 and an expenditure of £16,000.

Applications

In writing to the correspondent. An application form should be completed by those requesting grants for further education. Grants are given post-expenditure on receiving the receipts for items purchased.

Bingham

The Bingham Trust Scheme

£0

Correspondent: Gillian M Bailey, 20 Tithby Road, Bingham, Nottingham NG13 8GN (01949 838673)

Trustees: Joan Ward; Philip Bacon; Gillian Bailey; Janet Richie; Kathleen Quibell; Philip Jacques; Brian Richie; Rosemary Pigula; Mike Fish; Catherine Hobson; Ponniah Chandrakumar; Katherine Cox.

CC Number: 513436

Eligibility

People under the age of 21 living in Bingham.

Types of grants

Grants in the range of £50 and £150 to help with expenses incurred in the course of education, religious and physical welfare and so on. They are made in January and early July each year.

Annual grant total

In 2010/11 the scheme had an income of £162 and a total expenditure of £0.

Applications

Application forms are available from: Mrs R Pingula, 74 Nottingham Road, Bingham, Nottinghamshire NG13 8AW. They can be submitted directly by the individual or a family member by 30 April and 31 October each year.

Bingham United Charities

£1,500

Correspondent: Claire Pegg, 6 Park Road, Barnstone, Nottinghamshire NG13 9JG (01949 861181)

Trustees: Maurice Stockwood; Eric Sharp; Sally Abbey; Paul Durber.

CC Number: 213913

Eligibility

People in need who live in the parish of Bingham.

Types of grants

One-off grants in the range of £50 and £600. Grants are given for a range of educational purposes including school uniforms, books, school trips, Duke of Edinburgh expeditions and music lessons.

Annual grant total

In 2010/11 the charity had an income of £8,400 and an expenditure of £3,600.

Exclusions

No recurrent grants.

Applications

In writing to the correspondent, preferably directly by the individual; alternatively, they can be submitted through a social worker, Citizens Advice or other welfare agency. Applications are considered on the second Tuesday in alternate months, commencing in May. Details of the purpose of the grant and other grants being sought should be included.

Other information

Grants are also given to organisations and individuals for welfare purposes.

Carlton in Lindrick

The Christopher Johnson and the Green Charity

£1,000

Correspondent: C E R Towle, Hon. Secretary and Treasurer, 135 Windsor Road, Carlton in Lindrick, Worksop, Nottinghamshire S81 9DH (01909 731069; email: 1cert@tiscali.co.uk)

Trustees: Alistair Williams; Robin Johnson; Christine Connelly; Robin Towle; Christopher Smith; Jeanette Hurcon; Yvonne Jones; Jim Halpin; Gordon Greenwood; Michael Mills.

CC Number: 219610

Eligibility

Schoolchildren in need who live in the village of Carlton in Lindrick.

Types of grants

One-off grants ranging from £10 to £250 for school trips, books and so on.

Annual grant total

Grants usually total about £2,000 each year and are given for educational and welfare purposes.

Applications

In writing to the correspondent either directly by the individual, via a third party such as a social worker, doctor or district nurse or through a Citizens Advice or other welfare agency. Applications are considered throughout the year.

Collingham

William and Mary Hart Foundation
See entry on page 41

Mansfield

Faith Clerkson's Exhibition Foundation

£3,000

Correspondent: C P McKay, 67 Clumber Avenue, Beeston, Nottingham NG9 4BH (07771 978622)

Trustees: Bernard Ory; Jean Sparham; Joan Howson; John Carter; Keith Williams; Cllr Christine Smith; Margaret Munro; Cllr A. Fisher; Cllr Sharon Adey; Malcolm Sage.

CC Number: 528240

Eligibility

Boys and girls of school leaving age upwards who have for at least two years lived in the borough of Mansfield or the urban district of Mansfield Woodhouse.

Types of grants

Small cash grants, with no fixed maximum limit, to help students and others leaving school who are undertaking full-time education, with the cost of books, equipment, clothing and travel.

Annual grant total

In 2010/11 the foundation had an income of £3,000 and a total expenditure of £3,500.

Exclusions

No grants for fees.

Applications

In writing to the correspondent, including proof of income and details of any other grant applied for. Applications are considered in early June and early October.

North Muskham

The Mary Woolhouse Foundation

£4,000

Correspondent: Robert Patterson, Coniston, Main Street, North Muskham, Newark NG23 6HQ (01636 705517)

Trustees: David Mellors; Jennifer Hamilton; Ann Willey; Nicola Talbot.

CC Number: 528185

Eligibility

People under 25 who live in the parish of North Muskham and Bathley.

Types of grants

One-off grants are given to schoolchildren and college students towards books and equipment/instruments.

Annual grant total

In 2011 the foundation had an income of £6,300 and an expenditure of £9,500. Grants are made to individuals and local schools.

Applications

In writing to the correspondent. Applications should be submitted directly by the individual and are considered at any time.

Nottingham

The Audrey Harrison Heron Memorial Fund

£3,500

Correspondent: The Manager, Natwest Trust Services, 5th Floor, Trinity Quay 2, Avon Street, Bristol BS2 0PT (01179 403283)

Trustee: Nat West Trust Services.

CC Number: 504494

Eligibility

Girls and women who live in the city of Nottingham and are under the age of 25.

Types of grants

Grants of between £50 and £2,000 to help with books, equipment, clothing or travel, school, college or university fees or to supplement existing grants. Grants can be one-off or recurrent.

Annual grant total

In 2010/11 the fund had an income of £4,500 and an expenditure of £4,100.

Applications

On a form available from the correspondent. Applications can be submitted directly by the individual, through the individual's school/college/educational welfare agency or other third party, and are considered all year round.

The Peveril Exhibition Endowment Fund

£6,000

Correspondent: Graham Scott, Stone Cottage, 5 New Road, Burton Lazars, Melton Mowbray, Leicestershire LE14 2UU (01159 472541; fax: 01159 473636; email: peveril@chicco.co.uk)

Trustees: Paul Balen; Michael Bolton; Andrew Buchanan; David Wild; Tim Allen; Jeremy King; Nigel Hastings; Paula Hammond; Ian Malcolm; Michael Ackroyd; Jonathan Hirst; Carol Roberts; Steve Green; Bob Mardling; Martin Suthers; Rodney Exton; Margaret Renshaw; Mark Flanagan; Julia Bates.

CC Number: 528242

Eligibility

Applicants who (or whose parents) live within the city of Nottingham, aged 11 to 24. There is a minimum residential qualification period within the city of two years and the trustees will give preference to applicants who originate from, or who have long-term ties with, the Nottingham area rather than to those who are merely living there whilst completing an educational course locally.

Types of grants

One-off and recurrent grants tenable at any secondary school, college of education, university or other institution of further (including professional and technical) education approved by the trustees. Grants available up to £1,000. Larger grants may be given in exceptional circumstances.

Annual grant total

In 2010/11 the fund had an income of £8,000 and an expenditure of £7,000.

Applications

At any time on a form available from the correspondent. Applications should be submitted directly by the individual; parents will be requested to complete a means-test form if the applicant is still a dependant. Applications are considered all year around.

Tuxford

Read's Exhibition Foundation

£2,000

Correspondent: A A Hill, Sandy Acre, Eagle Road, Spalford, Newark NG23 7HA (01522 778250)

Trustees: Eric Bett; John Hempsall; Georgie Frost; Cynthia Smith; Lynn Sykes.

CC Number: 528238

Eligibility

Children and young people, including university students, who have lived in and attended a school in the parish of Tuxford.

Types of grants

Mainly help for students in further or higher education. Help is also given towards the cost of education, training, apprenticeship or equipment for those starting work and towards essentials for schoolchildren.

Annual grant total

In 2010/11 the trust had an income of £2,500 and an expenditure of £2,700.

Applications

In writing to the correspondent. Invoices for school equipment must be submitted on application before any grant is issued. Applications can be considered at any time.

Other information

All applications will be considered on receipt of an invoice.

Warsop

The Warsop United Charities

£2,500

Correspondent: Mrs J R Simmons, Newquay, Clumber Street, Warsop, Mansfield, Nottinghamshire NG20 0LX

Trustees: Peter Crawford; Alex Hague; Angela Price; Anthony Hague; Jean Simmonds; Joan Long.

CC Number: 224821

Eligibility

People in need who live in the urban district of Warsop (Warsop, Church Warsop, Warsop Vale, Meden Vale, Spion Kop and Skoonholme).

Types of grants

Grants for those at school, college or university.

Annual grant total

Previously about £5,000.

Applications

In writing to the correspondent. Trustees meet three or four times a year.

Other information

Grants are also made for relief-in-need purposes.

Shropshire

The Atherton Trust

£900

Correspondent: Paul Adams, Whittingham Riddell LLP, Belmont House, Shrewsbury Business Park, Shrewsbury SY2 6LG (01743 273273; email: pa@whittinghamriddell.co.uk)

Trustees: Frederick Morris; George Hall; Rodney Scott; Neville Lewis; John Pope; Stella Bridgewater.

CC Number: 515220

Eligibility

People in need who live in the parishes of Pontesbury and Hanwood and the villages of Annscroft and Hook-a-Gate in the county of Shropshire.

Types of grants

One-off grants given towards fees, living expenses or study or travel abroad for students in further and higher education and towards equipment or instruments for people starting work.

Annual grant total

In 2010/11 the trust had an income of £4,000 and a total expenditure of £5,000. Generally the trust gives around £900

annually to individuals for educational purposes.

Applications

On a form available from the correspondent, to be submitted directly by the individual. Applications are considered quarterly in February, May, August and November.

Other information

The trust also supports organisations that give, or agree to give when required, support and services to people who need aid due to loss of sight, limb or health by accident or inevitable causes.

Bowdler's Educational Foundation

£2,000

Correspondent: T Collard, Clerk to the Trustees, c/o Legal Services, Shropshire County Council, The Shire Hall, Abbey Foregate, Shrewsbury SY2 6ND (01743 252756; email: tim.collard@shropshire-cc.gov.uk)

Trustees: Yvonne Holyoak; Joyce Allaway; John Everall; Hazel Jones; Peter Jetson; Liz Parsons; Miles Kenny.

CC Number: 528366

Eligibility

People under the age of 25 who live in the county of Shropshire, but with a first priority for those living in the Shrewsbury area.

Types of grants

Grants, to a maximum of £100 to £200, for: (i) school pupils, to help with books, equipment, clothing or travel; (ii) help with school, college or university fees or to supplement existing grants; and (iii) help towards the cost of education, training, apprenticeship or equipment for those starting work.

Annual grant total

Expenditure for the trust averages out at £2,000 per year.

Applications

On a form available from the correspondent.

The Careswell Foundation

£10,000

Correspondent: Mrs B A Marshall, 24 The Crescent, Shrewsbury SY1 1TJ (01743 351332; fax: 01743 351844; email: solicitors@turnbullgarrard.co.uk)

Trustees: Christopher Conway; Richard Raven; John Hurst-Knight; Derek Peden; Sylvia Pierce; Stuart West; Lorna Withey.

CC Number: 528393

Eligibility

People under the age of 25 who live in Shropshire and have attended certain schools in the county, namely Shrewsbury School, Bridgnorth Endowed School, Adam's Grammar School (Newport), Idsall School (Shifnal), Thomas Adam's School (Wem) and the school or schools of secondary education by which Donnington, Shropshire is served.

Types of grants

Cash grants, to a usual maximum of about £150 a year for three years, to help with the cost of books and equipment, to be used at college or university or other establishments of further education.

Annual grant total

In 2010/11 the charity had both an income and expenditure of £11,000

Applications

On a form supplied by the headteacher of the relevant school to be submitted in August or September for consideration in October.

The Clungunford Educational Foundation

£1,500

Correspondent: Wendy Sheaman, Rose Cottage, Hopton Heath, Craven Arms, Shropshire SY7 0QD (01547 530447)

Trustees: Christine Tinker; Mary Bason; Mary Roberts; Robert Bywater.

CC Number: 505104

Eligibility

People under the age of 25 who live in the parish of Clungunford, that part of the parish of Onibury that used to be in Clungunford, and the former hamlet of Broome in the parish of Hopesay.

Types of grants

Help with the cost of books, clothing and other essentials for schoolchildren. Help is also available for students at college or university, and towards books, equipment, clothing and travel for people starting work. Grants range from £20 to £200.

Annual grant total

Around £1,500.

Applications

In writing to the correspondent or any trustee. An information sheet is distributed to each household in the parish at two or three-year intervals and to all newcomers.

Millington's Charity

£5,600 (12 grants)

Correspondent: Keith Fearnside, Clerk to the trustees, Copthorne Road, Shrewsbury, Shropshire SY3 8JW (01743 360904)

Trustees: Dick York; Geoffrey Cass; Ian Gillogaley; Daphne Capps; Martin Thorpe; Robin Case; Fiona Barnes; Helen Frostick; Jeremy Hawkey; Sally Sutton; Ryan Jervis; Elizabeth Merrifield.

CC Number: 213371

Eligibility

Preference for people who live in Shropshire. Applicants must be residents or have been educated in Shropshire, be aged between 15 and 25, and should be members, or their parents/guardian must be members, of the Church of England.

Types of grants

One-off grants ranging from £100 to £400 to help with incidental expenses associated with college or university attendance where there is a special need; to supplement existing grants; or to assist with funding a specific educational project. Grants are given towards the cost of books, equipment/instruments, maintenance/living expenses and study or travel abroad. Grants can also be awarded to people starting work.

Annual grant total

In 2010 twelve grants were made totalling £5,600.

Exclusions

Grants are not normally given towards fees.

Applications

Applications should be made on forms available from the correspondent upon written request. Details of parental income irrespective of the age of the applicant are obligatory. Decisions and awards are made at quarterly meetings in early March, June, September and December.

The Shropshire Youth Foundation

£5,000

Correspondent: Karen Nixon, The Shirehall, Abbey Foregate, Shrewsbury, Shropshire SY2 6ND (01743 252724; email: karen.nixon@shropshire.gov.uk)

Trustees: Alan Brice; Miss Gull; David Crowhurst; Sally Rhodes; Vince Hunt; Valerie Reynolds.

CC Number: 522595

Eligibility

People under the age of 25 years who live in Shropshire.

Types of grants

One-off grants, typically of £200, towards education through leisure time activities, such as voluntary service overseas and expeditions, may be given on occasions, so as to develop the physical, mental and spiritual capacities of individuals.

Annual grant total

In 2010/11 the foundation had an income of £9,100 and an expenditure of £13,000.

Exclusions

No grants are made towards educational courses.

Applications

Application forms are available from the foundation. The trustees meet twice yearly in June/July and January/February.

The Walker Trust

£77,000

Correspondent: Edward Hewitt, Clerk, 2 Breidden Way, Bayston Hill, Shrewsbury SY3 0LN (01743 873866)

Trustees: Malcolm Pate; A. E. Heber-Percy; Carolin Paton-Smith; Nicholas Bishop; David Lloyd; Shirley Reynolds.

CC Number: 215479

Eligibility

People who live in Shropshire. Preference is given to people who are leaving care, estranged from their families, single parents and those on low incomes or state benefits.

Types of grants

Grants have been made for gap year projects, music, drama and art costs. Higher education students are only assisted with medical or veterinary course related costs. Individual grants rarely exceed £2,000.

Annual grant total

In 2010/11 the trust had assets of £5.9 million and an income of £201,000. Grants to individuals totalled £77,000, broken down as follows:

music and drama	£40,000
university course	£20,000
college course	£14,000
foreign travel	£3,100
health and disability	£350

Exclusions

Higher education students eligible for help with tuition fees and student loans.

Applications

On a form available from the correspondent. Applications are considered in January, April, July and October. They must reach the correspondent at least one month before help is required. Decisions on urgent cases can be made between meetings.

Other information

Grants are also made to organisations.

Bridgnorth

The Bridgnorth Parish Charity

£2,000

Correspondent: Elizabeth Smallman, Clerk, 37 Stourbridge Road, Bridgnorth WV15 5AZ (01746 764149; email: eeesmallman@aol.com)

Trustees: Revd Simon Cawdell; Revd Angela Rogers; Dr Simon Martin; Elizabeth Smallman; Constance Baines.

CC Number: 243890

Eligibility

People living in Bridgnorth parish, including Oldbury and Eardington, who are in need.

Types of grants

One-off grants according to need, including those towards playgroup fees, school visits, funeral expenses and heating costs.

Annual grant total

In 2010 the charity had both an income and total expenditure of £5,500.

Applications

In writing to the correspondent either directly by the individual or through a doctor, nurse, member of the local clergy, social worker, Citizens Advice or other welfare agency.

Other information

Grants are also made to organisations.

Ercall Magna

The Ercall Magna Educational Endowment Fund

£400

Correspondent: Pauline Lloyd, 35 Talbot Fields, High Ercall, Telford, Shropshire TF6 6LY (01952 770353; email: geoff@gloyderdrome.com)

Trustees: Anita Bruckshaw; Louise Hughes; Margaret Picken; Shirley Lewis; John Sadler; Lynn Jackson; Christopher Hinks.

CC Number: 505544

Eligibility

People who live in the civil parish of Ercall Magna and have done so for at least one year and are aged between 16 and 25.

Types of grants

Recurrent grants of £20 to £40 for those at college or university towards costs such as books, equipment, fees/living expenses, equipment/instruments and study/travel abroad. Applicants must be staying in full-time education for at least one academic year after applying.

Annual grant total

The fund has an annual income of around £900 and makes grants totalling around £400.

Applications

On a form available from the correspondent. Applications should be submitted in time for consideration in September and the application must include an explanation of what the grant would help to achieve.

Hodnet

The Hodnet Consolidated Eleemosynary Charities

£1,000

Correspondent: Mrs S W France, 26 The Meadows, Hodnet, Market Drayton, Shropshire TF9 3QF (01630 685907)

Trustees: Janice Parker; Ann Taylor; John Powell; Gerald Mothershaw; Gillian Roberts; Dr James Mehta; David Morgan; Revd Charmian Beech.

CC Number: 218213

Eligibility

Students in need who live in Hodnet parish.

Types of grants

Grants for books to students in further/higher education.

Annual grant total

In 2010 the charities had an income of £3,500 and a total expenditure of £2,500. Grants usually total around £2,000.

Applications

In writing to the correspondent for consideration throughout the year. Applications can be submitted directly by the individual or through a social worker, Citizens Advice or other welfare agency.

Other information

This is essentially a relief-in-need charity that also gives money to students for books.

Hopesay

Hopesay Parish Trust

£500

Correspondent: David Evans, Park Farm, The Fish, Hopesay, Craven Arms, Shropshire SY7 8HG (01588 660545)

Trustees: Anne Weller; Judith Clarke; Caroline Habershon; Albert Evans; Christine Perkins; David Evans.

CC Number: 1066894

Eligibility

People in any level of education who live in the parish of Hopesay, Shropshire. Priority is given to those under 25 years old.

Types of grants

Grants are typically between £25 and £650 for an educational need. Except in cases of financial hardship, grants will not normally exceed half the cost of any activity. Trustees prefer not to enter into extended commitments, but will look favourably on repeat applications on an annual basis for extended periods of study.

Annual grant total

Grants usually total around £1,000 per year.

Exclusions

Grants are not made where the funding is the responsibility of central or local government, whether or not the individual has taken up such provision.

Applications

Preferably on an application form, available from the correspondent. The application form covers the essential information required, and the trustees will ask for further details if necessary. Applications can be made at any time, either directly by the individual, or by a third party on their behalf, such as parent/guardian, teacher or tutor, or through an organisation such as Citizens Advice or a school. They can be submitted at any time.

Other information

The trust gives priority to educational grants. At the trustees' discretion, any surplus income may be applied for other charitable purposes but only within the parish.

Newport

Charity of Annabelle Lady Boughey

£1,000

Correspondent: Stuart Barber, Merewood, Springfields, Newport TF10 7EZ (01952 814628; email: bougheyroddamha@btinternet.com)

Trustees: Eva Allen; Andy Burns; Brenda Flowers; Martin Pitchford; Phillip Norton; Tim Nelson; John Tyers; Geoff Clark.

CC Number: 213899

Eligibility

Individuals connected with the civil parish of Newport who require financial assistance with the costs of educational trips connected with non-vocational courses in any subject.

Types of grants

One-off grants for schoolchildren and students in further/higher education for study or travel abroad and instruments/equipment. Grants are also available to mature students for study or travel abroad.

Annual grant total

About £1,000

Applications

Initial telephone calls are welcomed and application forms are available on request. Applications can be submitted directly by the individual and are usually considered in March, June, September and November; completed applications should arrive in the preceding month.

Other information

Grants are also made to organisations.

Oswestry

John Matthews Educational Charity

See entry on page 143

Shrewsbury

John Allatt's Educational Foundation

£5,500

Correspondent: Peter Power, Sheinton House, Sheinton Street, Much Wenlock TF13 6HY (01952 727662; email: power535@btinternet.com)

Trustees: Richard Raven; B. Goodwin; John Wall; Jonathan Morris; M. A. K. Booth; Miles Kenny; Idris Owen; Tony Durnell; Steven Williams; Wendy Ford.

CC Number: 528294

Eligibility

People aged 11 to 25 who live in Shrewsbury and its immediate area, who are in need.

Types of grants

Help is available to schoolchildren for equipment/instruments and educational outings in the UK and further and higher education students for equipment/instruments, fees, books, living expenses, educational outings in the UK, gap year activities and study or travel abroad. Preference is given to: schoolchildren with serious family difficulties so that the child has to be educated away from home; people with special educational needs to help towards specialist equipment; and for specialist courses of education. Grants are usually one-off and range from £100 to £150.

Annual grant total

In 2010/11 the trust had an income of £6,800 and a total expenditure of £5,500.

Exclusions

No grants are made towards first degree courses.

Applications

On a form available from the correspondent. Applications are considered in January and July and should be submitted directly by the individual before 1 January and 1 July respectively. All applications must be supported by a letter from the applicant's educational establishment, or, if relevant, a medical practitioner or educational psychologist.

Telford

Maxell Educational Trust

£1,000

Correspondent: Ian Jamieson, Maxell Europe Ltd, Apley, Telford, Shropshire TF1 6DA (01952 522222)

Trustee: Mike Lowe.

CC Number: 702640

Eligibility

Young people aged 9 to 25 years who live, or whose family home is, in Telford, or who attend school or college there. Projects should ideally have an industrial or technological element.

Types of grants

One-off grants for schoolchildren, college students and people with special educational needs, towards books and equipment/instruments.

Annual grant total

Expenditure in recent years has been erratic, previously around £25,000 has been given in grants to individuals however in 2010/11 the trust had an income of £10,000 and a total expenditure was £1,500.

Applications

In writing to the correspondent. Applications are considered throughout the year and should be submitted either by the individual or a parent/guardian, through a third party such as a teacher, or through an organisation such as a school or an educational welfare agency.

Staffordshire

Consolidated Charity of Burton upon Trent

£39,000

Correspondent: Thomas J Bramall, Clerk, Talbot and Co., 148 High Street, Burton upon Trent, Staffordshire DE14 1JY (01283 564716; fax: 01283 510861; email: clerk@ consolidatedcharityburton.org.uk; website: www.consolidatedcharityburton. org.uk)

Trustees: Valerie Burton; Gwendoline Foster; Patricia Hill; Tom Dawn; Beryl Toon; Alison Parker; Dinsdale Salter; John Peach; Marie Nash; Peter Davies; Margaret Heather; Dennis Fletcher; Patricia Ackroyd; Gerald Hamilton; Elizabeth Staples; Ben Robinson; David Leese; Robert Styles; Leonard Milner.

CC Number: 239072

Eligibility

People who live in the former county of Burton upon Trent and the parishes of Branston, Stretton and Outwoods. Schools and colleges included in the scheme are Abbot Beyne School, Burton College, de Ferrers Specialist Technology College, John Taylor High School, Paget High School and Stapenhill Sixth Form Centre.

Types of grants

Undergraduate bursaries of £400 per annum for three years. One-off grants of up to £400 for further education and vocational training, overseas trips for personal development, sports activities and arts scholarships.

Annual grant total

In 2011 the trust had assets of £10.1 million and an income of £436,000. During the year the trust gave 30 bursaries to students totalling £36,000 (over three years) and 13 other grants to individuals totalling £3,200.

Exclusions

Grants are not awarded for postgraduate study.

Applications

On a form available from the website or the correspondent accompanied by a letter of support from a school or college.

Other information

The trust also makes grants to local organisations and to individuals for relief-in-need purposes.

Lady Dorothy Grey's Foundation

£17,000

Correspondent: John A Gloss, Walls Cottage, Kinver Road, Enville, Staffordshire DY7 5HE (01384 873691)

Trustees: Brian Edwards; John Redwood; Michael Scott-Bolton; Peter Williams; William Snelson; Dianna Williams; Richard Jones.

CC Number: 508900

Eligibility

People under 25 who live (or whose parents live) in the parishes of Enville, Bobbington or Kinver, with a preference for Enville.

Types of grants

One-off and recurrent grants to help further and higher education students with the cost of books, equipment/ instruments, fees, maintenance/living expenses, educational outings in the UK and study or travel abroad. Grants are in the range of £150 to £500.

Annual grant total

In 2010/11 the foundation had an income of £25,000 and a total expenditure of £18,000.

Applications

Directly by the individual or through a parent or guardian on a form available from the correspondent. Applications should be submitted by 31 August for consideration in October.

The Maddock, Leicester and Burslem Educational Charity

£7,000

Correspondent: Graham Hill, Grindeys LLP, Glebe Court, Stoke On Trent, Staffordshire ST4 1ET (01782 846441)

Trustees: John Beech; Edmund Yorke; Godfrey Heath; Raymond Reynolds; Helen Pegg; Nicholas Rugg.

CC Number: 528586

Eligibility

Students who have lived in Stoke-on-Trent or Newcastle-under-Lyme for at least seven years and are aged 15 to 21 inclusive (grants may occasionally be given to people outside this age range).

Types of grants

Help with the cost of books and educational outings for schoolchildren. Help is also available towards course fees for those at college or university. Grants are usually up to £200.

Annual grant total

In 2010/11 the charity had both an income and expenditure of £7,500.

Exclusions

No postgraduates or mature students are supported.

Applications

On a form available from the correspondent, to be submitted either directly by the individual or through the individual's school or educational establishment, for consideration in June. A circular is sent to over 20 local schools in the area. Applications must include details of what the grant is to be used for, what the student is aiming to achieve and what other funding is available. The school must also make a comment on the application.

Realise Foundation

£7,000

Correspondent: Steve Adams, Staffordshire Community Foundation, The Dudson Centre, Hope Street, Hanley, Stoke on Trent ST1 5DD (01782 683000; email: steve@staffsfoundation. org.uk; website: www.staffsfoundation. org.uk)

CC Number: 1091628

Eligibility

Students aged 18 and over who have been resident in North Staffordshire or Stafford town for at least five years and who are studying at any institute of further or higher education in the borough of Newcastle-under-Lyme, the city of Stoke on Trent, Stafford town or Leek town or a course related to a future employment aim.

Types of grants

One-off grants of up to £500 to help alleviate financial hardship where the student is at risk of being unable to immediately continue on their course.

Annual grant total

About £7,000

Exclusions

Students must be undertaking independent study, no funding for those financed by an employer.

Applications

On an application form available to download from the community foundation website. Proof of ID, excluding student ID, and permanent address should be provided with the application. You should also submit evidence of need for the item for which you are applying and any document you consider relevant to prove financial hardship. Applications must be countersigned by a representative from your university or college; details of the appropriate offices are available on the website.

The Strasser Foundation

£1,000

Correspondent: The Trustees, c/o Knights Solicitors, The Brampton, Newcastle-under-Lyme, Staffordshire ST5 0QW (01782 619225)

Trustees: Tony Bell; Alan Booth.

CC Number: 511703

Eligibility

Schoolchildren and students in the local area, with a preference for North Staffordshire.

Types of grants

Usually one-off grants for books, equipment and other specific causes or needs for educational purposes.

Annual grant total

In 2010/11 the trust had an income of £16,000 and a total expenditure of £26,000. Previously grants were made totalling £24,000, of which about £2,000 was given to individuals for educational and welfare purposes. The remaining £22,000 was awarded to organisations.

Exclusions

Grants are rarely made to people at doctoral level.

Applications

In writing to the correspondent. The trustees meet quarterly. Applications are only acknowledged if an sae is sent.

Bradley

The Bradley Trust

£2,400

Correspondent: Catherine Cartwright, 1 Elm Drive, Bradley, Stafford ST18 9DS (01785 780531)

Trustees: Peter Whittaker; Doreen Frost; Betty Metcalf; Graham Wright; Peter Wilks; James Brown; Karen Wilkes; Susannah Symons; Robert Turner; Stephen Furness; Timothy Powell.

CC Number: 528448

Eligibility

People from the parish of Bradley in Stafford who are in further and higher education.

Types of grants

Variable grants of amounts up to £2,000.

Annual grant total

In 2010/11 the trust had assets of £1.4 million, an income of £38,000 and made 'university grants' totalling £2,400.

Applications

On a form available from the correspondent. Applications are considered once a year in September and should be submitted along with proof of acceptance/attendance at university in August.

Other information

Village organisations and schools attended by Bradley children are also supported.

Leigh

Spencer Educational Foundation Trust

£1,500

Correspondent: Emma Beaman, 4 Bents Lane, Leigh, Stoke on Trent ST10 4PX (01889 502353)

Trustees: Christine Dickin; John Beaman; John Slater; Bernice Smallwood; David Brunt; David Heath; Edward Backhouse.

CC Number: 528442

Eligibility

People under 25 who live in the village of Leigh. No other applications will be considered.

Types of grants

Grants of around £150 each are given to further and higher education students and people starting work for books, clothing, equipment/instruments and fees.

Annual grant total

About £1,500.

Applications

On a form available from the correspondent. Applications are considered in September and should be received by August. Grants are paid in arrears after a reference from the educational body is received.

Rugeley

The Chetwynd Educational Foundation (part of the Chetwynd Charities)

£1,500

Correspondent: Carl Bennett, Sherwood, East Butts Road, Rugeley, Staffordshire WS15 2LU (01889 800727)

Trustees: Carl Bennett; Alan Loweth; Annie Walker; Gary Bennett; Patricia Tams; Irene Talbot; Paul Adams; Thomas Anderson; Geoffrey Martin; Michael Grocott.

CC Number: 234806

Eligibility

People going into higher education who live in the ancient parish of Rugeley.

Types of grants

To students who are proceeding to higher education, university, college or technical college. The correspondent states: 'There is no means test. All applications are considered on their merits. The grant is used mainly to buy books and other equipment. Any applicant who needs to purchase musical instruments or such equipment will also be considered for a further grant from our general fund. This would also apply to provision of special clothing.' Grants are also given towards study or travel abroad for students in further/higher education and towards fees for mature students. Grants are one-off and usually for amounts of £40 or £50 each.

Grants are usually made up to degree level, however, if the applicant intends to take a master's degree further help may be given.

Annual grant total

In 2010/11 the charity had an income of £3,400 and an expenditure of £2,700.

Applications

In writing to the correspondent. Applications are usually made directly by the individual and are considered in April and October. 'We normally expect to be informed of the applicant's results and the schools attended. Most applicants inform us of the course and subjects. We enjoy learning of their progress and the correspondence is friendly.'

Other information

Grants are also given for welfare needs.

The Rugeley Endowment

£42,000

Correspondent: The Trustees, c/o Staffordshire County Council, Finance Directorate, Wedgwood Buildings, Tipping Street, Stafford ST16 2DH (01785 276332; email: steveberisford@ staffordshire.gov.uk)

Trustee: Staffordshire County Council.

CC Number: 528603

Eligibility

People in need who are under 25 and live in the former urban district of Rugeley as constituted on 31 March 1974. Beneficiaries must have attended a voluntary, grant maintained or county school in the area of benefit.

Types of grants

One-off grants up to a maximum of £100 towards the cost of school clothing, books, travel, educational outings and equipment/instruments to schoolchildren, students in higher education or those preparing to enter a trade.

Annual grant total

In 2010/11 the trust had an income of £79,000 and gave £42,000 in grants.

Applications

Through the headteacher of the school attended.

Stafford

The Stafford Educational Endowment Charity

£10,000

Correspondent: Financial Directorate, Staffordshire County Council, Wedgwood Building, Tipping Street, Stafford ST16 2DH (01785 276333; email: steve.berisford@staffordshire.gov. uk)

Trustee: Staffordshire County Council.

CC Number: 517345

Eligibility

Pupils and former pupils of secondary schools in Stafford who are under 25 years of age.

Types of grants

Small one-off grants for books, travel, educational outings, educational equipment and similar expenses incurred by schoolchildren, students and people starting work. There is a preference to award grants for benefits not normally provided for by the LEA.

Annual grant total

In 2010/11 the charity had both an income and total expenditure of £18,000.

Exclusions

Grants are unlikely to be given for course fees or the ordinary living costs of students.

Applications

Through the headteacher of the secondary school attended.

Tamworth

The Rawlet Trust

£4,600

Correspondent: Christine Gilbert, 47 Hedging Lane, Wilnecote, Tamworth B77 5EX (01827 288614; email: christine. gilbert@mail.com)

Trustees: Revd Alan Barrett; Richard Hughes; Ian Perkins; David Milson; Vivian Khan; Jane Mallinson; Betty Bates; Kenneth Gant; Jeremy Oates; Michael Oates.

CC Number: 221732

Eligibility

Young people under the age of 25 who are in need and live, or have parents living, in Tamworth.

Types of grants

One-off grants ranging between £30 and £200 towards the cost of books, fees, living expenses, student exchange and study or travel abroad. Grants have also been made for equipment, instruments, clothing or travel for people starting work.

Annual grant total

In 2010/11 the trust had both an income and a total expenditure of £23,000. Previously, grants were made totalling £20,000, of which £4,600 was given in educational grants and £15,000 in non-educational grants.

Applications

On a form available from the correspondent, to be submitted either directly by the individual or through a third party such as a social worker or Citizens Advice. The clerk or one of the trustees will follow up applications if any further information is needed. The trustees meet in January, April, July and October to consider applications.

Other information

Grants are also made to organisations.

Trentham

The Lady Katherine and Sir Richard Leveson Charity

£500

Correspondent: Adam Bainbridge, 67 Jonathan Road, Stoke-on-Trent ST4 8LP (01782 643567)

Trustees: Neil Robinson; Revd Everton McLeod; Kevin Waters; Ross Irving; David Clarke; Adam Bainbridge.

CC Number: 1077372

Eligibility

People in need under 25 years who live in the ancient parish of Trentham.

Types of grants

One-off grants are given to: schoolchildren for equipment/instruments, educational outings in the UK and study or travel abroad; people starting work for equipment/instruments; and further and higher education students and postgraduates for books, equipment/instruments, educational outings in the UK and study or travel abroad.

Annual grant total

In 2010 the charity had an income of £2,000 and a total expenditure of £1,000.

Applications

In writing to the correspondent, either directly by the individual or through a third party such as an educational welfare office or school/college. Applications can be submitted at any time, though August is most popular.

Other information

The charity also makes grants to organisations and to individuals for relief-in-need purposes.

Tutbury

The Tutbury General Charities

£2,500

Correspondent: Jeanne Minchin, 66 Redhill Lane, Tutbury, Burton-on-Trent, Staffordshire DE13 9JW (01283 813310)

Trustees: Glenys Shenton; Arthur Tipper; David Stephenson; Owen Dyke; Eileen Mason; Juliana Bentley; Frank Turner; Alexandrina Mann; Francis Crossley; Janice Hamer; L. Evans.

CC Number: 215140

Eligibility

Students and people starting apprenticeships or other training who live in the parish of Tutbury.

Types of grants

One-off grants in the range of £40 and £80.

Annual grant total

In 2010/11 the charities had an income of £8,000 and an expenditure of £5,700 Grants are made for welfare and educational purposes.

Applications

The charities have application forms, available from the correspondent, which should be returned by 1 October for consideration in November. A letter of acceptance from the place of education is required.

Other information

The clerk of the trust states that details of the trust are well publicised within the village.

Warwick-shire

The Arlidges Charity

£2,000

Correspondent: Mrs A Pointon, 17 Ferndale Drive, Kenilworth, Warwickshire CV8 2PF (01926 855399)

Trustees: Alison Collet; Colin Ritchie; John Carrier; John Kelley; Peter Muckersie; Elizabeth Caswell; Gaynor Watkins.

CC Number: 528758

Eligibility

People under 25 who live in Kenilworth, Warwick and Leamington (the old county of Warwickshire). Applicants or their parent/guardian should be a member of a Congregational Church or United Reformed Church.

Types of grants

Help towards the cost of books, fees and travel or study abroad for students in further or higher education. Grants are recurrent if appropriate.

Annual grant total

The trust has an annual income and expenditure of around £2,000.

Exclusions

Grants are not given to schoolchildren or people starting work.

Applications

In writing to the correspondent, including details of the course to be taken and details of any other funding. Applications are considered in October.

The Dunchurch and Thurlaston Educational Foundation

£1,500

Correspondent: Paul Smith, Clerk, 11 Bilton Lane, Dunchurch, Rugby, Warwickshire CV22 6PY (01788 810635; email: paul.smith6@virgin.net)

Trustees: Paul Smith; Bob Fricker; Anne Gilbert; Malcolm Baugh; Paul Newsome; Rex Pogson; Gordon Collett; Tim Wainwright; Malcolm Garratt.

CC Number: 528738

Eligibility

People under 25 who live in the parishes of Dunchurch and Thurlaston.

Types of grants

One-off grants, rarely of more than £200. Schoolchildren, people starting work and people in further and higher education can receive support for books, equipment and instruments, educational outings in the UK and travel abroad in pursuit of education. In addition, people starting work and further and higher education students can be funded for fees and maintenance or living expenses.

Annual grant total

In 2010/11 the trust had an income of £2,600 and an expenditure of £3,400.

Applications

In writing to the correspondent, directly by the individual or their parent/guardian, at any time.

Other information

This trust also supports organisations providing benefits to people under 25 in the area.

The Hatton Consolidated Charities

£4,000

Correspondent: M H Sparks, Clerk, Weare Giffard, 32 Shrewley Common, Shrewley, Warwick CV35 7AP (01926 842533)

Trustees: Catherine Eleanor Price; Gillian Ward; Janet Lewis; Keith Mobberley; Sheila Light; Richard Wood.

CC Number: 250572

Eligibility

People who live in the parishes of Hatton, Beausale and Shrewley.

Applications from outside these areas will not be considered.

Types of grants

One-off grants usually in the range of £50 to £500. Recent grants have been given to college students, undergraduates, vocational and mature students towards books, equipment and instruments. People with special educational needs have also been supported.

Annual grant total

In 2010/11 the charity had an income of £9,800 and an expenditure of £9,300.

Exclusions

Grants are not given to schoolchildren.

Applications

In writing to the trustees or the correspondent, directly by the individual or a family member. Applications should include details of the course and envisaged expenditure.

The Leigh Educational Foundation

£25,000 (32 grants)

Correspondent: James Johnson, 3 Barford Woods, Barford Road, Warwick CV34 6SZ (01926 419300; email: johnson.jf@virgin.net)

Trustees: David Clark; Christopher Leigh; David Vaughan; Diana Holt; Richard Coates; Margaret Wallis; Katie Kingston.

CC Number: 701462

Eligibility

People in need who are under 26, and who live, or whose parents live, in the parishes of Stoneleigh, Ashow and Leek Wootton, Warwickshire.

Types of grants

One-off or recurrent grants according to need, ranging from £100 to £1,000. Grants are given to schoolchildren, college students, undergraduates, vocational students and people starting work. Grants given include those towards uniforms/clothing, fees, study/travel abroad, books, equipment/instruments and maintenance/living expenses.

Annual grant total

In 2010/11 the trust had assets of £787,000 and made 35 grants totalling £32,000, 33 of which were made to individuals.

Applications

On a form available from the correspondent (in hard copy or electronic format). Applications should be submitted directly by the individual.

They are considered in February, May, August and November.

The Middleton United Foundation Trust

£3,000 (15 grants)

Correspondent: E Foulkes, Horseshoes, Crowberry Lane, Middleton, Nr Tamworth, Staffordshire B78 2AJ (01213 083107)

Trustees: Joan Lea; Margaret Webb; Peter Rotherham; Robert Webb; Neil Wallace; Judith Davies.

CC Number: 528699

Eligibility

Young people under the age of 25 who are in need and live, or whose parents live, in the parish of Middleton or the immediate vicinity.

Types of grants

One-off and recurrent grants usually of amounts of up to £300 each. Schoolchildren, further and higher education students and postgraduates can be supported for books, equipment/instruments, educational outings in the UK and study or travel abroad. In addition, schoolchildren can be helped with uniforms/other school clothing and students in further and higher education can be supported with maintenance and living expenses. People starting work can be helped with books and equipment/instruments. Grants can also be made towards the costs of developing a hobby.

Annual grant total

In 2010/11 the trust had an income of £2,900 and an expenditure of £3,400. Fifteen grants to individuals were made during the year.

Applications

In writing to the correspondent, giving as many details as possible, for example, the purpose and size of grant requested, the cost of books/equipment, the age of the applicant and a description of the course.

Other information

Grants are occasionally made to organisations.

Perkins Educational Foundation

£13,000

Correspondent: The Clerk to the Governors, c/o Lodders Solicitors, 10 Elm Court, Arden Street, Stratford upon Avon CV37 6PA (01789 293259; website: www.williamperkinscharity.org)

Trustees: Stephen Roberts; Frank Spiers; Frederick Hiscocks; Michael John

Davies; Susan Juned; Susan Walker; Dilys King; Janet Satchwell; Sheila Jeffries.

CC Number: 528678

Eligibility

People aged 16 to 24 who have been living for at least two years, immediately prior to their application, in Salford Priors, Kings Broom, Bidford-on-Avon, Harvington or Cleeve Prior.

Types of grants

Grants towards the cost of books, fees/ living expenses and study or travel abroad for students in further/higher education, postgraduates or mature students under 25. Help may be given towards the cost of books, equipment/ instruments or travel for those involved in apprenticeships or those intending to acquire a profession or trade.

Annual grant total

Grants are made each year totalling around £13,000.

Applications

On a form available from the correspondent or to download from the website, to be returned by post-by mid-October for consideration in November. Telephone calls will not be accepted. An applicant's first application must be accompanied by a testimonial from his/ her headteacher, college principal, employer or other proper person recommending them as a suitable person to whom a grant might be made.

The Watson Scholarship for Chemistry

£800

Correspondent: Ruth Waterman, School Partnerships Support Officer, Learning and Achievement, Saltisford Office Park, Ansell Way, Warwick CV34 4UL (01926 742075; email: ruthwaterman@ warwickshire.gov.uk)

Eligibility

People who have a home address in Warwickshire, an A grade A-level in chemistry and a confirmed place on a first degree course in chemistry or one in which chemistry is the main subject.

Types of grants

Grants of up to £200, to be paid in the second semester of the first year of the course, after the university had confirmed the satisfactory progress of the student.

Annual grant total

In 2011/12 the trust gave £800 in grants to individuals. All those that applied were supported.

Exclusions

Students doing pharmacy or medicine will not be supported unless their main subject is chemistry.

Applications

Application forms are sent to schools/ colleges in the area in September/ October, or they are available from the correspondent. Forms must be signed by the headteacher of their school/college. The closing date for applications is 31 October.

Baginton

The Lucy Price Relief-in-Need Charity

£25,000

Correspondent: Delia Thomas, Clerk, 19 Holly Walk, Baginton, Coventry CV8 3AE (07884 182904)

Trustees: Jean Fawcett; Alan Brown; Louise Given; Nigel Thomas; Susan Williams; Roger Horsfall.

CC Number: 516967

Eligibility

Only people in need who live in the parish of Baginton, Warwickshire and who are under 25.

Types of grants

Grants are made for: (i) attendance at university, living away from home; (ii) attendance at university or colleges of further education, living at home; (iii) attendance at local schools or sixth form college or A-level courses; (iv) school uniforms; (v) travel or visits of an educational nature at home or abroad organised by school or university; (vi) occasionally for equipment, instruments or books specially required for people starting work; and (vii) special education needs requiring special courses or equipment.

Grants made under (i), (ii) and (iii) are for the academic year and are paid in three equal instalments. Grants made under (iv), (v), (vi) and (vii) may be applied for at any time.

Annual grant total

In 2011 the trust had an income of £5,100 and an expenditure of £26,000.

Applications

Application forms can be obtained from the correspondent either directly by the individual or by the applicant's parents if the individual is under 16 years old.

Barford

The Barford Relief-in-Need Charity

£4,000

Correspondent: Mr and Mrs T Offiler, 14 Dugard, Barford, Warwick CV35 8DX (01926 624153)

Trustees: Revd D. Jessett; Gerard Veness; Ian Webster; John Barrott; Philip Swallow; Philippa Mitchell; Lorraine Sayers.

CC Number: 256836

Eligibility

Young people who live in the parish of Barford.

Types of grants

Grants for those at school, college or university. Occasional financial assistance is provided for specific purposes such as Raleigh International and outward bound type courses.

Annual grant total

Around £8,000.

Exclusions

No loans are given.

Applications

In writing to the correspondent, directly by the individual or a family member. Applications are considered upon receipt. One of the trustees will visit to elicit all necessary information. Applications are usually considered in May and October.

Other information

Grants are also given to organisations.

Bilton

The Bilton Poor's Land and Other Charities

£2,000

Correspondent: Robin Walls, Trustee, 6 Scotts Close, Rugby CV22 7QY (01788 810930)

Trustees: Michael Goode; Revd Tim Cockell; Ish Mistry; Ian Lowe; Robin Walls; David Wright; Graham Gare; Lisa Parker; William Shields.

CC Number: 215833

Eligibility

People in need who live in the ancient parish of Bilton (now part of Rugby).

Types of grants

This charity is not primarily an educational charity, concentrating rather on the relief of need. However, some grants are made for books, fees and other costs.

Annual grant total

In 2010/11 the charity had assets of £399,000 and an income of £30,000. Grants to individuals and organisations totalled £6,700.

Applications

In writing to the correspondent, by the individual or through a relevant third party such as a minister, although often applications are forwarded by social services. They are considered in February, May and October.

Coleshill

The Educational Foundation of Simon Lord Digby and Others

£0

Correspondent: Juliet Bakker, The Vicarage, High Street, Coleshill, Birmingham B46 3BP (01675 462188)

Trustees: John Hoyle; Eileen Burton; John Wall; Bena Stuart; John Truman; Nick Parker; David Simkin.

CC Number: 528710

Eligibility

Students of secondary school or higher education age who live in the parish of Coleshill.

Types of grants

One-off grants are given to schoolchildren for school uniforms and other school clothing, books and educational outings, and to students in further/higher education for help with books. Preference is given to schoolchildren with serious family difficulties.

Annual grant total

In 2011 grants were made to local schools totalling £8,700, although no grants were made to individuals.

Exclusions

No grants to mature students.

Applications

On a form available from the correspondent. Applications should be submitted directly by the individual or parent/guardian for consideration in March or November, and include a breakdown of expenses, the amount requested and details of applications to any other grants.

Exhall

The Exhall Educational Foundation

£2,500

Correspondent: Alice Farnhill, St Giles' Parish Office, Church Hall, St Giles' Road, Ash Green, Coventry CV7 9GZ (02476 365258)

Trustees: Andrew Gandon; Ruth Westbrook; Roy Cogley; David Antcliffe; Royston Smith.

CC Number: 528663

Eligibility

People under 25 who live or whose parents live in the ancient parish of Exhall.

Types of grants

One-off and recurrent grants for educational purposes.

Annual grant total

In 2011 the trust had an income of £2,300 and an expenditure of £2,800.

Applications

On a form available from the correspondent. The trust advertises locally and considers applications in March and September.

Kenilworth

The William Edwards Educational Charity

£65,000 (130 grants)

Correspondent: John Hathaway, Heath and Blenkinsop Solicitors, 42 Brook Street, Warwick CV34 4BL (01926 492407; email: heath.blenkinsop@ btopenworld.com)

Trustees: Pauline Edwards; George Raper; John Hatfield; John Cooke; Michael Coker; Norman Vincett; Patrick Ryan; Roger Davies; Joanne Richmond.

CC Number: 528714

Eligibility

People under the age of 25 who live or whose parents live in the town of Kenilworth, or those who have attended a school in the town.

Types of grants

For educational purposes including uniforms and trips, each application is considered on its merits. Bursaries for postgraduate students are also made.

Annual grant total

In 2010/11 the trust had assets of £5.9 million and an income of £223,000. 127 grants to individuals were made totalling £30,000. Three bursaries to assist postgraduates were also made totalling £35,000.

Applications

On a form available from the correspondent.

Other information

In 2010/11 the trust also made five grants to schools totalling £185,000.

Shipston-on-Stour

Shipston-on-Stour Educational Charity

£2,000

Correspondent: D Squires, Pinnegar House, 49 Telegraph Street, Shipston on Stour CV36 4DA

Trustees: Richard Taylor; James Little; Amanda Stockley; Stephen Gray; Alison Dibbens; D. Thurburn-Huelin; Brian Punt.

CC Number: 507400

Eligibility

People under 25 who live, or whose parents live, in the parish of Shipston-on-Stour.

Types of grants

Grants are given to students undertaking further and higher education, postgraduates and apprenticeships. Support can be for uniforms/clothing, books, tools, instruments/equipment, educational outings in the UK or study or travel abroad.

Grants are one-off and range from £30 to £120.

Annual grant total

About £2,000.

Applications

On a form available from correspondent. Applications should be submitted directly by the individual by the first week of September for consideration at the end of that month.

Stoke Golding

Stoke Golding Boy's Charity

£5,500

Correspondent: Ruth Fisher, 21 Hinckley Road, Stoke Golding, Nuneaton, Warwickshire CV13 6DU (01455 212489)

Trustees: Ruth Fisher; Tony Smith; Roger Clifford; Alan Quinney.

CC Number: 519728

Eligibility

Young men and boys under the age of 25 who live in Stoke Golding. Some preference is given to people with special educational needs.

Types of grants

One-off grants, generally ranging from £150 to £200, depending on availability and circumstances.

Annual grant total

Around £5,500.

Applications

In writing to the correspondent directly by the individual. Applications should be submitted by mid-March for consideration in April.

Stratford upon Avon

The Stratford upon Avon Municipal Charities – Relief in Need

£250

Correspondent: Ros Dobson, Clerk to the Trustees, 6 Guild Cottages, Church Street, Stratford upon Avon, Warwickshire CV37 6HD (01789 293749; email: municharities@btinternet.com; website: www.municipal-charities-stratforduponavon.org.uk)

Trustees: Mary Nicol; Mick Love; Charles Bates; Colin McDowall; Maureen Beckett; Norman Price; Bill Dowling; Jenny Howard; Carole Taylor; Shelagh Sandle; Joy Seaman; Timothy Hewson; Tessa Bates; Rob Fradley; Stratford upon Avon Town Council.

CC Number: 214958

Eligibility

People in need living in the town of Stratford upon Avon.

Types of grants

Occasionally, one-off grants up to £500 are given towards the cost of: (i) school uniforms, other school clothing, books, maintenance and school fees for schoolchildren; (ii) books for students in further and higher education; and (iii) books, equipment and instruments for people starting work.

Annual grant total

In 2011 the charity gave £250 in educational grants.

Applications

On a form available from the correspondent, including details of the course costs and the financial circumstances of the applicant and parent(s) if appropriate. Applications for

schoolchildren must be made through the school.

Thurlaston

Thurlaston Poor's Plot Charity

£1,000

Correspondent: Mrs K Owen, Clerk, Congreaves, Main Street, Thurlaston, Rugby CV23 9JS (01788 817466)

Trustees: Jennifer Stokes; Roland Robinson; Colin Cook; Steven Watts; Claire Garside.

CC Number: 232356

Eligibility

Students in need who live in Thurlaston.

Types of grants

Grants are given for help with the cost of books.

Annual grant total

About £2,000 per year.

Applications

In writing to the correspondent directly by the individual. Applications are considered in January, September and November.

Other information

Welfare grants are also made to older people.

Warwick

The Austin Edwards Charity

£4,000

Correspondent: Jackie Newton, 26 Mountford Close, Wellesbourne, Warwick CV35 9QQ (01789 840135; website: www.warwickcharities.org.uk)

Trustees: Neil Thurley; John Henderson; Robin Ogg; Tony Atkins.

CC Number: 225859

Eligibility

People living in the old borough of Warwick.

Types of grants

Grants of up to £300 for students and mature students at college or university or for people starting work, towards clothing, equipment, books, travel expenses, course fees, overseas travel etc.

Annual grant total

In 2010/11 the charity had an income of £8,000 and a total expenditure of £7,500.

Exclusions

No grants for follow-on courses, postgraduate courses or second degrees.

Applications

In writing to the correspondent stating the purpose and amount of grant required plus details of any applications made to other charities. Applications are considered throughout the year.

The King Henry VIII Endowed Trust – Warwick

£10,000

Correspondent: Jonathan Wassall, Clerk and Receiver, 12 High Street, Warwick CV34 4AP (01926 495533; email: jwassall@kinghenryviii.org.uk; website: www.kinghenryviii.org.uk)

CC Number: 232862

Eligibility

People who live in the former borough of Warwick.

Types of grants

Grants are given to college students and undergraduates for study/travel overseas, to vocational students for fees and to schoolchildren for excursions.

Annual grant total

In 2011 the trust had assets of £24 million and an income of £1.5 million. There were 21 grants to individuals for education and welfare totalling £20,000.

Applications

On an application form available from the correspondent or from the trust's website. Though deadline dates are listed in the guidelines found on the trust website, applications can be submitted at any time. These can be submitted directly by the individual, a relevant third party or through a social worker, Citizens Advice or educational welfare agency.

Other information

Grants are also made to organisations.

Warwick Apprenticing Charities

£89,000

Correspondent: C R E Houghton, Clerk, Moore and Tibbits, Solicitors, 34 High Street, Warwick CV34 4BE (01926 491181; email: commercial@moore-tibbits.co.uk)

Trustees: Neil Thurley; Arthur Fitzmaurice; Jonathan Hearn; Terry Brown; Vaughan Roberts; Anthony

Atkins; Trudy Offer; Mary Kirkby; Jenny Morris; John Labrum.

CC Number: 528745

Eligibility

People aged 16 to 25 who live within the town boundaries of Warwick and are in need.

Types of grants

One-off grants are given for 'advancement in life', especially for the purchase of tools, equipment, books and travel for apprentices and students in further and higher education, and for outward bound courses and gap year projects.

Annual grant total

In 2011 there were 114 'advancement in life' awards totalling £82,000 made and £6,500 given towards Outward Bound places.

Applications

In writing to the correspondent. The trustees meet twice a year to approve and allocate grants.

Charity of Sir Thomas White, Warwick

£200,000

Correspondent: Belinda Shuttleworth, Clerk and Receiver, 12 High Street, Warwick CV34 4AP (01926 350555; email: connect@sirthomaswhite.org.uk; website: www.sirthomaswhite.org.uk)

Trustees: Neil Thurley; John McCarthy; Susan Rhodes; David Stephens; Sine Wyatt; John Edwards.

CC Number: 1073331

Eligibility

People between the ages of 18 and 35 who are ordinarily resident in the town of Warwick who are establishing a business or undertaking tertiary education.

Types of grants

Interest-free loans of up to £1,500 per year for three years for university students, or up to £10,000 for five years for young business people.

Annual grant total

About £200,000 a year in loans.

Applications

On a form available from the correspondent, or from the charity's website. Applications are considered upon receipt.

West Midlands

The Annie Bettmann Foundation

£5,000

Correspondent: John Kelley, Clerk to the Trustees, Alsters Kelley Solicitors, 1 Manor Terrace, Friars Road, Coventry CV1 2NU (0844 561 0100)

Trustees: Peter Cordle; Dorothy Brown; Jack Harrison; David Skinner; Raja Asif.

CC Number: 215973

Eligibility

People between 21 and 39 years of age who live in the city of Coventry or within three miles of the municipal boundary.

Types of grants

Grants for either people starting in business, or students in further education. Donations are usually in the range of £1,000.

Annual grant total

About £5,000.

Applications

Application forms are available from the clerk from the end of March to the end of May each year. The trust also advertises in the *Coventry Evening Telegraph*.

The Chance Trust

£1,500

Correspondent: Revd Anthony Perry, Trustee, St Mary's Vicarage, 27 Poplar Avenue, Edgbaston, Birmingham B17 8EG (01214 292165)

Trustees: Hayward Osborne; James Woodall; Revd Anthony Perry; Revd Andrew Smith; Madeline Page.

CC Number: 702647

Eligibility

People in need in the rural deaneries of Warley and West Bromwich.

Types of grants

One-off grants ranging from £50 to £400. Occasionally support can be made to university students for up to three years.

Annual grant total

The trust makes grants of between £2,500 and £3,000 per year to individuals for both educational and relief-in-need purposes.

Applications

In writing to the correspondent, outlining the need and the amount required. Applications are considered in January and July.

The W. E. Dunn Trust

£4,000 (22 grants)

Correspondent: Alan H Smith, Secretary, The Trust Office, 30 Bentley Heath Cottages, Tilehouse Green Lane, Knowle, Solihull B93 9EL (01564 773407)

Trustees: David Corney; C. P. King; Leita Smethurst; Jennifer Warbrick.

CC Number: 219418

Eligibility

People who live in the West Midlands who wish to further their education, but have special difficulties which prevent them from doing so. These can include, for example, prisoners who are using education as part of their rehabilitation, or students who are physically disabled or who have lived through particularly difficult circumstances.

Types of grants

One-off grants ranging from £50 to £200.

Annual grant total

In 2010/11 the trust had assets of £4.2 million and an income of £137,000. Grants totalling £44,000 were distributed to individuals in the following areas:

Clothing and furniture	119	£16,000
Convalescence and holidays	14	£2,500
Domestic equipment	90	£15,000
Education	22	£4,000
Radio, TV and licences	15	£2,000
Social and welfare	25	£4,000

Exclusions

Grants are not made to settle or reduce debts already incurred.

Applications

In writing to the correspondent. Applications for educational grants from mature students should be submitted directly by the individual and other applications should be submitted through the individual's parent/guardian or school/college/educational welfare agency. They are considered two or three times a month depending on the number of applications.

Other information

Grants are also made to organisations (£70,000 in 2010/11).

Grantham Yorke Trust

£11,400 (28 grants)

Correspondent: Christine Norgrove, Martineau, 1 Colmore Square, Birmingham B4 6AA (0870 763 2000; email: christine.norgrove@sghmartineau.com)

Trustees: Barbara Welford; Peter Jones; Pamela Ogilvie; Fred Rattley; Howard Belton; Patricia Mannion; Tim Clarke; Sam Monaghan.

CC Number: 228466

Eligibility

People under 25 who were born in what was the old West Midlands metropolitan county area (basically: Birmingham, Coventry, Dudley, Redditch, Sandwell, Solihull, Tamworth, Walsall or Wolverhampton).

Types of grants

One-off grants are given to:

- Schoolchildren and students for uniforms and other school clothing, books, equipment, instruments, fees, maintenance and living expenses, childcare, educational outings in the UK, study or travel overseas and student exchange
- Students leaving school or further education for equipment and clothing, which will help them enter, or prepare for, their chosen profession or trade
- People starting work for maintenance and living expenses and childcare
- Education focused on preventing unplanned pregnancies, drug, alcohol and gambling abuse, child abuse or youth offending

Annual grant total

In 2010/11 the trust held assets of £5.9 million and had an income of £196,000. £11,400 was made in 12 grants to individuals.

Applications

On a form available from the correspondent. Applications can be submitted either directly by the individual or a relevant third party; or through the individual's school, college or educational welfare agency.

Other information

The trust also makes grants to organisations and to individuals for welfare purposes.

The James Frederick and Ethel Anne Measures Charity

£5,000

Correspondent: The Clerk to the Trustees, Harris Allday, 2nd Floor, 33 Great Charles Street, Birmingham B3 3JN

Trustees: Rodney Watkins; Martin Green; Jeremy Wagg; David Seccombe.

CC Number: 266054

Eligibility

The following criteria apply:

1 Applicants must usually originate in the West Midlands
2 Applicants must show evidence of self-help in their application
3 Trustees have a preference for disadvantaged people
4 Trustees have a dislike for applications from students who have a full local authority grant and want finance for a different course or study
5 Trustees favour grants towards the cost of equipment
6 Applications by individuals in cases of hardship will not usually be considered unless sponsored by a local authority, health professional or other welfare agency

Types of grants

One-off or recurrent grants, usually between £50 and £500.

Annual grant total

In 2010/11 the charity had assets of £842,000 and an income of £38,000. Grants were made totalling £286,000 (this included a donation of £250,000 to Royal National Lifeboat Institution). Grants are awarded to individuals and organisations.

Applications

In writing to the correspondent. No reply is given to unsuccessful applicants unless an sae is enclosed.

The Mitchells and Butlers Charitable Trusts

£8,400 (52 grants)

Correspondent: Anne E Holmes, Clerk, Cobbetts LLP, 1 Colemore Square, Birmingham B4 6AJ (0845 404 2505; website: www.mbtrusts.org.uk)

Trustees: Mitchells and Butlers Trust Funds Ltd; Mitchells and Butlers Welfare Funds Ltd.

CC Number: 528922

Eligibility

Students over the age of 11 who live in the city of Birmingham and the borough of Smethwick. Preference is given to those who are children of an employee or ex-employee of the brewery industry including licensed retailing, catering and hotel management or who are undergoing training in these areas.

Types of grants

Grants in the range of £150 and £400 are given to: schoolchildren, college students, undergraduates, vocational students, mature students and people with special educational needs. Grants given include those towards uniforms/clothing, fees, books, equipment/instruments, and maintenance/living expenses.

Annual grant total

During the year the trust made 48 grants totalling £8,100 and four awards through Leeds Metropolitan University totalling £250.

Applications

Applications for the welfare fund can be made on a form available from the website. There is a preference for applications supported by a letter from a teacher or educational welfare officer etc. Applications can be submitted between April and June. Applications to the scholarship fund should be made through Leeds Metropolitan University.

The Perry Charitable Trust

£4,000

Correspondent: Michael Perry, 75 Park Walk, London SW10 0AZ (020 7351 9533; email: perrytrust@aol.com)

Trustees: William Stallard; Michael Perry; Carolyn Eyton; Joan Perry.

CC Number: 1094675

Eligibility

People in need under 25 whose parents or guardians have been resident in the West Midlands for not less than three years.

Types of grants

Grants for clothing, instruments, tools, books and so on.

Annual grant total

In 2010/11 the trust had assets of £110,000 and an income of £75,000. Donations to individuals and organisations totalled £24,000.

Applications

In writing to the correspondent.

Birmingham

The Birmingham Bodenham Trust

£10,000

Correspondent: Justin Pinkney, Finance (WS), PO Box 16306, Birmingham B2 2XR (01213 038744)

Trustees: R. Tulloch; David Osborne; Margaret Byrne; Judy Tizard; Keith Arnold; Jane Davies.

CC Number: 528902

Eligibility

People under 19 years of age who have special educational needs and live in the Birmingham area.

Types of grants

Grants are made for education and training, including for recreation and leisure, with the object of improving the quality of life of the individual.

Annual grant total

About £30,000 is available to be given in grants each year to organisations and individuals.

Applications

In writing to the correspondent. Applications are considered three times a year.

The Letisha and Charlene Education Awards

£4,000 (11 grants)

Correspondent: Yvonne Palmer, Operations Director, Birmingham Community Foundation, Nechells Baths, Nechells Park Road, Nechells, Birmingham B7 5PD (01213 225560; email: info@letishaandcharlene.com; website: www.letishaandcharlene.com)

Trustees: John Andrews; David Bucknall; Kay Cadman; Angela Henry; Shamiela Ahmed; David Scard; Richard Harris; John Matthews.

CC Number: 1048162

Eligibility

Young people aged sixteen and over living in Birmingham who are enrolled at an educational establishment.

Types of grants

Grants of around £400 towards course fees, computer equipment, accommodation fees, textbooks, travel expenses, childcare costs and so on.

Annual grant total

In 2011 grants totalling £4,000 were made to eleven students.

Applications

Application forms are available from the correspondent or to download from the website. Once funding has been fully allocated application forms will not be available until further funding has been set. Applications must include a reference from a professional person such as a teacher, tutor, social worker or youth worker.

Other information

This fund is administered by The Birmingham and Black Country Community Foundation.

Sir Josiah Mason's Relief in Need and Educational Charity

£800

Correspondent: Edward Kuczerawy, Financial Controller, Mason Court, Hillborough Road, Birmingham B27 6PF (01212 451002; fax: 01217 071090; email: enquiries@sjmt.org.uk; website: www.sjmt-rin.org.uk)

Trustees: A. B. Griffiths; Kenneth Meeson; Annabel Anderson; Hugh Dunn; Michael Shufflebotham; Roger Wood; Carol Jones; Michael Gahan; Betty Foster; Alison Crawley; Gareth Moore.

CC Number: 1073756

Eligibility

People under 25 who live or study in the West Midlands area and are in genuine financial hardship.

Types of grants

One-off grants of up to £500 for exam or tuition fees, study materials, books and equipment or tools for training or apprenticeships.

Annual grant total

In 2010/11 the charity had assets of £3.5 million and an income of £83,000. Grants to individuals totalled £800.

Exclusions

No grants for living costs.

Applications

On a form available from the website or from the correspondent to be returned by email or post. Applications are reviewed every three months, usually in March, June, September and December. The date of the next meeting is published on the website.

Other information

The charity made grants totalling £35,000 in 2010/11 to its connecting charities (which share trustees) including £1,300 for apprenticeship support, £28,000 for revenue deficit and £6,000 for building additions.

William Piddock Foundation

£7,000

Correspondent: Andrew Peet, Secretary, c/o Birmingham and Midland Institute, 9 Margaret Street, Birmingham B3 3BS (01212 363591; fax: 01212 124577; email: accounts@bmi.org.uk)

Trustees: Esther Boyd; Michael Sharpe; Janet Brookes; Robert Johnson; Simon Ramsay; Ann Morrison; Andrew Peet; Michael Jepson; Neil Riches; Maureen Cornish.

CC Number: 528920

Eligibility

People aged between 16 and 25 who are at secondary school or in further or higher education and live in Birmingham.

Types of grants

One-off and recurrent grants, usually ranging from £50 to £500 and loans are made to: further and higher education students and mature students to help with books, equipment/instruments, fees and maintenance/living expenses; and to postgraduates to help with study or travel overseas as part of their course.

Annual grant total

In 2010 the foundation had an income of £6,000 and an expenditure of £7,000.

Applications

Directly by the individual with a reference from a college/tutor on a form available from the correspondent. Applications are considered in August/September and should be submitted by the end of July. Applicants are required to attend an interview.

Joseph Scott's Educational Foundation

£1,000

Correspondent: Derek Duffield, 29 Jasmin Croft, Birmingham B14 5AX (01214 445479; email: joseph_scott_ef@hotmail.co.uk)

Trustees: Judith Gibbons; Christine Rowntree; Derek Duffied; H. Flinn; Malcolm Veitch; Mair O'Donovan; Jacky Homer; Robert Ash; Gordon Moyes; Ann Palmer; Lorna Pinches; Norman Gillhespy.

CC Number: 528919

Eligibility

People who live and were educated at primary level in the city of Birmingham.

Types of grants

One-off grants are given to students in further/higher education and mature students towards books and fees/living expenses.

Annual grant total

About £1,000.

Exclusions

No grants are given to postgraduates.

Applications

On a form available from the correspondent, for consideration in March, June, September and November.

Castle Bromwich

The Mary Dame Bridgeman Charity Trust

£500

Correspondent: Mr Jeremy Dutton, 60 Whateley Crescent, Birmingham, West Midlands B36 0DP

Trustees: Janet Richards; Jeremy Dutton; The Earl of Bradford; Alison Haywood; Ian Wright; P. Allen; Mark Smith; Revd Stuart Carter.

CC Number: 701557

Eligibility

People under 25 who are in need and living in the ecclesiastical parishes of St Mary, St Margaret and St Clement, Castle Bromwich.

Types of grants

One-off grants ranging from £100 to £400 towards clothing, books and educational outings for schoolchildren; and books, fees, living expenses and study or travel abroad for students in further/higher education. There is a preference for schoolchildren with serious family difficulties so that the child has to be educated away from home and people with special educational needs.

Annual grant total

About £1,000.

Exclusions

Grants are not given if they will affect any statutory benefits.

Applications

In writing to the correspondent either directly by the individual, through the individual's school, college, educational welfare agency or through a parent. The trustees meet twice a year in May and November.

Other information

This entry is an amalgamation of three separate charity funds which are administered as one.

Coventry

The Sir Charles Barratt Memorial Foundation

£2,500

Correspondent: Charley Russell, Chace Studio Centre, Robin Hood Road, Willenhall, Coventry CV3 3AN (02476 788575; email: admin@pas.coventry.gov.uk)

Trustees: Trevor Jones; Frank Vince; Gary Crookes; Catherine Miks; Rita Dawkins.

CC Number: 503108

Eligibility

People who live in the city of Coventry or those in full-time education at a school or place of further education in Coventry. There is a preference for applicants under the age of 18.

Types of grants

Grants to help those wishing to extend their musical education, whether in the UK or abroad. Grants generally range from £50 to £400.

Annual grant total

In 2010/11 the charity had an income of £3,800 and a total expenditure of £2,600.

Applications

The charity is advertised around October/November, usually in the *Coventry Evening Telegraph*. Applicants can then request an application form, which they must submit by the beginning of November. Applications are considered at the next meeting, usually in January.

The Children's Boot Fund

£15,000

Correspondent: Janet McConkey, Trustee, 123A Birmingham Road, Coventry CV5 9GR (02476 402837; email: martin_harban@btconnect.com)

Trustees: James Chapman; Janet McConkey; Martin Harban; Patricia Timmons; Peter Hancock; William Smith; Lucy Hancock.

CC Number: 214524

Eligibility

Schoolchildren in the city of Coventry, aged 4 to 16.

Types of grants

Grants for school footwear for children in need. No other type of help is given. Grants are made direct to footwear suppliers in the form of vouchers.

Annual grant total

In 2010/11 the fund had an income of £8,900 and an expenditure of £17,000.

Applications

Application forms are available from schools in the area and should be completed, verified and signed by the headteacher of the child's school. Applications are considered four times a year.

General Charities (City of Coventry)

£45,000

Correspondent: V A Tosh, General Charities Office, Old Bablake, Hill Street, Coventry CV1 4AN (02476 222769; email: cov.genchar@virgin.net)

Trustees: Richard Smith; David Mason; Michael Harris; Edna Eaves; Edward Curtis; Margaret Lancaster; Mavis Weitzel; Terence McDonnell; William Thompson; Nigel Lee; David Evans; Cllr Johnson; Terry Proctor; Caroline Rhodes; Gary Crookes; Marcus Lapsa; Vivian Kershaw; Catherine Miks.

CC Number: 216235

Eligibility

People in need living in the city of Coventry aged under 25.

Types of grants

Grants are given to students in further and higher education to help with the cost of fees, books or specialised equipment. Grants to support music education are also made.

Annual grant total

In 2011 the charity had assets of £8.3 million, an income of £1.3 million and gave education grants to individuals totalling £45,000, broken down as follows:

- Music awards: two grants totalling £10,000
- School fees: seven grants totalling £27,000
- Books and equipment: 83 grants totalling £8,700

Exclusions

Applications for fees or maintenance are never supported. Cash grants are not given.

Applications

Application forms can be collected from the correspondent in late August/early September and should be submitted for consideration in November. Replies will be sent out in December.

Other information

The charities receive income from Sir Thomas White's Charity, including the allocation for the Sir Thomas White's

Loan Fund in Coventry. Grants are also made for welfare purposes.

The Andrew Robinson Young People's Trust

£5,000

Correspondent: Clive Robinson, 31 Daventry Road, Coventry CV3 5DJ (02476 501579)

Trustees: Jonathan Veasey; Mark Crisp; Clive Robinson; Stella Robinson; Philip Gay.

CC Number: 1094029

Eligibility
Young people in Coventry who are in need.

Types of grants
One-off and recurrent grants to advance the religious education of young people and help their personal development.

Annual grant total
In 2010/11 the trust had an income of £15,000 and an expenditure of £10,000.

Applications
This trust has previously stated that its funds were fully committed.

Other information
The trust also makes grants to organisations and provides other support.

The Soothern and Craner Educational Foundation

£12,000

Correspondent: Gillian Waddilove, The Clerk, The Hollies, Priory Road, Wolston, Coventry CV8 3FX (02476 544255; email: admin@ soothernandcraner.org.uk; website: www. soothernandcraner.org.uk)

Trustees: Eleanor Nesbitt; Gillian Waddilove; Gyllian Brown; John Blundell; Pam Lunn; Faye Abbot.

CC Number: 528838

Eligibility
Girls and young women who are Quakers attached to Coventry Quaker Meeting, or girls and young women who live in the city of Coventry.

Types of grants
Mainly grants for further education, up to first degree level, to supplement existing grants or where no mandatory award is available. Grants have also been given towards school uniforms and school fees.

Annual grant total
In 2010/11 the foundation had an income of £11,000 and an expenditure of £15,000.

Exclusions
Grants are rarely given for study beyond a first degree.

Applications
There are two application forms available to download from the trust's website; one for those under the age of 16 and one for those over 16. Applicants should also have two references.

Dudley

The Baylies Educational Charity

£25,000

Correspondent: Alfred Austin, 5 Priory Close, Dudley, West Midlands DY1 3ED (01384 252310; fax: 01384 252310; email: fredaustin@btinternet.com)

Trustees: John Abbiss; Ian Cleland; Ken West; Cyril Woodall; Janet Dean; Carolyn Wickens; Pauline Gregory.

CC Number: 527118

Eligibility
People under 25 living in the area of Dudley Metropolitan Borough Council.

Types of grants
One-off grants for amounts of up to £1,000 each are given to schoolchildren for school uniforms and other school clothing, excursions and awards for excellence. Grants are also available to college students, undergraduates and vocational students for fees, study/travel abroad, books, equipment/instruments and maintenance/living expenses.

Annual grant total
In 2010/11 the trust gave grants (including book tokens) totalling £25,000.

Applications
In writing to the correspondent.

Daniel Parsons Educational Charity

£10,000

Correspondent: David Hughes, 53 The Broadway, Dudley, West Midlands DY1 4AP (01384 259277; email: parsonscharity@hotmail.com)

Trustees: John Abbiss; David Hughes; Ken West; John Wetherall; Arnold Jones; Robert Evans.

CC Number: 1068492

Eligibility
People under 25 who live, or whose parents live, or have attended a school in Dudley and district.

Types of grants
One-off grants in the range of £200 to £500.

Annual grant total
In 2011 the trust had an income of £13,000 and an expenditure of £12,000. Previously grants have totalled £10,000.

Applications
On a form available from the correspondent for consideration at any time.

The Sedgley Educational Trust

£3,000

Correspondent: Chris Williams, 12 Larkswood Drive, Dudley DY3 3UQ (01902 672880)

Trustees: Chris Williams; Alan Howes; Helen Jones; Stephen Buckley; Harry Grove; Tina Westwood.

CC Number: 1091563

Eligibility
People in need who live in the ecclesiastical parishes of All Saints Sedgley, St Mary The Virgin Sedgley and St Chad Coseley.

Types of grants
One-off and recurrent grants according to need to people in education, including Christian education.

Annual grant total
In 2011 the trust had an income of £2,600 and an expenditure of £4,200.

Applications
In writing to the correspondent.

King's Norton

The King's Norton United Charities

£2,500

Correspondent: Canon Rob Morris, The Rectory, 273 Pershore Road, Kings Norton, Birmingham B30 8EX (01214 590560)

Trustees: Annette Dickers; Geoffrey Sutton; Rob Morris; Alistair Dow; Roger Goodchild; Revd Jeremy Dussick; Revd David Warbrick; Revd Rebecca Clarke; Revd Catherine Grylls.

CC Number: 202225

Eligibility

People who live in the ancient parish of King's Norton in Birmingham and the West Midlands.

Types of grants

One-off and recurrent grants according to need.

Annual grant total

Grants usually total around £5,000.

Applications

Grants are made to named individuals only.

Other information

Grants are made for welfare and educational purposes.

Meriden

Meriden United Charities

£500

Correspondent: Alan Barker, 163 Avon Street, Coventry CV2 3GQ (02476 453342)

Trustees: Alan Gabbitas; David Bell; Christine Copper; Deborah Edwards; Grace Tuckey; Jennifer Harrison; Robert Hurton; Valerie Cotterrell.

CC Number: 234452

Eligibility

Young people who have lived in the parish of Meriden for at least two years.

Types of grants

Grants are given to schoolchildren, college students, undergraduates, vocational students and people with special educational needs. They include those for uniforms/clothing, fees, books and equipment/instruments.

Annual grant total

The charity has an income of about £1,500 a year. Grants are made for education and welfare purposes.

Applications

Applications can be submitted either directly by the individual or a family member or through a third party such as a social worker or teacher. The existence of the charities is made known by a notice in the Meriden magazine and by a notice in the library.

Oldbury

The Oldbury Educational Foundation

£5,000

Correspondent: Elaine Burke, c/o Shakespeare's Solicitors, 37 Temple Street, Birmingham B2 5DJ (01212 373000)

Trustees: Michael Darby; Owen Beale; Graham White; Roland Kay; Sylvia Milner.

CC Number: 527468

Eligibility

Pupils at schools in Oldbury.

Types of grants

Most grants are given to pupils at Warley High School, but pupils at other schools in Oldbury can also apply. Grants up to about £90 are available to help with books, clothing, equipment and travel for those at school, and grants of up to £300 are given to help with school, college or university fees or to supplement existing grants.

Annual grant total

In 2010/11 the foundation had an income of £6,400 and an expenditure of £6,600.

Applications

In writing to the correspondent by September of each year.

Rowley Regis

The Mackmillan Educational Foundation

£1,000

Correspondent: V J Westwood, Clerk, 18 Westdean Close, Halesowen, West Midlands B62 8UA (01216 022484; email: vicwestw@blueyonder.co.uk)

Trustees: Barbara Price; David Walker; Julie Webb; Robert Hamblett; Anne Shackleton; Iris Boucher.

CC Number: 529043

Eligibility

People under 25 who live in the ancient parish of Rowley Regis.

Types of grants

Grants to people at school and college.

Annual grant total

About £1,000 a year.

Applications

In writing to the correspondent.

Sandwell

The George and Thomas Henry Salter Trust

£20,000

Correspondent: J S Styler, Clerk, Lombard House, Cronehills Linkway, West Bromwich, West Midlands B70 7PL (01215 533286)

Trustees: Ann Maybury; David Payne; Hilary Pugh; Diana Wills.

CC Number: 216503

Eligibility

Students in further or higher education who are in need and resident in the borough of Sandwell.

Types of grants

Grants usually range between £100 and £1,000 and are given to help students pursue their education, including general, professional, vocational or technical training, in the UK and abroad.

Annual grant total

In 2011 the trust had assets of £1.3 million and an income of £30,000. Educational grants totalled £20,000 and relief in need totalled £8,200.

Applications

Initially by letter to the correspondent. Applicants must provide full written details of their circumstances and study courses. The trustees meet regularly and will occasionally interview applicants.

Stourbridge

The Palmer and Seabright Charity

£3,900

Correspondent: Susannah Griffiths, c/o Wall, James and Chappell, 15–23 Hagley Road, Stourbridge, West Midlands DY8 1QW (01384 371622)

Trustees: G. L. Partridge; David Rogers; Olive Calder; Robert Wilson; Suzanne Lowe.

CC Number: 200692

Eligibility

People living in the borough of Stourbridge.

Types of grants

One-off and recurrent grants are made to college students, undergraduates and mature students for fees, books, equipment/instruments and maintenance/living expenses. Grants are also given to schoolchildren for fees.

Annual grant total

The latest accounts available were for 2010 when the trust had assets of £230,000 and an income of £40,000. Grants for welfare and education totalled £7,800.

Applications

On a form available from the correspondent. Applications can be submitted either directly by the individual or a family member, through a third party such as a social worker or teacher, or through an organisation such as Citizens Advice or a school.

The Scott Educational Foundation

£1,000

Correspondent: Alan Cutler, 21 Primrose Hill, Stourbridge DY8 5AG (01384 443644)

Trustees: Audrey Green; G. Bells; S. Knowles; Alan Cutler; G. Partridge; David Mearman; David Hickman; M. Cowell.

CC Number: 511001

Eligibility

People under 25 who live in the old borough of Stourbridge (excluding Amblecote). Preference is given to those who have attended a maintained school in the area for more than two years.

Types of grants

Grants of £100 to £600 are given to schoolchildren towards school uniform, other school clothing, books, educational outings in the UK, maintenance and fees. Grants to students in further or higher education are given towards books, equipment/instruments, fees, living expenses and study or travel abroad; and grants to people starting work are for equipment or instruments.

Grants are mainly one-off, for recurrent grants a repeat application must be made.

Annual grant total

About £1,000.

Exclusions

Grants are rarely made to postgraduate students.

Applications

On a form available from the correspondent. Applications can be submitted either directly by the individual or a parent, guardian or local authority; or through the individual's school/college/educational welfare agency. Preferably they should be received by June or November for consideration in July and January, otherwise there is no requirement.

Sutton Coldfield

Sutton Coldfield Municipal Charities

£18,000 (342 grants)

Correspondent: Pauline John, Personal Assistant/Secretary, Lingard House, Fox Hollies Road, Sutton Coldfield, West Midlands B76 2RJ (01213 512262; fax: 01213 130651; email: pauline.john@ suttoncharities.org; website: www. suttoncoldfieldmunicipalcharities.com)

Trustees: David Roy; James Whorwood; John Gray; Susan Bailey; Jane Rothwell; Rodney Kettel; Michael Waltho; Freddie Gick; David Owen; Carole Hancox; Margaret Waddington; S. C. Martin; Malcolm Cornish; Neil Andrews; Linda Whitfield; Andrew Watson.

CC Number: 218627

Eligibility

People in need under the age of 25 living in the Four Oaks, New Hall and Vesey wards of Sutton Coldfield.

Types of grants

Grants are given to: schoolchildren for uniforms/other school clothing, books, equipment/instruments, fees and educational outings in the UK; and further and higher education students for books, equipment/instruments, fees, maintenance/living expenses, childcare, educational outings in the UK and study or travel abroad. Grants are also given to people with a wide range of special educational needs.

Annual grant total

In 2010/11 the charity had assets of £42 million and an income of £1.5 million. There were 33 grants to individuals in need, hardship or distress totalling £41,000, five grants for individual educational and personal needs totalling £10,000 and 340 school clothing grants totalling £13,000.

Exclusions

Grants are not given to individuals with a high parental income.

Applications

In writing or on a form available from the correspondent. Applications for educational grants should be made directly by the individual or through a parent or carer. They are considered every month, except April, August and December. Telephone enquiries are welcomed. Applications for school clothing are distributed to parents or carers through local schools before Easter each year.

Other information

The principal objective of the charities is the provision of almshouses, the distribution of funds and other measures for the alleviation of poverty and other needs for inhabitants and other organisations within the boundaries of the former borough of Sutton Coldfield.

Walsall

W. J. Croft for the Relief of the Poor

£1,000

Correspondent: Matthew Underhill, Constitutional Services, Walsall MBC, Civic Centre, Darwall Street, Walsall WS1 1EU (01922 652087; email: underhillm@walsall.gov.uk; website: cms.walsall.gov.uk/charities)

Trustees: Guy Svensson-Lockley; John Lea; Eileen Russell; Hilary Dunphy.

CC Number: 702795

Eligibility

Residents of the borough of Walsall who are in hardship, need or distress.

Types of grants

Grants for school uniforms including shoes.

Annual grant total

In 2010/11 the trust had an income of £2,000 and an expenditure of £2,300.

Applications

Contact the correspondent for an application form or download one from the website. Applications for school uniform grants are considered in July.

Other information

This organisation also makes grants for welfare purposes.

The Fishley Educational and Apprenticing Foundation

£22,000

Correspondent: Neil Picken, Constitutional Services, Walsall Council, Civic Centre, Darwall Street, Walsall WS1 1TP (01922 652018; email: charities@walsall.gov.uk; website: cms.walsall.gov.uk/charities)

Trustees: Michael Taylor; Keith Whittlestone; Mohammed Yaqub; Stella Petiffer; Stan Taylor; Najabit Ali.

CC Number: 529010

Eligibility

People under the age of 25 who live, work or are being educated in Walsall and who are in need.

Types of grants

Grants are available towards any educational need. Grants have been given towards books, fees, uniforms, clothing, educational outings and towards the study of music and the other arts.

Annual grant total

In 2010/11 the trust had an income of £19,000 and an expenditure of £23,000.

Applications

On a form available from the correspondent or the website. The trustees meet at least twice a year.

The C. C. Walker Charity

£1,500

Correspondent: Neil Picken, Clerk to the Trustees, Constitutional Services, Walsall Council, The Civic Centre, Darwall Street, Walsall WS1 1DQ (01922 652018; email: charities@walsall.gov.uk; website: cms.walsall.gov.uk/charities)

Trustees: Barbara McCracken; Kath Phillips; Gary Perry; Joan Baker.

CC Number: 528898

Eligibility

Individuals under the age of 25 (one of whose parents has died) who were born in Walsall.

In certain cases grants are available to individuals whose parents or surviving parent's fixed place of residence has at any time since the birth of the child been in Walsall (further information on eligibility for this specific criteria should be sought from the charity).

Types of grants

Grants according to need for any educational purpose. Grants have been given towards clothing for schoolchildren and books, fees, living expenses and equipment for students in further/higher education.

Annual grant total

In 2010/11 the charity had an income of £17,000 and an expenditure of £2,200.

Applications

On a form available from the correspondent or the website. Applications are considered in January, June and October.

Walsall Wood Charity

£10,000

Correspondent: Craig Goodall, Constitutional Services, Walsall Council, The Civic Centre, Darwall Street, Walsall WS1 1TP (01922 653317; email: goodallc@walsall.gov.uk; website: cms.walsall.gov.uk/charities)

Trustees: Alan Paul; Keith Sears; Rick Gamble; Michael Flower; Mike Bird.

CC Number: 510627

Eligibility

Residents of the borough of Walsall.

Types of grants

Grants for school uniforms including footwear.

Annual grant total

In 2010/11 the trust had an income of £23,000 and an expenditure of £30,000.

Applications

On a form available from the correspondent or the website. The inclusion of additional evidence that verifies personal circumstances such as proof of income (such as wage slips, benefits letters or bank statements) or letters of support from professional people who are familiar with the case will benefit the application. Trustees meet approximately six times a year.

The Blanch Woolaston Walsall Charity

£600

Correspondent: Mathew Underhill, Democratic Services, Walsall Council, Civic Centre, Darwall Street, Walsall WS1 1TP (01922 652087; email: underhillm@walsall.gov.uk)

Trustees: Geoffrey Barlow; Norman Mathews; Charles Underwood; Louise Harrison; Alan Paul.

CC Number: 216312

Eligibility

People in need living in the borough of Walsall. Educational grants will only be given to those under 21 years of age. There is no age limit for relief-in-need grants.

Types of grants

Around 20 one-off grants are made each year ranging from £50 to £300 for school uniforms and small household items. The trustees cannot undertake to repeat/renew any grants.

Annual grant total

Grants average around £1,200 per year.

Exclusions

No grants are made for the payment of rates, taxes or other public funds (including gas, electricity and so on).

Applications

On a form available from the correspondent. Applications are considered four times a year.

Warley

Palmer Educational Charity

£2,000

Correspondent: Miss Emma Lardner, Personal Assistant to the Diocesan Director of Education, Birmingham Diocesan Finance Office, 175 Harborne Park Road, Harborne, Birmingham B17 0BH (01214 260400; email: Emma. L@birmingham.anglican.org)

Trustees: Gerard Nixon; Anthony Perry; Nick Pelling; Jacqueline Hughes; Michael Wilkes.

CC Number: 508226

Eligibility

People under 25 who live in the rural deanery of Warley.

Types of grants

Schoolchildren and further and higher education students can receive help with the cost of books directly related to Christianity and religious education.

Annual grant total

In 2011 the charity had an income of £9,900 and an expenditure of £8,400.

Applications

On a form available from the correspondent. They should be submitted through the Parish Church Council or clergy of Warley Deanery and are considered in March and October.

Other information

Grants are also made to local schools, churches and organisations.

West Bromwich

The Akrill, Wilson and Kenrick Trust Fund and West Bromwich Educational Foundation

£100

Correspondent: Sandwell MBC, Young Peoples' Services, Shaftsbury House, 402 High Street, West Bromwich, West Midlands B70 9LT (01215 698283)

Trustee: Sandwell MBC.

CC Number: 528996

Eligibility

Students under 25 years of age, who are in need and live in West Bromwich.

Types of grants

(i) Scholarships and maintenance allowances for schoolchildren and students. (ii) Grants, clothing, tools, instruments and books for people leaving school or another educational establishment and starting work. (iii) Grants towards educational travel abroad. (iv) Grants for the study of music and other arts.

Annual grant total

In 2010/11 the foundation had an income of £1,700 and an expenditure of £100.

Applications

On an application form, available by writing to the correspondent.

Yardley

The Yardley Educational Foundation

£126,000

Correspondent: Derek Hackett, Edzell House, 121 Chester Road, Castle Bromwich, Birmingham B36 0AE (01212 463625; email: dhhackett@blueyonder.co. uk)

Trustees: Heather Jones; Penny Wagg; Brenda Capener; T. Wagg; Robert Jones; Michael Roden; William Sands; Mohammed Ansar.

CC Number: 528918

Eligibility

Children and young people aged 11 to 19 who have lived in the ancient parish of Yardley (virtually the whole of the east of Birmingham) for over two years.

Types of grants

Grants towards school uniforms, school clothing, sports equipment, educational outings in the UK and study or travel overseas. Donations are in the range of £50 to £200. Book vouchers are also given to those in years 7, 8 and 9.

Annual grant total

In 2010/11 the trust had assets of £4 million and an income of £149,000. Grants were given totalling £115,000 and book vouchers amounting to £11,000.

Exclusions

No grants to apprentices.

Applications

Application forms are available from the correspondent and should be submitted through the individual's school or college in May or June for consideration in July and August.

Worcester-shire

The Alfrick Educational Charity

£10,000

Correspondent: Andrew Duncan, Bewell, Alfrick, Worcestershire WR6 5EY (01905 731731; email: a.duncan@wwf.co. uk)

Trustees: Andrew Duncan; Andrew Bullock; Christine Williams; Gareth Lowe; Janet Proctor; Sheila Tolley; Clive Smith; Rosemary Harward; Dympna Jardine.

CC Number: 517760

Eligibility

People who live in the parish of Alfrick, Lulsley and Suckley and are under 25.

Types of grants

Grants are given to further and higher education students for books, maintenance/living expenses and educational outings in the UK.

Annual grant total

The trust has an income every year of around £8,500. In 2010/11 It had a total expenditure of £11,000.

Applications

In writing to the correspondent directly by the individual. Applications can be submitted at any time.

The Bewdley Old Grammar School Foundation

£7,500

Correspondent: Mrs Shana Kent, Clerk, Bewdley School and Sixth Form Centre, Stourport Road, Bewdley DY12 1BL (01299 403277)

Trustees: A. Scaplehorn; Susan Thompson; Julie Reilly; David Bishop; Susan Price; Lousie Edginton; John Latham.

CC Number: 527429

Eligibility

People under the age of 25 living in Bewdley, Stourport-on-Severn, and the parish of Rock and Ribbesford.

Types of grants

Help with the cost of books, clothing and other essentials for schoolchildren. Grants may also be available for those at college or university.

Annual grant total

Between £7,000 and £8,000 is given in grants each year.

Applications

In writing to the correspondent.

The Ancient Parish of Ripple Trust

£2,500

Correspondent: John Willis, Secretary, 7 Court Lea, Holly Green, Upton upon Severn, Worcestershire WR8 0PE (01684 594570; email: willis.courtlea@ btopenworld.com)

Trustees: Jane Crowther; Dorothy Marchant; Lady Jean Huntington-Whitely; Clive Astin; Revd Geoffrey Moore; Nicola Inchbald; Revd Frances Wookey; Gillian Sutton.

CC Number: 1055986

Eligibility

Students in higher education who live in the parishes of Ripple, Holdfast, Queenhill and Bushley.

Types of grants

Small cash grants are made.

Annual grant total

In 2010/11 the trust had an income of £11,500 and a total expenditure £13,000.

Applications

In writing to the correspondent. The trustees meet twice a year to consider applications, and the funds are advertised locally before these meetings.

Other information

Grants are also made to registered charities that serve local people.

Walwyn's Educational Foundation

£4,000

Correspondent: Charles Walker, 29 Brookmill Close, Colwall, Malvern, Worcestershire WR13 6HY (01684 541995; email: cdw1810@btinternet.com)

Trustees: Neil Bowring; Alexandra Berington; Elizabeth Clements; Susan Kennedy; Philip Probert; Paul Chambers; Susan Ling; John Cooney; Phillipa Mason.

CC Number: 527152

Eligibility

Young people who live in the parishes of Colwall and Little Malvern and are studying to first degree level. Grants may be available for secondary school, further education students and those on training courses. Some professions that insist on qualifications beyond first degree (for example, teaching profession) will be considered on their merits.

Types of grants

Grants of £160 each are given to students studying to first degree level, including those for books, fees/living expenses, study and travel abroad.

Annual grant total

About £4,000 each year.

Exclusions

No support will be given to mature students.

Applications

On a form available from the correspondent. Applications are considered in late September and should be submitted directly by the individual up to 15 September.

Worcester Municipal Exhibitions Foundation

£17,000 (266 grants)

Correspondent: Ian Pugh, 4 and 5 Sansome Place, Worcester WR1 1UQ (01905 726600; email: mary.barker@ hallmarkhulme.co.uk)

Trustees: Paul Griffith; D. A. Tibbutt; Brenda Sheridan; M. Jones; R. C. Peachey; M. Saunders; P. Denham; R. E. Berry; C. W. V. Lord; R. A. Kington; S. M. Osborne; S. G. Markwell; G. V. Hughes; C. M. Panter; A. J. Witcher; J. M. Whitehouse; Melanie Kirk; Jess Bird; R. H. Rust.

CC Number: 527570

Eligibility

People who are resident in, or have received education in, the city of Worcester and the parishes of Powick, Bransford and Rushwick, and the ancient parish of Leigh for at least two years.

Types of grants

One-off grants are given to schoolchildren, people starting work, further and higher education students and mature students for clothing, books, equipment/instruments, fees, maintenance/living expenses, childcare, educational outings in the UK, study or travel overseas and student exchanges. Grants can range from £20 to £1,000.

Annual grant total

The foundation receives 6% of the income of the Worcester Consolidated Municipal Charity each year, totalling £52,000 in 2011. £17,000 was awarded to 266 individuals in educational grants.

Exclusions

Help is not usually given to mature students and no grants are made to

foreign students studying in the UK or for private education.

Applications

Applications can be submitted by the individual or through a school, college or educational welfare agency on a form available from the correspondent. They are considered every month.

Other information

Grants are also given to schools and educational organisations.

Alvechurch

The Alvechurch Grammar School Endowment

£13,000

Correspondent: David Gardiner, 18 Tanglewood Close, Blackwell, Bromsgrove, Worcestershire B60 1BU (01214 453522)

Trustees: Kathleen Cholmondeley; Margaret Parry; Robert Fieldson; Jeremy Trafford; Karen Jordan; Derek Higgins; John Cypher; Wayne Thomas; Catriona Savage.

CC Number: 5274400

Eligibility

People who have lived in the civil parish of Alvechurch for at least three years and are under 25 on 30 June in the year of application.

Types of grants

Applications are invited from 'those needing help to enable them to pursue an academic or technical course whether at school or in some form of higher education and the governors are anxious to receive applications relating to education in its widest sense: young people undertaking projects designed to assist with their development, examples of which might be Sail Training Association or Outward Bound courses or language study courses abroad'.

In practice grants are given to those in further or higher education rather than schoolchildren, but they can be given for people starting work. Grants can be towards the cost of equipment, books and educational outings or travel in the UK or overseas.

Annual grant total

In 2010/11 the trust had an income of £18,000 and an expenditure of £14,000

Applications

On a form available from the correspondent, including parents' income, schools attended and record of examination results. Applications are

considered in January, May and September/October.

Other information

Grants are also made to youth-based organisations.

Cropthorpe

Randolph Meakins Patty's Farm and the Widows Lyes Charity

£1,500

Correspondent: Mrs J Ayliffe, Orchard House, Main Street, Cropthorne, Pershore, Worcestershire WR10 3LT (01386 860011)

Trustees: John Ayliffe; Garth Wood; Mary Blizard; Roger Hutchins; Sheila Smith.

CC Number: 500624

Eligibility

People in need who live in the village of Cropthorne (Worcestershire).

Types of grants

One-off grants according to need.

Annual grant total

Grants usually total about £3,000 per year.

Applications

In writing to the correspondent.

Evesham

John Martin's Charity

£224,000

Correspondent: The Clerk, 16 Queen's Road, Evesham, Worcester WR11 4JN (01386 765440; fax: 01386 765340; email: enquires@johnmartins.org.uk; website: www.johnmartins.org.uk)

Trustees: Nigel Lamb; Julia Westlake; Revd Mark Binney; Revd Barry Collins; Richard Emson; Catherine Evans; Gabrielle Falkiner; Diana Raphael; John Smith; Cyril Scorse; Joyce Turner; Revd Andrew Spurr; John Wilson.

CC Number: 527473

Eligibility

People resident in Evesham in Worcestershire. Applicants or a parent/ guardian must have lived in the town for at least 12 months at the date of application. Applications from those over 25 are income assessed.

Types of grants

Individual students, between the ages of 16 and state retirement age, may apply for educational grants to support study in a wide variety of courses at local colleges in addition to universities and colleges throughout the country and the Open University. Qualifying courses include HND, degree, postgraduate and part-time vocational courses. Grants are also made towards:

▶ School uniform costs – grants may be available to assist with the cost of school uniforms for children aged 4–18

▶ Educational visits and music, arts and sports activities – grants may be available to students aged 4–18 for activities including school trips, music lessons/instrument hire and sporting activities

▶ 'Standards of Excellence' awards – grants for students aged 4–18 for achieving a 'standard of excellence' in a sporting or arts/music area

Annual grant total

In 2010/11 the charity had assets of £18.7 million and an income of £766,000. Grants were made to individuals totalling £224,000 for the promotion of education.

Exclusions

The charity does not currently provide grants for full time courses below degree level.

Applications

On a form available from the correspondent or downloaded from the website, where criteria is also posted. Applications are considered from July to September for further and higher education grants. Grants for part-time vocational courses are available throughout the year.

Note the following statement from the charity: 'Since 1 July 2009 we have rejected 70% of all Student Grant Applications because the required evidence to prove residency in the town of Evesham was not supplied. Read the Application Form.'

Other information

Grants are also made to organisations and to individuals for welfare purposes. The charity has an informative website.

Feckenham

The Feckenham Educational Foundation

£2,000

Correspondent: J Bate, Clerk, Wychway, Droitwich Road, Hanbury, Nr Bromsgrove, Worcestershire B60 4DB (01527 821285)

Trustees: Arthur Price; Jane White; Phyllis Mote; Paul Richards; Jillian Rowe; J. Pulsford.

CC Number: 527565

Eligibility

People under 25 who live in the ancient parish of Feckenham.

Types of grants

Grants are given to schoolchildren and students, and towards the cost of outfits, tools and books to people preparing to enter a trade or profession.

Annual grant total

In 2010/11 the trust had an income of £3,300 and an expenditure of £2,200.

Applications

On a form available from the correspondent.

Worcester

The United Charities of Saint Martin

£2,900

Correspondent: Michael Bunclark, 4 St Catherine's Hill, London Road, Worcester WR5 2EA (01905 355585)

Trustees: Josephine Hodges; Bill Simpson; Lucy Hodgson; Revd Kenneth Boyce; Stephen Hodgson; Keith Burton; Jim Wheldon; Jabba Riaz; Robert Rowden.

CC Number: 200733

Eligibility

People in need who live in the parish of St Martin, Worcester.

Types of grants

One-off grants are given for general educational purposes.

Annual grant total

In 2010 the charities had an income of £6,000 and a total expenditure of £5,800.

Applications

In writing to the correspondent.

The Worcester Consolidated Municipal Charity

£17,000 (266 grants)

Correspondent: The Clerk to the Trustees, HallmarkHulme Solicitors, 3- 5 Sansome Place, Worcester WR1 1UQ (01905 726600; email: mary.barker@ hallmarkhulme.co.uk)

Trustees: Paul Griffith; D. A. Tibbutt; Brenda Sheridan; M. Jones; R. C. Peachy; M. Saunders; P. Denham; R. E. Berry; C. W. Lord; R. A. Kington; S. M. Osborne; S. G. Markwell; G. V. Hughes; C. M. Panter; A. J. Witcher; J. M. Whitehouse; Melanie Kirk; Jess Bird; Ron Rust.

CC Number: 205299

Eligibility

People in need who live in the city of Worcester, or the parishes of Powick, Bransford, Rushwick and Leigh, or have attended school in the city for at least two years.

Types of grants

One-off grants of £20 to £1,000, for educational needs including school clothing, tools/equipment and fees.

Annual grant total

In 2011 grants were made totalling £17,000 to 266 individuals for education including 252 grants for school clothing and 11 for course fees and equipment.

Applications

Applications are usually through a social worker, Citizens Advice or other welfare agency. Statutory sources must have first been exhausted. Applications are submitted on a form available from the correspondent and are considered every month.

Other information

The charity also gives grants to organisations and to individuals for welfare purposes and maintains almshouses, amongst other charitable activities in Worcester.

South West

General

The Adams Youth Trust

£50,000

Correspondent: Margaret Pyle, Greendale Court, Clyst St Mary, Exeter, Devon EX5 1AW (01395 233433)

Trustees: John Armson; Elizabeth Adams; Gerald Keay; Terence Adams.

CC Number: 1067277

Eligibility

Young people principally in the West Country.

Types of grants

Grants to provide opportunities for education, advancement of personal skills and training.

Annual grant total

In 2010/11 the trust had an income of £13,000 and a total expenditure of £107,000. Scholarships and bursaries usually total around £50,000.

Applications

In writing to the correspondent.

Other information

The trust also makes grants to other charities.

The Christina Aitchison Trust

See entry on page 151

Viscount Amory's Charitable Trust

£7,200 (13 grants)

Correspondent: The Trust Secretary, The Island, Lowman Green, Tiverton, Devon EX16 4LA (01884 254899)

Trustees: Sir Ian Amory; Catherine Cavender.

CC Number: 204958

Eligibility

People in need in the south west of England, with a preference for Devon.

Types of grants

One-off and recurrent grants according to need.

Annual grant total

In 2010/11 the trust had assets of £12 million and an income of £355,000. The trust made 13 grants to individuals totalling £9,000, mostly for educational purposes. A further £342,000 was given to organisations.

Applications

In writing to the correspondent, for consideration every month.

M. R. Cannon 1998 Charitable Trust

£16,000

Correspondent: Chris Mitchell, Trustee, 53 Stoke Lane, Westbury On Trym, Bristol BS9 3DW (01173 776540)

Trustees: Chris Mitchell; Michael Cannon; Sally Cannon.

CC Number: 1072769

Eligibility

Young people who wish to carry out vocational training or studies. There is a preference for North Devon, Dorset, Bristol, North Yorkshire and County Durham.

Types of grants

Grants given according to need.

Annual grant total

In 2010/11 the trust had an income of £3,000 and an expenditure of £80,000. Based upon previous years, grants to individuals probably totalled around £16,000.

Applications

In writing to the correspondent.

Other information

Grants are also made to medical/health charities and conservation and countryside related initiatives, as well as small local projects in the area of benefit.

Devon and Cornwall Aid for Girls' Trust

£13,000

Correspondent: Frederick Webb, 33 Downham Gardens, Tamerton Foliot, Plymouth, Devon PL5 4QF (01752 776612)

Trustees: Michael Brindley; Valena Jones; Paul Trevan; Helen Thom; Mary McNaughton; Sharon Privett.

CC Number: 202493

Eligibility

Girls or women between 16 and 23 years of age who live in the counties of Devon and Cornwall. There is a preference for people who have lost either or both parents, but any other girl in need can apply.

Types of grants

One-off and recurrent grants ranging from £100 to £350. Grants are given to help students in higher/further and vocational education with books, clothing, fees, equipment/instruments and living expenses.

Annual grant total

In 2010/11 the trust had an income of £12,300 and a total expenditure of £13,400.

Exclusions

Grants are not given for postgraduate, higher or second qualifications, home or part-time studies, mature students, or study outside of the UK.

Applications

On a form available from the correspondent, submitted directly by the individual. They are considered throughout the year.

The Dyke Exhibition Foundation

£2,500

Correspondent: Christopher Stanley-Smith, Grove View, Hodshill, Southstoke, Bath BA2 7ED

Trustees: Lady Acland; Gervase Channer.

CC Number: 306610

Eligibility

People under 25 who were born in Somerset, Devon or Cornwall and who have lived within the area for the past three years or who have been educated in the area for the past two years.

Types of grants

Awards, usually between £100 and £300 per year for up to three years, for educational purposes including fees, living costs, books and equipment. Applications are considered on merit, but preference is given to applicants who are, or are about to become, undergraduates of Oxford University or any other university, and those most in need.

Annual grant total

Grants usually total around £2,000 to £3,000 each year.

Applications

Application forms can be obtained by the individual, school or college, parent or guardian by sending an sae to the correspondent. Completed application forms must be submitted by the end of February for consideration in April.

The Elmgrant Trust

£5,200 (21 grants)

Correspondent: Angela Taylor, Elmhirst Centre, Dartington Hall, Totnes, Devon TQ9 6EL (01803 863160; email: info@ elmgrant.org.uk)

Trustees: Paul Elmhirst; Marian Ash; Mark Sharman; Sophie Young; David Young.

CC Number: 313398

Eligibility

Individuals living in the South West, especially in Devon and Cornwall. There is a preference for people with special education needs, and for schoolchildren with serious family difficulties causing the child to be educated away from home.

Types of grants

One-off grants of between £200 and £500 are made to schoolchildren for school clothing (not uniforms), books, equipment, fees and educational outings in the UK; people starting work for equipment; and further and higher education students, including mature students, for books, equipment, fees, maintenance/living expenses, childcare and educational outings in the UK.

Annual grant total

In 2010/11 the trust had assets of £1.9 million and an income of £51,000. 21 grants were made to individuals totalling £5,200.

Exclusions

Grants are not made for postgraduate study, expeditions, travel and study projects overseas, counselling courses, or to large-scale national organisations or overseas students.

People and organisations who have received a grant within the last two years are not eligible to reapply.

Applications

In writing to the correspondent at least one clear month before the trustees' meetings in March, July and November. Applications can be made directly by the individual, or through a third party such as a parent/guardian, school/college or educational welfare agency. They should include the individual's current financial circumstances (budget helpful), confirmation of place on course, letter in support (tutor, college or welfare worker) and information about the cost of items needed (if appropriate). An sae should also be included.

Other information

Grants are also made to local arts and community projects, disability and disadvantaged groups, and to medical causes.

A. B. Lucas Memorial Awards

£1,000

Correspondent: Martin Dare, Green Meadows, Lower Odcombe, Yeovil BA22 8TZ (01935 863522)

Trustees: John Lindley; Richard Lawrence; Terry Cox; Martin Dare; Michael Smale.

CC Number: 282306

Eligibility

People who are undertaking the study of dairy agriculture and live in the administrative counties of Cornwall, Devon, Somerset, Dorset and those parts of Avon that were previously part of Somerset.

Types of grants

One-off grants for the study of agriculture and particularly dairy farming. In practice the people who apply tend to be young people, aged under 30, who wish to study dairy agriculture overseas.

Annual grant total

Grants usually total around £1,000 each year.

Applications

In writing to the correspondent.

Bishop Wordsworth's Educational Trust

£0

Correspondent: Carolann Johnson, Clerk, Church House, Crane Street, Salisbury, Wiltshire SP1 2QB (01722 428420)

Trustees: John Wraw; Chris Shepperd; Andrew Cullis; Jenny Vokes; Edward Probert.

CC Number: 309502

Eligibility

Children who are under 18, members of the Church of England and live in the diocese of Salisbury (that is, most areas of Wiltshire and Dorset), whose parents are in need financially or through sickness, and so on. Children of both clergy and laity of the diocese of Salisbury are eligible.

Types of grants

Grants can be given to help with the cost of books, educational outings, educational tuition and music tuition. There is a preference for schoolchildren with serious family difficulties and schoolchildren with special education needs. Grants are not made for school fees or maintenance costs.

Annual grant total

Usually about 80% of the income is given to Church of England schools in the diocese and 20% to a small number of individuals. However in 2010/11 no grants were made to individuals.

Applications

Applications should be made by the parent or guardian to the correspondent. Information required includes applicant's name, occupation of guardian/parent, address, date of birth, name of school, educational expenses, details of income of applicant's parent/ guardian (i.e. financial status), amount applied for, for how long, source of other funds available, reasons for application, details of other children in family, church affiliation and a reference from the parish priest. Applications are usually considered around March and October. Telephone enquiries are welcomed.

Other information

Grants are also made to church schools in the diocese for Christian educational resources.

Avon

Bristol Trust for the Deaf

£500

Correspondent: A M Burrows, Clerk, 13 Wellington Walk, Bristol BS10 5ET (01179 505631)

Trustees: William Martin; David Morris; Jackie Norman; Margaret Shovelton; Susan Mason; Derek Pickup; Cathy Sander; Clare Burrows-Majithia.

CC Number: 311507

Eligibility

People with hearing impairments who live in and around the city of Bristol.

Types of grants

The trustees normally make grants to assist in the training of people working with people who are deaf to ensure that the greatest number of people benefit from the limited resources available. In certain circumstances applications from individuals are considered.

Grants range from £50 to £250 and are given for books, equipment/instruments and fees for students, mature students and postgraduates. Schoolchildren can receive grants for equipment/instruments.

Annual grant total

Grants are usually made to organisations, although there is marginal scope for grants to be made to individuals.

Applications

In writing to the correspondent, directly by the individual. Applications are considered in May and November and should be submitted in April and October, but special consideration can be given at other times to urgent needs.

Other information

This trust mainly supports Elmfield School for Deaf Children, Hearing Impaired Service and Bristol Centre for Deaf People.

Nailsea Community Trust Ltd

£2,000

Correspondent: Mrs Helen Owen, 42 Green Pastures Road, Wraxall, Bristol BS48 1ND (01275 856429)

Trustees: Robert Westlake; John Smithson; Karl Day; Nancy Elliott; Norman Baker; Patricia Robinson; Anthony Tavener; Philippa Taylor; Mary Jaggard; Alan Shaw; Dr Martin Elford.

CC Number: 900031

Eligibility

Grants are made to schoolchildren, college students and undergraduates for study/travel abroad.

Types of grants

One-off grants, usually up to £500.

Annual grant total

About £4,000 for educational and welfare purposes.

Applications

On a form available from the correspondent. Applications can be submitted either directly by the individual or via a relevant third party such as a school, social worker or Citizens Advice. Applications are considered at meetings held every three months.

Bath and North East Somerset

Richard Jones Charity

£2,500

Correspondent: Peter Godfrey, 'Two Shillings', 24d Tyning Road, Saltford, Bristol BS31 3HL (01225 341085; email: peter@godfreyfamily.org.uk)

Trustees: Raynor Nixon; Gillian Bueno de Mesquita; John Harvey; John Knibbs; Jon Wheatley; Nicolette Robson; Sheila Walker; Valerie Hardwick; John Sewart; Adrian Elvin; Sue Ford.

CC Number: 310057

Eligibility

People under 30 who live in the parishes of Chew Magna, Newton St Loe, Stanton Drew, Stanton Prior and Stowey-Sutton, all in the area of Bath and North East Somerset.

Types of grants

One-off and recurrent grants of £30 to £400 for:
(i) college and university students towards books, study or travel abroad, educational outings in the UK and equipment/instruments
(ii) schoolchildren towards school clothing, books and equipment/instruments
(iii) people starting work towards books, equipment/instruments
(iv) mature students and postgraduates up to the age of 30 for books and equipment/instruments.

Grants are also available for individuals in need at Christmas without any restriction of age. Schools, clubs and other organisations benefiting the youth of the above named parishes also receive grants towards equipment.

Annual grant total

The charity has an annual income and expenditure of between £2,500 and £4,000.

Exclusions

No grants are made to people attending private schools.

Applications

On a form available from the correspondent, submitted directly by the individual. Applications should be submitted in September/October and March/April, for consideration in October and April – actual dates of the meetings when applications are considered are advertised in parish magazines and on parish noticeboards. Completed application forms must be submitted to a parish trustee (details supplied on the form) and an interview arranged.

Other information

The correspondent states:

The majority of our beneficiaries are students at universities and colleges of further education. We would like to attract more applications from school leavers starting to learn a trade for grants towards tools and equipment … We do on occasions assist school pupils with the cost of extra music lessons and, if they can exhibit exceptional talent, towards the cost of musical instruments. We have also given grants to children for educational visits, camps etc. organised by their schools but it seems that most of the state schools in the area are able to fund needy pupils from their own resources for such activities. We do not, generally speaking, assist pupils at private schools. Very occasionally grants may be made towards the cost of school uniforms. Grants have also been given in the past few years to participants in Operation Raleigh expeditions, Outward Bound courses and other ventures of a similar nature.

Ralph and Irma Sperring Charity

£25,000

Correspondent: The Secretary, Thatcher and Hallam Solicitors, Island House, Midsomer Norton, Bath BA3 2HJ (01761 414646)

Trustees: S. A. Blanning; N. M. Busby; Revd C. G. Chiplin; E. W. Hallam; Dr P. Haxell; K. W. Saunders.

CC Number: 1048101

Eligibility

People in need who live within a five-mile radius of the Church of St John the Baptist in Midsomer Norton, Bath.

Types of grants

One-off and recurrent grants according to need.

Annual grant total

In 2010/11 the charity had assets of £5.7 million, which generated an income of £201,000. Awards to local causes amounted to £114,000. Further details were not available, however the charity makes grants to both individuals and organisations.

Applications

In writing to the correspondent, to be considered quarterly.

Bristol

Bagshaw Birkin Educational Trust

£2,500

Correspondent: Yvonne Craggs, 35 Barley Croft, Bristol BS9 3TG (01179 682435)

Trustees: Mrs Gulland; Robert Jennings; David McGregor; Mrs Down.

CC Number: 311676

Eligibility

Young people between the ages of 11 and 25 (preferably 11 to 18) who live within the boundaries of the city of Bristol and are studying at 'any school, university, college of education or other institution of further (including professional and technical) education approved for the purpose by the trustees', in the maintained education system.

Types of grants

Generally one-off cash grants to help with: essential clothing (not uniforms); school trips considered to have an educational or social value; and musical instruments. Grants are usually about £50, but can be up to £300.

In exceptional circumstances, applications from parents whose children are in private education will be considered, but there is a preference for children in the maintained education system.

Annual grant total

In 2010/11 the trust had an income of £3,000 and an expenditure of £3,300.

Exclusions

No grants will be considered for: year 11 clothing; baby clothing; furniture or other items; university or college fees; fees for children in private education; funding for the dependents of applicants; or maintenance allowances for years 12 and 13.

Applications

There are two types of applicant: individuals (usually through their parents), and schools who will make a block application for many pupils. The applicant's parents in each case will be required to complete a financial statement and give details of other children and whether they include wage earners. The applicant's full address must be provided to ensure the child lives within the Bristol city boundaries (the postcode is not necessarily sufficient). The trustees may wish to interview the parents.

Applications are considered at any time, if urgent, but usually at formal trustee meetings held in February, May and November, and applications for consideration at those meetings must be received by 28th of the previous month.

The Christ Church Exhibition Fund

£15,000

Correspondent: Ian Millsted, 1 All Saints Court, Bristol BS1 1JN (01179 292709; email: ascl.charity@virgin.net)

Trustees: Richard Morris; Chris Davies; David Moon; Stephen Parsons; Stephen Holliday; William Martin; Roger Kerridge; Martin Evans; Jonathan Price; P. C. L. Abraham; Theresa McGoldrick.

CC Number: 325124

Eligibility

(i) Boys and girls over the age of 11 who live in the city of Bristol and are attending fee-paying schools. Assistance is not, however, given on first entry to fee-paying education. Grants for schoolchildren are calculated in relation to family income and actual fees. (ii) Students in higher education up to the age of 25 who have received at least two years' secondary education in Bristol or who have long residential connections with the city.

Types of grants

(i) Grants, generally between £200 and £1,000 a year, for fee-paying secondary education, where parents are unable to maintain payments because of changed family or financial circumstances. Grants are to help with the cost of school uniforms, other school clothing, books and educational outings.

Occasional help is given to talented pupils at state schools who need help to pay for music lessons.

(ii) Grants of between £100 and £300 a year to students unable to obtain discretionary awards or for higher education courses not qualifying for grants. Grants are awarded only for courses in the UK. Grants can be to help with the cost of books and help with fees and living expenses.

Annual grant total

In 2010/11 the trust had an income of £24,000 and an expenditure of £16,000.

Exclusions

Grants are not given for trips abroad, for courses outside the UK or for postgraduate study.

Applications

On a form available from the correspondent from Easter onwards. Applications should be submitted directly by the individual (student) or by a parent (schoolchildren). Meetings are held in June/July for junior grants, and in September for seniors. Applications should include length of residence in Bristol, how long in present school (schoolchildren) and whether a definite place offer has been received (student).

Edmonds and Coles Scholarships

£2,000

Correspondent: Sandra Lampard, Merchants Hall, The Promenade, Bristol BS8 3NH (01179 73805; email: treasurer@merchantventurers.com; website: www.merchantventurers.com/charitable-activities/edmonds-and-coles-scholarships.html)

Trustees: Tim Pearce; David Poole; Ronald Singer; Christopher Jones; Peter Fraser; Felicity Brown; Alistair Perry; Bill Martin.

CC Number: 311751

Eligibility

People under the age of 25 who live in the ancient parishes of Henbury, Westbury-on-Trym or Horfield (Bristol) and have done so for at least three years.

Types of grants

Grants to help with educational expenses for those at school, college or university. This can include help with the study of music and other arts (which is outside the normal curriculum) and vocational training. Grants range from £100 to £1,000 and can be for books, equipment/instruments, travel costs, maintenance costs, educational outings in the UK and study or travel overseas. Grants can also be made for university fees, but not for school fees.

At primary and secondary school level, grants are not normally given to enable children to enter private education when parents cannot afford the cost. Help may be given in respect of children already in private education when there is a change in financial circumstances through, for example, death of a parent, marriage break-up, unemployment and so on, and there are good reasons for avoiding disruption of the child's education.

Annual grant total

In 2010/11 the charity had an income of £10,000 and an expenditure of £2,200.

Applications

On forms available from the correspondent or the website, submitted by the individual or a third party if the applicant is under 16. They are usually considered in February, July and September.

Other information

This charity consults and cooperates with Bristol Municipal Charities in some cases.

Anthony Edmonds Charity

£7,000

Correspondent: Fran Greenfield, 43 Meadowland Road, Henbury, Bristol BS10 7PW (01179 098308; email: fran. greenfield@blueyonder.co.uk)

Trustees: Dilys Naylor; Christine Payne; Leigh Mitchell; Marion Merrick; Morris Venables; Robert Gilmore; Wendy Roberts.

CC Number: 286709

Eligibility

Young people up to the age of 25 who live in any of the ancient parishes (as in 1898) of Henbury, Westbury-on-Trym or Horfield.

Types of grants

One-off grants up to £400 can be made for books, uniforms/school clothing, educational outings in the UK, study or travel overseas, equipment/instruments and fees. Grants are to help with activities of a broadly educational nature including apprentices, courses and less formal projects that can be academic; artistic; technical; social or sporting.

Annual grant total

Around £7,000.

Applications

On a form available from the correspondent, submitted directly by the individual. The trustees meet to consider applications in March and September.

The Gane Charitable Trust

See entry on page 145

The Redcliffe Parish Charity

£3,000

Correspondent: Paul Tracey, 18 Kingston Road, Nailsea, Bristol, North Somerset BS48 4RD (01275 854057)

Trustees: Angela Clayton; Andrew Clarke; Graham Briscoe; Alan Stevens; Paul Tracey; Susan Heller; Peter Cole; Bryan Anderson; Revd Dr Simon Taylor; Paul Jenking.

CC Number: 203916

Eligibility

Schoolchildren in need who live in the city of Bristol.

Types of grants

One-off grants usually of £25 to £50. 'The trustees generally limit grants to families or individuals who can usually manage, but whom are overwhelmed by circumstances and are in particular financial stress rather than continuing need.' Grants can be for children's school trips and school uniforms.

Annual grant total

In 2010/11 the charity had an income of £9,000 and a total expenditure of £7,000.

Exclusions

No support for adult education, school fees or repetitive payments.

Applications

In writing to the correspondent. Applications should be submitted on the individual's behalf by a social worker, doctor, health visitor, Citizens Advice or appropriate third party, and will be considered early in each month. Ages of family members should be supplied in addition to financial circumstances and the reason for the request.

Other information

Grants to schoolchildren occur as part of the trust's wider welfare work.

The Stokes Croft Educational Foundation

£20,000

Correspondent: Belinda Latham, 9 Chakeshill Close, Bristol BS10 6NX (01179 507906)

Trustees: Arthur Brown; Frances Webster; Sally Pugh; June Whitaker; Olga Jennings; Delydd McAdam; Frederick Ward; Peter Wildman; David Langley; William Hole; Angela Godwin; Dennis Ivory; Marie Eastman; Julia Lambert.

CC Number: 311672

Eligibility

People aged 11 to 50 with family connections with the Unitarian Church in Bristol, the Stokes Croft (Endowed) School or the Western Union of Unitarian and Free Christian Churches.

Types of grants

Cash grants for books and clothing on transfer from junior to secondary school. Grants are also given towards the cost of: (i) educational outings, school uniform, other school clothing, and books for schoolchildren, but not for fees or maintenance; (ii) books, fees/living expenses, study or travel abroad and exchange visits for students in further and higher education; (iii) books, equipment and instruments, and clothing, but not travel for people starting work; and (iv) books and fees, but not expenses such as childcare, for mature students. Grants range from £50 to £500.

Annual grant total

In 2010/11 the foundation had assets of £281,000 and an income of £18,000. Educational grants totalled £20,000.

Applications

Applicants must apply in writing for a form. Applications should be submitted directly by the individual or by a parent. They are considered in March and September.

Wraxall Parochial Charities

£7,000

Correspondent: Mrs A Sissons, Clerk to the Trustees, 2 Short Way, Failand, Bristol BS8 3UF (01275 392691)

Trustees: Anthony Tavener; Lorraine Marshfield; Raymond Llewellyn; Rosemary Hayes; Stephen Young; Rosey Lunn; Richard Smith.

CC Number: 230410

Eligibility

Residents of the parish of Wraxall and Failand, Bristol who are at any level of their education, in any subject, and are in need.

Types of grants

One-off grants in the range of £50 and £100.

Annual grant total

In 2010 the charity had an income of £13,500 and a total expenditure of £14,500.

Applications

In writing to the correspondent, directly by the individual. Applications are considered in February, June, September and November.

Other information

Grants are also made for welfare purposes.

North Somerset

Charles Graham Stone's Relief-in-Need Charity

£1,500

Correspondent: John Gravell, Easton Grey, Webbington Road, Cross, Axbridge BS26 2EL (01934 732266)

Trustees: Trevor Jones; John Hunt; Anthea Garley; Angela Walker; Ann Pursey; Peter Walker; Kenneth Young; Anthony Brown.

CC Number: 260044

Eligibility

Vocational students who live in the parishes of Churchill and Langford, North Somerset.

Types of grants

One-off grants of £50 to £150 towards fees, books, equipment and instruments.

Annual grant total

In 2010 the charity had an income of £4,000 and a total expenditure of £8,000. Grants are also made to individuals for welfare purposes.

Exclusions

No grants for payment of national or local taxes or rates.

Applications

In writing to the correspondent with a full explanation of the personal circumstances. Applications should be submitted by the end of February or August for consideration in the following month. Initial telephone calls are not welcomed.

Other information

Most of the trust's work involves making welfare grants within the parishes.

South Gloucestershire

Almondsbury Charity

£2,500 (10 grants)

Correspondent: Alan Gaydon, Chair, Highbank, 7a The Scop, Almondsbury, Bristol BS32 4DU (01454 613424; email: peter.orford@gmail.com; website: www. almondsburycharity.org.uk)

Trustees: Alan Gaydon; Ivor Humphries; Lewis Gray; Alan Bamforth; Diane Wilson; Michael Kirby; Sheila Fulton;

Jane Jones; Lucy Hamid; David Chandler; Roger Ducker.

CC Number: 202263

Eligibility

People in further or higher education who have a permanent residence or attend an educational establishment in the old parish of Almondsbury.

Types of grants

One-off grants are made, usually for buying books.

Annual grant total

In 2010/11 the charity had assets of £1.8 million and an income of £59,000. Grants were made to 20 individuals totalling £5,000.

Exclusions

No grants for school or course fees.

Applications

On a form available from the correspondent or the website. Cash grants are never made directly to the individual; the grant is either paid via a third party such as social services, or the trust pays for the item directly and donates the item to the individual. Trustees meet six times a year usually in January, March, May, July, September and November (exact dates available on the website) and applications should be submitted at least two weeks beforehand.

Other information

Grants were also made to schools and organisations totalling £21,000.

The Chipping Sodbury Town Lands

£20,000

Correspondent: Nicola Gideon, Clerk, Town Hall, 57–59 Broad Street, Chipping Sodbury, South Gloucestershire BS37 6AD (01454 852223; email: nicola.gideon@ chippingsodburytownhall.co.uk)

Trustees: Colin Hatfield; David Shipp; Jim Elsworth; Bill Ainsley; Bryan Seymour; Michelle Cook; Paul Robins; Wendy Whittle; Paul Tily.

CC Number: 236364

Eligibility

People in need who are aged up to 25 years and live in Chipping Sodbury or Old Sodbury.

Types of grants

One-off and recurrent grants according to need.

Annual grant total

In 2011 the charity had assets of £7.9 million, an income of £349,000 and gave grants totalling £20,000 for educational purposes.

Applications

In writing to the correspondent. Grant aid is advertised locally in schools, clubs, associations, churches and other religious orders, in the local press, and the Town Hall.

Cornwall

The Blanchminster Trust

£207,000 (347 grants)

Correspondent: Jane Bunning, Clerk to the Trustees, Blanchminster Building, 38 Lansdown Road, Bude, Cornwall EX23 8EE (01288 352851; fax: 01288 352851; email: office@blanchminster. plus.com; website: www.blanchminster. org.uk)

Trustees: Owen May; John Gardiner; Byron Rowlands; Gordon Rogers; Leonard Tozer; Julia Shepherd; Valerie Newman; Christine Bilsand; Christopher Cornish; Wilfred Keat; Chris Nichols; Ian Whitfield; Michael Worden.

CC Number: 202118

Eligibility

People who live (or have at least one parent who lives) in the parishes of Bude, Stratton and Poughill (the former urban district of Bude-Stratton). Current or immediate past pupils of Budehaven Community School living outside the area are also considered.

Types of grants

One-off grants are made to schoolchildren, people starting work, further and higher education students, mature students and postgraduates towards uniforms or other school clothing, books, equipment/instruments, fees, maintenance/living expenses, childcare, educational outings in the UK, study or travel overseas and student exchanges.

Annual grant total

In 2011 the trust had assets of £10 million, an income of £476,000 and made 347 educational grants totalling £207,000.

Exclusions

Grants are not given to foreign students studying in Britain.

Applications

On a form available from the correspondent. Applications are considered monthly and should be submitted directly by the individual. Where possible the application should include a request for a specific amount and be supported with quotes for the costs of items and so on needed and/or written support from a social worker or other welfare agency. Applications must include evidence of financial need.

Other information

Grants are also made to individuals for welfare and community projects.

The Elliot Exhibition Foundation

£1,000

Correspondent: Samantha Hocking, Student Services, Services for Children, Young People and Families, County Hall, Truro, Cornwall TR1 3AY (01872 324144; email: ask.elliott@cornwall.gov. uk)

Eligibility

Students going into higher education at any British university or higher education establishment, whose parents/guardians live in the city of Truro, the town council areas of Liskeard and Lostwithiel or the parish of Ladock.

Applicants must be under the age of 19 on 1 July preceding the award of the exhibition. Preference is given to applicants who have attended a maintained school for at least two years.

Applicants with parents/guardians who live in the county of Cornwall may also be considered if insufficient candidates meeting the above criteria apply.

Types of grants

Awards of up to £150.

Annual grant total

Grants usually total around £1,000.

Exclusions

No funding for postgraduate degrees, international students or travel abroad.

Applications

On a form available from the correspondent, to be submitted directly by the individual by 30 September for consideration in November.

The Ken Thomas Charitable Trust

£0

Correspondent: Christopher Riddle, Molesworth House, Wadebridge, Cornwall PL27 7JE (01208 815562; email: christopherriddle@royalcornwall. co.uk)

Trustees: John Newey; Paul Richards; Peter Thomas.

CC Number: 287260

Eligibility

Young people connected with the agricultural industry who live in Cornwall and the Isles of Scilly, aged from 20 to 30 years.

Types of grants

One-off cash grants, advice and assistance to enable beneficiaries to travel out of the county of Cornwall to further their experience in matters allied to agriculture and horticulture, either in this country or abroad.

Annual grant total

In 2010/11 the trust had an income of £1,000 and an expenditure of £0. The trusts states that it is operational, although small-scale in its operation.

Applications

Submitted by the individual, on a form available from the correspondent. Applications are considered throughout the year.

Linkinhorne

The Roberts and Jeffery Foundation

£1,000

Correspondent: Beryl Martin, The Old Dry, Minions, Liskeard, Cornwall PL14 5LJ (01579 362773; email: berylmartin@rocketmail.com)

Trustees: Beryl Martin; Christine Palfrey; Mark Clutson; John Turner; Richard Masson; Judith Rockliffe-King.

CC Number: 271577

Eligibility

All schoolchildren living in the parish of Linkinhorne who are in secondary education and/or training.

Types of grants

Grants are made to every eligible child; there is an option to return the money if it is not needed. Grants are for uniforms, other school clothing and educational outings in the UK.

Annual grant total

About £1,000.

Applications

In writing to the correspondent, directly by the individual or his or her parent/guardian; the trust is also sent a list from the primary school of those children who are moving to secondary school. Applications are considered in April and October.

St Newlyn East

The Trevilson Educational Foundation

£15,000

Correspondent: Marjorie Vale, Fiddlers Reach, 34 Station Road, St Newlyn East, Newquay, Cornwall TR8 5NE (01872 510318; email: maggie.vale@gmail.com)

Trustees: David Uren; Elizabeth Brimacombe; Marjorie Vale; David Laud; Martin Harvey; Matthew Davis; Graham Bone.

CC Number: 306555

Eligibility

People under 25 who live in the parish of St Newlyn East.

Types of grants

Help with the cost of books, educational outings and other essentials for schoolchildren, those at college or university, apprentices and people starting work. Grants usually range from £50 to £500.

Annual grant total

The foundation has an income of around £7,000 each year. Expenditure is irregular, £16,000 in 2010, the last year for which accounts were available.

Applications

In writing to the correspondent.

Devon

The Adventure Trust for Girls

£5,000

Correspondent: Beryl Cuff, 28 Lovelace Crescent, Exmouth, Devon EX8 3PR (01395 223606; email: ecuff@btinternet. com)

Trustees: Mary Tuckett; Susan Fowler; Susan Stubbings; Joan Barraclough; Marieke Biggs.

CC Number: 800999

Eligibility

Girls aged between 10 and 20 who live or attend school within eight miles of Exmouth Town Hall, excluding the areas west of the river Exe and north of the M5 motorway.

Types of grants

One-off grants ranging from £50 to £400 to assist applicants in their quest for adventure. Grants have been given towards Operation Raleigh, TEFL, school trips, ballet summer schools, sea scouts trips and a Department of Education campaigners camp. Grants have also been given to members of local table tennis, gymnastics and hockey teams. People taking part in a school exchange can be supported.

Annual grant total

In 2010/11 the trust had an income of £5,200 and an expenditure of £5,800.

Exclusions

Grants are not given towards organised school ski trips.

Applications

On a form available from the correspondent. Applications should be submitted two months before trustees' meetings, which are held in January, March, May, July, September and November.

The Albert Casanova Ballard Deceased Trust

£18,000 (121 grants)

Correspondent: Margaret Mary, Chair, Pengelly, 6 Victory Street, Keyham, Plymouth PL2 2BY (01752 569258)

Trustees: Audrey Houston; Joy Rendle; David Norris; Kenneth Banfield; Margaret Pengelly; Frances Norris; Lynn Smith; Stuart Brown.

CC Number: 201759

Eligibility

Boys entering or attending secondary schools between the ages of 11 and 16 years, who live within a seven-mile radius of Plymouth.

Types of grants

One-off grants are given towards school uniforms, books and equipment/instruments.

Annual grant total

In 2010/11 the trust had assets of £973,000 and an income of £49,000. Grants to 121 individuals totalled £18,000.

Applications

In writing to the correspondent directly by the individual or a parent/guardian. Applications are only considered once a year, in June – the deadline for applications is the end of May.

Other information

Grants are also made to organisations operating within the area of benefit.

Bideford Bridge Trust

£116,000

Correspondent: P R Sims, Steward, 24 Bridgeland Street, Bideford, Devon EX39 2QB (01237 473122)

Trustees: P. Christie; William Isaac; E. Junkison; E. Hubber; J. Baker; Oliver Chope; Angus Harper; Philip Pester; Trevor Johns; Brian Lacey; David Frics.

CC Number: 204536

Eligibility

People in need who live in Bideford and the immediate neighbourhood.

Types of grants

One-off grants ranging from £150 to £500 to: schoolchildren for books and equipment/instruments; people starting work for books; further and higher education students for books, equipment/instruments and fees; and mature students for books and equipment/instruments.

Annual grant total

In 2011 the charity had assets of £13 million and an income of £723,000. Book grants, student bursaries and grants and grants for vocational training courses and apprenticeships totalled £54,000. A further £62,000 was given in business start-up grants to people from disadvantaged backgrounds.

Exclusions

Grants are not given to postgraduates or for computers for personal use.

Applications

On a form available from the correspondent, to be submitted at any time during the year by the individual, although a sponsor is usually required. Applications are considered monthly.

Cranbrook Charity

£9,000

Correspondent: Stephen Purser, Venn Farm, Bridford, Exeter EX6 7LF (01647 252328; email: purseratvenn@hotmail.com)

Trustee: Stephen Purser.

CC Number: 249074

Eligibility

People in need who live in the parishes of Dunsford, Doddiscombeleigh and 'that part of the parish of Holcombe Burnel as in 1982 constituted part of the parish of Dunsford'.

Types of grants

One-off and recurrent grants to those in need. Recently, grants of £80 have been given every six months for relief-in-need and educational purposes.

Annual grant total

In 2010/11 the charity had both an income and expenditure of £9,500.

Applications

In writing to the correspondent.

Other information

Grants are also made for welfare purposes.

The Devon County Association for the Blind

£1,500

Correspondent: Martin Pallett, Station House, Holman Way, Topsham, Exeter EX3 0EN (01392 876666; fax: 01392 874442; email: enquiries@devoninsight.org.uk; website: www.devonblind.org.uk)

Trustees: Gwyn Dickinson; Rose Hewitt; Sandra Semmens; Marilyn Lant; Dr Alma Swan; Steve Muncer; Roger Ascough; Alun Gwernan-Jones; Rod Wilson.

CC Number: 203044

Eligibility

People in education who are blind and live in Devon (excluding the city of Exeter and Plymouth).

Types of grants

Grants of up to £250 to cover specific needs including equipment/instruments and excursions.

Annual grant total

In 2010/11 the charity had assets of £1 million and an income of £336,000. Grants were made totalling £3,000.

Applications

On a form available from the correspondent. Or call 01392 878802. Applications are considered quarterly and should be submitted either directly by the individual or through a third party such as a social worker or teacher. Applicants need to be in receipt of a means tested benefit or have income and savings of less than £10,000.

Other information

Grants are also made to organisations and for welfare purposes for individuals in need.

The Devon Educational Trust

£2,500

Correspondent: The Clerk to the Trustees, PO Box 86, Teignmouth TQ14 8ZT (email: devonedtrust@talktalk.net)

Trustees: Robin Wakinshaw; Frank Rosamond; Brian Wills-Pope; Bryn Evans; Judith Cook; William Forsythe; M. Gillett; P. Freeman.

CC Number: 220921

Eligibility

Pupils and students under the age of 25 who live, or whose parents' normal place of residence is, in Devon. Preference is given to applicants from low income families. Applicants or their parents must be living in Devon on a permanent basis for at least 12 months.

Types of grants

One-off grants of between £100 and £500 to schoolchildren for uniforms/clothing and equipment/instruments, to college students and undergraduates for special clothing, study/travel costs, books, equipment/instruments and maintenance/living expenses, to vocational students and people starting work for uniforms/clothing, books, equipment/instruments and maintenance/living expenses and to those with special educational needs.

Annual grant total

In 2011 the trust had assets of £24,000 and an income of £24,000. £2,500 was given in grants to individuals for course fees.

Exclusions

Assistance is not normally given to those embarking on a second or higher degree course. However, in some cases the trustees may make a small grant to assist with living costs or the purchase of books, equipment and so on. No assistance is available for the payment of fees and only in exceptional cases will the trustees consider paying school or boarding fees.

Applications

On a form available from the correspondent, including details of two references submitted directly by the individual in February, June and October for consideration by the trustees in March, July and November.

The Exeter Advancement in Life Charity

£5,500

Correspondent: M R King, Clerk, Chichester Mews, Exeter Municipal Charities, 22a Southernhay East, Exeter EX1 1QU (01392 201550; email: admin@exetermunicipalcharities.org.uk; website: www.exetermunicipalcharities.org.uk)

Trustees: C. Blong; J. Marshall; N. Long; Edna Norton; S. Force; Joan Blackmore; John Winterbottom; Richard Branston; Kate Caldwell; Roger Panter; Steven Sitch; Lesley Robson.

CC Number: 1002151

Eligibility

Schoolchildren and students aged under 25 who are in need and live in the city of Exeter or within 15 miles of the city centre. Preference may be given to schoolchildren with serious family difficulties so that the child has to be educated away from home.

Types of grants

Grants are one-off and recurrent and range from £100 to £500 a year. Schoolchildren may be supported with uniforms/school clothing, equipment/instruments, fees and educational outings in the UK. People starting work can receive help with equipment/instruments. People in further and higher education, mature students and postgraduates (if under 25 years) can be helped with books, equipment/instruments, fees and study or travel overseas.

Grants towards study or travel overseas are subject to a minimum study period of six months, unless it is an obligatory part of an approved course.

Annual grant total

In 2011 the charity had an income of £7,500 and an expenditure of £5,800.

Applications

On a form available from the correspondent or the website. Applications can be submitted directly by the individual or through a third party such as a parent/guardian or educational welfare agency. A reference, for example, from a tutor, and details of financial circumstances should be supplied. Applications are considered in February, May, August and November. Applicants or their personal representative must be prepared to attend an interview with the trustees.

Note, this charity is comprised of two educational trusts: John Dinam School Endowment and Lady Ann Clifford Trust. These two trusts have the same criteria, described above, with the exception that the Endowment can make grants outside of Exeter – up to 15 miles from the city centre. Applicants can only receive a grant from one of these trusts. Those living outside the city should apply to John Dinam School Endowment.

Other information

This charity is part of Exeter Municipal Charities.

The Gibbons Family Trust

£0

Correspondent: Cathy Houghton, Administrator, 14 Fore Street, Budleigh Salterton, Devon EX9 6NG (01395 445259; website: www.gibbonstrusts.org)

Trustees: Roger Dawe; John Frankish; Miles Joyner; Kerensa Pearson.

CC Number: 290884

Eligibility

People up to 25 in Devon and the Isle of Thanet area of Kent with a preference for those from East Devon.

Types of grants

Grants of on average £400 towards the maintenance and educational advancement, training and recreation of children and young people

Annual grant total

In 2010/11 the trust had assets of £1.9 million. Grants were made to organisations totalling £116,000. No grants to individuals were made during the year; however more recent information shows that in 2011/12 the average grant to individuals was £370.

Exclusions

No grants for private school fees, gap year projects or other types of overseas trips.

Applications

On a form available to download from the website with a short covering letter and a supporting statement from a third party such as a school, club, doctor or social worker. Applications must be posted and are not accepted by email.

The Heathcoat Trust

£115,000

Correspondent: Mrs C J Twose, Secretary, The Factory, Tiverton, Devon EX16 5LL

Trustees: Mark Drysdale; Sir Ian Heathcote-Amery; John Smith; Stephen Butt; Susan Westlake.

CC Number: 203367

Eligibility

Mainly students in secondary and further education who live and study in Tiverton and the mid-Devon area. Occasionally students can be supported for study outside the area if the courses are not available locally. Applicants need to have a personal connection with either the John Heathcoat or the Lowman Companies.

Types of grants

One-off and recurrent grants towards fees.

Annual grant total

In 2010/11 the trust had assets of £19.5 million and an income of £474,000. There were 4,501 grants made to individuals totalling £450,000 were distributed as follows:

In cases of hardship	4,000
Chiropody	18,000
Consolidated grant	220,000
Educational bodies	115,000
Hospital visiting	25,000
Death grants	26,000
Communication grant	5,500
Opticians' charges	21,000
Dentists' charges	13,500
Employees sickness	4,000

Applications

In writing to the correspondent. For A-level applicants who attend East Devon College, application forms are available and should be submitted between April and June each year.

Other information

Grants were also made to charitable organisations (£115,000 in 2010/11).

Hele's Exhibition Foundation

£1,500

Correspondent: Sally Luscombe, Trustee, Brook Cottage, 65 Fore Street, Plympton, Plymouth PL7 1NA (01752 344857)

Trustees: Sally Luscombe; Philip Clowes; Roger Newnham; Enid Hamlyn; Basil Cane; Robin Jones; Moss Pearson; Neville Edwards.

CC Number: 306657

Eligibility

People under 25 who live, firstly, in the former parishes of Plympton St Maurice, Plympton St Mary and Brixton, and, secondly, in other parts of Devon (excluding Plymouth) if there are insufficient applications from the initial areas. In practice, all grants are given in the first area and applications for grants from further afield in Devon cannot be considered.

Types of grants

Cash grants for school pupils to help with books, equipment, clothing or travel; grants to help with school, college or university fees or to supplement existing grants; and help towards the cost of education, training, apprenticeship or equipment for those starting work.

Annual grant total

In 2010/11 the foundation had an income of £4,800 and an expenditure of £1,900. £1,500 is usually given in grants each year.

Applications

In writing to the correspondent.

The Dulce Haigh Marshall Trust

£2,000

Correspondent: Colin Power, Well Park, Lustleigh, Newton Abbot, Devon TQ13 9TQ (01647 277276)

Trustees: Anne Kimber; Robert Marshall; Julian Marshall; Paul Mathews; Kenneth Parr; Colin Power; Alan Strowger.

CC Number: 286273

Eligibility

Violin, viola, cello and double bass players who are in need of financial assistance, live in Devon, and are under 25.

Types of grants

Grants of between about £200 and £500 towards buying an instrument or tuition fees.

Annual grant total

Usually about £2,000.

Exclusions

No grants to people whose parents (or their own) income is sufficient to meet needs. People who do not demonstrate sufficient commitment to learning their instrument will not be supported.

Applications

On a form available from the correspondent, to be returned before 1 May. Grants are usually distributed in August each year. Applications are made directly by the individual and should include a teacher's report. Students may be asked to attend an audition.

The Vivian Moon Foundation

£14,000

Correspondent: The Secretariat, c/o Simpkins Edwards, 21 Boutport Street, Barnstaple, Devon EX31 1RP (email: info@vivianmoonfoundation.co.uk; website: www.vivianmoonfoundation.co.uk)

Trustees: Thomas Bigge; Ross Moon; Keith Berry; David Atton; Anna May; Helena Murch; George Curry; Andrew Burke.

CC Number: 298942

Eligibility

People, over 18 years of age, with residential and/or family ties in the North Devon District or Torridge District Council areas. Support is favoured towards applicants who:

- Are likely to return to the beneficial area to practice their profession, ideally with an offer of employment at the end of their training with a company or firm in the beneficial area
- Have an offer of a place on a course of higher educational professional or vocational training, leading to employment or improvement in their vocational skills

Types of grants

One-off and recurrent grants in the range of £50 to £300 are given to help college students, vocational students, mature students, people starting work, and people with special educational needs.

Grants are given for fees, books and equipment/instruments.

Annual grant total

In 2010/11 the foundation had an income of £12,000 and an expenditure of £20,000. Grants to individuals total around £14,000 a year.

Applications

Applications are only received online via the foundation's website. One reference must be given. Anyone who is unable to complete the application online should contact the Pathfinder centre in Barnstaple (01271 345851).

The Pain Trust

£32,000

Correspondent: The Secretary, 15 Rolle Street, Exmouth, Devon EX8 1HA (01395 275443; email: applications@pain-trust.org.uk; website: www.pain-trust.org.uk)

Trustees: Ian Jay; John Chase; Douglas Upton; Peter Wilson; Christopher Brookbank; Iain Todd; Howard Mallett; Tom Moores.

CC Number: 276670

Eligibility

Young males aged between 11 and 21 on the day of the expedition or activity, not on the date of application, who live within eight miles of Exmouth Town Hall or in East Devon, excluding the area west of the estuary of the river Exe.

Types of grants

One-off grants towards travel and adventure to further physical development, character building, leadership training or fostering a team spirit. Examples of projects include: bungee jumping in New Zealand;

camping on Dartmoor; canoeing in Norway; assisting charity projects in Brazil and diving courses in Laos.

Annual grant total

In 2010/11 the trust made grants to 23 individuals and 28 groups totalling £32,000.

Exclusions

The grants are not issued during term time for those in full-time education. The trust does not support applications regarding competitive sport or the pursuit of excellence in sport. Grants cannot be made for the purchase of equipment.

Applications

An online application form is available on the trust's website. This should be submitted along with a covering letter. Applications must be submitted at least 6 days before a meeting, dates of which can be found on the website.

The Christine Woodmancy Charitable Foundation

£500

Correspondent: Jill Hill, Thompson and Jackson, 4–5 Lawrence Road, Plymouth PL4 6HR (01752 665037; email: jill@thompsonandjackson.co.uk)

Trustees: William Jones; Tony Daniel; Robert Embleton.

CC Number: 1012761

Eligibility

Children and young people under the age of 21 who live in the Plymouth area and are in need.

Types of grants

One-off grants to help maintain and educate young people in need.

Annual grant total

In 2010/11 the foundation had an income of £11,000 and a total expenditure of £7,500. However, in previous years grants have tended to be given mostly to organisations rather than individuals.

Applications

In writing to the correspondent, to be submitted either directly by the individual or via a school or educational welfare worker. Applications should include background information and provide evidence of financial need.

Bovey Tracey
Bovey Tracey Exhibition Foundation

£1,500

Correspondent: E A Crosby, 32 Churchfields Drive, Bovey Tracey, South Devon TQ13 9QU (01626 835524; email: ecrosby143@btinternet.com)

Trustees: Anna Klinkenberg; David Weddon; Fernley Holmes; George Gribble; Jill Coombes; Ronald Edwards; Susan Foot; Averil Kerslake.

CC Number: 306653

Eligibility

Full-time students in further or higher education, over 16, who live in Bovey Tracey and have done so for at least three years.

Types of grants

Grants ranging between £65 and £75 for students attending approved places of further and higher education to help with the cost of, amongst other things, books, fees and living expenses, equipment and uniforms. Grants can generally be spent on whatever is required by the recipient. Grants are generally recurrent.

Annual grant total

About £1,500.

Exclusions

Grants are not given to students on government sponsored schemes.

Applications

On a form available from the correspondent from 1 April, to be returned by 31 July for consideration in August. Applications should be made directly by the individual.

Braunton
Chaloner's Educational Foundation

£1,400

Correspondent: Louise Langabeer, Slee Blackwell Solicitors, 10 Cross Street, Braunton, Devon EX31 1BA (01271 349943; email: louise.langabeer@sleeblackwell.co.uk)

Trustees: David Roff; Derek Holland; Des Paul; Elizabeth; Spear; John Kelsey Howell; Tony Reed John Wensley; Stanley Dibble; John Squire.

CC Number: 286580

Eligibility

People under 25 who live in the parish of Braunton.

Types of grants

Grants of £100 are made towards equipment/instruments, books, fees, maintenance/living expenses and study or travel overseas for people who are starting work and for further and higher education students. The latter can also be supported for educational outings in the UK.

Annual grant total

In 2010/11 the trust had an income of £2,000 and an expenditure of £1,400.

Applications

On a form available from the correspondent, to be submitted directly by the individual for consideration in February, June or October.

Broadhempston
The Broadhempston Relief-in-Need Charity

£500

Correspondent: Mrs Rosalind H E Brown, Meadows, Broadhempston, Totnes, Devon TQ9 6BW (01803 813130)

Trustees: Revd Nicholas Pearkes; Daisy Cock; Keith Beer; Lot Sutcliffe; Thomas White.

CC Number: 272930

Eligibility

For educational purposes for children in need who live in the parish of Broadhempston.

Types of grants

One-off or recurrent grants ranging from £40 to £100. Grants are made towards children's educational trips and aids for educational purposes.

Annual grant total

Grants for both education and welfare total around £1,000 per year.

Applications

In writing to the correspondent directly by the individual to be considered in June and December.

Other information

The charity also gives welfare grants.

Colyton
The Colyton Parish Lands Charity

£500

Correspondent: The Bailiff, Colyton Chamber of Feoffees, Town Hall, Market Place, Colyton, Devon EX24 6JR

CC Number: 243224

Eligibility

Young people in need in the ancient parish of Colyton.

Types of grants

One-off and recurrent grants in support of education and training.

Annual grant total

In 2010/11 the charity had an income of £32,000. Grants totalled £4,500 which included grants made to the local primary school, local individuals and organisations.

Applications

In writing to the correspondent to be submitted either directly by the individual or a family member, through a third party such as a social worker or teacher, or through a welfare agency such as Citizens Advice. Applications are considered monthly.

Other information

The trust gives to both individuals and organisations.

Combe Martin

The George Ley Educational Trust

£3,000

Correspondent: James Williams, Brendon, Western Gardens, Combe Martin, Ilfracombe, Devon EX34 0EY

CC Number: 306788

Eligibility

People who live in Combe Martin who are in higher education.

Types of grants

Grants for books and equipment.

Annual grant total

About £3,000.

Exclusions

Grants are not given for main expenses such as fees or living costs.

Applications

In writing to the correspondent. A committee meets to consider

applications in May and September. Reapplications for future grants can be made by people who have already been supported by this trust.

Cornwood

Reverend Duke Yonge Charity

£5,000

Correspondent: Mrs J M Milligan, 8 Chipple Park, Lutton, Nr Cornwood, Ivybridge, Devon PL21 9TA

CC Number: 202835

Eligibility

People in need who live in the parish of Cornwood.

Types of grants

One-off grants according to need.

Annual grant total

In 2010 the charity had both and income and expenditure of around £13,500. Grants for education usually total about £5,000 a year.

Applications

In writing to the correspondent via the trustees, who are expected to make themselves aware of any need. Applications are considered at trustees' meetings.

Other information

Grants are also made to individuals in need and organisations.

Culmstock

Culmstock Fuel Allotment Charity

£1,500

Correspondent: Mrs J M Sheppard, Rexmead, Culmstock, Cullompton, Devon EX15 3JX (01823 680516)

CC Number: 205327

Eligibility

Students in need who live in the ancient parish of Culmstock.

Types of grants

Recurrent grants according to need. Previously, grants have ranged from £20 to £70 for books and equipment.

Annual grant total

In 2010/11 the trust had an income of £4,200 and a total expenditure of £3,600 Grants usually total around £1,500.

Applications

In writing to the correspondent directly by the individual.

Other information

Grants are also given for welfare purposes.

Great Torrington

The Great Torrington Town Lands Poors Charities

£1,500

Correspondent: Ian Newman, Town Hall Office, High Street, Great Torrington, Devon EX38 8HN (01805 625738; email: greattorringtoncharities@btconnect.com)

CC Number: 202801

Eligibility

People in need who live in Great Torrington.

Types of grants

Grants are usually made to students towards a year out (voluntary work). Requests are also considered for school uniform costs for schoolchildren and for other costs for mature students.

Annual grant total

In 2010/11 the charity had assets of £6.2 million, an income of £272,000 and gave educational grants totalling £1,500.

Applications

In writing to the correspondent, with all relevant personal information.

Other information

Grants are also made to organisations and to individuals for welfare purposes.

Plymouth

Joan Bennett's Exhibition Endowment

£0

Correspondent: Vanessa Steer, Clerk, 184 Mannamead Road, Plymouth PL3 5RE (01752 703280; email: v_steer@

yahoo.co.uk; website: www.plymouth. gov.uk)

CC Number: 306609

Eligibility

Young people resident in Plymouth.

Types of grants

Grants for further or higher education students, for tools, equipment, books, clothing and instruments to assist people starting apprenticeships or work. Assistance can also be given with travel costs.

Annual grant total

The fund has an annual income of £250 to £500. No grants have been made in recent years but the trust states that they are open to applications.

Applications

In writing to the correspondent.

John Lanyon Educational Foundation

£1,300

Correspondent: Frederick Webb, 33 Downham Gardens, Tamerton Foliot, Plymouth, Devon PL5 4QF (01752 776612)

CC Number: 306773

Eligibility

People in need who live within Plymouth city boundaries and are aged 16 to 23 years, with a preference for people from low-income families who are in higher education or leaving school or university and starting work.

Types of grants

One-off and recurrent grants ranging from £100 to £300, for instance, towards books, equipment/instruments, fees and maintenance/living expenses.

Annual grant total

About £1,300 is given annually in grants.

Exclusions

No grants for postgraduates, part-time or home study courses, mature students or study outside the UK.

Applications

On a form available from the correspondent, directly by the individual, for consideration in any month.

The Olford Bequest

£3,000

Correspondent: Robert Hughes Gaskin, Tredeague House, Devonport Hill, Kingsand, Torpoint, Cornwall PL10 1NJ (01752 823044)

CC Number: 306936

Eligibility

Young people from Plymouth schools.

Types of grants

Grants of £250 a year to students to help them 'more fully enjoy their stay at university – not for study'.

Annual grant total

About £3,000.

Applications

On a form available from the correspondent. Applications must be received by 30 June for consideration in August/September.

Orphan's Aid Educational Foundation (Plymouth)

£0

Correspondent: Vanessa Steer, 184 Mannamead Road, Plymouth PL3 5RE (01752 703280; email: v_steer@ yahoo.co.uk; website: www.plymouth. gov.uk)

CC Number: 306770

Eligibility

Children who live in the city and county borough of Plymouth of school age and from a one-parent family.

Types of grants

One-off grants of up to £250 for the purchase of school uniforms and shoes.

Annual grant total

The trust has an income of around £2,000 a year. No grants have been made in recent years but the trust states that it is open to applications.

Exclusions

No grants for school fees or maintenance, for people starting work or for mature students.

Applications

On a form available from the correspondent by email or post, including information about income,

expenditure and dependents. Applicants are usually interviewed.

Plymouth Charity Trust

£400

Correspondent: Susan Dale, Trust Manager, Charity Trust Office, 41 Heles Terrace, Prince Rock, Plymouth PL4 9LH (01752 663107; email: sdtm@ charity-trust.demon.co.uk)

CC Number: 1076364

Eligibility

People living in the city of Plymouth who are under the age of 25.

Types of grants

One-off grants ranging between £50 and £100 are made to people at all levels of education, including those towards school clothing, fees, books and equipment/instruments.

The trust usually makes the donation in the form of vouchers, credit at a relevant shop. They do not to give payments directly to the applicant.

Annual grant total

In 2010/11 grants to individuals totalled around £700 for educational and welfare purposes.

Exclusions

No grants are given to other charities, to clear debts or for any need that can be met by Social Services.

Applications

On a form available from the correspondent, to be submitted directly by the individual or through a school, educational welfare agency or other third party. Applications are considered on the first Monday of every month.

Other information

The trust also gives grants to individuals for welfare purposes.

Plympton

The Maudlyn Lands Charity

£2,000

Correspondent: Anthony Peter Golding, Clerk to the Trustees, Blue Haze, Down Road, Tavistock, Devon PL19 9AG (01822 612983)

David Tozer; Iris Wilson; Margaret Cameron; Maureen Diffy.

CC Number: 202577

Eligibility

People in financial need who live in Plympton St Mary and Sparkwell.

Types of grants

One-off grants to help with educational costs.

Annual grant total

Around £2,000.

Applications

In writing to the correspondent. Applications are considered in November.

Other information

This trust also gives grants to individuals for welfare purposes, and to organisations.

Sheepwash

The Bridgeland Charity

£1,300

Correspondent: Mrs D Tubby, Bramble Cottage, East Street, Sheepwash, Beaworthy, North Devon EX21 5NW (01409 231694)

Trustees: Charles Inniss; Brian Mayne; Graham Tidball; Jennifer Harris; John Newcombe; Michael Hearn; Tony Jones.

CC Number: 206377

Eligibility

Young people in need who live in the parish of Sheepwash.

Types of grants

One-off grants ranging from £50 to £500. Loans are also made.

Annual grant total

In 2010/11 the trust had an income of £3,400 and a total expenditure of £2,700.

Applications

In writing to the correspondent through a third party such as a social worker or teacher, for consideration throughout the year.

Other information

The trust also supports local schools and community projects.

Sidmouth

Sidmouth Consolidated Charities

£2,500

Correspondent: Ruth Rose, 22 Alexandria Road, Sidmouth, Devon

EX10 9HB (01395 513079; email: ruth. rose@eclipse.co.uk)

Trustees: Penelope Beatty; David James; Elizabeth Atkinson; Ann Liverton; Anthony Reed; Simon Pollentine; Richard Eley; Heather Ludford; Maureen Bess.

CC Number: 207081

Eligibility

People in need who live in Sidmouth, Sidford, Sidbury or Salcombe Regis.

Types of grants

One-off grants for educational needs such as computers and books for university students.

Annual grant total

Grants usually total around £5,000 for both educational and welfare purposes.

Applications

In writing to the correspondent, either directly by the individual, or through a social worker, Citizens Advice or welfare agency. Applications are considered at monthly meetings.

Silverton

The Richards Educational Charity

£29,000 (132 grants)

Correspondent: Geoffrey Knowles, Silvertrees, 26 Hederman Close, Silverton, Exeter EX5 4HW (01392 860109; email: johnmichael_thomas@ tiscali.co.uk)

Trustees: Donald Short; Michael Thomas; Jenny Payne; Joan Park; Alan MacDonald; Richard White; Geoffrey Knowles; Sarah Self.

CC Number: 306787

Eligibility

Young people under 25 who live in the parish of Silverton.

Types of grants

Recurrent grants in the range of £5 to £750 are given to schoolchildren and college students for study/travel abroad, books, equipment/instruments, maintenance/living expenses and excursions and to undergraduates, vocational students, mature students, and people starting work for fees, study/ travel abroad, books, equipment/ instruments, maintenance/living expenses and excursions

Annual grant total

Grants to individuals in 2010 totalled £29,000 distributed as follows:

- University students: 13 totalling £9,300
- Schoolchildren: 87 totalling £9,300
- Further education: six totalling £3,000

- Career training: ten totalling £3,000
- Pre-school: 16 totalling £2,300

Applications

On a form available from the correspondent. Applications should be submitted directly by the individual or a parent. They are considered monthly.

Other information

Some grants are also given to local educational groups.

Silverton Parochial Charity

£4,500

Correspondent: Michelle Valance, Secretary to the Trustees, 3 St Anne's Place, Silverton, Devon EX5 4NH (email: secretary@silvertonparochialtrust.co.uk)

Trustees: Alan MacDonald; Christine Walker; Arthur Williams; Jill Riggs; Robert Seward; Sue Tucker.

CC Number: 201255

Eligibility

People in need in the parish of Silverton only.

Types of grants

One-off grants, with no minimum or maximum limit.

Annual grant total

In 2010/11 the charity had an income of £28,000 and a total expenditure of £18,000. Grants to individuals for education and welfare purposes totalled £9,000.

Exclusions

No grants are made towards state or local authority taxes.

Applications

Application forms are available to download from the website. They can also be obtained from the Silverton Post-Office or the Community Hall, or prospective beneficiaries can write to the correspondent. Completed forms can be submitted to the correspondent by the individual or by a carer or welfare department, and so on. The trustees will need details of the applicant's financial situation. Applications are considered monthly.

Other information

Grants are also made to people in need who live in the parish and to organisations providing assistance for them.

The charity has an informative website.

South Brent

The South Brent Parish Lands Charity

£10,000

Correspondent: J I G Blackler, Luscombe Maye, 6 Fore Street, South Brent, Devon TQ10 9BQ (01364 646180)

Trustees: Anne Collier; David Winnington-Ingram; Philip French; Robert Savery; Roger Cockings; John Halliday; Colin Vallance; Greg Wall; Mary Andrew.

CC Number: 255283

Eligibility

Students in further education who live or have lived in the parish of South Brent.

Types of grants

One-off and recurrent grants in the range of £50 and £300.

Annual grant total

In 2010/11 the charity had an income of £46,000 and gave around £10,000 in educational grants.

Applications

On a form available from the correspondent which can be submitted at any time either directly by the individual or a family member, through a third party such as a social worker or teacher, or through an organisation such as Citizens Advice or a school.

Sowton

Sowton In Need Charity

£1,000

Correspondent: N Waine, Meadowsweet, Sowton, Exeter EX5 2AE (01392 368289; email: wn894@ btinternet.com)

Trustees: Mr N. Waine; Michael Fernbank; Joanna O'Donnell.

CC Number: 204248

Eligibility

Educational purposes for people in need who live in the parish of Sowton.

Types of grants

One-off grants for any specific educational or personal need. Grants have been given towards tuition fees.

Annual grant total

Grants total around £1,000 per year for educational purposes for individuals.

Applications

In writing to the correspondent, to be submitted either directly by the individual or through a social worker, Citizens Advice, other welfare agency or any third party.

Other information

Grants are also given to organisations and for individuals for welfare purposes.

Taunton Dean

Ayshford Educational Foundation

£500

Correspondent: Peter Walter, Clerk to the Trustees, Eastbrook, Burlescombe, Tiverton EX16 7JT (01823 672545; email: pwalter@talk21.com; website: sites.google.com/site/burlescombeparish/local-services/ayshford-trust)

Trustees: Desiree Butt; Graham Winterbourne; Katharine Brooke-Webb; Laraine Pengilley; Olive Pearce; Peter Costema; Rosalind Hignett; Jayne Neale; David Johnson-Garfield.

CC Number: 306659

Eligibility

Students over 18 resident in the parishes of Burlescombe, Holcombe Rogus and Uffculme.

Types of grants

Grants of up to £300 for books and equipment for further and higher education and apprenticeships.

Annual grant total

About £500.

Applications

In writing to the correspondent before 31 December for consideration by the Trustees in January. Awards will be made when receipts are submitted.

Dorset

Cole Anderson Charitable Foundation

£7,000

Correspondent: Martin Davies, Rawlins Davy, Rowlands House, Hinton Road, Bournemouth BH1 2EG (01202 558844; email: martin.davies@rawlinsdavy.com)

Trustees: Howard Alexander; Joyce Anderson.

CC Number: 1107619

Eligibility

Students studying medicine, architecture or music who live in Bournemouth and Poole.

Types of grants

Grants given according to need.

Annual grant total

About £14,000 for educational and welfare purposes.

Applications

In writing to the correspondent.

The Ashley, Churchill and Thorner Educational Trust

£9,000

Correspondent: Christine Bussell, Clerk to the Trustees, The Clerk's Office, Whetstone's, West Walks, Dorchester, Dorset DT1 1AW (01305 262662; email: act@whetstones.org.uk)

Trustees: Peter Mann; Tim Loasby; Carolyn Biggs; Robin Potter; Richard Nicholls.

CC Number: 306229

Eligibility

Young people under 25 who live either within five miles of the county hall in Dorchester, or in the civil parish of Crossways.

Types of grants

One-off grants are given to further and higher education students for uniforms and other school clothing, books, equipment and instruments, fees, educational outings in the UK, study or travel abroad and student exchanges. Apprentices can also receive grants towards materials, tools, travelling and any other support costs.

Annual grant total

In 2010/11 the trust had an income of £6,200 and a total expenditure of £9,600.

Applications

On a form available from the correspondent. Applications are considered in September, January and April, but urgent applications can be considered at any time. Applications should include details of parental income and confirmation from the tutor of the course being taken and how a grant would benefit the student. They can be submitted by the individual, or through the individual's school/college or educational welfare agency.

The Beaminster Charities

£3,000

Correspondent: John Groves, 24 Church Street, Beaminster, Dorset DT8 3BA (01308 862192)

Trustees: Janet Page; Audrey Bullock; Lynda Beazer; Margaret Harvey; Mike Beckett; Ralph Bugler; Richard Bugler; Sally Welsford; Robert Martin.

CC Number: 200685

Eligibility

Schoolchildren in need who live in Beaminster, Netherbury and Stoke Abbott.

Types of grants

Grants in the range of £50 and £1,000 are made to schoolchildren and college students for study/travel abroad, books and equipment/instruments. About 50 grants are made each year.

Annual grant total

In 2010 the charities had an income of £8,500 and a total expenditure of £6,500.

Applications

Applications can be submitted in writing to the correspondent by the individual or through a recognised referral agency such as social worker, Citizens Advice or doctor. The trustees meet throughout the year.

Other information

Grants are also made to organisations.

The Bridge Educational Trust

£37,000 (62 grants)

Correspondent: The Administrator, c/o Piddle Valley School, Piddletrenthide, Dorchester, Dorset DT2 7QL (01747 838131; email: admin@ bridgeeducationaltrust.org.uk; website: www.bridgeeducationaltrust.org.uk)

Trustees: Rex Goddard; Alan Zeal; John McCormack; Sue Nicholas; Tony Monds; Scilla Johnson; Peter Claxton; Coutts and Co.

CC Number: 1068720

Eligibility

People in need who were born in, or whose home is in, Dorset. Priority is given to:

- People who are from the parishes of Piddletrenthide, Plush, Piddlehinton and Alton Pancras
- Older people who are making a late start after interrupted education
- People with difficult family circumstances (including single mothers)
- Children with special education needs

Types of grants

Grants of £50 to £3,000, which can be one-off or recurrent (for a maximum of three years). Grants given include those towards fees, study/travel abroad, books, equipment/instruments, excursions and childcare.

Annual grant total

In 2010/11 the trust had an income of £20,000 and a total expenditure of £52,000. 62 grants to individuals were made totalling £37,000.

Exclusions

No loans are made. No grants for fees which can be covered by student loans.

Applications

On a form, available from the correspondent or by personal letter. Full details of the proposed course are required, together with a brief CV, some family background information and details of financial circumstances and costs. For applicants who are no longer resident in Dorset, documentary evidence of place of birth should accompany the application. Applications should be submitted in May for consideration in June, directly by the individual, or by the parent if the person is under 16 years.

The Cecil Charity

£20,000

Correspondent: Hon Anthony Cecil, Lytchett Heath House, Lytchett Heath, Poole BH16 6AE (email: charity@ lytchettheath.co.uk)

Trustees: James Rockley; Sarah Rockley; Anthony Cecil; Katherine Cecil; Sue Wizard; Francesca Moore.

CC Number: 306248

Eligibility

Young people, aged 10 to 21 years old, who live within a ten-mile radius of the parish church at Lytchett Matravers.

Types of grants

Grants, to a usual maximum of about £600 a year, to help with books or equipment, college or university fees and to schoolchildren with serious family difficulties so that the child has to be educated away from home. Other support may also be given to students whose parents are unable to help.

Annual grant total

In 2010/11 the charity had an income of £21,000 and an expenditure of £24,000.

Applications

An application form is available from the correspondent and can be submitted directly by the individual. Applications are considered in August, November and March.

Clingan's Trust

£49,000

Correspondent: John D H Richardson, Clerk, Avon House, 4 Bridge Street, Christchurch, Dorset BH23 1DX (01202 484242; email: enquiries@ williamsthompson.co.uk; website: www. clinganstrust.co.uk)

Trustees: John Sier; Yvonne Gerwat; Jane Hannifan; Paul Mills; Brian Woodifield; Linda Harcourt-Webster; Julian Macklin; Nicholas Geary.

CC Number: 307085

Eligibility

People under the age of 25 who live in the old borough of Christchurch which includes parts of Bournemouth and the surrounding areas. See the map on the website for the exact areas.

Types of grants

One-off grants of between £100 and £1,000 for any educational need for people under 25. Preference is given to schoolchildren with serious family difficulties where the child has to be educated away from home and people with special educational needs.

Annual grant total

In 2010 the trust had an income of £69,000 and gave grants to individuals totalling £49,000.

Applications

On a form available from the correspondent or to download from the website. Applications can be made directly by the individual unless under the age of 14. They are considered quarterly.

Other information

The trust also made £1,300 in grants to organisations.

The Dixon Galpin Scholarship Trust

£2,000

Correspondent: Business Support Team, Children's Services Directorate, Dorset County Council, County Hall, Colliton Park, Dorchester, Dorset DT1 1XJ (01305 228590)

Trustee: Dorset County Council.

CC Number: 306325

Eligibility

People born in Dorset or who have lived in the county for at least 12 months before the application (excluding people from the boroughs of Poole and Bournemouth).

Types of grants

Scholarships to assist people attending summer schools organised by a university; to people attending short courses or weekend schools organised by the Southern and Western Districts of the Workers' Education Association (or other similar body); or to students attending full or part-time courses at universities or other establishments of further education who are to undertake vacation study anywhere, to travel overseas for an educational purpose approved by the college authorities, or to buy books, instruments or equipment to further their education. Grants range from £100 to £150.

Annual grant total

Grants total around £2,000.

Applications

On a form available from the correspondent, to be submitted either directly by the individual or through the individual's school, college or educational welfare agency. Applications are considered in February, May and October and must include details of the student's financial circumstances, details of the course/expedition/vocation study, including costs, and what benefits they hope to gain from the course.

Other information

Dorset County Council also administers The Marras Prize – each year grants totalling up to £1,000 are given to people aged 16 to 19 who are assessed to be the most deserving from the point of behaviour, honesty and truthfulness. Two smaller trusts are also administered, each making grants totalling less than £500 a year.

The Gordon Charitable Trust

£5,000

Correspondent: Gerry Aiken, Hon. Clerk, 45 Dunkeld Road, Bournemouth BH3 7EW (01202 768337; email: gerry_aitken@hotmail.com)

Trustees: Stephen Chappell; Mark Constantine; Gerry Aiken; Kathy Bartlett; Len Carslake; Mary Aiken.

CC Number: 200668

Eligibility

Young people aged 15 to 25 years who live in the county of Dorset or the parishes of Ringwood, Burley, Ellingham, Harbridge and Ibsley, New Milton, Sopley and Bransgore in west Hampshire and are undergoing further education or an apprenticeship.

Types of grants

One-off and recurrent grants of up to £500 a year are made to further and higher education students towards books, equipment/instruments and maintenance/living expenses.

Annual grant total

In 2010/11 the trust had an income of £2,900 and an expenditure of £6,000.

Applications

On a form available from the correspondent, submitted directly by the individual, for consideration in March, June, September and December.

Other information

As the trust is reliant upon donations from other sources its income is limited and variable.

Lockyer's Charity Trust

£1,500

Correspondent: Richard J Tattershall, 89 Redwood Road, Upton, Poole BH16 5QG (01202 632505)

Trustees: Annie Gallimore; Elizabeth Collinson; Jeanne Hollard; Jean De Garis; David Ruston.

CC Number: 306246

Eligibility

People who live in Lytchett Minster, Upton and Organford, aged up to 25. Applicants must have lived in the parish for two years before applying and it must be their main residence.

Types of grants

Help towards books, equipment and educational outings in the UK for students in further or higher education, apprentices or people starting work.

Annual grant total

About £1,500.

Applications

On a form available from the correspondent, submitted directly by the individual or by a parent or guardian. Applications are considered in February, June and November and should be submitted in the preceding month.

Francis Ramage Prize Trust

£1,000

Correspondent: The Business Support Team, Children's Services, County Hall, Dorchester, Dorset DT1 1XJ (01305 224109; email: csbusinesssupport@dorsetcc.gov.uk)

Trustee: Dorset County Council.

CC Number: 1085755

Eligibility

Young people up to the age of 19 who live in the administrative area of Dorset

and attend a school maintained by Dorset Local Authority. Priority is given to children from low income families, then children with special educational needs.

Types of grants

One-off and recurrent grants according to need for study or travel abroad, study or experience in the UK, travel, training, coaching, rehearsals, books, equipment/tools, clothing and uniforms.

Annual grant total

About £1,000.

Applications

On a form available from the correspondent.

The William Williams Charity

£96,000

Correspondent: Ian Winsor, Steward, Stafford House, 10 Prince of Wales Road, Dorchester, Dorset DT1 1PW (01305 264573; email: enquires@williamwilliams.org.uk; website: www.williamwilliams.org.uk)

Trustees: Robert Cowley; Ray Humphries; Leo Williams; Carole Sharp; Haydn White; Richard Gillam; Richard Prideaux-Brune; Joe Rose.

CC Number: 202188

Eligibility

People in need who live in the ancient parishes of Blandford, Shaftesbury or Sturminster Newton (DT11 7, DT10 1, DT10 2 and SP7 8).

Types of grants

One-off grants of £500 to £1,000 for those embarking on higher education or recognised training schemes or apprentices.

Annual grant total

In 2011 the charity had assets of £7.9 million and an income of £292,000. Grants to 217 individuals totalled £146,000 with £50,000 given for welfare and £96,000 for education.

Applications

On a form available from the correspondent or the website along with guidelines. Applications are considered at least four times a year.

Other information

Grants are also made to organisations.

Blandford

The Blandford Children's Fund

£80

Correspondent: Trust Manager, Natwest Trust Services, 5th Floor, Trinity Quay 2, Avon Street, Bristol BS2 0PT (01179 403283)

Trustee: Natwest Private Banking.

CC Number: 249469

Eligibility

Children living in the borough of Blandford who were under 12 on 1 January in the year of application.

Types of grants

One-off or recurrent grants, on average of £100 each, for items such as clothing, school uniforms, books, educational outings and maintenance costs.

Annual grant total

In 2010/11 the fund had an income of £1,000 and an expenditure of £80. Over the past five years expenditure has fluctuated between £75 and £5,000.

Applications

On a form available from the correspondent. Applications are considered in January and must include details of parental occupation, net family income, purpose for which the grant will be used and a birth certificate. The Mayor of Blandford decides who will benefit.

Blandford Forum Charities

£4,000

Correspondent: Irene Prior, Barnes Homes, Salisbury Road, Blandford Forum, Dorset DT11 7HU (01258 451810)

Trustees: Heather Bracewell; Esme Butler; Lyn Lyndsay; Carole Sharp; Hayden White; Jean Balmer; John Barnes; Joseph Hitchings; Sara Loch; Colin Stevens; Rosemary Holmes.

CC Number: 230853

Eligibility

People under the age of 25 who are living, or who have been educated for at least two years, in the borough of Blandford Forum.

Types of grants

(i) Cash grants, to a usual maximum of about £400, for school pupils to help with books, equipment, clothing or travel.
(ii) Grants to a usual maximum of about £400 to help with school, college or university fees or to supplement existing grants.
(iii) Help towards the cost of education, training, apprenticeship, clothing or equipment for those starting work.

Annual grant total

In 2010/11 the charity had assets of £31,000, an income of £7,500 and made grants totalling £1,000.

Applications

In writing to the correspondent.

Other information

This fund is part of the Blandford Forum Almshouse Charity which also provides accommodation and relief in need.

Charmouth

The Almshouse Charity

£500

Correspondent: Mrs Anthea Gillings, Swansmead, Riverway, Charmouth, Bridport, Dorset DT6 6LS (01297 560465)

Trustees: Felicity Perkin; Mallory Hayter; Felicity Horton; Gillian Pile; Clare Perry; Richard Wyatt.

CC Number: 201885

Eligibility

People in further and higher education who, or whose immediate family, live in the parish of Charmouth.

Types of grants

One-off and recurrent grants, generally of £25 to £250 towards school uniforms, overseas voluntary/education work and university books.

Annual grant total

In 2010 the trust had an income of £3,000 and a total expenditure of £2,500.

Applications

In writing to the correspondent or other trustees. Applications can be submitted directly by the individual or through a third party such as a rector, doctor or trustee. They are usually considered at quarterly periods; emergencies can be considered at other times. Applications should include details of the purpose of the grant, the total costs involved, and an official letter or programme/itinerary.

Other information

Grants are also given to individuals for relief-in-need purposes and to youth clubs for specific purposes.

Corfe Castle

Corfe Castle Charities

£18,000 (16 grants)

Correspondent: Mrs J Wilson, The Spinney, Springbrook Close, Corfe Castle, Wareham, Dorset BH20 5HS (01929 480873)

Trustees: Mr F. Spooner; Mr M. Bond; Mr C. Thompson; Mr J. Sabben-Clare; Mrs A. Lardner; Mrs D. Reynolds; Revd I. Jackson; Revd G. Clemts; Revd G. Burrett.

CC Number: 1055846

Eligibility

People in need who live in the parish of Corfe Castle.

Types of grants

One-off grants or interest free loans to students in further or higher education. In recent years grants have been given for books, fees, maintenance/living expenses, educational outings in the UK and study or travel overseas. Schoolchildren have also received one-off grants for uniforms or other school clothing.

Annual grant total

In 2010/11 the charity had assets of £4.2 million and an income of £216,000. There were 16 educational grants made to individuals totalling £18,000.

Applications

On a form available from the correspondent, to be submitted directly by the individual. The trustees meet monthly, but emergency requests are dealt with as they arise.

Other information

Grants are also made to organisations.

Dorchester

Dorchester Relief-in-Need Charity

£1,000

Correspondent: R R E Potter, 8 Mithras Close, Dorchester, Dorset DT1 2RF (01305 262041)

Trustees: Derek Norris; Margaret Stephenson; Robert Potter; Revd Harold Stephens; Timothy Bullick; Mark Green.

CC Number: 286570

Eligibility

People in need who live in the ecclesiastical parish of Dorchester.

Types of grants

One-off grants to those in need. Recent grants have been given for school uniforms and excursions, and to people starting work for books and equipment.

Annual grant total

Grants for educational purposes usually total around £1,000 per year.

Applications

Application forms are available from the correspondent and can be submitted through a school/teacher, social worker, health visitor, Citizens Advice or social services.

Other information

This charity also gives grants for relief-in-need purposes.

Litton Cheney

The Litton Cheney Relief-in-Need Trust

£1,500

Correspondent: B P Prentice, Steddings, Chalk Pit Lane, Litton Cheney, Dorchester, Dorset DT2 9AN (01308 482535)

Trustees: Revd Bob Thorn; Brian Prentice; Margaret Thomas; Penelope Dewar; Freddie Spicer.

CC Number: 231388

Eligibility

University students and people starting work who live in the parish of Litton Cheney.

Types of grants

Grants of £100 are made each year for 16-year old people who are about to start a career and to 18-year olds who are about to start at university. Grants are towards books and equipment.

Annual grant total

About £3,000.

Exclusions

No grants for people taking A-levels, or for schoolchildren.

Applications

Applications, on a form available from the correspondent, should be submitted directly by the individual, and are considered throughout the year.

Poole

The Poole Children's Fund

£250

Correspondent: Julia Palmer, 52 Hennings Park Road, Poole BH15 3QX (01202 261921)

Trustees: Joan Hart; Pauline Shuttle.

CC Number: 277300

Eligibility

Children up to 18 who are disadvantaged, disabled or otherwise in need and live in the borough of Poole.

Types of grants

Help towards the cost of holidays and other recreational and educational facilities, including grants for educational outings for schoolchildren and for study or travel abroad for students in further and higher education. Grants can be in the range of £10 to £80 and are usually one-off.

Preference for children with behavioural and social difficulties who have limited opportunities for leisure and recreational activities of a positive nature, for schoolchildren with serious family difficulties so the child has to be educated away from home, and for people with special educational needs.

Annual grant total

About £500 for welfare and educational purposes.

Applications

On a form available from the correspondent completed by a third party such as a social worker, health visitor, minister or teacher. Applications are considered throughout the year. They should include details of family structure including: ages; reason for application; family income and any other sources of funding which have been tried; what agencies (if any) are involved in helping the family; and any statutory orders (for example, care orders) relating to the child or their family members.

Weymouth and Portland

The Sir Samuel Mico Trust

£28,000

Correspondent: C I Thompson, Clerk to the Trustees, 26 St Thomas Street, Weymouth, Dorset DT4 8OJ (01305 774666; email: info@ weymouthtowncharities.org.uk; website: www.weymouthtowncharities.org.uk)

Trustees: Alan Burt; Gary Hepburn; Steven Pitman; Kevin Vincent; Richard Shoulder; Andrew Prowse.

CC Number: 202629

Eligibility

People aged 16 to 25 who are normally resident in the area of Weymouth and Portland Borough Council.

Types of grants

One-off and recurrent grants are made to students in further or higher education or those undertaking apprenticeships.

Grants are given towards the cost of books, fees/living expenses, study or travel abroad and for student exchange. Grants are also given to people starting work towards the cost of books, equipment, tools, clothing and travel.

Annual grant total

In 2010/11 the trust had assets of £153,000, an income of £38,000 and gave grants totalling £28,000.

Applications

On a form available to download from the website or from the correspondent. Applicants must be able to show that they are in difficult financial circumstances and have a desire to extend their education.

Gloucestershire

Lumb's Educational Foundation

£13,000

Correspondent: Neville Capper, 54 Collum End Rise, Leckhampton, Cheltenham GL53 0PB (01242 515673)

Trustees: Katherine Holmes; Dennis Doctor; Margaret Wanless; Neville Capper; Terence Cox.

CC Number: 311683

Eligibility

People aged 16 to 25 who live in the borough of Cheltenham and surrounding parishes. Students from Gloucestershire, particularly art and music students, are also considered.

Types of grants

One-off grants of £50 to £1,000 to help with uniforms/other school clothing, books, equipment/instruments, fees, educational outings in the UK and study or travel abroad. People starting work can be helped with uniforms, books and equipment/instruments. People embarking on official gap-year projects are also supported.

Annual grant total

In 2010 the foundation had an income and expenditure of £14,000.

Exclusions

Grants are not made towards trips that are more of a holiday rather than educational, towards living expenses, or towards school fees.

Applications

On receipt of a written application a form is sent out, which must be completed and returned with a supporting letter, including details of income, expenditure, parental financial support and the purpose of the grant. The trustees usually meet in February, April, July, September and November. All applicants are interviewed. Each application is assessed according to need and funds available at the time.

Charlton Kings

Higgs and Coopers Educational Charity

£25,000

Correspondent: Martin Fry, 7 Branch Hill Rise, Charlton Kings, Cheltenham GL53 9HN (01242 239903; email: martyn.fry@dsl.pipex.com)

Trustees: Peter Ginns; Douglas Giraldi; Melanie Fletcher; Michael Palmer; Helena McCloskey; Duncan Smith; Michael Pigott; Catherine Cranna; Joan Collins.

CC Number: 311570

Eligibility

People under 25 who currently live, or were born, in the former urban district of Charlton Kings (as constituted prior to 1974). Preference is given to people in single parent families.

Types of grants

Grants to help with books, equipment/instruments, educational outings in the UK and study or travel overseas. People starting work and people in further and higher education can also be helped with fees.

Annual grant total

In 2010/11 the charity had an income of £14,000 and an expenditure of £22,000. Grants to individuals usually total around £12,000.

Applications

On a form available from the correspondent, submitted directly by the individual. Applications are considered six times a year. The charity publicises its grants locally in order to increase awareness, as sometimes there has been a lack of applications.

Other information

The trust supports schools, youth clubs, Guide and Scout groups, boys' and girls' brigades, and other voluntary organisations broadly connected with the education or recreational pursuits of young people in the area of benefit.

Cirencester

John Edmonds' Charity

£4,000 (10 grants)

Correspondent: Richard Mullings, 7 Dollar Street, Cirencester, Gloucestershire GL7 2AS (01285 650000)

Trustees: Raymond Fenton; Roger Brown; John Visser; Maureen Lloyd; Richard Reece; Simone Clark; Colin Illman; Canon Doolan; Patricia Lynskey.

CC Number: 311495

Eligibility

People under the age of 25, who were born of Cirencester parents or currently live in Cirencester or district, or were educated in Cirencester.

Types of grants

Help towards the cost of education, training, apprenticeship or equipment, including grants for schoolchildren, students and people starting work. Grants range from £100 to £500 and are one-off.

Annual grant total

Up to £4,000 is given in total each year to about ten individuals.

Applications

On a form available from the correspondent.

Highnam

William Andrews Foundation

£800

Correspondent: David Slinger, Clerk to the Trustees, 1 Wetherleigh Drive, Highnam, Gloucester GL2 8LW (01452 412936)

Trustees: Josephine Smith; Edward Felton; Joyce Dole; Sheila Humble; Sarah Smith.

CC Number: 311522

Eligibility

People in need aged under 25 years who live in the parish of Highnam.

Types of grants

One-off and recurrent grants ranging from £50 to £200 for schoolchildren, students and young people starting work. Help is specifically given towards school uniforms, textbooks, equipment, and educational visits in the UK, travel overseas and fees.

Annual grant total

Charitable expenditure in 2010 amounted to £1,000. The income for this trust continues to be around £800 per year.

Applications

In writing to the correspondent, directly by the individual or their parent, in time to be considered at the annual general meeting in July. Applications should include the reason for the request, place of residence, details of education, the age of the applicant and general financial information (for example, low income).

Stroud

The Stroud and Rodborough Educational Charity

£25,000

Correspondent: S Baker, Clerk to the Trustees, 14 Green Close, Uley, Dursley, Gloucestershire GL11 5TH (01453 860379; email: info@ stroudrodboroughed.org; website: www. stroudrodboroughec.org)

Trustees: Bryan Oosthuysen; Derek Jarvis; Elisabeth Bird; Len Tomlins; Myles Robinson; Roy Nicholas; Victor Lewis; John Parker; Nigel Cooper; Joanna Chapman; Dorcas Binns.

CC Number: 309614

Eligibility

People under 25 resident in the Stroud area.

Types of grants

Help is primarily for those in further and higher education towards equipment/instruments and foreign travel for educational purposes. Grants are also available for those at school, usually for extra-curricular activities such as music and drama lessons, special courses and field trips. Grants range from £10 to £500.

Annual grant total

In 2010/11 the charity had an income of £83,000 and gave grants to individuals totalling £25,000. Educational prizes totalled £1,000.

Exclusions

No grants for expenditure which, in the trustees' opinion, should be the responsibility of the Local Education Authority, such as travel to and from school or college or towards course fees.

Applications

On a form available from the correspondent or the website which should include a reference from a teacher. Applications are usually considered in February, April, June, September and November.

Other information

The priority of the charity is to provide financial help to the three secondary schools in the area. Any remainder is given to individuals. The charity also administers a number of prize funds tenable at the local schools.

Weston-sub-Edge

Weston-sub-Edge Educational Charity

£10,000

Correspondent: Rachel Hurley, Longclose Cottage, Weston-sub-Edge, Chipping Campden, Gloucestershire GL55 6QX (01386 841808)

Trustees: Kathleen Thorpe; Francis Robbins; Barrie Knight; Valerie Kemp; Sarah Hudson-Evans.

CC Number: 297226

Eligibility

People under 25 who live, or whose parents live, in Weston-sub-Edge, or who have at any time attended (or whose parents have attended) Weston-sub-Edge Church of England Primary School.

Types of grants

Grants range from £10 to £500. In cases of special financial need grants can be for uniforms or other clothing for schoolchildren. People at any stage of education who fit the criteria listed above (including people starting work) can be supported for books, equipment/instruments, fees, educational outings in the UK and study or travel abroad. Further and higher education may also be supported for maintenance/living expenses.

Annual grant total

In 2010/11 the charity had an income of £10,000 and an expenditure of £12,000.

Applications

On a form available from the correspondent, including details of the course, its duration and purpose. Applications should be submitted directly by the individual if over 16, or otherwise by the parent/guardian. Applications are considered in January, March, May, July, September and November.

Somerset

Huish's Exhibition Foundation

£3,500

Correspondent: Kate James, Porter Dodson Solicitors, Quad 4000, Blackbrook Park Avenue, Taunton TA1 2PX (01823 625800; email: kate.james@porterdodson.co.uk)

Trustees: John White; Robert Homeshaw; Ray Stokes; David Lowe; Patricia Hunt.

CC Number: 310245

Eligibility

Pupils of the following schools in the county of Somerset: Richard Huish College, Taunton; King's College, Taunton; Queen's College, Taunton; Taunton School, Taunton; Wellington School, Wellington who have a GCSE or A-level in Religious Studies.

Types of grants

Grants of £300 a year for students when they start at university. The grants are made for the duration of the university course.

Annual grant total

£3,000 to £4,000 a year.

Applications

Applications should be made through the various schools.

Ilminster Educational Foundation

£11,000 (41 grants)

Correspondent: Edward Wells, Clerk, 20 Station Road, Ilminster, Somerset TA19 9BD (01460 53029)

Trustees: Mary Davys; Stuart Shepherd; Jonathan Perry; Alan West; Doreen Brunt; Geoffrey Morgan; Gordon Twinberrow; Nigel Corbett; Roger Swan; Frederick Fisher Paul Whaites; Margaret Copley; Wendy Outram; Marie Jewson.

CC Number: 310265

Eligibility

People under 25 living in or educated in the ancient parish of Ilminster.

Types of grants

The foundation gives grants of £200 to £300 for two purposes: book grants to students in universities and to postgraduates; and for educational outings for schoolchildren and study or travel abroad for schoolchildren.

Annual grant total

In 2010/11 the foundation had an income of £96,000 and gave 41 grants to individuals for education totalling £11,000

Exclusions

Book grants are not available for A-Level courses.

Applications

On a form available from the correspondent. Applications are considered in October and November. Higher education grants should be submitted in September and October.

Other information

Grants are also made to schools.

Keyford Educational Foundation

£700

Correspondent: J R Pegg, The Blue House, The Bridge, Frome, Somerset BA11 1AP (01373 455338; email: bhouse1ap@btinternet.com)

Trustees: Colin Alsbury; Andrea Brooke; Brenda Hinton; Christine Potter; Clare Bonham-Christie; Hilary Daniel; Simon White; Mary Bawden; Marie-Louise MacLeay.

CC Number: 309989

Eligibility

Young people aged up to 25 who live in the parishes of Frome or Selwood.

Types of grants

One-off grants from £50 to £100. Schoolchildren and students in further and higher education can be helped with uniforms/other school clothing, books, equipment/instruments, fees, educational outings in the UK and study or travel abroad. Grants are also available for extracurricular activities such as music, arts and sport.

Annual grant total

About £700 a year to individuals. Half of the yearly income is designated to Frome College.

Applications

On a form available from the correspondent, to be submitted either directly by the individual, through the individual's school, college or educational welfare agency or through another third party such as their parent/guardian or social worker or Citizens Advice. The foundation requires a recommendation from the teacher or tutor and a telephone or personal interview. Applications are considered every other month, from January onwards.

Other information

This trust incorporates the Ancient Blue Coat Foundation.

The John Nowes Exhibition Foundation

£4,000

Correspondent: Lorraine Brown, c/o Battens Solicitors, Mansion House, Princes Street, Yeovil, Somerset BA20 1EP (01935 846000)

Trustees: Alan Tawse; Iris Coton; Bridget Dollard; Christine Salmon; Peter Seib.

CC Number: 309984

Eligibility

People under 25 who are in need, studying at a further, higher, or postgraduate level and live in the town of Yeovil and the parishes of Alvington, Barwick, Brympton, Chilthorne Domer, East Coker, Limington, Mudford, Preston Plucknett, West Coker and Yeovil Without.

Types of grants

Grants, ranging from £150 to £500, for general educational purposes to those in further and higher education, vocational and overseas students and for special educational needs.

Annual grant total

Around £4,000 a year.

Applications

By 31 August each year. A form is available from the correspondent and should be submitted with an academic reference.

Prowde's Educational Foundation

See entry on page 152

Blackford

Blackford Educational Trust

£4,500

Correspondent: Simon Kraeter, Secretary, c/o Hugh Sexey Middle School, Blackford, Wedmore, Somerset BS28 4ND (01934 710041; email: s. kraeter@virgin.net)

Trustees: Christopher McKinley; Rhoderick Stewart; Jackie Hipwell; Simon Kraeter; Mark Stanley-Smith; Martin Cahil; Liz Merryfield; Andrew Scott.

CC Number: 277339

Eligibility

People in primary, secondary, further or higher education who are aged 25 or under and live in the ecclesiastical parish of Blackford.

Types of grants

Grants are made to schoolchildren for equipment/instruments, educational outings in the UK and study or travel abroad, and to further and higher education students for books.

Annual grant total

In 2010/11 the trust had an income of £4,500 and an expenditure of £4,300. £4,000 to £5,000 is usually given in grants per year.

Applications

On a form available from the correspondent, submitted by the individual in January, May or September, for consideration by the trust in February, June or October. Applications must be accompanied by receipts and all expenses must have been incurred before an application can be submitted.

Other information

The trust also makes grants to primary and secondary schools in the Blackford area.

Draycott

Card Educational Foundation

£1,800

Correspondent: Helen Dance, Clerk and Treasurer, Leighurst, The Street, Draycott, Cheddar, Somerset BS27 3TH (01934 742811)

Trustees: David Sheldon; Gerald Dally; Graham Brown; Trish Corrick; Sue Hewish; Di Ginger; Mike Sealey; Jeff Astle; Sue Rose; Rachel Chard; Pat Sherlock.

CC Number: 309976

Eligibility

People in need in the hamlet of Draycott, aged between 4 and 30 years.

Types of grants

Grants range from £50 to £200 and can be for books, equipment/instruments, fees and study or travel abroad. Other grants can be made to: schoolchildren for uniforms or other school clothing, educational outings in the UK and student exchanges; people starting work for uniforms, maintenance/living expenses and educational outings in the UK; further and higher education students for maintenance/living expenses; and mature students and postgraduates for maintenance/living expenses, educational outings in the UK and student exchanges.

Annual grant total

Grants usually total around £1,800 each year.

Exclusions

No grants towards ski trips or school transport.

Applications

In writing to the correspondent including a clear statement of residence in the hamlet. Applications can be submitted either directly by the individual or through a third party such as a parent or teacher. They are considered at the end of November and should be submitted at least two weeks before.

Other information

Grants are also made to organisations.

Evercreech

The Arthur Allen Educational Trust

£5,000

Correspondent: Allison Dowding, Meadow's Edge, High Street, Stoney Stratton, Shepton Mallett, Somerset BA4 6DY (01749 831077)

Trustees: Allison Dowding; Barbara Biddescombe; Geoffrey Lawson; Robert Reed; Peter Rapsey; Raymond McGovern; S. Cradock; Michele Hole; Andrew Doble.

CC Number: 310256

Eligibility

People who were born or who live in the parish of Evercreech between 16 and 25 years old. Students attending technical college, university or sixth form college.

Types of grants

One-off grants in the range of £50 and £300 to college students, undergraduates and vocational students, towards clothing, fees, study/travel abroad, books, equipment/instruments, maintenance/living expenses and excursions.

Annual grant total

Around £5,000.

Applications

Awards are usually made in late October, so applications must be submitted in September. Applications can be submitted directly by the individual, including name, place and duration of course, eligibility, amount of local authority grant and parents' commitment, previous educational achievements and two references.

Ilchester

Ilchester Relief-in-Need and Educational Charity

£19,000

Correspondent: Wendy Scrivener, Milton House, Podimore, Yeovil, Somerset BA22 8JF (01935 840070)

Trustees: Philip Horsington; Alan Stephens; Greta Burke; Jonathan Coulson; Patricia Morley; Steven Marsh; Rachel Frampton.

CC Number: 235578

Eligibility

Students in financial need who live in the parish of Ilchester only.

Types of grants

One-off grants for educational expenses including travel, books/equipment and field trips.

Annual grant total

In 2011 the charity had an income of £34,000 and gave educational grants to individuals totalling £19,000.

Applications

On a form available from the correspondent. Applications can be submitted directly by the individual or through a third party such as their school or an educational welfare agency.

Unsolicited applications are not responded to.

Other information

Grants are also given for relief in need.

Rimpton

The Rimpton Relief-in-Need Charities

£750

Correspondent: J N Spencer, Secretary, Field End House, Home Farm Lane, Rimpton, Yeovil, Somerset BA22 8AS (01935 850530)

Trustees: Daphne Coombs; Gordon Diment; John Spencer; Sheila Fewkes; Revd Dr Michael Hayes; Robert McCreight.

CC Number: 239816

Eligibility

People who live in the parish of Rimpton only.

Types of grants

One-off or recurrent grants according to need. Recent grants have been made to cover student expenses, for exchange visits and to students representing their country at sport.

Annual grant total

Grants usually total about £1,500 each year for welfare and educational purposes.

Applications

On a form available from the correspondent, to be submitted either by the individual, a family member, or through a third party.

Taunton Deane

Taunton Heritage Trust

£26,000 (163 grants)

Correspondent: Clerk to the Trustees, Huish Homes, Magdalene Street, Taunton, Somerset TA1 1SG (01823 335348)

Trustees: John Ruff; Jean Allgrove; Beatrice Roberts; John Guy; John Richards; John Palmer; Richard Meikle; Michael Beer; Robert McKay; Alan Ladd; Mary Whitmarsh; Chris Cutting.

CC Number: 202120

Eligibility

People living in the borough of Taunton Deane that are of school age (up to the age of 16). Requests from the colleges of further education on behalf of individuals may also be considered, depending on circumstances and need.

Types of grants

Grants to schoolchildren are made according to need, towards school uniforms and in exceptional circumstances, computers.

Annual grant total

In 2011 the trust had assets of £5.1 million and an income of £518,000. Educational grants to 163 individuals totalled £26,000.

Applications

On a form available from the website, which must be typed not handwritten. Applications can be made throughout the year, via schools, an educational welfare agency, social services or Citizens Advice.

Other information

The prime role of the charity is to provide sheltered accommodation for older people. Grants are also made for welfare purposes.

Previously called 'Taunton Town Charity'.

Wiltshire

William (Doc) Couch Trust Fund

£9,300 (8 grants)

Correspondent: Carolyn Godfrey, Director for Children and Education, Wiltshire County Council, Department of Resources, County Hall, Trowbridge, Wiltshire BA14 8JJ (01225 718584; email: educationaltrusts@wiltshire.gov.uk)

CC Number: 1079040

Eligibility

Young people under the age of 18 who have a disability or are otherwise in financial need and live in Wiltshire.

Types of grants

Grants for schoolchildren and young people with special educational needs for lesson fees, books, equipment and educational outings in the UK. Grants for school trips, music, sport and drama.

Annual grant total

In 2010/11 the trust had an income of £122,000 and made grants to individuals for educational purposes totalling £9,300.

Exclusions

No funding for transport costs or fees.

Applications

On a form available from the correspondent. Applications can be submitted directly by the individual or through a social worker, Citizens Advice or other welfare agency.

Applications are invited in April with a closing date towards the end of May, early June and are promoted across the county.

Col. William Llewellyn Palmer Educational Charity

£8,000

Correspondent: Chief Accountant, Wiltshire County Council, Finance Department, County Hall, Trowbridge, Wiltshire BA14 8JN (01225 718584)

Trustee: Wiltshire Council.

CC Number: 1015681

Eligibility

Children attending schools maintained by the local education authority and grant maintained schools in Bradford-on-Avon. Support is also given to young people under 25 for further education.

Types of grants

One-off grants towards, for example, school uniforms, school trips and music lessons.

Annual grant total

Grants to organisations and individuals totalled £17,000.

Applications

Applications should not be made directly to the correspondent. Individual applications should be made on behalf of the child by his or her school, as part of a block application by the school on behalf of all of their pupils who wish to apply. Such block applications should be submitted to the correspondent, by the school, by 25 October, for consideration at a meeting on 20 November. Grants are then distributed via the school.

Other information

Grants are also made to local schools and to individuals and groups for the purchase of equipment, to help fund recreational projects and holiday schemes.

The Rose Charity

£10,000

Correspondent: Charles Goodbody, Trustee, 94 East Street, Warminster, Wiltshire BA12 9BG (01985 214444)
Trustees: Charles Goodbody; David Deacon; Howard Astbury; Paul Wells.
CC Number: 900590

Eligibility

Schoolchildren who live in Warminster and the surrounding villages.

Types of grants

One-off grants towards costs which cannot be met elsewhere, for example, school uniform, other school clothing, books, educational outings and music lessons. Grants range from £50 to £500.

Annual grant total

In 2010/11 the charity had an income of £16,000 and an expenditure of £11,000.

Applications

In writing to the correspondent, with the support of the social services or a school/college or other educational welfare agency, and so on. Applications are considered throughout the year.

Salisbury City Educational and Apprenticing Charity

£1,300

Correspondent: Clerk to the Trustees, Trinity Hospital, Trinity Street, Salisbury SP1 2BD (01722 325640; email: clerk@

almshouses.demon.co.uk; website: www. salisburyalmshouses.co.uk)
Trustees: Lady Benson; Alison Hatton; Josephine Bailey; Rodney Shipsey; Trevor Austreng; Alan Corkill; David Coulton; Gillian Ellis; Peter Moss; Anna Taylor; Patricia Lush; Alastair Brain; Fiona Green.
CC Number: 309523

Eligibility

Young people under 25 who live in the district of Salisbury (with a preference to those resident in the city of Salisbury, and/or in secondary education).

Types of grants

One-off grants ranging from £100 to £200 are made to schoolchildren for educational outings in the UK and study or travel abroad, and to further and higher education students (but not mature students or postgraduates) for books, equipment/instruments, educational outings in the UK and study or travel abroad.

Interest-free loans are also made towards the cost of tools and equipment needed to start a trade.

The charity interprets the term education in the widest sense, and offers help towards the cost of expeditions and other educational projects designed to develop character, such as Project Trust, scout jamborees and adventure training.

Annual grant total

In 2010/11 the charity made ten grants totalling £1,300.

Exclusions

Grants are not made for school uniform, maintenance/living expenses or student exchanges. There is no support for second degree courses.

Applications

On a form available, along with guidance notes, from the charity's website. Applicants are advised to contact the clerk as early as possible to discuss an application. Applications are considered monthly and can be submitted through the individual's school, college or educational welfare agency.

The Sarum St Michael Educational Charity

£39,000

Correspondent: The Clerk to the Governors, First Floor, 27A Castle Street, Salisbury SP1 1TT (01722 422296; email: clerk@sarumstmichael.org; website: www.sarumstmichael.org)
Trustees: June Osborne; Bill Merrington; Alec Knight; Michael Chamberlain; Jennifer Pitcher; Chris Shepperd; Lucinda Herklots; Samantha O' Sullivan;

Nicholas Holtam; John Cox; Katie Sporle; Jane Dunlop.
CC Number: 309456

Eligibility

People aged over 16 who live or study in the Salisbury diocese and adjoining dioceses including Bath and Wells, Exeter, Oxford and Winchester.

Types of grants

Grants for first degrees including mature students, diplomas, access courses, Open University courses, vocational courses, postgraduate courses and gap year courses and projects. Clergy can also apply for grants to attend conferences and travel grants

Bursaries for potential teachers of religious education are £1,000 for each year of the first degree and £2,000 for the PGCE (or equivalent) year, and a further £3,000 'golden handshake'.

Annual grant total

In 2011 the charity had assets of £4.7 million and an income of £175,000. Grants to 28 individuals totalled £39,000 including one receiving the religious education bursary.

Applications

On a form available from the correspondent. Applications are considered in January, April, July, September and November. Deadline dates for receiving applications are five weeks before the trustees' meetings. Applications should be submitted directly by the individual.

On forms available from the website. Governors meet four or five times a year to consider applications, see the website for meeting dates.

Other information

Grants are also given to schools, parishes and youth/educational organisations. Grants to individuals account for 40% of grantmaking.

Alfred Earnest Withy's Trust Fund

£7,000

Correspondent: The Chief Financial Officer, The Community Foundation for Wiltshire and Swindon, 48 New Park Street, Devizes, Wiltshire SN10 1DS (email: info@wscf.org.uk)
Trustee: Wiltshire Council.
CC Number: 1070264

Eligibility

Pupils aged 11 to 18 who are 'poor in pocket but rich in merit' and live in Wiltshire.

Types of grants

50% of the income accrued by the trust is passed over to the chief education officer to distribute. Priority is given towards the cost of school/field trips, games equipment, and so on. Grants are given for up to 80% of the cost, up to £100.

Grants will not be given retrospectively and will only exceed £500 in exceptional circumstances.

Annual grant total

In 2010/11 the trust had an income of £7,300 and an expenditure of £7,400.

Applications

On a form available from the correspondent, by or on behalf of the individual and should include details of the applicant's parents' income and expenses to ensure the 'poor in pocket' criterion is met. All applications must be accompanied by a reference and full educational record to substantiate the 'rich in merit' stipulation.

Chippenham

Chippenham Borough Lands Charity

£10,000

Correspondent: Catherine Flynn, Jubilee Building, 32 Market Place, Chippenham, Wiltshire SN15 3HP (01249 658180; fax: 01249 446048; email: admin@cblc.org. uk; website: www.cblc.org.uk)

Trustees: Jenny Budgell; Jack Konyenburg; Chris Dawe; Peter Kemp; Margaret Harrison; Michael Braun; Mark Packard; Peter Hutton; Graham Bone; Desna Allen; Terry Burke; Mary Pile.

CC Number: 270062

Eligibility

People in need who are living within the Parish of Chippenham at the date of application, and have been for a minimum of two years immediately prior to applying.

Types of grants

Usually one-off grants according to need, for things such as, help towards travel costs, the provision of equipment to undertake a course or help towards actual course fees, depending on the nature of the course and the individual's personal circumstances.

Annual grant total

In 2010/11 grants were given to 56 individuals totalling £21,000.

Exclusions

The charity is unable to help towards the cost of undergraduate degree courses. Equally, grants are not given in any

circumstances where the trustees consider the award to be a substitute for statutory provision.

Applications

On a form available from the correspondent. Once received the application will be looked at in detail by an education officer. It is possible that the charity will visit, or ask applicants to call in at this stage. Applications are considered every month and can be submitted directly by the individual or through a third party such as a teacher.

Other information

Grants are also given to organisations.

Conock

The Ewelme Exhibition Endowment

£81,000 (63 grants)

Correspondent: James Oliver, Clerk and Trust Manager, 126 High Street, Oxford OX1 4DG (01865 244661; email: office@ hmg-law.co.uk)

Trustees: Alice Penney; Derek Leonard; Neil Blake; Victor Angell; Rebecca Armstrong; Valerie Stattersfield; Sarah Maine.

CC Number: 309240

Eligibility

People under 21 who live in Ewelme and Marsh Gibbon, the other estate areas and the counties of Oxfordshire, Buckinghamshire and former Berkshire.

Types of grants

Grants of £600 to £1,200 for fees; uniform/clothing; tools/equipment; instruments; books and trips for schoolchildren, further and higher education students, apprentices and people staring work.

Annual grant total

In 2010/11 the fund had an income of £120,000 and gave 63 grants to individuals totalling £81,000.

Applications

On a form available from the correspondent. Applications should include attainments at school, details of parental income and a testimonial from the headteacher. They are considered in February and March.

East Knoyle

The East Knoyle Welfare Trust

£800

Correspondent: Miss Sabrina Sully, Old Byre House, Millbrook Lane, East Knoyle, Salisbury SP3 6AW

Trustees: Michael Hull; Sabrina Sully; Cliff Sully; Andrew Burton; Helen Lever; John Hacker; Margaret Browning; Revd S. Morgan; Sally-Anne Williams.

CC Number: 202028

Eligibility

People in need who are under the age of 25 and live in the parish of East Knoyle.

Types of grants

Any need is considered, including grants to school leavers for tools, working clothes and books.

Annual grant total

Grants usually total around £800.

Applications

At any time to the correspondent or any other trustee.

Other information

Grants are also made for welfare purposes.

Swindon

The W. G. Little Scholarship and Band Concert Fund

£30,000

Correspondent: Darren Stevens, Swindon Borough Council, Civic Offices, Euclid Street, Swindon SN1 2JH (01793 445500; email: customerservices@ swindon.gov.uk)

Trustee: Swindon Borough Council.

CC Number: 309497

Eligibility

Secondary school pupils who have lived in the Swindon Borough Council area for at least 12 months. The main priority is for pupils who are leaving primary school and transferring to secondary school. At the trust's discretion, support can also be given to students up to the age of 25 who wish to attend local colleges.

Types of grants

Grants of about £50 to help with school clothing.

Annual grant total

In 2010/11 the trust had an income of £22,000 and an expenditure of £33,000. Expenditure is usually all given in grants.

Applications

On a form available from the correspondent, to be submitted by the end of July. Successful applicants can only reapply every other year. Applicants are means tested.

Other information

Organisations are also supported, provided their service users are aged 11 to 21 and live within the borough boundary.

The Ethel May Trust

£1,250

Correspondent: Mrs Lesley Hodge, Trust Fund Administrator, Swindon Borough Council, Civic Offices, Euclid Street, Swindon SN1 2JH (01793 445500; email: customerservices@swindon.gov. uk)

Trustee: Swindon Borough Council.

CC Number: 1002739

Eligibility

Schoolchildren and students under the age of 25 of good character and studious application, who attend school or college full or part-time in the boundary of Swindon Borough Council.

Types of grants

One-off grants according to need. Grants are often £150 towards equipment or dancewear.

Annual grant total

The trust holds assets of around £50,000 and awards £1,000 to £1,500 a year.

Applications

In writing to the correspondent.

Tisbury

The Educational Foundation of Alice Coombe and Others

£2,000

Correspondent: Deborah Carter, Rosebank, Hindon Lane, Tisbury, Wiltshire SP3 6PU (01747 871311; fax: 01747 871311; email: debcarter311@ btinternet.com)

Trustees: Juliet Bowen; John Berkley-Matthews; Deborah Carter; Andrew Staley; Gillian Spiller.

CC Number: 309359

Eligibility

People under 25 years who live in the ancient parish of Tisbury and West Tisbury. Applications from outside this area will not be considered.

Types of grants

Cash grants for school uniforms, clothing, books, and educational visits for schoolchildren; nursery school fees; books and study or travel abroad for those in further or higher education; and books for mature students. People starting work can be give help towards books, equipment/instruments, clothing and travel to interviews.

Grants range from £20 to £250 and are one-off. Loans are rarely given.

Annual grant total

About £2,000 a year.

Applications

In writing to the correspondent, either directly by the individual or through their school, college or educational welfare agency, vicar, health visitor or any other third party. Applications are considered throughout the year.

Warminster

The Warminster Close School Trust Fund

£400

Correspondent: Chief Accountant, Department of Resources, Wiltshire County Council, County Hall, Bythesea Road, Trowbridge, Wiltshire BA14 8JN (01225 718584; email: studentfinance@ wiltshire.gov.uk; website: www.wiltshire. gov.uk)

Trustee: Wiltshire Council.

CC Number: 285097

Eligibility

People who live in Warminster.

Types of grants

Scholarships, allowances or grants towards any school, university, college of education or further education (professional or technical). Financial assistance towards school clothing, equipment or books, travel expenses, music or other arts.

Annual grant total

Around £400 a year.

Applications

On a form available from the correspondent. All applications for more than £100 must be supported by a reference and full educational record.

South East

General

Anglia Care Trust

£450

Correspondent: Jane Sharpe, 65 St Matthew's Street, Ipswich, Suffolk IP1 3EW (01473 213140; email: admin@ angliacaretrust.org.uk; website: www. angliacaretrust.org.uk)

Trustees: Ann Bryant; Chris Bally; Peter Heath; James Manning; Colin Reid; Gareth Roscoe; Colin Shiers; Alex Till; Mary Gibbons.

CC Number: 299049

Eligibility

People in need who live in East Anglia and are experiencing or have experienced a legal restriction on their liberty, and their families.

Types of grants

One-off grants towards rehabilitation and education. Grants usually range from £10 to £70 for students in higher/ further education to spend on fees, books, equipment or other learning aids. Sums of money are not usually paid direct, but itemised bills will be met directly.

Applicants are usually already being supported by, or are known to, ACT and should have exhausted all possible sources of statutory funds.

Annual grant total

Grants usually total around £900.

Exclusions

No money is available for schoolchildren.

Applications

In writing to the correspondent. All applications must be supported by a probation officer or other professional person.

Other information

For this entry, the information relates to the money available from ACT. For more information on what is available throughout East Anglia, contact the correspondent.

The Blatchington Court Trust

£84,000 (282 grants)

Correspondent: Geoffrey Lockwood, Ridgeland House, 165 Dyke Road, Hove, East Sussex BN3 1TL (01273 727222; email: info@blatchington-court.co.uk; website: www.blatchington-court.co.uk)

Trustees: Richard Martin; Roger Jones; Georgina James; Alison Acason; Jonathan Wilson; Daniel Ellman-Brown; Anna Hunter.

CC Number: 306350

Eligibility

People aged under 30 living in the Sussex area who are visually impaired.

Types of grants

Grants or allowances are made to young people who are visually impaired at any school, university, college of education or other institution of further education (including those providing professional or technical skills) which are approved by the trustees. Grants are also made towards the cost of equipment, mobility aids, books and other study aids (including those for the study of music and the arts) which will assist in the pursuit of the education, training and employment or business development of young people. Grants will also be made in connection with preparation for entry to a school, profession, trade, occupation or service. Occasionally the trust will fund one-to-one swimming or riding lessons if it is felt that this would be beneficial to the child.

One-off and recurrent grants are made as well as loans.

Annual grant total

In 2010/11 the trust had assets of £10.7 million and an income of £507,000. 282 grants to individuals were made totalling £84,000, consisting of £47,000 in 125 computer grants and £37,000 in 157 other personal grants.

Exclusions

The trust cannot provide funding for wheelchairs, building adaptations, bursaries, school fees, holidays or travel costs. It does not provide cash grants.

Applications

Contact the trust to request an application form. Applications should be made by 1 February, 1 June, 1 August and 1 October each year.

Other information

During the last financial year, grants totalling £49,000 were also made to organisations whose activities facilitate the education of young, vision impaired people.

The Chownes Foundation

£2,400 (3 grants)

Correspondent: Sylvia J Spencer, Secretary, The Courtyard, Beeding Court, Steyning, West Sussex BN44 3TN (01903 816699)

Trustees: Revd Stephen Ortiger; Mrs U. Hazeel; Mr M. Wooley.

CC Number: 327451

Eligibility

Individuals and small charities primarily in Sussex, particularly Mid-Sussex, being the former home of the founder.

Types of grants

One-off and recurrent according to need.

Annual grant total

In 2010/11 the foundation had assets of £1.6 million and an income of £68,000. Grants were made to three individuals for educational purposes totalling £2,400.

Applications

The trustees prefer a one page document and will request further information if they require it.

Other information

The majority of the charity's funds are committed to long-term support for poor and vulnerable beneficiaries, so only very few applications are successful.

The Eric Evans Memorial Trust

£8,000

Correspondent: John Kinder, Trustee, 55 Thornhill Square, London N1 1BE (email: info@ericevanstrust.com; website: www.ericevanstrust.com)

Trustees: John Kinder; Cyril Henry Flajsner; Amelia Evans.

CC Number: 1047709

Eligibility

People who live in East Anglia or London.

Types of grants

Educational grants linked to sport.

Annual grant total

In 2010/11 the trust had an income of £0 and an expenditure of £8,400.

Applications

In writing to the correspondent, either directly by the individual or through the individual's school, college or welfare agency, or any other third party. Applications are considered quarterly.

The Ewelme Exhibition Endowment

See entry on page 277

The Hale Trust

£12,000 (12 grants)

Correspondent: J M Broughton, Secretary, Rosemary House, Woodhurst Park, Oxted, Surrey RH8 9HA

Trustees: Sheila Henderson; John Tuke; Diana Whitmore; John Burns; Jocelyn Broughton; Julia Cole; David Macfarlane.

CC Number: 313214

Eligibility

Young people under 25 years of age who live in Surrey, Sussex, Kent or Greater London.

The trust helps children whose lives are affected by the following issues:
(i) mental, physical or sensory disabilities
(ii) behavioural or psychological problems
(iii) living in poverty or situations of deprivation
(iv) illness, distress, abuse or neglect.

Bursaries are given to children under the age of 18 where there are medical requirements, family problems, special educational needs or limited funding.

Types of grants

Grants are usually one-off and given towards: (i) school fees, educational outings and books for schoolchildren; and (ii) books for students in further and higher education. Bursaries of £400 per term are also available for people under 18, but they cannot exceed £1,200 a year per individual, or last for more than three years. Grants are paid to the school and not the individual.

Annual grant total

In 2010/11 the trust had assets of £1.1 million and an income of £38,000. 12 bursaries were made totalling £12,000.

Exclusions

No grants for unspecified expenditure, deficit funding, the repayment of loans or second degrees/postgraduate work.

Applications

Applications can be submitted through the individual's school, college or educational welfare agency. Applicants for one-off grants should write to the correspondent, at the address below. They should preferably be submitted in time for the trustees' meetings in February, June and October.

Applicants for bursaries should apply to: Mrs Sheila Henderson, Foyle Farm, Merle Common, Oxted, Surrey RH8 9PN. The trust aims to interview all applicants for bursaries. Grants are paid to the school.

Other information

This trust also supports charities concerned with the advancement of education of children who are disabled or disadvantaged.

The Walter Hazell Charitable and Educational Trust Fund

£10,000

Correspondent: Rodney Dunkley, 20 Aviemore Gardens, Northampton NN4 9XJ (01604 765925)

Trustees: Michael Pegge; Rodney Dunkley; Terence Stewart.

CC Number: 1059707

Eligibility

Employees and past employees of the printing trade in Buckinghamshire and Berkshire. Spouses, widows, widowers and children and any other financial dependents can also be supported.

Types of grants

Grants are given to university students towards the cost of books and other course-related expenses.

Annual grant total

In 2010/11 the trust had an income of £19,000 and an expenditure of £14,000.

Exclusions

No grants are made towards course fees.

Applications

In writing to the correspondent.

Other information

This trust also awards Christmas payments to ex-employee pensioners of BPC Hazells.

Kentish's Educational Foundation

£15,000

Correspondent: Margery Roberts, Clerk to the Trustees, 7 Nunnery Stables, St Albans, Hertfordshire AL1 2AS (0172 856626)

Trustees: David Ridgeway; Joan Ripley; B. H. Henson; Hilary Burningham; Alison Steer; Michael Highstead; Robin Younger; Will Dickinson; David Nice.

CC Number: 313098

Eligibility

Young People aged 11 to 35 who have the name Kentish or who are related to the founder Thomas Kentish (died 1712 and require financial help. There are also opportunities to award grants to children/young people not named Kentish from Hertfordshire and Bedfordshire only (Thomas Kentish was associated with these counties).

Types of grants

One-off and recurrent grants ranging from £200 to £1,000. Grants for young people at secondary school for uniforms, clothing, book, educational outings, equipment and special help with disabilities which affect education. Further/Higher awards are towards books, fees, equipment, study or travel abroad or student exchange. Grants for people starting work can be for travel, books, equipment/instruments or expense arising from apprenticing. Due to the limited number of grants available grants for postgraduate study are awarded only in special cases.

Annual grant total

In 2010/11 the foundation had an income of £25,000 and an expenditure of £27,000. Grants to individuals usually total around £15,000.

Applications

A form is supplied on request and can be submitted by the individual or their parents/guardians. A copy of a school or tutor's report is required, together with copies of birth or marriage certificates if the applicant claims kinship with the founder but does not have the surname Kentish. Applications are to be submitted by the end of August for consideration in October.

The Mijoda Charitable Trust

£650

Correspondent: Jacquie Hardman, Oak House, 38 Botley Road, Chesham, Buckinghamshire HP5 1XG (01494 783402)

Trustees: Jacquie Hardman; David Stephenson; Michael Hardman.

CC Number: 1002565

Eligibility

People who live in Buckinghamshire, Bedfordshire and Hertfordshire who are undertaking further, higher or postgraduate education in music, the arts or medicine. Beneficiaries are usually under 40 years of age.

Types of grants

One-off and recurrent grants of up to £250 towards fees and study or travel overseas.

Annual grant total

About £650 to individuals.

Applications

In writing to the correspondent. A reply will only be sent if an sae is enclosed.

The Nichol-Young Foundation

£21,000

Correspondent: The Clerk, Bates Wells and Braithwaite, 27 Friars Street, Sudbury, Suffolk CO10 2AD (01787 880440)

Trustees: John Mitson; Carol Mitson.

CC Number: 259994

Eligibility

Individuals in need who are in full-time education, with a preference for those who live in East Anglia.

Types of grants

One-off and recurrent grants ranging from £100 to £2,000 for educational trips, medical electives and other such projects undertaken by individuals, usually during the course of full-time education. Grants are also given for computers, equipment and tools.

Annual grant total

In 2011 the foundation made grants to individuals totalling £21,000.

Applications

In writing to the correspondent. Applications are considered on a weekly or fortnightly basis. Unsuccessful applicants will only be contacted if an sae is provided. The trust does not accept telephone enquiries.

Other information

The foundation also gives grants to organisations.

Bedfordshire

Ashton Schools Foundation

£16,000

Correspondent: Mrs Yvonne E Beaumont, Grove House, 76 High Street North, Dunstable, Bedfordshire LU6 1NF (01582 890619)

CC Number: 307526

Eligibility

People under 25 years old who are in need and live within a radius of six miles from the parish church of the ecclesiastical parish of St Peter, Dunstable, in Bedfordshire

Types of grants

One-off and recurrent grants according to need.

Annual grant total

In 2010/11 the foundation had an income of £22,000 and a total expenditure of £18,000.

Applications

In writing to the correspondent.

Chew's Foundation at Dunstable

£14,000

Correspondent: Yvonne Beaumont, Grove House, 76 High Street North, Dunstable, Bedfordshire LU6 1NF (01582 660008; email: dunstablecharity@yahoo.com)

Trustees: P. V. Hughes; Joan Bailey; Sally Newton; Brenda Boatwright; Christina Scott; Audrey Rees; David Clarke; Eric Bullock; Hugh Garrod; Richard Andrews; Ann Hathaway; Terry Beaumont; Ann Sparrow.

CC Number: 307500

Eligibility

Beneficiaries must be resident in the borough of Dunstable and surrounding villages, borough of Luton or the parish of Edlesborough. Their parents must not be dissenters of the Church of England. Preference will be given to those families in need, whose beneficiaries are under 25. A certificate of baptism is required.

Types of grants

To support children in their education with the cost of books, school uniforms, school trips, equipment etc.

Annual grant total

In 2010/11 the foundation had an income of £17,000 and an expenditure of £15,000. In previous years, about 20 to 25 grants were awarded to individuals with the amount depending on parental income and the number of dependent children of school age.

Applications

On a form available from the correspondent on request. Completed applications must be received by the end of May. Grants are awarded in July but late applications may be considered in December.

The Harpur Trust

£67,000

Correspondent: Lucy Bardner, Grants Manager, Grants Manager, Princeton Court, The Pilgrim Centre, Brickhill Drive, Bedford MK41 7PZ (01234 369500; fax: 01234 369505; email: grants@harpurtrust.org.uk; website: www.bedfordcharity.org.uk)

Trustees: David Palfreyman; Ian David McEwen; Hugh Murray Stewart.

CC Number: 1066861

Eligibility

Adults who are returning to study after a minimum of five years away from formal education and are resident in the borough of Bedford. Schoolchildren, who are in receipt of free school meals, in need of school uniform when transitioning from state upper school to middle school.

Undergraduate bursary applicants should meet the criteria set by their school or college.

Types of grants

Grants are made to help with the cost of continuing and further education courses leading to career development and school uniform grants.

The charity also provides bursaries at the schools it runs as well as undergraduate bursaries for school leavers at the partner schools. Contact the school directly to discuss.

Annual grant total

In 2010/11 the charity had an income of £52 million and gave grants to individuals totalling £67,000.

Exclusions

No grants for PGCE courses and certificates of education or for recreational courses, including academic courses taken for recreational purposes only.

Applications

Adults returning to education may use the form available with guidelines from the website, to be submitted by the end of April for courses beginning in September of that year after which you will be invited for an interview if your application is successful. The trust recommends contact with the grants manager before an application is made and also for courses starting at other times in the year. Applicants must determine their entitlement to statutory funding before making an application.

Applicants for the university bursaries should apply via their schools. Applicants for the college bursaries may apply by making enquiries directly with the college. The school uniform grants scheme is advertised to all eligible families in the borough by the Bedford schools.

Other information

The trust has recently incorporated and was previously registered with the charity commission under charity number 204817.

The David Parry Memorial Trust

£0

Correspondent: Ann Swaby, The Mary Bassett Lower School, Bassett Road, Leighton Buzzard, Bedfordshire LU7 1AR (07710 272520)

Trustees: Ann Swaby; Marian Smith; Paul Harris.

CC Number: 1020762

Eligibility

Schoolchildren aged 5 to 18, in the areas centred around Leighton Buzzard and Linslade whose families are experiencing severe financial hardship.

Types of grants

Grants ranging to enable pupils to take part in extra-curricular activities and visits. Help towards books may also be given.

Annual grant total

The trust has had an expenditure of £0 for the past two years.

Applications

Applications can only be made on behalf of the families by the head of the school that the pupil attends and not directly by the parents. They are considered all year round.

The Sandy Charities

£3,000

Correspondent: P J Mount, Clerk, Woodfines Solicitors, 6 Bedford Road, Sandy, Bedfordshire SG19 1EN (01767 680251; email: pmount@woodfines.co.uk)

Trustees: Christine Summerfield; Revd Derwyn Williams; William Bickerdike; Robert Browning; Barbara Arnold; David Stevinson; David Sharman; Jonathan Pym.

CC Number: 237145

Eligibility

People in need who live in Sandy and Beeston.

Types of grants

One-off grants only, ranging from £100 to £1,000. Schoolchildren can receive grants towards school uniforms and other school clothing and educational outings; and college students, undergraduates and vocational students towards books and equipment/instruments.

Annual grant total

In 2010/11 the charities had an income of £9,200 and a total expenditure of £8,300.

Applications

In writing to the correspondent who will supply a personal details form for completion. Applications can be considered in any month, depending on the urgency for the grant; they should be submitted either directly by the individual or via the individual's school, college or educational welfare agency.

Other information

Grants are also made to organisations and to individuals for welfare purposes.

Bedford

Alderman Newton's Educational Foundation (Bedford branch)

£1,500

Correspondent: David Baker, Committee Services Officer, Bedford Borough Council, Borough Hall, Cauldwell Street, Bedford MK42 9AP (01234 228778; email: david.baker@bedford.gov.uk)

Trustees: Randolph Charles; Sylvia MacDowell; Stanley Pullinger; Keith Fossey; Peter Squire.

CC Number: 307471

Eligibility

People aged 13 to 25 who live in the town of Bedford.

Types of grants

Grants are given to schoolchildren, people starting work and further and higher education students. Grants given include those for school uniforms, books, equipment/instruments and childcare costs.

Annual grant total

About £1,500.

Applications

On a form available from the correspondent. Applications can be submitted at any time.

Clapham

The Ursula Taylor Charity

£2,000

Correspondent: Mavis Nicholson, 79 High Street, Clapham, Bedford MK41 6AQ (01234 405141; email: mavis.nicholson1@ntlworld.com)

Trustees: Douglas Tomkins; Nigel Sparrow; Steven Liley; Keith Crane; Norman Hurst; Daphne Kitchen.

CC Number: 307520

Eligibility

Young people who live in the parish of Clapham, between the ages of 13 and 25.

Types of grants

Grants are made to schoolchildren, people starting work and students in further/higher education for books, educational outings, school fees, equipment/instruments and other educational needs.

Annual grant total

About £2,000.

Exclusions

No grants are given for bus passes.

Applications

On a form available from the correspondent, submitted either directly by the individual or through the charity's trustees. Applications are considered in February, April, June and October. Applications should include receipts for items purchased.

Clophill

Clophill United Charities

£1,500

Correspondent: Gillian Hill, 10 The Causeway, Clophill, Bedford MK45 4BA (01525 860539)

Trustees: Ray Sharp; Julie Benson; Revd Dean Henley; Andrew Hicks; Richard Pearson.

CC Number: 200034

Eligibility

People who live in the parish of Clophill and are in need.

Types of grants

One-off and recurrent grants according to need.

Annual grant total

Grants usually total around £3,000 per year.

Exclusions

No grants are given where statutory funds are available (e.g. no school fees).

Applications

On a form available from the correspondent.

Flitwick

The Flitwick Town Lands Charity

£4,000

Correspondent: David Empson, Trustee, 28 Orchard Way, Flitwick, Bedford MK45 1LF (01525 718145; email: Deflitwick8145@aol.com)

Trustees: Ann Lutley; David Empson; Revd Michael Bradley.

CC Number: 233258

Eligibility

Students between 18 and 25 who live in the parish of Flitwick.

Types of grants

Grants are awarded to students of around £100 to £250. As a general rule, educational grants are awarded to students at the start of their second year of study in higher education. In exceptional circumstances, one-off grants may be given, for reasons such as providing sports equipment to a youth group.

Annual grant total

In 2010/11 the charity had both an income and total expenditure of £8,800. Grants are given for education and welfare purposes.

Applications

On a form available from the correspondent.

Kempston

The Kempston Charities

£1,000

Correspondent: Mrs Christine Stewart, 15 Loveridge Avenue, Kempston, Bedford MK42 8SF (01234 302323)

Trustees: Susan Oliver; Revd Stephen Huckle; Lance Blacklock; Philip Catteril; Richard Hyde; Kay Burley; Adrien Beardmore; George Lambert; Fiorentino Manocchio.

CC Number: 200064

Eligibility

People in need who live in Kempston (including Kempston rural).

Types of grants

One-off grants according to need.

Annual grant total

Grants average around £3,000 per year.

Exclusions

No recurrent grants are made.

Applications

In writing to the correspondent. Applications should be made either directly by the individual or through a social worker, Citizens Advice or other welfare agency. They are considered in March, July and November.

Other information

Grants are also given to local schools and other local institutions.

Oakley

The Oakley Educational Foundation

£2,000

Correspondent: Louise Tunley, 4 Beanfield Close, Riseley, Bedford MK44 1ES (01234 708156)

Trustees: Patricia Olney; Dorothy Palmer; Jane Walker; John Saunders; Linda Bond; Hilarie Worley.

CC Number: 307464

Eligibility

People between the ages of 16 and 25 who live in the parish of Oakley.

Types of grants

Grants are made to people starting work, further and higher education students, mature students and postgraduates. Awards include those for books, equipment/instruments, educational outings in the UK and study and travel abroad.

Annual grant total

About £2,000 to individuals.

Exclusions

No grants for travel fares.

Applications

In writing to the correspondent requesting an application form. Applications should be submitted by 1 May and 1 November for consideration in those months respectively, and must include receipts of purchase.

Potton

The Potton Consolidated Charities

£18,300

Correspondent: Christine Hall, 1a Potton Road, Everton, Sandy, Bedfordshire SG19 2LD (01767 680663; email: pot.concha@tiscali.co.uk)

Trustees: Mrs J. M. Norton; Mr F. W. Jakes; Mrs J. M. Way; Mr M. Horgan; Mr M. Ansell; Mrs R. Burmo; Mr C. Belcher; Revd Mrs G. Smith.

CC Number: 201073

Eligibility

People between 18 and 25 who live in the parish of Potton.

Types of grants

Book grants of about £200 for students in further or higher education.

Annual grant total

In 2010/11 grants to individuals for educational purposes totalled £18,300.

Applications

Directly by the individual on a form available from the correspondent. Applications are considered in November and should be received by 31 October.

Berkshire

Crowthorne Trust
See entry on page 17

The Polehampton Charity

£2,500

Correspondent: Miss E Treadwell, Assistant Clerk, 114 Victoria Road,

283

Wargrave, Berkshire RG10 8AE (website: www.thepolehamptoncharity.co.uk)

Trustees: Douglas Norris; James Weaver; Richard Fort; Janet Potter; Rosemary Pratt; David Turner; Robert Collett; William Treadwell; Simon Howard; Nic Downes; Rosie Chapman.

CC Number: 1072631

Eligibility

People who live in the ecclesiastical parishes of Twyford and Ruscombe.

Types of grants

(i) Educational grants – these cover the purchase of books, tools, instruments and so on which are essential for the completion of courses or training at universities, colleges of further education and other recognised educational establishments, including apprenticeships. They also cover assistance to allow young people to study music or other arts, and to make provision for recreational and sports training, not normally provided by local authorities. Grants are also given for school uniforms and school educational outings.

(ii) Educational bursaries – these are to assist those who are under 25 and are undertaking courses of further education for which no local authority or similar grants is available.

Grants are in the range of £100 to £250.

Annual grant total

In 2011 the charity had assets of £2.3 million and an income of £97,000. Grants to individuals for education totalled £2,500 and for other purposes totalled £2,200.

Applications

Applications should be submitted either directly by the individual or a family member, through a third party such as a social worker or teacher, or through and organisation such as Citizens Advice or a school. They should include a list of the books and/or equipment needed. Applications can be made at any time and are considered at trustee meetings.

Other information

Grants are also made to local schools and organisations.

Reading Dispensary Trust

£1,000

Correspondent: Walter Gilbert, Clerk, 16 Wokingham Road, Reading RG6 1JQ (01189 265698; email: admin@rdt. btconnect.com)

Trustees: Ian Hammond; Jim Durlin; Jean Horrocks; Norman Ross; A. Hendry; Jean Turton; Barbara Hirst;

Denis Jones; Erina Titcomb; Judy Warwick; Geoff Chivers; Tom Lynch; Janet Wignall; Francis Read.

CC Number: 203943

Eligibility

People in need who are in poor health, convalescent or who have a physical or mental disability and live in Reading and the surrounding area (roughly within a seven-mile radius of the centre of Reading).

Types of grants

One-off grants towards course fees, computer equipment and software.

Annual grant total

In 2011 the trust had assets of £1.1 million and an income of £46,000. There were 163 grants to individuals totalling £25,000 with the majority being given for welfare purposes, and some for education.

Applications

On a form available from the correspondent. Applications should be submitted directly by the individual or through a social worker, Citizens Advice or other third party. They are considered on a monthly basis.

Other information

Grants are also made to organisations and to individuals for a wide range of welfare needs.

The Spoore Merry and Rixman Foundation

£209,000

Correspondent: Helen MacDiarmid, PO Box 4229, Slough SL1 0QZ (email: clerk@smrfmaidenhead.org; website: www.smrfmaidenhead.org.uk)

Trustees: Grahame Fisher; Ann Redgrave; Dorothy Kemp; Leo Walters; Tony Hill; Ian Thomas; David Coppinger; Asghar Majeed; Barbara Wielechowski; Philip Love.

CC Number: 309040

Eligibility

People under 25 who live in the old (pre-1974) borough of Maidenhead and the ancient parish of Bray, including Holyport and Woodlands Park.

Types of grants

Grants for (i) school pupils to help with books, equipment, clothing or travel, and for sporting activities, music, drama, dance and so on; (ii) college or university fees or to supplement existing LEA funding; and (iii) books, equipment, clothing and travel expenses for people starting work. People with special educational needs are also supported and grants are made to enable

people to travel abroad as part of their education. Grants are for amounts of up to £5,000 each, although in special cases, such as death of parents, this figure can be exceeded.

Annual grant total

In 2010 the trust had assets of £9.1 million and an income of £293,000. 153 grants to individuals were made totalling £209,000

Applications

On forms available from the website. Applications can be made either directly by the individual or through a school, college or educational welfare agency. Parents are required to provide a statement of their annual income. Meetings of the trustees are held in mid-January, April, July and October.

Other information

Grants are also made to schools and youth clubs.

The Winchcombe Charity

£2,000

Correspondent: Mrs V Druce, 113 Sagecroft Road, Thatcham, Berkshire RG18 3AX (01635 865339; email: thatchamcharities@btinternet.com)

Trustees: David Wootton; Brian Wheeler; Robert Tayton; Erika Tipton; Stephanie Skelly; Sheila Ellison; Christine Leake; Julian Gadsby; Rita Ball; Dominic Boeck; Mark Bennet.

CC Number: 309045

Eligibility

People who live in the parishes of Thatcham, Bucklebury or Cold Ash whose children have attended a local school for at least two years. Applicants should be aged between 16 and 25.

Types of grants

Grants to (i) three Church of England Sunday Schools, (ii) young people leaving school at 16 and entering further or higher education for books, help with fees or travel or study abroad and (iii) people starting work for books, equipment, clothing, travel etc.

Grants are one-off and range from £75 to £200.

Annual grant total

About £2,000.

Applications

On a form available from the correspondent, to be completed by the parents or guardian. Applications should be submitted by June for consideration in July.

The Wokingham United Charities

£5,000

Correspondent: P Robinson, Clerk, 66 Upper Broadmoor Road, Crowthorne, Berkshire RG45 7DF (01344 351207; email: peter.westende@btinternet.com)

Trustees: Mr G. Cockroft; Mr R. Wyatt; Mr J. Tobin; Mr G. Brown; Mr D. Auger; Mrs P. Cox; Mr J. Ellis; Mr D. Eyriey; Mr M. Hall; Dr C. Gallagher; Mr A. King; Mrs G. Hewetson; Mr G. Veitch.

CC Number: 1107171

Eligibility

Schoolchildren in need who live in the civil parishes of Wokingham, Wokingham Without, St Nicholas, Hurst, Ruscombe and that part of Finchampstead known as Finchampstead North.

Types of grants

One-off grants between £25 and £150. Grants have been given towards school uniforms and educational visits.

Annual grant total

Grants usually total around £10,000 a year.

Applications

On a form available from the correspondent. Applications are considered each month (except August) and can be submitted directly by the individual, or through a social worker, school liaison officer or similar third party.

Pangbourne

The Breedon Educational and Vocational Foundation

£750

Correspondent: Richard Stone, Westfields, Woodview Road, Pangbourne, Reading RG8 7JN (01189 844452; email: stonerc@aol.com)

Trustees: Pamela Bale; Heather Parbury; Matilda Oppenheimer; Rochard Stone; Edward Wardle; Pam Hiller-Brook; Edward Goddard; Terence Relf; Felicity Pethica; Heather Leighton-Jones.

CC Number: 309069

Eligibility

Children and young people who live in the civil parish of Pangbourne, Berkshire who are in full-time or further education.

Types of grants

One-off and recurrent grants: (i) to help with books, equipment, clothing or travel for schoolchildren, students or people starting work; or (ii) to help with school, college or university fees or to supplement existing grants.

Annual grant total

In 2010/11 the trust had an income of £1,200 and an expenditure of £2,300.

Applications

On a form available from the correspondent. Applications are considered in March, July and December each year.

Windsor and Maidenhead

The Prince Philip Trust Fund

£2,000

Correspondent: Kevin M McGarry, Secretary, 10 Cadogan Close, Holyport, Maidenhead, Berkshire SL6 2JS (01628 639577; email: kmmcgarry@talktalk.net; website: www.rbwm.gov.uk/web/members_grants_prince_philip_trust.htm)

Trustees: Marcia Twelftree; K. M. McGarry; Headmaster of Eton College; Lady Palmer; Deputy Ranger; Prince Philip.

CC Number: 272927

Eligibility

Young people undertaking voluntary work or training schemes from the royal borough of Windsor and Maidenhead. Support is also given to individual pupils selected to represent their district, county or country in an activity considered worthy of the trust's support.

Types of grants

One-off grants.

Annual grant total

In 2010/11 the trust had assets of £1.4 million and an income of £66,000. Grants to individuals totalled £2,000.

Exclusions

Grants are not made for tuition fees.

Applications

In writing to the correspondent, including details of the project, the amount of grant sought, amount in hand, budget projection and the names of two referees. Trustees meet twice a year to consider applications.

Other information

Grants are mainly made to organisations.

Buckingham-shire

The Amersham United Charities

£0

Correspondent: C Atkinson, 25 Milton Lawns, Amersham, Buckinghamshire HP6 6BJ (01494 723416)

Trustees: Miss P. A. Appleby; Mrs G. Bungey; Mr E. Newhouse; Miss B. Webber; Revd T. Harper; Mrs L. Hollett; Mr S. Partridge; Mr P. Gray.

CC Number: 205033

Eligibility

People under the age of 21 who live in the parishes of Amersham and Coleshill.

Types of grants

One-off grants for those at school, college or university, or about to start work, to help with the cost of fees (students only), books, equipment, clothing and travel.

Annual grant total

Although no grants have been made in recent years, the correspondent has stated that the charity is open to applications from individuals for relief in need and education.

Applications

In writing to the correspondent.

Other information

The main work of the charity is the administration and management of 13 almshouses.

Norman Hawes Memorial Trust

£2,500

Correspondent: Sue Bruce, Schools Support Officer, Milton Keynes Council, Education Department, 502 Avebury Boulevard, Milton Keynes MK9 3HS (01908 253614; fax: 01908 253289; email: sue.bruce@milton-keynes.gov.uk)

Trustees: Bruce Abbott; Vivien Thompson; David Hildreth; Dennis Silverton; Bryan Watson; Lynda Cockerall; Milton Keynes Council; Bucks County Council.

CC Number: 310620

Eligibility

Young people aged between 15 and 18 who are in full-time education and live in Milton Keynes and north Buckinghamshire.

Types of grants

Grants for international study visits, ranging between £50 and £200.

Annual grant total

In 2010/11 the trust had an income of £3,600 and an expenditure of £2,600.

Applications

On an application form available from the correspondent to be submitted directly by the individual or through the school/college/educational welfare agency. Applications can be submitted in September/October and January/February for consideration in November and February/March.

The Marlow Educational Foundation

£5,000

Correspondent: Rennie Miller, LGP Solicitors, Lacemaker House, 5–7 Chapel Street, Marlow, Buckinghamshire SL7 3HN (01628 404620)

Trustees: Anthony Roderick; Patrick Land; Dani Trivino; Debbie Cooper.

CC Number: 310650

Eligibility

People under 25 who live or were born in the parish of Great Marlow or the urban districts of Marlow, and are attending, or for not less than one year have attended, any school in that parish or urban district.

Types of grants

Grants range from £200 to £700 and are given to individuals at further education institutions and for travel for educational purposes. Grants are also given for tools, clothing and the like for individuals starting work, training or apprenticeships, and for assistance to study music or the arts.

Annual grant total

About £5,000 per annum.

Applications

On a form available from the correspondent. Applications can be submitted directly by the individual or a parent/guardian, through a teacher, or an organisation such as a school or an educational welfare agency. They are considered two or three times a year.

The Salford Town Lands

£500

Correspondent: Julian Barrett, South Cottage, 18 Broughton Road, Salford, Milton Keynes MK17 8BH (01908 583494)

Trustees: Julian Barrett; Revd Hugh; Kathleen Draycott; Christopher Hall; Kevin Burke; Robert Harrison.

CC Number: 256465

Eligibility

People in need who live in the parish of Hulcote and Salford.

Types of grants

Grants are one-off and range from £100 to £200. They will be considered for the following: the cost of school uniforms, school clothing, books, educational outings and maintenance for schoolchildren; books and help with fees/living expenses for students in further or higher education; books, travel and fees for mature students; and books, equipment/instruments, clothing and travel for people starting work.

Annual grant total

Previously about £5,000, although this was mostly for welfare purposes.

Applications

In writing to the correspondent. Applications can be submitted directly by the individual or through any other parishioner.

Other information

Grants are also made to organisations supporting the community.

The Saye and Sele Foundation

£14,000

Correspondent: R T Friedlander, Clerk, Parrot and Coales, Solicitors, 14 Bourbon Street, Aylesbury, Buckinghamshire HP20 2RS (01296 318500)

Trustees: Peter Avery; Celia Prideaux; P. Jackman; Revd Mears; K. J. Smith; V. M. Craker; Kathleen Blanchard.

CC Number: 310554

Eligibility

People under 25 who live in the parishes of Grendon Underwood and Quainton.

Types of grants

One-off grants to help school, college or university students with books, equipment and training costs. Grants have been made towards computers for people from low-income families and equipment for people with disabilities. Grants are generally around £200, but can be for any amount.

Annual grant total

In 2010 the foundation had an income of £15,000 and an expenditure of £15,000.

Applications

In writing to the correspondent, to be considered in January, April, July and October.

The Stoke Mandeville and Other Parishes Charity

£20,000

Correspondent: Caroline Dobson, 17 Elham Way, Aylesbury HP21 9XN (01296 431859)

Trustees: Angela Norris; Barbara Ezra; David Brown; Peter Pugh; Robin Hunt; Stuart Allen; Paul Walter.

CC Number: 296174

Eligibility

People in need who live in the parishes of Stoke Mandeville, Great and Little Hampden and Great Missenden.

Types of grants

Help with the cost of books, clothing and other essentials for schoolchildren, people at college or university and for people starting work. Grants for schoolchildren are up to a maximum of £300 a year and grants for people in further or higher education are up to a maximum of £600 a year. Individuals must reapply each year for additional grants.

Annual grant total

In 2011 the charity had assets of £1.8 million and an income of £85,000. Educational grants totalled £20,000.

Applications

On a form available from the correspondent, considered in January, April, July and October.

Other information

The charity also gives grants to organisations and to individuals for welfare.

Aylesbury

William Harding's Charity

£110,000 (152 grants)

Correspondent: John Leggett, Clerk to the Trustees, 14 Bourbon Street, Aylesbury HP20 2RS (01296 318501; email: doudjag@pandclip.co.uk)

Trustees: Les Sheldon; Anne Brooker; Freda Roberts; Bernard Griffin; Penni Thorne; Roger Evans; William Chapple; Lennard Wakelam; Susan Hewitt.

CC Number: 310619

Eligibility

People who live in the town of Aylesbury under 25 years of age.

Types of grants

One-off grants are made to schoolchildren for uniforms/school clothing, fees, study/travel overseas, books, equipment/instruments and educational outings in the UK, to college students, undergraduates, vocational students and mature students for fees, study/travel overseas, books, equipment/instruments and maintenance/living expenses and to individuals with special educational needs for uniforms/clothing, books, equipment/instruments and excursions.

Annual grant total

In 2011 the charity had assets of £22 million and an income of £776,000. Pupil support to 152 individuals totalled £110,000.

Applications

On a form available from the correspondent to be submitted directly by the individual or a family member, through a third party such as a social worker or teacher or through an organisation such as Citizens Advice. Trustees meet ten times each year to consider applications. Applications should include details of family income.

Thomas Hickman's Charity

£25,000

Correspondent: John Leggett, Parrott and Coales, 14–16 Bourbon Street, Aylesbury, Buckinghamshire HP20 2RS (01296 318500; email: doudjag@ pandclip.co.uk)

Trustees: Graham Aylett; Tim Voss; Shane Wood; Elizabeth Mossford; Roger Harwood.

CC Number: 202973

Eligibility

People in need who live in Aylesbury town.

Types of grants

Grants for school uniforms.

Annual grant total

In 2011 the charity had assets of £16 million and an income of £601,000. Grants were made to 144 individuals totalling £53,000.

Applications

On a form available from the correspondent. Applications should be submitted either directly by the individual or a family member, through a third party such as social worker or school, or through an organisation such

as Citizens Advice or a school. Trustees meet on a regular basis and applications are considered as they arise.

Other information

The charity also provides almshouses.

Aylesbury Vale

Charles Pope Memorial Trust

£800

Correspondent: Roger Kirk, 77 Aylesbury Road, Bierton, Aylesbury, Buckinghamshire HP22 5BT (01296 415312)

Trustees: Roger Kirk; D. Crook; E. Mortimer; Diana Golder; C. Beattie; S. M. Baxter; L. Cheshire; R. F. Cook; L. Orchard; J. Benson.

CC Number: 287591

Eligibility

People in need who have lived or been educated in the area administered by Aylesbury Vale District Council for at least two years.

Types of grants

Grants are awarded for musical education, including tuition, instruments, scores etc. Grants will not normally exceed £300.

Annual grant total

In 2010/11 the trust had an income of £2,400 and an expenditure of £400.

Applications

On a form available from the correspondent, submitted directly by the individual or by a parent or guardian. Applications are usually considered in March, June and November and should be received in the middle of February, May and October. A reference is required from a relevant music tutor. If it is close to the time when applications are to be considered, it is helpful if the reference can be sent with the application. In other cases the secretary will contact the referee direct. Applicants need to show some musical competence and commitment.

Calverton

Calverton Apprenticing Charity

£1,000

Correspondent: Karen Phillips, 78 London Road, Stony Stratford, Milton Keynes MK11 1JH (01908 563350; email: karen.phillips20@yahoo. co.uk)

Trustees: Ross Northing; Charles Sherwood; Martin Luckett; Diane West; Judy Hildreth; Judy Hayter.

CC Number: 239246

Eligibility

People under the age of 21 who have lived in the parish of All Saints, Calverton for at least five years.

Types of grants

Grants in the range of £100 to £150 are available to college students, undergraduates, apprentices and people starting work for uniforms/clothing, fees, books and equipment/instruments.

Annual grant total

Grants for educational purposes usually total around £1,000 each year.

Applications

On a form available from the correspondent to be submitted directly by the individual or a family member.

Other information

The charity also makes grants to organisations and for welfare purposes to older people in need.

Cheddington

Cheddington Town Lands Charity

£10,000

Correspondent: Stuart Minall, 10 Hillside, Cheddington, Leighton Buzzard LU7 0SP (01296 661987)

Trustees: Patricia Bannister; Stephen Fox; Stuart Minall; Revd Robert Wright.

CC Number: 235076

Eligibility

People in need who live in Cheddington.

Types of grants

One-off and recurrent grants according to need.

Annual grant total

Grants usually total around £10,000.

Applications

In writing to the correspondent, directly by the individual or a family member.

Other information

Grants are also made for the benefit of the community and individuals in need.

Emberton

Emberton United Charity

£1,500

Correspondent: Jeremy Howson, Trustee, 14 Gravel Walk, Emberton, Olney MK46 5JA (01234 712042)

Trustees: Jeremy Howson; W. Clarke; Gerald Mann; Susan Soul; Judith Taylor.

CC Number: 204221

Eligibility

People under 25 in higher education who live in the parish of Emberton.

Types of grants

One-off and recurrent grants, usually of up to £350, towards books and equipment/instruments, but not fees.

Annual grant total

In 2011 the charity had an income of £22,000 and an expenditure of £11,000. Previously educational grants have totalled around £1,500.

Applications

In writing to the correspondent, directly by the individual.

Other information

Grants are also given for welfare purposes.

Great Linford

The Great Linford Advancement in Life Charity

£2,000

Correspondent: M Williamson, Treasurer, 2 Lodge Gate, Great Linford, Milton Keynes, Bucks MK14 5EW (01908 605664)

Trustees: J. Wilson; Michael Williamson; Ted Pawley; David Enticknap; Peter Ballantine; Sandie Jenner.

CC Number: 310570

Eligibility

People under 25 who live in the civil parish of Great Linford.

Types of grants

Grants of up to £200 are given for many educational purposes, such as scholarships and bursaries, clothing, equipment, musical instruments, books and travel. Grants are also awarded for young people preparing to enter a trade or profession after leaving school or university.

Annual grant total

The trust has both an income and a total expenditure of approximately £2,000 per annum, most of which is distributed in grants to individuals.

Applications

In writing to the correspondent, either directly by the individual or through their school, college or educational welfare agency. Applications must include details of the purpose for which the request is being made and official estimates. They are considered in January, May and September.

Other information

Consideration may be given to groups provided that their membership comprises of eligible people.

Olney

The Olney British School Charity

£0

Correspondent: Donald Saunders, 17 Long Lane, Olney, Buckinghamshire MK46 5HL (01234 711879)

Trustees: Donald Saunders; Thomas James; Carol Crouch; Michael Eaton; Richard Sargent.

CC Number: 310538

Eligibility

People under the age of 25 who live, or whose parents live, in Olney, who are involved in further education or training after leaving school.

Types of grants

Grants to those 'who are preparing for, entering upon or engaged in any profession, trade, occupation, or service, by providing them with outfits, or by paying fees, travelling or maintenance expenses, or by such means for their advancement in life or to enable them to earn their living'. Students in further/higher education can receive grants for books or study or travel abroad.

Annual grant total

Usually about £2,500 but in 2010/11 there was no expenditure.

Applications

In writing to the correspondent. Applications must be received by 31 August for consideration in September.

Radnage

Radnage Poor's Land Educational Foundation

£1,300

Correspondent: Ian Blaylock, Clerk to the Trustees, Hilltop, Green End Road, Radnage, High Wycombe, Buckinghamshire HP14 4BY (01494 483346)

Trustees: Nigel Lacey; Caroline Strange; Lindsay Wilcox.

CC Number: 310582

Eligibility

People in need below 25 years, who live in the parish of Radnage.

Types of grants

One-off grants ranging from £100 to £500. Grants are given to schoolchildren and further and higher education students including those for uniforms, books, equipment/instruments, fees, maintenance/living expenses, educational outings in the UK, study or travel abroad and student exchanges. Grants are also given to people starting work for books.

Annual grant total

In 2011 the charity had an income of £2,800 and an expenditure of £1,300.

Applications

In writing to the correspondent, either directly by the individual or through a school, college or education welfare agency, for consideration in February, June, September and December.

Other information

Local schools are also supported.

Stoke Poges

Stoke Poges United Charities

£1,500

Correspondent: Anthony Levings, Clerk, The Cedars, Stratford Drive, Wooburn Green, High Wycombe HP10 0QH (01628 524342)

Trustees: Trevor Egleton; Susan Lynch; Michael Dier; Chris Morris; Raymond Aldridge; Henry Latham; Hemantha Kumar.

CC Number: 205289

Eligibility

Children in primary and secondary school and apprentices/people starting work who live in the parish of Stoke Poges.

Types of grants

Grants of £30 to £1,500 are given for tools, clothing, books and other school equipment.

Annual grant total

In 2011 the charity had assets of £431,000 and an income of £29,000. Grants to six individuals for welfare and education totalled £3,500.

Applications

In writing to the correspondent, to be submitted either directly by the individual or through a social worker, Citizens Advice, other welfare agency or any third party.

Stokenchurch

The Stokenchurch Education Charity

£43,000

Correspondent: Martin Sheehy, Fish Partnership LLP, The Mill House, Boundary Road, Loudwater, High Wycombe HP10 9QN (01928 527956)

Trustees: Mary Shurrock; Anthony Saunders; Frank Downes; Andrew Palmer; Alistair France; Camilla Baker.

CC Number: 297846

Eligibility

People under 25 who live in the parish of Stokenchurch.

Types of grants

Grants range from £5 to £500 and are for educational expenses including clothing, equipment/instruments and tools.

Annual grant total

In 2010/11 the charity had assets of £1.5 million and an income of £56,000. Grants to individuals totalled £43,000.

Exclusions

No grants are made for private tuition, or where statutory grants are available. Applicants from outside the Parish of Stokenchurch are not supported.

Applications

On a form available from the correspondent. In August the trustees place an advertisement in the local press, and two public places in Stokenchurch, inviting applications. Educational applications must be received by 30 November of each academic year and grants are paid in April. Applications from outside the parish are not responded to.

Other information

Any excess in income is given to village groups which benefit local inhabitants.

Stony Stratford

The Ancell Trust

£5,500

Correspondent: Karen Phillips, Secretary, 78 London Road, Stony Stratford, Milton Keynes MK11 1JH (01908 563350; email: karen.phillips20@yahoo.co.uk)

Trustees: Rosemary Dytham; Susan Starr; Michael Benham; Patricia Eales; Brian Faulkner; Lawrence Francis; Robert Ayers; Sheila Brazell; Wendy Cowley; Barbara Bird; Dr Kenneth Chambers.

CC Number: 233824

Eligibility

People in need in the town of Stony Stratford.

Types of grants

Grants are given to students for books and are occasionally made to individuals for welfare purposes and to organisations.

Annual grant total

In 2010/11 the trust had an income of £8,200 and a total expenditure of £11,000.

Applications

In writing to the correspondent at any time.

Arnold's Education Foundation

See entry on page 222

Winslow

Rogers Free School Foundation

£2,500

Correspondent: T B Foley, 16 Buckingham Road, Winslow, Buckinghamshire MK18 3DY (01296 713904; email: g4fyo@tesco.net)

Trustees: David Rowlands; Hilary Thornton; Gordon Wiseman; Geoffrey Ball; Lorraine Honor; Terence Capstick.

CC Number: 310557

Eligibility

People in any stage of education who live in the parish of Winslow.

Types of grants

Grants are given towards help with school uniforms, other school clothing, educational outings in the UK, books, fees and study or travel abroad.

Annual grant total

Around £2,500.

Applications

On an application form, available from the correspondent. Applications can be submitted either directly by the individual or through a parent.

Wolverton

Wolverton Science and Art Institution Fund

£4,000

Correspondent: Karen Phillips, 78 London Road, Stony Stratford, Milton Keynes MK11 1JH (01908 563350; email: karen.phillips20@yahoo.co.uk)

Trustees: Gerald Stimpson; Eric Swannell; Peter Hill; Maureen Higgins; Susan Sprittles.

CC Number: 310652

Eligibility

People who live in the Wolverton and Stanningbury parishes which include all of Wolverton, New Bradwell, Bradville, Stantonbury, Bradwell Common, Bradwell, Stacey Bushes and Hodge Lea.

Types of grants

Recurrent grants in the range of £100 to £500. Grants are given to schoolchildren, people starting work, further and higher education students, mature students and postgraduates for uniforms/other school clothing, books, equipment/instruments, fees and educational outings in the UK.

Annual grant total

In 2010/11 the fund had an income of £5,700 and an expenditure of £8,500.

Exclusions

Grants are not made to cover the salary expenses of a project.

Applications

On a form available from the correspondent, either directly by the individual or through a school/college/educational welfare agency. Applications are considered in February, April, August and October and should be received in the preceding month.

Other information

Grants are also made to educational organisations.

Cambridge-shire

Bishop Laney's Charity

£26,000 (109 grants)

Correspondent: Richard Tyler, 8 Barton Close, Witchford, Ely, Cambridgeshire CB6 2HS (01353 662813; email: richard_i_tyler@hotmail.com; website: www.whitingandpartners.co.uk/Content/Bishop_Laney_Charity_Grants.htm)

Trustees: R. Bamford; Hamish Ross; Brian Ashton; Nik Mumford; Geoffrey Fisher; Timothy Jones.

CC Number: 311306

Eligibility

People in need under 25 who live in the parishes of Soham and Ely. Consideration will be given to people under 25 who live in other parts of Cambridgeshire where funds permit.

Types of grants

Grants are given to people starting work for general purposes. Preference is given to apprentices. Grants are also given to students in further/higher education for uniforms/clothing, books and equipment/instruments and the charity will consider grants for study or travel abroad, excursions in the UK and maintenance/living expenses. Support for schoolchildren is also considered for excursions in the UK and maintenance/living expenses. Grants to individuals are for either £150 or £250.

Annual grant total

In 2010/11 the trust had assets of £2.7 million and an income of £109,000. A total of £26,000 was awarded in one hundred and nine grants to individuals.

Applications

On a form available from the web page or the correspondent, to be submitted directly by the individual, for consideration usually in July, September, October and December. Applications must include a copy of the applicant's birth certificate, proof of attendance at college/university etc. and details of the book shop/music shop etc. In the latest accounts the trustees stated that they were looking at ways to increase the number of applications they receive.

Other information

The trust also gives grants to educational establishments.

The Leverington Town Lands Educational Charity

£10,000

Correspondent: R Gagen, 78 High Road, Gorefield, Wisbech, Cambridgeshire PE13 4NB (01945 870454; email: leveoffees@aol.com)

Trustees: David Newling; John Maxey; Kitty Hall; Mervyn Baker; Robert Littlechild; Susan Robb; B. T. Hunt; M. Lenton; R. Gent; Michael Humphrey; S. Fisher; E. Newling; Angela Kett; Jennifer Everall.

CC Number: 311325

Eligibility

Schoolchildren and people in further/higher education who live in Leverington, Parson Drove and Gorefield.

Types of grants

One-off grants according to need.

Annual grant total

In 2010/11 the trust had an income of £20,000 and an expenditure of £23,000.

Applications

On a form available from the correspondent for consideration in September.

Other information

Grants are also made to local schools.

The Henry Morris Memorial Trust

£5,000

Correspondent: Heather Mepham, Hon. Secretary, 4 Ryecroft Lane, Fowlmere, Royston, Herts SG8 7TT (01763 208620; email: mail@henrymorris.plus.com; website: www.henrymorris.plus.com)

Trustees: Geoffrey Morris; Peter Hains; David Rooney; David Farnell; Diana Cook; Jonathan Holmes; Sue Bryan; June Cannie; Andrew Allsworth; Janet Aves; Heather Mepham.

CC Number: 311419

Eligibility

Students between the ages of 13 and 19 who live, attend, or have attended, school or college in Cambridge or east or south Cambridgeshire.

Types of grants

Grants of up to £300 (usually £20 to £200) are given to help finance 'short expeditions or projects with purpose'. For example in the past the trust has funded: a comparison between Coventry's and Dresden's old cathedrals; a journey to investigate the history of the piano at the Paris Museum; a bird-spotting trip to Land's End and home-based projects such as making a RAKU kiln and interview of a local artist.

Annual grant total

About £5,000.

Exclusions

No grants are given towards organised courses, excursions or projects, for example, Raleigh International.

Applications

On a form available from local schools or from the trust's website. Applications should be submitted directly by the individual by 31 January for consideration in February/March.

Other information

Applicants must make independent travel and accommodation arrangements.

The Charities of Nicholas Swallow and Others

£800

Correspondent: Nicholas Tufton, Clerk, 11 High Street, Barkway, Royston, Hertfordshire SG8 8EA (01763 848888)

Trustees: June Bater; Carol Abson; Chris McSweeney; David Toop; John Jennings; Kenneth Winterbottom; Tim Teversham; Karen Wright; Martyn Postle; Robert Cassels; Llandre Pickup.

CC Number: 203222

Eligibility

People in need who live in the parish of Whittlesford (near Cambridge) and adjacent area.

Types of grants

One-off grants according to need.

Annual grant total

In 2010/11 the charities had assets of £603,000 and an income of £46,000. Educational grants totalled £800.

Applications

In writing to the correspondent directly by the individual.

Other information

The principal activity of this charity is as a housing association which manages bungalows and garages.

Elsworth

The Samuel Franklin Fund

£1,000

Correspondent: Helen Oborne, Low Farm, 45 Brook Street, Elsworth, Cambridge CB23 4HX (01954 267197; email: helenobornesft@googlemail.com)

Trustees: Ian Maddison; Annie Howell; Sue Taylor; Fiona Windsor; John Hicks; Lorna Knight.

CC Number: 228775

Eligibility

People at any level or stage of their education, studying any subject, who live in the parish of Elsworth.

Types of grants

One-off and recurrent grants in the range of £10 to £1,000.

Annual grant total

In 2011 the trust had an income of £32,000 and gave grants to 31 individuals totalling £12,000, most of which was given in welfare grants.

Applications

In writing to the correspondent including brief details of requirements.

Hilton

Hilton Town Charity

£1,500

Correspondent: Mr Stephen Sheppard, 20 Chequers Croft, Hilton, Huntingdon PE28 9PD

Trustees: Ralph Slater; Joanne Turner; B. Ward; Revd David Busk; Elizabeth Bush.

CC Number: 209423

Eligibility

People who live in the village of Hilton, Cambridgeshire, at any stage or level of their education, undertaking study of any subject.

Types of grants

Only a limited number of grants are given for educational purposes.

Annual grant total

In 2010 the charity had an income of £5,000 and a total expenditure of £7,500. On average about £3,000 is available in grants.

Applications

In writing to the correspondent.

Other information

Grants are also available for organisations which serve the direct needs of the village.

Little Wilbraham

The Johnson Bede and Lane Charitable Trust

£1,500

Correspondent: Mrs J Collins, The Gate House, Church Road, Little Wilbraham, Cambridge CB21 5LE (01223 811465)

Trustees: Mrs J. Collins; Gillian Clifford; Monica Wells; Prudence Addecott; Madhu Davies; Linda Stead.

CC Number: 284444

Eligibility

People in need who live in the civil parish of Little Wilbraham.

Types of grants

One-off grants usually between £50 and £150. Grants given include those to schoolchildren and college students, including those towards fees, equipment/instruments, excursions, music lessons and school outings.

Annual grant total

In 2010/11 the trust had an income of £4,400 and a total expenditure of £4,000. Grants to individuals usually total around £3,000.

Applications

In writing to the correspondent directly by the individual or by a third party such as a social worker, Citizens Advice or neighbour. Applications are considered on an ongoing basis.

Other information

Grants are also made to organisations and for welfare purposes.

Sawston

John Huntingdon's Charity

£2,500

Correspondent: Revd Mary Irish, Charity Manager, John Huntingdon House, Tannery Road, Sawston, Cambridge CB2 4UW (01223 492492; email: office@johnhuntingdon.org.uk)

Trustees: Thomas Butler; Susan Reynolds; Reg Cullum; Christine Ingham; Eugene Murray; Eleanor Clapp; Catherine Gilmore; Alan Partridge; David Baslington; Eileen Wheatley.

CC Number: 1118574

Eligibility

Schoolchildren, college students and people with people with special educational needs who live in the parish of Sawston in Cambridgeshire.

Types of grants

One-off grants, usually ranging from £25 to £250 and occasionally up to £500 or more. About 100 grants are made each year. Grants are given to: schoolchildren for uniforms/clothing, school trips and books; college students for books and equipment/instruments; and people with special educational needs for uniforms/clothing, books, equipment/instruments and excursions.

Annual grant total

In 2011 the charity had assets of £7.3 million and an income of £329,000. Bursary awards allocated in previous years totalled around £2,500.

Applications

On an application form available from Sawston Support Services at the address above or by telephone. Office opening hours are 9am to 2pm Monday to Friday. Grants are considered on an ongoing basis.

Other information

Grants are also made for welfare purposes and to organisations.

Werrington

The Werrington Educational Foundation

£1,000

Correspondent: John Burrell, Clerk, 15 Gildale, Werrington, Peterborough PE4 6QY (01733 577652)

Trustees: Helen Bradley; George Rogers; Steve Bateman; Jennie Edis; Rachel Lidgett.

CC Number: 311838

Eligibility

People under 25 who live in the parish of Paston (Werrington).

Types of grants

Grants towards the cost of essentials for schoolchildren, books, fees/living expenses and study or travel abroad for students, and towards books, equipment and clothing for people starting work. The trustees are required to have regard to the promotion of education in accordance with the principles of the Church of England.

Recently the trust has had few individual applications and has given grants to the schools in the beneficial area. When individual applications are received they are given priority.

Annual grant total

In 2010/11 the trust had both an income and expenditure of £1,000.

Applications

On a form available from the correspondent. Applications are considered in May and October.

Whittlesey

The Whittlesey Charity

£2,000

Correspondent: P S Gray, 33 Bellamy Road, Oundle, Peterborough PE8 4NE (01832 273085)

Trustees: Gordon Ryall; Ralph Butcher; Pearl Beeby; David Green; David Wright; Geoffrey Oldfield; Andrew Whitehouse; Philip Oldfield; Gill Lawrence; Claire Smith.

CC Number: 1005069

Eligibility

People under the age of 25 who live in the ancient parishes of Whittlesey Urban and Whittlesey Rural.

Types of grants

Any grant is considered, but the trustees say they would have to be satisfied that all alternative sources had been investigated. Previously grants have been made to allow people to travel abroad for trips such as a scouts jamboree and travel to the World Martials Arts Championships.

Annual grant total

In 2010 educational grants totalled £2,000.

Applications

Applications can be submitted directly by the individual, school or college, or other third party. Applications are usually considered in February, May and September, but urgent applications could be dealt with at short notice. Note, the trust will not respond to ineligible applicants.

Other information

The charity makes grants to organisations and individuals, for relief in need, educational purposes, public purposes and it also makes grants to churches.

Wisbech

Elizabeth Wright's Charity

£4,000

Correspondent: Sylvia Palmer, Beechcroft, 124 Fridaybridge Road, Elm,

Wisbech PE14 0AT (01945 861312; email: wisbchar@aol.com)

Trustees: Richard Barnwell; Ian Mason; Jean Bowser; Janet Stevens; Keith Aplin; Paul West.

CC Number: 203896

Eligibility

People who live in the parishes of SS Peter and Paul and St Augustine, Cambridgeshire.

Types of grants

Grants for students of music, the arts, vocational education or training amongst other areas. Secondary, primary and further education grants for projects in the areas of RE, citizenship, the arts, music and drama and vocational education and Christian and youth work.

Annual grant total

In 2010/11 the trust had assets of £951,000 and an income of £38,000. Grants to individuals totalled about £4,000 including £1,100 for music lessons.

Exclusions

No grants for people starting work.

Applications

In writing to the correspondent. Applications can be submitted directly by the individual at any time.

Other information

The trust also makes grants to schools and organisations, and to adults for welfare purposes.

East Sussex

The Catherine Martin Trust

£13,000

Correspondent: The Secretary, c/o the Parish Office, The Vicarage, Wilbury Road, Hove, East Sussex BN3 3PB (email: audrey_t@hotmail.com)

Trustees: Baron Sanders; Arlene Rowe; Beryl Thei; Jennifer Barnard-Langston; Leslie Hamilton; Phil Ritchie.

CC Number: 258346

Eligibility

Young people under 21 who are British born, in financial need and resident in the old borough of Hove and Portslade for at least one year.

Types of grants

Recurrent grants according to need are made to schoolchildren and further and higher education students. Grants can be for clothing, books, equipment,

educational outings in the UK, fees or living expenses.

Annual grant total

In 2010/11 the trust had an income of £12,000 and an expenditure of £14,000.

Applications

In writing to the correspondent, either by the individual or through the individual's school, college, educational welfare agency, or a third party such as health or social worker, solicitor, friend or relative. Applications are usually considered in March, June, August, September and December.

The Mrs A. Lacy Tate Trust

£8,000

Correspondent: The Trustees, Heringtons Solicitors, 39 Gildredge Road, Eastbourne, East Sussex BN21 4RY (01323 411020)

Trustees: Mr I. Stewart; Mrs L. Macey; Mrs J. Roberts; Mrs L. Burgess.

CC Number: 803596

Eligibility

Schoolchildren in need who live in East Sussex.

Types of grants

One-off and recurrent grants according to need.

Annual grant total

In 2010/11 the trust made 159 grants to individuals for both welfare and educational purposes totalling £16,000.

Applications

In writing to the correspondent.

Other information

Grants are also made to individuals in need for relief-in-need purposes and to organisations.

Brighton and Hove

The Brighton Educational Trust

£4,000

Correspondent: Mary Grealish, Brighton and Hove City Council, Central Accounting, Kings House, Grand Avenue, Hove, East Sussex BN3 2SR (01273 291259)

Trustees: Jeane Lepper; Mo Marsh; Andrew Wealls; Ruth Buckley; Sue Shanks.

CC Number: 306963

Eligibility

People under 25 who live in Brighton and Hove and are pursuing a course of study.

Types of grants

One-off grants between £10 and £250 are available for a whole range of educational needs and activities, including: books, clothing and equipment; living costs; the cost of studying music or other arts; and travel and educational visits in UK or abroad.

Annual grant total

In 2010/11 the trust had an income of £3,800 and an expenditure of £4,800.

Exclusions

Grants are not made towards course fees, maintenance or to foreign students studying in the UK.

Applications

Applications should be made on a form available from the correspondent for consideration in September and April. Applicants should provide a letter of support from the place of study.

The Brighton Fund

£3,000

Correspondent: The Secretary, Brighton and Hove Council, Democratic Services, Room 121, Kings House, Grand Avenue, Hove BN3 2LS (01273 291077; email: steven.clare@brighton-hove.gov.uk; website: www.brighton-hove.gov.uk)

Trustees: Cllr Anne Meadows; Cllr Geoffrey Bowden; Cllr Jeane Lepper; Cllr Anne Norman; Cllr Stephanie Powell.

CC Number: 1011724

Eligibility

People in need who live in Brighton and Hove administrative boundary.

Types of grants

One-off cash grants are given for nursery childcare costs, excursions and school uniforms.

Annual grant total

In 2010/11 the fund had assets of £1.1 million and an income of £43,000. Grants totalled £14,000 and were distributed between: individuals in need over 60 (£7,000); individuals in need under 60 (£3,000); and exception awards (£4,000).

Applications

On a form, available from the correspondent or the website, to be submitted either through an organisation such as Citizens Advice or a school or through a third party such as a social worker or teacher. Applications are considered upon receipt.

The Oliver and Johannah Brown Apprenticeship Fund

£15,000

Correspondent: Mary Grealish, Brighton and Hove Council, Central Accounting, Room 201 Kings House, Grand Avenue, Hove, East Sussex BN3 2SU (01273 291259; fax: 01273 291659; email: mary.grealish@brighton-hove.gov.uk)

Trustees: Jeane Lepper; Mo Marsh; Andrew Wealls; Ruth Buckley; Sue Shanks.

CC Number: 306335

Eligibility

People under the age of 25 who live in Brighton and Hove and are pursuing a recognised course of study or serving an apprenticeship. They must either have been born there or have lived there for five years immediately before 1 May in the year in which the application is made.

Types of grants

One-off grants of £10 to £600 are made for a wide range of educational needs e.g. clothing, books, tools and travel. Grants are also given for apprenticeships.

Annual grant total

The income of this fund is steady at around £11,000–£12,000 per annum. The expenditure has steadily increased over the past five years from £9,000 to £16,000 in 2010/11.

Exclusions

No grants towards course fees, maintenance or overseas students studying in Britain.

Applications

On a form available from the correspondent, submitted by the individual, for consideration in September and April. Applicants should provide a letter of support from the place of study/apprenticeship.

The Hallett Science Scholarship

£2,000

Correspondent: Mary Grealish, Brighton and Hove City Council, Central Accounting, Kings House, Grand Avenue, Hove, East Sussex BN3 2SR (01273 291259)

Trustees: Jeane Lepper; Mo Marsh; Andrew Wealls; Ruth Buckley; Sue Shanks.

CC Number: 306361

Eligibility

People under 25 who have lived in Brighton and Hove for at least two years and are undertaking a course or a research project in pure or applied science.

Types of grants

One-off grants of £250 to £500 are given for materials and equipment and occasionally travel.

Annual grant total

In 2010/11 the fund had an income of £1,600. The trust states that there is around £2,000 available for distribution each year.

Applications

On a form available from the correspondent, submitted directly by the individual. Applications are considered in April and September.

Other information

Recent low expenditure is due to the difficulty in finding eligible applicants, the trust is definitely active and open for applications.

Soames Girls Educational Trust

£6,000

Correspondent: Mary Grealish, Brighton and Hove City Council, Central Accounting, Room 201, Kings House, Grand Avenue, Hove, East Sussex BN3 2SR (01273 291259; email: mary.grealish@brighton-hove.gov.uk)

Trustees: Jeane Lepper; Mo Marsh; Andrew Wealls; Ruth Buckley; Sue Shanks.

CC Number: 306962

Eligibility

Girls or young women under 25 years of age who are living, or have recently lived in, Brighton and Hove.

Types of grants

One-off grants are usually to a maximum of £500 a year, for school pupils, college students or university undergraduates, to help with books, equipment, specialist clothing or travel.

Annual grant total

In 2010/11 the charity had an income of £5,500 and an expenditure of £6,900.

Exclusions

No grants for course fees or for basic day to day living expenses.

Applications

On a form available from the correspondent. Applications are considered in April and September.

Hastings

Isabel Blackman Foundation

£11,000 (17 grants)

Correspondent: D J Jukes, Trustee and Secretary, Stonehenge, 13 Laton Road, Hastings, East Sussex TN34 2ES (01424 431756)

Trustees: Margaret Haley; Denis Jukes; John Lamplugh; Patricia Connolly; Christine Deacon; Evelyn Williams.

CC Number: 313577

Eligibility

People in need who live in Hastings and the surrounding district.

Types of grants

Grants can be made to schoolchildren for educational outings in the UK and further and higher education, mature and postgraduate students for books, equipment/instruments, fees and maintenance/living expenses. Mature students can also be supported towards the costs of childcare.

Annual grant total

In 2010/11 the foundation had assets of £4.9 million and an income of £287,000. Approximately £11,000 was given in grants to 17 individuals for educational purposes.

Applications

In writing to the correspondent, directly by the individual. 'Applications for grants are more likely to succeed where it can be shown that the applicants are helping themselves as well as seeking assistance.'

Other information

The foundation mainly supports organisations and also makes grants to individuals for welfare purposes.

The Magdalen and Lasher Educational Foundation

£42,000

Correspondent: Gill Adamson, Administrator, 132 High Street, Hastings, East Sussex TN34 3ET (01424 452646; email: mlc@oldhastingshouse.co.uk; website: www.magdalenandlasher.co.uk)

Trustees: Clive Morris; Keith Donaldson; Gareth Bendon; Ian Steel; Jenny Blackburn; Joy Waite; John Bilsby; Michael Foster; Susan Parsons; Donald Burrows; John Hodges; Nikki Port; Richard Stevens; Robert Featherstone; Sue Phillips.

CC Number: 306969

Eligibility

People under 25 who live in the borough of Hastings.

Types of grants

Up to 25 bursaries of £1,000 each to undergraduates plus grants for assistance with course fees and other expenses for individuals. Grants are means tested.

Annual grant total

In 2010/11 the foundation had assets of £3.7 million and an income of £310,000. 25 bursaries totalling £25,000 and individual grants totalling £17,000 were made.

Applications

On a form available from the correspondent. The trustees meet every three months.

Other information

The foundation also supports state schools in Hastings.

Mayfield

The Mayfield Charity

£1,000

Correspondent: Brenda Hopkin, Appletrees, Alexandra Road, Mayfield, East Sussex TN20 6UD (01435 873279)

Trustees: Ann Adam; Fiona Bickerton; John Logan; Mary Pennington; Father Nigel Prior.

CC Number: 212996

Eligibility

People in need who live in the ancient parish of Mayfield.

Types of grants

One-off grants of £50 to £1,000 to: schoolchildren for uniforms, clothing, equipment, instruments and excursions; college students for study/travel abroad and equipment/instruments; and undergraduates for study/travel abroad.

Annual grant total

Grants are made for relief-in-need and educational purposes and total about £2,000 each year.

Applications

In writing to the correspondent at any time either directly by the individual or a family member, through a third party such as a social worker or teacher, or through an organisation such as Citizens Advice or a school. Proof of need should be included where possible.

Newick

The Lady Vernon Trust

£3,000

Correspondent: Colin Andrews, 30 Leveller Road, Newick, Lewes BN8 4PL (01825 723696)

Trustees: Colin Andrews; Patrick Cumberlage; Stella Hill; Sylvia Armitage; Jennie Smerdon; Liz Duncton.

CC Number: 306410

Eligibility

People under 25 living in and/or attending school in Newick only.

Types of grants

One-off and recurrent grants of £100 to £200 to help satisfying the residential/school requirements with education or starting work. This includes help towards the cost of school uniforms, other school clothing, books, educational outings and study/travel abroad for schoolchildren; fees, books, and study or travel abroad for students in further education and books for students in higher education, mature and vocational students, postgraduates and people starting work.

Annual grant total

About £3,000 each year.

Applications

In writing to the correspondent, either directly by the individual if aged 18 or over, or by the parent/guardian for girls under 18 or through an organisation such as a school or educational welfare agency. Details of the purpose of the grant and the amount anticipated to be spent should be included in the application. They are considered in April and October and should be received in the preceding month.

Warbleton

Warbleton Charity

£500

Correspondent: John Leeves, 4 Berners Court Yard, Berners Hill, Flimwell, Wadhurst, East Sussex TN5 7NE (01580 879248)

Trustees: Christopher Wells; Richard Reading; Lionel Daw; Caroline Rees; Revd Marc Lloyd.

CC Number: 208130

Eligibility

People living in the parish of Warbleton who are either taking part in vocational training courses in further education or starting apprenticeships.

Types of grants

One-off grants according to need. Recent awards have been made for books and equipment.

Annual grant total

Grants usually total about £1,000 each year.

Exclusions

Students on academic courses are not eligible.

Applications

In writing to the correspondent either directly by the individual or through a third party. Applications are considered on a regular basis.

Other information

Grants are also made for welfare purposes.

Essex

The Hervey Benham Charitable Trust

£11,000 (17 grants)

Correspondent: J Woodman, Clerk to the Trustees, 3 Cadman House, off Peartree Road, Colchester CO3 0NW (01206 561086; fax: 01206 561086; email: jwoodman@aspects.net)

Trustees: Andrew Phillips; Keith Mirams; Martyn Carr; Mike Ellis.

CC Number: 277578

Eligibility

Individuals whose home is in Colchester or North East Essex, who have exceptional artistic talent (especially in music) and are disadvantaged in a way which affects their development.

Types of grants

One-off and recurrent grants ranging from £150 to £2,000. Schoolchildren can be supported for equipment/instruments and fees; further and higher education students can receive grants for equipment/instruments, fees and study or travel abroad; and postgraduates may be supported for fees and study or travel abroad.

Annual grant total

In 2010/11 the trust had assets of £1.2 million and an income of £32,000. 17 grants to individuals were made totalling £11,000.

Exclusions

Applications are not accepted from outside the beneficial area, or for mainstream education.

Applications

On a form available from the correspondent, submitted directly by the individual in time to be considered by the trustees in January, April, July and October. Applications should include information about total funds needed and all other sources of funding available, including from the individual's family.

Other information

The trust also gives to organisations.

Billericay Educational Trust

£8,000

Correspondent: Richard Lambourne, Clerk to the Trustees, Brentwood School, Ingrave Road, Brentwood, Essex CM15 8AS (01277 243252; email: info@ billericayeducationaltrust.co.uk; website: www.billericayeducationaltrust.co.uk)

Trustees: Geoffrey Buckingham; Anthony Page; James Bacchus; Ian Bruton; Michael Ginn; Frances Hutt.

CC Number: 310836

Eligibility

University students under the age of 25 years who live within a six-mile radius of Billericay.

Types of grants

Recurring grants may be given for up to three years for a variety of purposes including tuition fees, clothing, tools, musical instruments, artistic equipment, books etc. Grants may also be given for travel for educational purposes in the UK or abroad.

Annual grant total

In 2010/11 the trust had an income of £15,000 and an expenditure of £9,000.

Applications

Application forms can be downloaded from the trust's website and should be submitted by the second week of June for consideration in July.

The Butler Educational Foundation

£8,000

Correspondent: Nicholas Welch, Duffield Stunt, 71 Duke Street, Chelmsford, Essex CM1 1JU (01245 262351)

Trustees: Margaret Martin; Brian Cook; John Galley; Pat Breeze; Wendy Godden; John MacAllister; Fiona Walker; Gill Cooch; Lee Batson.

CC Number: 310731

Eligibility

People who live in Boreham and Little Baddow who have attended a state elementary school in the area for at least two years.

Types of grants

Grants have been awarded mostly after parental application towards the cost of items as diverse as school visits, music lessons, examination fees and special equipment for projects required on certain courses. Grants are also available for students in higher and further education, apprentices and people starting work.

Annual grant total

In 2010/11 the foundation had an income of £7,300 and an expenditure of £9,000.

Applications

On a form available from the correspondent. The trustees meet three times a year, usually in January, April and October. One of the trustees normally visits the applicant.

George Courtauld Educational Trust

£2,000

Correspondent: Bryony Wilmshurst, c/o Cunningtons, Great Square, Braintree, Essex CM7 1UD (01376 326868)

Trustees: Graham Butland; David Mann; Pat Purdy; David Baugh.

CC Number: 310835

Eligibility

People under the age of 21 who live in, or have attended a school in, the parishes of Braintree, Bocking, Black Notley, Great Notley, Rayne and Cressing.

Types of grants

One-off grants up to £250 are given to schoolchildren and further and higher education students for uniforms/other school clothing, books and equipment/ instruments. Grants given include those in the areas of music and other arts and individuals preparing to enter a profession or trade after leaving school or higher education.

Annual grant total

In 2011 the trust had an income of £1,600 and an expenditure of £2,300.

Applications

On a form available from the correspondent. Applications can be submitted at any time, directly by the individual, including an independent letter of support and a written quotation.

The Earls Colne and Halstead Educational Charity

£11,000 (76 grants)

Correspondent: Martyn Woodward, St Andrews House, 2 Mallows Field, Halstead C09 2LN (01787 479960; email: earlscolnehalstead.edcharity@yahoo.co.uk)

Trustees: Margarita James; Angela Paramor; Oliver Forder; Patricia Taylor; Susan Thurgate; John Panayi; Mike Murray; David Finch; Chris Siddall; Frank Williams; David Hume; Fiona Lee-Allan; Julie Winstanley; Joe Pike.

CC Number: 310859

Eligibility

People under 25 who have lived for at least one year or attended school, in the former catchment areas of Halstead and Earls Colne grammar schools.

Types of grants

One-off grants are made to: schoolchildren for educational outings in the UK and study or travel abroad; and further and higher education students and postgraduates for books, equipment/instruments, education outings in the UK and study or travel abroad.

Grants previously awarded include purchase of a cello for a young musician, residential training courses for a footballer and travel to a forestry project in Uganda. Grants range from £100 to £250.

Annual grant total

In 2010/11 the charity had assets of £1.2 million and an income of £51,000. Grants to 76 individuals totalled £11,000.

Applications

On a form available from the correspondent, which must include the signature of a relevant person in authority. Applications are considered in February, May, October and December.

Other information

Voluntary organisations offering opportunities to young people and schools can also receive grants. The following parishes were in the former Halstead and Earls Colne grammar schools catchment areas: Alphamstone, Ashen, Birdbrook, the Bumpsteads, Bures, Coggeshall, the Colnes, Foxearth, Gestingthorpe, Gosfield, Greenstead Green, Halstead Rural, the Hedinghams, the Henns, Lamarsh, the Maplesteads, Middleton, Pebmarsh, Pentlow, Ridgewell, Stambourne, Stisted, Sturmer, Toppesfield, Twinstead, Wickham St Paul, the Yeldhams and the town of Halstead, all in the district of Braintree; and the parishes of Chappel, Mount Bures and Wakes Colne, all in the district of Colchester.

Essex Awards Trust

£700

Correspondent: Samantha Taylor, Essex County Council, Corporate Resources, PO Box 4, Chelmsford CM1 1JZ (01245 434057)

Trustee: Essex County Council.

CC Number: 310842

Eligibility

Applicants must have lived in Essex for at least two years prior to application, and must be undergoing a course of study in further or higher education beyond school-leaving age or are in attendance at a secondary school in Essex.

Types of grants

Grants are given to those in financial need in secondary school, further or higher education for fees, books and equipment, study abroad, living expenses and educational outings.

Annual grant total

In 2010/11 the trust had an income of £220 and a total expenditure of £730.

Applications

On a form available from the correspondent. Applications should be made by the 15th of June, October and February.

Other information

Two small trusts, the Florence Knapton Scholarship and the Cicely Courtauld and Ashdown Scholarships, have been incorporated into this trust.

The Fawbert and Barnard's Educational Foundation

£1,000

Correspondent: Christine Baxter, Fawbert and Barnards (Undl) Primary School, London Road, Harlow CM17 0DA (01279 429427; email: admin@fawbert-barnards.essex.sch.uk)

Trustees: Sue Livings; Joyce Vincent; Paul Sztumpf; Christine Baxter; Richard Morgan; Eddie Johnson.

CC Number: 310757

Eligibility

People under the age of 25 who live in Harlow and surrounding villages.

Types of grants

(i) Grants, to a usual maximum of about £25, for school pupils to help with books, equipment, clothing or travel. Grants are not given for school fees.

(ii) Grants, to a usual maximum of about £25, to help with school, college or university fees, books or equipment or to supplement existing grants.

(iii) Help towards the cost of education, training, apprenticeship or equipment for those starting work.

Annual grant total

The foundation usually has an income and a total expenditure of approximately £1,000, most of which is allocated to Fawbert and Barnard School. Grants are not usually made directly to individuals.

Applications

In writing to the correspondent. The trustees usually meet in February, June and October.

Other information

Larger grants are given to schools within the beneficial area.

Hart's and Nash's Education Foundation

£2,000

Correspondent: Peter Bricknell, Stonehams Solicitors, 68 High Street, Saffron Walden, Essex CB10 1AD (01799 527299)

Trustees: Peter Bricknell; Alison Tills; Elizabeth Marshall; Nicholas Boyle; Susan Ross.

CC Number: 310727

Eligibility

Schoolchildren and students who live in the parishes of Great Chesterford and Little Chesterford.

Types of grants

One-off and recurrent grants to schoolchildren towards uniforms, other school clothing, books, educational outings, maintenance and extra-curricular activities, and to students in further/higher education towards books.

Annual grant total

In 2010/11 the foundation had both an income and an expenditure of £2,500. Grants are usually made totalling £2,000

Applications

In writing to the correspondent.

The Canon Holmes Memorial Trust

£12,000

Correspondent: The Revd Canon John D Brown, Secretary, 556 Galleywood Road, Chelmsford CM2 8BX (01245 358185; fax: 01245 268209; email:

secretary@canonholmes.org.uk; website: canonholmes.org.uk/index.html)

Trustees: J. F. Aldridge; John Brown; Philip Wilson; Sheila Charrington; Peter Mockford; Richard Tufnell; Jason Whiskerd; Annie Oxley.

CC Number: 801964

Eligibility

Young people aged 7 to 13 living in the Roman Catholic diocese of Brentwood or the Anglican diocese of Chelmsford, Essex whose families have experienced a change in circumstances causing them to be unable to meet financial commitments to children's education, such as illness or death of a parent or guardian, employment crisis or marital breakdown.

Types of grants

Grants for private school fees.

Annual grant total

In 2010/11 the trust had an income of £12,000 and an expenditure of £8,000

Applications

On a form available from the website. Applications must come from parents or guardians and grants will be paid directly to the school.

Ann Johnson's Educational Foundation

£20,000

Correspondent: J P Douglas-Hughes, Clerk, 58 New London Road, Chelmsford, Essex CM2 0PA (01245 493939; fax: 01245 493940)

Trustees: Graham McGhie; Laura Lewis; Margaret Bardsley; Paul Foulger; Peter Turrall; Elizabeth Marshall; Yvonne Spence; Jean Patterson; Marie-Jean Bradford; Noreen Hiom.

CC Number: 310799

Eligibility

People living or educated in Chelmsford and the surrounding parishes, who are under 25.

Types of grants

Help with the cost of books, clothing and other essentials for schoolchildren, including school fees. Grants are also available for those at college or university and towards the cost of books, equipment and instruments, clothing and travel for people starting work.

Annual grant total

In 2010 the trust made grants to 18 individuals (11 boys and 8 girls) totalling £20,000.

Applications

On a form available from: Ravenscroft, Stock Road, Galleywood, Chelmsford,

Essex CM2 8PW (01245 260757). The governors meet quarterly to consider applications.

Other information

The trust also gives funding to local schools (£5,500 in 2010).

The Paslow Common Educational Foundation

£500

Correspondent: The Finance Directorate, Essex County Council, PO Box 4, Chelmsford CM1 1JZ (01245 434057)

Trustee: Essex County Council.

CC Number: 310821

Eligibility

People under the age of 25 who are in need and live in the parishes of Blackmore, Bobbingworth, Doddinghurst, Fyfield, High Ongar, Kelvedon Hatch, Magdalen Laver, Moreton, Ongar, Stondon Massey and Willingale, or who have attended a county or voluntary school in any of the above parishes for at least two years.

Types of grants

One-off grants are made to secondary schoolchildren, college students, undergraduates, vocational students and people starting work, including those for fees, books, study/travel abroad, equipment/instruments, maintenance/living expenses and excursions.

Annual grant total

In 2010/11 the foundation had an income of £3,800 and an expenditure of £500.

Applications

On a form available from the Student and Pupil Financial Support Service. Applications are considered at meetings held in March, July and November, the deadlines for which are 15 February, 15 June and 15 October respectively.

Pilgrim Educational Trust

£2,000

Correspondent: Bryony Wilmshirst, Cunningtons, Great Square, Braintree, Essex CM7 1UD (01376 326868)

Trustees: Anthony Fenton; David Drake; Johanna Withams.

CC Number: 1083109

Eligibility

People aged between 16 and 20 who attend a Braintree or Bocking senior school, namely Alec Hunter High School, Tabor High School, Notley High

School or Braintree College of Further Education.

Types of grants

One-off grants are given to costs incurred in connection with A-level courses.

Annual grant total

In 2010/11 the trust had an income of £4,000 and an expenditure of £2,000.

Applications

On a form available from the correspondent, to be submitted by the individual at any time. Applications must include an independent letter of support.

The British and Foreign School Society - Saffron Walden

£6,000

Correspondent: Imogen Wilde, Director, Maybrook House, Godstone Road, Caterham, Surrey CR3 6RE (01883 331177; email: director@bfss.org.uk; website: www.bfss.org.uk)

Trustees: Graham Kingsley; Stephen Orchard; David Swain; Steve Hodkinson; Roger Howarth; David Tennant; Brian York; Stephen Ross; Emily Tomlinson; David Zahn; David Stephens; Shubhi Rao; Jaz Saggu; Ben Ramm; E. J. Weale.

CC Number: 314286

Eligibility

Young people in education under the age of 25 who live, or whose parents/guardians live, in Saffron Walden and neighbourhood.

Types of grants

For the promotion of education but not to relieve public funds. Previously, a grant of £2,000 was made to Newport Free Grammar School and three individual grants were made, including one to two children of a Lebanese refugee family.

Annual grant total

Around £6,000.

Applications

Using the application form available on the British and Foreign School Society website.

Other information

Grants are also awarded to schools and educational establishments within the beneficial area.

Canewdon

The Canewdon Educational Foundation

£4,300 (44 grants)

Correspondent: Alan Lane, Trust House, Anchor Lane, Canewdon Essex SS4 3PA (01702 258258)

Trustees: Molly Stalker; Anne Bromley; Ian Puzey; Joyce Smith; Michael Wright; Timothy Clay; Trevor Stewart; Geraldine Lunn; Nigel Wallace; A. Nickolls; M. S. Buffett; L. D. Van Houten.

CC Number: 310718

Eligibility

People under 25 who live in the parish of Canewdon only.

Types of grants

Grants to assist with the purchase of books, tuition in music, dance, drama and swimming, extra tuition, boarding costs, travel expenses, dyslexia assessment, school uniforms and school trips, for both secondary and further education. Grants to assist apprentices and people staring work.

Annual grant total

In 2011 the charity had assets of £631,000, an income of £31,000 and gave grants to 44 individuals totalling £4,300.

Exclusions

Individuals from outside the parish of Canewdon will not be supported.

Applications

In writing to the correspondent. Information sheets have been delivered to each household in the parish giving details of how, and to whom, applications should be made. The trustees meet 11 times a year. Unsolicited applications will not be responded to.

Other information

Grants are also made to organisations including youth clubs, and the Canewdon Poor's Charity.

Chelmsford

The Chelmsford Educational Foundation

£8,000

Correspondent: Richard Emsden, 19 Rushleydale, Chelmsford CM1 6JX (07941 958652; email: remsden@gmail.com)

Trustees: Stewart Martin; Brian Frost; Eric Hardy; Karen Jackson; Peter Sawyer; Janet Chaplin; Pam Fitch; Tony Sach; Peter Jackson; Jacqueline Arnot; Gwen Hudson; Peter Cousins.

CC Number: 310815

Eligibility

People who live, and those educated in, the borough and rural district of Chelmsford.

Types of grants

Grants of up to £500, are given to students of any age to help with books, equipment, clothing or travel; to help with college or university fees; or to supplement existing grants, plus travel grants, including travel abroad.

Annual grant total

In 2011 the foundation had an income of £18,000 and an expenditure of £16,000. Grants are made to individuals and organisations.

Exclusions

Grants are not given for school fees.

Applications

On a form available from the correspondent. Initial applications are considered in December/January, Easter and August/September. Candidates are then interviewed before a decision is made.

Coggeshall

Sir Robert Hitcham's Exhibition Foundation

£7,000

Correspondent: C D Sansom, 76 Church Street, Coggeshall, Colchester, Essex CO6 1TY (01376 561277)

Trustees: Elwyn Bishop; Barry Gibson; Bryan Hockridge; Editha Tebbutt; Roy Howitt; Stanley Haines; Vivien Patience; Philip Banks; Peter Hutton; Sarah Glossop; Brian Stapley; Nicholas Johnson.

CC Number: 1095014

Eligibility

Students under the age of 25 who live in Coggeshall and have left school and are moving on to higher education or training.

Types of grants

Grants in the range of £50 to £150 are given towards books, equipment/ instruments and living costs.

Annual grant total

In 2010/11 the trust had an income of £6,500 and a total expenditure of £7,000.

Applications

On a form available from the correspondent. Applications are considered in early September and should be submitted by the end of August.

Finchingfield

Sir Robert Kemp's Education Foundation

£2,300

Correspondent: Jo Davies, Bramble Cottage, Mill End, Spains Hall Road, Finchingfield, Essex CM7 4NH (01371 810642)

Trustees: Edwin Collar; Joanna Davies; Ann Kerr; Judith M'Elligott; Linsay Hamilton; Alec James.

CC Number: 310804

Eligibility

People in need who are under 25 and live, or whose parents live, in the parish of Finchingfield.

Types of grants

Grants can be towards books, equipment, educational trips, music and so on for individual students or people staring work. Grants can also be made to organisations providing an educational element in their activities, as well as educational providers if the benefits of the grants relate directly to under 25 year olds.

Annual grant total

In 2010/11 the trust had an income of £2,200 and an expenditure of £2,300.

Applications

On a form available from the correspondent. Applications should be submitted in April and October for consideration in May and November.

Other information

Grants are also made to organisations.

Gestingthorpe

The Gestingthorpe Educational Foundation

£1,500

Correspondent: Jane Winmill, The Secretary, Dower House, Gestingthorpe, Halstead, Essex CO9 3BL (01787 460631)

Trustees: Alice Nolda; Ashley Cooper; Corrina Brown; Deborah Nott; Steve Bolter; Peter Nice.

CC Number: 310725

Eligibility

People who live in the ancient parish of Gestingthorpe, preference being given to those under 25.

Types of grants

One-off grants are given to: schoolchildren and further education students for books equipment/instruments, fees, educational outings in the UK and study or travel abroad; to mature and vocational students for books and fees; and to higher education students for books. Grants are in the range of £10 to £225.

Annual grant total

Grants usually total £1,500.

Applications

In writing to the correspondent directly by the individual, including receipts for any payments made. Applications are usually considered in April and October.

Other information

Grants are also made to organisations for educational purposes.

Ongar

Joseph King's Charity

£30,000

Correspondent: Catherine E M Kenny Maat, 36 Coopers Hill, Ongar, Essex CM5 9EF (01277 366167)

Trustees: Margaret Herring; Anne Sydenham; Margaret Evans; Roger King; Peter Mockett; F. H. Hart; S. M. Cooper; Peter Richardson; M. Love; Diane Stratton; Jeremy Lewis.

CC Number: 810177

Eligibility

People under 25 years of age who live in the civil parish of Chipping Ongar.

Types of grants

Help with the cost of books, clothing and other essentials for schoolchildren. Help may also be available for students at college or university. Preference is given to the advancement of the Christian religion.

Annual grant total

In 2011 the trust had assets of £1.8 million and an income of £75,000. Grants to individuals for education totalled £30,000.

Applications

In writing to the correspondent.

Other information

The trust also gives grants to local schools.

Thaxted

Lord Maynard's Charity

£1,000

Correspondent: Michael Chapman, Wade and Davies Solicitors, 28 High Street, Great Dunmow, Essex CM6 1AH (01371 872816)

Trustees: Peter King; Daniel Fox; Lord Braybrooke.

CC Number: 278579

Eligibility

People under 25 who live in the parish of Thaxted.

Types of grants

£50 to £100 towards the cost of education, training, apprenticeship or equipment for those starting work.

Annual grant total

About £2,500 for education and welfare.

Applications

In writing to the correspondent. Applicants traditionally queue in the local church on the first Saturday in August for the money to be handed out, but postal applications prior to this are accepted.

Other information

Although records at the Charity Commission are very overdue, the correspondent has confirmed that the trust is active.

Hampshire

Aldworth Trust Foundation

£1,000

Correspondent: Mrs D M Reavell, Clerk, 25 Cromwell Road, Basingstoke, Hampshire RG21 5NR (01256 473390; email: reavell@btinternet.com)

Trustees: Robert Fergie; Christopher Evans; Roger Gardiner; Sheila Knight; Peter Davis; Joanna Stoker; Linda Lawson; Evelyn Marion Boult; Janet Cippico; Valerie Marwood.

CC Number: 307259

Eligibility

Young people who require financial help with needs that are broadly educational. Applicants must also be educated, formerly educated, resident or formerly resident in the Borough of Basingstoke and Deane

Types of grants

(i) Grants for school pupils to help with educational outings, uniforms and equipment but not for fees, maintenance or books.

(ii) Grants to students to help with books and study or travel abroad, but not for fees/living expenses or for student exchanges.

(iii) Grants to people starting work for books, equipment and clothing, but not for travel.

Annual grant total

In 2010/11 the trust had an income of £1,900 and an expenditure of £1,100.

Applications

On a form available from the correspondent. Applications are considered in February, June and October.

The Ashford Hill Educational Trust

£5,500

Correspondent: Graham Swait, Oakview, Yeomans Lane, Newtown, Newbury RG20 9BL (01635 276098)

Trustees: D. Chamings; Lucy Thirtle; D. Fowler; K. Chapman; Bob Lawrence; Ann Hoddinott.

CC Number: 1040559

Eligibility

People who live in the parish of Ashford Hill with Headley or the surrounding area.

Types of grants

Grants are generally given to promote social and physical education. They are given towards the cost of formal education, enhancement of employment prospects, group activities, music, adult education and sporting and recreational activities.

Annual grant total

Around £5,500 a year is given in grants.

Applications

On a form available from the correspondent. Applications are considered in January, March, July and October.

Bramshott Educational Trust

£4,000

Correspondent: Richard Weighell, 107 Haslemere Road, Liphook GU30 7BU (01428 724289; email: info@bramshotteducationaltrust.org.uk; website: www.bramshotteducationaltrust.org.uk)

Trustees: Mary Eyre; Richard Weighell; Sarah Sear; Valentine Inglis-Jones.

CC Number: 277421

Eligibility

People under 25 who live or have a parent who lives in the parish of St Mary the Virgin, Bramshott and Liphook.

Types of grants

Grants up to £200. Grants are given for educational needs including physical, social, musical education and travel and equipment necessary in the pursuit of such aims. Some travel scholarships of up to £250 may also be awarded for adventure travel such as Raleigh International.

Annual grant total

In 2010/11 the trust had an income of £6,400 and a total expenditure of £4,300.

Applications

On a form available from the website. Applications are considered in July and November, with the closing dates for applications being 30 June and 31 October each year. Applications should include full details of courses/projects and an sae.

The Cliddesden and Farleigh Wallop Educational Trust

£10,000

Correspondent: Ms Alison Mosson, 11 Southlea, Cliddesden, Basingstoke RG25 2JN

Trustees: Caroline O'Herlihy; Quentin Wallop; Stephen Mourant; Alison Cecil.

CC Number: 307150

Eligibility

People under 25 who live within the original boundaries of the parishes of Cliddesden and Farleigh Wallop only.

Types of grants

One-off and recurrent grants. Education is considered in its broadest sense, from help with school projects and trips to college/university courses to music lessons.

Annual grant total

In 2010 the trust had an income of £10,000 and an expenditure of £16,000.

Applications

In writing to the correspondent. Applications should be submitted through a school or directly by the individual or their guardian to reach the secretary by the end of April, August or December, accompanied by fully documented receipts.

Dibden Allotments Charity

£700 (5 grants)

Correspondent: Harvey Mansfield, 7 Drummond Court, Prospect Place, Hythe, Southampton SO45 6HD (02380 841305; email: dibdenallotments@btconnect.com; website: daf-hythe.org.uk)

Trustees: Judith Saxby; Malcolm Fidler; Mrs M. McLean; Mike Harvey; Pat Hedges; Peter Parrott; Chris Harrison; Rosemary Dash; Jill Tomlin.

CC Number: 255778

Eligibility

People in need who live in the parishes of Hythe, Dibden, Marshwood and Fawley.

Types of grants

One-off and recurrent grants according to need. Recent grants have been awarded for school uniforms, other school clothing, books, equipment, fees and living expenses for students in further and higher education, educational outings for schoolchildren and childcare for mature students.

Annual grant total

In 2010/11 the charity had assets of £8.1 million and an income of £328,000. There were five grants made for educational purposes totalling just over £700.

Applications

On a form available on the fund's website, where the fund's criteria, guidelines and application process are also posted.

Other information

Grants are also made to charitable and voluntary organisations.

The Gordon Charitable Trust

See entry on page 269

The Robert Higham Apprenticing Charity

£6,000

Correspondent: Roy Forth, PO Box 7721, Kingsclere RG20 5WQ (07796 423108; email: kclerecharities@aol.co.uk)

Trustees: G. Swait; D. Chamings; Jean Turner; Penny Stewart; Rachel Theaker; Lucy Thirtle; Patrick Dring; Marie Gundry; Irene Powers.

CC Number: 307083

Eligibility

People aged between 16 and under 25 who live in the parishes of Kingsclere, Ashford Hill and Headley, Hampshire.

Types of grants

Grants towards books, specialist equipment and clothing or travelling expenses for those preparing for or engaged in any profession, trade, occupation, service or towards books, study or travel abroad for those studying for A-levels. Grants can be one-off or recurrent and are given according to need.

Annual grant total

The charity has an annual income of around £7,000 and expenditure of £6,000.

Applications

On a form available from the correspondent. Applications must include a letter outlining the applicant's further education plans. Applications are not accepted from parents. The trustees meet five times a year, applications must be with the correspondent by 31 January, 31 March, 30 May, 31 August and 31 October.

The Foundation of Sarah Rolle

£5,000

Correspondent: G P McCann, Mount View, East Dean Road, Lockerley, Romsey, Hampshire SO51 0JQ (01794 340698)

Trustees: Ronald Corne; Anthony Robins; Barbara Boby; Caroline Monro; James Pitkin; John Smith; Hugh Dalgety; Jayne Perry.

CC Number: 307157

Eligibility

Schoolchildren, people starting work and further and higher education students under 25 who live, or whose parents live in the parishes of East Tytherley and Lockerley.

Types of grants

Grants for uniforms/other school clothing, books, equipment/instruments, educational outings in the UK and study or travel abroad. Grants range from £50 to £250.

Annual grant total

In 2011 the foundation had both an income and expenditure of £11,000.

Exclusions

Grants are not given for school or college fees or living expenses.

Applications

On a form available from the correspondent, to be submitted either directly by the individual or through a parent. Applications should be submitted by January or July for consideration in February or August respectively.

Other information

Grants are also awarded to local schools.

The Earl of Southampton Trust

£1,000 (3 grants)

Correspondent: Mrs S C Boden, Clerk to the Trustees, 24 The Square, Titchfield, Hampshire PO14 4RU (01329 513294; email: earlstrust@yahoo.co.uk; website: eost.org.uk)

Trustees: Sally Loretto Hopton; Dennis Arthur Hignell; Constance Hockley; Frances Charlotte Knight; David Nation; Paul Vincent Cousins; Ann Hammond; John Stewart Peterkin.

CC Number: 238549

Eligibility

People in need who live in the ancient parish of Titchfield (now subdivided into the parishes of Titchfield, Sarisbury, Locks Heath, Warsash, Stubbington and Lee-on-the-Solent).

Types of grants

One-off grants ranging from between £25 and £1,000 to schoolchildren, college students, mature students and to people with special educational need towards tuition fees, uniforms and books.

Annual grant total

In 2010/11 the trust had assets of £1.5 million and an income of £85,000. There were 97 grants made totalling £25,000 for welfare and educational purposes.

Exclusions

Grants are not given for study or travel abroad, student exchange, tertiary and postgraduate education.

Applications

In writing to the correspondent through a school, other educational establishment, an educational welfare agency or another third party. Applications must include details of the extent of the need and the full address of the applicant or nominee. Applications are considered on the last Tuesday of every month. Forms are available to download from the website.

Other information

The trust runs almshouses and a day centre for old people.

Sir Mark and Lady Turner Charitable Settlement

£5,000

Correspondent: Louise Marsden, Kleinwort Benson, 30 Gresham Street, London EC2V 7PG (020 3207 7000; email: louise.marsden@kleinworthbenson.com)

Trustee: Kleinwort Benson Trustees Ltd.

CC Number: 264994

Eligibility

People in need, with a preference for those in further education who live in north London and Hampshire

Types of grants

One-off and recurrent grants up to £300 for fees, books and equipment/instruments.

Annual grant total

In 2010/11 the trust had an income of £7,900 and an expenditure of £12,000.

Applications

In writing to the correspondent, including either a telephone number or email address. Applications must be received by the end of April or October for consideration in early June or December. Only successful applicants are notified of the trustees' decision.

Other information

Grants are also made for welfare purposes.

Alverstoke

The Alverstoke Trust

£500

Correspondent: Mrs Jane Hodgman, 5 Constable Close, Gosport, Hampshire PO12 2UF (02392 589822)

Trustees: Aleck Hayward; Julia Grant; Timothy Hall.

CC Number: 239303

Eligibility

People in need who live in Alverstoke or nearby.

Types of grants

One-off grants, usually of amounts of up to £200, to college students, undergraduates, vocational students and people with special educational needs. Grants given include those for fees, study/travel abroad and books.

Annual grant total

In 2010 the trust had an income of £1,500 and a total expenditure of £1,100.

Exclusions

The trust does not make loans, grants to other charities or recurring awards.

Applications

In writing to the correspondent, either directly or through a third party such as a Citizens Advice, social worker, welfare agency or other third party. Applications are considered at any time.

Andover

Miss Gales Educational Foundation

£7,000

Correspondent: John Butcher, Barker Son and Isherwood, 32 High Street, Andover SP10 1NT

Trustees: Zilliah Brooks; Joan Bruce; Susan Evans; David Drew; John Harkin; John Butcher.

CC Number: 307145

Eligibility

Children and young people under the age of 25 who live in or are being educated in the Andover district. Preference is given to schoolchildren with serious family difficulties.

Types of grants

Grants are given towards the cost of: (i) school uniforms, other school clothing, books and educational outings for schoolchildren; (ii) books and study or travel overseas for students in further and higher education; and (iii) books, equipment and instruments for people starting work. Grants range from £10 to £300 and are one-off.

Annual grant total

In 2011 the trust had an income of £8,400 and an expenditure of £7,700.

Exclusions

Grants are not given for school or college fees or living expenses.

Applications

In writing to the correspondent, either directly by the individual or through the individual's school, college or an educational welfare agency. Applications should include information on what the grant is required for, the applicant's date of birth and the circumstances which make it impossible for the family to provide for themselves. Applications are considered quarterly.

Fareham

The William Price Charitable Trust

£14,000 (84 grants)

Correspondent: Christopher Thomas, 24 Cuckoo Lane, Fareham, Hamps PO14 3PF (01329 663685; email: clerk@ pricestrust.org.uk; website: www. pricestrust.org.uk)

Trustees: Tessa Short; Revd Peter Hall; John Bryant; John Coghlan; John Westbrook; Bruce Thomas; Robert Miller; Rodney Baker; Trevor Howard; Anne Butcher; Christina Ahern; Jill Rattle; June Waller; June Powell; Revd Sally Davenport; Pamela Bryant; Donna Irving; William Price Trust Company.

CC Number: 307319

Eligibility

The benefit area consists of the town parishes of Fareham in Hampshire, namely those of St Peter and St Paul, Holy Trinity with St Columba and St John the Evangelist (note that this area does not cover the larger area of Fareham borough as a whole). Only those under the age of 25 living in the Fareham benefit area, or schools substantially serving that area, are eligible for grants.

Types of grants

Grants usually of up to £300 each to help with the education of individuals who are in financial need, under 25 and resident in the benefit area, with fees, educational trips, travel, outfits, clothing, books etc. Also promoting education in the doctrines of the Church of England and providing schools in or substantially serving the benefit area with educational benefits not normally provided by the local education authority.

Annual grant total

In 2010/11 the trust had assets of £6.2 million and an income of £171,000. Grants to individuals totalled £14,000, distributed as follows:
- Minor 'hardship' grants: 79 grants totalling £8,900
- College/university fees/overseas project: four grants totalling £3,100
- Private school fees: one grant of £1,500

Applications

Whenever possible applications should be made through a school or college. Application forms are used and can be downloaded from the website or sent on request. Larger grants are considered by trustees twice each year, usually in May/ June and November/December. Smaller grants for individual assistance are considered more quickly and normally in less than one month.

Other information

Grants are also made to churches, schools/colleges and welfare organisations.

Gosport

Thorngate Relief-in-Need and General Charity

£3,000

Correspondent: Kay Brent, 16 Peakfield, Waterlooville PO7 6YP (02392 264400; email: kay@brentco.co.uk)

Trustees: Roy Dyer; Alexander Burns; John Eager.

CC Number: 210946

Eligibility

People in need who live in Gosport.

Types of grants

One-off grants mostly between £100 and £500.

Annual grant total

In 2010/11 the charity had an income of £9,000 and a total expenditure of £14,000. Grants are made for both welfare and educational purposes.

Exclusions

No grants are made towards legal expenses.

Applications

On a form available from the correspondent. Applications can be made either directly by the individual or through a social worker, Citizens Advice, Probation Service or other welfare agency.

Other information

Grants are also made to organisations.

Isle of Wight

The Broadlands Home Trust

£2,000

Correspondent: Mrs M Groves, 2 Winchester Close, Newport, Isle of Wight PO30 1DR (01983 525630; email: broadlandstrust@btinternet.com)

Trustees: June Cox; Hilary Spurgeon; Caroline Baston; Revd Graham Morris; Revd Michael Weaver.

CC Number: 201433

Eligibility

Girls and young single women (under the age of 22) in need who are at school, starting work or are in further or higher education.

Types of grants

One-off grants of £100 to schoolchildren, vocational students, people with special needs and people starting work, including those for uniforms/clothing, books, equipment/ instruments and educational trips.

Annual grant total

In 2010/11 the trust had an income of £11,500. Grants were made totalling £10,500 and were distributed as follows:

Pensions	£7,000
Advancement of life grants	£2,000
Christmas boxes to pensioners	£800

Exclusions

No grants for married women or graduates.

Applications

On a form available from the correspondent, to be submitted either directly by the individual or a family member. Applications are considered quarterly in January, April, July and October.

Portsmouth

The Bentley Young Person's Trust

£2,000

Correspondent: The Secretary, Portsmouth City Council, Civic Offices, Guildhall Square, Portsmouth PO1 2QR (02392 834057; email: joanne. wildsmith@portsmouthcc.gov.uk)

Trustees: Alex Bentley; Brian Webb; Gwendoline Shaw; John Turner; Elaine Baker.

CC Number: 1069727

Eligibility

People under the age of 26 who live in Portsmouth and surrounding areas, or who have a connection with the area.

Types of grants

Grants to help develop the 'physical, mental and spiritual capacities' of young people.

Annual grant total

In 2010/11 the trust had an income of £3,000 and a total expenditure of £2,300.

Applications

In writing to the correspondent.

Other information

Grants are also made to organisations.

The Zurich Insurance Travelling Scholarships

£1,500

Correspondent: Local Democracy Manager, Civic Offices, Portsmouth City Council, Guildhall Square, Portsmouth PO1 2AL (02392 834056; email: teresa. deasy@portsmouthcc.gov.uk)

Trustees: April Windebank; Cheryl Buggy; Gerald Vernon-Jackson.

CC Number: 275519

Eligibility

Students who are studying (or have studied within the previous year, and are under 20) at least one modern foreign language to A-level at a Portsmouth school and who wish to go to the country of that language.

Types of grants

Grants to help with the costs of travel and educational visits abroad, and to help with the cost of study at an overseas educational institution for those studying a foreign language. Examples of scholarships include attending an organised course abroad, attending a foreign school as a full-time pupil for a short period, undertaking a work placement or preparing a project to discover some aspect of life in a foreign country. There is usually a maximum of two scholarships awarded each year of between £750 and £1,000 each.

Annual grant total

In recent years the scholarship has had an income of around £2,500 to £3,000 per year. Previously, scholarships have amounted to £1,500.

Applications

On a form available from the correspondent, to be submitted directly by the individual, including statements on the intended project and how the scholarship will contribute to their studies. Applications should be received by the end of November for consideration in February/March.

Wield

The Wield Educational Trust

£7,000

Correspondent: Teresa Burnhams, The Dairy, Upper Wield, Alresford, Hampshire SO24 9RT

Trustees: Mark Kemp-Gee; Barbara Wells; Claire Hutchinson; Teresa Burnhams.

CC Number: 288944

Eligibility

People aged 5 to 18 who live in the parish of Wield.

Types of grants

One-off and recurrent grants are given towards books and educational outings for schoolchildren. Preference is given to people with special education needs.

Annual grant total

In 2010/11 the trust had an income of £7,200 and an expenditure of £7,400.

Exclusions

Grants are not given for school fees or maintenance.

Applications

On a form available from the correspondent.

Hertfordshire

The 948 Sports Foundation

£7,000

Correspondent: J Dekker, Old Albanian Sports Club, Woollam Playing Fields, 160 Harpenden Road, St Albans AL3 6BB (01727 864476)

Trustees: Geraint Morton John; Bryan Short; Dick Dunn; Peter Dredge; Alexander Bell; Angela Byrne.

CC Number: 1088273

Eligibility

Young people participating in sport and recreation who attend schools, colleges and universities in St Albans and the surrounding areas.

Types of grants

Grants given according to need.

Annual grant total

In 2010/11 the foundation had an income of £16,000 and an expenditure of £14,000. Grants are also made to organisations.

Applications

In writing to the correspondent.

The Digswell Arts Trust

£1,500

Correspondent: Howard Cropp, 10 Old Garden Court, St Albans, Hertfordshire AL3 4RQ (01727 811412; email: sje_rogers@hotmail.com; website: www.digswellartstrust.com)

CC Number: 305993

Eligibility

Young people living in Welwyn, Hertfordshire and the surrounding areas

'who intend to or have become artists or craftsmen who are in need of financial assistance by the provision of materials or the payment of fees, travelling expenses or maintenance allowances or by other means for their advancement in life and to enable them to earn their living.'

Types of grants

One-off and recurrent according to need.

Annual grant total

Grants to fellows average between £1,000 and £2,000 each year.

Applications

In writing to the correspondent.

The Fawbert and Barnard School Foundation

£5,000

Correspondent: P Rider, Clerk, 22 Southbrook, Sawbridgeworth, Hertfordshire CM21 9NS (01279 724670)

Trustees: Carol Croft; Harold Rawlings; Pamela Rider; Patricia Bovaird.

CC Number: 310965

Eligibility

People between 16 and 25 years of age who live, or have attended a school, within three miles of Sawbridgeworth for at least four years.

Types of grants

Grants to assist those students wishing to continue their studies by way of full-time education at either a college or university. The bursary is awarded for use by the student to purchase books or materials associated with the course. Grants are usually in the range of £100 to £200.

Annual grant total

In 2011 the foundation had both an income and expenditure of £9,000. Previously grants to individuals totalled around £5,000.

Applications

On a form available from the correspondent. The closing date for applications is 30 September and they are considered in October.

Other information

As the grant is awarded once only, students who do not apply during their first year can apply at any time during their period of study.

The Hertfordshire County Nursing Trust

£7,300

Correspondent: A D Shand, Timber Hall, Cold Christmas Lane, Thundridge, Ware SG12 7SN (01920 466086)

Trustees: Dennis Hussey; Jill Eames; Nicholas Tufton; Joy Norris; Susan Stephens; Richard Dawkins; Robert Chambers; William Thorwer; Caroline Cherry; Kate De Boinville; Violet Beazley; Jayne Dingemans.

CC Number: 207213

Eligibility

Education for community nurses, either practising or retired, who work or have worked in Hertfordshire.

Types of grants

One-off and recurrent grants for course fees and expenses.

Annual grant total

In 2010/11 the trust had assets of £708,000 and an income of £49,000. Grants to individuals totalled £7,300.

Applications

In writing to the correspondent.

The Hertfordshire Educational Foundation

£10,000

Correspondent: The Honorary Secretary, c/o Finance Accountancy Group, 3rd Floor, North West Block, County Hall, Hertford, Herts SG13 8DN (01992 588525; website: www.hersdirect.org/hef)

Trustees: Peter Jackson; John Harris; Gillian Tattersfield; Donald MacKean; Robert Stephens; Joyce Lusby; Basil Flashman; Graham Bliss; Geoff Churchard; Terry Price; John Gardener; Christine Hood; Richard Thake.

CC Number: 311025

Eligibility

Pupils and students up to 21 years who have a home address in Hertfordshire.

Types of grants

The foundation administers three types of grant scheme:
1 Travel scholarships to individuals aged 17 to 21 to undertake approved courses of study, expeditions, voluntary work and other projects in overseas countries. The usual duration is for a minimum of one month and individuals should be able to demonstrate how their project will benefit the local community they are visiting. Scholarships range between £100 and £500

2 Grants for school visits, usually ranging between £25 and £50. Help for pupils in exceptional circumstances, whose parents have difficulty in paying the board and lodging cost of visits arranged by their schools
3 The Sir George Burns Fund. Grants to enable young people who are disabled or underprivileged aged 16 to 21 to participate in expeditions, educational visits and so on, or to purchase special items of equipment needed for them to become involved in recreational and educational activities. Grants are usually in the range of £50 to £700 and previous awards have covered the costs of laptops and computer software, travel expenses, courses and conferences

Annual grant total

In 2010/11 the trust had an income of £19,000 and an expenditure of £13,000. Educational grants to individuals total around £10,000 each year.

Applications

On forms available from the correspondent. Applications should be submitted at least a month before the individual travels. The deadlines for travel scholarships and Sir George Burns Fund applications are the end of February, May and October. Guidelines and application forms are available from the foundation's website.

Other information

The Foundation has also provided grants to organisations.

The Hitchin Educational Foundation

£39,000

Correspondent: Brian Frederick, 33 Birch close, Broom, Biggleswade, Bedfordshire SG18 9NR (01767 313892)

Trustees: Archie Kingston-Splatt; D. Hitchcock; Derrick Ashley; Nigel Brook; C. Minton; Jean Wood; M. Roden; D. Chapallaz; Sarah Wren; D. Miller; Susan Cracknell.

CC Number: 311024

Eligibility

People who live in the former urban district of Hitchin and surrounding villages, aged under 25. The grants are means tested so income and size of family are taken into account.

Types of grants

One-off grants are given towards the cost of uniforms, other school clothing and educational outings for schoolchildren; equipment and clothing for people starting work; and studying

and travelling abroad for people in further/higher education. Preference is given to children with serious family difficulties, and people with special educational needs.

Annual grant total

In 2010/11 the trust had assets of £1.3 million and an income of £102,000. £39,000 was made in grants to individuals consisting of £6,000 in grants of less than £400 and £33,000 in grants of over £400.

Exclusions

Grants are not available for books, fees, travel, living expenses or mature students.

Applications

On a form available from the correspondent, either directly by the individual, or through the individual's school, college, educational welfare agency or any third party. They are considered monthly.

Other information

Grants are also made available to three local secondary schools.

The James Marshall Foundation

£92,000 (136 grants)

Correspondent: Teresa Whittle, Trustees Office, Unit 6 17 Leyton Road, Harpenden, Hertfordshire AL5 2HY (01582 760735; email: jmfoundation@ btconnect.com)

Trustees: N. D. Clements; C. J. Grenside; D. D. Mills; J. A. Turner; J. R. Coad; T. A. Reason; Annie Atton; P. F. Kent.

CC Number: 312127

Eligibility

People under 25 who live in Harpenden and Wheathampstead and are in financial need.

Types of grants

Grants to help with the cost of education, training, apprenticeships or work-related expenses. The awards are very wide ranging in scope, and have included all of the following courses, occupations and activities: GCSE; A-levels; acting; art and design; beauty therapy; BTEC; business studies; carpentry; conservation; electrician; fashion design; hairdressing; law; GNVQ; first degrees; postgraduate studies; medicine; motor mechanics; music; nursing; painting and decorating; plumbing; teaching; theology; and travel and tourism.

Grants are given to schoolchildren, people starting work, further and higher education students, mature students and postgraduates. Grants given include those for uniforms/other school clothing, books, accommodation, equipment/instruments, fees, educational outings in the UK and study or travel abroad. No grants are made towards university tuition fees.

All applications are based on family income, unless the applicant is fully self-supporting.

Grants generally range from £50 to £2,000, but can be for up to £4,000.

Annual grant total

In 2010/11 136 grants were made totalling £92,000. The number of grants made in each category was:

- 69 primary/secondary/further education
- 33 degree courses
- 10 personal development
- 8 computer
- 7 vocational/apprentices/tools
- 7 other
- 2 medical student

Exclusions

Grants are not given for university tuition fees.

Applications

On a form available from the correspondent which can be submitted directly by the individual at any time; they are considered every six to eight weeks. Applicants must give details of their parental or other income and confirmation of the purpose for the requested grant.

The Platt Subsidiary Foundation

£11,000

Correspondent: Alan Taylor, Secretary, 57a Loom Lane, Radlett, Hertfordshire WD7 8NX (01923 855197)

Trustees: John Beardwell; Robert Fletcher; Rosamund Gray; Ron Worthy; Gill Balen; William Hogg; James Fowler; Neil Payne.

CC Number: 272591

Eligibility

People under the age of 25 who live in the parishes of St John the Baptist, Aldenham, and Christ Church, Radlett.

Types of grants

The charity aims in particular to provide: (i) 'financial assistance, outfits, clothing, tools, instruments or books to assist such people to pursue their education (including the study of music and other arts), to undertake travel in furtherance thereof and to prepare for and enter a profession, trade or calling on leaving school, university or other educational establishment.' (ii) 'facilities not normally provided by the local

education authority for recreation and social and physical training including the provision of teaching in athletics, sports and games for such persons who are receiving primary, secondary or further education.'

Annual grant total

In 2011 the foundation had an income of £8,200 and an expenditure of £12,000.

Applications

On a form available from the correspondent. Applications are considered in January, May and September.

The Ware Charities

£12,500

Correspondent: Mrs S Newman, 3 Scotts Road, Ware, Hertfordshire SG12 9JG (01920 461629; email: suedogs@hotmail.com)

Trustees: Alan Wiffen; Kathleen Sanders; Jacqueline Harrison; Terence Milner; Colin Millett; David Perman; Ann Hammond; Alan Mills; Peter Rolfe.

CC Number: 225443

Eligibility

Schoolchildren, college students and people starting work who live in the area of Ware Town Council, the Parish of Ware side and the parish of Tunbridge.

Types of grants

Grants are given to schoolchildren, college students, people with special educational needs, people starting work and overseas students, including those for uniforms/clothing, fees, study/travel abroad, books, equipment/instruments and excursions. Grants are also made to undergraduates and vocational students for uniforms/clothing.

Annual grant total

In 2010/11 the charities had assets of £1.1 million and an income of £57,000. There were 47 grants made to individuals totalling £25,000.

Applications

In writing to the correspondent at any time, to be submitted directly by the individual or a family member. Applications must include brief details of the applicant's income and savings and be supported and signed by a headteacher, doctor, nurse or social worker.

Other information

Grants are also made to local organisations.

Berkhamsted

Bourne's Educational Foundation

£1,500

Correspondent: Priscilla Watt, Flat 11, Cavalier Court, Chesham Road, Berkhamsted HP4 3AL (01442 863804; email: priscilla.watt@googlemail.com)

Trustees: Michael Bowie; David Pearce; Michael Hart; Jenny Habib; Jonathan Gordon; Philippa Seldon; Edward de la Salle; Phillippa O'Shea; Ian Reay; Anne Bull.

CC Number: 310996

Eligibility

People under the age of 25, who live in the ecclesiastical parish of Great Berkhamsted or are, or have been, in attendance at the Berkhamsted Victoria Church of England Primary School.

Types of grants

Grants to students in primary, secondary, further and higher education for books, equipment/instruments, uniforms and other school clothing, educational outings in the UK and study or travel abroad.

Annual grant total

In 2010/11 the trust had an income of £1,000 and a total expenditure of £1,700.

Exclusions

No grants for people starting work, mature students or maintenance and school fees for schoolchildren.

Applications

On a form available from the correspondent. Applications can be submitted directly by the individual or through a social worker, Citizens Advice or other welfare agency and should include information on parental income. Applications are usually considered in March and October.

Salter's Educational Foundation

£3,500

Correspondent: Priscilla Watt, Flat 11, 11 Cavalier Court, Chesham Road, Berkhamsted HP4 3AL (01442 863804; email: priscilla.watt@googlemail.com)

Trustees: Michael Bowie; Jenny Habib; Rachel Swaffield; Phil Gibbs; Edward Delasalle; Phillippa O'Shea; Ian Gent; Caroline Bailey.

CC Number: 311081

Eligibility

People under the age of 25, who live in the ancient parish of Berkhamsted St Peter.

Types of grants

Grants in the range of £100 to £200 to help: schoolchildren with the cost of school uniforms and other school clothing, books, equipment/instruments, educational outings in the UK and study or travel abroad; and further and higher education students with books, equipment/instruments and study or travel abroad and in the UK.

Annual grant total

In 2010/11 the foundation had an income of £1,700 and an expenditure of £4,100.

Exclusions

No grants for people starting work, mature students or maintenance and school fees for schoolchildren.

Applications

On a form available from the correspondent. Applications can be submitted directly by the individual or through a social worker, Citizens Advice or other welfare agency and should include information on parental income. Applications are usually considered in March and October.

Cheshunt

Robert Dewhurst's School Foundation

£5,000

Correspondent: Jill Hemplman, 215 Northbrooks, Harlow, Essex CM19 4DH (01279 425251)

Trustees: Peter Hicks; Alan Felstead; Roy Lee; Rosemary King; Christopher Robinson; John Williams; Derek Cockman; Peter Hutchinson; Pauline Orchard; Stephen Sell; Steve Latham.

CC Number: 310972

Eligibility

People who live in the ancient parish of Cheshunt, between the ages of 5 and 24. Preference is given to people who have studied for at least two years at Dewhurst St Mary's Church of England Primary School, although any applicant from the parish will be considered.

Types of grants

One-off grants to schoolchildren and further and higher education students to help with the costs of books, equipment, clothing, travel, fees and educational outings in the UK.

Annual grant total

In 2010/11 the trust had an income of £11,000 and an expenditure of £9,100.

Applications

In writing to: P H Hutchinson, 88 Church Lane, Cheshunt, Hertfordshire EH8 0EA. Applications can be submitted directly by the individual or through a school or welfare agency or another third party e.g. social services or headteacher. Applications are considered throughout the year and should state details of hardship.

Dacorum

The Dacorum Community Trust

£15,000

Correspondent: The Grants and Finance Officer, Cementaprise Centre, Paradise, Hemel Hempstead HP2 4TF (01442 231396; email: admin@dctrust.org.uk; website: www.dctrust.org.uk)

Trustees: Tony Williams; Brian Ivory; Mike Edis; John Carlton-Ashton; Gill Chapman; Jill Clarke; David Furnell; Sue Pesch; Mog Phillips; Stuart Wesley.

CC Number: 272759

Eligibility

People in need who live in the borough of Dacorum.

Types of grants

Generally one-off grants up to £500 to schoolchildren for uniforms/clothing, equipment/instruments and excursions, to college students, undergraduates and people starting work for clothing and equipment/instruments and to vocational students, mature students and those with special educational needs for uniforms/clothing, equipment/ instruments and childcare.

Annual grant total

In 2010/11 the trust had assets of £192,000 and received an income of £61,000. Grants totalling £39,000 were given to 465 individuals and families.

Exclusions

Grants are not normally given for the costs of further or mainstream education and only in exceptional circumstances for gap-year travel.

Applications

On a form available from the correspondent or to download from the website. Applications can be submitted by the individual, through a recognised referral agency (such as Social Services or Citizens Advice) or through an MP, doctor or school. Applications are considered in March, June, September and December. The trust asks for details

of family finances. A preliminary telephone call is always welcome.

Harpenden

The Harpenden Trust

£12,000

Correspondent: Dennis Andrews, The Trust Centre, 90 Southdown Road, Harpenden AL5 1PS (01582 460457; email: admin@theharpendentrust.org.uk; website: www.theharpendentrust.org.uk)

Trustees: Dennis Andrews; Roy Brimblecombe; Jan Seager; Geoff Kelly; Teresa Heritage; John Goodson; Rodger Livesey; Sue Coad.

CC Number: 1118870

Eligibility

Children in need who live in the 'AL5' postal district of Harpenden.

Types of grants

One-off grants are available for school field trips, special equipment and to help towards involvement in charitable work.

Annual grant total

In 2010/11 the trust had assets of £3.5 million and an income of £197,000. Grants were made to 845 individuals totalling £56,000 and were distributed as follows:

Grants	511	£29,000
Utilities Grants	76	£14,000
Christmas Parcels	187	£1,500
Youth Grants	71	£12,000

A further £32,000 was given to local organisations.

Applications

In writing to the correspondent, either directly by the individual or through a third party such as a social worker or Citizens Advice.

Other information

The trust has an informative website.

Hatfield

Wellfield Trust

£3,000

Correspondent: Mrs Jeanette Bayford, Birchwood Leisure Centre, Longmead, Hatfield, Hertfordshire AL10 0AN (01707 251018; email: wellfieldtrust@aol.com; website: www.wellfieldtrust.co.uk)

Trustees: Adrian Ashby; Maggie Haynes; Howard Morgan; Bernard Prestion; John Dean; Margaret White; Mick Clark; Anthony Bailey; Sheila Jones.

CC Number: 296205

Eligibility

People in need who live in the parish of Hatfield and are undertaking vocational courses, such as computer or hairdressing training. Schoolchildren in the parish may also be supported.

Types of grants

One-off grants of £100 to £500 to schoolchildren, college students, mature students, people with special educational needs and people starting work, including those towards, the cost of uniforms/clothing, fees, books, equipment/instruments, excursions and childcare.

Annual grant total

In 2010/11 grants to individuals totalled £14,000, with a further £7,400 given towards projects.

The majority of grants are given for welfare purposes.

Exclusions

Grants are not made for council tax arrears, rent or funeral costs.

Applications

On a form available from the correspondent or to download from the website, only via a third party such as social services or Citizens Advice. Most of the local appropriate third parties also have the application form. Applications are considered monthly and should be received by the first Monday of every month.

Other information

The trust has an informative website.

Hertford

The Newton Exhibition Foundation

£8,000

Correspondent: Anne Haworth, 117 Ladywood Road, Hertford, Hertford SG14 2TA (01992 550121; email: clerk@ newtonexhibitionfoundation.co.uk)

Trustees: Richard Taylor; Jill Geal; Peter Ruffles; Henry Sargent; Jacqueline Gudgin; Hugh Stewart; Sally Newton; Brenda Haddock; Jo Loveridge; Jackie Lawn; Russell Radford.

CC Number: 311021

Eligibility

Young people between the ages of 5 and 25 attending, or having attended, any school in the town of Hertford, with preference for members of the Church of England. Grants may also be awarded to young people under 25 who are, or have been, resident in the town of Hertford but who, because of special learning difficulties or other disability, are

attending or have attended schools outside the town.

Types of grants

Grants in the range of £20 to £400 are given to schoolchildren, further and higher education students and postgraduates. Grants given include those for uniforms/other school clothing, books, equipment/instruments, educational outings in the UK and study or travel overseas.

Annual grant total

About £8,000.

Applications

On a form available from the correspondent, including name(s) of schools attended, details of educational project, including cost, for which application is being made, and information as to other grants obtained or applied for. Applications should be submitted through the individual's school or welfare agency, directly by the individual, or through a social worker. They are considered in February, May, July and October, and at other times when necessary.

Hertingfordbury

Walter Wallinger Charity

£3,000

Correspondent: R France, 24 Castle Street, Hertford SG14 1HP

Trustees: Karen Murphy; Mary Jansen; Roger Morris; Rosemary Caruana; Hugh Stewart; John Cook; Shoba Edgell.

CC Number: 312137

Eligibility

People aged 6 to 24 who lived, or were educated, for at least two years in the ancient parish of Hertingfordbury, Hertford and are in financial need.

Types of grants

(i) Grants to help with books or educational outings for schoolchildren and towards books and study or travel abroad for students. (ii) Help towards the cost of education, training, apprenticeship or equipment for those starting work.

Grants to a usual maximum of £300.

Annual grant total

About £3,000.

Applications

On a form available from the correspondent to be submitted by the individual or a parent/guardian. For consideration in May and November.

Hexton

The Hexton Village Trust

£500

Correspondent: Patrick Cooper, Hexton Manor, Hitchin, Hertfordshire SG5 3JH (01582 882991)

Trustees: Patrick Cooper; Richard price; David Brittain.

CC Number: 285832

Eligibility

People who live in the parish of Hexton.

Types of grants

The trust 'supports individuals and community activities within its charitable objects'. This probably includes help with the cost of books, clothing and other essentials for schoolchildren. Grants may also be available for those at college or university.

Annual grant total

In 2010/11 the trust had an income of £900 and an expenditure of £1,000. Grants to individuals for education usually total around £500.

Applications

In writing to the correspondent.

Letchworth Garden City

The Letchworth Civic Trust

£48,000

Correspondent: Sally Jenkins, Broadway Chambers, Letchworth Garden City SG63 AD (07785 104357; email: letchworthct@gmail.com; website: letchworthct.org.uk)

Trustees: Jenny Green; Keith Emsall; Mary Deary; William Armitage; Neville Brammer; Patricia Walker; Lynda Needham; Ian Cotterill; Monica Bloxham; Sally Jenkins.

CC Number: 273336

Eligibility

Schoolchildren and students attending college or university who are in need and have lived in Letchworth Garden City for two years or more.

Types of grants

Grants are one-off and range from £50 to £500; loans are also made. Schoolchildren can receive help with the cost of educational trips and study or travel abroad where their parents cannot afford the whole amount. People starting work may be supported for equipment/ instruments. Further and higher education students, mature students and postgraduates can be helped with books and equipment/instruments.

Annual grant total

In 2010/11 the trust had assets of £583,000 and an income of £69,000. Grants totalled £48,000 distributed as follows:

- 182 university students received average grants for educational learning materials of £225 totalling £41,000
- 50 school students with disadvantaged home backgrounds received average grants of £50 totalling £2,500
- 9 other individuals received average grants for educational or medical support of £496 totalling £4,500

Applications

On a form available from the website for university students or people applying through third parties. Other applicants should apply in writing. Applications are considered in January, March, June, September, October and December and can be submitted either directly by the individual or through a third party such as a headteacher, probation officer or social worker.

Other information

Grants are also made to people who are in need, sick or requiring accommodation, and to groups and societies, but not religious or political groups.

Royston

The Leete Charity

£6,000

Correspondent: Susan Thornton-Bjork, Royston Town Council, Town Hall, Melbourn Street, Royston, Hertfordshire SG8 7DA (01763 245484; email: enquires@roystontowncouncil.gov.uk; website: www.roystontowncouncil.gov. uk)

Trustee: Royston Town Council.

CC Number: 311084

Eligibility

People under 25 who are seeking further education and live in, or attend a school in, Royston.

Types of grants

One-off and recurrent grants to help with books, equipment/instruments, fees and travel expenses for students in further or higher education. Grants range from £50 to £150.

Annual grant total

In 2010/11 the charity had an income of £3,600 and an expenditure of £6,600.

Exclusions

No grants are given for people starting work or mature students.

Applications

On a form available from the town council or its website. Applications can be submitted directly by the individual at any time.

Wormley

The Wormley Parochial Charity

£3,000

Correspondent: Mrs C Proctor, 5 Lammasmead, Broxbourne, Hertfordshire EN10 6PF

Trustees: Peter Lardi; Prof. Stanley Earles; Carol Procter; Barbara Burgess; Iris Banerjee; Christopher House.

CC Number: 218463

Eligibility

Students of any age in the parish of Wormley as it was defined before 31 March 1935.

Types of grants

Grants to schoolchildren or college students, people undertaking training or apprentices, towards essential clothing, equipment, instruments or books.

Annual grant total

About £6,000

Exclusions

The trust does not give loans.

Applications

In writing to the charity either directly by the individual or through a social worker, Citizens Advice, welfare agency or a third party such as a friend who is aware of the situation. Applications are considered in April and October.

Kent

The Reverend Tatton Brockman's Charity

£1,000

Correspondent: Janet Salt, Greatfield House, Ivychurch Road, Brenzett, Romney March, Kent TN29 0EE (01797 344364)

Trustees: Keith Fazzani; Hilary Jones; David Body; Jean Thompson; Colin Johnson.

CC Number: 307681

Eligibility

People under the age of 25 who are in full-time education and live in the ancient parishes of Brenzett, Cheriton, and Newington-next-Hythe in the county of Kent.

Types of grants

One-off grants to help with the cost of fees, study or travel abroad, books, equipment and instruments for schoolchildren, students in further/ higher education, vocational students and people with special educational needs. Grants are in the range of £100 to £500.

Annual grant total

In 2010/11 the charity had an income of £20,000 and a total expenditure of £23,000

Applications

In writing to the correspondent, directly by the individual. Applications are considered in May and November.

Other information

The charity's main financial concern is its support of four Church of England primary schools in the area of benefit. However, the correspondent states: 'We would very much like to make a greater number of grants to individuals but efforts to encourage more applications have, so far, met with very limited success.' Furthermore, 'it should be stated that in allocating grants the trustees shall have regard to the principles and doctrines of the Church of England'.

The John Collings Educational Trust

£17,000

Correspondent: Anthony Herman, 11 Church Road, Tunbridge Wells, Kent TN1 1JA (01892 526344)

Trustees: Alexander Helm; Anthony Herman; Thomas Simpson.

CC Number: 287474

Eligibility

Children up to the age of 14 who are in need.

Types of grants

Help with the cost of books, fees and other essentials for schoolchildren.

Annual grant total

In 2010/11 the trust had an income of £28,000 and made grants totalling £61,000, although grants to individuals usually only total around £17,000.

Exclusions

No grants are available for those at college or university.

Applications

In writing to the correspondent, however, the trust states that income is accounted for and new applicants are unlikely to benefit.

The Mike Collingwood Memorial Fund

£2,500

Correspondent: Peter Green, Trustee, Acorn House, 12 The Platt, Sutton Valence, Maidstone, Kent ME17 3BQ (01622 843230)

Trustees: Peter Green; Clifford Stossel; Peter Sutton; Norman McGill; Rodney Davis.

CC Number: 288806

Eligibility

Young people who live within a 20-mile radius of 'The Who'd a Thought It' pub in Grafty Green, Kent.

Types of grants

Grants or loans according to need to provide further experience in, or facilities for, education or vocational training and for similar purposes. The fund aims to give learning opportunities which may not be essential for a course, but are a good learning experience. For example, supporting a trip for a doctor who wants to travel abroad to carry out research. Applications for assistance with Outward Bound or similar courses can also be considered.

Annual grant total

In 2010/11 the trust had an income of £600 and an expenditure of £3,200.

Applications

In writing to the correspondent including a brief CV, details of the course or activity the candidate wishes to attend and an sae. Applications must be submitted before 31 December each year for consideration in the following month.

Wykeham Stanley Lord Cornwallis Memorial Fund

£3,200

Correspondent: R D Bushrod, Honorary Secretary, Dundurn House, St Fillans, Crieff PH6 2NH (email: secretary@cornwallisfunds.org.uk; website: www.cornwallisfunds.org.uk)

Trustees: Fiennes Cornwallis; J. Pemberton; Chris Cowdrey; Allan

Willett; Matthew Fleming; Charles Philipson; Charlotte Cornwallis; Michael Firmin.

CC Number: 291426

Eligibility

Any person who lives in Kent who is attending or intending to attend a course of study at a school, college or university to pursue their sporting ambitions, or serving or intending to serve an apprenticeship relating to agriculture or horticulture.

Types of grants

One-off grants or recurring grants in the range of £100 to £500. Grants are given to schoolchildren, further and higher education students, mature students and postgraduates for fees.

Annual grant total

In 2009/10 the fund had an income of £4,100 and an expenditure of £7,500, of which around half is given in grants to individuals.

Applications

On a form available from the correspondent, on receipt of an sae. Applications can be submitted either directly by the individual, or via the individual's school or college or another third party. Sporting applications should be submitted via Kent County Playing Fields Association. Applications are considered in March and should be submitted four weeks in advance.

Other information

Grants are also made to organisations. The fund has a sister charity (CC no. 220391) that gives welfare grants to individuals.

Headley-Pitt Charitable Trust

£10,500

Correspondent: Thelma Pitt, Old Mill Cottage, Ulley Road, Kennington, Ashford, Kent TN24 9HX (01233 626189; email: thelma.pitt@headley.co.uk)

Trustees: H. C. Pitt; J. R. Pitt; R. W. Pitt; Mrs S. D. Pitt.

CC Number: 252023

Eligibility

Individuals in need who live in Kent, with a preference for those residing in Ashford.

Types of grants

One-off grants usually in the range of £100 and £300. Recent grants have been given to schoolchildren, college students, undergraduates, vocational students, mature students, people with special educational needs, people starting work

and overseas students, for various educational purposes.

Annual grant total

In 2010/11 the trust had assets of £2.5 million and an income of £64,000. Grants made to individuals totalled £21,000.

Applications

In writing to the correspondent, either directly by the individual or through a third party.

Other information

Grants are also made to organisations and to individuals for welfare purposes.

The Hothfield Educational Foundation

£8,000

Correspondent: Pater Patten, The Paddocks, Hothfield, Ashford TN26 1EN (01233 620880)

Trustees: Marianne Highwood; Penny Sutcliffe; Shirley Whittington; Peter Patten; Peter Howard; Tessa Flood.

CC Number: 307670

Eligibility

People under the age of 25 who live in, or attended the primary school at, the parish of Hothfield and the part of the parish of Westwell which forms part of, or nearly adjoins, Hothwell Heath. People over 25 may be supported if there are surplus funds.

Types of grants

One-off and recurrent grants to help with the cost of books, school clothing and other essentials for schoolchildren; and books, fees, living expenses and study or travel abroad for those at college or university. Grants have been given for music and other university courses. People starting work may receive grants towards books, equipment, instruments and clothing.

Annual grant total

In 2010 the foundation had an income of £6,800 and an expenditure of £8,800.

Applications

In writing to the correspondent. Applications are considered on an ongoing basis.

The Hugh and Montague Leney (Travelling) Awards Trust

£5,000

Correspondent: Lyn Edwards, Awards Group, Education and Libraries, Bishops

Terrace, Bishops Way, Maidstone, Kent ME14 1AF (01622 605111; email: leneytrust@hotmail.co.uk)

Trustees: Nick Jordan; Catherine James; Teresa Buckley; Stephen Manion.

CC Number: 307950

Eligibility

Children and young people aged 16 to 19 who attend, or have attended within the previous 12 months, any county, voluntary or independent school in Kent (as constituted on 31 March 1965).

Types of grants

Bursaries or maintenance allowances to enable travel to all parts of the world for educational and humanitarian purposes. Grants are for amounts of up to £2,500.

The purpose is to extend the knowledge of young people in subjects related to their future occupations by travel or expeditions arranged by recognised bodies in the UK or abroad, or to broaden their general knowledge and confidence before they go on to higher education or employment.

Annual grant total

About £5,000.

Applications

On a form available from the correspondent. Applications should be submitted by a headteacher, or come through an educational welfare agency. The closing date is 31 January each year.

The Rebecca McNie Foundation

£4,000

Correspondent: Wilkins Kennedy, Stourside Place, Station Road, Ashford TN23 1PP

Trustees: Melanie McNie; Symon James McNie; Carol Pack.

CC Number: 1108739

Eligibility

Children and young people in Kent who are involved in the performing arts.

Types of grants

Grants given according to need.

Annual grant total

In 2010/11 the foundation had an income of £5,800 and an expenditure of £4,600.

Applications

In writing to the correspondent.

The William Strong Foundation

£9,000

Correspondent: Brian Barkley, 5 Blatchington Road, Tunbridge Wells TN2 5EG (01892 525047)

Trustees: David Power; Barbara Cobbold; John Brokker; Nigel Blackburn; Peter Burgess; Joseph Simmons; Brian Barkley; David Aikman.

CC Number: 307944

Eligibility

People under the age of 25 who live in the former borough of Tunbridge Wells, the former urban and rural districts of Tonbridge, and the former urban district of Southborough. Preference is given to beneficiaries who intend to take up a nautical career or occupation.

Types of grants

Mainly one-off grants in the range of £60 to £250 are given to: (i) schoolchildren for uniforms/other school clothing, books and equipment/instruments; (ii) people starting work for books, clothing and equipment/instruments; and (iii) further and higher education students for books, equipment/instruments and maintenance/living expenses.

Annual grant total

In 2010/11 the foundation had both an income and total expenditure of £9,000.

Exclusions

No grants are given for gap year activities.

Applications

Applications can be submitted in writing directly by the individual or a parent, including details of the applicant's (and parents') total income and annual outgoings. Applications are considered in June and July and should be submitted between January and March.

Tomorrow's Child Trust

£1,000

Correspondent: Katrina Ashton, Trustee, 53 Park Road, Sittingbourne ME10 1DY (01795 558795)

Trustees: Gillian Foreman; Karen Davies; Katrina Ashton; Lyn Gallagher; Michelle Winter; Lou Gallagher.

CC Number: 802222

Eligibility

Women who are undertaking midwifery courses, which they will use in their work to benefit people living in the Medway and Swale districts.

Types of grants

One-off grants according to need.

Annual grant total

In 2010/11 the trust had an income of £9,700 and an expenditure of £3,800.

Applications

This trust has previously stated that due to a very low income, grants were not being issued.

The Yalding Educational Foundation

£5,000

Correspondent: Kim Keeler, Hamilton, Vicarage Road, Yalding, Maidstone, Kent ME18 6DR (01622 817919)

Trustees: Clare Hudson; Andrew Thurston; Paul Filmer; Michael Stewart; Hilary Reeve; Paulina Stockell.

CC Number: 307646

Eligibility

Former pupils of schools in Yalding, Laddingfield and Courier Street who attended for at least two years.

Types of grants

One-off grants towards anything necessary for study at college or university. Grants are also given to local schools.

Annual grant total

In 2008/09 the foundation had an income of £7,100 and an expenditure of £6,700.

Applications

In writing to the correspondent giving details of the school attended in the parish, the college or university to be attended, course to be taken and length of the course. Applications should be received by 31 October for a December meeting.

Other information

The foundation also sponsors a spoken English competition in local primary schools.

Benenden

The Gibbon and Buckland Charity

£5,000

Correspondent: David Harmsworth, Trustee, Hemsted Oaks, Cranbrook Road, Benenden, Cranbrook TN17 4ES (01580 240683)

Trustees: Simon Brown; Aurea Gregory; David Harmsworth; Mary Kellett; Charles Hill; Anthony Fullwood.

CC Number: 307682

Eligibility

People under 25 who have lived in Benenden for three years.

Types of grants

Grants are given to students entering further and higher education and people starting work and apprentices.

Annual grant total

In 2011 the trust had an income of £25,000 and an expenditure of £13,000.

Applications

In writing to the correspondent in September. The charity is advertised locally.

Other information

The trust also supports a local primary school, and provides bibles to pupils.

Borden

The William Barrow's Charity

£18,000

Correspondent: Stuart Mair, George Webb Finn, 43 Park Road, Sittingbourne, Kent ME10 1DY (01795 470556; email: stuart@georgewebbfinn. com)

Trustees: Denis Jarrett; Donald Jordan; Edmund Doubleday; Peter Mair; Jeremy Jefferiss; Pauline Cole; Janet Scott; John Lewis; Stephen Batt; Christine Ford.

CC Number: 307574

Eligibility

People under 25 who live in the ancient ecclesiastical parish of Borden or have lived in the parish and now live nearby.

Types of grants

One-off grants and twice-yearly allowances may be given to schoolchildren for uniforms/clothing, study/travel overseas, books, equipment/ instruments and excursions, to college students and undergraduates for study/ travel overseas, books, equipment/ instruments and maintenance/living expenses, to vocational students for books, students with special educational needs for equipment/instruments and people starting work for clothing, books and equipment. Grants typically range from £350 to £500.

Annual grant total

In 2011 the trust had assets of £5.9 million, an income of £190,000 and gave £18,000 in educational grants to individuals.

Applications

On a form available from the correspondent. Applications are considered in January, April, July and October.

Canterbury

The Canterbury United Municipal Charities

£3,000

Correspondent: Aaron Spencer, Furley Page, 39–40 St Margaret's Street, Canterbury, Kent CT1 2TX (01227 863140; email: aas@furleypage.co.uk)

Trustees: Marjorie Lyle; Ann Burgess; Mercia Powell; Canon Michael Bunce; Clive Bowley; Catherine Hellman; Joan Pritchard; Gina Langford-Allen; Gill Prett; Revd Iain Taylor; Fred Powell; Susan Dawkins.

CC Number: 210992

Eligibility

People in need who have lived within the boundaries of what was the old city of Canterbury for at least two years.

Types of grants

Small one-off and recurrent grants are made to further and higher education students for books and equipment/ instruments.

Annual grant total

In 2010 the charities had an income of £8,500 and a total expenditure of £6,000. Approximately £3,000 was given towards educational purposes.

Applications

In writing to the correspondent through the individual's school/college/ educational welfare agency or directly by the individual. Applications are considered on an ongoing basis and should include a brief statement of circumstances and proof of residence in the area.

Other information

Grants are also given to individuals for welfare purposes and to organisations with similar objects.

Streynsham's Charity

£2,600

Correspondent: The Clerk to the Trustees, PO Box 970, Canterbury, Kent CT1 9DJ (0845 094 4769)

Trustees: Alicia Pentin; Alasdair Hogarth; David Bentley; James Lees; Philippa Trewby; William Mearns; Anne Ovenden; Jacqui Webber. Mark Ball; Gavin Kennett; Jeanie Armstrong; Leonore Edwards.

CC Number: 214436

Eligibility

Young people who live or attend school in the ancient parish of St Dunstan's, Canterbury, and are under the age of 21.

Types of grants

One-off grants up to a maximum of about £300. Help with the cost of books, clothing, educational outings, maintenance and other essentials can be given to schoolchildren. Grants are also available for those at college or university, (including mature students), for books, fees, travel and living expenses. People starting work can receive help towards books, equipment/ instruments, clothing and travel.

Annual grant total

In 2011 grants for education totalled £2,600.

Applications

In writing to the correspondent. Applications can be made directly by the individual, through the individual's school/college/educational welfare agency or through other third party on behalf of the individual. They are usually considered in March and October but can be made at any time and should include an sae and telephone number if applicable.

Dover

The Casselden Trust

£1,000

Correspondent: Leslie Alton, 26 The Shrubbery, Walmer, Deal, Kent CT14 7PZ (01304 375499)

Trustees: John Morgan; Martin Husk.

CC Number: 281970

Eligibility

People in need who live in the Dover Town Council area.

Types of grants

One-off and recurrent grants, up to a maximum of £250.

Annual grant total

Grants usually total around £2,000 each year.

Applications

In writing to the correspondent.

Fordwich

The Fordwich United Charities

£5,000

Correspondent: Aaron Spencer, Furley Page Solicitors, 39 St Margaret's Street,

Canterbury CT1 2TX (01227 863140; fax: 01227 863220)

Trustees: Roger Green; Peter Cornish; David Keegan; June Hardcastle; Elizabeth Lewis; Sylvia McNally.

CC Number: 208258

Eligibility

People who live in the parish of Fordwich, aged 16 to 25.

Types of grants

One-off grants of £150 are given towards books for college students.

Annual grant total

In 2010 the charity had an income of £19,000 and an expenditure of £11,000.

Applications

In writing to: M R Clayton, Ladywell House, Fordwich, Canterbury CT2 0DL. The deadline for applications is 1 September and a decision will be made within a month.

Godmersham

Godmersham Relief in Need Charity

£3,000

Correspondent: David T Swan, Feleberge, Canterbury Road, Bilting, Ashford, Kent TN25 4HE (01233 812125)

Trustees: Christine Luckhurst; Gregory Ellis; Patricia Fletcher; Revd Ian Campbell; David Jones.

CC Number: 206278

Eligibility

Students who live in the ancient parish of Godmersham in Kent.

Types of grants

One-off and recurrent grants to help with the costs of equipment, instruments, books, study or travel overseas and extra-curricular activities, such as music lessons and sports coaching.

Annual grant total

In 2010 the charity had both an income and total expenditure of £6,000. Grants are given for both educational and relief-in-need purposes.

Applications

In writing to the correspondent, either directly by the individual or through a third party.

Hawkhurst

Dunk's and Springett's Educational Foundation

£5,000

Correspondent: Mrs B Van Winkelen, Rydale Water, Coptall Avenue, Hawkhurst, Cranbrook TN18 4LR (01580 754463)

Trustees: Anne Wheelhouse; Brian Piper; C. R. Dewing; Liz Weatherly; Jon Addyman; Samantha Cornish; Nigel Radford; Valerie Martin.

CC Number: 307664

Eligibility

People under 25 who live in the ancient parish of Hawkhurst.

Types of grants

One-off and recurrent grants to students on any full-time educational course.

Annual grant total

In 2010 the trust had an income of £6,600 and a total expenditure of £5,100. Grants usually total around £5,000.

Applications

In writing to the correspondent after the grants are advertised in a local newspaper.

Hayes

Hayes (Kent) Trust

£5,200

Correspondent: Richard Marlin, 43 Eastry Avenue, Hayes, Bromley, Kent BR2 7PE (020 8462 1363; email: hayes.kent.trust@btinternet.com)

Trustees: Revd David Graham; Carol Truelove; Alison Naish; Susan Rogers; Brian Lightoller; Richard Marlin.

CC Number: 221098

Eligibility

Students who live in the parish of Hayes and can demonstrate that they are in need.

Types of grants

One-off grants, generally in the region of £75 to £1,500, are given according to need.

Annual grant total

In 2010/11 the trust had assets of £890,000 and an income of £44,000. Grants totalling £5,200 were given to individuals for educational needs.

Applications

In writing to the correspondent. Applications should include the full name of the applicant, postal address in Hayes (Kent), telephone number and date of birth. Applications can be made either directly by the individual, or through a third party such as the individual's college, school or educational welfare agency.

Other information

The trust also makes grants to organisations and to individuals for welfare purposes.

Hythe

Anne Peirson Charitable Trust

£5,000

Correspondent: Mrs Ina Tomkinson, Trustee/Secretary, Tyrol House, Cannongate Road, Hythe, Kent CT21 5PX (01303 260779)

Trustees: Ina Tomkinson; Kenneth Crowe; Revd Tony Windross; Richard Carroll; Capt. Karen Layton.

CC Number: 800093

Eligibility

People who live in the parish of Hythe who are at any level of their education, in any subject, who are in need.

Types of grants

One-off grants ranging between £50 and £600 given mainly to early years children and schoolchildren for books, educational outings, fees and equipment.

Annual grant total

In 2010 the trust had an income of £11,300 and a total expenditure of £10,300.

Exclusions

No grants are made where statutory support is available.

Applications

In writing to the correspondent via either Citizens Advice, a social worker, health visitor, school headteacher or other third party. Grants are considered at quarterly meetings of the trustees, but emergency applications can be considered in the interim.

Other information

Grants are also made to organisations.

Isle of Thanet

The Gibbons Family Trust

See entry on page 261

Medway

Arthur Ingram Trust

£104,000 (82 grants)

Correspondent: Margaret Taylor, Charities/Treasury Management Officer, Business Support Department, Finance Support (level 2), Gun Wharf, Dock Road, Chatham, Kent ME4 4TR (01634 732876; fax: 01634 732835; email: margaret.taylor@medway.gov.uk)

Trustees: Edward Baker; Julia Bell; Simon Decker; Mick Hayward; Fiona Miller.

CC Number: 212868

Eligibility

People aged between 14 and 21 and in full time education who are in need and live in the Medway council area.

Types of grants

Grants are made from three funds:
(i) The general grant scheme is for students aged between 14 and 16 whose parents are on a low income and need assistance with school uniform, books and towards school trips which are identified as being linked to exam-related studies. The maximum general grant is £300.

(ii) The continuing education scheme is for students aged between 16 and 18 and in financial need but who are continuing at school or in further education establishments/training. Grants are dependent on the applicant having attendance of at least 90% unless there are exceptional reasons for absence, such as long-term illness (proof is required). The maximum continuing education grant is £400. Students aged 19 to 21 can also be considered.

(iii) Advanced payments in kind can be made to schools/colleges for students whose courses have been recognised as requiring specialist equipment. The maximum grant is £150.

Independent students can be supported if parental assistance is not possible or appropriate and the student is independent through no fault of their own.

Bursary grants are also given to sixth form students. These students are nominated by the school and applications cannot be requested directly from the trust.

Annual grant total

In 2010/11 the trust had assets of £2 million and an income of £83,000. Grants were made totalling £104,000 in the following categories:
- Bursary grants: £83,000 in twenty eight grants
- Continuing education: £12,000 in thirty one grants
- School field trips: £6,700 in nine grants
- Uniforms: £1,800 in twelve grants
- School equipment/books: £400 in two grants

Applications

On a form available from the correspondent. Applications can be made by the individual, through a third party such as a teacher or through a school, college, or educational welfare agency. Continuing education applications should be submitted between July and March; bursaries can be applied for from April to June. General grants can be submitted at any time and are considered on an ongoing basis. Each application is means tested and evidence of income is required with every application.

Other information

The trust also gives emergency grants to school voluntary funds.

New Romney

Southland's Educational Charity

£3,000

Correspondent: U Whiting, Clerk, c/o Town Hall, High Street, New Romney, Kent TN28 8BT (01797 362348)

Trustees: Anthony Smart; Edward Holton; Edward Smith; Gladys Spink; Spencer Buck; Valerie Tully; P. Butchers; Mrs Newton; Sally Maycock; J. Field.

CC Number: 307783

Eligibility

People who live in the parish of New Romney under the age of 25.

Types of grants

Grants are given towards the cost of books, equipment, instruments, fees, maintenance/living expenses, educational outings in the UK and study or travel overseas for students in further and higher education. Grants are in the range of £100 to £500.

Annual grant total

About £3,000 to individuals.

Applications

On a form available from the correspondent. Applications are considered in October.

Rochester

Cliffe at Hoo Parochial Charity

£2,300

Correspondent: Paul Kingman, Clerk, 52 Reed Street, Cliffe, Rochester, Kent ME3 7UL (01634 220422; email: paul.kingman@btopenworld.com)

Trustees: Marie Vyse; Diane Forman; Revd Edward Wright; Christopher Fribbins; Kenneth Kentell; Linda Jones; Yvonne Kingman; Doreen Ellis; Lynne Bush.

CC Number: 220855

Eligibility

People in need who live in the ancient parish of Cliffe-at-Hoo.

Types of grants

One-off grants according to need for any educational purpose.

Annual grant total

In 2010/11 the charity had an income of £3,600 and a total expenditure of £4,600. Around £2,300 worth of grants were given for educational purposes.

Applications

In writing to the correspondent, to be submitted either directly by the individual or a family member, or through a third party such as a social worker or teacher.

Richard Watts and The City of Rochester Almshouse Charities

£19,000

Correspondent: Jane Rose, Clerk, Watts Almhouses, Maidstone Road, Rochester, Kent ME1 1SE (01634 842194; email: admin@richardwatts.org.uk; website: www.richardwatts.org.uk)

Trustees: Roger Hill; Juliet Wright; David Bradley; Donald Troup; Ian Robinson; Michael Bailey; Daphne MacDonald; Eunice Tober; Jean Lingham; Ronald Kettle; Roger Hawkes; Hilary Moore; Terence Burton; Anthony Clayton; Brian Cox; Hilary Harwood.

CC Number: 212828

Eligibility

People who are in need and live in the city of Rochester.

Types of grants

One-off grants towards school uniforms, books, tours, musical equipment and other 'indirect' support.

Annual grant total

In 2011 the charity had assets of £18 million and an income of £1.7 million. Educational grants totalled £19,000.

Applications

In writing to the correspondent, directly by the individual or a family member. Applications can be submitted at any time and are considered on a monthly basis.

Other information

Grants are also given to organisations which benefit the local community and the charity also runs an almshouse.

Sandgate

The James Morris Educational Foundation

£2,000

Correspondent: Maria Wells, Trustee, 4 Bybrook Field, Sandgate, Folkestone, Kent CT20 3BQ (01303 248092; email: robjhudson@ntlworld.com)

Trustees: Rob Hudson; Annette Sutcliffe; Ian Adams; Maria Wells; Vivienne Rumbold; Margaret Butler; Jo Robertson; Margaret Hudson.

CC Number: 307559

Eligibility

Young people who live within the boundaries of Sandgate on a permanent basis.

Types of grants

Grants of about £75 to £275 to help further and higher education students with fees/living expenses, books, equipment/instruments and maintenance/living expenses; towards the cost of school uniform, books and equipment/instruments for schoolchildren; and towards books and fees for people starting work. Mature students can receive help towards books, fees and maintenance/living expenses and vocational students can receive help towards fees. Grants can be one-off or recurrent.

Annual grant total

About £2,000.

Applications

In writing to the correspondent, either directly by the individual or through their school, college or educational welfare agency. Applications should include particulars of the university or college that the applicant is attending or planning to attend, together with details of the course of study and ultimate ambitions. Applications should be submitted by 15 September for consideration in October.

314

Sevenoaks

The Kate Drummond Trust

£1,000

Correspondent: David Batchelor, The Beeches, Packhorse Road, Sevenoaks, Kent TN13 2QP (01732 451584)

Trustees: David Batchelor; Revd Angus MacLeay; Carlton Andrews; Janet Batchelor.

CC Number: 246830

Eligibility

Young people, especially girls, living in Sevenoaks.

Types of grants

One-off grants are given towards education, recreation or training.

Annual grant total

Grants tend to total around £2,000 each year.

Applications

In writing to the correspondent, with an sae if a reply is required.

Wilmington

The Wilmington Parochial Charity

£1,500

Correspondent: Derek Maidment, 23 The Close, Dartford DA2 7ES (01322 224829)

Trustees: Ann Allen; Chris Settle; Michael Iveson; Richard Arding; Shelagh Longstaff; Tom Maddison; Jenny Rickwood.

CC Number: 1011708

Eligibility

People in need, living in the parish of Wilmington, who are receiving a statutory means-tested benefit, such as Income Support, Housing Benefit or help towards their council tax.

Types of grants

One-off grants according to need. Grants are awarded to: (i) schoolchildren for books and educational outings but not clothing, uniforms or fees; (ii) students in further/higher education for books, fees, living expenses and study and travel abroad, but not to foreign students or for student exchange; and (iii) mature students for books and travel but not fees or childcare.

Annual grant total

Educational grants total about £1,500 each year.

Applications

Applications should be submitted by the individual, or through a social worker, Citizens Advice or other welfare agency. The trustees meet in February and November. Urgent applications can be considered between meetings in exceptional circumstances.

Other information

Grants are also given to local schools at Christmas and to individuals for welfare.

Norfolk

Anguish's Educational Foundation

£322,000 (2,655 grants)

Correspondent: David Walker, Clerk to the Trustees, 1 Woolgate Court, St Benedicts Street, Norwich NR2 4AP (01603 621023; email: david.walker@ norwichcharitabletrusts.org.uk)

Trustees: David Fulham; Brenda Ferris; Geoffrey Loades; Philip Blanchflower; Pam Scutter; Ian Brooksby; Jeremy Hooke; Roy Blower; Jeanne Southgate.

CC Number: 311288

Eligibility

Permanent residents of Norwich and the parishes of Costessey, Hellesdon, Catton, Sprowston, Thorpe St Andrews and Corpusty, aged under 25. Applicants must be on a low income. Preference is given to individuals who live in the city of Norwich and have lost either one or both parents.

Types of grants

The main beneficiaries are pupils of state schools. A small proportion of grants are made to college or university students under the age of 25, mostly for books and equipment, but also for small maintenance grants. A few grants are made each year for educational travel including school trips and occasional overseas visits, for example, attending the world scout jamboree. Grants are made for the costs of music, other arts or sports studies. The trustees believe, however, that the most urgent need of parents is help with the cost of school clothing and the majority of grants are made for this purpose.

Annual grant total

In 2010/11 the foundation had net assets of £17.7 million and an income of £646,000. Educational grants totalled £322,000, which were broken down as follows:

- School clothing £162,000 (51%)
- School trips £87,000 (27%)
- University student support £42,000 (13%)

- Further education and school fees £26,000 (8%)
- Dyslexia and scotopic therapy and child minding £2,000 (1%)
- Musical training £1,400
- Books and equipment £1,200

Exclusions

Postgraduates are not supported.

Applications

In writing to the correspondent directly by the individual. Applications are considered at five meetings held throughout the year. Parents or individuals will generally be required to attend the office for a short interview.

Other information

£50,000 was also given in grants to organisations.

The Brancaster Educational and Almshouse Charity

£2,000

Correspondent: Dorothy Wooster, Strebla, Mill Road, Brancaster, Norfolk PE31 8AW (01485 210645; email: rodolf@btinternet.com)

Trustees: Alan Townshend; James Petchey; Mervyn Nudds; Eileen Muntzer; Colin Mitchell; Stephen Bocking.

CC Number: 311128

Eligibility

People living in the ancient parishes of Brancaster, Titchwell, Thornham, and Burnham Deepdale only.

Types of grants

Grants to schoolchildren for excursions and to undergraduates for books.

Annual grant total

In 2010 the charity had an income of £10,000 and an expenditure of £4,200.

Applications

In writing to the correspondent.

Other information

Grants are also given to Brancaster School towards the cost of equipment.

The Norfolk (le Strange) Fund and Provincial Charities

£3,400

Correspondent: Michael Spalding, Secretary, 23 Woodfield Close, Shadingfield, Beccles, Suffolk NR34 8PD (01502 575722; email: mike@thespaldings50.fsnet.co.uk)

Trustees: John Rushmer; Stephen Allen; Roy Skinner; Anthony Bothway; Richard

Thurston; Michael Hedges; Mike Gooderson; Russell Carter; Charles Hall; Philip Hunt; Michael Spalding.

CC Number: 209020

Eligibility

Dependents of Freemasons of the Province of Norfolk.

Types of grants

Help with the cost of books, clothing and other essentials for schoolchildren. Grants may also be available for those at college or university. The trust will ensure that all eligible people will be supported throughout their education.

Annual grant total

In 2010 the fund had an income of £32,000 and made grants to individuals for welfare and educational purposes totalled £6,800.

Applications

In writing to the correspondent. Applications are considered every two months. The trust does not respond to unsuccessful applications made outside of its area of interest and prefers applicants to enquire and apply by post or email, rather than by phone.

The Norwich French Church Charity

£10,000

Correspondent: Samantha Loombe, Hansells Solicitors, 13–14 The Close, Norwich NR1 4DS (01603 275814; email: samanthaloombe@hansells.co.uk)

Trustees: Charles Martineau; Graham Smith; David White; Antony Jarrold; Peter Duval; Lucy McCarraher; Patrick Harris.

CC Number: 212897

Eligibility

Children and young people primarily of French Protestant descent who are under the age of 25 and live in Norwich. Applicants from Norfolk can also be considered.

Types of grants

Grants, ranging from £250 to £500, for schoolchildren and college students for uniforms/other school clothing, books, equipment/instruments, maintenance/living expenses, childcare, educational outings in the UK, study or travel abroad, etc. A preference is given to applicants with a Huguenot descent.

Annual grant total

In 2010 the charity had both an income and expenditure of £12,500.

Applications

On a form available from the correspondent which can be submitted directly by the individual or through the

individual's college or educational welfare agency, or another third party, at any time.

The Sir Philip Reckitt Educational Trust Fund

See entry on page 19

Red House Youth Projects Trust

See entry on page 12

The Charity of Joanna Scott and Others

£41,000

Correspondent: G H Smith, Clerk, Hansells, 13–14 The Close, Norwich NR1 4DS (01603 615731)

Trustees: R. S. Rathbone; Iris Voegeli; Cym Cant; Evelyn Collishaw; Mary Rae; Richard Snowden.

CC Number: 311253

Eligibility

People under the age of 25 who are being educated or live within five miles of Norwich City Hall. Preference is given to families in financial need.

Types of grants

Grants are given towards the costs of uniforms/other school clothing, books, equipment/instruments, fees, maintenance/living expenses, childcare, educational outings in the UK, study or travel abroad and student exchanges. Grants range between £15 and £2,000. The trust also offers interest-free loans.

Annual grant total

In 2010/11 the foundation had assets of £1.9 million, an income of £65,000 and made grants to individuals totalling £41,000.

Applications

On a form available from the correspondent. Applications are usually considered in March, July, September and November, but smaller applications are considered daily. Supply a copy of the appropriate circular from the school or college to assist the trustees.

Other information

Grants are also given to organisations and schools.

The Shelroy Trust

£4,300 (11 grants)

Correspondent: Roger Wiltshire, 4 Brandon Court, Brundall, Norwich NR13 5NW (01603 715605)

CC Number: 327776

Eligibility

Youth of East Norfolk and Norwich for voluntary services overseas. Projects must have a Christian and/or humanitarian objective.

Types of grants

One-off grants, ranging from £200 to £300.

Annual grant total

In 2010/11 the trust had both an income and total expenditure of £32,000. Grants for young people totalled around £4,300.

Applications

In writing to the correspondent at any time. Individuals applying for grants must provide full information and two referees are required. Applications can be made directly by the individual or through a social worker, Citizens Advice or other third party. They are considered at the trustees' quarterly meetings in March, June, September and December. The trust is not able to reply to unsuccessful applicants unless an sae is provided.

Other information

Grants are also made to organisations.

West Norfolk and King's Lynn Girls' School Trust

£20,000

Correspondent: Miriam Aldous, Clerk to the Trustees, The Goodshed, Station Road, Little Dunham, Kings Lynn PE32 2DJ (01760 720617)

CC Number: 311264

Eligibility

Girls and young women over the age of 11 who are at a secondary school or in their first years after leaving school or further education, who live in the borough of King's Lynn and West Norfolk and the parishes of Beeston with Bittering, Beetley, Brisley, Great Dunham, Gressenhall, Horningtoft, Kempstone, Langham, Lexham, Litcham, Little Dunham, Mileham, Narborough, Rougham, Stanfield, Tittleshall, Weasenham All Saints, Weasenham St Peter, Wellingham, Wendling and Whissonsett.

Types of grants

One-off and recurrent grants of between £100 and £1,000 are given to (i) schoolchildren for help with school uniforms, other school clothing, books equipment/instruments and educational outings in the UK and overseas, but not for maintenance or fees; (ii) students in further/higher education for help with books, fees, equipment, instruments, living expenses, study or travel overseas and student exchange but not for foreign students; and (iii) mature students for books, travel, fees, living expenses and childcare. Grants are also available for music, sports and creative arts education. The trustees hope the trust can enable a girl to undertake some course or venture of an educational nature that she would otherwise not have been able to do.

Annual grant total

About £20,000 to individuals.

Applications

On a form available from the correspondent. Applications should include parental income, details of course or educational need, two references including one from a teacher or lecturer, and a supporting letter from the applicant. They are considered in January, April and September.

Other information

This trust also gives grants to secondary schools within the area.

Burnham Market
The Harold Moorhouse Charity

£7,500

Correspondent: Christine Harrison, 30 Winmer Avenue, Winterton-on-Sea, Great Yarmouth, Norfolk NR29 4BA (01493 393975; email: haroldmoorhousecharity@yahoo.co.uk)

CC Number: 287278

Eligibility

Individuals in need who live in Burnham Market in Norfolk only.

Types of grants

One-off grants are made ranging from £50 to £200 for education equipment and school educational trips.

Annual grant total

About £15,000 for educational and welfare purposes.

Applications

In writing to the correspondent. Applications should be submitted directly by the individual in any month.

Burnham Thorpe
Richard Bunting's Educational Foundation

£3,500

Correspondent: Anthony Taylor, Grints Cottage, Walsingham Road, Burnham Thorpe, King's Lynn PE31 8HN (01328 738902)

CC Number: 311175

Eligibility

People in need under the age of 25 who live in the parish of Burnham Thorpe.

Types of grants

Grants of up to £400 are made to help schoolchildren with the cost of uniforms, books, equipment/instruments, fees, educational outings in the UK, study or travel abroad and student exchanges. Grants are also made to help towards clothing costs for people starting work, further and higher education students and mature students.

Annual grant total

In 2010/11 the foundation had an income of £4,100 and an expenditure of £3,500.

Applications

In writing to the correspondent either directly by the individual (if over 18) or by a parent/guardian. Applications are considered in February and September, but emergencies can be dealt with on an ongoing basis.

Buxton with Lammas
Picto Buxton Charity

£1,000

Correspondent: Stephen Pipe, Clerk, The Beeches, Coltishall Road, Buxton, Norwich NR10 5JD (01603 279771)

CC Number: 208896

Eligibility

People in need who live in the parish of Buxton with Lamas.

Types of grants

One-off grants of £100 to £200 to schoolchildren for uniforms/clothing, books and excursions and to college students, undergraduates, vocational students, mature students and people starting work towards books.

Annual grant total

In 2010/11 the trust made charitable donations totalling £22,000. Grants totalling £2,000 were given to individuals.

Applications

In writing to the correspondent directly by the individual or a family member, or through a third party such as a social worker or teacher. Applications are considered at any time.

Other information

Grants are also available for relief-in-need purposes and to organisations or groups within the parish boundary.

Diss

The Diss Parochial Charities Poors Branch

£500

Correspondent: Cyril Grace, 2 The Causeway, Victoria Road, Diss, Norfolk IP22 4AW (01379 650630; email: cj. grace@btinternet.com)

Trustees: John Maskell; Adrian Kitchen; Tony Billett; Graham Elliott; Barbara Roberts; Terence Gilbert; Trevor Venman.

CC Number: 210154

Eligibility

People in need who live in the town and parish of Diss.

Types of grants

One-off grants to schoolchildren towards fees, books and excursions and to college students and undergraduates towards fees and books. Grants range from £30 to £200.

Annual grant total

In 2011 the charity had assets of £678,000 and an income of £29,000. Grants to individuals totalled £2,000. Previously the majority of grants have been welfare-related, with a couple of awards made for educational purposes.

Applications

In writing to the correspondent directly by the individual, through the individual's school/college/educational welfare agency or through another third party on behalf of the individual. They are considered upon receipt.

Other information

The charity also supports local organisations.

East Tuddenham

The East Tuddenham Charities

£800

Correspondent: Janet Guy, 7 Mattishall Road, East Tuddenham, Dereham, Norfolk NR20 3LP (01603 880523)

Trustees: Colin Cram; Leslie Anderson; Maurice Marchant; Tilly Taylor; Audrey Ratcliffe; Binnie Lenihan.

CC Number: 210333

Eligibility

People in further and higher education who live in East Tuddenham.

Types of grants

Help with the cost of books, clothing and other essentials.

Annual grant total

Grants are usually made totalling £1,800 a year, mostly for welfare purposes.

Applications

In writing to the correspondent.

Feltwell

Sir Edmund Moundeford's Educational Foundation

£1,800

Correspondent: Barry Hawkins, The Estate Office, 15 Lynn Road, Downham Market, Norfolk PE38 9NL (01366 387180)

Trustees: Edmund Lambert; P. Garland; Tim Fox; Martin Storey; Josephine Leveridge; Leslie Ward; Christopher Cock.

CC Number: 1075097

Eligibility

Individuals in need who live in Feltwell.

Types of grants

One-off cash grants and grants in kind are made to schoolchildren, college students and vocational students, including those for clothing/uniforms, books and equipment/instruments.

Annual grant total

In 2011 the charity had assets of £3.8 million and an income of £123,000. Student grants totalled £1,100 and school leavers grants totalled £650.

Applications

In writing to the correspondent either directly by the individual or through an organisation such as Citizens Advice or a school. Applications are considered at meetings held quarterly.

Other information

Fuel grants are also made to individuals.

Garboldisham

The Garboldisham Parish Charities

£1,000

Correspondent: P Girling, Treasurer, Sandale, Smallworth Common, Garboldisham, Diss, Norfolk IP22 2QW (01953 681646)

Trustees: Mr P. Girling; Revd D. Sheppard; Mr T. Lambert; Revd M. Bull; Mr D. Atkins; Mrs B. Sears; David Hance.

CC Number: 210250

Eligibility

People under 25 who have lived in Garboldisham for at least two years.

Types of grants

One-off and recurrent grants including gifts in kind are made to schoolchildren, college students, undergraduates, vocational students, people with special needs and people starting work. Grants given include those for uniforms/clothing, study/travel abroad, books, equipment/instruments and maintenance/living expenses. Grants are in the range of £30 to £600.

Annual grant total

Educational grants usually total around £1,000 per year.

Applications

Applications can be submitted directly by the individual including specific details of what the grant is required for. They are usually considered in July and December.

Other information

This charity also makes grants to organisations.

Harling

Harling Town Lands Educational Foundation

£1,700

Correspondent: David Gee, Clerk, Hanworth House, Market Street, East Harling, Norwich NR16 2AD (01953 717652; email: gee@harlingpc.org.uk)

CC Number: 311209

Eligibility

Young people resident in Harling who are in need.

Types of grants

One-off grants for those attending higher or further education (including professional and technical education) for books, clothing, equipment and so on.

Annual grant total

Grants average around £1,700 per year.

Applications

In writing to the correspondent at any time from any source. A brief financial statement will also be required.

Hempnall

The Hempnall Town Estate Educational Foundation

£5,000

Correspondent: Marjorie Joyce Emery, 17 Roland Drive, Hempnall, Norfolk NR15 2RB (01508 499460)

CC Number: 311218

Eligibility

People who live in Hempnall and have done so for a year.

Types of grants

Grants are made to help with: (i) costs of educational outings for schoolchildren; (ii) expenses incurred while at college or university such as books, help with fees and study or travel abroad; and (iii) help with the cost of vocational courses. Grants are also available for a wide range of other activities, including athletic expenses and the study of the arts.

Grants to individuals are usually made on a percentage basis on production of receipts for courses, books and so on, with a maximum ceiling which is reviewed annually. Each application is considered entirely on merit, but if a grant is made to one person on a particular course, then everyone making an application for the same course receives exactly the same amount or percentage.

Annual grant total

In 2010/11 the foundation had an income of £17,000 and an expenditure of £24,000. About £10,000 is given a year in educational grants to individuals and to village organisations.

Applications

In writing to the correspondent, including evidence of the course being taken and relevant receipts. Applications should be made by 1 March, 1 July and 1 November to be considered during these months.

Other information

Further information on the foundation and how to make an application is available in the Parish News Letter, published annually in January.

Hilgay

The Hilgay Feoffee Charity

£1,500

Correspondent: P Golds, 1 St James Drive, Downham Market, Norfolk PE38 9SZ (01306 388496)

CC Number: 208898

Eligibility

People starting an apprenticeship or work who live in the parish of Hilgay.

Types of grants

One-off and recurrent grants according to need, including fuel vouchers and help towards costs of apprenticeship or training.

Annual grant total

In 2011 the charity had an income of £21,000 and an expenditure of £18,000. Grants to individuals generally total around £2,000 with 75% for education, training and apprenticeships and the remainder for general grants.

Applications

In writing to the correspondent, directly by the individual. Applications are considered in June each year.

Other information

The trust also gives to local schools.

Horstead with Stanninghall

The Horstead Poor's Land

£1,500

Correspondent: W B Lloyd, Watermeadows, 7 Church Close, Horstead, Norwich NR12 7ET (01603 737632; email: chadlloyd@btopenworld.com)

CC Number: 364730

Eligibility

People in need who live in Horstead with Stanninghall.

Types of grants

One-off grants up to a maximum of £2,000 can be made for any purpose.

Annual grant total

The latest figures available were for 2009/10 when the trust had an income £7,800 and an expenditure of £7,200. Grants are given for both welfare and educational purposes, and to local organisations.

Applications

Applications can be submitted directly by the individual, through a school or college, or other third party giving details of the applicant's financial resources. Applications are considered a any time.

King's Lynn

The King's Lynn General Educational Foundation

£1,000

Correspondent: Andrew Cave, Wheelers 16 North Street, Wisbech, Cambridgeshire PE13 1NE (01945 582547; email: andrew.cave@wheelers-accountants.co.uk)

CC Number: 311104

Eligibility

People aged under 25 who have lived in the borough of King's Lynn for not less than two years, or those who have attended school in the borough for not less than two years, who are going on to further education.

Types of grants

One-off grants of £75 to £200 for people at school, college or university or any other further education institution towards the cost of books, equipment, fees and living expenses.

Annual grant total

The foundation awards around £1,000 in grants each year.

Applications

On a form available from R G Pannell, 21 Baldwin Road, King's Lynn, Norfolk PE30 4AL, to be submitted by 30 August each year. The application should be supported by the applicant's previous educational establishment.

Norwich

Norwich Town Close Estate Charity

£65,000

Correspondent: David Walker, Clerk to the Trustees, 1 Woolgate Court, St Benedicts Street, Norwich NR2 4AP (01603 621023; email: david.walker@ norwichcharitabletrusts.org.uk)

Trustees: Nigel Back; Eddie Burton; Anthony Hansell; Richard Gurney; Michael Quinton; Michael G. Quinton; Robert Self; John Rushmer; John Symonds; Brenda Arthur; Philip Blanchflower; David Fullman; Brenda Ferris; Pamela Scutter; Geoffrey Loades; Heather Tyrrell; Jeanne Southgate.

CC Number: 235678

Eligibility

Freemen of Norwich and their dependents.

Types of grants

Grants are given to schoolchildren, further and higher education students, mature students and postgraduates for fees and maintenance/living expenses.

Annual grant total

In 2010/11 the charity made grants to individuals totalling £178,000, these were broken down as follows:

- Pension: £104,000
- Educational: £65,000
- TV licence: £3,600
- Relief in need: £5,500

Applications

In writing to the correspondent by June/ early July each year. Applications are considered in August.

Sir Peter Seaman's Charity

£3,000

Correspondent: Kevin Pellatt, Great Hospital, Bishopgate, Norwich NR1 4EL (01603 622022)

Trustees: Elizabeth Crocker; Jolyon Heaton Harris; Michael Brookes; Peter Jarrold; Alexandra de Bunsen; Paul King; James Powell; David Buck; Julie James; Pamela Peterson; David Marris; Stuart Holmes; Sarah Callaghan; Catherine Jeffries; John Walker; Jon Stanley.

CC Number: 311101

Eligibility

Young people up to the age of 21 who live in Norwich.

Types of grants

One-off and recurrent grants generally between £100 and £300. Grants can be towards all kinds of educational purposes, including starting a new job/ career or to help with educational trips such as Duke of Edinburgh Award Scheme, Raleigh International etc.

Annual grant total

Around £3,000.

Applications

In writing to the correspondent. Applications can be submitted directly by the individual and are considered quarterly in March, June, September and December.

Outwell

The Outwell Town Lands Educational Foundation

£3,000

Correspondent: Debbie Newton, 90 Wisbech Road, Outwell, Wisbech, Cambridgeshire PE14 8PF (01945 774327; email: outwellpc@btinternet. com)

Trustees: John Wake; Harry Humphrey; Peter Cutting; Janet Edgson; Daniel Cuckow; Alan Jesson; Stephen Lawrence; Dale Boyce; David Murfitt.

CC Number: 311211

Eligibility

People who live in the ancient parish of Outwell.

Types of grants

Recurrent grants are usually made to: (i) those staying at school beyond normal school-leaving age; (ii) those attending courses of further education at technical colleges, other colleges (e.g. agricultural

and teacher training) and universities; and (iii) those taking an apprenticeship course or other work leading to a trade qualification. Grants range from £50 to £200 and are for general educational purposes.

Annual grant total

About £3,000.

Applications

On a form available from the correspondent. Applications should be submitted directly by the individual in September for consideration in October. Proof of satisfactory attendance may be requested. Grants are paid at the end of January.

Oxborough

The Hewars Educational Charity

£500

Correspondent: E Mason, 31 Oxborough Village, Oxborough, King's Lynn PE33 9PS (01366 328874)

Trustees: Christopher Chalcraft; Henry Lambert; Valerie O'Dwyer; C. Ashley; Elizabeth Mason.

CC Number: 311184

Eligibility

People who live in the ancient parish of Oxborough who are under the age of 25.

Types of grants

Educational grants for those at school, college or university. The maximum grant is usually £200.

Annual grant total

About £500.

Applications

In writing to the correspondent. Applications are usually considered in November.

Saxlingham

The Saxlingham United Charities

£2,000

Correspondent: Mrs Jane Turner, 4 Pitts Hill Close, Saxlingham, Nethergate NR15 1AZ (01508 499623)

Trustees: Anthony Hook; Linda Durrant; David Moore.

CC Number: 244713

Eligibility

People under 21 who have lived in Saxlingham Nethergate for at least five years.

Types of grants

Grants of £50 to £100 towards the cost of books, clothing or tools to young people starting work or in further or higher education.

Annual grant total

In 2010/11 the charities had an income of £4,200 and a total expenditure of £4,000. Grants are made for welfare and educational purposes.

Applications

In writing to the correspondent. Applications can be submitted directly by the individual and are usually considered in October.

Snettisham

Halls Exhibition Foundation

£60,000 (95 grants)

Correspondent: Christopher Holt, 4 Bewick Close, Snettisham, Kings Lynn, Norfolk PE31 7PJ (01485 541534; email: administrator@hallsfoundation.co.uk; website: www.hallsfoundation.co.uk)

Trustees: Andrew Cave; Edward Stanton; Ian Goddard; Janice Eells; Beryl Wardlow; Paul Norris; Sybil Melton; Ian Devereux.

CC Number: 325128

Eligibility

People in need who are aged 11 to 25 and have resided in the village of Snettisham for at least one year.

Types of grants

The following types of grant are available:

- For young people aged 11+ going into secondary school (£200)
- For young people of 16+ staying on at school to take A-levels or to attend equivalent further education courses. A grant is available for each year of the course (£200 per year)
- For students of 18+ attending a University or an equivalent higher educational course. A grant is available for each year of the course. All students are eligible for this grant, regardless of parental income. The grant is awarded as £1,000 at the start of the academic year, and £1,000 at the end

Grants will be considered to students over the age of 18 years following a recognised course of study or other form of musical scholarship acceptable to the trustees. A grant may be made up to half the cost of an instrument (to a maximum of £500) plus an interest free loan for the other half (up to £500).

Additional grants, up to half the costs, may be available for students having to travel abroad as part of their studies.

Annual grant total

In 2010/11 the foundation held assets of 1.4 million and had an income of £60,000. £60,000 in grants was distributed as follows:

- Pupils moving from primary/middle schools: 18 grants of up to £200 were made totalling £3,600
- Students undertaking 6th form/ further education courses at 16+: 38 grants of up to £200 were made totalling £7,600
- Students undertaking university/ higher education courses: 29 grants of up to £2,000 were made totalling £48,000
- Other grants awarded totalled £700

Exclusions

No additional grants will be made for word processors, computers, textbooks, normal travelling expenses or work experience costs. Grants must be returned if any year of the course is not completed.

Applications

On a form available from the correspondent or to download from the website. Applications can be submitted either directly by the individual or a parent/guardian, through a third party such as a teacher, or through an organisation such as a school or an educational welfare agency.

Other information

The foundation also makes grants to organisations, although not in the year 2010/11.

South Creake

The South Creake Charities

£2,000

Correspondent: Miss Sarah Harvey, The Vicarage, 18 Front Street, South Creake, Fakenham, Norfolk NR21 9PE (01328 823234)

Trustees: Barbara Allen; Christopher Gardner; Rodney Wakeman; Sara Freakley.

CC Number: 210090

Eligibility

People in further or higher education who are in need and live in South Creake.

Types of grants

One-off grants range from £100 to £200 and are given to help schoolchildren and further and higher education students with the cost of books, equipment/

instruments, fees and educational outings in the UK.

Annual grant total

In 2010/11 the charities had an income of £4,700 and a total expenditure of £4,300.

Applications

In writing to the correspondent. Applications should be submitted directly by the individual and are considered in November; they should be received before the end of October.

Other information

Grants can also be given to schools and playgroups.

South Walsham

Harrold's Charity

£3,000

Correspondent: Jane Clamp, Ivy Cottage, Burlingham Road, South Walsham, Norwich NR13 6DJ (01603 270425; email: paulinejames@aol.com)

Trustees: Dorothy Dean; Jane Clamp; John Debbage; Nicholas Garrard; Arthur Lawn.

CC Number: 311107

Eligibility

People aged 13 to 25 who live in the parish of South Walsham.

Types of grants

Grants are given towards the cost of school uniforms/clothing, books, equipment, educational outings and study or travel abroad for schoolchildren. Students in further/ higher education, apprentices and students on training courses can receive grants towards general education costs. Grants can be one-off or recurrent and range from £25 to £250.

Annual grant total

The trust consistently has both an annual income and total expenditure of around £3,000.

Applications

In writing to the correspondent. Applications are considered in January, April and September and must include receipts for any expenditure incurred, confirmation of college course etc.

Swaffham

Swaffham Relief In Need Charity

£1,000

Correspondent: Richard Bishop, The Town Hall, Swaffham, Norfolk

PE37 7DQ (01760 722922; email: reliefinneed@swaffhamtowncouncil.gov.uk)

Trustees: Ian Sherwood; Shirley Mathews; David Harman; Pamela Buxton; David Butters; David Cannon; Paul Ison; Anne Greaves; Terry Jennison; Paul Darby.

CC Number: 1072912

Eligibility

People in need who live in Swaffham.

Types of grants

Grants are given for welfare purposes, including for school uniforms.

Annual grant total

In 2010/11 the charity had an income of £12,000 and a total expenditure of £8,000.

Applications

In writing to the correspondent.

Other information

Grants are also made to organisations.

Walpole

The Walpole St Peter Poor's Estate

£750

Correspondent: Edward Otter, 1 Sutton Meadows, Leverington, Wisbech, Cambridgeshire PE13 5ED (01945 565018)

Trustees: Gerard Fletcher; Revd Michael Chesher; Clive Melton; George Baty; John Bliss; Jack Bowers; Kenneth Horspole; William Brooks.

CC Number: 233207

Eligibility

People in need aged 16 and over who are at college or university and live in the old parishes of Walpole St Peter, Walpole Highway and Walpole Marsh.

Types of grants

Recurrent grants ranging from £10 to £50 to help buy books.

Annual grant total

The trust distributes about £1,500 each year.

Applications

In writing to the correspondent. Applications should be submitted directly by the individual and are considered in November.

Other information

Grants are also made to older people.

Wiveton

The Charities of Ralph Greenway

£500

Correspondent: Mr Robert Harris, East Barn, Hall Lane, Wiveton, Holt, Norfolk NR25 7TG (01263 740090)

Trustees: Mr J. Woodhouse; Dinah Comins; Hazel Clift; Janet Harcourt; Philippa Stancomb; Revd Neil Batcock; Margaret Bennett.

CC Number: 207605

Eligibility

Young people living in the parish of Wiveton or associated closely with it, up to university age, including young people who are starting work.

Types of grants

One-off grants are given towards books, equipment, clothing, study/travel abroad, excursions and so on.

Annual grant total

In 2010/11 the charities had an income of £2,700 and a total expenditure of £3,300. Grants for educational purposes are generally under £500 in total.

Applications

Applications, on a form available from the correspondent, should be submitted directly by the individual and are considered twice a year. However, if a need arises, a special meeting can be convened.

Other information

Grants are also available for individuals in need who are over 60 and live in the village.

Woodton

Woodton United Charities

£1,500

Correspondent: P B Moore, 6 Triple Plea Road, Woodton, Bungay, Suffolk NR35 2NS (01508 482375)

Trustees: Jane Bond; Christine Taylor; Peter Moore; Michael Beckett; Liz Billett.

CC Number: 207531

Eligibility

People in need who live in the parish of Woodton.

Types of grants

One-off and recurrent grants according to need for books and equipment. Recent grants include tools for an apprentice and books for an A-level student.

Annual grant total

In 2010/11 the charities had an income of £4,000 and a total expenditure of £3,400.

Applications

In writing to the correspondent directly by the individual, including details of the nature of the need. Applications can be submitted at any time.

Oxfordshire

The Bampton Exhibition Foundation

£3,000

Correspondent: Gerald Mills, 21 Southlands, Aston, Bampton OX18 2DA (01993 850670)

Trustees: David Hawkins; David Pullman; David Lloyd; Edward Baughan; J van den Berge; M. Dowding; Gerald Mills; Brenda Sapsford; Beate Howitt.

CC Number: 309238

Eligibility

People under 25 who live in Bampton, Aston, Cote, Weald or Lew and are in need.

Types of grants

Grants are given to schoolchildren, people with special educational needs, students in further/higher education, vocational students and postgraduates for projects/courses which would be otherwise beyond the means of applicants. Support that can be given includes books, equipment/instruments, fees, maintenance/living expenses, educational outings in the UK, study or travel abroad and so on.

Annual grant total

In 2010/11 the foundation had an income of £5,100 and an expenditure of £3,500.

Applications

In writing to the correspondent at any time, including details regarding the proposed project/course, any expenses involved and relevant references. Applications can be submitted either directly by the individual, through the individual's school, college or educational agency, or through another third party such as a teacher or parent.

Charney Bassett and Lyford Educational Trust

£1,000

Correspondent: Mrs F Rothwell, Russets, Buckland Road, Charney Bassett, Wantage OX12 0ES (01235 867358)

Trustees: Christopher Lewis; David Douglas; Joycelyn Bath; Colin McGuire; Geoffrey Rumble; Robin Pike; Nicholas Milne.

CC Number: 1076943

Eligibility
People who live in Charney Bassett and Lyford who are in need.

Types of grants
Grants towards educational need.

Annual grant total
About £1,000 is given each year in grants.

Applications
In writing to the correspondent.

Other information
Grants are also made to organisations.

The Culham Educational Foundation

£8,000 (1 grant)

Correspondent: Mark Chater, Flat 1, 16 Church Hill, Arnside, Cumbria LA5 0DQ (01865 284885; fax: 01865 284886; email: enquiries@culham.ac.uk; website: www.culham.ac.uk)

Trustees: Anthony Williamson; Norman Russell; Geoffrey Paine; Jo Fageant; John Hughesdon; Karen Gorham; Leslie Stephen; John Keast; John Pritchard.

CC Number: 309671

Eligibility
Grants are available to Anglicans who are pursuing personal study, or undertaking projects or research primarily relating to religious education, theology or religious studies taught in schools. Consideration will be given only to applicants who live or work in the Diocese of Oxford. Endorsement by a diocesan or LEA officer is required, or in the case of clergy, the area bishop or archdeacon.

Types of grants
Grants up to a maximum of £1,500 are made towards books, fees and living expenses. A few grants are made to corporate bodies; the main work of the foundation is the support of the Culham College Institute.

Annual grant total
In 2010/11 the trust had assets of £6.5 million and an income of £419,000. One grant of £8,000 was given to an individual.

Exclusions
Applicants must be living or working in the diocese of Oxford.

Applications
On a form available from the correspondent. Applications must be submitted by 31 March for courses commencing in the autumn.

Other information
Grants are also made to organisations.

Ducklington and Hardwick with Yelford Charity

£300

Correspondent: Mrs Joyce Parry, 16 Feilden Close, Ducklington, Witney, Oxfordshire OX29 7XB (01993 705121)

Trustees: Diana Scott; Edmund Strainge; Philip Rogers; Revd Bob Edy; Glyn Rees.

CC Number: 237343

Eligibility
People in need or hardship who live in the villages of Ducklington, Hardwick and Yelford.

Types of grants
Grants of £75 to £200 to: schoolchildren for educational outings in the UK; people starting work for equipment; people in further/higher education for books and study or travel overseas and vocational students for books.

Annual grant total
Educational grants usually total around totalled £300.

Applications
In writing to the correspondent. Applications are considered in March and November, but emergency cases can be dealt with at any time.

Other information
Grants are also made to organisations such as clubs, schools and so on.

The Faringdon United Charities

£6,000

Correspondent: Vivienne Checkley, Bunting and Co., 7 Market Place, Faringdon, Oxfordshire SN7 7HL (01367 243789; fax: 01367 243789)

Trustees: B. Barber; J. Carter; D. Keeling; David McKay; Peter Eyre-Brook; Revd Charles Draper; Alan Hickmore; Jill Woodward; Julie Farmer.

CC Number: 237040

Eligibility
People in need who live in the parishes of Faringdon, Littleworth, Great and Little Coxwell, all in Oxfordshire.

Types of grants
One-off grants to: schoolchildren for study/travel abroad, equipment/instruments and excursions; mature students for books; people with special educational needs for equipment/instruments; and people starting work for equipment/instruments.

Annual grant total
In 2010/11 the trust had both an income and total expenditure of £13,500.

Applications
In writing to the correspondent throughout the year. Applications can be submitted either through Citizens Advice, a social worker or other third party, directly by the individual or by a third party on their behalf for example a neighbour, parent or child.

Other information
Grants are also made for welfare purposes and to organisations.

The Henley Educational Charity

£25,000

Correspondent: Claire Brown, Clerk, Syringa Cottage, Horsepond Road, Gallowstree Common, Reading, Berkshire RG4 9BP (01189 724575; email: henleyeducationalcharity@ hotmail.co.uk; website: www. henleyeducationalcharity.com)

Trustees: William Parrish; Colin Homent; Marjorie Hall; Rosalind Whittaker; Martyn Griffiths; Maureen Smith; Pamela Mayor; Stephan Gawrysiak; William Hamilton.

CC Number: 309237

Eligibility
People under the age of 25 who live in the town of Henley or parishes of Bix, Rotherfield Greys or Remenham, or attend a publicly maintained school or college in the region, or have done so for at least two years.

Types of grants
Grants are awarded to schoolchildren for uniforms, educational outings, pre-school fees, music lessons and instruments and educational extra-curricular activities on an income-based assessment. Young people under 25 can apply for assistance with books, studying or voluntary work abroad but not for

university courses or accommodation costs. Assistance may be provided for people starting work to buy equipment. The maximum grant for a primary schoolchild is £75 and £120 for secondary.

Annual grant total

In 2010/11 the trust had assets of £2.9 million and an income of £119,000. There were 107 grants to individuals made totalling £25,000.

Exclusions

No funding for school fees.

Applications

Application forms are downloadable from the website and can be submitted by the individual, or through their school/college, parent/guardian, educational welfare agency or social services. The trustees meet eight times a year to consider grant applications, however no meetings are held in April, July August and December.

Other information

One third of the trust's income may be given in special benefits to publicly maintained schools in the region. The charity states: 'You may need help in some other way not mentioned. The charity would like to assist you if it possibly can. Do not be afraid to ask!' The trust also administers the Mary Clarke Music Award which offers support for musical activities.

The Hope Ffennell Trust

£8,000

Correspondent: Louis Letourneau, Church End, Wytham Abbey, Wytham, Oxon OX2 8QE (01865 203475)

Trustees: Louis Letourneau; K. F. Day; Lady Piper; A. Cresswell; A. Dawson; R. Beckwith.

CC Number: 309212

Types of grants

Help towards outings and educational visits, books and the study of music.

Annual grant total

In 2011 the trust had an income of £7,200 and an expenditure of £8,500.

Applications

In writing to the correspondent.

The Stevens Hart and Municipal Educational Charity

£4,000

Correspondent: Jean Pickett, Henley Municipal Charities, Rear, 24 Hart

Street, Henley-on-Thames, Oxfordshire RG9 2AU (01491 412360; email: henleymcharities@aol.com)

Trustees: Jean Sichel; David Tate; Gillian Ovey; Inez Hemsley; Joyce Walden; Elizabeth Hodgkin; Martyn Griffiths; Michael Forsdike; Peter Ashby; Richard Tomlins; Pamela Phillips; Tristan Stubbs; Lousie Lloyd.

CC Number: 292857

Eligibility

Children and young people who live in the parishes of Bix and Rotherfield Greys and the town of Henley-on-Thames.

Types of grants

Grants up to a maximum of £300 towards the cost of books, clothing and other essentials for schoolchildren. Help may also be available for students at college or university.

Annual grant total

About £4,000.

Applications

On a form available from the correspondent.

The Thame Welfare Trust

£12,000

Correspondent: J Gadd, 2 Cromwell Avenue, Thame, Oxfordshire OX9 3TD (01844 212564)

Trustees: Ann Midwinter; Cecil Wiggs; David Youens; David Dodds; Jane Hussey; Helen Fickling; Dr Patricia Markus; Rosalie Gibson; Dr Timothy Mitchell; Karen Vear; Alan Garratt; Mrs J. Mander.

CC Number: 241914

Eligibility

People in need who live in Thame and immediately adjoining villages.

Types of grants

One-off grants of amounts up to £1,000 are given to help towards a wide variety of needs to schoolchildren, college students, undergraduates, vocational students, mature students, people with special educational needs and people starting work.

Annual grant total

In 2010/11 the trust had an income of £20,500 and a total expenditure of £77,000. Grants are made to organisations and individuals for relief-in-need and education.

Applications

In writing to the correspondent mainly through social workers, probation officers, teachers, or a similar third party, but also directly by the applicant.

Banbury

The Banbury Charities

£60,000

Correspondent: Anthony Andrews, 36 West Bar, Banbury, Oxfordshire OX16 9RU (01295 251234)

Trustees: Craig Brodey; Janet Justice; Fred Blackwell; Judy May; Julia Colgrave; Angela Heritage; Nigel Morris; Helen Madeiros; Colin Clarke; Martin Humphris; Jamie Briggs; Keiron Mallon.

CC Number: 201418

Eligibility

People under 25 who live in the former borough of Banbury, as it was in 1974.

Types of grants

Grants are given to people preparing for or entering a profession or trade and students in higher and further education, particularly for books and equipment. Also grants are given to assist young persons under the age of 25 who are studying the arts, literature or science.

Annual grant total

In 2010 the charities had assets of £4.4 million and an income of £374,000. Grants were made to 428 individuals for both education and welfare purposes at an average of £279 per grant, totalling £119,000.

Applications

In writing to the correspondent. Applicants are encouraged to obtain a letter of support from their social worker, carer, teacher or other person in authority to give credence to their application.

Other information

The Banbury Charities contains six constituent charities: Bridge Estate Charity, Countess of Arran's Charity, Banbury Almshouse Charity, Banbury Sick Poor Fund, Banbury Arts and Educational Charity and Banbury Welfare Trust.

The charities give to organisations as well as individuals and also maintain almshouse accommodation for six people.

Barford

The Shepherd and Bakehouse Charity

£3,000

Correspondent: Lucy Warner, Mead Farm Bungalow, Mead Road, Barford St John, Banbury OX15 0PW (01295 720202)

CC Number: 309173

Eligibility

Young people under 25 who live or whose parents live in the parish of Barford St John and Barford St Michael and have done so for at least three years.

Types of grants

Grants of £150 to £300 towards the cost of education, training, apprenticeship or equipment for those starting work.

Annual grant total

In 2010/11 the charity had both an income and an expenditure of £3,500.

Exclusions

Grants are not made for schoolchildren.

Applications

Applications can be submitted directly by the individual by 30 September.

Bletchington

The Bletchington Charity

£5,000

Correspondent: Sue Green, Causeway Cottage, Weston Road, Bletchington, Kidlington, Oxon OX5 3DH (01869 350895)

CC Number: 201584

Eligibility

People in need who live in the parish of Bletchington.

Types of grants

Grants to students and apprentices to help with the purchase of books, instruments or tools necessary for their course.

Annual grant total

In 2010 the charity had an income of £11,000 and a total expenditure of £12,000.

Applications

Applications can be made in writing to the correspondent by the individual.

Other information

The charity also seeks to support any medical and social needs that will benefit the village community as a whole.

Charlbury

The Charlbury Exhibition Foundation

£3,500

Correspondent: Kate Gerrish, Secretary, The Byre, 8 Lyneham Farm Cottages, Lyneham, Chipping Norton OX7 6QP (01993 832845)

CC Number: 309236

Eligibility

Students in higher/further education who live in the ancient township of Charlbury.

Types of grants

Recurrent grants of about £100 per applicant per annum (depending on income), paid in the first and then subsequent years to students on three-year courses to be spent on books, equipment and so on.

Annual grant total

In 2010/11 the foundation had an income of £9,300 and an expenditure of £3,700. The grant total varies from year to year and is for educational purposes only.

Exclusions

No grants to schoolchildren.

Applications

In writing to the correspondent by 1 October to be considered annually.

Eynsham

Bartholomew Educational Foundation

£2,000

Correspondent: R N Mitchell, Clerk, 20 High Street, Eynsham, Witney, Oxfordshire OX29 4HB (01865 880665; website: www.eynsham.org)

CC Number: 309278

Eligibility

People under 25 who live in the parish of Eynsham and are in need.

Types of grants

The foundation makes one-off grants to schoolchildren, people starting work, further and higher education students and postgraduates for general education needs. Donations are usually in the range of £50 to £200 and include those for uniforms/other school clothing, books, equipment/instruments, fees, maintenance/living expenses, educational outings in the UK, study or travel abroad and so on.

Annual grant total

In 2010 the foundation had an income of £4,000 and a total expenditure of £2,200. Grants usually total about £2,000.

Applications

Applications for people under 18 should be made by a parent or guardian. Write to the correspondent with full details of the person the grant is requested for (name, address, age, what the grant is for, costings).

Apprentices and trainees should send a list of tools, books, instruments or whatever the items needed may be with their prices and the date that the training will commence.

Trustees meet four times a year, usually in February, May, August or September and November. Applications should be submitted in the month before the next meeting.

Oxford

The Thomas Dawson Educational Foundation

£1,800

Correspondent: K K Lacey, Clerk, 56 Poplar Close, Garsington, Oxford OX44 9BP (01865 368259)

CC Number: 203258

Eligibility

Children and young people in need who have lived in the city of Oxford (postcodes OX1 to OX4) for three years, with a preference for those resident in the parish of St Clements.

Types of grants

Help with the cost of books, clothing, fees and other essentials for schoolchildren and for people at college or university. Grants also for people preparing for entering or engaging in a profession, trade, occupation or service. Grants generally range from £40 to £1,500.

Annual grant total

In 2011 the charity had an income of £334,000 and made grants to individuals totalling £1,800.

Exclusions

No grants are given for medical sponsorships or electives, or towards accommodation, travel or living expenses.

Applications

In writing to the correspondent, with evidence regarding course fees. Note: applicants can only apply for one degree course.

Other information

Grants are also made to schools and youth, family and volunteer organisations.

The City of Oxford Charities

£14,000

Correspondent: The Administrator, 11 Davenant Road, Oxford OX2 8BT (01865 247161; email: enquiries@ oxfordcitycharities.fsnet.co.uk; website: www.oxfordcitycharities.org)

Trustees: Judith Iredale; Robin Birch; Diana Pope; Dorothy Tonge; Tony Woodward; John Gould; Verena Brink; Jean Fooks; Jason Tomes; Richard Whittington; Michael Lancashire; Ben Lloyd-Shogbesan; Roger Smith; Susan Bright; Alan Armitage; Ivan Coulter; Gillian Sanders.

CC Number: 239151

Eligibility

Students under 25 who have lived in the city of Oxford for at least five years.

Types of grants

One-off grants are given to: schoolchildren for uniforms, fees, books, equipment and school trips; students for books and equipment/instruments; undergraduates for books and equipment/instruments; and mature students under 25 for fees, books and equipment/instruments.

Annual grant total

In 2011 educational grants to 34 individuals totalled £14,000.

Applications

Application forms are available from the correspondent or can be downloaded from the website. Applications are considered quarterly in March, June, September and December.

Other information

Grants are also made to schools.

Rotherfield Greys

The Rotherfield Greys Educational Charity

£250

Correspondent: Sam Samuels, Cowfields Farm, Rotherfield Greys, Henley-on-Thames RG9 4PX (01491 628819; email: samsamuels@btconnect.com)

Trustees: Richard Ovey; Brendan Bailey; Sam Samuels; Graham Ethelson.

CC Number: 284643

Eligibility

People aged between 5 and 25 who live in the ecclesiastical parish of St Nicholas, Rotherfield Greys.

Types of grants

One-off grants are available to schoolchildren and further and higher education students to cover the cost of books, equipment/instruments, fees, educational outings in the UK, and study and travel abroad. There is a preference for Church of England-oriented education.

Grants are given in the range of £100 to £250.

Annual grant total

In 2010/11 the charity had an expenditure of £250.

Applications

On a form available from the correspondent for consideration in March and September. Applications must include proof of residential qualification.

Wallingford

The Wallingford Municipal and Relief-in-Need Charities

£2,000

Correspondent: A Rogers, Town Clerk, 9 St Martin's Street, Wallingford, Oxfordshire OX10 0AL (01491 835373; email: wallingfordtc@btconnect.com)

Trustees: Patricia Granados; David Kershaw; Jacqueline Payne; Elizabeth Atkins; Elizabeth Lee; Chris Tyndall; Elizabeth Vaisey; Rose Owen; Mrs J. Castle; Mrs A. Willis; Pat Hayton; Revd David Rice; Theresa Jordan.

CC Number: 292000

Eligibility

People in need who live in the former borough of Wallingford.

Types of grants

Help with the cost of bills, clothing and other essentials. The trust gives one-off grants only.

Annual grant total

Grants total approximately £8,000 per year.

Applications

On a form available from the correspondent, submitted either directly by the individual or through a local organisation. Trustees meet about every three months, although emergency cases can be considered. Urgent cases may require a visit by a trustee.

Other information

The majority of grants are given for welfare needs.

Wheatley

The Wheatley Charities

£3,800

Correspondent: R F Minty, 24 Old London Road, Wheatley, Oxford OX33 1YW (01865 874676)

Trustees: P. J. Targett; D. A. S. John; R. F. Minty; Graham Colverson.

CC Number: 203535

Eligibility

People who are under 25 and live in the parish of Wheatley.

Types of grants

Grants are given to help young people prepare for any trade or occupation or to promote their education.

Annual grant total

About £3,800.

Applications

In writing to the correspondent.

Wootton

The Parrott and Lee Educational Foundation

£1,500 (5 grants)

Correspondent: Charles Ponsonby, Woodleys House, Woodstock, Oxford OX20 1HJ (01993 811717)

Trustees: Curtis Price; Charles Ponsonby; John Harwood; Mary Tuely; Stephen Jones.

CC Number: 309586

Eligibility

People under the age of 25 who attended Wootton-by-Woodstock Primary School and/or live in Wootton-by-Woodstock.

Types of grants

Annual grants of about £200, in particular towards course fees, maintenance, travel, outfits, books and equipment to people in tertiary education.

Annual grant total

In 2011 there were five grants to individuals totalling £1,500, made in the following areas: childcare, forensic science, drama, social work and zoology.

Applications

On a form available from the correspondent, which should be submitted directly by the individual. They are considered half yearly, normally in March and September.

Suffolk

The Calthorpe and Edwards Educational Foundation

£10,000

Correspondent: R G Boswell, Clerk, Chegwidden, Beauford Road, Ingham, Bury St Edmunds IP31 1NW (01284 728288)

Trustees: Hermione Scrope; Keith Boswell.

CC Number: 310464

Eligibility

People between the ages of 18 and 25 who live in the parishes of Ampton, Great Livermere, Little Livermere, Ingham and Timworth, Troston, Ixworth, Culford, Great Barton, West Stow, Wordwell, Fornham St Genevieve and Fornham St Martin.

Types of grants

Grants for schoolchildren, university students and people starting work to help with the cost of books, equipment, clothing and study or travel overseas.

Annual grant total

In 2010/11 the trust had an income of £8,600 and an expenditure of £11,000.

Applications

Applications can be submitted directly by the individual. They are usually considered in October.

The Fauconberge Educational Foundation

£2,000

Correspondent: Barry Darch, Trustee, The Moorings, 9 Waveney Road, Beccles NR34 9NW (01502 711318)

Trustees: Bill Jenner; Colleen Paterson; Denys Simpson; Vivienne Osborne; John Beauchamp; Barry Darch; Judy Hunt; Jack Walmsley; Alan Thwaites.

CC Number: 310459

Eligibility

Children and young people between the ages of 11 and 19 who live within a five-mile radius of Beccles Town Hall and who are 'engaged in a course of study intended to prepare them for higher or further education or for an advanced qualification'.

Types of grants

Grants for schoolchildren and further education and vocational students to help with school fees, books, equipment, educational outings in the UK and study or travel abroad. Schoolchildren can also receive help for uniform and clothing. The grants are given as one-off payments and range from £50 to £500.

Annual grant total

In 2010/11 the trust had an income of £1,700 and an expenditure of £2,500.

Exclusions

University students are not eligible.

Applications

Vacancies are advertised in local papers and area noticeboards, and application forms are available from the correspondent. Applications are considered at any time. They can be submitted directly by the parent/guardian or through a teacher and should include the family's financial position and number of children.

Other information

The trust also makes occasional grants to local secondary schools.

Hope House and Gippeswyk Educational Trust

£6,000

Correspondent: John Clements, 4 Church Meadows, Henley, Ipswich IP6 0RP

Trustees: Peter Grimwade; Diana Lewis; William Pipe; John Clements; Mark Piper; Susanne Scott; William Coe; Pauline Thomas; Peter Shepherd.

CC Number: 1068441

Eligibility

People under 21 who live in Ipswich and the surrounding area.

Types of grants

One-off grants are made. Schoolchildren can receive grants towards the cost of school uniforms, other school clothing, books, educational outings, maintenance

costs and school fees. Students in further or higher education can be given grants towards books, fees/living expenses and study or travel abroad. Preference can be given to schoolchildren with serious family difficulties.

Annual grant total

In 2010/11 the charity had an income of £11,000 and a total expenditure of £12,000. Grants to individuals usually total around £6,000.

Applications

On a form available from the correspondent, submitted through the individual's school, college or educational welfare agency. Applications are considered throughout the year.

Other information

The trust also makes grants to organisations.

The Mills Educational Foundation

£1,500

Correspondent: Deborah Stace, The Chairman of the Trustees, 45 Saxmundham Road, Framlingham, Suffolk IP13 9BZ (01728 724370; email: info@themillscharity.co.uk; website: www.themillscharity.co.uk)

Trustees: Howard Wright; Kenneth Musgrave; Mr Kelleway; C. Wright; P. C. Booth; Revd Vipond; Kate Hunt; Nick Corke.

CC Number: 310475

Eligibility

Children and young people up to the age of 24 who live in Framlingham and the surrounding district, or attend a school there.

Types of grants

One-off grants ranging from £50 to £550. Schoolchildren and further/higher education students can be supported for uniforms, other school clothing, books, equipment, instruments, educational outings in the UK and study or travel abroad. People starting work can receive grants for uniforms, other clothing, equipment and instruments.

Annual grant total

In 2010/11 the foundation gave grants to individuals totalling £6,100.

Applications

In writing to the correspondent, either directly by the individual or through a third party such as a social worker or the individual's school/college/educational welfare agency. Applications are considered every two months, unless it is an emergency situation.

Other information

Local primary schools are also supported.

The Stowmarket Educational Foundation

£1,500

Correspondent: Colin Hawkins, Clerk to the Trustees, Kiln House, 21 The Brickfields, Stowmarket, Suffolk IP14 1RZ (01449 674412; email: colinhawkins@aol.com)

Trustees: David Hopgood; Raymond Taylor; William Smith; Hazel Burl; Ron Snell; Lesley Mayes; Michael Eden; Kathleen Butt; Kate Riddleston; Keith Edward.

CC Number: 802573

Eligibility

People in need who are under 25 and live or attend a school or other educational establishment, or whose parents live, in the town of Stowmarket and the civil parishes of Badley, Combs, Greeting St Peter, Great Finborough, Haughley, Old Newton with Dagworth, Onehouse and Stowupland, all in the county of Suffolk.

Types of grants

One-off grants of £50 to £200 towards uniforms, clothing and educational outings for schoolchildren. Students, including mature students, in further/higher education can receive assistance with books, equipment and instruments.

Annual grant total

About £1,500.

Applications

On a form available from the correspondent, for consideration throughout the year. Applications should be submitted by a school or college, a social worker or other professional.

Annie Tranmer Charitable Trust

£13,000 (37 grants)

Correspondent: M R Kirby, Clerk to the Trustees, 51 Bennett Road, Ipswich, Suffolk IP1 5HX (01473 743694)

Trustees: John Miller; Valerie Lewis; Nigel Bonham-Carter; Patrick Grieve.

CC Number: 1044231

Eligibility

Young people in education who live in within a 15 mile radius of Woodbridge in Suffolk.

Types of grants

One-off and recurrent grants according to need, towards for example,

educational outings, fees, equipment/instruments and travel overseas. Grants range from £40 to £1,000.

Annual grant total

In 2010/11 the trust had assets of £3.4 million and an income of £109,000. Grants to individuals totalled £13,000.

Applications

In writing to the correspondent, including details of the specific need, finances and alternative funding sources.

Other information

Grants are also made to other local agencies for the benefit of individuals.

Brockley

The Brockley Town and Poor Estate (Brockley Charities)

£650

Correspondent: Jane Forster, Brooklands, Chapel Lane, Brockley, Bury St Edmunds IP29 4AS (01284 830558)

Trustees: Ian Robertson; Peter Miller; Geoffrey Baber; Sue Parker; Jane Forster.

CC Number: 236989

Eligibility

Schoolchildren who live in Brockley village.

Types of grants

Grants are given for the purchase of uniforms. In previous years an educational book has also been given to all students in the village on reaching the age of 15.

Annual grant total

In 2010 the trust had an income of £1,700 and a total expenditure of £1,300. Grants are made for educational and welfare purposes.

Applications

In writing to the correspondent to be submitted directly by the individual or a family member.

Bury St Edmunds

Old School Fund

£3,000

Correspondent: Michael Dunn, 121 Southgate Street, Bury St Edmunds, Suffolk IP33 2AZ (01284 769483)

Trustees: Michael Phillips; Marie MacInnes; Malcolm Rogers; Malcolm Dale; Brenda Humpage; Frances Ward; Valerie Moore.

CC Number: 310348

Eligibility

Persons under 25 who live in, or whose parents live in, Bury St Edmunds and are undertaking further or higher education in any subject and are in need.

Types of grants

One-off and recurrent grants of between £100 and £250 towards the cost of books, fees and living expenses.

Annual grant total

About £3,000.

Exclusions

Grants are not made for benefits which are normally provided by the local education authority.

Applications

An introductory letter and reference to the correspondent is preferred, requesting an application form. Deadlines for applications are subject to dates of trustee meetings.

Other information

Grants are also given to local schools.

Dennington

The Dennington Consolidated Charities

£500

Correspondent: Dr W Blakeley, Clerk, Thorn House, Saxtead Road, Dennington, Woodbridge, Suffolk IP13 8AP (01728 638031)

Trustees: Robert Rous; Elizabeth Hickson; Revd Jonathan Olanczu; Robert Wardley; Mandy Sayer; Adrian Neill; Keir Wyatt.

CC Number: 207451

Eligibility

Grants are awarded to those embarking on tertiary education and vocational training living in the village of Dennington.

Types of grants

One-off and recurrent grants.

Annual grant total

In 2010 the charities had an income of £13,000 and a total expenditure of £10,000. The charities give approximately £500 each year for educational purposes and £3,000 for welfare.

Exclusions

The trust does not make loans, nor does it make grants where public funds are available unless they are considered inadequate.

Applications

In writing to the correspondent. Applications are considered throughout the year and a simple means test questionnaire must be completed by the applicant.

Grants are only made to people resident in Dennington (a small village with 500 inhabitants). The charities do not respond to applications made outside this specific geographical area.

Dunwich

The Dunwich Town Trust

£8,400

Correspondent: John Cary, Black Pig Studio, Dunwich, Saxmundham, Suffolk IP17 3DR (01728 648927)

Trustees: John Salusbury; Veronica Donovan; Nick Mayo; David Cook; Angela Abell; Linda Prior; Keith Maunder; Crispin Clay.

CC Number: 206294

Eligibility

People in need who live in the parish of Dunwich.

Types of grants

All grants are to individuals. Grants for education range from £600 to £3,500 depending on the needs and type of course.

Annual grant total

In 2011 grants to individuals for education totalled £8,400.

Applications

Write to the correspondent and request an application form.

Other information

Formerly known as 'Dunwich Pension Charity'.

Earl Stonham

Earl Stonham Trust

£2,000

Correspondent: San Wilson, College Farm, Forward Green, Stowmarket, Suffolk IP14 5EH (01449 711497; email: sam_wilson@talk21.com)

Trustees: Sam Wilson; Jennifer Griffiths; Cynthia Collins; Barry Rice; Colin Woods; Phil Hurt.

CC Number: 213006

Eligibility

People with educational needs who live, or whose parents live, in the parish of Earl Stonham.

Types of grants

One-off grants up to a maximum of £200.

Annual grant total

In 2010/11 the trust had an income of £6,800 and an expenditure of £4,200. Grants can be made for both educational and welfare needs.

Applications

In writing to the correspondent, to be submitted directly by the individual.

Other information

The trust also makes grants to organisations.

Gislingham

The Gislingham United Charity

£5,000

Correspondent: Robert Moyes, 37 Broadfields Road, Gislingham, Eye, Suffolk IP23 8HX (01379 788105; email: r.moyes1926@btinternet.com)

Trustees: Jane Franklin; Andrew Dickson; Betty Cunningham; Geoffrey Laurence; Pamela Shorten; Ron Pye; Alan Harding; Geoff Mason; Peter Neale; Christopher Wells.

CC Number: 208340

Eligibility

Children who attend Gislingham Church of England School.

Types of grants

Grants are given to schoolchildren for excursions and to college and mature students for books.

Annual grant total

In 2011 the charity had an income of £21,000 and an expenditure of £23,000.

Applications

Applications can be submitted directly by the individual or verbally via a trustee. Applications must include reasons for the application, the amount requested and the applicant's address.

Other information

The charity also gives grants to individuals in need and supports village organisations and ecclesiastical causes.

Hadleigh

Ann Beaumont's Educational Foundation

£9,900 (75 grants)

Correspondent: R Welham, 55 Castle Road, Hadleigh, Suffolk IP7 6JP (01473 822718)

Trustees: David Grutchfield; John Everitt; Martin Cork; John Bloomfield;

Laurie Munson; Martin Thrower; Lesley Turner.

CC Number: 310397

Eligibility

People under the age of 25 years who are in need of financial assistance and live in the parish of Hadleigh.

Types of grants

Grants to help with course books, equipment or travel for people at school, college, university or for those starting work.

Annual grant total

In 2010/11 the charity had assets of £1.2 million, an income of £31,000 and made 75 grants totalling £9,900.

Applications

In writing to the correspondent, together with evidence of the cost of the books or equipment required. Applications are considered four times a year.

Other information

75 grants were made to individuals and eight to organisations.

Halesworth

The Halesworth United Charities

£1,000

Correspondent: Janet Staveley-Dick, Clerk, Hill Farm, Primes Lane, Blyford, Halesworth, Suffolk IP19 9JT (01986 872340)

Trustees: Edward Hyde-Clarke; Joan Lee; Janet Wright; Annette Dunning; Anne Wilkinson; Mary Hussey; Paul Widdowson.

CC Number: 214509

Eligibility

People in need who live in the ancient parish of Halesworth.

Types of grants

One-off grants according to need. Recent examples include travel abroad for educational purposes, medical equipment or tools needed for a trade.

Annual grant total

Grants usually total between £2,000 and £3,000.

Applications

In writing to the correspondent, directly by the individual or through a social worker, Citizens Advice or other welfare agency. Applications can be submitted at any time for consideration in January, July and December, or any other time if urgent.

Other information

Grants are also made to individuals for welfare purposes.

Hundon

The Hundon Educational Foundation

£7,000

Correspondent: Bernard Beer, Beauford Lodge, Mill Road, Hundon, Sudbury, Suffolk CO10 8EG (01440 786942)

Trustees: Desmond Notley; Jock Whitehouse; Paul Turner; Peter Blair; Jane Midwood; Stuart Mitchell; Lynda Burrows.

CC Number: 310379

Eligibility

People under 25 living in the parish of Hundon.

Types of grants

Grants ranging from £50 to £500 are given to schoolchildren and further and higher education students including those for uniforms, books, equipment/instruments, fees, maintenance/living expenses, educational outings in the UK and study or travel abroad and to people starting work for books and equipment/instruments.

Annual grant total

In 2011 the trust had an income of £7,300 and an expenditure of £7,900.

Applications

On an application form available from the correspondent, either directly by the individual or by their parent/guardian. Applications are considered in March, July and November and should be received in the preceding month.

The foundation is well advertised in the village. It does not respond to applications made outside of its area of interest.

Kirkley

Kirkley Poor's Land Estate

£1,700

Correspondent: Lucy Walker, 4 Station Road, Lowestoft, Suffolk NR32 4QF (01502 514964)

Trustees: Jennifer Pelt; Andrew Shepherd; Michael Cook; Ralph Castleton; Elaine High; Rose Hudson; Revd Andrew White.

CC Number: 210177

Eligibility

Individuals in need who live in the parish of Kirkley.

Types of grants

One-off grants ranging from £200 to £300 to help towards university expenses.

Annual grant total

In 2010/11 the charity had assets of 1.9 million and an income of £84,000. Grants were made totalling £39,000 and were distributed as follows:

Grants to individuals (education)	£1,700
Grocery voucher scheme	£15,000
Grants to organisations	£22,000

Applications

In writing to the correspondent.

Lakenheath

The Charities of George Goward and John Evans

£7,000

Correspondent: Laura Williams, 8 Woodcutters Way, Lakenheath, Brandon, Suffolk IP27 9JQ

Trustees: Horace Parsons; John Gentle; Mrs Shipp; Robert Rolph; Kevin Wickham; Steve Hills.

CC Number: 253727

Eligibility

People under 25 in the parish of Lakenheath in Suffolk.

Types of grants

Grants in the range of £25 and £300, for school leavers and students in further and higher education to help with living expenses and books. Schoolchildren can receive grants towards uniforms, clothing and educational outings. Grants are also given to people starting work for books and equipment.

Annual grant total

In 2010 the charity had both an income and total expenditure of £15,000.

Applications

In writing to the correspondent. Applications can be submitted either directly by the individual or a family member, through a third party such as a social worker or teacher, or through an organisation such as Citizens Advice. They should be received by February and August for considered in March and September respectively. Applications should include a brief financial situation and receipts are required for book grants.

Other information

Grants are also made to organisations and to individuals for educational purposes.

Lowestoft

The Lowestoft Church and Town Educational Foundation

£7,000

Correspondent: J M Loftus, Clerk, 148 London Road North, Lowestoft, Suffolk NR32 1HF (01502 718700)

Trustees: John Allen; Jill Collins; June Chapman; Edith McLean; Elizabeth Hudd; Gerda Buckley; Myrtle Wigg; Mary Rudd; Sandra Keller; Roy Stebbings; Ian Graham; John Parle; Michael Asquith.

CC Number: 310460

Eligibility

People in need aged between 5 and 25 who have either lived or attended school in the area of the old borough of Lowestoft for at least three years.

Types of grants

One-off grants of £150 each are given to: schoolchildren towards the cost of uniforms/other school clothing, childcare, educational outings in the UK, and study and travel abroad; and students in further/higher education towards the cost of books, equipment/instruments, maintenance/living expenses and study or travel abroad.

Annual grant total

In 2010/11 the foundation had an income of £22,000 and an expenditure of £14,000.

Applications

Applications, on a form available from the correspondent, should be submitted directly by the individual. Forms need to be verified by the applicant's place of education; the closing date is 30 November. Grants are paid in the following January.

Other information

Grants are also made to local schools.

Mendlesham

The Mendlesham Education Foundation

£16,000 (41 grants)

Correspondent: S C Furze, Beggars Roost, Church Road, Mendlesham, Stowmarket IP14 5SF

Trustees: Hugh Cutting; James Baker; Philip Gray; Dawn Smith; Raymond Fenning; David Nunn; Andrew Stringer; Paul Head.

CC Number: 271762

Eligibility

People under 25 who live in the parish of Mendlesham.

Types of grants

One-off and recurrent grants are given towards pre-school fees for children with serious family difficulties, and books and equipment for students in further/higher education or apprenticeships.

Annual grant total

In 2011 the foundation had an income of £48,000 and made 41 grants to further education students totalling £16,000.

Exclusions

Grants are not given for school fees or maintenance. They are not normally available towards the cost of school educational outings or for special education needs.

Applications

On a form available from the correspondent, including details of education to date, details of course to be taken, other grants applied for, estimated expenditure, parents' financial position and other dependent children in the family. Applications should be made by the individual or through a parent/guardian by mid-September.

Other information

Grants are also made to organisations and Mendlesham CP School.

Pakenham

The Pakenham Educational Trust

£2,000

Correspondent: Christine Margaret Cohen, Clerk, 5 St Mary's View, Pakenham, Nr Bury St Edmunds, Suffolk IP31 2ND (01359 232965)

Trustees: Marion Sargent; Derek Dorling; Richard Bacon; Nigel Farthing; Katherine Valentine.

CC Number: 310364

Eligibility

Students in post-16 education or training who are in need and who live in Pakenham.

Types of grants

Grants are given to people attending university and college courses for a variety of educational needs. Mature students may receive help towards fees. Grants are also given towards activities

such as Duke of Edinburgh Award Scheme, cathedral camps, sports scholarships etc. Grants can be one-off or recurrent and range from £50 to £300.

Annual grant total

About £4,000 to organisations and individuals.

Applications

Applications should be sent directly by the individual to the correspondent by 31 October. They are considered in November.

Other information

Grants are also given to local organisations.

Risby

The Risby Fuel Allotment

£1,000

Correspondent: Penelope Wallis, 3 Woodland Close, Risby, Bury St Edmunds, Suffolk IP28 6QN (01284 81064)

Trustees: Bernard Abrey; Penelope Wallis; Heather Wagner; Eric Tennant.

CC Number: 212260

Eligibility

People in need who live in the parish of Risby.

Types of grants

Grants are given to higher education students.

Annual grant total

In 2010/11 the charity had an income of £5,700 and an expenditure of £4,600. Grants are given primarily for relief-in-need purposes and fuel costs.

Applications

In writing to the correspondent. Applications can be submitted by the individual and are considered in March and October. Applications made outside the specific area of interest (the parish of Risby) are not acknowledged.

Stutton

The Charity of Joseph Catt

£3,000

Correspondent: Keith R Bales, 34 Cattsfield, Stutton, Ipswich, Suffolk IP9 2SP (01473 328179)

Trustees: Revd Geoffrey Clement; Dr Jane Pavitt; Keith Bales; Karl Baxter.

CC Number: 213013

Eligibility

People in need who live in the parish of Sutton.

Types of grants

One-off grants and loans according to need.

Annual grant total

In 2010 the trust had an income of £9,000 and a total expenditure of £10,000.

Applications

Applications can be submitted by the individual, or through a recognised referral agency (e.g. social worker, Citizens Advice or doctor) and are considered monthly. They can be submitted to the correspondent, or any of the trustees at any time, for consideration in May and November.

Other information

The charity also supports local almshouses.

Walberswick

The Walberswick Common Lands

£4,000

Correspondent: Jayne Tibbles, Lima Cottage, Walberswick, Southwold, Suffolk IP18 6TN (01502 724448; website: walberswick.onesuffolk.net/walberswick-common-lands-charity/)

Trustees: Nigel Hunt; Kate Goodchild; Brian Fisher; James Darkins; Clive Brynley-Jones; Madeline Dabbs; Keith Graham Webb.

CC Number: 206095

Types of grants

Grants are given in the range of £35 and £1,200 to schoolchildren for maintenance/living expenses and to college students for study/travel abroad, maintenance/living expenses and equipment.

Annual grant total

In 2011 educational grants totalled £1,100. A further £5,800 was given in personal loans.

Applications

In writing to the correspondent, either through the individual's school/college/educational welfare agency, or directly by the individual or through a parent or relative. Applications are considered in February, April, June, August, October and December.

Other information

Grants are also made to organisations.

Surrey

The Archbishop Abbot's Exhibition Foundation

£6,000

Correspondent: Richard Middlehurst, 17 Ashdale, Bookham, Leatherhead, Surrey KT23 4QP (01483 303678; email: rhm@awb.co.uk)

Trustees: Christopher Fox; Michael Wills; Derek Holbird; Nicholas Brougham; Richard Hemingway; John Trigg; Geoffrey Wilson.

CC Number: 311890

Eligibility

People aged between 11 and 29 who (i) live in the area administered by the Guildford Borough Council or the Waverley Borough Council (except that part of Waverley formerly within the urban district of Farnham), or (ii) attend, are about to attend or have for at least three years attended a school in the borough of Guildford as constituted on 1 April 1974. Preference is given to male applicants.

Preference is given to low-income families, to schoolchildren with serious family difficulties so that the child has to be educated away from home and to people with special educational needs.

Types of grants

One-off grants are given to: schoolchildren towards books, equipment, instruments and fees; and people starting work or at any level of further or higher education towards equipment, instruments, books, fees and living expenses. Students in further or higher education can also be supported in their study or travel abroad. Grants are given to assist students in their future careers.

Grants range from £250 to £800 and are one-off.

Annual grant total

About £6,000 a year.

Applications

On a form available from the correspondent which requests details of information about parents'/guardians' income and expenditure and details of any savings. Applications can be submitted directly by the individual, through the individual's school, college or educational agency or through a relative or friend. Applications are considered in January, May and September and should be received in the preceding month.

The Egham Education Trust

£3,000

Correspondent: Max Walker, 33 Runnemede Road, Egham TW2 9BE (01784 472742; email: eghamunicharity@aol.com)

Trustees: Betty Wheeler; Jill Reynolds; John Ashmore; Yvonna Lay; Christine Searle; Diana Brickell.

CC Number: 311941

Eligibility

People under 25 who have lived in the electoral wards of Egham, which is now Egham, Engerfield Green, Virginia Water and Hythe, for at least five years.

Types of grants

One-off and recurrent grants in the range of £100 and £500 are made to schoolchildren, undergraduates, vocational students, mature students and people with special educational needs. Grants may also be given for activities such as the Duke of Edinburgh Award Scheme.

Annual grant total

About £3,000.

Applications

On a form available from the correspondent. Applications must include details of other grants and loans. The deadline for applications is the 15th of each month.

The Mary Stephens Foundation

£10,000

Correspondent: John Stephenson, Doghurst Cottage, Doghurst Lane, Chipstead, Surrey CR5 3PL (01737 556548)

Trustees: Simon Kolesar; Katy Deragon; Timothy Humm; Madeleine MacCallum; Jean Pearce; Dinah Mabbutt; John Stephenson.

CC Number: 311999

Eligibility

People under the age of 25 who live, or whose parents live, in the ancient parish of Chipstead and Hooley, or who have attended Chipstead County First School.

Types of grants

One-off and recurrent grants up to a maximum of £1,200 a year. Help to people in further education is in the form of books, uniforms and travel expenses. Limited help is given towards fees on a scholarship basis.

Grants are given to those qualifying to obtain further education in the broadest possible way, such as for music lessons and field courses.

Annual grant total

In 2010/11 the foundation had an income of £5,600 and an expenditure of £13,000.

Exclusions

The trust does not issue grants to pre-schoolchildren or provide loans.

Applications

Applications are considered at quarterly meetings and should be made directly by the individual, or by the individual's head of school or church leader.

The Witley Charitable Trust

£1,300

Correspondent: Daphne O'Hanlon, Triados, Waggoners Way, Grayshott, Hindhead, Surrey GU26 6DX (01428 604679)

Trustees: Daphne O'Hanlon; Pamela Pile; Peter Herring; John Withers; John Cable; Dr David Pollard.

CC Number: 200338

Eligibility

Children and young people aged under 20 who are in need and who live in the parishes of Witley and Milford.

Types of grants

One-off grants ranging from £25 to £300.

Annual grant total

Around £3,000 each year.

Exclusions

The trust does not give loans or for items which should be provided by statutory services.

Applications

In writing to the correspondent, to be submitted through social workers, schools, Citizens Advice and so on but not directly by the individual. Applications are usually considered in early February and September, although emergency applications can be considered throughout the year.

Charlwood

John Bristow and Thomas Mason Trust

£0

Correspondent: Marie Singleton, Trust Secretary, 3 Grayrigg Road, Maidenbower, Crawley RH10 7AB (01293 883950; email: trust.secretary@jbtmt.org.uk; website: www.jbtmt.org.uk)

Trustees: R. Parker; William Campen; Martin James; Feargal Hogan; Howard Pearson; Alison Martin; J. King; C. Jordan.

CC Number: 1075971

Eligibility

Only people who live in the ancient parish of Charlwood (as constituted on 17 February 1926).

Types of grants

Grants are given to schoolchildren, college students, undergraduates, vocational students, mature students, people with special educational needs and to people starting work. Help is given for the cost of uniforms/other school clothing, books, equipment/instruments, fees, maintenance/living expenses, childcare, education outings in the UK, study or travel abroad and student exchanges.

Annual grant total

In 2011 the trust had assets of £2.3 million, an income of £76,000 and made grants totalling £66,000, of which £300 went to individuals for welfare purposes. No grants to individuals for education were made during the year.

Applications

On a form available from the correspondent or to download from the website. Applications can be submitted directly by the individual or through a third party. They will normally be considered within two weeks but can be dealt with more quickly in urgent cases.

Chertsey

The Chertsey Combined Charity

£1,250

Correspondent: M R O Sullivan, Secretary, PO Box 89, Weybridge, Surrey KT13 8HY

Trustees: Malcolm Loveday; Christopher Norman; David Harding; John Gooderham; Judith Norman; Michael Everett; Peter Austin; Richard Fleming; Revd Timothy Hillier; Claire Gant; Derek Cotty; David Frith; John Leach.

CC Number: 200186

Eligibility

People in need who live in the electoral divisions of the former urban district of Chertsey.

Types of grants

Grants are often given to help towards the cost of books, clothing and other essentials for those at school. Grants may also be given to people at college or university.

Annual grant total

In 2010/11 the charity had an income of £62,000 and a total expenditure of £68,000. Grants to individuals were made totalling £2,500.

Applications

On a form available from the correspondent.

Other information

The charity also makes grants to organisations (£45,000 in 2010/11).

Chessington

Chessington Charities

£2,000

Correspondent: Mrs L Roberts, St Mary's Centre, Church Lane, Chessington, Surrey KT9 2DR

Trustees: Revd Peter Jenner; Jackie Bone; Michael Brook; Revd Sara Oakland; Marjorie Redding; Joy Fogg.

CC Number: 209241

Eligibility

People in need who live in the parish of St Mary the Virgin, Chessington. Applicants must have lived in the parish for at least one year.

Types of grants

Recent grants included those for school uniforms, shoes and school trips. Grants are given in the range of £30 to £250 and are usually one-off.

Annual grant total

In 2010 the charities had both an income and total expenditure of £5,400.

Exclusions

Grants are not given to pay debts. Applicants must live in the Parish of St Mary the Virgin; this excludes those that live in the rest of the Chessington postal area.

Applications

On a form available from the correspondent to be submitted either directly by the individual or through a social worker, Citizens Advice or other agency. Christmas gifts are distributed in November. Other applications are considered throughout the year. A home visit will be made by a trustee to ascertain details of income and expenditure and to look at the need.

Other information

Grants are also given to local organisations which help people who are elderly or disabled such as Chessington Voluntary Care and Arthritis Care. Individual welfare grants are also available.

Chobham

Chobham Poor Allotment Charity

£3,000

Correspondent: Mrs Elizabeth Thody, 46 Chertsey Road, Windlesham GU20 6EP

Trustees: David Elliott; Violet Tedder; Winifred Patterson; Jennifer Stratford; Antony Astall; Sue Bush; Edward Bentall

CC Number: 200154

Eligibility

Residents of the ancient parish of Chobham.

Types of grants

Grants for school uniforms and school trips.

Annual grant total

In 2010/11 the charity had an income of £43,000 and gave £3,000 in grants to individuals for education.

Applications

In writing to the correspondent.

Other information

The charity's main activities are the maintenance of allotments and relief in need; however a small amount is given each year to assist with school uniform and school trip expenses.

East Horsley

Henry Smith's Charity (East Horsley)

£500

Correspondent: Mr R Deighton, East Horsley Parish Council Office, Kingston Avenue, East Horsley, Surrey KT24 6QT (01483 281148; email: henrysmithcharity@easthorsley.net)

Trustees: Olive Ridler; Stephen Skinner; Roy Proctor; Revd Elisabeth Bussmann.

CC Number: 200796

Eligibility

Children from poor or disadvantaged backgrounds who have lived in East Horsley for at least two years.

Types of grants

Grants can be given to children to support them through their schooling and to orphaned children for small scholarships.

Annual grant total

Each year the trust receives about £1,000, allocated by Henry Smith's (General Estate) Charity which is divided ccording to need between welfare and ducational grants.

Applications

n writing to the correspondent through third party such as a social worker, eacher or vicar. Applications are onsidered in December.

Elmbridge

The R. C. Sherriff Trust

£5,500

Correspondent: Dean Blanchard, High treet, Esher, Surrey KT10 9SD (01372 74140; email: arts@rcsherrifftrust.org. k; website: www.rcsherrifftrust.org.uk)

Trustees: Nigel Cooper; James Vickers; annia Shipley; Shweta Kapadia; Penny Harris; Claire Gibbins; Barry Cheyne; Wendy Smithers; Alison Clarke; Elizabeth Cooper; Ruth Lyon.

CC Number: 272527

Eligibility

Composers, craftspeople, curators, esigners, directors, film-makers, nusicians, performers, producers, romoters, theatre technicians, visual rtists, writers and other individual arts ractitioners in Elmbridge.

Types of grants

Grants and bursaries, usually of up to 500 to assist with:
- Professional development and training (including travel grants) e.g. short courses in specific skills, work placements with other artists, specified periods of travel and/or study
- Research and development for arts projects
- The publication or production of a specific piece of work
- Capital items e.g. equipment

Annual grant total

n 2010 the trust had assets of 3.6 million and an income of £181,000. Grants to individuals totalled around 5,500.

Exclusions

No retrospective grants or funding for igher education courses, long-term ocational training e.g. Drama School, or ngoing training programmes (e.g. piano essons, regular dance classes).

Applications

On a form available from the orrespondent or the trust's website. The rustees meet quarterly to consider pplications, after the deadlines which re usually in January, April, July and October.

Other information

Grants are also made to organisations.

Epsom

The Epsom Advancement in Life Charities

£1,500

Correspondent: Patricia Vanstone-Walker, 42 Canons Lane, Tadworth, Surrey KT20 6DP (01737 361243; email: vanstonewalker@ntlworld.com)

Trustees: Robert Leach; Gillian Heym; John Steward; Joan Harridge; A. R. M. Watson; Christine Long; Simon Talbott; David Eggett; Colin Bird; Neil Dallen.

CC Number: 200571

Types of grants

One-off and recurrent grants according to need are given to: schoolchildren, college students, undergraduates, vocational students, mature students, people starting work and people with special educational needs, including those towards clothing/uniforms, fees, books, equipment/instruments maintenance/living expenses and excursions.

Annual grant total

In 2010 grants for education totalled £1,500.

Applications

On a form available from the correspondent, to be submitted directly by the individual. Applications are considered in March, June, September and December and should be submitted in the preceding month.

Other information

Grants are also given from Epsom Parochial Charities for relief in need.

Leatherhead

The Leatherhead United Charities

£8,500

Correspondent: David Matanle, Homefield, Fortyfoot Road, Leatherhead, Surrey KT22 8RP (01372 370073; email: luchar@btinternet.com)

Trustees: John Buchanan Henderson; Bridget Lewis-Carr; Alan Wright; Graham Osborne; Michael Ward; David Sharland.

CC Number: 200183

Eligibility

People in need who live in the area of the former Leatherhead urban district council.

Types of grants

One-off grants in the range of £100 and £750. This charity does not deal with educational needs only, 'grants are made for the relief of need generally'.

Annual grant total

In 2011 the charity gave 54 grants to individuals. No grants total was available but in previous years grants to individuals have totalled around £20,000, for welfare and educational purposes.

Applications

On a form available from the correspondent to be submitted directly by the individual or a family member. Applications are considered throughout the year.

Other information

The charity also makes grants to organisations.

Reigate

The Pilgrim Band Trust

£8,000

Correspondent: Gregory Andrews, Clevelands, 13 Furzefield Road, Reigate RH2 7HG (01737 244134; email: pilgrim. band@virgin.net)

Trustees: Gregory Andrews; Natalie Lennon; Annie Smith; Anthony Upton; Peter White; James Wood.

CC Number: 1140954

Eligibility

Young musicians, particularly of classical religious and folk music, who are in need in Reigate and the surrounding area, with particular emphasis on children with disabilities.

Types of grants

Grants are given towards tuition fees.

Annual grant total

This trust was removed and reregistered with the Charity Commission, therefore no accounts or annual return have been submitted yet. However previously the trust has given £8,000 in scholarships and donations.

Applications

In writing to the correspondent.

Other information

Grants are also made to schools to purchase musical equipment.

Thorpe

The Thorpe Parochial Charities

£1,000

Correspondent: Mrs D Jones, 9 Rosefield Gardens, Ottershaw, Chertsey, Surrey KT16 0JH (01932 872245)

Trustees: Diana Andrews; Brian Relph; Doris Mackie; Jane Nadin; Margaret Harnden; Susan Knight.

CC Number: 205888

Eligibility

People in need under 21 years who live in the ancient parish of Thorpe.

Types of grants

Grants are occasionally given towards books for students in further or higher education. Relief-in-need grants are also available.

Annual grant total

About £2,000.

Applications

In writing to the correspondent by the end of October. Applications are usually considered in November. The grants are usually given out at Michaelmas.

Woking

The Deakin Charitable Trust

£1,400

Correspondent: William Hodgetts, Station House, Connaught Road, Brookwoood, Woking GU24 0ER (01483 485444)

Trustees: Paul Deakin; William Hodgetts; Geraldine Lawson.

CC Number: 258001

Eligibility

People studying music who are living in the immediate Woking area.

Types of grants

Bursaries are given to students of music.

Annual grant total

In 2010/11 the trust had assets of £1 million and an income of £51,000. Music bursaries for individuals totalled £1,400.

Applications

In writing to the correspondent.

Other information

Most of the trusts income goes in grants to organisations.

West Sussex

The Hooper and Downer Educational Foundation

£9,000

Correspondent: Peter Smith, Smith and White Accountants, 28 Downside Avenue, Storrington, Pulborough RH20 4PS (01903 742684)

Trustees: Diane Line; Malcolm Acheson; Bernard Lavin; Garry Smart; Ray Hunt; Alison Murphy.

CC Number: 306423

Eligibility

People under 25 who live, or whose parents live, in the area of benefit, which is the parishes of Amberley with Stoke, Ashington with Buncton, Ashurst, Bramber with St Botolphs, Greatham, Parham, Pulborough, Steyning, Storrington, Sullington, Thakeham with Warminghurst, Upper Beeding, Washington, West Chiltington, Wiggonholt and Wiston, all in West Sussex.

Types of grants

One-off grants according to the nature of assistance requested. Grants can be given towards books, tools, equipment, travel expenses, course fees and so on.

Annual grant total

Grants are usually made to around 50 to 70 individuals annually totalling around £9,000.

Applications

On a form available from the correspondent. An endorsement by a teacher or tutor is required if applicable, and also information on family circumstances.

Other information

Funds are also used to maintain and improve the Old School in Storrington, the trust's historic property, which is in use for educational and cultural purposes.

The Betty Martin Charity

£8,500

Correspondent: Madeleine Crisp, 46 Guillards Oak, Midhurst, West Sussex GU29 9JZ (01730 813769)

Trustees: Alison Cunnington; David McCahearty; Elizabeth Moore; Joanna Green; Noel Simpson; Shelagh Legrave.

CC Number: 1029337

Eligibility

People who live in Sussex, with a preference for those who live within a 1 mile radius of the Parish Church in Midhurst, West Sussex

Types of grants

Grants are given to people, including mature students, in further/higher education and apprentices towards the cost of books, fees, living expenses, study and travel overseas, travel and childcare. Grants range from £100 to £500.

Annual grant total

In 2010/11 the trust had assets of £537,000, an income of £29,000 and gave £8,500 in grants.

Applications

An application form is available from the correspondent which is then submitted directly by the individual along with a reference.

The Bassil Shippam and Alsford Charitable Trust

See entry on page 19

Angmering

William Older's School Charity

£3,000

Correspondent: Hon. Secretary, School Charity Parish Office, Church House, Arundel Road, Angmering, Littlehampton BN16 4JS

Trustees: Peter Gayler; Richard Hobden; Shelagh Downing; Andrew Forbes.

CC Number: 306424

Eligibility

People aged 23 or under who live in the ecclesiastical parish of Angmering. The applicant's parents must reside in Angmering.

Types of grants

One-off and recurrent grants up to £500 towards the cost of equipment/instruments and fees for schoolchildren and towards books, equipment/instruments, childcare and educational outings in the UK for students in further or higher education.

Grants/loans are also given to local schools, pre-school playgroups and other educational foundations towards the rent of premises, provision of books, equipment etc.

Annual grant total

About £3,000 to individuals with further grants given to organisations.

Applications

In writing to the correspondent giving details of income and expenditure, course being studied and residence in Angmering. Applications are considered in January, May and October.

Crawley

Crawley and Ifield Educational Foundation

£2,000

Correspondent: Hilary Ward, St Marys Rectory, Forester Road, Crawley, West Sussex RH10 6EH (01293 547261)

Trustees: Tim Wilson; Malcolm Liles; Bob Burgess; Simon Newham.

CC Number: 1042834

Eligibility

People under 25 who live in Ifield, Southgate, Crawley or Rusper and are in financial need.

Types of grants

One-off and recurrent grants, with a preference for those which will promote the individuals religious education, such as Sunday School.

Annual grant total

Expenditure is erratic but in 2010 totalled £11,000, the majority of which probably went in grants to organisations.

Applications

In writing to the correspondent.

Other information

Grants are also made to local schools.

London

General

The Aldgate and Allhallows Barking Exhibition Foundation

£31,000 (30 grants)

Correspondent: The Clerk, 31 Jewry Street, London EC3N 2EY (020 7488 2518; email: aldgateandallhallows@ sirjohncass.org; website: www. aldgateallhallows.org.uk)

Trustees: Denise Jones; David Mash; Robin Hazlewood; D. J. Ross; Bertrand Olivier; Graham Forbes; John Hall; William Hamilton-Hinds; Marianne Fredricks; Billy Whitbread; Paul James; Susan Knowles; Sirajul Islam; Laura Burgess; Kevin Everett.

CC Number: 312500

Eligibility

Young people under the age of 25 who are permanent residents of Tower Hamlets or City of London (and have been for at least three years) and are from financially disadvantaged backgrounds, studying full-time in further, higher or postgraduate education on a course of at least one year in length that will result in the awarding of a recognised qualification.

Individuals from a refugee background are welcome to apply, providing they have been granted indefinite leave to remain in the UK or full refugee status.

Types of grants

Most grants are made by way of undergraduate bursaries to students at Queen Mary, University of London and Birkbeck, Stratford. A small number of other grants are made to individuals studying at other colleges and universities.

Grants can be made for education costs, maintenance and tuition fees.

Annual grant total

In 2010 the foundation had assets of £6.8 million and an income of £48,000.

Grants to 30 individuals totalled £31,000.

Exclusions

Grants are not given for courses at private colleges, fees at independent schools, repeated years of study, study for a qualification at the same or lower level than those an individual already possesses, fees for higher education courses, unless they are for second degrees or medical electives. Individuals with time limited leave to remain in the UK are not eligible to apply.

Applications

Initially in writing to the correspondent by the individual, through a third party such as a teacher or through an organisation such as a school or educational welfare authority detailing circumstances and purpose of grant. Those meeting the correct criteria are then sent an application form to complete and return. Applications are considered throughout the year.

The foundation welcomes informal contact via phone or email prior to application.

Application guidelines are available on the website.

Other information

Grants were also made to 20 institutions (£298,000).

Sir William Boreman's Foundation

£4,500 (5 grants)

Correspondent: Andrew Mellows, Head of Charities, Drapers' Hall, Throgmorton Avenue, London EC2N 2DQ (020 7588 5001; fax: 020 7628 1988; email: charities@thedrapers.co.uk; website: www.thedrapers.co.uk)

Trustee: The Drapers' Company.

CC Number: 312796

Eligibility

Full or part-time students under the age of 25 who live in the London boroughs of Greenwich and Lewisham, and have been resident there for at least the last

three years (prior to the start of the course). Applicants must be a UK national or have full refugee status. Parental joint residual income must be in the region of £25,000 per annum or less.

Types of grants

The main aim of the foundation is to make educational grants to schoolchildren and students at institutions of further and higher education. For those in further or higher education support is available towards the costs of books, travel fares, equipment/stationery, maintenance, student fees/living expenses and costs for mature students such as childcare. Grants are made up to £1,000.

Schoolchildren may be eligible for a small hardship grant towards the cost of school uniforms, sports kit, travel costs and educational excursions.

Annual grant total

In 2010/11 the foundation had assets of £3.1 million and an income of £109,000. Five grants to individuals were made totalling £4,500.

Exclusions

No grants are made for:

- Students aged over 25 or pre-schoolchildren
- Non-UK citizens and asylum seekers (only those with full refugee status may apply)
- Postgraduate students who have attained a 2.2 in their first degree (unless there are extenuating circumstances)
- Grants to purchase computers (with the exception of disabled students)
- Overseas study
- Retrospective grants
- Tuition fees
- Non-educational related loans or debts
- Business ventures
- High course fees (i.e. Acting, Dance or Drama courses) where a student provides no clear indication on how the course will be funded
- Private school fees – unless there is a case of unexpected and considerable hardship arising since the child's

entry to the school and where the child is due to sit either GCSEs or A-levels in the current academic year

Applications

On a form available from the correspondent or the website, together with proof of income and parental income, evidence of age, an academic reference and for non-UK citizens only, proof of refugee status. Applicants are expected to have applied for a grant from their Local Education Authority and to have received a decision on this before applying to the foundation. Some applicants will be asked to attend a brief interview with the governors. Applicants are advised to read the guidelines, also available from the website, before making an application. Meetings which take place three times a year, usually in February, June and October and applications should be made at least four weeks beforehand.

Other information

The foundation also gave £55,000 in grants to organisations.

Sir John Cass's Foundation

£14,500 (21 grants)

Correspondent: Richard Foley, Deputy Clerk, 31 Jewry Street, London EC3N 2EY (020 7480 5884; fax: 020 7480 4268; email: contactus@sirjohncass.org; website: www.sirjohncass.org)

Trustee: The Board of Governors.

CC Number: 312425

Eligibility

People in need aged under 25 who, for the last three years, have been a permanent resident for Inner London (namely Camden, City of London, City of Westminster, Greenwich, Hackney, Hammersmith and Fulham, Islington, Kensington and Chelsea, Lambeth, Lewisham, Newham, Southwark, Tower Hamlets and Wandsworth) and are from a financially disadvantaged background. Preference is given to people aged over 19.

Types of grants

The foundation now only runs the scholarship programme in conjunction with the City of London.

Annual grant total

In 2010/11 the foundation had assets of £4 million and an income of £5.9 million. 21 grants to individuals were made totalling £14,500. Of these 21 individuals, all but one were studying at a higher education level.

Exclusions

No grants are made towards one year courses, which only offer qualifications at a level already attained from a different course or repeating/resitting a year of study.

Applications

Via the trust's website.

Other information

In 2011 the foundation established a £1.5 million five year scholarship programme to fund students higher education.

This trust also administers The Aldgate and Allhallows Barking Exhibition Foundation with identical criteria except being open only to people in the City of London and the borough of Tower Hamlets.

The foundation also gives grants to organisations (£525,000) and schools (£106,000).

The Castle Baynard Educational Foundation

£6,000

Correspondent: Anthony Rogers, Trustee, Quinces, Hosey Common Road, Westerham TN16 1PP (01959 564370; fax: 020 7354 9225; email: csmcguiness@aol.com)

Trustees: Ian Luder; Nigel Challis; Catherine McGuinness; David Levin; Raymond Catt; Anthony Rogers; Guy Treweek.

CC Number: 312502

Eligibility

People in need with a connection to the City of London or the former county of Middlesex.

Types of grants

Grants in the range of £100 and £500 for those at school, college or university, people starting work and people with special educational needs. Grants are more suited towards meeting expenses such as specific books, items of equipment or events.

Annual grant total

In 2010/11 the foundation had an income of £7,000 and an expenditure of £6,400.

Exclusions

Grants are not normally for course fees or general maintenance.

Applications

In writing to the correspondent. Applications should include: details of the purpose for which the grants is requested; a CV setting out age, schools and colleges attended and educational attainments to date; proof of financial need; a written reference in support of the application confirming current educational status and financial need; and an sae. Applications are considered in March, June, September and December.

The City and Diocese of London Voluntary Schools Fund

£19,000 (311 grants)

Correspondent: Inigo Woolf, London Diocesan Board for Schools, 36 Causton Street, London SW1P 4AU (020 7932 1163; email: inigo.woolf@london.anglican.org; website: www.london.anglican.org/schools)

Trustee: The London Diocesan Board for Schools.

CC Number: 312259

Eligibility

Any person under 25 who has attended Church of England voluntary aided school in the diocese of London (i.e. north of the river) for at least two years

Types of grants

Grants are given towards educational activities which do not form part of the usual school day or curriculum. Pupils still at school can receive support for music, dance, specialist sport (such as national team places), field trips and other forms of educational enrichment, and for pupils whose personal circumstances are difficult. Occasional grants are given for special needs.

Grants are also given to students in further/higher education for books, fees and travel abroad, and to people starting work for books, equipment and occasionally clothing. Grants range from £50 to £500 and are usually one-off, but are sometimes recurrent.

Annual grant total

In 2010/11 the trust had assets of £650,000 and an income of £161,000. 311 grants were made totalling £19,000.

Exclusions

Grants are not given for school fees or other costs for schoolchildren except those above. Retrospective applications are not considered.

Applications

On a form available from the correspondent by request. Applications should include references and details on the proposed purpose of the grant. Applications for individuals under 16 should be completed by a parent/guardian. Two references must be included. They are considered quarterly

The City of London Corporation Combined Education Charity

£3,000

Correspondent: Barbara Hamilton, Head of Adult Education, Community and Children's Services, City of London, PO Box 270 EC2P 2EJ (020 7332 1755; email: adulteducation@cityoflondon.gov. uk; website: www.cityoflondon.gov.uk/ corporation/lgnl_services/advice_and_ benefits/grants/student_awards.htm# hersef)

Trustees: Joy Hollister; Billy Dove; Martin Raymond.

CC Number: 312836

Eligibility

People aged 14 to 18 who are in need and are following special technical courses full-time at secondary schools or establishments of further education in the area formerly under the control of the London County Council (ex-ILEA area). Priority will be given to courses related to civil engineering and construction, but other branches of engineering, building studies, manufacturing, IT and design will also be considered. A list of approved courses is available from the correspondent.

Types of grants

Support may take the form of: a bursary over an academic year, with possible renewal for further years during the period of eligibility (living, travel and/or tuition expenses); specific grants to assist in the completion of short course or educational project work; and help with the costs of attendance at courses or conferences in the UK or overseas. Grants can be up to £500.

Annual grant total

In 2010/11 the fund held assets of £440,000 which represents the total assets for the combined funds (see other information). There was an income of £16,000 for this fund alone. £3,000 is available for grants each year but no grants were made in 2010/11.

Applications

On a form available from the correspondent, submitted either directly by the individual, or via their school, college or educational welfare agency. Applications must show evidence of financial hardship and be accompanied by a covering letter of support from the head of the institution. Applications should be submitted before March.

Other information

This fund was previously called the Higher Education Research and Special Expenses Fund (HERSEF), which received no applications in the year 2010/11. In 2011 a new scheme was approved whereby this fund merged with Archibald Dawnay Scholarships, Robert Blair Fellowships for Applied Science and Technology and Alan Partridge Smith Trust to form the City of London Corporation Combined Education Charity (retaining the charity registration number for HERSEF).

John Edmonds

£1,500

Correspondent: Stephen Willmett, Battersea United Charities, Battersea District Library, Lavender Hill, London SW11 1JB (01273 202730)

Trustees: Barbara Hayr; Peter Barnshaw; Tessa Strickland; S. Tester; Lorna Windmill; Philip Beddows; Pamela O'Reilly; Dee Platt; Stephen Willmett.

CC Number: 312153

Eligibility

People under 25 who live in the former metropolitan borough of Battersea, with a preference for those whose families have lived in Battersea for a long time.

Types of grants

One-off and recurrent grants of £50 to £500. Schoolchildren can receive help towards uniforms, school clothing, books, equipment/instruments, educational outings in the UK and study or travel abroad. Students in further and higher education, including postgraduates and vocational students can receive grants towards books, equipment/instruments, excursions, fees, maintenance and childcare.

Annual grant total

In 2010/11 the charity had an income of £3,700 and an expenditure of £1,700.

Applications

On a form available from the correspondent, to be submitted at any time directly by the individual or through their school, college or university. Applications are considered bi-monthly.

The Eric Evans Memorial Trust
See entry on page 280

Francon Trust

£14,000

Correspondent: Derek Ivy, Smithtown, Kirkmahoe, Dumfries DG1 1TE (01387 740455)

Trustees: David Eldridge; Terry Nemko; Joe Herzberg; Gordon Gentry.

CC Number: 10033592

Eligibility

People in need aged up to 20, who were born or brought up in London and still live there, particularly those studying in the professions of medicine, architecture, accountancy, insurance, banking, law or other professional business or trade fields, including science and engineering. Applicants must have expected (or obtained) grades of at least one A and two Bs for their A-levels.

Types of grants

Grants range between £10,000 and £15,000 in the form of interest-free loans which become gifts on completion of the course after six months of employment in a related occupation. Grants can be spent on the costs of university training. Grants awarded are not necessarily restricted to course fees, but may cover other aspects of necessary expenditure including living expenses (all items should be listed in the detailed financial analysis to be provided). Grants may be in the form of a single payment, or a series of successive payments, depending upon circumstances. Approximately seven students per annum are supported.

Annual grant total

In 2010/11 the trust had assets of £1.1 million, an income of £27,000 and awarded grants totalling £14,000 to give educational, welfare and social support to needy students in London.

Applications

The trust does not invite 'unsolicited applications' and states that 'all funds are committed'. The trusts annual report states that 'potential students for first degree courses are selected in accordance with the guidelines, based upon applications and recommendations from headteachers in support of bright students who have little or no financial means. Potential students are identified by contact with headteachers and then, after due application, are interviewed by the trustees to decide those who should receive support'.

The Hale Trust
See entry on page 280

The Hornsey Parochial Charities

£21,000

Correspondent: Lorraine Fincham, Clerk to the Trustees, PO Box 22985, London N10 3XB (020 8352 1601; fax: 020 8352 1601; email: hornseypc@blueyonder.co.uk)

Trustees: Peter Kenyon; Ann Jones; Barbara Simon; Eddie Griffith; John

Hudson; Lorraine Marshall; Patrick Henderson; Vivienne Manheim; Ann Gillespie; Carol O'Brien; Katy Jones; Paula Lanning.

CC Number: 229410

Eligibility

People under 25 who have lived for at least one year in the ancient parish of Hornsey (that is the London postal area of N8, and parts of the London postal areas of N4, N6 N10 and N16 in Haringey and Hackney).

Types of grants

Grants of £200 to £1,400 for students to help with books, equipment, clothing or travel. Grants to help with school, college or university fees or to supplement existing grants. Help towards the cost of education, training, apprenticeship or equipment for those starting work.

Annual grant total

In 2011 the charity made 65 educational grants to organisations and individuals. Grants to individuals averaged £600.

Applications

Individuals can write requesting an application form that, on being returned, can usually be dealt with within a month.

Other information

Grants are also made for welfare purposes.

The Island Health Charitable Trust

£0

Correspondent: Sonia Lapwood, Island Health Trust Ref: JFC/3873, Carter Lemon Camerons LLP, 10 Aldersgate Street, London EC1A 4HJ (020 7406 1000; email: info@islandhealthtrust.org; website: www.islandhealthtrust.org)

Trustees: Roger Squire; Stephen Molyneaux; Alan Holam; Suzanne Goodband; Christopher Exeter.

CC Number: 1127466

Eligibility

People who are involved in providing primary healthcare and want to continue training, living or working in the London boroughs of Tower Hamlets and Newham.

Types of grants

One-off grants and recurrent grants according to need for up to three years. The maximum grant available is £5,000.

Annual grant total

In 2010/11 the trust had assets of £3.2 million and an income of £289,000. Although grants were made to nine organisations totalling £27,000 it appears

no grants to individuals were made during the year.

Exclusions

Grants are not given to university students for living expenses or tuition fees, to cover the travel costs of training abroad, or are made in any case where statutory funding is available.

Applications

On the application form available with guidance notes on the trust's website.

The London Youth Trust (W. H. Smith Memorial)

£15,000

Correspondent: The Worshipful Company of Carpenters, Carpenters' Hall, Throgmorton Avenue, London EC2N 2JJ (020 7588 7001; fax: 020 7382 1683; email: info@carpentersco.com; website: www.londonyouthtrust.org.uk)

Trustee: The Worshipful Company of Carpenters.

CC Number: 224484

Eligibility

People under 25 resident in London and studying at the Building Crafts College.

Types of grants

There are three grants schemes (i) LYT scholarships: £6,500 for students enrolled at the Building Crafts College (ii) LYT bursaries: £15–£20 a week to support students in training and during the transition to employment for tools or travel (iii) LYT prizes: two prizes of £250.

Annual grant total

In 2010/11 the trust had assets of £635,000 and an income of £64,000. Grants to individuals and organisations totalled £33,000.

Applications

Apply via the Worshipful Company of Carpenters, see their website for details. Grants for students at the Building Crafts College are considered in May, all other applications in July.

Other information

In September 2012 the trust fund was passed over to the Worshipful Company of Carpenters. It remains as a restricted fund but is administered by the Company via the Norton Folgate fund.

Need and Taylor's Educational Charity

£3,000

Correspondent: Julia Cadman, St Paul's Church Office, St Paul's Road, Brentford, Middlesex TW8 0PN (020 8568 7442; email: bcmcharity@yahoo.co.uk)

Trustees: Revd Derek Simpson; Mel Collins; Peter Williams; Matt Harmer; Andrew Dakers; Steve Curran.

CC Number: 312269

Eligibility

Children, under the age of 21, who live in the former boroughs of Brentford and Chiswick.

Types of grants

One-off grants of £80 to £100 to schoolchildren towards uniforms and other school clothing including PE kits, coats and shoes, equipment, instruments, fees and educational outings in the UK.

Annual grant total

In 2010/11 the charity had an income of £14,000 and an expenditure of £11,000.

Applications

On a form available from the website along with the 'applicants letter' which must be signed by the child's headteacher. Applications are considered at any time.

Other information

Grants are also made to schools.

The Philological Foundation

£17,000

Correspondent: J Slack, Clerk, 1 Luxborough Tower, Luxborough Street, London W1U 5BP (email: philological@gmail.com)

Trustees: Gerald Margolis; Gwyneth Hampson; Peter Sayers; David Jones; Margery Hall; Serena Standing; John Leys; Rita Brightmore; Carolyn Keen.

CC Number: 312692

Eligibility

People aged 16 to 25 who attended a secondary school in the London borough of Camden or the City of Westminster, including those who are living elsewhere for their studies.

Types of grants

One-off and recurrent grants of £150 to £1,000 are given to: schools and young people for educational outings in the UK, student exchange and study or travel abroad; further and higher education students for books, equipment, fees, living expenses, study or travel overseas and student exchange; equipment/tools and travel costs for people starting work and postgraduates (but not people undertaking research degrees) for books, fees, living expenses and study or travel abroad.

Grants for education are considered at the following levels: GNVQ; GCSE; A-level; Access; Foundation; Diploma; First Degree and Postgraduate Taught Degrees.

Annual grant total

In 2010/11 the foundation had assets of £877,000 and an income of £79,000. Grants to individuals totalled £17,000.

Exclusions

The foundation does not give bursaries, scholarships or loans.

Applications

On a form available from the correspondent. Applications are considered in February, April, July, September and December and completed forms (with a covering letter) must be submitted a month before these meetings. Applicants must provide: (i) proof of attendance at a Westminster or Camden school; (ii) support for the figures quoted in the amount of grant requested; (iii) exam results; and (iv) details of income and expenditure. Applicants should also have applied for a statutory loan.

The correspondent stated: 'If non-eligible students apply (for example, those aged over 25 or those who did not attend a secondary school in Westminster or Camden) the application will not be acknowledged.'

Other information

Grants are also made to schools within the area of benefit for journeys and educational visits, performing arts and books and play and environmental improvement.

The Pocklington Apprenticeship Trust (Acton, Ealing and Hammersmith and Fulham branch)

£750

Correspondent: Mary Church, 48 St Dunstans Avenue, London W3 6QB (02089928311)

Trustees: Mary Church; M. Gallagher; Abdullah Gulaid; Kate Crawford.

CC Number: 312186

Eligibility

Young people aged 25 or under who have lived in Acton, Ealing or Hammersmith and Fulham for at least five years. Special consideration is given to people who have a disability or special educational needs.

Types of grants

Grants in the range of £100 and £300 are given towards tools, equipment, training course fees, textbooks, stationery, computer accessories, special clothing etc.

Annual grant total

About £500 to £1,000 is available each year.

Applications

On a form available from the correspondent, for consideration in May/June. Applicants should provide evidence of financial hardship; this could be being in receipt of state benefits or because of personal circumstances. Applicants can apply on their own behalf or through a sponsor who might be a teacher, tutor, youth leader or social worker.

Other information

Although it is primarily for the benefit of young people, the fund has stated that it will also be worth older people applying who, because of a disabling condition later in life, have had to consider an alternative job to that which they have been used to.

Richard Reeve's Foundation

£260,000 (611 grants)

Correspondent: The Clerk to the Governors, 2 Cloth Court, London EC1A 7LS (020 7726 4230; email: clerk@ richardreevesfoundation.org.uk; website: www.richardreevesfoundation.org.uk)

Trustees: Billy Dove; Mavis Hughesdon; P. J. Tickle; S. Dewing; Sarah Betteley; Michael Bennett; Charlynne Pullen; Mark Jessett; Shannon Farrington.

CC Number: 1136337

Eligibility

Applicants must be under the age of 25 (in exceptional cases this may be extended to 40) and either: (a) they or their parent(s) must have lived, studied or worked for the last twelve months in the London Boroughs of City of London (Square Mile), Camden or Islington or(b) they must have lived, studied or worked in the London Boroughs of City of London (Square Mile), Camden or Islington for at least two of the last ten years.

Applications from refugees with exceptional and indefinite leave to remain are welcome. The foundation is also, depending on individual circumstances, able to make grants to people whose asylum claims are still being processed.

Types of grants

Grants of up to £1,000 are available to help with:

- Maintenance costs (e.g. travel, books, equipment)
- The cost of special tuition or treatment (e.g. music or dyslexia)
- UK based field trips that are required as an essential part of the course
- The cost of training, apprenticeship or tools/equipment for those starting work
- Course fees (depending what course you are studying and your individual circumstances)

Annual grant total

In 2010/11 the foundation had assets of £15.7 million and an income of £716,000. Grants were made totalling £260,000 to 611 students of whom 346 were in further education.

Exclusions

The foundation will not consider grants for the following:

- Computers
- Holidays
- Clothing
- Child care costs
- Fees at private schools or colleges (except in some exceptional cases and where we agree that education within the state system would be inappropriate)
- Overseas trips or placements
- Second degrees
- Postgraduate courses (except those that are essential for certain careers)
- International students who are resident in the UK on a student visa

Applications

Forms and guidelines can be downloaded from the website or by telephone or email. Applications are considered at meetings in March, June, October and December. Deadlines for each meeting are published on the website.

Students studying at Birkbeck, University of the Arts, City and Islington College, Guildhall School of Music and Drama or Westminster Kingsway College should see their welfare advisor to discuss making an application via the partnership funds.

The Sheriffs' and Recorders' Fund

£17,400 (107 grants)

Correspondent: The Chair, c/o Central Criminal Court, Old Bailey, Warwick Square, London EC4M 7BS (020 7248 3277; email: secretary@srfund.net; website: www.srfund.org.uk)

Trustees: Christopher Thomas; David Biddle; Lady Prue Davies; James Harman.

CC Number: 221927

Eligibility

People on discharge from prison, and families of people imprisoned. Applicants must live in the Greater Metropolitan area of London.

Types of grants

One-off grants for education and training at any level. In 2010/11 the average grant was £124.

Annual grant total

In 2010/11 the fund had assets of £719,000 and an income of £179,000. Grants were made to 1,040 individuals totalling £130,000. There were 107 grants totalling £17,000 made for education and training purposes.

Applications

On a form available from the correspondent, submitted through probation officers or social workers. They are considered throughout the year.

Other information

Grants are also made for welfare purposes and for special projects.

St Clement Danes Educational Foundation

£13,000

Correspondent: Ann Baron, St Clement Danes School, Drury Lane, London WC2B 5SU (020 7641 6593; email: abaron@stcd.co.uk)

Trustees: Inigo Woolf; David Jarvis; Richard Carey; Somin Grigg; Stephen Twining; William Bailey; Kumar Iyer; Cameron Thomson.

CC Number: 312319

Eligibility

After meeting the needs of St Clement Danes Primary School, grants are awarded to, in order of priority: (i) ex-pupils of St Clement Danes Church of England Primary School; and (ii) people who are under 25 years of age and have lived within the diocese of London, with preference for the City of Westminster, for the majority of their education.

Types of grants

Grants to assist with the costs of books, materials, travel, uniform and associated costs for study at college or university.

Annual grant total

In 2011 the foundation had assets of £2.7 million and an income of £142,000. Educational grants to 29 individuals totalled £13,000.

Exclusions

Grants towards fees are not usually given to pupils in primary and secondary education. No grants to overseas students.

Applications

On a form available from the correspondent. Applications can be submitted directly by the individual, or by a parent/guardian if the individual is under 18, for consideration in February, May, October or November. They need to be submitted six weeks before the committee meeting.

Sir Walter St John's Educational Charity

£5,300

Correspondent: Melanie Griffiths, Office 1A, Culvert House, Culvert Road, London SW11 5DH (020 7498 8878; email: manager@swsjcharity.org.uk; website: www.swsjcharity.org.uk)

Trustees: Daphne Daytes; Tony Tuck; Martin Stratton; Sarah Rackham; Julian Radcliffe; Barry Fairbank; John O'Malley; Peter Dyson; Sheldon Wilke; Godfrey Allen; Jenny Scribbins; Peter Dawson; Simon Butler; Adedamola Aminu; Wendy Speck.

CC Number: 312690

Eligibility

People under 25 who live in the boroughs of Wandsworth and Lambeth and have lived there for at least six months. There is a preference for those who live in the Battersea area. All applicants must provide evidence that they and their parent(s) are in receipt of benefit or very low income.

Grants will only be awarded to students who are following a validated, approved or recognised course.

Types of grants

Grants are one-off and are for a range of educational needs; this can include social and physical training as well as study on college courses. Student grants are towards costs that are necessary for attendance on the course, such as registration fees, travel, books and equipment. The normal upper limits for grants are £500 for students aged 16 to 18, and £750 for students aged 19 to 24.

Lone parents who are in receipt of benefit can receive grants of up to £1,800 towards childcare. Grants of up to £1,500 (and above in exceptional circumstances) can be made to students on foundation or access courses in arts, dance and drama. Disabled students are eligible for grants to meet additional education/training expenditure.

Grants are made to students under 18 and to full-time students on university degree courses only in exceptional or unforeseen circumstances.

Annual grant total

In 2010/11 the charity had assets of £3.5 million and an income of £123,000. Grants to individuals totalled £5,300. Grants are mostly given to organisations.

Exclusions

Grants are not made to pupils at independent schools or to students on postgraduate courses. Grants are not given towards general living expenses, study or travel abroad or student exchanges.

Applications

All applicants must provide evidence that they have a good prospect of successfully completing the course. Students attending courses at South Thames College should apply to their college student advice service.

Students attending courses at other colleges should email, write or telephone, providing their full name, date and place of birth, present address and length of time they have lived there, the name of their college or school and the title of the course of study or training, including start and finish dates. Applicants who then appear eligible for an award will be asked to complete an application form. The office is normally staffed on Tuesdays and Thursdays.

The Truro Fund

£8,000

Correspondent: John Ansell, The Clerk to the Trustees, Parish Church of St Clements, 1 St Clements Court, London EC4N 7HB (020 7623 5454; email: lm800aat@hotmail.com)

Trustees: Roger Cooper; Pamela Clarke; David Parrott; Alastair Collett.

CC Number: 312288

Eligibility

Young people under the age of 21 living or attending school or college in the area previously within the Inner London Education Authority.

Types of grants

The fund's policies are laid out in a clear and simple leaflet. Small grants may be awarded for the purchase of tools, books

r other equipment for young people
ntending to start their own business,
ollow a trade or profession or enter an
pprenticeship. The trust also gives
ursaries or scholarships to help those
vishing to further their education.
Grants to individuals rarely exceed £500
nd are non-renewable. The trustees take
 strong personal interest in all
pplicants and prefer to make small
rants to individuals rather than
rganisations.

Annual grant total
n 2010/11 the fund had an income of
8,700 and an expenditure of £8,700.

Exclusions
No grants for school fees, maintenance
r travel costs. Grants to organisations
vill only be made where the organisation
an identify the young people who will
e assisted by funding. The aim has to
e to improve the employment prospects
r the education of the beneficiaries.

Applications
On a form available from the
orrespondent. Applications should
nclude: three references, at least one of
vhich should be from college; evidence
f date of birth; full financial details; and
ny information concerning immigration
tatus (if necessary). Applications are
onsidered in May and November.

The British and Foreign
School Society Trust
Fund

£3,500 (10 grants)

Correspondent: Imogen Wilde, Director,
Maybrook House, Godstone Road,
Caterham, Surrey CR3 6RE (01883
331177; email: director@bfss.org.uk;
vebsite: www.bfss.org.uk)

Trustees: Graham Kingsley; Stephen
Orchard; David Swain; Steve Hodkinson;
Roger Howarth; David Tennant; Brian
ork; Stephen Ross; Emily Tomlinson;
David Zahn; David Stephens; Shubhi
Rao; Jaz Saggu; Ben Ramm; E. J. Weale.

CC Number: 314286

Eligibility
Students in Bermondsey, Bethnal Green,
Poplar, Southwark and Stepney. In
ractise students need to be studying at
London South Bank University, who
urrently administer grants from this
und.

Types of grants
Grants of £150 to £1,300.

Annual grant total
n 2011 ten grants to individuals
otalling £3,500 were made.

Exclusions
Grants are not given for private
education.

Applications
Applications should be made directly to
the University Welfare Fund at London
South Bank University.

Sir Mark and Lady
Turner Charitable
Settlement
See entry on page 301

The Turner Exhibition
Fund

£2,000

Correspondent: Mrs J M Cuxson, Veale
Wasbrough Vizards, Barnards Inn,
86 Fetter Lane, London EC4A 1AD (020
7405 1234; email: jcuxson@vwv.co.uk)

Trustee: Audrey Hogston.

CC Number: 312891

Eligibility
Girls and women who are members of
the Church of England, have attended a
school wholly or partly maintained out
of public funds for at least two years and
are now living in the diocese of London
or that part of the diocese of Southwark
which lies within the London boroughs
of Greenwich, Lambeth, Lewisham,
Southwark and Wandsworth.

Types of grants
Small cash grants, from £250 to £1,000,
to assist candidates in meeting the
expenses of, and incidental to, their
education or training at any stage after
leaving primary school, such as fees, and
the purchase of books and equipment.
Grants are also made for travel costs to
and from college. The fund prefers to
award grants to those undertaking a first
course of education or training, rather
than postgraduate students.

Annual grant total
About £2,000.

Applications
In writing to the correspondent,
including the nature of the course of
education and training which the
applicant intends to pursue and
availability of other funding.
Applications are usually considered in
June and October and application forms
are issued on request approximately two
months before each meeting.

The Wiseman and
Withers Exhibition
Foundation

£1,500

Correspondent: David Fisher, Clerk,
5 Upton Road, Bexleyheath, Kent
DA6 8LQ (020 8306 0278)

Trustees: Brian Siderman; Brian
O'Sullivan; Janet Gillman; Grahame
Stephens.

CC Number: 312820

Eligibility
People who live in the London borough
of Greenwich and that part of the
London borough of Newham which was
formerly in the metropolitan borough of
Woolwich. Applicants must be under the
age of 26.

Types of grants
Grants of between £50 and £200, to
provide equipment needed for courses of
further education.

Annual grant total
About £1,500.

Exclusions
No grants towards travel or major
awards to finance full-time education.

Applications
In writing to the correspondent. The
trustees meet twice a year.

Barking and
Dagenham

The Catherine Godfrey
Association for those
with Learning and other
Disabilities

£0

Correspondent: Hilda Bastable,
25 Wraglings, Beldams Lane, Bishop's
Stortford CM23 5TB

Trustees: Kathryn Pettitt; Patricia
Beverly.

CC Number: 207370

Eligibility
People who have learning difficulties
and/or other disabilities, including
physical disabilities, and people with
mental health issues. Applicants must be
in financial need and live in Barking and
Dagenham and the surrounding areas.
Support is also given to carers.

Types of grants

Grants for outdoor activities and holidays in Britain to those who cannot afford them.

Annual grant total

In 2010/11 the trust had an income of £2,000. There has been no expenditure for the past three years.

Applications

In writing to the correspondent. Applications need to be co-signed by a social worker or similar and have to be submitted between September and December for consideration in January.

Barnet

The Elizabeth Allen Trust

£12,000

Correspondent: Mrs Helen Rook, PO Box 270, Radlett, Herts WD7 0DJ (01923 853966; email: elizabethallentrust@fsmail.net)

Trustees: Liz Ratcliffe; Peter Ziman; Valerie Johnston; Ruth Dyer; Wilf Nichols; Marylin Kirtan.

CC Number: 310968

Eligibility

People in need under 25, who live in the borough of Barnet and who have not already gained a first degree. Priority is given to applicants from the pre-1965 urban district of (High) Barnet.

Types of grants

One-off grants of up to £300 are made for specific needs (such as books, equipment and fees) and maintenance grants of up to £250 a term are paid for an academic year. Grants for educational outings in the UK are considered in exceptional circumstances.

Annual grant total

In 2009/10 the trust had an income of £22,000 and an expenditure of £19,000. Grants usually total around £12,000.

Exclusions

No grants are made towards private school fees, for gap year activities or for purposes funded by the LEA.

Applications

On a form available from the correspondent upon receipt of a stamped addressed envelope. Forms can also be obtained by leaving a message (including telephone number) on the trust's answer phone. Applications must include details of parental finances and the use of the applicant's student loan. The trustees meet five times a year to consider applications.

344

The trust states that the trustees' April meeting is realistically the last at which applications for the current year can be considered.

The Mayor of Barnet's Benevolent Fund

£1,000

Correspondent: The Grants Unit, London Borough of Barnet, North London Business Park, Oakleigh Road South, London N11 1NP (020 8359 2020; fax: 020 8359 2685; email: ken. argent@barnet.gov.uk)

Trustees: Brian Coleman; Andrew Travers; Jeffrey Lustig.

CC Number: 1014273

Eligibility

Schoolchildren who live in the London borough of Barnet and have done so for at least six months and whose parents are on an income-related benefit.

Types of grants

One-off grants of up to £100 can be given towards school uniforms.

Annual grant total

In 2009/10 the trust had an income of £3,000 and a total expenditure of £2,000.

Applications

Applications should preferably be submitted directly by the individual, but may also be made directly by a supporting agency. All requests should include a quotation for the items required.

Other information

Grants are also made for welfare purposes.

The Hyde Foundation

£11,000 (19 grants)

Correspondent: Robin Marson, 1 Hillside, Codicote, Hitchin SG4 8XZ (020 8449 3032; email: marson36@ homecall.co.uk)

Trustees: Barbara Taylor; Nigel Baker; Revd Canon Hall Speers; Averill Lovatt; Ann Evans; Jennifer Smith; Judy Burstow; Bob Burstow; Sarah Lloyd-Winder; Katherine Morris; Tim Bennett.

CC Number: 302918

Eligibility

People in education up to first degree level in the ancient parishes of Chipping Barnet and Monken Hadley.

Types of grants

One-off grants in the range of £100 to £6,000. Grants are given to college students, undergraduates, vocational students, mature students, people with special educational needs and people starting work. Grants given include those for music lessons, fees, travel abroad, books, equipment and maintenance/ living expenses.

Annual grant total

In 2011 the trust had assets of £648,000 and an income of £42,000. Grants to 19 individuals totalled £11,000.

Applications

In writing to the correspondent, who will forward an application form. Trustees meet quarterly in January, April, July and October to consider applications and applications should be received at the end of December, March, June and September respectively.

Other information

Grants are also given to local schools and organisations.

The Valentine Poole Charity

£0

Correspondent: Victor Russell, Clerk, The Forum Room, Ewen Hall, Wood Street, Barnet, Hertfordshire EN5 4BW (020 8441 6893; email: vpoole@ btconnect.com)

Trustees: Hall Speers; Tony Alderman; Stephen Lane; Helena Davis; Brenda Sandford; I. Butcher; June Hughes; M. Jamieson; Susan McKenzie; Brian Salinger.

CC Number: 220856

Eligibility

Young people in need under the age of 26 who live in the former urban district of Barnet and East Barnet (approximately the postal districts of EN4 and EN5).

Types of grants

One-off grants to schoolchildren for uniforms and people starting work for books, equipment and instruments.

Annual grant total

In 2011 the trust had assets of £508,000 and an income of £66,000. Welfare grants and pensions totalled £30,000 but no educational grants were made during the year.

Applications

On a form available from the correspondent for consideration in March, July and November. Applications should be submitted by a school, welfare agency or other relevant third party, not directly by the individual.

Other information

Grants are also made to local organisations.

Bexley

Bexley United Charities

£600

Correspondent: Kenneth Newman, 13 High Street, Bexley, Kent DA5 1AB (07831 838054)

Trustees: John Waters; Mrs Broadhurst; Neil Sayers; Martin Lea; Sylvia Malt; Peter Wilson; Barbara Graham.

CC Number: 205964

Eligibility

People under the age of 25 who live in the borough of Bexley.

Types of grants

Grants tend to be less than £500 and are given towards books for students at school, college or university, and towards books, equipment and instruments for people starting work or apprentices.

Annual grant total

Grants totalled £600 in 2010/11.

Applications

In writing to the correspondent.

Brent

The Wembley Samaritan Fund

£2,000

Correspondent: Jack Taylor, c/o Sudbury Neighbourhood Centre, 809 Harrow Road, Wembley, Middlesex HA0 2LP (020 8908 1220)

Trustees: Mary Steele; Ron Dawson; Gill Barrons; Kath Barrett; Betty Harvel; Jean Hows; Mona Gregory; Anne Lake; Janet Bartlett.

CC Number: 211887

Eligibility

People in need who live in the electoral wards of Wembley (Tokyngton, Alperton, Sudbury, Sudbury Court and Wembley Central). The charity is particularly aimed at children.

Types of grants

One-off grants mostly for school uniforms, warm clothing, nursery equipment and the costs of school outings.

Annual grant total

About £4,000 for education and welfare.

Applications

By telephone or in writing to the correspondent.

Other information

Grants are also made to local organisations.

Bromley

The Downham Feoffee Charity

£5,100

Correspondent: Jo Howard, 35 Fieldside, Ely, Cambridgeshire CB6 3AT (01353 665774; email: downhamfeoffees@hotmail.co.uk)

Trustees: Philip Laver; Carole Hall; Helen Last; Bruce Smith; Caroline Frankland; Pat Golding; Debbie Adams-Payne; Owen Winters; Margaret Talbot; Marilyn Oldfield; Nathaniel Missin.

CC Number: 237233

Eligibility

Residents of the ancient parish of Downham.

Types of grants

Grants for students attending higher education or other education or training.

Annual grant total

Grants to individuals for education totalled £5,100.

Applications

In writing to the correspondent.

Other information

The charity also makes grants to schools and to individuals for welfare purposes.

Camden

Bromfield's Educational Foundation

£20,000

Correspondent: Charlotte Malzels, Grant Officer, St Andrew's Holborn, 5 St Andrew Street, London EC4A 3AB (020 7583 7394; email: info@ standrewholborn.org.uk; website: www. standrewholborn.org.uk)

Trustees: Lyle Dennen; John Booth; Brian Hanson; Jane Cruse.

CC Number: 312795

Eligibility

People in need under 25 who live (or whose parents or guardians live) in the Holborn area of the London borough of Camden for at least two years.

Types of grants

One-off and termly grants of £600 for clothing, books, equipment/instruments, computers and maintenance/living expenses.

Annual grant total

In 2011 the foundation had assets of £1.4 million and an income of £49,000. Grants to individuals totalled £22,000. 21 families received termly grants from the foundation, almost all of which included a child with a disability. Two grants were also given for the cost of music lessons and 64 for school uniform.

Exclusions

No grants for school, college or university fees.

Applications

On a form available from the website, to be submitted directly by the individual or through a school/college/educational welfare agency or a parent or guardian. Details of income and expenditure and personal information are required, supported by documentary evidence which will be treated in the strictest confidence. Applications can be submitted at any time, and will be considered within 21 days.

Other information

Priority is given to families of children with disabilities. Grants are also given to organisations.

Hampstead Wells and Campden Trust

£4,700

Correspondent: Sheila Taylor, Director and Clerk, 62 Rosslyn Hill, London NW3 1ND (020 7435 1570; email: grant@hwct.co.uk; website: www.hwct. org.uk)

Trustees: Ms Chung; Jocelyne Tobin; Diana Dick; Ian Harrison; Geoffrey Berridge; Gaynor Bassey; Alistair Voaden; Christina Williams; Dennis Finning; Francoise Findlay; Gaynor Humphreys; Ted Webster; Mike Bieber; Stephen Tucker; Alistair Jacks; Charles Perrin; Ilan Jacobs; Michael Katz.

CC Number: 1094611

Eligibility

People in need who live in the former metropolitan borough of Hampstead.

Types of grants

Grants of up to £3,000 are given to people at any stage of their education, or who are entering a trade or profession, for uniforms and other clothing, books, equipment, instruments, maintenance, living expenses, childcare and educational outings in the UK.

Annual grant total

In 2010/11 the trust had assets of £15 million, an income of £611,000 and gave grants to 3,642 individuals totalling £224,000, including 18 education grants totalling £4,700. 95 pensions totalling £74,000 were also awarded.

Exclusions

The trustees are unable to offer assistance with course or school fees.

Applications

Applications may be made by letter or on the trust's application form which can be downloaded from its website. Applications by letter will only be accepted if they include the following details: the client's name, date of birth, occupation, address and telephone number, details of other household members, other agencies and charities applied to, result of any applications to the Social Fund, household income, and details of any savings and why these savings cannot be used. Applications should be supported by a statutory or welfare agency. Decisions are made within two weeks.

St Andrew Holborn Charities

£28,000

Correspondent: The Grants Officer, 5 St Andrew Street, London EC4A 3AB (020 7583 7394; email: info@ standrewholborn.org.uk; website: www. standrewholborn.org.uk)

Trustees: Lyle Dennen; John Booth; Edward Lord; Nasim Ali; Brian Hanson; Jeremy Simons; Janie Spring; Jane Cruse; Ian Wilson; Tom Deidun; Abdul Hai.

CC Number: 1095045

Eligibility

People who live or attend an educational institution in Holburn, and have done for at least two years. See the map on the website for the beneficial area.

Types of grants

One-off grants up to £500 for educational needs including books, computers, instruments, uniforms, travel and living costs. Recurrent grants can be made for children with disabilities.

Annual grant total

In 2011 the charity had assets of £7.8 million and an income of £209,000. There were 91 grants totalling £37,000 and 121 annual awardees, totalling

£76,000. Altogether funding for individuals totalled £113,000.

Exclusions

No grants for private school fees.

Applications

On a form available from the correspondent or to download from the website. There are separate forms for under 18s and over 18s. Once received, applicants may be visited by a grants officer. Applications generally take about 21 days.

Other information

This charity is the result of an amalgamation of three trusts: The City Foundation, The Isaac Duckett Charity and The William Williams Charity. Grants are also made to local organisations.

City of London

The Thomas Carpenter Educational and Apprenticing Foundation

£24,000 (12 grants)

Correspondent: Thomas F Ackland, Secretary, 59 Broadfields Avenue, Winchmore Hill, London N21 1AG (020 8360 5296; fax: 020 8360 5296; email: thomas.ackland@talktalk.net)

Trustees: Rodney Fitzgerald; Michael Evans; Michael Savory; Barry Davis; Roger Alderman; George Bush.

CC Number: 312155

Eligibility

People under 25 who live, or whose parents have lived or worked for three years, in Bread Street and adjoining wards in the City of London.

Types of grants

Grants of £500 to £3,000 to people at school, college or university towards costs which are directly related to the course, including fees, books, equipment, instruments, uniforms, travel abroad to pursue their education and help with the costs of studying music or other arts.

Annual grant total

In 2010/11 the foundation had assets of £844,000 and an income of £30,000. Grants were made to 12 students totalling £24,000.

Exclusions

No grants are given towards electives or field trips which are not part of a full-time study course.

Applications

On a form available from the correspondent. Applications should be submitted before 31 July by the individual's parent or guardian, details of whose financial circumstances should be provided.

The Cutler Trust (the Worshipful Company of Makers of Playing Cards)

£1,000

Correspondent: David Barrett, Cutler Trust Secretary, 256 St Davids Square, LONDON E14 3WE (020 7531 5990; email: clerk@makersofplayingcards.co. uk; website: www.makersofplayingcards. co.uk)

Trustees: David Warner; Peter Cregeen; Roger Howells; Mark Ladd; Nigel Nicholson; Tony Carter; Mark Winston; Lance Whitehouse.

CC Number: 232876

Eligibility

'Deserving students', the trust has some preference for the City of London.

Types of grants

One-off and recurrent grants according to need.

Annual grant total

In 2010/11 the trust had assets of £627,000 and an income of £50,000. Grants to individuals usually total £1,000.

Applications

The trust invites applications for funding of grants from members of the Worshipful Company of Makers of Playing Cards, from educational bodies connected with the City of London, and from members of the public. The Marshall of Appeals considers the merits of the applications and seeks further information before submitting recommendations to the trustees' meeting, which happens twice a year.

The Mitchell City of London Educational Foundation

£91,000 (55 grants)

Correspondent: Lucy Jordan, Ash View, High Street, Orston, Nottingham NG13 9NU (01949 835632; email: mitchellcityoflondon@gmail.com)

Trustees: Charles Link; Billy Dove; Dennis Cotgrove; David Levin; Derek Balls; Eleanor Stanier; Alan Cornwell; John Barker; Michael Sherlock; Michael

Chesterton; Peter Borrowdale; Rodney East; Pamela Beevers; John Marshall; Diana Vernon; Donald Payne.

CC Number: 312499

Eligibility

People aged 11 to 19 who are either attending a City of London school or whose parents have lived or worked there for at least five years.

Types of grants

Grants ranging from £1,200 to £1,400 each are given as sixth form bursaries for A-level students or grants for school fees for children from single parent families. Awards are also made to needy students.

Annual grant total

In 2010/11 the foundation had an income of £104,000 and gave £91,000 to individuals consisting of forty two sixth form bursaries, eleven single parent family grants and two awards for needy students.

Applications

On a form available from the correspondent, to be submitted either directly by the individual or a parent/guardian, or through an organisation such as a school or an educational welfare agency. They are considered in March and September.

City of Westminster

St Giles-in-the-Field and William Shelton Educational Charity

£0

Correspondent: Pam Nicholls, Clerk to the Trustees, The Rectory, 15a Gower Street, London WC1E 6HW (020 7323 1992; email: pam.nicholls@london. anglican.org; website: www. stgilescharities.org.uk)

Trustees: Bill Jacob; Peter David; Julian Sharpe; David Peebles; Peter Bloxham; Nicholas Peters; Vanessa Samuel.

CC Number: 1111907

Eligibility

Children and young people living or being educated in the ancient parishes of St Giles in the Fields, St Martin in the Fields and St Paul, Covent Garden.

Types of grants

Grants to help with the cost of books, clothing, tuition and other essentials for schoolchildren.

Annual grant total

In 2011 the trust had assets of £6 million and an income of £36,000. Grants to individuals were only made via other organisations.

Applications

On a form available from the charity's website. Applications are considered at trustees' meetings, which take place approximately every three months. Emergency applications from individuals for up to £750 can be considered in between meetings. Applications should ideally be received at least two weeks in advance of the meeting. Meeting dates are published on the trust's website.

Croydon

Church Tenements Charity – Education Branch

£8,200 (27 grants)

Correspondent: June Haynes, Croydon London Borough Council, Taberner House, Park Lane, Croydon CR9 3JS (020 8760 5768; email: june.haynes@croydon.gov.uk)

Trustees: Colin Boswell; Janet Marshall; Jason Perry; Marlene Bourne; Gail Winter,.

CC Number: 312554

Eligibility

People under the age of 25 who are living or studying in the London borough of Croydon, including people from overseas studying in Croydon.

Types of grants

'The trustees have a limited amount of funds at their disposal. They are therefore inclined to apply the trust income to exceptional or extraordinary cases of hardship or circumstance. They will generally favour an application below £500 where a grant has not been given previously by the local education authority. Grants are wide ranging but mainly cover primary, secondary or post-school education and training. Grants may also be given towards the cost of uniforms, equipment, musical instruments and tuition etc.' Grants can also be for books, stationery, school fees, educational outings in the UK and study or travel abroad. They range from £50 to £500.

Whilst no preference is given to any type of application, the trustees will be encouraged to give grants if the applicant has made some effort to raise some finance him/herself.

Annual grant total

In 2010/11 the fund made grants to 27 individuals totalling £8,200.

Applications

On a form available from the correspondent. Applications are considered quarterly in January, April, July and October. The charity asks for as much supporting information as possible.

Other information

The charity also gives to youth services and ecclesiastical organisations.

Frank Denning Memorial Charity

£5,000

Correspondent: Gerry Hudson, Assistant Honorary Secretary, Croydon Council, Chief Executive's Office, Taberner House, Park Lane, Croydon CR9 3JS (020 8726 6000; email: gerry.hudson@croydon.gov.uk; website: www.croydon.gov.uk)

Trustees: Edward Handley; Peter Champion; Julie Dakin; Jojo Monney.

CC Number: 312813

Eligibility

Full-time students at colleges of further education who live or whose parents/guardians live in the London Borough of Croydon. Applicants must be between the ages of 19 and 25 on 30 March in the year the application is considered.

Types of grants

One-off travelling scholarships of up to £1,000 each for travel abroad to carry out projects which have specific educational objectives. Beneficiaries must have every intention of returning to the UK at the end of their overseas visit.

Annual grant total

In 2010/11 the fund had an income of £4,300 and an expenditure of £6,000.

Applications

On a form available from the website. Forms are available from June and must be returned by the individual by 2 March for consideration in March/April. A handout is sent to all Croydon students giving information on the charity. Interviews are held each year during the Easter holidays.

Ealing

Acton (Middlesex) Charities

£2,000

Correspondent: Revd David Brammer, The Rectory, 14 Cumberland Park, London W3 6SX (020 8992 8876; email: acton.charities@virgin.net; website: www. actoncharities.co.uk)

CC Number: 312312

Eligibility

Students whose home residence is in the former ancient parish of Acton. They must be between 18–25 years of age and have entered a full-time course in the UK, usually of at least three years, which will lead to a recognised qualification.

Types of grants

Grants of £200 per year to assist with books or equipment.

Annual grant total

In 2011 the trust had an income of £10,000 and an expenditure of £6,300.

Applications

On a form available from the correspondent. Proof that the student is entered on an educational course is required.

Other information

The trust also provides welfare and arts grants and supports local schools and carnivals.

The Francis Courtney Educational Foundation

£500

Correspondent: Janis Gaylor, Clerk, 5 Holly Farm Road, Southall UB2 5SY (020 8574 5980)

Trustees: Leslie Lawrence; Maureen Crosby; Brian Hutnell; Michael Coombe; Michael Johnson.

CC Number: 312547

Eligibility

People under 25 who live in Southall.

Types of grants

One-off grants are given to assist in further education only. Help may be given towards books, fees/living expenses and study or travel abroad. Mature students may also receive help in special circumstances.

Annual grant total

The trust has an annual income of around £3,000. Expenditure has dropped in the past couple of years to £750 in 2010.

Exclusions

No grants for clothing, equipment or childcare.

Applications

On a form available from the correspondent, indicating the size of contribution the individual can make and an indication of what the grant is for. The applicant's place of study must approve the completed form, which should be submitted directly by the individual. Applications are considered before the individual begins further education.

The Educational Foundation of William Hobbayne

£2,000

Correspondent: Caroline Lumb, Clerk, Community Centre, St Dunstan's Road, London W7 2HB (020 8810 0277; email: hobbaynecharity@btinternet.com)

Trustees: Nicholas Robinson; Allison Rockley; Angela Wallis; John Sawyer; Mark Cosstick; Matthew Grayshon; Roy Price; David Muir; Robert Coomber.

CC Number: 312544

Eligibility

Children and young people who live in Hanwell (W7 area) in the London borough of Ealing. There is a preference for children in junior school.

Types of grants

Grants generally of up to £100 for the costs of school trips, educational outings, books/equipment and travel. Students including those taking Open University/long-distance courses can also be supported.

Annual grant total

In 2010/11 the foundation had an income of £3,000 and an expenditure of £2,500.

Applications

In writing to the correspondent. Applications must be supported by a sponsor (usually the school, Scout or Guide group and so on), and are considered monthly.

Other information

Grants are also made to organisations.

Enfield

The Enfield Church Trust for Girls

£4,000

Correspondent: Revd Michael M Edge, Enfield Vicarage, Silver Street, Enfield, Middlesex EN1 3EG (020 8363 8676)

Trustees: Revd Michael Macleod Edge; Graham Eustance; Margaret Pateman; Maureen Anderson; Nancy Hands; Tanya Orr; Amanda Young.

CC Number: 312210

Eligibility

Young women in need under the age of 25, who live, work or attend school, college or university in the ancient parish of Enfield.

Types of grants

Grants to help individuals to lead as fulfilling lives as possible by helping with the costs of their education, recreation, leisure and social welfare. For example, the trust bought a radio-linked hearing aid to enable a deaf 12-year-old girl to continue normal schooling.

Grants have also been given towards course fees when local education authority grants are not available and to students for books and study or travel abroad. Grants for childcare and other child costs have been given to single-parents who are studying, training or early on in their careers, and the trust will consider grants for books, equipment and clothing for women starting work. The trustees are particularly concerned to help disadvantaged young women and girls. Grants usually range from £70 to £300. Grants are generally one-off although beneficiaries are free to re-apply each year.

Annual grant total

In 2011 the trust had an income of £3,700 and an expenditure of £4,500.

Exclusions

No grants for mature students or for school fees, though grants for school uniform, books, educational outings and maintenance are considered for schoolchildren.

Applications

On a form available from the correspondent. Applications are considered all year.

The Old Enfield Charitable Trust

£52,000

Correspondent: The Trust Administrator, The Old Vestry Office, 2 The Town, Enfield, Middlesex EN2 6LT (020 8367 8941; email: enquiries@toect.org.uk; website: www. toect.org.uk)

Trustees: Gordon Smith; Colin Griffiths; Audrey Thacker; Clive Parker; Horace Brown; Jim Eustance; Michael Braithwaite; Nicholas Taylor; Dr Patrick O'Mahony; Phyllis Oborn; Richard Cross; Susan Attwood; Chris Bond; Sam Bell; Bob Sander.

CC Number: 207840

Eligibility

People in need who live in the ancient parish of Enfield.

Types of grants

For students and other residents who are undertaking education or training, help is given with living costs, equipment, stationery, childminding and other general expenses during their course of study.

Annual grant total

In 2010/11 the trust had an income of £547,000. A total of £141,500 was given in grants to 292 individuals, of which £52,000 was given for educational purposes. A further £1,000 was donated to organisations.

Exclusions

The trust cannot help with costs that are the responsibility of the local authority or central government. No support is given for second degrees or master's degree courses.

Applications

On a form available on request from the correspondent. Applicants are then interviewed by a committee.

Greenwich

The Greenwich Blue Coat Foundation

£15,000

Correspondent: M I Baker, Clerk, 36 Charlton Lane, London SE7 8AB (020 8858 7575)

Trustees: Christina Stanley; David Tewson; Gillian Page; Michael Leader; Barbara Lane; Susanna Bloomfield.

CC Number: 312407

Eligibility

Young people up to 25 years of age who live, or who are being educated in, the borough of Greenwich.

Types of grants

One-off and recurrent grants towards educational needs, usually for less than £1,000 each.

Annual grant total

In 2010/11 the foundation had an income of £22,000 and an expenditure of £39,000.

Applications

In writing to the correspondent.

Other information

Grants are also given to organisations, namely schools.

Hackney

The Hackney Parochial Charities

£24,000

Correspondent: Robin Sorrell, Clerk to the Trustees, c/o Sorrells Solicitors, 157 High Street, Chipping Ongar, Essex CM5 9JD (01277 365532; email: rsorrell@sorrells.org.uk)

Trustees: Fr R. Wickham; Mrs M. Cannon; G. Taylor; C. Kennedy; Ms N. Baboneau; Ms V. Belfon; Mr D. Horder; Mr P. Cofie.

CC Number: 219876

Eligibility

People in need who live in the former metropolitan borough of Hackney.

Types of grants

Help towards the cost of books, equipment, tools and examination fees for apprentices and young people at college or university who are not in receipt of a full grant. Grants are one-off, although applicants can re-apply annually.

Annual grant total

In 2010/11 the charities had assets of £4.9 million and an income of £185,000, of which £136,000 was distributed in grants mainly to organisations.

Applications

In writing to the correspondent. The trustees meet in March, June, September and November and as grants cannot be made between meetings it is advisable to make early contact with the correspondent.

Other information

In 2008 the Charities took over the administration of Hackney District Nursing Association. In 2010/11 the trustees made no grants out of the Hackney District Nursing Association's funds.

Hammersmith and Fulham

Dr Edwards' and Bishop King's Fulham Charity

£2,300

Correspondent: The Clerk to the Trustees, Percy Barton House, 33–35 Dawes Road, London SW6 7DT (020 7385 9387; fax: 020 7610 2856; email: clerk@debk.org.uk; website: www. debk.org.uk)

Trustees: Michael Clein; Charles Treloggan; Allen Smith; Ronald Lawrence; Michael Waymouth; Susan O'Neill; Carol Bailey; Lindsey Brock; Adronie Alford; P. V. R. Richards; Mark Osbourne.

CC Number: 1113490

Eligibility

People undertaking training courses who live in the old metropolitan borough of Fulham. This constitutes all of the SW6 postal area and parts of W14 and W6.

Types of grants

One-off grants are made to individuals for accredited training courses which are likely to lead to employment, support with childcare and other needs.

Annual grant total

In 2010/11 grants to individuals totalled £125,000 with 264 grants given for relief in need and five for education or training.

Exclusions

The charity does not fund postgraduate courses or give cash grants (unless they are to be administered by an agency).

Applications

Application forms are available from the correspondent or on the charity's website. Applications must be submitted in hard copy either directly by the individual or through a third party. Though, it is important to note that individuals applying directly for a grant will be visited at home by the grants administrator.

The committee which considers relief-in-need applications, including educational grant applications, meets ten times a

349

year, roughly every 4–5 weeks. The charity suggests that applications be submitted around two to three weeks before the next meeting.

Other information

The fund gives money to both individuals and organisations, with its main responsibility being towards the relief of poverty rather than assisting students.

Haringey

Tottenham Grammar School Foundation

£283,000

Correspondent: Graham Chappell, Clerk, PO Box 34098, London N13 5XU (020 8882 2999; email: info@tgsf.org.uk; website: www.tgsf.org.uk)

Trustees: Frederick Gruncell; Keith Brown; Keith McGuiness; Paul Compton; Peter Jones; Terry Clarke; Victoria Phillips; John Fowl; Roger Knight; Andrew Krokou; Graham Kantorowicz.

CC Number: 312634

Eligibility

People under 25 who, or whose parents, normally live in the borough of Haringey, or who have attended a school in the borough.

Types of grants

The foundation has three types of award and there are different eligibility criteria for each:

▶ The Somerset Award is £200 for students on full time courses at colleges of further education (or equivalent)

▶ The Somerset Undergraduate Award is £200 a year for students at university following a full time degree or an equivalent higher education course of at least two years' duration

▶ The Somerset Special Award covers a wide range of grants and examples of potential applicants include the following: postgraduate students; young sportsmen and women who are at county standard or higher; musicians who are at conservatoire standard; students or children with special needs

Annual grant total

In 2010/11 the foundation had assets of £17.8 million and an income of £372,000. Grants, scholarships and bursaries to individuals totalled £373,000.

Exclusions

No awards to support apprenticeships.

Applications

Application forms for the separate awards can be downloaded from the foundation's website. The closing date for applications for Somerset Awards is 30 November.

Other information

Grants are made to schools in Haringey and other voluntary organisations in Haringey for equipment and activities not provided by the local authority, totalling £245,000 in 2010/11.

The Wood Green (Urban District) Charity

£1,250

Correspondent: Mrs Carolyn Banks, Clerk, PO Box 365, Laughton, Essex IG10 9EY (07758 730078; email: charities@virginmedia.com)

Trustees: Sylvia Acott; John Broadhurst; Cheery McAskill; Khaled Moyeed; John Hawting; Pauline Gibson; Hannah Essex.

CC Number: 206736

Eligibility

People in need who have lived in the urban district of Wood Green (as constituted in 1896, roughly the present N22 postal area) for at least three years.

Types of grants

Assistance to schoolchildren, college students, undergraduates, vocational students, children with special educational needs, people starting work and overseas students for clothing (including uniforms), books and equipment/instruments.

Annual grant total

About £2,500 for welfare and educational purposes.

Applications

On a form available from the correspondent, to be submitted by a school, social worker, Citizens Advice or other welfare agency or third party. Applications are considered all year round.

Hillingdon

Uxbridge United Welfare Trusts

£23,000

Correspondent: David W Routledge, Chair, Trustee Room, Woodbridge House, New Windsor Street, Uxbridge UB8 2TY (01895 232976; email:

enquires@uuwt.org; website: www.uuwt. org)

Trustees: Cheryl Evans; John Childs; Pauline Crawley; David Routledge; Peter Ryerson; Gerda Driver; Duncan Struthers; Alan Morris; Ray Graham; Michael Cater; Susan James.

CC Number: 217066

Eligibility

People in need who live in the Uxbridge area (bordered by Harefield in the north, Ickenham in the east, Uxbridge in the west and Cowley/Colham Green in the south).

Types of grants

One-off grants for people in school or further or higher education. Grants can be towards course costs, books, uniforms, trips, travel and equipment and sometimes living expenses and so on.

Annual grant total

In 2011 the trust had assets of £6.7 million and an income of £462,000. Grants for education were given to 17 individuals totalling £23,000.

Exclusions

No grants for school fees.

Applications

On a form available from the correspondent. Applications can be submitted directly by the individual or through a social worker, Citizens Advice or educational welfare agency. They are considered each month.

Other information

Grants are also given for welfare purposes.

Islington

The Worrall and Fuller Exhibition Fund

£8,500

Correspondent: Christine Shephard, 90 Central Street, London EC1V 8AJ (07799 282413; website: www. worrallandfuller.org.uk)

Trustees: Katharine Rumens; Erika Rowe; Ian Moore; Nicola Brokker; Paul Bagott; Amanda Lee; David Bradbury.

CC Number: 312507

Eligibility

Young people aged 5 to 25 who live work or study in the Old Borough of Finsbury (now part of Islington), with a preference for those resident in, or whose parents have, during the preceding year had their business or employment in the Parish of St Luke.

Types of grants

The fund covers a wide range of educational purposes giving grants towards, for instance, school, college or university fees and books, travel and other equipment expenses, for people wishing to study music and the arts and for those preparing to start work.

Annual grant total

In 2010/11 the fund had both an income and a total expenditure of £17,000.

Applications

On a form available from the correspondent.

Other information

The fund gives grants for the maintenance of local schools.

Kensington and Chelsea

The Campden Charities

£437,000 (306 grants)

Correspondent: Christopher Stannard, Clerk, 27a Pembridge Villas, London W11 3EP (020 7243 0551, Grants officer: 020 7313 3797; website: www.cctrustee.org.uk)

Trustees: Revd Gillean Craig; David Banks; Susan Valerie Lockhart; Dr Kit Davis; Cllr Richard Walker-Arnott; Terry Myers; Elisabeth Brockmann; Tim Martin; Sam Berwick; Dr Christopher Calman; Ben Pilling; Marta Rodkina; Michael Finney.

CC Number: 1104616

Eligibility

Individuals applying for funding must:
- Be living in the former parish of Kensington
- Have been living continuously in Kensington for two years or more,
- Are a British or European citizen or have indefinite leave to remain in Britain
- Be renting their home

Working age members of the family must also be in receipt of an out-of-work benefit (e.g. Income Support, Jobseeker's Allowance, Pension Credit Guarantee or Incapacity Benefit) or on a very low income.

Types of grants

The charity considers funding to all ages of applicant, however it divides its funding into three basic categories:
- Young people (16–24)
- People of working age
- People of retirement age

The charity will give grants for many direct and indirect educational causes, including course and training fees, childcare costs, travel expenses and equipment.

Annual grant total

In 2010/11 grants made directly to individuals for educational purposes totalled £437,000, of which 257 grants were made for vocational education (£284,000), with a further 49 grants (£152,000) being awarded to encourage academically able young people from disadvantaged backgrounds to attend university.

Exclusions

The charity will not give funding for:
- Direct payment of council tax or rent
- Debt repayments
- Fines or court orders
- Foreign travel or holidays
- Career changes
- Personal development courses
- Postgraduate studies
- Computers
- Individuals whose immediate goal is self-employment
- Goods and services catered for by central government

Applications

Preliminary enquiries should be made by telephone or in writing to the education assistant, who will then informally interview applicants. The trustees of the education committee, who meet monthly, then make final decisions, based on the formal interviews of the applicants.

Applicants should also be willing for a grants officer to visit them at home.

Other information

Grants are also awarded to organisations and individuals for welfare purposes.

The Pocklington Apprenticeship Trust (Kensington)

£1,500

Correspondent: Andrew Tagg, Floor 1 Room 127, Town Hall, Hornton Street, London W8 7NX (email: andrew.tagg@rbkc.gov.uk)

Trustees: Merrick Cockell; Daniel Moylan; Judith Blakeman.

CC Number: 312943

Eligibility

Young people in need, aged 21 years or younger who were either born in Kensington and Chelsea or who have lived there for at least ten years.

Types of grants

One-off grants, usually of between £200 and £300 are awarded to schoolchildren, students in further/higher education,

vocational students, people starting work and special educational needs for books, equipment, instruments and commuting expenses. People starting work may also receive support for uniforms and clothing.

Annual grant total

About £1,500.

Exclusions

Help is only given to attend classes outside the borough if the classes are unavailable within it.

Applications

On a form available from the correspondent, for consideration at any time.

Westway Development Trust

£18,000

Correspondent: Martyn Freeman, Chief Executive, 1 Thorpe Close, London W10 5XL (020 8962 5720; fax: 020 8969 5936; email: info@westway.org; website: www.westway.org)

Trustees: Cynthia Dize; Pat Healy; Terence Buxton; David Lindsay; Fiona Buxton; David Oliver; Peter Wilson; Mary Roser; Joanna Farquharson; Mary Gardiner; Mike Jones; Abdul Towolawi; Timothy Davis; James Caplin; Rock Feilding-Mellen; Ruth Hilary; Ken Scott.

CC Number: 1123127

Eligibility

People who live in the Borough of Kensington and Chelsea working towards qualifications which will assist them in gaining employment. Applicants must not be in full time employment, or be able to get a grant from a statutory body to cover their expenses.

Types of grants

Grants of up to £1,000 each towards the costs course fees, required books, equipment and materials, travel costs, child-minding costs.

Annual grant total

In 2010/11 the trust had assets of £29 million and an income of £7.2 million. The trust gave £16,000 in education grants and £1,700 in sports grants to individuals.

Applications

On a form available from the trust's website. Applicants must be able supply the names of a referee on their course and any other information reasonably required by the trust. A report on the use of the grant is also expected.

Other information

This operational charity also makes grants to local community organisations.

Lambeth

The Walcot Foundation

£70,000 (122 grants)

Correspondent: Daniel Chapman, Grants Manager, 127 Kennington Road, London SE11 6SF (020 7735 1925; fax: 020 7735 7048; email: office@ walcotfoundation.org.uk; website: www. walcotfoundation.org.uk)

Trustee: The Walcot and Hayle's Trustee.

CC Number: 312800

Eligibility

People in need who live in the borough of Lambeth. Individuals currently living outside of the area but who are still considered to be Lambeth residents will also qualify for assistance.

Types of grants

Student grants: Up to £2,000 per academic year to help young people from low-income households with the costs of post-secondary education, whether academic or vocational, that has a strong likelihood of leading to work. Grants can be given for: course fees (not for private institutions); associated travel costs; books; special clothing; equipment; study/field trips; childcare; and, reasonable general living expenses.

Benefits-to-work grants: One-off grants for vocational training and related activities for people who are trying to move from benefits to work. This can include the costs associated with taking on work experience.

Annual grant total

In 2010/11 the foundation had assets of £67 million and an income of £2.2 million and gave grants to 122 individuals for educational purposes totalling £70,000, broken down into the following two categories:
- Students pursuing post-secondary academic or vocational education: 105 grants totalling £58,000
- Schoolchildren and young people to support the development of special talents or to overcome difficult circumstances: 17 grants totalling £12,000

Exclusions

No grants for: postgraduate studies or second degrees, personal development courses, study at private institutions, or career changes; course fees in cases where it is not clear that the applicant will be able to raise the balance of funds to complete the entire course; or the cost of goods or services already purchased.

If the applicant already has significant work experience with a reasonable level of responsibility, the trust will not fund further study.

Applications

On a form available from the correspondent or to download from the website. Applications can be made at any time and should be submitted through a recognised referral agency such as a social care agency, voluntary organisation, health worker, clergy or teacher. The trust aims to respond to applications from individuals within six weeks.

Other information

The foundation is made up of four charities, the Walcot Educational Foundation, the Walcot Non-Educational Charity, Hayle's Charity and the Cynthia Mosley Memorial Fund.

The foundation also provides additional services to beneficiaries including careers advice, debt and budgeting advice, capacity building and low cost psychotherapy.

Lewisham

Lewisham Education Charity

£400

Correspondent: Emily Roberts, Clerk, Clerk's Office, Lloyd Court, Slagrove Place, London SE13 7LP (020 8690 8145)

Trustees: Alan Till; Gloria Phillips; Veronica Shirfield; Omega Jackson; Julia Pring; Julian Watson; Susan Luxton; Stella Jeffrey; Scott Anderson.

CC Number: 1025785

Eligibility

People aged 25 or under who are in need and live in the ancient parish of Lewisham (which does not include Deptford or Lee).

Types of grants

One-off grants for any educational need. There are no specific restrictions except where statutory bodies should be responsible. Applications are preferred for specific items rather than contributions to large fee costs.

Annual grant total

In 2010/11 the trust had an income and an expenditure of £400. Previously, grants have totalled £1,000.

Applications

On a form available from the correspondent, either directly by the individual, or via their school, college or educational welfare agency. Applications are considered regularly.

Other information

Some support is also occasionally given to local schools.

Merton

A. and H. Leivers Charity Trust

£10,000

Correspondent: The Trustees, PO Box 112, Worcester Park, Surrey KT4 7YY

Trustees: Kevin Young; Roger Young.

CC Number: 299267

Eligibility

Young people in need up to the age of 18 who live or attend school in the London borough of Merton.

Types of grants

One-off and recurrent grants to help with the cost of books, clothing, educational outings and other essentials for those at school.

Annual grant total

Around £10,000 is given in grants annually.

Applications

On a form available from the correspondent. Applications can be submitted by the individual, his/her headteacher or a social care worker. Applications should include full details of what funds are requested, and are usually considered between April and June although urgent cases can be considered at any time.

Richmond upon Thames

The Barnes Workhouse Fund

£12,000 (14 grants)

Correspondent: Miranda Ibbetson, PO Box 665, Richmond, Surrey TW10 6YL (020 8241 3994; email: mibbetson@barnesworkhousefund.org. uk; website: www.barnesworkhousefund. org.uk)

Trustees: Nicolas Phillips; Peter Siddall; Wendy Kyrle-Pope; Philip Conrath; John Brocklebank; K. Pengelley; Timothy Besley; Lucy Hine; Paul Hodgins.

CC Number: 200103

Eligibility

tudents and schoolchildren who have een resident in the ancient parish of arnes (in practice SW13) for at least six onths. Applications are actively ncouraged from individuals looking to eturn to education.

Types of grants

ne-off grants of up to £1,000 are vailable for students in further ducation where local or national uthority assistance is unavailable for osts such as fees, maintenance, ducational equipment and books, travel osts and childcare.

Annual grant total

n 2011 the fund had assets of 11 million and an income of £603,000. rants were made to 14 individuals for ducation totalling £12,000.

Applications

n a form available from the website, to e submitted directly by the individual. pplications are considered upon eceipt. If students apply for more than 750 this will be considered at bi-onthly trustee meetings held in anuary, March, May, July, September nd November.

tudents under the age of 25 must rovide details of their parents'/carers' ncome.

Other information

rants are also made to organisations nd for other purposes, such as welfare.

The Hampton Wick United Charity

£10,000

Correspondent: Roger Avins, Hunters odge, Home Farm, Redhill Road, obham, Surrey KT11 1EF (01932 96748)

Trustees: Miss M. Kearn; A. Arbour; Mr 1. McDougall; Dr P. Butterworth; Revd . Warner.

CC Number: 1010147

Eligibility

eople under 25 who are in need and ve in Hampton Wick and most of outh Teddington, within the parishes of t John the Baptist, Hampton Wick and t Mark, South Teddington.

Types of grants

ne-off cash grants (with the possibility f future reapplication) to help with the ost of, for example, books, equipment, lothing and course fees.

Annual grant total

reviously over £20,000 a year in ducational and welfare grants. Recent nformation was not available.

Applications

In writing to the correspondent. The trustees normally meet three times a year to consider applications.

The Petersham United Charities

£2,500

Correspondent: The Clerk, The Vicarage, Bute Avenue, Richmond TW10 7AX (020 8940 8435)

Trustees: Richard Robinson; Arthur Carter; Ivy Faulks; Charles Archer; James Kimble; Revd Timothy Marwood.

CC Number: 200433

Eligibility

People under 25 who live in the ecclesiastical parish of Petersham, Surrey as constituted in 1900.

Types of grants

One-off grants of £75 to £500 are given for any educational need.

Annual grant total

In 2010 the trust had an income of £4,000 and a total expenditure of £6,000.

Applications

In writing to the correspondent. Applications are considered in January, April, July and October and can be submitted either directly by the individual or through a social worker, Citizens Advice or other welfare agency.

Other information

Grants are also given for relief-in-need purposes and to organisations.

The Richmond Parish Lands Charity

£110,000 (119 grants)

Correspondent: The Clerk to the Education Committee, The Vestry House, 21 Paradise Road, Richmond, Surrey TW9 1SA (020 8948 5701; fax: 020 8332 6792; website: www.rplc.org. uk)

Trustees: Rita Biddulph; Ashley Casson; Colin Craib; Clare Head; Jeffery Harris; Kate Ellis; Lisa Blakemore; Paul Coles; Niall Cairns; Ros Sweeting; Rosie Dalzell; Sue Jones; Susan Goddard; Dr Vivienne Press; Tim Sketchley.

CC Number: 200069

Eligibility

People above school age who are in need and have lived in the TW9 TW10 or SW14 areas of Richmond for at least six months prior to application and have no other possible sources of help.

Types of grants

One-off and recurrent grants to help people obtain vocational, professional or academic qualifications or to retrain after employment. Grants can range from £50 towards course books to larger recurrent grants over several years for course fees.

Annual grant total

In 2010/11 the charity made grants to over 1,000 individuals totalling £220,000. Grants for educational purposes were given to 119 individuals and totalled £110,000.

Exclusions

No grants to schoolchildren.

Applications

On a form available from the Clerk to the Education Committee, to be submitted directly by the individual. This includes details of current employment, income and expenditure, details of the course/expenses applied for and a statement in support of the application. Two references are required and applicants are usually asked to attend an interview. Applications should be based on financial need and parental income is taken into account up to the age of 25 years. There are two trusts which are also administered by the Richmond Parish Lands Charity:

The Barnes Relief in Need Charity (BRINC) – cc.no 200318

BRINC small grant forms are available for existing RPLC small grants referral agencies. In addition some Mortlake based organisations will be invited to become referral agencies for individuals in need. Application forms for organisational and individual grants are available from the correspondent.

The Bailey and Bates Trust – cc.no 312249

Grants are made for relief in need purposes for individuals living in the postcode area SW14. Contact the correspondent for further details of how to apply. However, note that charitable expenditure for this trust has been particularly low since 2005.

Other information

Grants are also made to organisations. The charity has an informative website.

The Thomas Wilson Educational Trust

£18,000

Correspondent: Karen Hopkins, 23 Tranmere Road, Whitton, Middlesex TW2 7JD (020 8893 3928)

Trustees: D. Stockford; Lesley Secker; Colin Mills; Sharon Kay; Trevor Wright.

CC Number: 1003771

Eligibility

People under 25 who live in Teddington and neighbourhood.

Types of grants

Grants of £100 to £4,500 are given to schoolchildren towards clothing, books, educational outings and fees (only in exceptional circumstances) and to students in further or higher education, including overseas students (depending on how long they have been a resident in Teddington), towards books, fees, living expenses and study or travel abroad. Help may also be given to mature students under 25.

Annual grant total

In 2010 the trust made nine grants totalling £18,000.

Applications

On a form available from the correspondent. Applications can be submitted directly by the individual or by a parent or guardian. They are considered throughout the year.

Southwark

The Christchurch Church of England Educational Foundation

£2,000

Correspondent: The Administrator, Christ Church, 27 Blackfriars Road, London SE1 8NY (020 7928 4707; email: admin@christchurchsouthwark.org.uk; website: www.christchurchsouthwark. org.uk)

Trustees: Janet Amery; Jean Vigar; Terry McLeman; Timothy Scott; Leigh Hatts.

CC Number: 312363

Eligibility

People aged under 25 who live in the following areas (in order of priority): (i) the parish of Christchurch, Southwark; and (ii) the former borough of Southwark.

Types of grants

Grants are for promoting education 'in accordance with the principles of the Church of England'. Grants are made towards (i) school uniforms, other school clothing, books and educational outings for schoolchildren, (ii) books, study or travel abroad and student exchanges for students in further and higher education, (iii) books, equipment and instruments, clothing and travel for people starting work and (iv) books and travel for mature students. Grants range from £50 to £150 and are one-off.

Preference is given to schoolchildren with serious family difficulties so the child has to be educated away from home and to people with special education needs.

Annual grant total

In 2011 the foundation had an income of £5,200 and an expenditure of £2,200.

Exclusions

Grants are not made for fees or maintenance costs for schoolchildren or for fees/living expenses for students.

Applications

In writing to the correspondent, including details of other applications made. Applications are considered in May and November.

Charity of Thomas Dickinson

£3,000

Correspondent: David Freeman, Flat 99 Andrewes House, Barbican, London EC2Y 8AY (020 7628 6155)

Trustees: David Freeman; David Pape; Charles Moore; Katharine Rumens; Doris Webb; Kathleen Sheen; Ray Andrews.

CC Number: 802473

Eligibility

Young people aged 25 or under and in financial need who are living in, studying in or have at least one parent working in the ancient parishes of: St Giles, Cripplegate; St Sepulchre, St George the Martyr, Southwark; or St Mary Magdalene, Bermondsey.

Types of grants

One-off grants ranging from £100 to £500 are given to: schoolchildren for uniforms and educational outings in the UK and overseas; students in further or higher education for books; vocational students for equipment and instruments; and to individuals with special educational needs for uniforms/clothing.

Annual grant total

About £3,000.

Applications

On a form available from the correspondent, submitted either directly by the individual or via their school/college/educational welfare agency. Applications are considered in February/March, June/July and October/November.

The Newcomen Collett Educational Foundation

£25,000 (102 grants)

Correspondent: Catherine Dawkins, Clerk to the Governors, 66 Newcomen Street, London SE1 1YT (020 7407 296; fax: 020 7403 3969; email: grantoffice@ newcomencollett.org.uk)

Trustees: Richard Edwards; Sylvia Morris; Bruce Saunders; John Spencer; Robin Lovell; Edward Bowman; Barbara Lane; Andrew Covell; Robert Ashdown; Alexander Leiffheidt; Helen Cockerill; Michael Ibbott.

CC Number: 312804

Eligibility

People under the age of 25 who have lived in the London borough of Southwark for at least two years. There is a preference for those living in the parish of St Saviour's.

Types of grants

Grants for students undertaking tertiary education or apprenticeships and to people pursuing courses in arts, music, dancing and so on. Grants are also available for uniforms. Grants are one-off and of up to £1,000, but are usually about £500 for individuals.

Annual grant total

In 2010/11 the trust had assets of £2.7 million and an income of £239,000. Around £20,000 was given in 49 grants to individuals. A further 53 grants totalling £5,000 were given by referral through Southwark Education Welfare Office.

Exclusions

No grants for school fees, domestic bills, childcare or debts.

Applications

On a form available from the website or the correspondent along with a supporting statement from a tutor or other qualified person confirming they are undertaking the specified course. Applications are considered four times year in March, June, September and December and should be submitted a month beforehand, check the website for deadlines.

St Olave's United Charity, incorporating the St Thomas and St John Charities

£38,000

Correspondent: Angela O'Shaughnessy, 6–8 Druid Street, off Tooley Street,

London SE1 2EU (020 7407 2530; email: st.olavescharity@btconnect.com)

Trustees: F. Colley; J. Lynch; P. John; I. Donovan; D. Brasier; C. Bennett; G. Johnson; S. Broughton; L. Rowe; D. Hams; D. Trescher; B. Albin-Dyer.

CC Number: 211763

Eligibility

People under the age of 24 who live in the ancient parishes of Southwark St Olave and St Thomas, and Bermondsey Horsleydown St John. In practice this means residents of Bermondsey (part SE1 and all SE16).

Types of grants

Grants for schoolchildren for items such as clothing, travel and fees are only given in very exceptional circumstances. Grants to college students and mature students for books.

Annual grant total

In 2010/11 the charity had assets of almost £12.1 million and an income of £304,000. Educational grants to individuals totalled £38,000.

Applications

In writing outlining the need. Applications should be made through a school or similar organisation.

Other information

Grants are also made to organisations and to individuals for relief-in-need purposes.

Tower Hamlets

Stepney Relief-in-Need Charity

£3,000

Correspondent: Mrs J Partleton, Clerk to the Trustees, Rectory Cottage, 5 White Horse Lane, Stepney, London E1 3NE (020 7790 3598)

Trustees: Ms V. Jenkins; Mrs C. Horlor; The Revd C. Burke; Mrs V. Hullyer; Capt. N. Coke; Mrs B. Harris; Mrs J. Yeatman.

CC Number: 250130

Eligibility

People in need who live within the old Metropolitan Borough of Stepney.

Types of grants

One-off grants of £200 to £500, including those for uniforms/clothing, books and fees for attendance at college or university.

Annual grant total

In 2010/11 the charity had an income of £36,000 and a total expenditure of £34,000. Grants totalled £13,000 and are made for relief-in-need and educational purposes.

Applications

An application form is available from the correspondent and may be submitted either directly by the individual or through a relative, social worker or other welfare agency. The trustees usually meet four times a year, but some applications can be considered between meetings at the chair's discretion.

The Tower Hamlets and Canary Wharf Further Education Trust

£103,000 (79 grants)

Correspondent: David Stone, London Borough of Tower Hamlets, Mulberry Place, 5 Clove Crescent, London E14 2BG (020 7364 4888; email: david.stone@towerhamlets.gov.uk)

Trustees: Abdal Ullah; Howard Sheppard; John Garwood; Abdul Asad.

CC Number: 1002772

Eligibility

Students (but not schoolchildren) who have lived in the London borough of Tower Hamlets for at least three years. Applicants must be ordinarily resident in the UK, have been granted exceptional leave to remain in the UK or have refugee status. The three year residency is waived for people with full refugee status, or people whose parents have lived in the borough for the last three years and have returned home.

Types of grants

The trust gives grants for fees and maintenance, paid in three termly instalments. There is a means-tested system for deciding which applicants qualify for help with fees, maintenance support and those who can claim for both. Grants also cover books and equipment/instruments. Grants to a maximum of £3,300. Preference is given to education and training in technical and managerial skills relevant to commerce and industry.

Annual grant total

In 2010/11 grants totalled £103,000, broken down as follows:

- Tuition fees: 45 grants totalling £80,000
- Maintenance: 34 grants totalling £23,000

Grants were also broken down in the trust accounts by type of course assisted:

- Postgraduate: 26 grants totalling £68,000
- Advanced Education: 47 grants totalling £30,000
- First degree: five grants totalling £5,000
- A-level studies: one grant of £280

Exclusions

Courses of religious study are not supported, regardless of religion.

Applications

On a form available from the correspondent with full guidelines. Completed forms must be submitted directly by the individual and include details of family income, proof of residency in the borough and confirmation by the college or university of intention to study. The closing date is usually in June in the preceding academic year for the grant to be made when the course commences. Forms are normally available from March each year.

Waltham Forest

The Henry Green Scholarship Fund

£3,500

Correspondent: Duncan Pike, Head of Resources for Children, Silver Birch House, Uplands Business Park, Blackhorse Lane, London E17 5SD (email: sandra.edenborough@walthamforest.gov.uk)

Trustees: Nicholas Russell; Maria Holmden; Clyde Kitson; Pat Gough; Milton Martin; Jenny Sullivan; John Marks; Vicar of Leyton; Anna Mbachu; Sylvia Poulssen.

CC Number: 310918

Eligibility

People under 25 who live in Waltham Forest and are studying at the universities of Cambridge, London or Oxford and attended one of the following schools: Connaught Girls' High School, Norlington Boys' High School, Leyton Sixth Form College, George Mitchell High School, Tom Hood Senior High School and Leytonstone School.

Types of grants

Grants ranging from £50 to £200 to help with books, equipment or living expenses.

Annual grant total

In 2010/11 the fund had an income of £3,300 and an expenditure of £3,500. Grants to individuals usually total between £1,000 and £5,000.

Applications

On a form available from the correspondent. Applications must be submitted directly by the individual by the end of May for consideration by August.

Sir William Mallinson Scholarship Trust

£3,000

Correspondent: Alice Everett, Waltham Forest College, 707 Forest Road, London E17 4JB (020 8501 8134)

Trustees: David Ranger; Terence Mallinson.

CC Number: 312489

Eligibility

People under 21 who live in the London Borough of Waltham Forest.

Types of grants

Grants of £150 to £500 to people starting work for equipment, instruments and travel expenses and students in further or higher education for study or travel overseas and student exchange.

Annual grant total

The trust has an average income of between £1,500 and £2,000. Expenditure is erratic but in 2010/11 totalled £3,800.

Applications

On a form available from the correspondent, to be submitted by the end of February through the individual's school, college or educational welfare agency for consideration in March/April.

The Sir George Monoux Exhibition Foundation

£2,000

Correspondent: Duncan Pike, Silver Birch House, Uplands Business Park, Blackhorse Lane, Walthamstow, London E17 5SD (020 8496 3592; email: sandra. edenborough@walthamforest.gov.uk)

Trustees: D. Hainsworth; R. Darvill; D. Carey; J. Lewis; Simon Heathfield; Steve Newton; Karen Bellamy; Sylvia Poulsen.

CC Number: 310903

Eligibility

Further and higher education students aged under 25 who live in the London Borough of Waltham Forest and are pupils or former pupils of the following schools: Aveling Park School, Leyton Sixth Form College, Walthamstow Academy, Connaught School For Girls, Leytonstone School, Tom Hood School, George Mitchell Community School, Norlington School For Boy,

Walthamstow School For Girls, Highams Park School, Rush Croft School, Warwick School For Boys, Holy Family Technology College, Sir George Monoux Sixth Form College, Willowfield School, Kelmscott School, the Lammas School and Waltham Forest College.

Types of grants

One-off awards ranging from £50 to £100 are available for activities not normally covered by local authority grants. Such activities include student exchanges and other educational visits overseas, as well as educational visits in the UK. The fund also aims to 'encourage students to develop their project work'.

Annual grant total

About £2,000.

Applications

On a form available from London Borough of Waltham Forest.

Wandsworth

The Peace Memorial Fund

£500

Correspondent: Gareth Jones, Town Hall, Room 153, Wandsworth High Street, London SW18 2PU (020 8871 7520; email: garethjones@wandsworth. gov.uk)

Trustee: Gordon Passmore.

CC Number: 213167

Eligibility

Children aged 16 or under who live in the borough of Wandsworth.

Types of grants

Grants of £40 to £75 towards the cost of holidays and educational visits (mainly in the UK).

Annual grant total

About £1,000 for education and welfare purposes.

Applications

Through a welfare agency on a form available from the correspondent. Applications should be submitted in February/March and May/June.

Supporting Children of Wandsworth Trust (SCOWT)

£1,500

Correspondent: Adrian Butler, 82 Reigate Road, Epsom KT17 3DZ (020

8393 5344; email: adrian.butler2@ ntlworld.com)

Trustees: Adrian Butler; David Hopkinson; John Grove; Lois Lees; Tina Thompson.

CC Number: 1063861

Eligibility

Children aged between 3 and 18 who have lived in the borough of Wandsworth for at least two years.

Types of grants

Grants to a maximum of £200 towards items such as musical instruments, sporting equipment, special clothing and educational trips. Grants are made for educational and welfare purposes to 'help children to achieve their full potential'.

Annual grant total

About £1,500.

Applications

On a form available from the correspondent. Applications should include recommendation letters from clubs, social workers and so on if possible. The trustees meet every two to three months, although urgent applications can be considered between meetings.

Westminster

The Hyde Park Place Estate Charity (Civil Trustees)

£4,500

Correspondent: Shirley Vaughan, Clerk, St George's Hanover Square Church, The Vestry, 2a Mill Street, London W1S 1FX (020 7629 0874)

Trustees: Revd Roderick Leece; Mark Hewitt; Michael Beckett; Mrs R. Bottinge; Lady Rees-Mogg; Lady Clare Howes; Mrs J. Prendergast; Mrs H. Acton.

CC Number: 212439

Eligibility

People under 25 who are residents of the borough of Westminster and are studying at schools or colleges in Westminster.

Types of grants

Grants of £50 to £500 for schoolchildren college students and vocational students towards clothing, books, living expenses and excursions.

Annual grant total

In 2010/11 the civil trustees had an income of £458,000 and made grants totalling £107,000 for the relief of hardship, the relief of sickness and the advancement of education, of which £98,000 went to organisations and £9,000 to 106 individuals.

Exclusions

Refugees, asylum seekers and overseas students are not eligible.

Applications

All applications should be made through a recognised third party/organisation and include a case history and the name, address and date of birth of the applicant. Applications are considered on an ongoing basis.

The Paddington Charitable Estates Educational Fund

£18,000

Correspondent: Nicholas Maxwell, 14th Floor, Westminster City Hall, 64 Victoria Street, London SW1E 6QP (020 7641 2135)

Trustees: Michael Brahams; Gary Bradley; Tim Cowell; Alistair Thom; Jan Prendergast.

CC Number: 312347

Eligibility

People aged under 25 for the duration of their course who live in the former metropolitan borough of Paddington (roughly the north west corner of the City of Westminster bounded by the Edgware Road and Bayswater Road).

Types of grants

The fund has a number of schemes that support both individuals and organisations.

The pocket money scheme allocates a block grant to the admissions and benefits office of the education department of Westminster City Council, which then distributes about 25 to 30 grants to individuals nominated by schools and educational welfare officers, of £2 per week for children aged 11 to 14 and £2.50 for children aged over 14.

Long-term recurrent grants are made for school and course fees for children who are particularly gifted, or in need of special tuition, to enable them to attend special schools.

One-off grants are also made towards one-off course fees and maintenance, travel, clothing and other expenses.

Scholarships and bursaries are available towards educational trips and to allow people to enter into a trade or profession or to study music and other arts.

Annual grant total

In 2010 grants totalling £18,000 were made to individuals for education.

Applications

Applications should be made in writing by a social services or welfare organisation on behalf of an individual. If in doubt a telephone call to the correspondent would be useful to establish whether a case is eligible.

Other information

Grants are also made to schools, organisations and individuals for welfare purposes.

The Saint Marylebone Educational Foundation

£58,000

Correspondent: Caroline Grant, Clerk, c/o St Peter's Church, 119 Eaton Square, London SW1W 9AL

Trustees: Helen Wells; Michael Wrottesley; Sarah Woolman; Lucy Dennett; Nicholas Papadopulos; Canon Evans.

CC Number: 312378

Eligibility

People aged between 8 and 18 who, for at least two years, have lived or been educated in the former borough of St Marylebone and the City of Westminster. Preference is given to those who have embarked on a course of education the run into unforeseen circumstances affecting their financial situation, such as parental illness and to those for whom boarding school is a preferred option, due to parental illness or a specific educational need.

Types of grants

Generally recurrent grants for school pupils to help with fees. Grants range from £500 to £5,500.

Annual grant total

In 2010/11 grants totalling £58,000 were made to 11 pupils.

Exclusions

No grants for higher education.

Applications

Initially by writing to the correspondent, requesting an application form. These should be completed by the applicant's parent/guardian or by the individual if aged over 18. Applications can also be made by a third party such as a teacher, or come through an organisation such as a school or welfare agency. Applications are considered in January and July.

Other information

Grants are also made to independent schools.

Statutory grants and student support

A comprehensive guide to benefits is beyond the scope of this book. There are a number of organisations which provide comprehensive guides, information and advice to students wishing to study in the UK and overseas. Contact details for these organisations can be found in the 'Contacts and sources of further information' section on page 375.

The following is a basic guide to the statutory entitlements for people in education. The situation is extremely complex and changes continually, but the state is still the largest provider of educational support and will continue to be so. Potential applicants should check the situation before applying. Note that this information is correct as of February 2013. You are advised to check the relevant sources (signposted in this section) for the latest information.

This chapter covers:

- **Schoolchildren** (aged 16 and under) – free school meals, school clothing grants, and school transport
- **Further Education** – Discretionary Learner Support, Residential Support Scheme, Care to Learn, 24+ Advanced Learner Loans and Adult Entitlement to Learning
- **Welfare reforms**
- **Student support** – from the government, LEAs, supplementary grants, NHS bursaries, social work bursaries and teacher training funding

Schoolchildren (aged 16 and under)

The following benefits are all separately administered by individual local education authorities (LEAs) which set their own rules of eligibility and set the level of grants. The following information covers the basic general criteria for benefits, but you should contact your LEA directly for further information and advice (see 'Education authority contacts' on page 379 to find your local LEA).

Free school meals
In England and Wales, LEA-maintained schools must provide a free midday meal to pupils if they or their parents receive:
- Income Support
- Jobseeker's Allowance
- Employment and Support Allowance
- Support as asylum seekers

The school must also provide a free meal if a pupil's parents receive Child Tax Credit and their income is below a certain level or if they get the Guarantee Credit part of the Pension Credit. Children who receive a qualifying benefit in their own right are also entitled to free school meals.

School clothing grants
All schools are expected to consider cost a high priority when deciding on a uniform policy, as no school uniform should be so expensive that families feel excluded.

In England, LEAs have the discretion to give grants to help towards the cost of buying school uniforms for pupils in maintained schools, colleges for further education and sixth form colleges. They will set their own criteria for eligibility; this can include uniform and non-uniform clothes, shoes and sports kits. In some schools and colleges, help may be available from the governing body or parents' association.

Some LEAs, however, do not give financial help to buy school uniforms on the grounds that there is no legal basis for a pupil to wear a school uniform. In this instance, you may have to challenge your LEA if the school requires a pupil to wear a uniform and you cannot afford the cost. Information on challenging an LEA can be found on the Citizens Advice Adviceguide website (www.adviceguide.org.uk).

It is worth remembering that many schools address the issue of the cost of school uniforms by selling good quality second-hand items directly to parents. Some schools also have hardship funds to enable parents to purchase uniforms, while others run schemes for purchasing uniforms through the school, where uniforms can be paid for in weekly instalments. Contacting the school before buying new items may significantly help to reduce the cost.

You can check if your local authority provides school clothing grants on the www.gov.uk website.

transport

, children who are between 5 and 16 years old qualify for free school transport if they go to their nearest suitable school and live at least two miles from the school if they are under 8 years old or three miles from the school if they are over 8 years old, or if there is no safe walking route to school. There are lower requirements for families on low incomes and some LEAs may provide free transport for other reasons. Check with your local LEA for more information (for a list of LEAs, see 'Education authority contacts' on page 379).

People who are over 16 years old and in further education may qualify for help with transport costs; this varies by LEA.

Local authorities also have to consider any disability or special educational needs when deciding whether transport is necessary for a child. If a child has a statement of special educational needs (SEN) and has transport requirements written into their statement, the local authorities must meet them. Discretionary grants may also be available from LEAs to cover travel expenses for parents visiting children at special schools.

Pupils living in London can also qualify for free transport on London buses and trams if they are in full-time education or work-based learning. For more information, a helpline is available on 0845 330 9876, or information can be found online at www.tfl.gov.uk.

Further education

Discretionary Learner Support

You may be eligible for Discretionary Learner Support if you are over 19 years old, on a further education course and facing financial hardship. This can help to pay for childcare, accommodation and travel, course materials and equipment and other hardship needs. Contact your learning provider, as each institution administers this scheme individually.

Residential Support Scheme

If you have to live away from home to attend a level 2 or 3 qualification course you can be eligible for up to £4,000, depending on household income and where the course is located.

Care to Learn

You can get grants of up to £175 per week if you are a parent under the age of 20 at the start of your course (which must be publicly funded). Contact the Learner Support helpline on 0800 121 8989 to get an application form and guidance notes.

24+ Advanced Learning Loans

If you are 24 years old or older you can apply for a loan to help with the costs of a college or training course at level 3 or above. Similar to higher education loans, you don't pay anything back until you are earning more than £21,000 a year. Contact your training organisation or college for more details on this loan, which is available from August 2013.

Adult Entitlement to Learning

Eligible adults aged 19 and over have access to a range of qualifications from basic English and maths to level 3 qualifications that can be studied with no course fees to pay. Contact the National Careers Service for advice and information on 0800 100 900.

Further information

Department for Education: Castle View House, East Lane, Runcorn, Cheshire WA7 2GJ (tel: 03700 002288; website: www.education.gov. uk).

Department of Business, Innovation and Skills (further and higher education): 1 Victoria Street, London SW1H 0ET (tel: 020 7215 5000; email: enquires@bis.gsi.gov.uk; website: www.bis.gov.uk).

Welsh Assembly Education and Skills: Cathays Park, Cardiff CF10 3NQ (tel: 03000 603300/03000 604400; email: learningwales@wales. gsi.gov.uk; website: www.learning. wales.gov.uk).

Education Scotland: Denholm House, Almondvale Business Park, Almondvale Way, Livingston

EH54 6GA (tel: 01412 825000; email: enquires@educationscotland.gov.uk; website: www.educationscotland.gov. uk).

Department of Education for Northern Ireland: Rathgael House, Balloo Road, Rathgill, Bangor, County Down BT19 7PR (tel: 02891 279279; email: mail@deni.gov.uk; website: www.deni.gov.uk).

Welfare reforms

The coalition government is implementing drastic welfare reforms. As well as reassessing everyone on Employment and Support Allowance, most means-tested benefits are being rolled into one single means-tested benefit called Universal Credit, which is being piloted in some areas of England starting in April 2013.

- Disability Living Allowance is being replaced with Personal Independence Payments, with pilot schemes starting in April 2013
- Council Tax Benefits will now be the responsibility of local authorities, rather than being worked out according to a national formula
- A benefits cap is being introduced which puts a limit on the total amount of money from benefits you can receive if you are of working age

Other changes include amendments to the rules about appealing against a benefits decision, new conditions about looking for work and means-testing for Child Benefit. Also, large parts of the Social Fund are being abolished.

If you think you might be affected by any of these changes, we advise you to contact your local Citizens Advice for information and advice. There is a list of local advice centres and some self-help guides at www.adviceguide. org.uk. The Department for Work and Pensions also provides a general advice line on 0800 882 200 (not for personal claims information).

Student support

Following drastic changes in the way universities are funded in England, different rules apply depending on whether you started university pre-2012 when the old funding system was in place, or 2012 or after when the new system came in.

Advice is available from your LEA (see 'Education authority contacts' on page 379). However, note that the busiest time for LEAs is the period between mid-August (when A-level results come out) and about mid-November (by which time most awards have been given). It is probably best not to contact your LEA for detailed advice at this time unless absolutely necessary. Students should also check with their university or college for other available funds.

Students who began university before September 2012

Full-time students are entitled to a Tuition Fee Loan of up to £3,500 per year, a Maintenance Loan of up to £4,950 (£6,928 in London), and a Maintenance Grant of up to £2,984. Most of this is dependent upon your household income and whether or not you are living at home. Funding is slightly different for part-time students.

Repayments are automatically deducted from your pay when your income is over £15,795 a year and payments are at a rate of 9% of any given income over this amount. Check www.gov.uk for more information.

Students who began university after September 2012

As tuition fees have tripled, you are entitled to a Tuition Fee Loan of up to £9,000 (less for part-time students) and a Maintenance Loan of up to £5,500 (up to £7,765 in London). You are also entitled to a Maintenance Grant of up to £3,354; this is dependent upon household income and will reduce the amount of Maintenance Loan to which you are entitled.

Repayments are linked to your income and begin when you are earning more than £21,000, with 9% of everything above this amount being deducted.

Funding is slightly different for part-time students. See the www.gov.uk website for more information.

Supplementary grants

Some students are entitled to extra help, and this can be applied for through supplementary grants:

- **National Scholarship Programme:** If your household income is less than £25,000 a year, you can apply for this bursary which could provide up to £1,000 of help with tuition fees and accommodation or a free foundation year. Contact your college or university to find out how and when to apply.
- **Access to Learning Fund:** If you are in financial hardship you can apply for help from this fund to start a course or stay in higher education. Your college or university decides who gets the money and how it is paid.
- **Childcare Grant:** Full-time higher education students with children can apply for a childcare grant of up to 85% of childcare costs (maximum amounts apply), dependent upon income. Apply as part of your main student finance application and include an estimation of your childcare costs.
- **Parents' Learning Allowance:** Full-time students with children can get up to £1,500 a year to help with costs such as books, study materials and travel. Applications are made as part of the main student finance application.
- **Adult Dependents' Grant:** Students can apply for a grant of up to £2,642 if they have an adult who depends upon them financially. The amount given varies according to the student and the dependent's income and can be applied for as part of the main student finance application.
- **Disabled Students' Allowance:** If you have a disability, long-term health condition, mental health condition or specific learning disability, you can apply for specialist equipment allowance, a non-medical helper allowance and

a general allowance using the Disabled Students' Allowance form available from the www.gov.uk website.

Information and applications for student finance in England can be found on the www.gov.uk website. You can also contact your LEA, a list of which can be found on page 379. Further useful contacts include:

- **Student Finance England:** 100 Bothwell Street, Glasgow G2 7JD (tel: 01413 062 000; website: www.slc.co.uk)
- **Student Finance Wales:** (tel: 0845 602 8845; website: www.studentfinancewales.co.uk)
- **Student Finance Northern Ireland:** (tel: 0845 600 0662; website: www.studentfinanceni.co.uk)
- **Student Awards Agency for Scotland:** (tel: 0300 555 0505; website: www.sass.gov.uk)
- **For students from other EU countries:** (tel: 01412 433570; website: www.gov.uk/studentfinance)

NHS bursaries

Full-time NHS students can apply for a bursary and a grant from the NHS. Part-time students are eligible for reduced bursaries and grants. Grants are for £1,000 and bursaries can be up to £5,460 depending on course intensity, where you study and live and your household income.

Eligible courses that lead to professional registration are:

- Medicine or dentistry
- Chiropody, podiatry, dietetics, occupational therapy, orthoptics, physiotherapy, prosthetics and orthotics, radiography, radiotherapy, audiology and speech and language therapy
- Dental hygiene or dental therapy
- Nursing, midwifery or operating department practice

Social Work Bursaries

Social Work Bursaries do not depend upon your household income and can help with living costs and tuition fees.

For students in England: NHS Student Bursaries, Hesketh House, 200–220 Broadway, Fleetwood, Lancashire FY7 8SS (tel: 0300 330 1345; website: www.nhsbsa.nhs.uk)

For students in Wales: Care Council for Wales (CCW), South Gate House, Wood Street, Cardiff CF10 1EW (tel: 0300 3033 444; email: info@ccwales. org.uk; website: www.ccwales.org.uk)

For students in Scotland: Scottish Social Services Council (SSSC), Compass House, 11 Riverside Drive, Dundee DD1 4NY (tel: 0845 603 0891; email: enquiries@sssc.uk.com; website: www.sssc.uk.com)

For students in Northern Ireland: Social Service Inspectorate (SSI), The Department of Health, Social Services and Public Safety, Castle Buildings, Stormont, Belfast BT4 3SJ (tel: 02890 520500; website: www.dhsspsni.gov. uk)

Teacher Training Funding

Funding is available for full-time or part-time students on initial teacher training (ITT), postgraduate certificate in education (PGCE) and school-centred initial teacher training (SCITT) courses through the main student finance avenue. Training bursaries are available from the Teaching Agency to students who achieved at least a 2:2 at undergraduate level. These bursaries are dependent upon what subject or phase is being studied, as some are priority areas. They can range from £4,000 up to £20,000 for a trainee with a first class degree who is training to teach physics, chemistry or maths.

Teaching Agency: (tel: 0800 389 2500; website: www.education.gov.uk/ teachregister)

Further advice and information services are listed in the 'Contacts and sources of further information' on page 375).

Types of schools in the UK and their funding

This section contains information about and details of the types of schools that exist in the UK, how they are funded and how funding can be obtained to attend them.

Local authority maintained schools

These schools are funded by the local education authority and include foundation schools, community schools, voluntary-controlled schools, voluntary-aided schools, nursery schools and some special schools. They all follow the national curriculum and are inspected by Ofsted.

The gov.uk website supplies some information about the different types of schools, how to find one and apply for a place. See: www.gov.uk/types-of-school/overview for more information.

Academies

Academies are independently managed schools which are funded directly by the Education Funding Agency and operate outside the control of the local authority. They are set up by sponsors from business, faith or voluntary groups in partnership with the Department for Education and the local authority. In January 2013 more than half of all secondary schools had converted, or were in the process of converting, to academy status. Many factors have caused academies to be a controversial current issue; therefore there exists a wide range of information available about academies from all perspectives. The Department for Education supplies some here: www.education.gov.uk/schools/leadership/typesofschools/academies.

Free schools

These schools are non-profit, independent, state-funded schools which are not controlled by the local authority. They are similar to academies but are usually new schools, set up as a response to a demand that is not being met by existing schools.

The New Schools Network provides advice about free schools, including how to set one up. See www.newschoolsnetwork.org or call 020 7537 9208 for more information.

Independent schools

Independent schools are independent in their finances and governance, and are funded by charging parents fees (on average £10,500 a year, or £25,000 for boarders). They set their own curriculum and admissions policies and are inspected by Ofsted or other approved inspectorates. According to the Independent Schools Council, around 6.5% of schoolchildren in the UK are educated in independent schools, with the figure rising to 18% of pupils for those over the age of 16.

Most independent schools offer scholarships and bursaries to some applicants, ranging from 10% of fees to full fees paid (very occasionally). They are subject to fierce competition and are usually awarded on the basis of academic merit, as well as individual need.

A number of independent schools also offer music scholarships, varying from 10% of fees to full fees paid (including free musical tuition). Candidates are usually expected to offer two instruments at at least grades 6 to 8. Contact the Director of Music at the school you are interested in for more details.

The Independent Schools Directory

The Independent Schools Directory lists all the UK independent schools.

Tel: 020 8906 0911

Email: info@indschools.co.uk

Website: www.indschools.co.uk

The Independent Schools Council Information Service

The Independent Schools Council Information Service is the main source of information on independent schools. It has a website containing detailed information to help families to select the right school and find possible sources of funding.

Tel: 020 7766 7070

Website: www.isc.co.uk

The Independent Schools Yearbook

The Independent Schools Yearbook contains details of schools with a membership of one or more of the Constituent Associations of the Independent Schools Council. It is published by A&C Black and can be bought online.

Tel: 020 7631 5988

Email: isyb@acblack.com

Website: www.isyb.co.uk

The Independent Association of Prep Schools

The Independent Association of Prep Schools is the professional association for head teachers of the leading 600 independent prep schools in the UK and worldwide.

Tel: 01926 887833

Email: iaps@iaps.org.uk

Website: www.iaps.org.uk

The Council of British International Schools

The Council of British International Schools is a membership organisation of British schools of quality, Europe and worldwide which provide a British education.

Tel: 020 8240 4142

Email: executivedirector@cobis.org.uk

Website: www.cobis.org.uk

Boarding schools

Boarding Schools Association

The Boarding Schools Association serves and represents boarding schools and promotes boarding education in the UK, including both state and private boarding schools.

Very occasionally the local authority may pay for a child's boarding fees, if they have a particularly difficult home situation. Seventy-five children were supported in this way in 2011/12, and the new Assisted Boarding Network, which is backed by the government, is pushing for this number to rise to 1,000 by 2018.

Contact the Director of Education or the Chief Education Officer for the area in which you live, or if you live outside the UK, the area with which you have the closest connection.

Tel: 020 7798 1580

Email: bsa@boarding.org.uk

Website: www.boarding.org.uk

Maintained boarding schools

These are state schools that take boarders as well as day pupils; they only charge for the cost of boarding, not for tuition. Boarding costs are generally between £8,000 and £13,000 a year. There are 39 state boarding schools in England and one in Wales. They are a mix of all-ability comprehensive schools, academies and grammar schools. They all follow the national curriculum and take the same examinations as pupils in day state schools.

State Boarding Schools Association

Tel: 020 7798 1580

Email: info@sbsa.org.uk

Website: www.sbsa.org.uk

Music, dance and stage schools

Choir schools

Choir Schools Association

The Choir Schools Association is a group of 44 schools which are attached to cathedrals, churches and college chapels around the country. The majority are fee-paying, with 9 out of 10 choristers qualifying for financial help with fees through the schools or through the government' Access to Excellence scheme (see details of this scheme below).

Tel: 01359 221333

Email: info@choirschools.org.uk

Website: www.choirschools.org.uk

Music schools

There are various specialist music schools in the UK, with no overall umbrella body. Contact the school directly for information about fees and funding.

Access to Excellence

The government's Access to Excellence scheme helps identify and assist children with exceptional potential to enable them to progress towards self-sustaining careers in music and dance. Information can b found on the Department for Education website, which also lists music schools in the UK.

Website: www.education.gov.uk/ schools/teachingandlearning/ curriculum/subjects/b0068711/mds

MMA

MMA is the national association for music teaching professionals. It publishes the *MMA Music Directory* annually, a comprehensive guide to music departments and music scholarships in the UK, which can b purchased on its website.

Tel: 01227 475600

Email: admin@mma-online.org.uk

Website: www.mma-online.org.uk

Foundations for Excellence

The Foundations for Excellence website provides information, guidance and signposting in the area of health and wellbeing for young musicians and dancers.

ebsite: www.foundations-for-
cellence.org

ance schools

**ouncil for Dance and Education
aining**

formation on dance education and
aining can be obtained from the
ouncil for Dance and Education
raining. It is the quality-assurance
dy of the dance and musical theatre
dustries and provides information
n its recognised schools and
achers.

el: 020 7240 5703

mail: info@cdet.org.uk

ebsite: www.cdet.org.uk

ance Schools UK

ance Schools UK provides a
rectory of dance schools and
achers across the UK and Ireland.

ebsite: www.danceschools-uk.co.uk

tage schools

rama UK

rama UK was formed out of the
ational Council for Drama and the
onference of Drama Schools and
rovides accreditation for vocational
rama courses and support for
rganisations which offer accredited
aining. It acts as an advocate for the
ctor and encourages the industry
nd training providers to work
gether. Its website provides
formation about drama training.

el: 020 7529 8794

mail: info@dramauk.co.uk

ebsite: www.dramauk.co.uk

ree Index

ree Index provides a list of stage
chools in the UK.

ebsite: www.freeindex.co.uk/
ategories/entertainment_and_
festyle/performing_arts/stage_
chools

Other possible sources of help with fees

Allowances for Crown Servants

The Foreign and Commonwealth
Office gives grants to enable children
of diplomats and other government
servants working abroad to attend
boarding schools in the UK.

Tel: 01908 515580

Allowances for Armed Forces Personnel

The Children's Education Advisory
Service (CEAS) provides expert and
impartial advice about the education
of Service children.

Children whose parents are members
of Her Majesty's Forces are eligible
for an allowance towards boarding
education, whether their parent(s) is
(are) serving at home or abroad. This
is the Continuity of Education
Allowance which is available for
children who are 8 years old and
older. Families are expected to
contribute a minimum of 10%
towards the fees. Contact CEAS to
obtain advice and the relevant
application form.

Address: Trenchard Lines, Upavon,
Pewsey, Wiltshire SN9 6BE

Tel: 01980 618244 (civilian)/
GPTN 94 344 8244 (military)

Extra funding is also available for
day-school allowances, special
educational needs, guardian's
allowances and children's visits to
parents serving overseas.

Multinational companies

Some multinational companies and
organisations help with school fees if
parents have to work overseas. A few
firms make grants, run scholarship
schemes or provide low-interest loans
for employees who are resident in the
UK. Consult your employer for
further information.

Company sponsorship and career development loans

This chapter looks at two possible sources of finance for some students.

1. Company sponsorships: these apply particularly to people in their last year at school who are intending to study a business-related, engineering, or science-based subject at university.

2. Career development loans: these can be a useful means of helping to finance vocational courses for periods of up to two years, particularly if the course offers the prospect of obtaining a steady, reasonably well-paid job at the end.

Company sponsorships

Sponsorship of degree courses

A number of companies sponsor students who are taking degree courses at universities, usually in business, engineering, technology or other science subjects. These are generally for students who are resident in the UK and are taking a first degree course (or a comparable course).

Sponsorship generally takes the form of cash support (i.e. a bursary or scholarship) while at university, with a salary being paid during pre-university and vacation employment or during periods of industrial training at the company concerned. (If the sponsorship is for a sandwich course the placements will be for longer than the vacation and will form an integral part of the course.) Sponsorships are highly competitive but can be of great value to students who, for any reason, do not receive the full grant. They may also help students avoid having to take out a loan.

Each company has its own sponsorship policy. Some sponsorships are tied to a particular course or institution; others are only given for specific subjects. The value of the sponsorship also varies. Additional help can be available in the form of discretionary educational gifts or degree prizes.

Sponsorships do not necessarily offer a permanent job at the end of the course (unless the student is classed as an employee). Equally, the student does not usually have to take up a job if offered by the company, although there may be at least a moral obligation to consider one.

Students should not decide on a course simply because there may be sponsorship available, they should choose the course first and seek sponsorship afterwards if appropriate.

In most sponsorships it is the student, not the company, who has to make arrangements to get on the course. Indeed some companies will only sponsor students who have already been accepted on a course. However, most university departments have well-established links with industry and actively encourage students who are seeking sponsorship.

Students should apply for sponsorships as early as possible in the autumn term of the final academic year before moving to university.

Year in Industry

This is an option for students to take a year between school and university to earn money and gain work experience. It can help you to clarify which course you want to take, and to decide what you want to do once you have completed it.

367

The Year in Industry is an education charity which finds placements for students in all areas of engineering, science, IT, e-commerce, business, marketing, finance and logistics. It offers the chance of sponsorship, paid vacation work or a combination package, where students can combine their work experience with voluntary work, expeditions and summer camps abroad. It is available nationwide and is open to any students interested in a career in industry. The package includes 'off the job' training to develop interpersonal skills and business awareness.

Applications for pre-degree places in industry can be made directly to the company or through the scheme. It is recommended that applications are made as early as possible in the final year of A-levels, Highers, Advanced GNVQ and so on. There is a non-refundable £25 registration fee for applying.

For further information you should contact one of the regional centres that administer the scheme. Details can be found by visiting the website (www.etrust.org.uk/year_in_industry).

Further information

The main guide on company sponsorships is *Engineering Opportunities*. This is published by the Institution of Mechanical Engineers, 1 Birdcage Walk, London SW1H 9JJ (tel: 020 7222 7899; email: library@imeche.org; website: www.imeche.org). It is published annually and you can get a copy free of charge by contacting the institution, or online at www.engopps.com.

Details of company sponsorship for other industries are a little sketchy. Individuals are best advised to identify major institutions working in the industry they intend to follow and see what schemes are available.

Professional and career development loans

Professional and career development loans are available through an arrangement between the Skills Funding Agency (SFA) and participating high-street banks. The interest during the duration of the course (and one month afterwards) is met by the SFA and so the learner does not have to make any repayments until after the course is completed. The loan is then repaid by the former student to the bank over an agreed period at a fixed rate of interest.

To be eligible, you must be:
- 18 years old or over at the point of application
- 'Settled' (i.e. have either indefinite leave to enter or remain or have the right of abode) in the UK and have been ordinarily resident in the UK for at least the three years prior to the start of your learning programme
- Intending to work in the UK, the EU or the EEA when the course finishes

Remember: even if you meet these conditions, the decision on whether you have been successful in your application remains with the bank. The bank's decision will depend on you meeting their specific lending criteria.

Courses must:
- Only last up to two years, or three years if they include one year of work experience
- Be provided by an organisation on the Professional Career and Development Loan Register, or the organisation must be willing to become registered with the programme
- Help with your career (they don't have to lead to a qualification)

Professional and career development loans cannot be given for:
- Foundation or access courses that are being used as a step towards a degree course (however, a stand-alone foundation course that leads

to employment in its own right would be eligible)
- Graduate Diplomas in Law, otherwise known as the Common Professional Examination or CPE, as this is a course that can lead to the Legal Practice Course or Bar Vocational Course
- Careers advice or help with job hunting
- The costs of running or starting up a business such as marketing or buying a franchise licence

Amount available

The amount available ranges from £300 to £10,000. Remember, a professional and career development loan isn't right for everyone – make sure you have looked at the full range of funding options. You may be able to get financial support that you do not have to pay back such as Discretionary Learner Support, which may be available from your college.

Repayments

Repayments begin one month after the completion of the course. This is interpreted as the intended finishing date at the start of the course, which is either on the day the learner withdraws from the course or when an extension has been provided due to ill health or similar unforeseen circumstances. Extensions given for other reasons, such as late submission of a dissertation, are not accepted as a new finishing date. Similarly, submitting a dissertation before a deadline, for example, does not affect the referral date.

There are options to postpone the start of repayments if you are receiving a statutory means-tested benefit at the end of the course, although this must be agreed by the bank. People actively looking for employment and receiving Jobseeker's Allowance or Employment and Support Allowance, for instance, may be able to defer, whereas people opting to spend a year travelling before looking for work cannot.

The rate of interest is agreed when the loan is taken out and a plan for repayments is made. These can be spread over one to five years. Banks can offer different interest rates within the scheme.

Further information

Order an application pack from the National Careers Service (tel: 0800 585 505 or 0800 100 900; website: www.nationalcareersservice.direct. gov)

Repayment details can be obtained from branches of the two participating banks (at the time of writing):

1   Barclays Bank PLC (0845 609 0060)

2   The Co-operative Bank (0800 346 494)

Funding for gap years and overseas voluntary work

Gap years have traditionally been a popular choice with school-leavers looking to travel, volunteer, work or broaden their horizons in some other way before embarking on university life. However, in order to avoid the tuition fees hike which came into effect in 2012, many prospective students forsook gap years and applied to universities in record numbers in order to afford tuition. An increasingly popular option is to take a 'mini-gap' during the summer holidays which can be organised for current undergraduate volunteers; this can add valuable experience and skills to a CV and is looked upon by many universities and potential employers as an advantage in what is a very competitive job market.

There are some opportunities to participate in voluntary work, expeditions and other activities which can be funded or partly funded through trusts, bursaries and schemes. For further information on trust giving in this area see 'Gap year/voluntary work overseas' on page 16. The trusts in this section are divided into two categories:

1 Those with full entries – these mainly fund gap-year activities
2 Those that are cross-referenced – these prefer to give more widely in other areas as part of their charitable objectives

Generally, most trusts have quite specific criteria which they apply to all eligible applicants; it is important to keep this in mind and not assume that you can apply just because you wish to travel to a particular area or place. Likewise, many may have a particular preference for a certain type of project such as conservation or one that involves childcare. They may also give within a specific catchment area, so it can be useful to look at local trusts first. Many of the local trusts in this guide will give grants under terms such as 'travel overseas' or 'personal development activities'. This allows them to give broadly to a number of different activities which may fall into these categories, such as gap-year projects, voluntary work overseas and so on.

It cannot be over-emphasised that it is your responsibility to check that you are eligible for funding from any trust to which you intend to apply. Please do not apply if you are in doubt of your eligibility; where appropriate, contact the trust for further clarification.

If you are successful in gaining financial support, remember that it is always good practice to keep trusts informed of the progress of your project and what you have achieved by doing it. This might even be a requirement of accepting their funding. You may also be asked to act as an ambassador to the trust when returning to the UK by giving talks or presentations on your experiences.

This might be something to think about when making your application, particularly if the organisation is keen to involve past participants in promoting its scheme.

It may help your cause if you raise some of the funds yourself; this might give you an edge over other applicants and prove how dedicated and determined you are to succeed. You may also find it useful to break down the total cost of your application and apply to several different trusts for smaller amounts of money, as this could increase your chances of securing the right amount of funding.

There are other alternatives to funding gap-year projects and voluntary work overseas. There are many large volunteer organisations that provide funded or partly funded volunteering and exchange schemes that will allow you to take part in voluntary work at minimum cost. Many can offer bursaries to cover specific costs such as the project fee or flight fare, and some will ask you to fundraise a block amount of money but will pay for all your necessary costs in return. For example, the International Citizen Service programme requires most of its participants to fundraise £800 towards the project and the organisation will pay for all other costs in return.

Below is a list of funded or partly funded voluntary schemes available to young people living in the UK.

The European Voluntary Service (EVS)

EVS is a fully funded youth volunteering scheme run by the British Council, the UK's national agency for the Youth in Action programme. EVS provides opportunities for young people to volunteer in another European country for two weeks to twelve months.

The scheme is open to all young people aged 18 to 30 who are:

▶ Resident in one of the European member states
▶ Members of the European Economic Area
▶ Resident in any country in Eastern Europe and the Mediterranean area that are applying for membership of the European Union

EVS placements take place in all member countries of the European Union, the European Economic Area and pre-accession countries such as Turkey, and it is also possible to take part in EVS projects in countries of the South East European area, such as the Balkan states and the Caucasus.

Most placements last from six to twelve months and priority is given to longer-term placements; however, short-term placements from two weeks to twelve months are also available. Placements can be organised in variety of sectors, such as social, cultural, environmental and sports and are selected by the volunteers themselves.

All EVS projects are fully funded by European Commission grants, which are applied for by the applicant's sending organisation. The grant covers the costs of travel, food and accommodation, insurance, training and living expenses and provides volunteers with a modest living allowance.

In order to take part in an EVS project, volunteers have to find a suitable host organisation to volunteer with and a sending organisation from their own country to sponsor them. A list of sending organisations, host organisations, projects and other information regarding EVS can be found on their website: www.britishcouncil.org.

However, applicants are advised to plan their projects in advance (preferably six months), as the process can take this long to complete.

In addition to applying for a volunteer placement with EVS directly, it is also possible to organise a placement through certain volunteering organisations that are linked to the EVS programme. The Inter-Cultural Youth Exchange (www.icye.org.uk) and International Voluntary Service (www.ivsgb.org) will help volunteers through application processes and will sometimes carry out administration work on their behalf. If you are interested in volunteering with EVS, it may be worthwhile contacting one of these organisations for help.

Lattitude Global Volunteering

Lattitude Global Volunteering is a UK-based volunteering organisation and registered charity (272761) that organises volunteer placements for young people in developing countries and offers bursaries and funded projects for applicants in need of financial help. Volunteers can take part in a number of different projects such as camps and outdoor education, and environmental, medical and community projects. Lattitude Global Volunteering can also offer graduate placements that focus on a specific skill or professional area, which can be designed by the applicant themselves.

General bursary scheme

Bursaries of £500 to £1,000 can be given to UK applicants aged 17 to 25. Applicants must be able to prove why they would have difficulty in raising money in comparison to other Lattitude candidates.

There are also specific bursary schemes for young people from the West Midlands, the North East and Scotland.

Full details of all these schemes can be found on Lattitude's website.

Lattitude Global Volunteering, 42 Queen's Road, Reading, Berkshire RG1 4BB; tel: 01189 594914; website: www.lattitude.org.uk, email: volunteer@lattitude.org.uk

The Jack Petchey Foundation

The foundation wants to support young people who have to raise money in order to be involved in a voluntary project or participate in events that will benefit others in society. Grants are only available to those aged 11 to 25 who live in Essex or London. Full details of eligibility criteria and how to apply can be found on the foundation's website (www.jackpetcheyfoundation.org.uk).

VSO

VSO is an international development charity working with volunteers in developing countries. They currently offer the part funded International Citizen Service programme in partnership with the Department for International Development

This programme runs until 2014 and is available for 18 to 25 years olds from the UK. Projects are usually for 12 weeks, working on issues in a community organization in groups of between 5 and 20. Volunteers must fundraise £800 to take part and receive food, accommodation and an allowance whilst they are on the project.

Further details on these schemes can be found at VSO's website: www.vso-ics.org.uk; alternatively enquiries are taken by email: enquiry@ics-uk.org.uk, or telephone: 020 8780 7500.

Other helpful contacts

www.igapyear.com

iGapyear.com provides advice on how to put together a proposal for a funding application.

www.gapyear.com

A social network where travellers can meet, chat and share experiences.

www.idealist.org

Idealist.org is an independent, online network of non-profit and voluntary organisations that provide information on voluntary opportunities worldwide.

www.wwv.org.uk

Worldwide Volunteering has a search-and-match database of voluntary organisations and volunteer placements worldwide.

Volunteer organisations

www.vso.co.uk

www.frontier.ac.uk

www.raleigh.org.uk

Contacts and sources of further information

Many people in education and training need financial advice and help from time to time. It is usually best to contact the following people or organisations as a starting point:

The educational institution you are studying at

Your local education authority (addresses are in the previous section of this guide)

Your local Citizens Advice or other welfare agencies

These should point you in the right direction for more specialist advice if you need it. However, the following organisations and publications may be useful and should be available from all main libraries. Readers should also look at the specialist sections of this guide where relevant.

General

Citizens Advice

England: 0844 411 1444

Wales: 0844 477 2020

Scotland: 0808 800 9060

Provides free, independent, confidential and impartial advice to everyone on their rights and responsibilities. Find your local bureau at www.citizensadvice.org.uk or get advice online at www.adviceguide.org.uk.

Department for Education

Castle View House, East Lane, Runcorn, Cheshire WA7 2GJ (tel: 03700 002288; website: www.education.gov.uk)

Department of Business, Innovation and Skills (further and higher education)

1 Victoria Street, London SW1H 0ET (tel: 020 7215 5000; email: enquires@bis.gsi.gov.uk; website: www.bis.gov.uk)

Department of Education for Northern Ireland

Rathgael House, Balloo Road, Rathgill, Bangor, County Down BT19 7PR (tel: 02891 279279; email: mail@deni.gov.uk; website: www.deni.gov.uk)

Educational Grants Advisory Service (EGAS)

501–505 Kingsland Road, London E8 4AU (tel: 020 7254 6251; website: www.family-action.org.uk).

EGAS offers guidance and advice on funding for those studying for post-16 education and training.

Education Scotland

Denholm House, Almondvale Business Park, Almondvale Way, Livingston EH54 6GA (tel: 01412 825000; email: enquires@educationscotland.gov.uk; website: www.educationscotland.gov.uk)

Gov.uk

Website: www.gov.uk

General advice and information on government services.

The Money Advice Service

Holborn Centre, 120 Holborn, London EC1N 2TD (tel: 0300 500 5000; typetalk: 18001 0300 500 5000 [Mon–Fri, 8am–8pm, Sat, 9am–1pm]; email: enquiries@moneyadviceservice.org.uk; website: www.moneyadvice.org.uk; an online chat facility is also available.)

The Prince's Trust

0800 842 842; email: sarah.haidry@princes-trust.org.uk; website: www.princes-trust.org.uk

A youth charity that helps change young lives. The trust can help people under 30 who are not expecting to achieve 5 GCSEs grades A–C or who are not in education, training or not working more than 16 hours a week.

Welsh Assembly Education and Skills

Cathays Park, Cardiff CF10 3NQ (tel: 03000 603300/03000 604400; email: learningwales@wales.gsi.gov.uk; website: www.learning.wales.gov.uk)

Children

Child Poverty Action Group (CPAG)

Child Poverty Action Group, 94 White Lion Street, London N1 9PF (tel: 020 7837 7979; email: info@cpag. org.uk; website: www.cpag.org.uk)

CPAG publishes a number of guides which include information on state benefit and entitlements for both schoolchildren and students.

National Youth Advocacy Service

Egerton House, Tower Road, Birkenhead, Wirral CH41 1FN (tel: 01516 498700; helpline: 0300 330 3131 Mon–Fri, 9am–8pm, Sat, 10am–4pm; email: main@nyas.net or help@nyas.net; website: www.nyas. net)

Youth Access

1–2 Taylors Yard, 67 Alderbrook Road, London SW12 8AD (tel: 020 8772 9900; email: admin@ youthaccess.org.uk; website: www. youthaccess.org.uk – an online directory of information, advice and support services for young people).

Further and continuing education

City & Guilds

1 Giltspur Street, London EC1A 9DD (tel: 0844 543 0033; email: learnersupport@cityandguilds.com; website: www.cityandguilds.com)

Department for Business, Innovation, and Skills

Department of Business, Innovation and Skills (further and higher education): 1 Victoria Street, London SW1H 0ET (tel: 020 7215 5000; email: enquires@bis.gsi.gov.uk; website: www.bis.gov.uk)

National Institute of Adult Continuing Education (NIACE)

Chetwynd House, 21 De Montford Street, Leicester LE1 7GE (tel: 01162 044200; email: enquiries@niace.org. uk; website: www.niace.org.uk).

National Institute of Adult Continuing Education Wales

3rd Floor, 33–35 Cathedral Road, Cardiff CF11 9HB (tel: 02920 370900; email: enquiries@niacedc.org.uk; website: www.niacedc.org.uk).

NIACE is the national organisation for adult learning.

Higher Education

The National Union of Students (NUS)

NUS, HQ, 4th Floor 184–192 Drummond Street, London NW1 3HP (tel: 0845 521 0262; website: www.nus.org.uk).

NUS Scotland

29 Forth Street, Edinburgh EH1 3LE (tel: 01315 566598; email: mail@nus-scotland.org.uk)

NUS-USI

42 Dublin Road, Belfast BT2 7HN (tel: 02890 244641 email: info@ nistudents.org)

NUS Wales

2nd Floor, Cambrian Buildings, Mount Stuart Square, Cardiff CF10 5FL (tel: 02920 435390 email: office@nus-wales.org.uk)

The Open University (OU)

The Open University, PO Box 197, Milton Keynes MK7 6BJ (tel: 0845 300 6090; email: online form; website: www.open.ac.uk).

Scholarship Search

Website: www.scholarship-search.org. uk

Search scholarships in the UK for pre-university, undergraduate and postgraduate learning.

Student Award Agency for Scotland

Gyleview House, 3 Redheughs Rigg, Edinburgh EH12 9HH (tel: 0300 555 0505; website: www.saas.gov.uk).

Student Cashpoint

Website: www.studentcashpoint.co.uk

Information on student grants, loans, bursaries, scholarships and awards.

University and Colleges Admissions Service (UCAS)

PO Box 28, Cheltenham, Gloucestershire GL52 3LZ (tel: 08714680468; email: enquiries@ucas. ac.uk; website: www.ucas.ac.uk).

Applications for full-time university degree courses must be made throug UCAS (part-time degree courses and the Open University are not covered by UCAS – apply directly to the university).

Careers

National Careers Service

Website: www.nationalcareersservice. direct.gov.uk; tel: 0800 100 900

Provides information, advice and guidance to help people make decisions on learning, training and work opportunities. The service offer confidential and impartial advice, supported by qualified careers advisers.

Not Going to Uni

www.notgoingtouni.co.uk

Opportunities for school and college leavers outside of the traditional university route, including apprenticeships, sponsored degrees, diplomas, gap years, distance learnin and jobs.

Prospects

www.prospects.ac.uk

Graduate careers website for jobs, postgraduate courses, work experience and careers advice.

Students with disabilities

Disability Rights UK

12 City Forum, 250 City Road, London EC1V 8AF (tel: 0800 328 5050; email:students@disabilityrights.org; website: www.disabilityrightsuk.org)

National pan-disability organisation led by disabled people that provides advice to disabled students.

Lead Scotland

Princes House, 5 Shandwick Place, Edinburgh EH2 4RG (tel: 01312 289441; email: enquires@lead.org.uk; website: www.lead.org.uk)

Set up to widen access to learning for disabled young people and adults and carers across Scotland.

Study overseas

The British Council

10 Spring Gardens, London SW1A 2BN (tel: 01619 577755; email: general.enquiries@britishcouncil.org; website: www.britishcouncil.org).

Advice and publications on educational trips overseas.

Erasmus

British Council, Erasmus Team, 1 Kingsway Cardiff CF10 3AQ (tel: 02920 924311; email: erasmus@ britishcouncil.org; website: www. britishcouncil.org/erasmus).

Erasmus enables higher education students, teachers and institutions in 31 European countries to study for part of their degree in another country.

Overseas students

Refugee Women's Association

Print House, 18 Ashwin Street, London E8 3DL (tel: 020 7923 2412; email:info@refugeewomen.org.uk; website: www.refugeewomen.org.uk)

Provides advice and guidance on education, training, employment, health and social care for refugee women.

United Kingdom Council for International Students' Affairs (UKCISA)

9–17 St Albans Place, London N1 0NX (tel: 020 3131 3576; website: www.ukcisa.org.uk).

UKCISA provides information for overseas students on entering the UK, as well as general advice.

Other funding or sources of help

Community Foundations

Tel: 020 7713 9326; website: www. communityfoundations.org.uk

These local organisations sometimes have a pot of money available for individuals to apply for.

Money Saving Expert

Website: www.moneysavingexpert. com

British consumer finance information and discussion website providing information and journalistic articles enabling people to save money.

Prisoners Education Trust

Tel: 020 8648 7760; website: www. prisonerseducation.org.uk

Access to a grants programme to enable prisoners in England and Wales to study through distance learning. Also provides advice and support, and influences policy and best practice.

Education authority contacts

This section provides a list of council offices and of the main government departments. Check online for specific education departments or for further information relating to children and young people in education.

Government departments

England

Department for Business, Innovation and Skills: 1 Victoria Street, London W1H 0ET (tel: 020 7215 5000; email:enquiries@bis.gsi.gov.uk; website: www.bis.gov.uk).

Department for Education: Castle View House, East Lane, Runcorn, Cheshire WA7 2GJ (tel: 03700 02288; email: online enquiry form; website: www.education.gov.uk).

Isle of Man

Department of Education and Children: Hamilton House, Peel Road, Douglas IM1 5EZ (tel: 01624 85820; email: admin@doe.gov.im; website: www.gov.im/education).

Northern Ireland

Department of Education for Northern Ireland: Rathgael House, 3 Balloo Road, Bangor, Co. Down T19 7PR (tel: 02891 279279; email: mail@deni.gov.uk; website: www.deni. gov.uk).

Scotland

Education Scotland: Denholm House, Almondvale Business Park, Almondvale Way, Livingston EH54 6GA (tel: 01412 825000; email: enquires@educationscotland.gov.uk; website: www.scotland.gov.uk).

Wales

Children, Education, Lifelong Learning and Skills Department: Cathays Park, Cardiff CF10 3NQ (tel: 0845 010 3300; website: www.wales. gov.uk).

Local education authorities

England

London

Barking and Dagenham: Civic Centre, Rainham Road North, Dagenham RM10 7BN (tel: 020 8215 3004; website: www.barking-dagenham.gov. uk).

Barnet: North London Business Park (NLBP), Oakleigh Road South, London N11 1NP (tel: 020 8359 2000; website: www.barnet.gov.uk).

Bexley: Civic Offices, Broadway, Bexleyheath, Kent DA6 7LB (tel: 020 8303 7777; website: www.bexley.gov. uk).

Brent: Town Hall, Forty Lane, Wembley HA9 9HD (tel: 020 8937 1200; website: www.brent.gov.uk).

Bromley: Education Department, Civic Centre, Stockwell Close, Bromley BR1 3UH (tel: 020 8464 3333; website: www.bromley.gov.uk).

Camden: Camden Town Hall, Judd Street, London WCH1 9JE (tel: 020 7278 4444; website: www.camden.gov. uk).

City of London: PO Box 270, Guildhall, London EC2P 2EJ (tel: 020 7606 3030; website: www. cityoflondon.gov.uk).

Croydon: Education Offices, Taberner House, Park Lane, Croydon CR9 3JS (tel: 020 8726 6000; website: www. croydon.gov.uk).

Ealing: 5th Floor, Percival House, 14–16 Uxbridge Road, Ealing W5 2HL (tel: 020 8825 5000; website: www.ealing.gov.uk).

Enfield: Civic Centre, Silver Street, Enfield EN1 3XY (tel: 020 8379 1000; website: www.enfield.gov.uk).

Greenwich: Town Hall, Wellington Street, Woolwich, London SE18 6PW (tel: 020 8854 8888; website: www. greenwich.gov.uk).

Hackney: Hackney Service Centre, 1 Hillman Street, London E8 1DY (tel: 020 8356 3000; website: www. hackney.gov.uk).

Hammersmith and Fulham: Town Hall, King Street, London W6 9JU (tel: 020 8748 3020; website: www. lbhf.gov.uk).

Haringey: Education Dept, Civic Centre, High Road, Wood Green, London N22 8LE (tel: 020 8489 0000; website: www.haringey.gov.uk).

Harrow: Civic Centre, PO Box 57, Station Road, Harrow HA1 2XF (tel: 020 8863 5611; website: www.harrow. gov.uk).

Havering: Town Hall, Main Road, Romford RM1 3BB (tel: 01708 434343; website: www.havering.gov. uk).

Hillingdon: Civic Centre, High Street, Uxbridge UB8 1UW (tel: 01895 250111; website: www.hillingdon.gov.uk).

Hounslow: Civic Centre, Lampton Road, Hounslow TW3 4DN (tel: 020 8583 2000; website: www.hounslow.gov.uk).

Islington: 222 Upper Street, Islington, London N1 1XR (tel: 020 7527 2000; website: www.islington.gov.uk).

Kensington and Chelsea: The Town Hall, Hornton Street, London W8 7NX (tel: 020 7361 3000; website: www.rbkc.gov.uk).

Kingston upon Thames: Guildhall, High Street, Kingston-upon-Thames, Surrey KT1 1EU (tel: 020 8547 5000; website: www.kingston.gov.uk).

Lambeth: Town Hall, Brixton Hill, London SW2 1RW (tel: 020 7926 1000; website: www.lambeth.gov.uk).

Lewisham: Town Hall, Catford, London SE6 4RU (tel: 020 8314 6000; website: www.lewisham.gov.uk).

Merton: Merton Civic Centre, London Road, Morden, Surrey SM4 5DX (tel: 020 8274 4901; website: www.merton.gov.uk).

Newham: Dockside1000, Dockside Road, London E16 2QU (tel: 020 8430 2000; website: www.newham.gov.uk).

Redbridge: London Borough of Redbridge, PO BOX No.2, Town Hall, 128–142 High Road, Ilford, Essex IG1 1DD (tel: 020 8554 5000; website: www.redbridge.gov.uk).

Richmond-upon-Thames: Civic Centre, 44 York Street, Twickenham TW1 3BZ (tel: 0845 612 2660; website: www.richmond.gov.uk).

Southwark: PO BOX 64529, London SE1P 5LX (tel: 020 7525 5000; website: www.southwark.gov.uk).

Sutton: Civic Offices, St Nicholas Way, Sutton SM1 1EA (tel: 020 8770 5000; website: www.sutton.gov.uk).

Tower Hamlets: Education and Community Services, Town Hall, Mulberry Place, 5 Clove Crescent, London E14 2BG (tel: 020 7364 5020; website: www.tower hamlets.gov.uk).

Waltham Forest: Town Hall, Forest Road, London E17 4JF (tel: 020 8496 3000; website: www.lbwf.gov.uk).

Wandsworth: Education Dept, Town Hall, Wandsworth High Street, London SW18 2PU (tel: 020 8871 6000; website: www.wandsworth.gov.uk).

Westminster: Westminster City Hall, 64 Victoria Street, London SW1E 6QP (tel: 020 7641 6000; website: www.westminster.gov.uk).

Midlands

Derbyshire
Derby City Council: Derby City Council, Council House, Corporation Street, Derby DE1 2FS (tel: 01332 293111; website: www.derby.gov.uk).

Derbyshire County Council: Education Offices, County Hall, Matlock DE4 3AG (tel: 0845 605 8058; website: www.derbyshire.gov.uk).

Herefordshire
Herefordshire Council: Brockington, 35 Hafod Road, Hereford, Herefordshire HR1 1SH, (tel: 01432 260000; email: info@herefordshire.gov.uk; website: www.herefordshire.gov.uk).

Leicestershire and Rutland
Leicester City Council: New Walk Centre, Welford Place, Leicester LE1 6ZG (tel: 01162 527000; website: www.leicester.gov.uk).

Leicestershire County Council: County Hall, Glenfield, Leicester LE3 8RA (tel: 01162 323232; website: www.leics.gov.uk).

Lincolnshire County Council: Education Department, County Offices, Newland, Lincoln LN1 1YL (tel: 01522 552222; website: www.lincolnshire.gov.uk).

North East Lincolnshire Council: Municipal Offices, Town Hall Square, Grimsby DN31 1HU (tel: 01472 313131; website: www.nelincs.gov.uk).

North Lincolnshire Council: Pittwood House, Ashby Road, Scunthorpe, North Lincolnshire DN16 1AB (tel: 01724 296296; website: www.northlincs.gov.uk).

Rutland District Council: Catmose, Oakham, Rutland LE15 6HP (tel: 01572 722577; website: www.rutland.gov.uk).

Northamptonshire
Northamptonshire County Council: John Dryden House, 8–10 The Lakes,

Northampton NN4 7DD (tel: 01604 236236; website: www.northamptonshire.gov.uk).

Nottinghamshire
Nottingham City Council: Loxley House, Station Street, Nottingham NG2 3NG (tel: 01159 155555; website: www.nottinghamcity.gov.uk).

Nottinghamshire County Council: County Hall, West Bridgford, Nottingham NG2 7QP (tel: 0844 980 8080; website: www.nottinghamshire.gov.uk).

Shropshire
Shropshire County Council: Shirehall, Abbey Foregate, Shrewsbury SY2 6ND (tel: 0845 678 9000; website: www.shropshire.gov.uk).

Telford and Wrekin Council: Civic Offices, Coach Central, Telford TF3 4HD (tel: 01952 380000; website: www.telford.gov.uk).

Staffordshire
Staffordshire County Council: St Chad's Place, Stafford ST16 2LR (tel: 0300 111 8000; website: www.staffordshire.gov.uk).

Stoke-on-Trent City Council: Civic Centre, Glebe Street, Stoke-on-Trent ST4 1RN (tel: 01782 234567; website: www.stoke.gov.uk).

Warwickshire
Warwickshire County Council: Shire Hall, Warwick CV34 4SA (tel: 01926 410410; website: www.warwickshire.gov.uk).

West Midlands
Birmingham City Council: Education Office, The Council House, Victoria Square, Birmingham B1 1BB (tel: 01213 031111; website: www.birmingham.gov.uk).

Coventry City Council: Earl Street, Coventry CV1 5RS (tel: 02476 833333; website: www.coventry.gov.uk).

Dudley Borough Council: Dudley Metropolitan Borough Council, Council House, Priory Road, Dudley, West Midlands DY1 1HF (tel: 01384 812345; website: www.dudley.gov.uk).

Dudley Metropolitan Borough Council: Council House, Priory Road, Westox House, 1 Trinity Road, Dudley DY1 IHF (tel: 01384 812345; website: www.dudley.gov.uk).

ndwell Borough Council: Sandwell ouncil House, Oldbury, West idlands B69 3DE (tel: 0845 358 ?00; website: www.lea.sandwell.gov. k).

lihull Borough Council: Education d Children's Department, PO Box ?, Council House, Solihull B91 9QU el: 01217 046000; website: www. lihull.gov.uk).

alsall Borough Council: Education ept, Civic Centre, Darwall Street, 'alsall WS1 1TP (tel: 01922 650000; ebsite: www.walsall.gov.uk).

olverhampton Borough Council: lucation Services, Civic Centre St ?ter's Square, Wolverhampton 'V1 1RR (tel: 01902 556556; website: ww.wolverhampton.gov.uk).

orcestershire

*orcestershire County Council: lucation and Lifelong Learning, ?unty Hall, Spetchley Road, *orcester WR5 2NP (tel: 01905 ?3763; website: www.worcestershire. ?v.uk).

orth East

ounty Durham

arlington Borough Council: Town all, Feethams, Darlington, County urham DL1 5QT (tel: 01325 380651; mail: enquiries@darlington.gov.uk; ebsite: www.darlington.gov.uk).

urham County Council: County all, Durham DH1 5UL (tel: 01913 ?3000; website: www.durham.gov. k).

ast Yorkshire

ast Riding of Yorkshire Council: ?ounty Hall, Cross Street, Beverley U17 9BA (tel: 01482 393939; ebsite: www.eastriding.gov.uk).

ull City Council: Guildhall, Alfred elder Street, Hull HU1 2AA (tel: 1482 300300; website: www.hullcc. ?v.uk).

orth Yorkshire

?orth Yorkshire County Council: ?ounty Hall, Northallerton, North ?orkshire DL7 8AD (tel: 01609 ?0780; website: www.northyorks.gov. k).

orthumberland

?orthumberland County Council: ?ounty Hall, Morpeth NE61 2EF (tel: ?670 533000; website: www. ?rthumberland.gov.uk).

City of York Council: The Guildhall, York Y01 9QN (tel: 01904 551550; website: www.york.gov.uk).

South Yorkshire

Barnsley Borough Council: Town Hall, Barnsley S70 2TA (tel: 01226 770770; website: www.barnsley.gov. uk).

Doncaster Borough Council: Council House, College Road, Doncaster DN1 1BR, (tel: 01302 736000; website: www.doncaster.gov.uk).

Rotherham Borough Council: Civic Building, Walker Place, Rotherham S65 1UF (tel: 01709 382121; website: www.rotherham.gov.uk).

Sheffield City Council: Town Hall, Pinstone Street, Sheffield S1 2HH (tel: 01142 726444; website: www. sheffield.gov.uk).

Teesside

Hartlepool Borough Council: Civic Centre, Victoria Road, Hartlepool TS24 8AY (tel: 01429 266522; website: www.hartlepool.gov.uk).

Middlesbrough Borough Council: PO Box 99, Town Hall, Middlesbrough TS1 2QQ (tel: 01642 245432; website: www.middlesbrough.gov.uk).

Redcar and Cleveland Borough Council: Redcar and Cleveland House, Kirkleatham Street, Redcar TS10 1YA (tel: 01642 774774; website: www.redcar-cleveland.gov.uk).

Stockton-on-Tees Borough Council: PO Box 11, Church Road, Stockton-on-Tees TS18 1LD (tel: 01642 393939; website: www.stockton-bc.gov.uk).

Tyne and Wear

Gateshead Borough Council: Civic Centre, Regent Street, Gateshead NE8 1HH (tel: 01914 333000; website: www.gateshead.gov.uk).

Newcastle upon Tyne City Council: Civic Centre, Barras Bridge, Newcastle upon Tyne NE9 1RD (tel: 01912 328520; website: www. newcastle.gov.uk).

North Tyneside Borough Council: Quadrant, The Silverlink North, Cobalt Business Park, North Tyneside NE27 0BY (tel: 0345 2000 101; website: www.north tyneside.gov.uk).

South Tyneside Borough Council: Town Hall and Civic Offices, Westoe Road, South Shields NE33 2RL (tel:

01914 271717; website: www. southtyneside.info).

Sunderland City Council: Education and Community Services, Civic Centre, Burdon Road, Sunderland SR2 7DN (tel: 01915 205555; website: www.sunderland.gov.uk).

West Yorkshire

Bradford District Council: Education Bradford, Future House, Bolling Road, Bradford, West Yorkshire BD4 7EB (tel: 01274 385500; website: www.bradford.gov.uk).

City of Bradford Metropolitan District Council: City Hall, Centenary Square, Bradford BD1 1HY (tel: 01274 432111; website: www. bradford.gov.uk).

Calderdale Borough Council: Education Department, Crossley Street, Halifax HX1 1UJ (tel: 0845 245 6000; website: www.calderdale. gov.uk).

Calderdale Council: Town Hall, Crossley Street, Halifax HX1 1UJ (tel: 01422 357257; website: www. calderdale.gov.uk).

Kirklees Council: Civic Centre 3, Market Street, Huddersfield HD1 1WG (tel: 01484 221000, website: www.kirklees.gov.uk).

Leeds City Council: Civic Hall, Calverley Street, Leeds LS1 1UR (tel: 01132 348080; website: www.leeds. gov.uk).

Wakefield District Council: Town Hall, Wood Street, Wakefield WF1 2HQ (tel: 0845 850 6506; website: www.wakefield.gov.uk).

North West

Cheshire and Chester

Cheshire East Council: Westfields, Middlewich Road, Sandbach CW11 1HZ, (tel: 0300 123 55 00); website: www.cheshireeast.gov.uk).

Cheshire West and Chester Council: HQ, 58 Nicholas Street, Chester CH1 2NP (tel: 0300 123 8 123; website: www.cheshirewestandchester. gov.uk.

Halton Borough Council: Municipal Building, Kingsway, Widnes, Cheshire WA8 7QF (tel: 0303 333 4300; website: www3.halton.gov.uk).

Warrington Borough Council: Education and Lifelong Learning, New Town House, Buttermarket

Street, Warrington WA1 2NH (tel: 01925 443322; website: www.warrington.gov.uk).

Cumbria

Cumbria County Council: The Courts, Carlisle CA3 8NA (tel: 01228 606060; email: information@cumbriacc.gov.uk; website: www.cumbria.gov.uk).

Greater Manchester

Bolton Borough Council: Bolton Metro, Town Hall, Victoria Square, Bolton BL1 1RU (tel: 01204 333333; website: www.bolton.gov.uk).

Bury Council: Town Hall, Knowsley Street, Bury, Lancashire BL9 OSW (tel: 01612 535000; website: www.bury.gov.uk).

Manchester City Council: Town Hall, Albert Square, Manchester M60 2LA (tel: 01612 345000 Fax: 01612 347007; website: www.manchester.gov.uk).

Oldham Council: Education and Leisure Services, Civic Centre, West Street, Oldham OL1 1UG (tel: 01619 113000; website: www.oldham.gov.uk).

Rochdale Metropolitan Borough Council: Municipal Offices, Smith Street, Rochdale OL16 1XU (tel: 01706 647474; website: www.rochdale.gov.uk).

Salford City Council: Civic Centre, Chorley Road, Swinton, Salford M27 5AW (tel: 01617 944711; website: www.salford.gov.uk).

Stockport Metropolitan Borough Council: Stockport Council, Town Hall, Edward Street, Stockport SK1 3XE (tel: 01614 804949; website: www.stockport.gov.uk).

Tameside Council: Council Offices, Wellington Road, Ashton-under-Lyne OL6 6DL (tel: 01613 428355; website: www.tameside.gov.uk).

Trafford Council: Trafford Town Hall, Talbot Road, Stretford, Manchester M32 OYT (tel: 01619 122000; website: www.trafford.gov.uk).

Wigan Borough Council: Town Hall, Library Street, Wigan WN1 1YN (tel: 01942 244991; website: www.wigan.gov.uk).

Lancashire

Blackburn with Darwen Borough Council: Town Hall, King William Street, Blackburn, Lancashire BB1 7DY (tel: 01254 585585; website: www.blackburn.gov.uk).

Blackpool Council: Town Hall, Blackpool FY1 1AD (tel: 01253 477477; website: www.blackpool.gov.uk).

Lancashire County Council: PO Box 78, County Hall, Fishergate, Preston PR1 8XJ (tel: 0845 053 0000; website: www.lancashire.gov.uk).

Merseyside

Knowsley Borough Council: Municipal Buildings, Cherryfield Drive, Kirkby, Knowsley L32 1TX (tel: 01514 896000; website: www.knowsley.gov.uk).

Liverpool City Council: Municipal Buildings, Dale Street, Liverpool L69 2DH (tel: 01512 333000; website: www.liverpool.gov.uk).

St Helens Council: Town Hall, Victoria Square, St Helens, Merseyside WA10 1HP (tel: 01744 456789; website: www.sthelens.gov.uk).

Sefton Borough Council: Town Hall, Southport PR8 1DA (tel: 0845 140 0845; website: www.sefton.gov.uk).

Wirral Borough Council: Town Hall, Brighton Street, Wallasey, Wirral CH44 8ED (tel: 151 606 2000; website: www.wirral.gov.uk).

South East

Bedfordshire

Central Bedfordshire Council: County Hall, Cauldwell Street, Bedford MK42 9AP (tel: 0300 300 8000; website: www.centralbedfordshire.gov.uk).

Luton Borough Council: Town Hall, George Street, Luton, Bedfordshire LU1 2BQ (tel: 01582 546000; website: www.luton.gov.uk).

Berkshire

Bracknell Forest Council: East Hampstead House, Town Square, Bracknell RG12 1AQ (tel: 01344 352000; website: www.bracknell-forest.gov.uk).

Reading Borough Council: Civic Centre, Reading RG1 7AE (tel: 01189 373737; website: www.reading.gov.uk).

Slough Borough Council: Landmark Place, High Street, Slough SL1 1JL (tel: 01753 475111; website: www.slough.gov.uk).

West Berkshire Council: Market Street, Newbury, Berkshire RG14 5LD (tel: 01635 42400; website: www.westberks.gov.uk).

Windsor and Maidenhead: Education Dept, Town Hall, St Ives Road, Maidenhead SL6 1RF (tel: 01628 683800; website: www.rbwm.gov.uk).

Wokingham District Council: Education and Cultural Services, Shute End, Wokingham RG40 1BN (tel: 01189 746000; website: www.wokingham.gov.uk).

Buckinghamshire

Buckinghamshire County Council: County Hall, Walton Street, Aylesbury HP20 1UA (tel: 0845 370 8090; website: www.buckscc.gov.uk).

Milton Keynes Council: Civic Offices, 1 Saxon Gate East, Central Milton Keynes MK9 3HQ (tel: 01908 69169; website: www.milton-keynes.gov.uk).

Cambridgeshire

Cambridgeshire County Council: Shire Hall, Castle Hill, Cambridge CB3 0AP (tel: 0345 045 5200; website: www.cambridgeshire.gov.uk).

Peterborough City Council: Town Hall, Bridge Street, Peterborough PE1 1QT (tel: 01733 747474; website: www.peterborough.gov.uk).

East Sussex

Brighton and Hove City Council: King's House, Grand Avenue, Hove BN3 2LS (tel: 01273 290000; website: www.brighton-hove.gov.uk).

East Sussex County Council: County Hall, St Anne's Crescent, Lewes BN7 1SG (tel: 0345 60 80 190; website: www.eastsussex.gov.uk).

Essex

Essex County Council: County Hall, Market Road, Chelmsford CM1 1LX (tel: 0845 743 0430; website: www.essex.gov.uk).

Southend-on-Sea Borough Council: Civic Centre, Victoria Avenue, Southend-on-Sea SS2 6ER (tel: 0170 215000; website: www.southend.gov.uk).

Thurrock Council: Civic Offices, New Road, Grays, Thurrock, Essex RM17 6SL (tel: 01375 652652; website: www.thurrock.gov.uk).

Hampshire

Hampshire County Council: Education County Office, The Castle, Winchester SO23 8UJ (tel: 0845 603 5638; email: info@hants.gov.uk; website: www.hants.gov.uk).

Isle of Wight Council: Education Dept, County Hall, High Street, Newport PO30 1UD (tel: 01983 821000; website: www.iwight.gov.uk).

Portsmouth City Council: Civic Offices, Guildhall Square, Portsmouth PO1 2BG (tel: 02392 822251; website: www.portsmouth.gov.uk).

Southampton City Council: Civic Centre, Southampton SO14 7LY (tel: 02380 833000; website: www.southampton.gov.uk).

Hertfordshire

Hertfordshire County Council: County Hall, Pegs Lane, Hertford SG13 8DQ (tel: 0300 123 4040; website: www.herts direct.org).

Kent

Kent County Council: County Hall, Maidstone, Kent ME14 1XQ (tel: 0845 824 7247; email: county.hall@kent.gov.uk; website: www.kent.gov.uk).

Medway Council: Gun Wharf, Dock Road, Chatham, Kent ME4 4TR (tel: 01634 306000; website: www.medway.gov.uk).

Norfolk

Norfolk County Council: County Hall, Martineau Lane, Norwich NR1 2DH (tel: 0844 800 8020; website: www.norfolk.gov.uk).

Oxfordshire

Oxfordshire County Council: County Hall, New Road, Oxford OX1 1ND (tel: 01865 792422; website: www.oxfordshire.gov.uk).

Suffolk

Suffolk County Council: Endeavour House, 8 Russell Road, Ipswich, Suffolk IP1 2BX (tel: 01473 583000; website: www.suffolkcc.gov.uk).

Surrey

Surrey County Council: County Hall, Penrhyn Road, Kingston-upon-Thames KT1 2DJ (tel: 0845 600 9009; website: www.surreycc.gov.uk).

West Sussex

West Sussex County Council: Education Department, County Hall, Chichester PO19 1RQ (tel: 01243 777100; website: www.westsussex.gov.uk).

South West

Avon

Bath and North East Somerset Council: The Guildhall, High Street, Bath BA1 5AW (tel: 01225 477000; website: www.bathnes.gov.uk).

Bristol City Council: The Council House, College Green, Bristol BS1 5TR (tel: 01179 222000; website: www.bristol-city.gov.uk).

North Somerset Council: Town Hall, Walliscote Grove Road, Weston-Super- Mare BS23 1UJ (tel: 01934 888888; website: www.n-somerset.gov.uk).

South Gloucestershire Council: Badminton Road, Council Offices, Badminton Road, Yate BS37 5AF (tel: 01454 868009; website: www.southglos.gov.uk).

Cornwall

Cornwall County Council: County Hall, Treyew Road, Truro, Cornwall TR1 3AY (tel: 0300 1234 100; email: enquiries@ cornwall.gov.uk; website: www.cornwall.gov.uk).

Council of The Isles of Scilly: Town Hall, St Mary's, Isles of Scilly TR21 0LW (tel: 01720 422537; website: www.scilly.gov.uk).

Devon

Devon County Council: County Hall, Topsham Road, Exeter EX2 4QD (tel: 0845 155 1015; website: www.devon.gov.uk).

Plymouth City Council: Armada Way, Plymouth PL1 2AA (tel: 01752 668000; website: www.portsmouth.gov.uk).

Torbay Borough Council: Town Hall, Castle Circus, Torquay, Devon TQ1 3DR (tel: 01803 201201; website: www.torbay.gov.uk).

Dorset

Bournemouth Borough Council: Town Hall, Bourne Avenue, Bournemouth BH2 6DY (tel: 01202 451451; email: enquiries@ bournemouth.gov.uk; website: www.bournemouth.gov.uk).

Dorset County Council: County Hall, Colliton Park, Dorchester DT1 1XJ (tel: 01305 251000; website: www.dorsetfor you.com).

Borough of Poole Council: Education Dept, Civic Centre, Poole, Dorset BH15 2RU (tel: 01202 633633; website: www.poole.gov.uk).

Gloucestershire

Gloucestershire County Council: Shire Hall, Westgate Street, Gloucester GL1 2TG (tel: 01452 425000; website: www.gloucestershire.gov.uk).

Somerset

Somerset County Council: Children and young people's service, County Hall, Taunton, Somerset TA1 4DY (tel: 0845 345 9122; website: www.somerset.gov.uk).

Wiltshire

Swindon Borough Council: Civic Offices, Euclid Street, Swindon SN1 2JH (tel: 01793 445500; website: www.swindon.gov.uk).

Wiltshire County Council: Education Dept, County Hall, Bythesea Road, Trowbridge, Wiltshire BA14 8JN (tel: 01225 713000; website: www.wiltshire.gov.uk).

Northern Ireland

Belfast: Education and Library Board, 40 Academy Street, Belfast BT1 2NQ (tel: 02890 564000; website: www.belb.org.uk).

CCMS (Council for Catholic Maintained Schools): 160 High Street, Holywood, County Down BT18 9HT (tel: 02890 426972; website: www.onlineccms.com).

North Eastern: Education Welfare Office, 76 Trostan Avenue, Ballymena BT43 7BL (tel: 28 2564 5687; website: www.neelb.org.uk).

South Eastern: Education and Library Board, Grahamsbridge Road, Dundonald, Belfast BT16 2HS (tel: 02890 566200; website: www.seelb.org.uk).

Southern: Education and Library Board, 3 Charlemont Place, The Mall, Armagh BT61 9AX (tel: 02837 512200; website: www.selb.org).

Western: Education and Library Board, Campsie House, 1 Hospital Road, Omagh, Co. Tyrone BT79 0AW (tel: 02882 411411; website: www.welbni.org).

Scotland

Aberdeen City Council: Culture and Learning, Aberdeen City Council, 2nd Floor, St Nicholas House, Broad Street, Aberdeen AB10 1BY (tel: 0845 608 0910; website: www.aberdeencity. gov.uk)

Angus Council: Education Department, Angus House, Orchardbank Business Park, Forfar DD8 1AE (tel: 01307 476300) website: www.angus.gov.uk).

Argyll and Bute Council: Education Dept, Kilmory, Lochgilphead, Argyll PA31 8RT (tel: 01546 602127; website: www.argyll- bute.gov.uk).

Clackmannanshire Council: Greenfield, Alloa, Clackmannanshire FK10 2AD (tel: 01259 450000; website: www.clacksweb.org.uk).

Comhairle nan Eilean Siar: Council Offices, Sandwick Road, Stornoway, Isle of Lewis HS1 2BW (tel: 01851 703773; website: www.w-isles.gov.uk).

Dumfries and Galloway Council: Council Headquarters, Council Offices, English Street, Dumfries DG1 2DD (tel: 030 33 33 3000; website: www.dumgal.gov.uk).

Dundee City Council: Education Dept, 8th Floor, Tayside House, Crichton Street, Dundee DD1 3RZ (tel: 01382 433111; website: www. dundeecity.gov.uk).

East Ayrshire Council: Council Headquarters, London Road, Kilmarnock KA3 7BU (tel: 0845 724 0000; website: www.east-ayrshire.gov. uk).

East Dunbartonshire Council: Tom Johnston House, Civic Way, Kirkintilloch G66 4TJ (tel: 0845 045 4510; website: www.eastdunbarton. gov.uk).

East Lothian Council: Education and Community Services, John Muir House, Haddington EH41 3HA (tel: 01620 827827; website: www. eastlothian.gov.uk).

East Renfrewshire Council: Council Offices, Education Dept, Eastwood Park, Rouken Glen Road, Glasgow G46 6UG (tel: 01415 773001; website: www.east renfrewshire.gov.uk).

Edinburgh City Council: Education Dept; Waverley Court, 4 East Market Street, Edinburgh EH8 8BG (tel: 01312 002000; website: www. edinburgh.gov.uk).

Falkirk Council: Municipal Building, West Bridge Street, Falkirk FK1 5RS (tel: 01324 506070; website: www. falkirk.gov.uk).

Fife Council: Education service, Fife Council, Fife House, North Street, Glenrothes KY7 5LT (tel: 01592 583372; website: www.fife-education. org.uk).

Glasgow City Council: Education Dept, 25 Cochrane Street, Glasgow G1 1HL (tel: 01412 872000; website: www.glasgow.gov.uk).

Highland Council: Glenurquhart Road, Inverness IV3 5NX (tel: 01463 702000; website: www.highland.gov. uk).

Inverclyde Council: Municipal Buildings, Greenock PA15 1LY (tel: 01475 717171; website: www. inverclyde.gov.uk).

Midlothian Council: Midlothian House, Buccleuch Street, Dalkeith EH22 1DN (tel: 01312 707500; website: www.midlothian.gov.uk).

Moray Council: Educational Services, Council Offices, High Street, Elgin IV30 1BX (tel: 01343 543451; website: www.moray.gov.uk).

North Ayrshire Council: Cunninghame House, Friars Croft, Irvine KA12 8EE (tel: 0845 603 0590; website: www.north- ayrshire.gov.uk).

North Lanarkshire Council: Education Dept, Municipal Buildings, Kildonan Street, Coatbridge ML5 3BT (tel: 01236 812222; website: www. northlan.gov.uk).

Orkney Islands Council: Council Offices, School Place, Kirkwall, Orkney KW15 1NY (tel: 01856 873535; website: www.orkney.gov.uk).

Perth and Kinross Council: 2 High Street, Perth PH1 5PH (tel: 01738 475000; website: www.pkc.gov.uk).

Renfrewshire Council: Renfrewshire House, Cotton Street, Paisley PA1 1UJ (tel: 01418 425000; website: www.renfrewshire.gov.uk).

Scottish Borders Council: Lifelong Learning, Council Headquarters, Newtown St Boswells, Melrose TD6 0SA (tel: 01835 824000; website: www.scotborders.gov.uk).

Shetlands Islands Council: Education Services, Hayfield House, Hayfield Lane, Lerwick, Shetland ZE1 0QD (tel: 01595 744000; website: www. shetland.gov.uk).

South Ayrshire Council: County Buildings, Wellington Square, Ayr KA7 1DR (tel: 01292 601 202; website: www.south-ayrshire.gov.uk).

South Lanarkshire Council: Education Dept, 5th Floor, Council Offices, Almada Street, Hamilton ML3 0AA (tel: 01698 454444; website: www. southlanarkshire.gov.uk).

Stirling Council: Viewforth, Stirling FK8 2ET (tel: 0845 277 7000; website: www.stirling.gov.uk).

West Dunbartonshire Council: Learning and Education, Council Offices, Garshake Road, Dumbarton G82 3PU (tel: 01389 737000; website: www.west-dunbarton.gov.uk).

West Lothian Council: West Lothian House, Almondvale Boulevard, Livingston, West Lothian EH54 6QG (tel: 01506 775000; website: www. westlothian.gov.uk).

Wales

Blaenau Gwent County Borough Council: Education/Lifelong Learning, Municipal Offices, Civic Centre, Ebbw Vale NP23 6XB (tel: 01495 35055; website: www.blaenau-gwent.gov.uk).

Bridgend County Borough Council: Education, Leisure and Community Services, Civic Offices, Angel Street, Bridgend CF31 4WB (tel: 01656 643643; website: www.bridgend.gov. uk).

Caerphilly County Borough Council: Directorate of Education and Leisure, Woodfieldside Business Park, Blackwood NP12 2DG (tel: 01443 815588; website: www.caerphilly.gov. uk).

The City and County Council of Cardiff: Education Dept, County Hall, Atlantic Wharf, Cardiff CF10 4UW (tel: 02920 872087; website: www.cardiff.gov.uk).

Carmarthenshire County Council: County Hall, Carmarthen SA31 IJP (tel: 01267 234567; website: www. carmarthenshire.gov.uk).

Ceredigion County Council: Canolfan Rheidol, Rhodfa Padarn, Llanbadarn Fawr, Aberystwyth, Ceredigion

Y23 3UE (tel: 01970 617911; website: www.ceredigion.gov.uk).

Conwy County Borough Council: Bodlondeb, Conwy, North Wales LL32 8DU (tel: 01492 574000; website: www.conwy.gov.uk).

Denbighshire County Council: Education Services, Denbighshire County Council, County Hall, Wynnstay Road, Ruthin LL15 1YN (tel: 01824 712777; website: www. denbighshire.gov.uk).

Flintshire County Council: Education and Children's Services, County Hall, Mold CH7 6NB (tel: 0845 607 7577; website: www.flintshire.gov.uk).

Gwynedd Council: Gwynedd-Ni, Caernarfon Library, Pavilion Hill, Caernarfon, Gwynedd LL55 1AS (tel: 1286 675570; website: www. gwynedd.gov.uk).

Isle of Anglesey County Council: Council Offices, Llangefni, Anglesey LL77 7TW (tel: 01248 750057; website: www.anglesey.gov.uk).

Merthyr Tydfil County Borough Council: Civic Centre, Castle Street, Merthyr Tydfil CF47 8AN (tel: 01685 725000; website: www.merthyr.gov. uk).

Monmouthshire County Council: Lifelong Learning and Leisure, County Hall, Cwmbran NP44 2XH (tel: 01633 644644; website: www. monmouthshire.gov.uk).

Neath Port Talbot County Borough Council: Education Dept, Civic Centre, Port Talbot SA13 1PJ (tel: 01639 686868; website: www.neath-porttalbot.gov.uk).

Newport County Borough Council: Education Dept, Civic Centre, Newport NP20 4UR (tel: 01633 656656; website: www.newport.gov. uk).

Pembrokeshire County Council: Education Dept, County Hall, Haverfordwest SA61 1TP (tel: 01437 764551; website: www.pembrokeshire. gov.uk).

Powys County Council: Education Dept, County Hall, Llandrindod Wells, Powys LD1 5LG (tel: 01597 827460; website: www.powys.gov.uk).

Rhondda Cynon Taff County Borough Council: Ty Bronwydd, Bronwydd Avenue, Porth CF39 9DL

(tel: 01443 744000; website: www. rhondda-cynon-taff.gov.uk).

City and County of Swansea: Education Dept, County Hall, Swansea SA1 3SN (tel: 01792 636000; website: www.swansea.gov.uk).

Torfaen County Borough Council: Torfaen County Borough Council, Civic Centre, Pontypool NP4 6YB (tel: 01495 762200; website: www. torfaen.gov.uk).

The Vale of Glamorgan County Borough Council: Education Dept, Civic Offices, Holton Road, Barry CF63 4RU (tel: 01446 700111; website: www.valeofglamorgan.gov. uk).

Wrexham County Borough Council: Learning and Achievement Department, 16 Lord Street, Wrexham LL11 1LG (tel: 01978 297505; website: www.wrexham.gov. uk).

Index